W9-CAO-381

In the Shadow of the Poorhouse:
A Social History of Welfare in America

Improving Poor People

The Undeserving Poor:
From the War on Poverty to the War on Welfare

Reconstructing American Education

Poverty and Policy in American History

The Social Organization of Early Industrial Capitalism
(with Mark J. Stern et al.)

The Irony of Early School Reform:
Educational Innovation in Mid-Nineteenth Century Massachusetts

Class, Bureaucracy, and Schools:
The Illusion of Educational Change in America

The People of Hamilton, Canada West:
Family and Class in a Mid-Nineteenth-Century City

THE PRICE OF CITIZENSHIP

THE PRICE OF CITIZENSHIP

REDEFINING THE AMERICAN WELFARE STATE

MICHAEL B. KATZ

METROPOLITAN BOOKS

Henry Holt and Company

New York

Metropolitan Books
Henry Holt and Company, LLC
Publishers since 1866
115 West 18th Street
New York, New York 10011

Metropolitan Books™ is an imprint of
Henry Holt and Company, LLC.

The prologue to this book is a condensation
of an article coauthored by Michael B. Katz and Lorrin R. Thomas,
"The Invention of 'Welfare' in America," published
in the *Journal of Policy History,* 1998.

Library of Congress Cataloging-in-Publication Data

Katz, M. B.
    The price of citizenship : redefining the American welfare state / Michael B. Katz.—1st ed.
    p.   cm.
    Includes index.
    ISBN 0-8050-5208-9
    1. Public welfare—United States—History.   2. Welfare state.   3. United States—Social
policy—History.   I. Title.
HV91 .K37   2001
361.6'5'0973—dc21   00-046906

First Edition 2001

DESIGNED BY FRITZ METSCH

Printed in the United States of America
1   3   5   7   9   10   8   6   4   2

TO THE MEMORY OF

GEORGE J. KATZ

(1913–1999)

CONTENTS

THE INVENTION OF WELFARE

In 1950 the British sociologist T. H. Marshall described the triumph of the welfare state as "the subordination of market price to social justice." In recent decades that trajectory has been reversed. While the tension between capitalism and equality remains as powerful as ever, today it is social justice that is subordinate to market price.

Welfare once signified a broad and progressive program with wide public support; the welfare state embodied a generation's hopes and aspirations for universal economic security and protection from the worst consequences of life's ordinary hazards. But by the 1960s this meaning of *welfare* and *welfare state* had changed completely. No longer understood to protect everyone against risk, "welfare" had become a code word for public assistance given mainly to unmarried mothers, mostly young women of color, under Aid to Families with Dependent Children. No other public benefits carried the stigma of welfare. The political left, right, and center all attacked it. In the early 1990s, when President Bill Clinton promised to "end welfare as we know it," everyone knew that he meant AFDC—the most disliked public program in America.

Thus it was not surprising that most of the country—eight out of ten Americans—applauded when Clinton honored his pledge to "end welfare" by signing the 1996 welfare reform bill. In practical terms, the bill ended the sixty-year-old entitlement of the poorest Americans to public assistance, put time limits on benefits, tied aid closely to work, transferred the authority to set benefits and administer programs from the federal government to the states, and greatly reduced or eliminated eligibility for legal immigrants and the disabled.

The new legislation signaled the victory of three great forces—the war on dependence, the devolution of public authority, and the application of market models to public policy— that redefined not only welfare but all of America's vast welfare state. The story of how these forces transformed public policy is important not only because the welfare state consumes a large share of the nation's income and influences the life of every American. It is important as well because the idea of the welfare state codifies our collective obligations toward one another and defines the terms of membership in the national community. By tightening the links between benefits and employment, the late-twentieth-century welfare state has stratified Americans into first- and second-class citizens and undermined the effective practice of democracy. Everywhere market price has superseded social justice.

. . . .

The word *welfare* initially meant "well-being." In the U.S. Constitution, the promotion of the "general welfare" referred to government's advancement of the well-being of the entire population. Early-twentieth-century references to "welfare" in social policy usually meant "child welfare"—the provision of services to orphaned, neglected, and abandoned children. In the second decade, county superintendents of the poor proudly renamed themselves public welfare officials, and state governments replaced boards of state charities with departments of public welfare that centralized and modernized the administration of welfare. In those years, *welfare* rang with a progressive tone; it signified the increased assumption of public responsibility for dependence, the professional administration of programs, the rejection of charity, and the initial steps of the recognition of entitlement.[1]

Thus, in his second biennial report, the Pennsylvania Secretary of Welfare proudly observed that his department, created in 1921, "embodied the most advanced social policy in state administration in the field of charities and correction." When New York City reorganized its Department of Public Charities in 1920, it chose to call it the Department of Public Welfare to express its "broader purpose" and the rejection of outmoded ideas of philanthropy. In 1923, the *Annals of the American Academy of Political and Social Science* devoted a special issue to public welfare. In his foreword, *Annals* editor Clyde King remarked on the recent emergence of public welfare as a modern replacement for outmoded methods of relief. "A decade ago," he wrote, "the Department of Public Welfare was a new ideal just finding official favor in cities and in states" as "the older idea of charities and corrections" retreated before "the newer conception of protection and . . . public welfare."[2]

The early state public welfare departments bundled together a variety of tasks previously performed by several state agencies. For instance, the Massachusetts Public Welfare Department, founded in 1919, oversaw "mental diseases, correction, hospitals and schools, aid and relief." City departments applied the term "public welfare" to an even more diverse set of activities than did either states or counties.[3] The concept of welfare extended beyond the public to the private sector, where it referred to a broad array of activities intended to promote the well-being of workers. These functions included help with buying a home; stock purchase plans; insurance against accident, illness, old age, and death; old-age pensions; medical services; classes and sports programs; land for gardening; improved plant working and safety conditions; and assistance with a variety of personal problems. Together, these activities were known as "welfare work." In the early-twentieth century, welfare work became a national movement as employers experimented with methods designed to reduce labor turnover, boost production, and counteract attempts to unionize their workforces. The National Civic Federation, an employers' organization, even formed its own Welfare Department in 1903, while large corporations appointed "welfare secretaries" to administer their programs and universities began to train students in welfare work.[4]

"Welfare" clearly retained its Progressive Era association with modernity, progress, science, and efficiency and with services rather than relief. In the 1930s, the word *welfare* rarely appeared alone. More frequent were discussions of "social welfare" or "public welfare," terms that stood for a broad array of programs designed to ensure economic security for all. In June 1934, President Franklin Delano Roosevelt appointed the Committee on Economic Security to determine the best way to safeguard Americans "against misfortunes which cannot be wholly eliminated in this man-made world of ours." The committee called for a far-reaching program that included insurance against unemployment, old age, and sickness; expanded public health programs; pensions for the uninsured elderly; and aid for "fatherless children." The Economic Security Act of 1935—the charter of the federal welfare state—embraced the committee's comprehensive understanding of welfare, which encompassed both public assistance—that is, means-tested relief programs such as Old Age Assistance and Aid to Dependent Children—and social insurance, which included contributory programs whose benefits were not tied to income or assets, such as Old Age Insurance (popularly known as Social Security) and unemployment insurance.[5] With these programs, Roosevelt sought to create a system of economic security that replaced the old poor laws and their invidious distinctions with the entitlements of citizenship.

This broad definition of welfare persisted into the years after World War II. In 1946, a Brookings Institution report described federal welfare responsibilities as "education, health, employment and relief, and social security." In 1947, Congress's definition of "public welfare" included services designed to meet a wide array of needs, from helping families reach self-support to overcoming "problems resulting from parental neglect" and foster care. The positive connotations of "welfare state" were so entrenched that the *Saturday Evening Post*'s editors advised critics to avoid the term when discussing President Truman's plans to extend social benefits. "The opponents of such a system," they wrote, "have an excellent case, but they do not help it by adopting precisely the words which put it in a favorable light. 'Welfare' is the key word. Who's against welfare: Nobody. . . . Fighting an election by opposing welfare is on a par with taunting an opponent for having been born in a log cabin."[6]

And yet within a decade, *welfare* had lost this inclusive and positive meaning. The American public welfare state had split linguistically along two of the tracks that divided it administratively: public assistance and social insurance.[7] Welfare now signified only public assistance—which to most people meant Aid to Dependent Children—while Social Security, along with other social insurance programs, was no longer viewed as a form of welfare. Welfare was a despised program of last resort primarily for the "undeserving" poor—unmarried mothers, many of them black and Hispanic. The stigmas of race and sex hovered over public assistance; the aura of work and saving surrounded social insurance. Social Security, with its articulate middle-class supporters, absorbed the "deserving poor" and remained unassailable. These differences in valuation carried enormous consequences. Social insurance programs often lifted their beneficiaries out of poverty; public assistance almost never did—it just helped them to survive.

The process of bifurcation was gradual and, paradoxically, rooted in optimism. The federal officials who administered America's early social welfare programs promoted social insurance and tried to differentiate it from public assistance. They expected public assistance to "wither away" as more and more Americans became paid-up members of the social insurance system. And they believed that the unitary idea of welfare advocated by the Committee on Economic Security threatened to retard the progress of social insurance by tainting it with the historic stigma of "the dole" carried by public assistance.[8] In addition, between 1939 and 1956, Congress aided the devaluation of public assistance by extending social insurance from just the unemployed and retired workers to more and more groups: widows and dependents, the self-employed; domestic, agricultural, and railroad workers; and the disabled. Public assistance began to appear increasingly residual—a category of aid for those few left over.

Initially, the new insurance system for the elderly proved a hard sell. In 1940, Old Age Assistance, the major form of public assistance at the time, paid benefits to 2.07 million people, while Social Security's elderly beneficiaries numbered only 131,000. Even as late as 1949, Old Age Assistance beneficiaries outnumbered those of Social Security by a third—2.49 to 1.67 million. In 1940, Old Age Assistance paid benefits to almost twice as many persons as ADC, and during World War II, a time of full employment, the number on ADC fell while the number of elderly receiving benefits continued to rise. "Relief" conjured up a destitute old person, not an unmarried mother with children.[9]

Although by 1950, the expectation that social insurance would supplant public assistance did not appear unreasonable, events soon overturned predictions. Within a decade, the belief that public assistance would wither away appeared a quaint notion of the recent past. In 1955, for the first time, more persons received benefits under Aid to Dependent Children than Old Age Assistance. The 1960s proved the catalytic decade for AFDC—as of 1962 the new name for ADC—with an astonishing 169 percent rise. Between 1970 and 1975, while Old Age Assistance plummeted 99 percent and nearly disappeared, AFDC grew another 30 percent.[10]

As one group after another left public assistance for social insurance, those who remained—mainly single mothers with children—inherited the degraded mantle of "outdoor relief." First, hostility to ADC increased in some states when voters learned that families with "several children" often received benefits larger than the average earnings of workers "living in the same communities."[11] As a result, at least one midwestern state lowered its benefits. Then, the relief scandals of the late 1940s and early 1950s furthered the equation of public assistance, women, and immorality. A 1947 headline in the *New York Times* proclaimed, "Woman in Mink with $60,000 Lived on Relief in a Hotel"; the "woman in mink" was an unmarried mother. A 1949 *Saturday Evening Post* piece, "Detroit Cracks Down on Relief Chiselers," used only women or families with children as examples; in 1951 another *Saturday Evening Post* article on Oklahoma, "The Relief Chiselers Are Stealing Us Blind," described only abuses under ADC.[12]

But alleged fraud did not yet equate relief with welfare. Nor did welfare yet conjure a narrowly conceived image of morally suspect women. Instead, welfare became controversial in the 1950s because of its correlation with the welfare state—and through the welfare state with socialism. Welfare fell from its protected shelf as one more victim of the cold war.

American critics associated the welfare state with the regimentation, loss of freedom, and heavy-handed state paternalism they equated with socialism. In New York, Governor Dewey warned an audience, "The self-feeding, ever-growing, nobody-can-feed-you-but-us philosophy of the welfare state is not to be confused with the ever-present motive and power of the free modern state to serve its people." A writer in the *Catholic World* argued, "The support of something called welfare now has led to a far more formidable institution, namely the Welfare State, which provides not merely for aid to the helpless but undertakes to enlist all in a great national economic organization supervised by the State. . . . This is Socialism—British Fabian Socialism." An editorial writer in the *Saturday Evening Post* admonished, "Nearly forty years ago, Hilaire Belloc called the Welfare State by a more accurate name, 'the Servile State,' judging correctly that the masses under any managed economy would wind up as slaves—petted and pampered slaves, if they were docile, but slaves in the sense that they would own nothing but a license to earn a living, revokable by someone else." In 1950, members of Congress made speeches titled "The Creeping Shadow of Socialism" and "The Case against the Welfare State."[13]

President Truman deplored the campaign to characterize the "welfare state" as un-American and subversive. In Truman's administration welfare retained its broad and general meaning. His 1948 budget report, for instance, referred to the funds set aside for both Old Age Insurance and Unemployment Insurance as "welfare trust funds." In 1949, he warned against "a new set of scare words" deployed by "the selfish interests" who had opposed his proposals for economic security. Earlier, he pointed out, opponents of Franklin Delano Roosevelt and the New Deal had tried to scare voters with terms like "socialism" and "regimentation." But when these failed to arouse the electorate, critics turned to "bureaucracy" and "bankruptcy." "Now," Truman said, smarting from another lost election, "they're talking about 'collectivism,' and 'statism,' and 'the welfare state.' "[14]

Neither Truman's inclusive use of "welfare" nor his refusal to stigmatize the welfare state prevailed. Instead, by the late 1950s, all the pieces needed for a narrow, derogatory definition of welfare had fallen into place. Public policy had cemented a wall between public assistance and social insurance. Social insurance had drained public assistance of most of the sympathetic or "deserving" poor. Scandals had tainted the image of public assistance, increasingly seen as a program for unmarried mothers and their children. And the cold war association of the welfare state with socialism stripped away the favorable meaning that welfare had held for many Americans. "Welfare" now emerged as a term ready for application to programs that aided the "undeserving poor."

Four related trends accelerated the transmutation of welfare into a synonym for AFDC. First, the social work profession underwent a radical transformation from its origins in helping poor people find food, shelter, clothing, medical care, and jobs to an emphasis on practicing psychotherapy, which increased the divide between public assistance and social insurance. As social workers became increasingly professionalized, public assistance offices were staffed largely by untrained workers; in 1950, only one in twenty-five public assistance workers had a professional degree.[15] The split between social work and the administration of AFDC widened the separation of services from relief and, later, "welfare."

The second trend was the ever-tighter equation of AFDC with race. The proportion of black ADC recipients increased sharply during the late 1940s and 1950s. By 1961, it had reached about 40 percent, which is where it more or less has remained. In some places, the number was much larger, reinforcing the association of ADC and race. The third trend was the rising number of out-of-wedlock births to mothers on AFDC. Between 1950 and 1960, the proportion of children on the ADC rolls who were "illegitimate" increased 25 percent, to 34 percent of black and 10.9 percent of white children—both figures much higher than those for the whole population. The explosive increase of the ADC caseload was the fourth trend. Between 1950 and 1970, the number of AFDC recipients grew by 333 percent—not only as a consequence of the rising number of single mothers but also as a result of Supreme Court decisions and the efforts of welfare rights activists that dramatically increased the proportion of eligible women who actually received AFDC.[16]

By the mid-1960s, the idea of "welfare rights" illustrated the unquestioned equation of welfare with AFDC by the political left as well as the right. In 1966, when poor women joined together to advocate for more generous AFDC benefits and more humane administration of politics, they called themselves the National Welfare Rights Organization. The association of "welfare" with "rights" reflected a strategy designed to link welfare with the civil rights movement and break the lingering association of public assistance with charity and poor relief. The strategy found support in an influential article in the *Yale Law Journal* by Charles Reich, who argued that welfare represented one among several forms of "new property" guaranteed by the Constitution. In a series of major decisions, the U.S. Supreme Court supported the idea of welfare as a right by asserting the entitlement of AFDC recipients to due process and other procedural guarantees of fair and equitable treatment from public authorities. As a result, the proportion of eligible recipients who received benefits rose from about a third in the 1960s to 90 percent in 1971. But the Supreme Court could not abolish the stigma attached to welfare, nor did it make welfare a permanent right.[17]

Instead, the narrow and derogatory definition of welfare directed discussions of public policy along separate tracks. With the exception of Medicare, social insurance programs tied benefits to employment. Their association with work—and the benefits they delivered to the middle class—solidified their hold on public support, and they provided the most generous benefits in America's public welfare state. Welfare, or public assistance, traveled a different route. Tied increasingly to people out of work, unmarried mothers, and people of color, welfare exchanged its early favorable connotation for an association with the undeserving poor. The pejorative connotation of welfare was reinforced by the private sector, which, after World War II, replaced the language of welfare work with that of employee benefits, which no one now calls welfare.

The division of welfare and social insurance along separate discursive as well as policy tracks created fictive distinctions between categories of need and set the beneficiaries of public social provision against one another, leaving them politically vulnerable. The restriction of welfare to the nonworking poor left many workers who were struggling to stay self-sufficient hostile to anyone who appeared to get cash and other benefits without working. More broadly, struggles over welfare directed attention away from the falling wages, growing inequality, and erosion of public benefits that threatened everyone except a fortunate minority. Today, the condemnation of welfare continues to inhibit the development of coherent policy. It permits a president to claim that abolishing AFDC and eliminating entitlements to public assistance represent "ending welfare as we know it," when the most extensive and costly parts of American welfare remain scarcely touched. And it justifies a "welfare reform" that heightens the risks and worsens the poverty that welfare was invented to remedy.

THE AMERICAN WELFARE STATE

By focusing attention on public assistance, the language of welfare has obscured the true size and scope of America's welfare state. In reality, it is neither public nor private, but an enormous structure that combines the two. A public branch with three divisions—public assistance, social insurance, and taxation—intersects in a myriad of ways with a huge private branch divided between the independent sector—charities and social services—and employee benefits. In the 1970s, fissures began to appear in the edifice of this rickety structure; by the 1980s, the fissures had turned into giant cracks. By the end of the twentieth century, the war on dependence, the devolution of authority, and the application of market models to social policy had infiltrated every one of its corners. To understand how this occurred, we must look back at how the welfare state was constructed and elucidate the forces that shook its foundation.

The Architecture of the American Welfare State

The term "welfare state" refers to a collection of programs designed to assure economic security to all citizens by guaranteeing the fundamental necessities of life: food, shelter, medical care, protection in childhood, and support in old age. In America, the usual restriction of the definition of welfare state to government programs mistakenly excludes the vast array of private activities that address economic security and the needs associated with poverty and dependence. Thus, "state," as in welfare state, means not only the agencies of federal, state, and local government; it includes both government funding of nominally private organizations to carry out public tasks and private activities heavily regulated by public authorities. "State" is a shorthand for a web of government programs and the quasi-public, quasi-private organizations they finance and regulate. Understood this way, a vast and intricate American welfare state emerges.[1]

The American welfare state resembles a massive watch that fails to keep very accurate time. Some of its components are rusty and outmoded; others were poorly designed; some work very well. They were fabricated by different craftsmen who usually did not consult with one another; they interact imperfectly; and at times they work at cross-purposes. Neither a coherent whole nor the result of a master plan, the public and private programs of America's welfare state originated at different times and from different sources; they remain loosely coupled at best. Yet together they are the means by which America delivers security and support to its citizens. This modern welfare state touches everyone. Because few people can afford to pay the full cost of their medical care or retirement, some welfare state benefits—Social Security and Medicare—are universal and reach beyond the poor. Other programs extend into the ranks of the employed, where many people earn wages too low to lift themselves above poverty through work alone. The welfare state nonetheless has boundaries, however imprecise. Indeed, even though the national government provides huge subsidies to business and the wealthy, the concept of the welfare state should not include all government benefits.[2] To embrace all government subsidies would rob the term "welfare state" of its historic focus on economic security, poverty, and dependence.

Welfare is as old as the Colonies and as American as Thanksgiving. Public assistance, the original component of America's welfare state, began with early colonial poor laws adapted from British practice. Variously called outdoor relief and poor relief, sometimes just relief, later general relief, and, as we have seen, after the 1960s, welfare, it has proved inescapable and unavoidable; for centuries, all attempts to do away with it have failed. The stigma attached to public assistance has proved equally enduring; its beneficiaries have consistently composed the "undeserving poor."

Public assistance is marked by two other characteristics. First, it has always been, and remains, administered and funded locally rather than federally, at least in part. Originally, counties and towns operating under loose state laws bore almost exclusive responsibility for poor relief. During the nineteenth century, states increased their involvement and oversight. The federal government, however, ran large public assistance programs for only a few years during the Great Depression. The two federal programs introduced in 1935—Aid to Dependent Children and Old Age Assistance—were administered by the states, which were allowed to set benefit levels, and which drew their funding from their own as well as federal treasuries. As a consequence, benefits varied greatly throughout the nation.

Second, public assistance has always been inexpensive. Governments complain about its cost, but it is a bargain compared to other programs, and its low cost is one key to its staying power. Throughout American history, it is hard to imagine a cheaper means of keeping people alive. Though public assistance has caught most of the hostility to welfare, it forms a very small part of the welfare state. In 1995, the total cost of AFDC was $22 billion, of which the federal government paid $12 billion and the states the rest. AFDC amounted to less than 1 percent of the gross domestic product (GDP). Together, in 1995, the three major federal and federal-state public assistance income support programs— AFDC, food stamps, and Supplemental Security Income—amounted to 4.4 percent of the federal budget. About 14 million individuals, more than 9 million of them children, received support from AFDC, 27 million from food stamps, and 6.5 million, roughly 80 percent of whom were disabled, from SSI. (The number of recipients of the program that replaced AFDC fell dramatically after 1996.)[3]

The cost of social insurance programs dwarfs public assistance. Called "insurance" because they require the payment of "premiums" by individuals or employers, these programs provide uniform benefits to everyone who meets fixed criteria (such as age), regardless of income or assets. Public social insurance began with workers' compensation in the early-twentieth century. By the 1930s, a few states had taken tentative steps toward unemployment and old age insurance as well. With the Economic Security Act of 1935, often referred to as the Social Security Act, the federal government launched social insurance as a series of national programs—the first were Unemployment Insurance and Old Age Insurance. In 1956, Congress added disability insurance, and, in 1965, Medicare.

In the mid-1990s, workers' compensation amounted to about $43 billion a year, twice the cost of Aid to Families with Dependent Children. In 1995, unemployment compensation paid benefits to 7.9 million individuals at a cost of $21.3 billion.[4] Medicare covered about 38 million individuals at a cost of $180 billion, and Social Security benefits reached 43.4 million individuals at a cost of $336 billion, or 21.8 percent of the U.S budget of $1.54 trillion. In 1995, Social Security alone cost five times as much as AFDC, food stamps, and SSI combined. Low to begin with, the real value of AFDC benefits had declined steeply—by 47 percent in constant dollars from 1970 to 1995—while Social Security benefits, which are indexed, kept pace with inflation.[5]

Social Security and Medicare are national programs; benefits do not vary by state. All social insurance programs provide much more generous benefits than do any public assistance programs. "Insurance," however, describes them imperfectly because they are financed not by accumulated contributions but primarily with the payroll taxes of currently employed workers. Because they are universal and share, even if inaccurately, the mantle of insurance, they remain by far the most popular programs in America's public welfare state. And they deserve their esteem: Social Security has cut poverty among the elderly by about two-thirds, while Medicare has vastly improved the access of the elderly to health care.[6]

Social insurance programs, like public assistance, also inscribed race and gender hierarchies into public policy. Social Security and unemployment insurance originally excluded agricultural and domestic workers—in other words, most African Americans and women, who found themselves relegated most often to public assistance, while state governments discriminated against blacks in awarding Aid to Dependent Children. Despite the expansion of "covered" occupations, unemployment insurance continued to discriminate against women and blacks, penalizing them for their customary work histories. And Social Security still tilts away from equitable treatment for married women and widows. Current formulas do not credit the contributions of many previously employed married women toward higher benefits, and they maintain a very large gap between the benefits of couples and of survivors. Nevertheless, Social Security has worked a revolution in the experience of elderly women, who compose the majority of its beneficiaries. African Americans confront the irony that programs that serve them less adequately than whites nevertheless assure many a level of regular support previously unknown and remain the only shield between them and economic disaster.[7]

The public welfare state's use of taxation to promote economic security is much less well known and less appreciated or disliked than either social insurance or public assistance. With good reason, political scientist Christopher Howard calls taxation the "hidden welfare state." The tax code delivers benefits indirectly through incentives and directly through tax credits and deductions. Employers who offer health and retirement benefits are allowed to deduct their expenses from their incomes. (Of course, this benefits all workers, not just those with low incomes.) The tax code is designed to stimulate the construction of low-income housing and jobs by offering developers and businesses tax credits, such as the Low Income Tax Credit, worth $495.5 million in 1994. Tax-based incentives also underlie recent urban policies designed to revive inner cities by attracting businesses and investment. In 2000, Republicans proposed using tax credits to extend health insurance to many of the uninsured. The federal Work Opportunity Tax Credit, the

Welfare to Work Tax Credit, and various other state subsidies and tax credits all encourage employers to hire welfare recipients. In 1993, the cost of "tax breaks for social purposes"—cash equivalents and deductions for pensions and private social benefits—was more than twice the amount spent on AFDC.[8]

The Earned Income Tax Credit is a dramatic example. It delivers benefits directly: individuals receive checks for the amount owed to them by the federal government. As a result of President Bill Clinton's expansion of EITC, in 1996 the federal government predicted that 18 million people would claim the credit, at a cost of $25.1 billion. The EITC, which paid money to more people and at a greater cost than that of AFDC, emerged as the federal government's primary means of boosting the working poor over the poverty line. With virtually no opposition, the Clinton administration engineered a massive increase in an income transfer program at a time when other forms of social welfare faced only real or proposed cutbacks.[9]

The private welfare state is as complicated and varied as the public one. The charity and social services sphere, or "independent sector," encompasses everything from small soup kitchens to the massive Catholic Charities USA, with an annual budget of about $2 billion. It also includes foundations, social services like Meals-on-Wheels and foster care, and organizations devoted to single issues, such as the American Heart Association. Although the independent sector has never met all the needs of poor or otherwise dependent Americans, its essential components—charity, voluntarism, and philanthropy—can claim a long history and an essential role in American social welfare. In the mid-1990s, the best estimate put the independent sector's annual cost at $568 billion (roughly the cost of Social Security and Medicare combined) and the number of its institutions at more than one million.[10]

Employee benefits exceed even those of the independent sector. Most Americans receive their health care and part of their retirement income through this private welfare state. To be sure, benefits contingent on employment and, to some extent, on the goodwill or enlightened self-interest of employers are an imperfect replacement for universal public entitlements. But they amount to significant spending that in other countries often comes from the public treasury. International comparisons of U.S. social spending frequently fail to include private benefits. At 7.82 percent of GDP, America's 1993 "voluntary private social expenditures" far exceeded those of other advanced nations: 3.19 percent in the United Kingdom, 0.97 percent in Sweden, and 1.47 percent in Germany. The importance of the private welfare state cannot be underestimated, not only because of its impact on the security and well-being of Americans, but also because of its cost—in 1992, $824 billion.[11]

American social policy has always carried out public purposes through private agencies. In the early-nineteenth century the state of New York contributed public funds to a private philanthropy for the education of New York City's poor children. Some state governments tried to meet the growing demand for secondary education by chartering and subsidizing private academies. State governments paid private orphanages to care for needy children and hospitals to treat the sick. They granted private agencies—the Society for the Prevention of Cruelty to Children, for instance—police powers to intervene in cases of suspected child abuse and neglect. American government, in Alan Wolfe's trenchant phrase, has always operated partly as a "franchise state." It is the way the nation builds missiles and delivers social services; increasingly, it is the way it punishes convicted criminals. Indeed, in recent years social service agencies and charities have drawn even closer to public authorities as providers for the state. Nor is the private welfare state of employee benefits exempt from government influence: enormously complicated regulations and legislation govern the administration of private pension plans and other benefits, such as health and family leave policies.[12]

America's welfare state not only retains a mixed economy, it also remains remarkably local and decentralized. Recent welfare reform not only preserved the vast variation in benefit levels among states, it encouraged yet more variety by devolving significant authority to state governments, which, in turn, are at liberty to cede much of the administration and rule setting for public assistance to counties. Although Social Security, Medicare, food stamps, and the Earned Income Tax Credit are national programs, two crucial components of social insurance—workers' compensation and unemployment compensation—are partially or wholly state programs that differ widely in eligibility rules and benefits. Medicaid, a key component of the public assistance safety net, is also a joint federal-state program that allows states discretion in setting benefits and reimbursement amounts. Block grants for child welfare are another example of the way the federal government promotes local variation in the welfare state. And, of course, the private welfare state provides benefits and services through literally millions of agencies and employers, which, despite federal and state regulations and the strings attached to grants, retain a great deal of autonomy.

Its links to employment, as well as its decentralization, distinguish the American welfare state from its counterparts in other industrial nations.

For most nonelderly Americans, access to health care depends on having a job with medical benefits, or being a dependent of someone who does. In no other modern industrial nation is health care an earned privilege rather than a human right. Throughout American history, welfare reformers have tried to couple public assistance and private charity with employment by devising work tests to separate the deserving from the undeserving poor. Nineteenth-century Charity Organization Societies sent men who applied for help out to cut wood or break stone. Poorhouses tried, without much success, to put their inmates to work. During years of great industrial upheaval, public officials and the leaders of private philanthropy demonized out-of-work men as lazy tramps. For many years, the opposite was true for working mothers: advocates of mothers' pensions in the years 1910–19 and Aid to Dependent Children in the 1930s hoped public benefits would permit mothers to stay at home with their children, or at least work only part-time. They viewed full-time work among mothers as a source of family pathology, not a means for overcoming it. In recent years, of course, all this has changed. With the passage of "welfare reform" in 1996, the links between employment and public assistance tightened. Welfare reform transmuted survival itself into a privilege contingent on work.[13]

The American welfare state also stands out for what it lacks. America has what I have called a "semi-welfare state"; others have referred to it as incomplete or truncated or have called America a welfare laggard. Whatever the label, the evidence is clear and familiar: America, unlike other advanced nations, lacks national health insurance. It has no family allowance. It permits more of its children to remain in poverty than does any comparable country. It offers unmarried mothers less help with either day-to-day survival or the transition to independence than do most other industrial nations. It provides far fewer of its citizens with publicly supported housing than do European nations, and it restricts what Europeans calls "social housing" to the very poor. It spends far less on active labor market policies, such as job training and job creation. In 1990, among eight advanced countries, only Japan, at 11.2 percent of GDP, ranked lower than the United States at 11.5 percent in public outlays on pensions, health insurance, and other income maintenance. For France, spending amounted to 23.5 percent of GDP and for Germany, 19.3 percent. Although European nations have recently moved in the direction of American practice, the distinction between continents remains unmistakable, at least for the present. With the United States considered as 1, the 1993 ratios of public social spending were:

United Kingdom   1.50
Sweden   2.54
Germany   1.91

However, with private social benefits included, the ratios drop and the United States seems less of an outsider, although it still ranks last compared with advanced European nations.

United Kingdom   1.16
Sweden   1.73
Germany   1.35

Including tax deductions and credits would reduce the disparity even more.[14] Still, the United States remains distinct because it spends less on social programs and because it calibrates the balance between public and private in a different way than European nations do.

The results of public intervention in labor markets highlight other differences between U.S. and European social policy. In the 1980s and 1990s, U.S. unemployment rates remained consistently lower than those in most western European countries. This enviable situation, it was usually argued, resulted from the lighter hand of government and freer markets—specifically, the far less regulated American labor market and a low and falling rate of unionization. In Europe, the theory went, unionization kept wages artificially high and depressed employment, and welfare states that influenced the supply and demand of labor had the perverse effect of increasing unemployment.

Contrary to this conventional story, however, official unemployment rates in the United States appear lower only because they omit inmates of prisons and jails. The United States incarcerates a far higher proportion of its population than does any western European country. The average rate of incarceration in sixteen Organization for Economic Development and Cooperation countries in 1992–93 was 78 per 100,000 population. In the United States it was 519—1,947 for blacks and 306 for whites. This extraordinary U.S. figure bears no relation to differences in violent crime rates. Rather, it reflects changes in criminal justice practices, including tougher sentencing and the criminalization of drug-related activity. By correcting unemployment for incarceration, Bruce Western and Katherine Beckett have shown that the U.S. rate rises by about 2 percentage points. This corrected rate approaches rates in some European countries and exceeds those of others. Factoring in incarceration also raises the rate of joblessness and qualifies the image of economic recovery in the 1990s. About 40 percent of African American men over the age of twenty have been out of the labor force at all times during the last two decades, through prosperous times as well as recessions.

This high rate of incarceration does more than mask real unemployment and joblessness; it contributes to both by reducing the job prospects of ex-convicts. Not surprisingly, they have more difficulty finding work, and they often end up back in prison. This perverse effect of imprisonment proves especially long lasting for youth. It is true that European welfare states reduce labor force participation by making it possible to live without work. But in the process they also redistribute income and increase equality. In Europe, tax and transfer policies lift about half the nonelderly poor out of poverty. In the United States, where the figure is much lower, the dynamic is reversed. There, the impact of incarceration registers most heavily on those with the least power in the labor market—young, unskilled minority men, who are imprisoned at a far higher rate than that of any other group. As a consequence, America's de facto labor market policy, administered through the penal system, heightens poverty and increases inequality.[15]

Still, the frustrating limits that hobble America's welfare state should not obscure its achievements. Compared to the situation at the start of the last century, public programs have dramatically alleviated the consequences of poverty and dependence. In America's cities, millions of women and men who at the start of the twentieth century would have suffered desperate poverty now, at the turn of the next century, live with a sense of security and in modest comfort. Others, although they remain poor, find survival incomparably more assured than they would have a century ago. Without Social Security and Medicare, old people suffered extraordinary poverty and lacked access to adequate health care. Without AFDC or food stamps, single mothers with children could only beg a pittance from the suspicious agents of charity. Without unemployment insurance, workers' compensation, and disability insurance, employees injured on the job or thrown out of work lacked any public source of assistance other than tiny, sporadic amounts of relief, accommodation in a poorhouse, or temporary lodging in a police station or homeless shelter; they found it hard, if not impossible, to locate private charity, which remained uncertain and inadequate. Poverty and dependence in America have never been easy or pleasant to endure, but a century ago they were immeasurably worse.[16]

Welfare and the Conservative Ascendancy

The resurgence of conservatism in late-twentieth-century politics and culture inspired attacks on the huge, imperfectly articulated American welfare state. Building on a demographic base in the South and the sub-urbs, conservatism responded to the anger and confusion of ordinary Americans experiencing economic insecurity and a new racial order. The movement drew strength from its affiliation with evangelical and fundamentalist Protestantism, from ideas disseminated by conservative think tanks underwritten by big money, and from the perceived failures of government and the collapse of communism.[17]

Conservative policy was one among the possible responses to real problems. Its ascendance signaled first of all a victory for international business. In the 1970s, relentless international competition forced busi-nesses to reduce costs by downsizing, restraining wages, attacking unions, reducing benefits, and pressuring governments to cut back on welfare states. The welfare state, they believed, increased the costs of business by raising taxes and forcing business to raise wages to attract workers who found an alternate source of support in public benefits. All over the globe—in Europe, Asia, and Latin America as well as in the United States—the need to control the cost of labor in a global economy ranked high among the influences prompting nations to redefine their welfare states.[18]

National budgets and changing demographics also put pressure on welfare states. The problem was worldwide. In Europe the cost of increased unemployment challenged the fiscal capacity of governments to continue current levels of social spending. Although unemployment was lower in the United States, the situation paralleled Europe's. There, too, a similar contradiction between escalating need and seemingly unsustainable expense overburdened the welfare state, threatening to raise taxes. In addition, a demographic crisis loomed: as the population aged, the number of elderly citizens in need of support grew faster than the number of workers whose taxes supported them. Even though the relative size of the aged population was smaller in the United States than in Europe, its projected cost drove attempts to redesign the welfare state's most expensive programs: Social Security, Medicare, and Medicaid.[19]

In the United States, the cost of both hot and cold war also drew funds away from social programs. Despite his promise of "guns and butter," President Lyndon Johnson's escalation of the Vietnam War in the 1960s undermined the War on Poverty. In the 1970s, the military buildup occa-sioned by competition with the Soviet Union drained funds that might have been spent on domestic programs. In the 1980s, the Reagan admin-istration's "Star Wars" initiative and its massive military spending again diverted limited federal funds away from the welfare state.

In the same years, the economic stress felt by ordinary workers fueled a hostility toward welfare and the dependent poor, driving politics in a conservative direction. Resentments welling up among traditionally Democratic voters led many of them to support George Wallace and, later, Ronald Reagan. As income inequality widened after the early 1970s, workers found themselves running harder just to stay even. With their real wages falling, families needed multiple jobs and income from both husbands and wives. Hundreds of thousands found themselves laid off as a result of downsizing and restructuring. They watched as jobs migrated to Asia, Mexico, or anywhere wages remained lower, and they resented government "handouts" that seemed to reward nonwork and loose morals. Women forced by economic necessity to work, even when they had young children, could not understand why their taxes went to support women who stayed at home.[20]

Desegregation and affirmative action added race to the brew of resentments. In many places, whites objected when court-ordered busing brought black children to their neighborhood schools or forced their own children to travel to distant schools. They watched angrily when federal and local governments used civil rights laws, housing subsidies, and public assistance to support blacks who wanted to move into their neighborhoods. They identified welfare, public housing, and housing subsidies with minorities and wondered at the justice of these benefits when they worked so hard to pay their own mortgages, rent, and grocery bills. White workers thought themselves disadvantaged because, they believed, less qualified blacks were hired or promoted in their place. Government programs associated with liberals or Democrats became the villains, and blue-collar workers moved decisively to the right, where conservative politicians played on their fears. Instead of directing anger at the wealthy and powerful, the fusion of race and taxes deflected the hostility of hard-pressed lower- and middle-class Americans away from the source of their deteriorating economic position and toward disadvantaged minorities—and, in the process, eroded support for the welfare state. This working-class move to the right did not confine itself to the United States, as the popularity of Margaret Thatcher in Britain and the rise of right-wing populist political movements in continental Europe reveal. There, too, racial animus, directed mainly toward immigrant workers and their families, joined economic insecurity to propel politics rightward and weaken popular support for welfare states.[21]

The increasing prominence of the Sunbelt in electoral politics strengthened conservatism's influence. Southern and western conservatism arose not only from lower- and middle-class whites angry at competition from blacks, scared by economic insecurity, and upset at the transformation of the old racial order. It also received strong support,

and leadership, from business interests alienated by Democratic economic and natural resource policies.[22] Middle-class suburbanization in
the Sunbelt—indeed, throughout the nation—also fueled the new conservative politics. Many suburbanites were the children of white Catholic
immigrants, who were angry at busing, threatened by affirmative action,
and offended by the behaviors they associated with African American
newcomers to their cities. "Suburbia," reported political commentator
Kevin Phillips, "did not take kindly to rent subsidies, school balance
schemes, growing Negro migration or rising welfare costs. . . . The great
majority of middle-class suburbanites opposed racial or welfare innovations." Together, the Sunbelt and the suburbs provided the demographic and political base for the new conservatism, assured the
rightward drift of politics among both Republicans and Democrats, and
reinforced hostility to public social programs that served the poor—especially where those poor were thought to be mainly black or Hispanic.

As the writing on the political wall became clearer, Democrats, eager
to win back business support, "acquiesced in, and in many cases helped
promulgate, the right turn in public policy," as Thomas Ferguson and
Joel Rogers put it in *Right Turn.* By the 1990s, no administration that
wanted to remain in office could propose higher taxes for social spending,[23] and with the New Democrats led by President Bill Clinton, the
campaign to redefine the welfare state had become truly bipartisan.

The politics of evangelical Protestants intensified the movement to
redefine the welfare state. In the 1970s, appalled at government support
for what they considered rampant immorality and threats to funding for
Christian schools, they entered politics. With remarkable speed, they
built an infrastructure of grass-roots organizations and media outlets.
Although they focused on social and moral issues, they made common
cause with free-market conservatives and became a powerful force in the
movement of American politics to the right and in the attack on the welfare state.[24]

Historically, evangelicals had for the most part stayed out of politics.
Before the early 1970s, conservative Christians (a term that includes
evangelicals and fundamentalists) distrusted politics, and studies
showed even an inverse relation between religious conservatism and
involvement in political activities. All this reversed in the 1970s, when
conservative Christians entered politics largely to protect families. Only
through politics, they came to believe, could they guard their interests
and reverse the moral corruption of the nation. Welfare, they thought,
weakened the institution of family by encouraging out-of-wedlock births,
rewarding sex outside of marriage, and allowing men to escape the
responsibilities of fatherhood.[25] Although the Christian right drew its

real inspiration from social and moral issues—abortion, school prayer, the teaching of evolution, gay civil rights, and the Equal Rights Amendment—it also forged links with free-market conservatives and conservative opponents of the Soviet Union. Indeed, militant anticommunism fused the strands of the conservative movement around opposition to a common enemy.[26]

Fiscal conservatives won the support of middle-class fundamentalists, first, by linking social programs to moral issues and, second, by appealing to conservative Christians whose "economic fortunes depend more on keeping tax rates low by reducing government spending than on the social welfare programs that poorer fundamentalists might desire," argued Robert Wuthnow and Matthew P. Lawson. The result was a fundamentalist politics opposed to the social and moral tendencies of modern government "but in support of economic policies favorable to the middle-class"—a movement crucial for building both the electoral and financial base of conservatism.[27]

Evangelicals and fundamentalists constitute a powerful political force: in the South, they make up about a third of the white electorate; in the North, a little more than a tenth. In 1980, a leading evangelical strategist, Paul Weyrich, urged evangelical ministers to mobilize their congregations to vote for Republican candidates, especially Ronald Reagan, who had asked evangelicals to help win him the presidency that year. With the support of evangelicals, the New Right won stunning electoral victories throughout the country. By the 1990s, evangelicals and fundamentalists constituted the largest and most influential grass-roots movement in American politics.[28] Its great breakthrough came with the 1994 congressional elections, when, for the first time, a majority of evangelicals identified themselves as Republicans and only one-third claimed to be Democrats. The Christian right, according to one estimate, mobilized 4 million activists and reached 50 million voters. The outcome of the election proved the success of its organizing: the Christian right supported candidates in at least 120 contests for the House of Representatives, and its candidates won 55 percent of them.[29] They were a crucial element in the Congress that voted to "end welfare as we know it."

Political and social movements need money as well as passion. The cash to pay for the rightward movement of American politics and culture and bankroll the attack on the welfare state derived primarily from two sources. Through political action committees the militant right marshaled money for use in elections, referenda, and lobbying, and through the support of nonprofit research centers—"think tanks"—it gathered funds for the production and dissemination of ideas. With funding from conservative foundations and corporations, older institutes reorganized, while newer ones formed to challenge liberalism. The American Enterprise Institute, founded in 1943, reorganized in 1953; the Hoover Institution, started in 1919, severed formal ties with Stanford University in 1959; the Heritage Foundation, originally supported by Colorado brewer Joseph Coors, opened in 1973; and the libertarian Cato Institute opened in 1977.[30]

Within a year of its founding, the Heritage Foundation received funds from eighty-seven corporations and large contributions from six or seven major foundations. Along with other conservative think tanks—notably the Hudson Institute, the American Enterprise Institute, the Adolph Coors Foundation, and Empower America—Heritage worked hard to discredit the welfare state. Concentrated funding streams linked conservative foundations, think tanks, and public policy scholars in a tight and powerful network—a web of foundations, fund-raising organizations, direct mail operations, publications, and mass media connections. The same funders nourished the development of conservative policy on a number of related issues: English only, immigration reform, affirmative action, welfare, tort reform, and campus wars over educational and cultural issues. From 1992 to 1994 twelve conservative foundations with assets of $1.1 billion awarded $300 million in grants. The top five conservative groups worked with revenues of $77 million in 1995, compared to $18.6 million for "their eight political equivalents on the left."[31]

Conservative think tanks not only produce ideas—they market them. The Manhattan Institute funded Charles Murray's anti–welfare state polemic, *Losing Ground*, and spent heavily to promote it to the press and public. In the 1970s, metaphors of "science and disinterested research," prominent during the early history of think tanks, gave way to market metaphors. According to historian James Smith, "marketing and promotion" did "more to change the think tanks' definition of their role (and the public's perception of them)" than did anything else. Conservative funders paid "meticulous attention to the entire 'knowledge production process,' " wrote Smith, which they portrayed as a "conveyor belt" stretching from "academic research to marketing and mobilization, from scholars to activists," and they developed "sophisticated and effective media outreach strategies." In 1995 alone, Citizens for a Sound Economy "produced more than 130 policy papers, conducted 50 different advertising campaigns, appeared on 175 radio and television shows, placed 235 op-ed articles, and received coverage in more than 4,000 news articles." In 1989, the Heritage Foundation spent 36 percent of its budget on marketing and 15 percent on fund-raising, including direct mail to 160,000 individual supporters. Liberal organizations did not begin to match the outreach efforts of conservatives, whose ideas, often unchallenged and based on inaccurate data, powerfully shaped public opinion about politics, the economy, and the welfare state.[32]

The right circumvented the liberal politics of most leading social scientists in the United States first by channeling "lavish amounts of support on scholars willing to orient their research" in conservative directions, and second by adopting a "grow-your-own approach." Conservatives funded "law students, student editors, and campus leaders with scholarships, leadership training, and law and economics classes aimed at ensuring that the next generation of academic leaders has an even more conservative cast than the current one."[33]

In their attack on the welfare state, conservative foundations and think tanks drew on a body of ideas articulated with force and clarity. Martin Anderson, a Republican economist and public policy expert who had worked in both the Nixon and Reagan administrations, described Reagan's 1980 election and subsequent events as the political results of an international intellectual movement that had started in the United States in the 1950s and 1960s. Anderson described the movement to Godfrey Hodgson as "an intellectual revolution moving with the power and speed of a glacier"—proof that "ideas do move the world."[34]

The new conservatism wove together three intellectual strands—economic, social, and nationalist. Its economics stressed free markets and minimal government regulation. Its social impulse led toward the restoration of social order and private morals by authoritarian government. Conservatism's nationalist streak favored heavy public spending on the military. It focused on both the enemy without—the Soviet Union and communism—and the enemy within—anything or anyone that facilitated the socialist takeover of America. Incompatibilities, even contradictions, had threatened to keep the strands of conservatism separate, unable to twist together into a powerful and unified force.[35] The history of conservative thought tells the story of how these incompatible strands fused into a powerful intellectual movement.

Conservative thought found acceptance because it resonated with interests, fears, and hopes as varied and contradictory as the strands that composed it. Some of these have been discussed already: the economic strains on ordinary Americans, the anger and fear aroused by the end of the racial order in the South and affirmative action in the North, the needs of international business, the wage pressures felt by American firms, and the resurgent evangelical Protestantism that spread outward from the South. Hodgson points as well to the belief in American exceptionalism—a patriotism violated, conservatives believed, by the political left, which seemed to take pleasure in the denigration of America. He also stresses the odd populism that fed conservative thought: America's troubles had been brought on by elite easterners who disdained the values and interests of ordinary Americans. A true conservatism would return government to the people.[36]

Conservative thought gained strength, too, from the widespread sense that the federal government's massive social programs launched in the 1960s had failed. Aside from higher taxes, more poverty, dying cities, increased crime, and moral rot, what was there to show for the money and effort? The sense that federal social policy had failed was reinforced by a rejection of the Keynesian economic theories that had justified social spending, an antipathy to politics, and a distrust of government, including the large bureaucracies that administered social programs and institutions. The theoretical attack on activist government, led by University of Chicago economist Milton Friedman, brought great sophistication to the cause of the economic conservatives. "By 1980 the climate of economic thinking in the United States," reports Hodgson, "had changed utterly from the orthodoxy of 1965." Keynesian economics, which had sustained the welfare state, appeared dead.[37]

On a more popular level, distrust of government found expression in Charles Murray's enormously influential *Losing Ground* (1984)—sometimes referred to as the Reagan administration's new bible. Murray, who argued for the withdrawal of government from social welfare, assaulted welfare from a market-based, libertarian, antigovernment perspective. Despite massive government social spending since 1965, he contended, both poverty and antisocial behavior—crime and out-of-wedlock births—had increased. Neither could be traced to economic conditions. Rather, they resulted from rational responses to the perverse, short-term economic incentives built into federal welfare policy. His solution lay in changing the incentives by ending welfare.

Unlike Murray, Lawrence Mead, author of *Beyond Entitlement: The Social Obligations of Citizenship* (1986)—the other major conservative book on welfare published during the 1980s—justified big government in conservative terms. His preferred philosophers were Hobbes, Burke, and Tocqueville, not Adam Smith; he focused on society, not the individual; and he worried more about moral order than liberty. Mead advocated enforced social obligations for the poor. The major problem with government social programs, claimed Mead, lay in their permissiveness, not their size. Although he wanted to inject people into the marketplace, not shield them from it, he still stressed the tutelary role of government. "Government is really a mechanism by which people force themselves to serve and obey *each other* in necessary ways." Social order demanded that government "must take over the socializing role."[38]

Popular conservative books and articles exuded confidence that seemingly intractable national problems could be solved with common sense, sound values, and faith in the capacity of ordinary Americans. At a time when unemployment and inflation together produced a new phenomenon—"stagflation"; when the nation reeled from the humiliation inflicted by Iran's seizure of American hostages; when feminism and affirmative action seemed to threaten traditional family values and opportunity structures; and when crime appeared to rule city streets, the optimism of conservative thought proved one of its most potent appeals. Liberals, by contrast, appeared unable to offer a new vision of America's future, a prescription free of complex government, that could rise above a gloomy and incapacitating account of the structural origins of America's interconnected and intractable problems.

Ronald Reagan's successful 1980 presidential campaign wove together the three strands of conservatism: the social, economic, and nationalist. Ronald Reagan may have used Murray as his bible on welfare reform, but the major welfare legislation of his term in office owed much more to Mead. Reagan's cheerful theoretical eclecticism characterized his administration, and his optimism reflected the upbeat tone of much conservative literature. Reagan attacked the perceived excesses of liberalism, championed the replacement of the public by the private sector, and responded to the anger at the decline of America's international power and prestige. The collapse of the Soviet Union, which discredited communism, appeared to vindicate both his foreign policy and his distrust of the state. It seemed to offer living proof that the ideas championed by conservatives were destined to sweep all others into history's trash. The reality was more complex, as subsequent events revealed. The unrestrained capitalism that invaded the former Soviet bloc showed the dislocation and misery that unbridled markets and the shredding of social safety nets could create. Still, in the United States, not only communism and socialism but social democracy and its offspring, the welfare state, seemed anachronisms, vestiges of a discredited and outmoded political philosophy.

The Soviet collapse did not prove an unmixed blessing for conservatives, however. Hostility toward the Soviet Union and communism had given conservatism an enemy that intensified commitment to its cause and fused its internal contradictions into a single movement. With the common enemy removed, what else could provide the glue, the focus, and the energy? To some extent, Islam took the place of communism, and Iraq and Iran replaced the Soviet Union. But they were enemies of a lesser order. Republicans lacked a great enemy, the strain of arguments over strategy eroded their unity, and the Democratic Party, captured by the New Democrats, adopted many of their key ideas. As a result, the Republican Party began to fracture as the old strain between social and economic conservatives, papered over but never mended, reappeared.[39]

Whatever happens to the Republican Party should not obscure the larger story: the ascendancy of conservative ideas in American politics at the close of the twentieth century. The New Democrats, led by a Southern Baptist president and vice president, advocated smaller government, encouraged the devolution of federal authority to the states, asserted the superiority of markets, and joined the war on dependence. Thirty years earlier, it would have been unthinkable that a Democratic president would sign a bill ending the entitlement of the poorest Americans to public assistance. With great clarity, President Bill Clinton's endorsement of the "welfare reform" legislation of 1996 signaled the erosion of the principles that had guided the Democrats since the New Deal.[40] Republicans may have lost the battles for the presidency in 1992 and 1996, but conservatives had won the war. One consequence was the redefinition of America's welfare state.

Dependence, Devolution, and Markets

In the 1980s public social policy coalesced around three great objectives that began to redefine the American welfare state. The first was the war to end dependence—not only the dependence of young unmarried mothers on welfare, but all forms of dependence on public and private support and on the paternalism of employers. The second was to devolve authority, that is, to transfer power from the federal government to the states, from states to counties, and from the public to the private sector. The third was the application of market models to social policy. Everywhere, the market has triumphed as the template for a redesigned welfare state. None of these forces originated in the 1980s, but in those years they burst through older tendencies in public policy and joined to form a powerful tide. As a result, with only a few exceptions, political arguments about the welfare state now revolve more around details than great principles.

In the brave new market-governed world, dependence—reliance for support on someone else—signifies failure and the receipt of unearned benefits. Dependents clog the working of markets; they interfere with relations between productive, working citizens. The tendency of capitalism, as Harry Braverman argued in his dystopian account of the future of work, is to clear the market of all but active and able citizens.[41] This reaction against dependence has worked its way into every corner of the welfare state.

Historically, dependence has had various meanings: legal, domestic, economic, and behavioral. According to philosopher Nancy Fraser and historian Linda Gordon, current-day discussions of American social policy, however, have narrowed dependence to stand for the reliance of poor unmarried mothers on public assistance. This new idea of dependence and the "cultural panic" that surrounds it have been reinforced by the association of dependence with sickness in medical and psychological literature, the equation of dependence with immaturity, especially among women, and the American Psychiatric Association's 1980 identification of Dependent Personality Disorder.[42]

In the 1980s and 1990s, political debate reflected this heightened and widespread anxiety about dependence. "Dependency at the bottom of society," writes political scientist Lawrence Mead, "not economic equality is the issue of the day." Dependency politics arose out of Americans' preoccupation with the "nonworking underclass" responsible for "the decay of the inner city."[43] Mead accurately identified a note in American politics that grew louder and more shrill in the debates over welfare reform, but, like Fraser and Gordon, he missed the hostility to dependence that also has surfaced in attempts to reengineer employee benefits, health care, and Social Security by forcing individuals to rely on themselves rather than on the unhealthy paternalism of employers, charity, or the state.

The war on dependence coincided with a new emphasis on the devolution of authority. In the 1960s, an earlier assault on centralization had attacked the great educational fortresses that oversaw school systems. This movement toward educational devolution sputtered and nearly died of some of its own excesses. By the late 1980s, however, amid growing dissatisfaction with the performance of urban schools, it gained renewed strength. All over the country, school systems granted authority to individual schools as reformers pressed hard for autonomy, which they sometimes, as in Chicago, won to a stunning degree. As corporations realized the disadvantages of large size and command-and-control management, they also decentralized decision making to local sites and reorganized along more flexible lines.[44]

Across the nation, state governors also championed devolution. Influenced by market models and frustrated at the rising costs of public assistance, they chafed at federal regulations that, they said, violated the constitutional separation of powers and prevented them from reforming welfare. Everywhere, "one size fits all" became one of the harshest criticisms of social policies and programs. In the 1980s the federal government began to acquiesce and transfer to states many of the services it had funded since the 1970s, leaving states to pay for them as they could. The

1996 welfare bill replaced the federal entitlement to public assistance with block grants to the states, which allowed the states great latitude in designing their own welfare rules and benefits. State governments, in turn, devolved varying degrees of authority—in some states a great deal of authority—to counties to plan and implement their own welfare systems. They also increasingly handed the administration of public assistance and prison management to both nonprofit and for-profit private entities.

The growing reliance on market models in public policy, the third great force redefining the welfare state, also encouraged devolution. In markets, points out economics writer Robert Kuttner, prices rise and fall "instantly and change continually, as they adjust to shifting tastes and costs. . . . Markets epitomize decentralized, atomized decision-making." The values associated with markets have never drifted far from the center of American public policy. What marks the post-1980 period is their hegemony—their replacement of alternative templates in both the public and private sectors. In recent years, writes Kuttner in *Everything for Sale*, "enthusiasts of markets have claimed that most human activity can and should be understood as nothing but a series of markets, and that outcomes would be improved if constraints on market behavior were removed. . . . A more complex view of society has given way to the claim that most issues boil down to material incentives, and most social problems are best resolved by constructing or enhancing markets. And, indeed, fewer people today enjoy protections against the uglier face of the market, or social income as a right of citizenship. More aspects of human life are on the auction block. Champions of market society insist that all of this makes us better off."[45]

"The move to the market is beyond doubt a truly global phenomenon," assert Daniel Yergin and Joseph Stanislaw. During most of the twentieth century, they point out, the state remained ascendant, "extending its domain further and further into what had been the territory of the market." The mixed economy that resulted remained "virtually unchallenged" until the early 1970s, when, with stunning speed, a reaction set in. By the 1990s, government was in retreat everywhere as the focus shifted from "market failure" to "government failure," the consequences that occur "when the state becomes too expansive and too ambitious and seeks to be the main player, rather than a referee, in the economy." This "decamping of the state from the commanding heights marks a great divide between the twentieth and twenty-first centuries."[46]

There are many varieties of markets. All of them, however, are systems of exchange guided, for the most part, by a set of underlying assumptions. Markets assume rationality: rational individuals act in ways that serve their self-interest. Their collective and unimpeded interactions, the theory goes, yield the greatest public good. Because markets enhance both individual freedom of choice and the optimal allocation of scarce resources, they are the ultimate source of liberty and prosperity. It follows—the extreme version of market philosophy—that governments should interfere with markets as little as possible; the ideal government policy toward markets is laissez-faire.[47] Although the welfare economics literature offers a much more sophisticated view of markets and the rationale for regulation, this stark and unqualified version permeates discussions of the welfare state in politics and the media.

In the United States the shift from government to market found bipartisan support. President Clinton's 1997 *Economic Report* emphasized the "advantages of markets" and the circumscribed, if still crucial, role of government. "At the center of the U.S. Economy," claims the report, stands the market: "vibrant competition among profit-maximizing firms has enhanced economic efficiency and generated innovation, giving the United States one of the highest standards of living in the world." Markets process information more efficiently than government, which cannot "duplicate and utilize the massive amount of information exchanged and acted upon daily by the millions of participants in the marketplace." At the same time, markets provide incentives unavailable to governments. "In private markets, buyers and sellers directly reap the benefits and bear the costs of their demand and supply decisions." Incentives not only shape the uses of resources, they encourage the development of innovations that increase efficiency and "new products that raise living standards." Governments, therefore, should limit their role in the private economy. "Initiatives to increase our economy's reliance on markets, and to improve the efficiency of regulation through market mechanisms, reflect an awareness of the tremendous benefit that market forces can bring to bear by employing private incentives to achieve social goals."[48] "Social goals" here include the objectives of the welfare state.

Markets exist in an uneasy tension with welfare states. The act of exchange at the center of the market experience means "that no market goods are available without some effort or sacrifice." Nothing, in other words, is free. The idea that an individual should receive unearned benefits contradicts the core assumptions on which markets rest. The recent application of market models to public policy is an attempt to resolve the contradiction between markets and welfare states by linking benefits more closely to employment, reducing dependence, and privatizing services.[49]

Legislators, journalists, public officials, and representatives of the private welfare state all now apply market models to public policy, with varying degrees of rigor. While economists attempt to work out the implications with mathematical exactness, public officials more often rely on superficial versions of market models that turn into little more than vacuous slogans. Everywhere, though, the language of the market dominates public policy. It has met stiffest resistance in public education, although advocates of vouchers and private school choice have moved from the fringe to the respectable center of debate.[50] It has found more success throughout the welfare state.

The language of the welfare state and public policy too often reifies markets. Markets appear as outside history, culture, and social structure—a force of nature ineluctably leading to a single inevitable set of results. This easy reification obscures the variability of markets that results from the nature of commodities and forms of capital, relations of power between participants, cultural restraints that define what may and may not be sold, and the conditions under which exchanges may take place. "The human economy," wrote the economic historian and social theorist Karl Polanyi and his colleagues, remains "embedded and enmeshed in institutions, economic and non-economic. The inclusion of the non-economic is vital. For religion or government may be as important to the structure and functioning of the economy as monetary institutions or the availability of tools and machines themselves that lighten the load." The literature of economic sociology explores the rich complexity of markets—current economic sociologists view "their primary task to be to show that markets do not simply consist of homogeneous spaces where buyers and sellers enter into exchange with one another"—but political discussions of the welfare state and other public policy issues remain by and large content with loose metaphors and abstract assumptions that rationalize the actions of those who hold power.[51]

Narrowly applied, market models naturally favor certain answers to key questions about the welfare state—questions about the preferred source of benefits and services, the mechanisms for assuring quality and controlling costs, the criteria for deciding who receives help, the role of guarantees and safety nets, and the source of the ultimate responsibility for ensuring economic security. According to market logic, benefits should originate with private, rather than public, agencies wherever possible, and competition between providers should be relied on to improve the quality and efficiency of service. When governments must provide benefits, authority should rest with state and local officials, rather than with Congress or federal agencies, while only those who earn benefits should receive them. Demonstrated need, socially useful labor (for example, volunteering or child raising), or even good behavior do not by themselves earn benefits: only work for pay counts. Benefits are rewards, not entitlements; there should be no guarantees. Ultimately, the responsibility for economic security should rest not with charity, employers, or the state, but with autonomous individuals taking charge of their lives.

This unreflective application of market models to the welfare state ignores crucial and uncomfortable questions. Whom do market-based policies really serve? What are the forms of capital and who controls them? Who actually participates in the exchange, and does it create casualties? The turn to managed care in health policy is a particularly clear example of the imbalance of power inherent in market-based policies. Proponents of managed care predicted that the injection of market practices into health care would lower costs and improve quality. However, when health care reorganized into managed care with astonishing speed, consumers howled in protest at the result. What happened was not what economists call "market failure." To the contrary, the results represented market success because the real consumers in this case were not patients, but businesses. More than any other force, the drive of business to lower the cost of employee health benefits drove the managed care revolution. And managed care served its customers well; costs leveled off for a while; the market worked. A health care market controlled by consumers-as-patients would produce a very different outcome. A similar story could be told about public assistance. The women forced to claim public assistance in order to survive exert little if any influence over the design of newly "marketized" welfare policies. The real exchange links politicians and their constituencies. The commodity is votes, and the desired outcome is reduced welfare rolls, regardless of what happens to those rejected for benefits or terminated from assistance.

An unreflective application of market models to the welfare state suffers, first, from a failure to explore where markets are appropriate and where they are not. And it also fails to appreciate the possible markets that might be constructed within the welfare state to lessen asymmetries of power and redefine the buyers and sellers of its commodities.

The application of market models to the welfare state has proceeded with a cheery enthusiasm that has excluded any serious and sustained debate over their strengths and limits.[52] What public policy needs desperately is a thorough exploration of where market models work, and where they misfire; what they can achieve, and where the hurt they inflict outweighs their benefits; where they do indeed enhance freedom, and where they redefine democracy and citizenship in ways that violate America's best traditions.

A reevaluation is urgently needed—not only because of the scope and expense of the welfare state but also because of its weakened capacity to respond constructively to new forms of poverty and inequality. Recent public policy has focused on the size of welfare rolls, not the sources of poverty among single mothers; the need of homeless people for shelter, not the crisis in affordable housing; the cost of medical care, not its capture by the marketplace. Confronted with a new American city embodying the contradictory legacy of public policy, urban capitalism, and racism, the welfare state has staggered, incapacitated by the forces—the war on dependence, the clamor for devolution, and the reliance on market models—driving its recent history.

[2]

POVERTY AND INEQUALITY
IN THE NEW AMERICAN CITY

There is a new American city. Its features are inscribed in the miles of abandoned factories visible from the window of a train passing through North Philadelphia on its way to New York City and in the blocks of abandoned housing, resembling nothing so much as the aftermath of war. The new American city can be found in the Korean, Mexican, and other immigrant neighborhoods that punctuate a trip across Los Angeles, the minicities anchored by shopping malls where highways intersect, the segregated towers of public housing, the new immigrant sweatshops, and in both the endless suburbs stretching out from central cities and revitalized downtowns with their festival markets, gentrified housing, and international skylines.

It is tempting—but misleading—to think of the new American city as lacking either social or spatial coherence. An urban form unlike any other in history, this city defies representation by a single image or metaphor. Neither the gleaming skylines of office towers nor the stark silhouettes of high-rise public housing projects embody its meaning. Rather, it is their conjunction that defines the new American city. Its logic lies precisely in its contradictions.

The revolutions in economy, demography, and space that have shaped this new American city have also made it a site of great inequality and new forms of poverty. These developments are pregnant with meaning for America's welfare state.

Economies

The economic transformation of the American city—as profound and radical as the industrial revolution of earlier centuries—reconstructed labor markets in ways that heightened the risks that welfare states had been built to reduce. Between the 1890s and the 1920s, the American industrial city flourished in the North and Midwest. As early as the 1930s, however, industries began to leave the cities of the industrial heartland for the South. Although by the 1950s a close observer could have found signs of trouble in older industrial cities, it was in the 1960s, 1970s, and 1980s that cities began to hemorrhage manufacturing jobs. In a national sample, 30 percent of manufacturing plants that had more than one hundred employees in 1969 had closed by 1976. These closings were spread almost equally across the country, but the loss of manufacturing hit older cities hardest. Between 1954 and 1977 Detroit lost about half of its manufacturing jobs; between 1947 and 1982 the number of manufacturing jobs in Chicago plummeted from 668,000 to 277,000. This deindustrialization reflected the spectacular foreign growth of industries such as electronics and automobiles, as well as corporate America's search for lower wage and production costs in the suburbs, the Sunbelt, and Third World countries. As businesses competing in the new global economy shed workers, cut wages, and reduced benefits, millions of formerly secure employees found themselves redundant—flotsam on the tide of industrial restructuring.[1]

Drained of industrial jobs, many small older cities shriveled. Empty factory hulks, downtowns bereft of commerce, boarded-up houses, and open spaces overgrown with weeds marked cities such as Camden, New Jersey; Flint, Michigan; or East St. Louis, Illinois, as casualties of economic transformation. In one incarnation, the new American city serves as a reservation for the minority poor. Like Native American reservations, some older cities even began to look to casinos to rescue their economic futures. Formerly industrial cities that also performed other economic functions—government, banking, commerce, medicine, education, and culture—fared better. Their nonindustrial heritage cushioned them against the full consequences of the loss of manufacturing. With some difficulty, cities such as Chicago, New York, Boston, and San Francisco survived the transition to a new form of urbanism; others, like Philadelphia and Baltimore, teetered uncertainly between revival and decline.[2]

Government policy fueled the redefinition of city economies. In the 1940s and 1950s, for example, New York City began to lose industrial jobs partly as a result of planning decisions that viewed factories and warehouses as "urban blight." Housing development pushed 100 large manufacturing firms (and 330 firms of all sizes) from the city between 1946 and 1954. At the same time, governments also created massive numbers of city jobs. Between 1929 and 1974, government employment grew more than any other category in the national economy. These jobs were concentrated in central cities as state and local governments, often with federal funds, assumed new responsibilities in housing, social services, medical care, and education. New "government centers" and other public buildings sprouted alongside the institutions of commerce and finance. The expansion of "third-sector" institutions (education, medicine, nonprofit agencies), also energized by federal funds, accelerated central city economic transformation.[3]

By themselves, however, government and third-sector growth proved unable to revive most city economies, and in the late 1970s observers wondered if old central cities retained any purpose. With population, manufacturing, services, and entertainment scattered to suburbs and exurbs, did big older cities still have any importance? In 1980, an urban commission appointed by President Jimmy Carter encouraged older cities to accept their senescence and advised against offering them federal life support. "The nation can no longer assume that cities will perform the full range of their traditional functions for the larger society. They are no longer the most desirable settings for living, working, or producing."[4]

Like other observers, the commission underestimated cities' capacity for redefinition. A new generation of urban economists argued that cities remained important because they concentrated the people and services essential to commerce and finance, and they asserted that suburban well-being depended on the health of central cities. America, they contended, had become a nation of metropolitan *regions,* anchored by central cities. "Regional economies, with cities at the heart, are now the primary engines of our national prosperity," claimed the U.S. Department of Housing and Urban Development.[5]

Indeed, with the economic recovery of the mid-1990s, cities began to experience modest economic improvement. The central city's share of the growth of retail and service jobs increased, while unemployment and poverty rates declined.[6] This modest revival, however, did not reverse the underlying trends that had reconfigured urban economies, leaving them fragile and vulnerable with a great many residents underemployed and poor.

This contradictory aspect of American cities—the coexistence of downtown redevelopment and gentrification with extreme poverty and deterioration—has grown out of their roles as lead actors in the new world economy. In the 1950s international trade consisted primarily of raw materials and resource-based manufacturing. By the 1980s the capital and services industries began to dominate a redefined international economic order, and major cities became, urbanist Saskia Sassen claims, its "command points." Other cities serve the same purpose on a smaller scale. Not just centers of control, cities are also production sites and markets for the "advanced corporate services" that underpin the new international economy: investment, banking, accounting, management consulting, law, and advertising. Cities may not manufacture as many goods as earlier in their histories, but their financial products and services still fuel world trade.[7]

As these new forms of production replace manufacturing, office towers have become the urban factories of the twenty-first century. But they do not provide the opportunity or the security that industrial factories once did. Service jobs are often nonunionized and do not offer the same pay or benefits as the manufacturing jobs they replaced. Moreover, cities, though integrated into the world economy, have also developed local informal economies—activities that generate income "outside the framework of public regulation." This definition, which excludes crime, includes a range of activities from work out of the home to gypsy cabs. In New York City, for example, informal work is found in apparel, accessories, construction, special trade contracting, footwear, toys, sporting goods, furniture and woodwork, electronic components, packaging, and transportation. Grim sweatshops have also reappeared. "From Philadelphia's Chinatown to New York City's Garment District, workers paint a bleak portrait of the industry as a place where earning less than the federally mandated minimum wage is common, overtime pay is rare, and there is no guarantee of a paycheck at the end of a long week of sewing."[8]

Poorly paid, low-skilled work in services and manufacturing is not an occupational atavism. It is crucial to the economies and social structures of modern cities. Indeed, low-wage employment has expanded as a result of recent economic growth. The key to understanding what at first seems paradoxical—the expansion of low-tech work in a modern international city—lies in distinguishing the characteristics of jobs from the industries in which they are found. In other words, the most dynamic, technologically sophisticated industries all include jobs that pay poorly, lack benefits, and lead nowhere. Stock clerks, maintenance workers, and office cleaners work in advanced industries along with actuaries, lawyers, and engineers.

In the new American city the office tower embodies the same economic processes as the sweatshop. Finance, insurance, and other corporate services, as well as retail trade—all growing sectors—pay less money, employ more part-time and female workers, usually lack unions, and show greater income inequality than did the old manufacturing industries. In myriad ways, they encourage informal work. The substitution of services for manufacturing has thus eroded the private welfare state, thereby magnifying the effects of reductions in public benefits.

The manufacturing that remains in cities has not been immune to the forces reshaping labor markets either. In the late 1970s and the 1980s, as manufacturing employers tried to lower costs by organizing production more flexibly, they too began to rely on involuntary part-time and temporary work and outsourcing, which allowed them to lower wages and benefits. These actions—like the expansion of the service sector—hastened the decline of unions and enlarged the informal economy. The spread of informal work detaches more and more people from the protections associated with steady jobs—health, unemployment, and disability insurance; workers' compensation; and pensions—at the very time when the welfare state has restricted access to public assistance and social insurance.[9]

The social and labor structures of the American city have thus split into two vastly unequal but intimately linked economies—intimately linked because only the informal sector can supply the trappings of prosperity that make urban life attractive to the affluent. Affluent urban workers have created lifestyles that depend on a large pool of low-wage workers. They demand personal services, specialty shops, food individually prepared rather than mass-produced, custom-crafted goods, expensive restaurants, and household help. They want doormen for their condos, cleaning services for their apartments, parking attendants for their cars, and delivery boys for their groceries. And their numbers ensure a viable market for these shops and services. The result, David Cay Johnston observes, is a new "servant class." Like corporations, affluent urbanites have outsourced their domestic tasks for much the same reasons of economy and flexibility and with much the same results. The people they hire often work for poverty wages and suffer full exposure to the risks that, in the formal economy, are covered by employers and the state.[10]

Even the explosive growth of services, local retailing, and small-scale manufacturing cannot supply work for all the low-skilled women and men who want it. In Harlem, two researchers discovered, fourteen people apply for every opening in fast-food restaurants. Cities are full of the unemployed, the underemployed, and the marginally employed working for poverty wages, receiving few benefits, vulnerable to the moods of the economy, and hopeless about the future. Economic recovery began to improve circumstances slightly in 1997 and 1998 as unemployment fell. But central city unemployment is still high, and the underlying conditions that make many central city residents vulnerable remain in place—threatening to reverse modest progress during an economic downturn.[11]

In the past, most unemployment among healthy, working-age adults reflected periodic downturns in the economy, seasonal layoffs, or other temporary factors. Now superimposed on these conventional sources of unemployment is a new phenomenon: relatively permanent isolation from the regular labor force, or chronic joblessness. Very large numbers of people have not worked for a very long time, at least in the regular economy; they may in fact never work there, and their life prospects grow ever dimmer. This is another aspect of inequality in the new American city.

Joblessness—whether the product of economic transformation, as William Julius Wilson contends, or the result of individual willfulness, as Lawrence Mead asserts—underlies the concentration of poverty in inner cities and the emergence of an "underclass." Since the 1960s the share of the chronically jobless among the poor and among African Americans has increased steeply. By 1990, 43 percent of adult men and 56 percent of adult women living in high-poverty census tracts were jobless. The tight labor markets of the late 1990s improved prospects unevenly across groups. In May 1998, for example, the unemployment rate among minority youths in central cities remained five times the average unemployment rate for their white peers. In American cities, there is a connection between race, poverty, and chronic joblessness new in the nation's history.[12]

The distance between the regularly employed and the marginally employed; the young lawyer in his condo and the young man who delivers his pizza; or the stockbroker in her office and the woman who empties her wastebasket exemplify the inequalities inherent in the social structure of the new American city. These examples are extreme, but they represent the income inequality that has increased since the early 1970s.[13]

The disassociation of productivity growth from wages also fueled income inequality. For the first time in American history, productivity gains did not translate into rising real wages. Instead, productivity rewarded shareholders and senior management while workers' pay stagnated. This income inequality contributed to the growth of poverty. Between 1979 and 1992, the official poverty rate grew 23.9 percent. Even including inflation and all noncash benefits, such as health insurance, reduces the increase to only 23.6 percent. As a result, in 1992, 14.5 percent of the population, or 36.8 million people, were poor. Even though the economic expansion after 1993 reduced poverty to 12.7 percent in 1998, the rate was still higher than it had been at the end of the last economic expansion in 1969. "For the first time in recent history," two experts on poverty trends wrote in 1995, "a generation of children has a higher poverty rate than the preceding generation, and a generation of adults has experienced only a modest increase in its standard of living."[14]

Not surprisingly, poverty affects children and minorities disproportionately. The rates are staggering. In 1996, 28.4 percent of all blacks and 31 percent of blacks living in central cities were poor. The outlook for children under eighteen was even bleaker. In 1996, more than one in five

(20.5 percent) was poor—up from 16.4 percent in 1979. And with cuts in public assistance, the severity of child poverty worsened. During the economic expansion between 1995 and 1998, the "child poverty gap"— the total amount of money by which the incomes of all poor children fell below the poverty line—declined only 2 percent while the amount that the average poor child fell below the poverty line rose from $1,471 to $1,604. Among blacks the child poverty rate was 39.9 percent and among Hispanics, 40.3 percent. Overall, the young-child poverty rate in central cities was 36 percent, compared to 16 percent in suburbs. Among states the figure varied greatly, from under 12 percent in New Hampshire and Vermont to 40 percent or more in Louisiana and West Virginia. As a group, American children were worse off economically than children in fifteen of eighteen Western industrialized nations.[15]

Economists do not agree on the reasons for the growth in inequality and poverty, and it is clear that no single factor can account for the trends. The culprit is not government social welfare spending, as Charles Murray and other conservatives argue; nor is it the size of the baby-boom generation, the business cycle, or even declining skills. Instead, beneath the increasing inequality and poverty lie profound changes in the structure of the American economy. The transition from manufacturing to services, the shift from permanent, full-time employment to temporary and part-time work, and the growth of chronic joblessness have all helped to create a class of vulnerable Americans who cannot find economic security in work. For these people, the public safety net has gained more importance, even as it frays beneath them.

Demography

Demographic transformation also played a dramatic role in the emergence of the new American city. The modern story begins with the first Great Migration of African Americans to the North. For impoverished southern blacks, northern and midwestern cities beckoned as "lands of hope," and from World War I to 1920, between 700,000 and 1 million blacks moved north while another 800,000 made the journey during the 1920s. The enormous labor demands of the war opened industrial jobs, and reductions in immigration—first by war, later by acts of Congress— created new opportunities as well. Most black migrants went to cities, men at first to the industrial Midwest, women in greater numbers to older cities in the East, where they worked as domestic servants. As a result, black ghettos emerged and expanded in cities across the nation.[16]

The first Great Migration paled in size before the second. Between 1940 and 1970, 5 million more African Americans left the South, mainly

for northern cities. They left for several reasons. The results of the Agricultural Adjustment Act (1933) pushed sharecroppers off their land, and
the mechanization of cotton harvesting in southern agriculture after the
1940s made their labor increasingly redundant. In fact, the demand for
unskilled labor in the Mississippi Delta plummeted 72 percent between
1949 and 1952. Blacks found economic opportunities more abundant in
the North, even though they were relegated to the worst jobs; they wel-
comed escape from southern violence, the relative availability of public
services, and access to the ordinary rights of citizens.[17]

The second Great Migration reshaped the demography of cities
across the country. Between 1940 and 1970 the size of San Francisco's
black population grew from 4,846 to 96,078 and Chicago's from 277,731
to 1,102,620. In 1940, fewer than one in ten Chicago residents were
African American—compared to about four in ten in 1980. As a consequence, the relatively small ghettos of the first Great Migration
expanded, intensifying residential segregation. The second Great Migration ended in the 1970s, when blacks followed whites in leaving central
cities, moving west, even back to the South, and in modest but increasing numbers to the suburbs.[18]

As blacks moved into cities, whites moved out. Between 1950 and
1970, 7 million white people left central cities. Urban housing shortages,
inexpensive suburban housing, cheap government-backed mortgages,
and the interstate highway system all conspired to lure families out of
cities. As a result, the African American share of central city populations
increased dramatically. Washington, D.C., became the first majority-
black city in the nation, and Detroit and Newark shifted from mostly
white to predominantly black in one generation. In northern cities,
which became increasingly poor as well as black, the consequences of
the Great Migration tightened the association of welfare with race.[19]

Even the number of African American newcomers did not equal the
number of departing whites, and central-city populations stagnated or
declined in the North and Midwest. Between 1957 and 1990, the population of Rustbelt cities dropped from 25 to 20 million. The size of Sunbelt
cities, in sharp contrast, jumped from 8.5 to 23 million—a result largely
of the annexation of suburbs as well as of migration. And everywhere,
suburban growth outstripped the growth of central cities. Between 1950
and 1970, American cities grew by 10 million people overall, while the
suburbs increased by 85 million. In Los Angeles and Houston, the outer
rings grew more than three times as fast as the core. Consequently, many
older cities experienced serious depopulation—from 1950 to 1980, for
instance, St. Louis lost 47 percent of its residents and Detroit lost 35 percent. Of the thirty largest American cities, only eleven contained more

residents in 1998 than in 1970. The depopulation of old cities reduced their density and returned stretches of urban space to nature as untended fields of weeds grew up around the abandoned buildings where housing, retailing, or industry once had stood. The brilliant photographer José Camilo Vergara has labeled this landscape the "green ghetto." Complementing this is Vergara's "institutional ghetto," an area where the institutions of criminal justice and public assistance are concentrated, emphasizing their affiliation with race, social control, and the undeserving poor.[20]

Vergara also described a new "immigrant ghetto." The Hart-Celler Act of 1965 eliminated the discriminatory quotas dating from the 1920s and repealed the barriers to Asian entry that originated in the 1880s. The 13,615,895 people who entered the United States legally between 1961 and 1989 were second in number for a thirty-year period only to the immigrants in 1891–1920. The 1980s saw the most immigration, about 6 million people. In fact, if return migration is taken into account, the 1980s was the decade of greatest net immigration in American history. Undocumented or illegal immigrants lift the real number in the 1980s much higher—by 2 to 3 million, according to Census Bureau estimates. This resurgent immigration built new ghettos and redefined the ethnic makeup of many cities. In some cities immigration stanched, and even reversed, population loss, increased the supply of low-wage labor, and fostered new businesses and services. It also put new pressures on local welfare states.[21]

Immigrants not only arrived in greater numbers; they came from different parts of the world as well. In 1900, 90 percent of immigrants arrived from Europe; in the 1980s, only 11 percent originated there. Latin Americans and Asians composed the majority of the new immigrants after 1970, with Asian immigrants making up nearly half by the early 1980s. Among Latin American countries, Mexico contributed the most immigrants. Nonetheless, the total number of nations sending immigrants increased, and the result was the largest variety of arriving nationalities in American history.[22]

Like their predecessors, the great majority of immigrants—in the 1980s about four of every five settled in metropolitan areas, most in central cities. In America's largest cities immigrants, their children, and African Americans formed a majority of the population. Immigrants did not distribute themselves evenly among the nation's urban areas, however; rather, they clustered in "gateway cities": Los Angeles, Miami/Dade County, New York City, and San Francisco. In 1990, the county with the greatest proportion of foreign-born residents, 45 percent, was Dade County, Florida; immigrants made up 60 percent of Miami's population. Immigrants from Vietnam, Cambodia, and Laos chose to settle in California; Los Angeles, already the world's second largest Mexican city, became the main destination of Koreans. By the 1980s, more than two-thirds of new immigrants entered through the South and the West, and with the exception of New York City, the Sunbelt contains all the gateway cities into which new immigrants poured after 1965. Los Angeles International Airport was the Ellis Island of the late-twentieth century.[23]

The new immigrants probably were a net economic gain for the nation. Their taxes flowed into the federal treasury; their work effort increased productivity; their youthfulness offset the expense of an aging population. They took jobs that no one else wanted. But they also strained the economies of the cities in which they clustered. Their children overcrowded schools. Usually lacking health insurance, they taxed the resources of local emergency rooms and hospitals. When they were out of work or homeless, they claimed help from state and local authorities, while their income taxes and social insurance contributions went mainly to the federal government. State and local governments, in other words, paid most of the bills; the federal government collected most of the money. Not all groups of immigrants did equally well, either. Among Hispanics, poverty rates and other indicators of economic hardship increased alarmingly. The local economic pressure from the new immigrants intensified latent anti-immigrant feelings, now reinforced by the newcomers' cultural differences and dark skins. In the welfare state, anti-immigrant sentiment was written into law in the 1996 welfare bill, which stripped even legal immigrants of the right to many social benefits—an action that was modified, but far from completely reversed, by a later Congress.[24]

The transformation of urban family structure, as well as urban ethnicity, also helped shape the new American city. Women began delaying marriage and childbearing, fewer married at all, and many more worked outside their homes. Only 26 percent of households now consist of married couples with children. Small households organized around work and consumption sustain revitalized entertainment and shopping districts. These concentrations of well-educated women and men with disposable income and few family responsibilities have fueled the multiplication of private cultural/commercial institutions—the coffee bars and superbookstores that help to define the transformed downtowns of American cities, which have become singularly unwelcoming to the homeless and beggars, and singularly unaffordable by any except the affluent.[25]

New family arrangements have also helped to define inner-city neighborhoods. Increasing numbers of white and Hispanic children, and most

African American children, are born out of wedlock. In 1960, single mothers headed about 8 percent of families with children; by 1990, the proportion had increased to nearly 25 percent. Demographers project that one of every two American children born after 1990 will live for some time in a family headed by a single mother. The increase in single-parent families both increased public assistance rolls and instigated the backlash against them: the object of welfare critics became out-of-wedlock births rather than the poverty of poor young mothers.

In 1960, single mothers were often divorced or separated, and many were widows; now, although a majority are still divorced, nearly 40 percent have never married. The proportion varies by race and ethnicity: 21 percent for whites, 56 percent for blacks, and 37 percent for Hispanics. These trends are most dramatic in impoverished areas of cities. In extreme poverty zones, 73 percent of African American families are headed by single women with children. Nonetheless, even in the extreme poverty tracts of central cities only one-third of families received public assistance in 1990. The rise in the minimum wage, the strong economy, and the tight labor market improved the situation somewhat during the 1990s: the median income of black single mothers increased 21 percent, from $12,765 to $15,530 in inflation-adjusted dollars between 1993 and 1996. Still, in 1995, the poverty line for a family of three was a little over $13,000, which means that these increased wages, welcome as they were, did not lift most families far from official poverty.[26]

Poor African American children often die young in American cities. Infant mortality, although it has declined to record lows for the United States, remains unacceptably high among African Americans—twice the level among whites. In several large cities, the African American figure rivals or exceeds the rate in some Third World countries. Nor do the dangers end with infancy. In Harlem, a fifteen-year-old boy has less chance of reaching the age of forty-five than his white peer has of living to sixty-five. In the late-twentieth century, black men in Harlem were less likely to reach age sixty-five than were men in Bangladesh. "Daily life in the inner city can be harrowing," commented *New York Times* columnist Bob Herbert. "Residents are beset with the uncertainty and anxiety that accompany their efforts to cope with poverty, unsafe neighborhoods and persistent racism. . . . Those kinds of stresses evolve in complicated ways into diseases that are killing people." Drug- and gang-related murders are also a source of early death. Between the periods 1957–60 and 1988–90 in Philadelphia, which sadly is not unusual in this respect, the average homicide victimization rate for nonwhite boys soared from 42.6 to 153.0 per 100,000. Among white boys it rose from 2.6 to 33.5. It is much lower for girls. Although urban crime decreased in the 1990s—in some places dramatically—crime rates remain above their levels of thirty years ago. For poor black children the American city is a dangerous place.[27]

Space

The new urban economy and demography occupy transformed space. Architecture critic Michael Sorkin describes it as "a wholly new kind of city, a city without a place attached to it"—an "ageographical city" projected across the nation. "Globalized capital, electronic means of production, and uniform mass culture," he writes, "abhor the intimate, undisciplined differentiation of traditional cities."[28] But they coexist easily with suburbs. Although there are real differences between cities and suburbs, the distinctions between them are shrinking. Cities and suburbs are joined inescapably as different faces of the new American city. More than they realize, suburbanites are clients of the welfare state, and its redefinition hits them as hard, if in different ways, as it does residents of inner cities.

Suburbanization enjoyed its greatest growth after World War II, but its roots stretch far back in American history, when transportation, affluence, and land development began to transform older cities. The Census Bureau gave suburbs official recognition in 1910. Then, for the first time, in the 1920s the suburbs grew faster than cities. By 1950, the suburban population was increasing ten times faster than urban populations. Housing developments, industrial and business parks, shopping malls, and even entertainment complexes now cluster in "minicities" or "edge cities," an urban form unlike any other in history.

Several influences joined to stimulate the exodus from cities. However, in the early stages, the desire to escape blacks generally was not one of them. Rather, with a national housing shortage and cities densely packed, suburbs held a great attraction for young families seeking homes they could own and open space for their children. The federal government helped by underwriting cheap, long-term mortgages with low down payments in the suburbs and refusing to underwrite them in central cities or in desegregated or black neighborhoods. It also hastened suburban growth with federal highway subsidies and the development of the interstate highway system. In the same years, technology facilitated suburbanization as builders learned to mass-produce houses inexpensively and developed mass marketing techniques to sell them.[29]

The benefits of suburban homeownership included more than security and lifestyle. By accumulating equity in their homes, the white suburban middle class built assets. Most blacks, excluded from suburbs and the mortgage market, were unable to replicate white success. Without home equity, they were massively outstripped by whites in capital accumulation. As a consequence, they found themselves far more vulnerable to the common risks of life and far closer to the edge of dependence, with public assistance rather than a home equity loan their likely safety net in times of unemployment.

As industries as well as families left cities, suburbs became the centers of American manufacturing. By 1977, two-thirds of the manufacturing industry in the Philadelphia area was located in the suburbs; in San Francisco, more than 75 percent of the industry; and in Denver, over half. In Chicago, manufacturing employment dropped nearly 50 percent, while manufacturing jobs in the city's outlying region nearly doubled from 278,000 to 521,000. Giant industrial districts surround Los Angeles, while the nation's second largest manufacturing region lies within a sixty-mile radius of New York City.

Retailing and services soon followed the movement of population and manufacturing. Between 1977 and 1982, suburban service jobs grew four times faster than service work in central cities, and by 1988, 59 percent of the nation's office space was located in the suburbs. The suburbanization of employment moves work away from inner-city residents, which means that those who need jobs the most are literally farthest away from them. Without automobiles, and stymied by public transportation designed to take commuters into cities rather than in the other direction, many inner-city residents depend on public assistance because they cannot get to work.[30]

Collectively, suburbs wield real power. They are where most Americans live, and since 1975, their representatives constitute the largest voting bloc in Congress. Individually, they shape their own demographies because they are minigovernments. By world standards, these small communities possess extraordinary capacities to define land use, organize institutions, and tax residents. Because so many services are financed in whole or in part by local property taxes, the economic disparity among suburban tax bases and between suburbs and cities translates into dramatic inequalities. In 1997–98, for instance, the four counties surrounding Philadelphia spent an average of $1,900 more per pupil for schooling than the city did. As suburbs hoard their resources, shielding them from cities, they become central agents in the reproduction of segregation and poverty in America. The invisible walls suburbs erect to keep poor people within city limits concentrate poverty and increase the burdens on the welfare state, while suburban legislators wield their political power to reduce the public benefits that their exclusiveness helped make more necessary.[31]

Suburbs are not nearly as independent of cities as their residents think, however, and a growing body of literature traces the economic links that join them. "To compete in the global economy," argues the Department of Urban Housing and Development's *State of the Cities, 1998* report, "cities and their suburbs must cooperate more than they compete." Metropolitan economies depend on "urban strengths and have a huge stake in city job growth."[32] Cities and suburbs blend in other ways as well. With the advent of the downtown shopping mall, suburban architectural and retail forms have come to central cities, where they have hastened the privatization and control of public space. Meanwhile, the city's problems have infiltrated the suburbs with traffic congestion, aging infrastructure, strained finances, and even increased poverty. As central city and suburb increasingly turn toward each other, the differences between them blur. Affluent suburbanites may pick up stakes and move farther outward, but they cannot avoid this process forever, or even for long. Nor are suburbs independent of the welfare state. Suburbanites are laid off from their jobs and lose their benefits. They worry about paying for their parents in nursing homes. They try to imagine how they will keep their standard of living in retirement. As American suburbanites face these problems, they find themselves as dependent on the welfare state as a single mother in the inner city.

Americans migrated south and west as well as to the suburbs. Together, federal government spending, economic opportunity, and an appealing lifestyle fueled explosive job growth and urban development in the region south of the thirty-seventh parallel, stretching from the Carolinas to Silicon Valley. The Sunbelt, the name given to this new region, captured the glamour and the sense of possibility in the nation's reordered urban hierarchy.[33]

The American mobilization for World War II accelerated the Sunbelt's development. Between 1940 and 1943, expanded defense production and huge military facilities pumped money, jobs, and infrastructure into the region and tilted the national economy toward the southern Atlantic, Gulf, and Pacific coasts. After the war, the federal government nourished Sunbelt growth with about 60 percent of the military budget and a disproportionate share of defense production facilities and military bases. It also located more civilian jobs in the Sunbelt than elsewhere. The Sunbelt states offered less expensive labor and other operating costs, fewer unions, and more Republican votes. When population growth strained the resources of Sunbelt cities, the federal government responded with grants for infrastructure construction, such as highways, water and sewage plants, and mass transit. Federal urban renewal money helped reconstruct aging downtowns. There is a delicious irony in the conservative, antigovernment, antiwelfare politics of a region dependent upon federal spending for its growth and prosperity.[34]

Another irony is this: the federal government increased the attractiveness of the Sunbelt as a place to live, work, and invest by imposing unwanted change on the region. By forcing southern cities to desegregate public facilities and honor the civil rights of African Americans, the federal government helped them to shed their image as centers of racial bigotry, which moderate southern politicians and business leaders realized detracted from the South's appeal.[35]

Consequently, Sunbelt cities grew at an astonishing pace. In the 1960s, 62 percent of the nation's metropolitan growth occurred in the South and West; in the 1970s, the proportion rose to 96 percent. In the 1970s, while the North lost 60.1 jobs for every thousand population, the South gained 92.1 and the West 128.4.[36] This population boom tipped the balance of national political power toward the Sunbelt, thereby reducing political support for welfare state programs, such as public assistance, that did not serve the middle class and elderly.

In some ways, Sunbelt cities gained disproportionately from the increasing importance of foreign trade in the American economy. By 1975, nearly two-thirds of American trade entered or left through West Coast, Gulf, or southern Atlantic ports. Tourism is harder to measure, but self-reporting by Sunbelt states lists it often as the second or third largest industry.[37] Retirees also promoted the fortunes of Sunbelt cities. Census data show large increases in the number of residents over the age of sixty-five in southern and western states, and the flow of their Social Security and Medicare dollars links the health of Sunbelt economies to the welfare state.

In the decades after the war, the progrowth coalitions that controlled Sunbelt cities attracted investment with cheap nonunion labor, low taxes, and limited social welfare spending, as well as minimal zoning, land-use regulation, and building codes. Houston, for instance, spent $1.16 per capita on public welfare in 1970, compared to $9.09 in Chicago; Phoenix spent five cents, compared to $31.90 in Newark. As a result, many Sunbelt cities had underdeveloped social services and shoddy public facilities and infrastructure. Nor did urban prosperity translate into greater income equality. Indeed, poverty was widespread within the region's cities.[38] Nevertheless, major Sunbelt cities of the 1960s and 1970s offered a stunning contrast to the old industrial cities of the North and Midwest. With their booming economies, mushrooming populations, and thriving downtowns, they seemed poised for a golden future—new engines of American prosperity and new sites for the realization of American dreams.

But the 1980s held a different fate for Sunbelt cities. Population figures from 1980 to 1984 showed a sharp reduction in growth. Whereas in the 1970s the number of high-poverty census tracts in the South and Southwest had declined, in the 1980s, with the collapse of oil prices and the shock of the savings and loan debacle, they increased. Sunbelt cities now confronted deteriorating infrastructure, strained municipal resources, corporate downsizing, defense industry reductions, and increased poverty, homelessness, and crime—many of the same issues that were forcing cities in the Rustbelt to develop new strategies for growth and to redefine their social obligations. As with the suburb and the city, the economies and problems of Sunbelt and Rustbelt have been converging. The two regional faces of the new American city increasingly dissolve into one: Sorkin's "ageographical" city, where location collapses into irrelevance and is replaced by the office towers, malls, fast-food restaurants, festival markets, and international airports of the new American city.[39]

Sunbelt and Rustbelt cities also share another defining feature of American urbanism: racial segregation. In American cities, racial segregation—or "American apartheid," in the words of Douglas Massey and Nancy Denton—has not only persisted, but grown. The segregation of African Americans differed fundamentally from the experience of white immigrants from Europe in the nineteenth and early-twentieth centuries. Immigrants never lived in enclaves as ethnically homogeneous as the black ghettos of post–World War II America. And immigrant ghettos did not prove to be permanent. Indexes of segregation and spatial isolation among European immigrant groups declined rapidly after 1910 as economic mobility increased and the native-born children of immigrants moved away from the neighborhoods of their parents.[40]

By contrast, the segregation of African Americans survives at extraordinary levels throughout the nation, although it is generally a little worse in the North and in larger, more modern cities. It is much higher now than in 1860 or 1910. In 1930, in northern cities, except for Chicago and Cleveland, the average African American lived in a neighborhood dominated by whites; by 1970, this was totally reversed, and blacks in all northern cities lived far more often with other African Americans than with whites. The average African American in major northern cities lived in a neighborhood that rocketed from 31.7 percent black in 1930 to 73.5 percent in 1970.[41]

Although it is often equated with poverty, racial segregation afflicts affluent as well as poor African Americans. Indexes of segregation remain about as high for them as for poor blacks. In northern metropolitan areas, the degree of segregation for African Americans with annual incomes of less than $2,500 was the same as for those with incomes of $50,000 or more in 1980. According to Massey and Denton, one of every three African Americans in sixteen metropolitan areas was living under conditions of intense racial segregation they call "hypersegregation."[42]

By no means does segregation signify uniform poverty, run-down housing, or trash-strewn streets. Tidy, well-kept blocks of single-family homes populate the black as well as the white districts of metropolitan America. But the failure of social scientists to document the spaces and neighborhoods of black America has unwittingly reinforced this stereotype, which is sustained by the media, by politicians, and by the unwillingness of most nonblack Americans to acquaint themselves firsthand with the facts. Even so, as Massey and Denton show, segregation by itself can initiate a vicious process that concentrates poverty and intensifies its impact, and by concentrating poverty, segregation vastly increases the burdens on America's welfare state.[43]

All levels of government share responsibility for perpetuating and intensifying racial segregation. In the 1930s the underwriting practices of federal agencies ruined central city housing markets, denied mortgage money to blacks, and promoted the development of white suburbs. Governments used road and highway construction to manipulate or confine racial concentrations. The first federal public housing regulations in the 1930s permitted no project to disturb the "neighborhood composition guideline"—that is, the racial status quo. As a result, before World War II, two-thirds of all public housing with black occupants remained wholly segregated. After the war, local governments used public housing to segregate blacks even more completely.[44]

In addition to racial segregation, economic segregation, which exists independently of race, has also increased among African Americans—as well as among whites and Hispanics in cities of all sizes across the nation. The economic segregation of whites grew most in the 1970s, as deindustrialization and rising income inequality left poor whites concentrated in urban neighborhoods. Blacks and Hispanics caught up in the 1980s. Together with racial segregation, economic segregation mapped the processes that have shaped the new American city and created a new geography of public assistance. Another of these processes was urban redevelopment.[45]

Unless land is vacant, reconfiguring urban space cannot be a benign process. There are people, businesses, and institutions to be moved out, buildings to be demolished, trees to be uprooted. Displacement rarely operates in a socially neutral way: those forced out are disproportionately poor or working class. They appear to be making marginal and unproductive use of valuable land; sometimes, because of their poverty, lifestyle, or race, they seem a nuisance. This process of displacement has a long history. Nineteenth- and early-twentieth-century housing reformers, for instance, wrote about slums, not ghettos, and in both New York City and Philadelphia settlement houses—bastions of reform—played an active part in slum clearance. Along with business and real estate interests, they saw slum clearance not only as the path to better housing for the poor but as the key to developing cities by putting valuable land to more productive uses.[46]

After World War II, slum clearance acquired a new name: urban redevelopment. Real estate interests wanted to use downtown land for development; institutions wanted the room to expand; politicians wanted city growth. Unlike their predecessors, this postwar growth coalition relied on the federal government for help. As a shorthand for the problem they planned to attack, politicians and commentators began to refer to "blight," which became the reigning metaphor for urban distress during the 1940s and 1950s. Growth coalitions stressed the elimination of blight with revived downtowns full of new offices and residences for the well-to-do. Housing for the poor played a subsidiary role in their plans. As in the nineteenth and early-twentieth centuries, reformers who wanted to sweep away slums and their denizens seem to have given remarkably little thought to one important question: where would displaced people go?[47]

With only a few exceptions, public authorities in America did not build housing before the Great Depression of the 1930s. Although the absence of public housing increased the hardships of the poor, the ill housed, and families displaced by slum clearance, most reformers and public officials resisted constructing public housing for a very long time. Only the terrible housing crisis of the Great Depression overcame their reluctance to interfere with real estate markets and their fear of socialism. In 1937, Congress authorized the construction of the first federal public housing. Bitterly opposed by the real estate industry, the legislation did not produce much housing, but it did set a precedent for federal action in public housing.[48]

Congress assumed that public housing should serve only those families too poor to find shelter in the private market, but setting strict income limits, which seemed fair to liberals concerned with distributing scarce resources, had unfortunate consequences. For twenty-five years the nation's major housing program was unable to serve one group of people with real housing needs—the working poor. It also penalized public housing tenants for modest upward economic mobility by evicting them when their incomes rose above an arbitrary ceiling. Eviction often worsened their financial condition and robbed housing projects of stable community leaders. (Finally, in the late 1990s, federal policy makers began trying to modify the income mix among public housing tenants.)[49]

In 1949 the Taft-Ellender-Wagner Housing Act, long sought by housing reformers, set an unprecedented goal for the American welfare state: "a decent home and suitable living environment" for every American family. The act committed federal funds for use by local redevelopment agencies to acquire and redevelop sites. It required that sites be predominantly residential either before or after redevelopment and gave redevelopment agencies the authority to level residential areas labeled slums and replace them with offices, housing, shopping areas, and parking lots. The law also authorized the building of 801,000 public housing units in the next six years and mandated the relocation of displaced families in equivalent housing. The jubilation of housing reformers, however, did not last long. In 1951, New York City's master developer Robert Moses showed how the law could be manipulated to leverage $26 million of federal money to build a coliseum and luxury apartments. By 1952, only 85,000 units of public housing were under construction; eventually, only one-quarter of the authorized housing was actually built.[50]

In the more conservative Eisenhower years, Congress weakened the already fragile link between redevelopment and housing by eliminating the requirement for residential housing in some portions of redeveloped areas. It also introduced the term *urban renewal*, which earned its epithet "Negro removal" by destroying African American neighborhoods. By 1967, urban renewal had replaced 404,000 dwelling units, most of them occupied by low-income residents, with 41,580 units—only 10 percent of the original number, located primarily in racially segregated high-rise public housing towers. For the most part shoddily constructed warehouses for the poor, this early public housing reflected the inability of architects and planners to foresee the drawbacks of high-rise living for impoverished families or the social consequences of segregation and concentrated poverty.[51]

If segregated public housing was the ugliest face of urban redevelopment, gentrification was its prettiest. Gentrification—"the rehabilitation of working-class and derelict housing and the consequent transformation of an area into a middle-class neighborhood," as two scholars defined it—not only renovated houses and transformed cityscapes, it also brought a remarkably uniform population to central cities: young, white, childless urbanites with professional or managerial jobs and above-average incomes. (It is a myth that gentrification attracts many suburbanites back to cities.)[52] Gentrification was the residential arm of urban revitalization, paralleling efforts to bring corporate offices, business services, retailing, and tourism back to city centers. Like other forms of redevelopment, it necessitated the cooperation of local elites with city, state, and federal governments. They cooperated because it served all their interests well. Local governments benefited directly because gentrification raised the taxable value of property, attracted affluent consumers who circulated income through local economies, enhanced tourism, and helped hold corporations in central cities. Financial, real estate, and business interests gained in many ways—from commissions on increased transactions, speculation in land and buildings, higher rents, mortgage interest and loans, retail sales, and entertainment spending. Urban professionals profited from attractive housing that suited their lifestyle. Nonetheless, gentrification produced losers as well as winners—most often the poor, displaced by gentrification, facing steeper rents in tight real estate markets.[53]

Conversely, large urban districts often deteriorated because they were pushed outside the market, and poor people found themselves homeless in a sea of abandoned housing. Declining real estate values and the inability of poor people to pay high rents made much inner-city residential real estate unprofitable—unappealing to landlords, unresponsive to market-based public policies, and dependent for improvement or development on infusions of capital from government, philanthropy, or local community economic development strategies.[54]

In the early 1980s urban social critics linked abandonment and gentrification as complementary phases in the history of urban land markets and capital accumulation. For urban planner Peter Marcuse, the twin processes gave geographic form to the economic polarization of the city. They created a "vicious circle . . . in which the poor are continuously under pressure of displacement and the well-to-do continuously seek to wall themselves . . . within gentrified neighborhoods." The effect of displacement from abandonment and gentrification is not trivial. In New York City in the early 1980s Marcuse estimated displacement from abandonment at 60,000 households, or 150,000 people each year. He put annual displacement from gentrification, which is harder to measure, at 10,000 to 40,000 households. Total annual displacement in the United States has been estimated at 2.5 million persons.[55]

In the mid-1980s, homelessness, one consequence of displacement, suddenly surfaced as a public issue. Rising joblessness, increased poverty, the destruction of cheap lodging in skid rows, and the deinstitutionalization of the mentally ill rank high among the factors that have inscribed homelessness into urban landscapes. Homelessness often originates in neighborhoods marked by poverty, unemployment, abandoned housing, overcrowding, female-headed families with young children, and few social and family supports—the neighborhoods created by the great transformations of urban economy, demography, and space.[56]

Another powerful force in the transformation of public and private space was highway construction. When its full history is written, highway construction may emerge as even more destructive than urban renewal. Major federal support of highways resulted from two federal laws passed by Congress in 1956, which fixed the federal contribution to the cost of interstate highways at 90 percent, to be financed through gasoline taxes. Ten times more expensive than urban renewal, new highways were supposed to help cities by channeling traffic downtown; instead, they spurred the growth of suburbs. They also caused massive displacement; whole districts had to be leveled to accommodate roadways and interchanges. Congress did not require local or federal authorities to find housing for the mainly low-income families whose homes were to be destroyed. "Black communities," writes historian Raymond Mohl, "were uprooted in virtually every big city to make way for the new urban traffic arteries." The path of construction did not run through poor and black neighborhoods by chance. Often, local authorities, fixated on remaking downtowns, wanted to wipe out poor neighborhoods or to use highways as barriers between these neighborhoods and the redeveloping sections of their cities.[57]

Urban redevelopment and highway construction altered the physical appearance of American cities and cut the templates for future downtown development. They built an urban infrastructure for the emergent world economy of the information age and formalized mechanisms for turning the always mixed public/private economy of urban development into a major force for the reconstruction of cities. As a result of federal housing initiatives, the amount of substandard housing decreased, especially during the Great Society, when Congress greatly expanded federal construction of public housing and authorized money for housing rehabilitation and rent supplements.[58] Nonetheless, urban redevelopment and highway construction also hastened the deterioration of local neighborhoods and fueled a new social geography of public assistance based on the concentration of poverty into large, racially segregated, and isolated districts where residents lived in substandard housing or the new postwar public housing slums. The office tower and the high-rise public housing project are both products of post–World War II urban redevelopment, and they are linked causally, not accidentally.

. . . .

The new American city dazzles with its wealth and opulence. Count the expensive restaurants; watch the shoppers in the exclusive stores; look at the price of real estate and the high rents. But the new American city also depresses with its poverty. Step over the homeless men and women sleeping on grates; avoid the beggars; drive through neighborhoods of abandoned or neglected housing; look at the men and women lined up for shelters or free food. Income inequality and poverty worsened between the early 1970s and the early 1990s and hardly budged thereafter. More people are poor; the geographic concentration of poverty in cities is greater than ever before; poor people lead more isolated lives. By the 1990s, this concentrated poverty had spread to cities across the nation, from Rustbelt to Sunbelt.

Mike Davis calls Los Angeles, emblematic for him of the new American city, "fortress L.A." Security dominates urban design in its privatized spaces. Active life takes place away from the streets. Underground passages, skyways, and malls—private spaces where beggars can be barred, unpleasant or threatening encounters avoided, and movement monitored with video cameras—assure workers and shoppers minimal contact with the rougher, unpredictable, uncontrollable diversity of the streets.[59]

Fortress America was built on fear—the belief that crime, violence, and danger stalked the city. Until recent decades, urban architecture exuded a confidence incompatible with deep concerns about crime: stores opened directly onto public streets, homes and buildings could be entered with little difficulty, and schools had several entrances, which remained unlocked. At the beginning of the twenty-first century, this earlier urban architecture seems naïve, and retrofitting older homes and buildings with security systems, stronger locks, and window bars has become a minor urban industry.

There are as many anecdotes about urban crime as there are people who live in cities. Everyone has a story, if not about his or her own mugging or break-in, then about a friend's or neighbor's. City people feel besieged; crime dominates talk at dinner parties as well as on the nightly news. Although trends in crime do not conform to popular beliefs— crime rates dropped dramatically in most cities in the middle and late 1990s, for example—it is perception that has fueled the construction of Fortress America.

Crime opens a window on how the great transformations in urban economy, demography, and space register in the daily lives of people in cities. It embodies the translation of poverty, hopelessness, and frustration into rage; it records the acting out of blocked aspirations in robbery; it traces the consequences of low wages and joblessness in drug dealing. It follows heightened poverty and inequality as they arc back toward the affluent in the form of street mugging, burgled homes, and smashed windshields. It maps the consequences of urban redevelopment that have turned city centers into places of danger by leaving them devoid of activity after dark. In 1961 urban critic Jane Jacobs described the conditions for safe and healthy city streets—multiage dwellings, density, short blocks, mixed uses of space. Her book created a sensation, but mainstream urban redevelopment ignored its prescription, and the statistics of urban crime reflect the results.[60]

The gleaming corporate complexes transforming downtowns encase the heart of the new American city in glass, steel, and concrete. However, even cities that negotiated economic transition with some success have not avoided the problems of Camden or East St. Louis. Rather, the new urbanism has superimposed a social geography, architecture, economy, and lifestyle on top of deteriorated neighborhoods, concentrated poverty, and economic redundance. The architecture of downtown faces forward, toward the global city; the architecture of poor and modest neighborhoods faces backward, toward the defunct industrial city.

The privileges of wealth—private guards, expensive security systems, secure buildings, isolation from the street—separate redeveloped downtowns and rich residential districts from poorer neighborhoods that cannot afford the price of safety. Wealth also buys cleanliness and well-maintained streets. Downtown businesses and property owners, as in Philadelphia and New York City, organize and pay for their own special service districts, whose employees clean and monitor the streets.

Inner-city neighborhoods, by contrast, show no signs of privilege. Despite the occasional modern school, hospital, prison, or housing project, most buildings date from earlier eras. Once-gracious homes of the upper-middle class trace white flight and increased poverty in their neglect and multiple mailboxes. Vacant buildings, pawn shops, check-cashing agencies, and struggling small businesses populate the old stores in now depressed blocks of formerly vibrant neighborhood shopping districts. Trash-filled streets signify the poverty of city governments unable to pay for their cleaning and the inability of residents to hire private services. Weeds surround the broken benches in local parks.

It is easy to leave the study of recent urban history overwhelmed by a sense of inevitability and despair. But there are antidotes to nihilism. Everywhere, modest but hopeful signs appear. A new grass-roots politics of community development has scored significant victories. Exciting examples of urban revitalization exist in cities around the country. Some indications of distress, notably poverty rates and unemployment, have leveled off or declined a bit. Cities remain vibrant centers of arts, culture, education, and research, and the new immigration has rekindled the diversity that lies at the core of the urban experience and constitutes its great appeal.[61]

Policy options, it is crucial to remember, always exist. The new American city emerged as the result of political choices as well as great impersonal forces. It represents human agency as well as structural transformation, and it embodies decisions made at every stage of its construction. The existence of urban alternatives—of the possibility of different urban outcomes even in the modern era—abound in Canada and Europe. Unfortunately, the coalitions that guided urban reconstruction in the United States chose paths that favored large commercial and real estate interests and disadvantaged poor and minority residents. The contradictions inherent in their strategies furthered the deterioration of vast stretches of inner cities, increased racial segregation, intensified poverty, and created huge problems for the welfare state, which inherited the responsibility for responding to the human consequences of the new American city. There is no reason why the same choices must be repeated now and in the future.

THE FAMILY SUPPORT ACT
AND THE ILLUSION
OF WELFARE REFORM

With the right turn in American politics, federal and state government efforts to reform welfare in the 1980s did not attempt to reverse the trends in poverty, inequality, and joblessness associated with the new American city. Instead of leading a new charge against poverty and its causes, they focused on trimming the number of people on welfare and cutting benefits, a crusade against "dependence"—in particular, the reliance of young unmarried mothers on AFDC and the pittance provided by the remaining state public assistance programs.

To be sure, AFDC did need reform. A host of counterproductive regulations, together with the absence of child care and medical insurance for clients who left the rolls, worked against moving AFDC recipients from welfare to work. Strict limits on the assets that clients were allowed to retain in order to receive benefits—such as the value of a car or any appreciable saving—meant that many could not reach jobs, save for emergencies, or acquire the modest capital necessary to buy a house or start a small business. And the steep reduction in benefits that followed from almost any earned income discouraged clients from taking jobs to supplement their welfare benefits. Because former AFDC clients usually took low-wage jobs without benefits, "independence" meant the loss of medical insurance and the inability to afford medical care. In addition to these practical considerations, conservatives complained that benefits carrying neither work requirements nor time limits encouraged long-term dependence. Liberals, on the other hand, objected to low benefits that varied drastically from state to state and to the often punitive and stigmatizing manner in which they were administered. Clients, meanwhile, found the benefits they did receive inadequate and the administrative procedures demeaning.

The Family Support Act of 1988 (FSA) addressed some of these issues. As well as introducing work obligations, the FSA enhanced the collection of child support from noncustodial parents and strengthened federal support for child care, education, and job training as part of public assistance. However, by failing to create jobs or address the inadequacy of wages, the FSA repeated the historic failure of American social policy to link public assistance with labor markets. At most, the FSA promised to reduce the AFDC rolls and increase child support payments; it offered little hope of reducing poverty or promoting lasting economic independence. And even these limited goals were compromised: inadequate federal funding and reluctant state governments prevented any valid test of the FSA's real potential while reliance on positive incentives and supports marked it as an anachronism in the new, punitive, market-directed era of welfare reform.[1]

The FSA looked toward both the past and future of social policy. The first major legislative overhaul of AFDC since the 1930s, it brought together three important strands in the history of public welfare: the centuries-old attack on outdoor relief, the failed search for ways to link welfare to work, and the ineffective struggle to collect child support from noncustodial parents.

Outdoor Relief

The story of American welfare begins in the colonial era with "outdoor relief," for most of the nation's history the common term for what, in America today, is usually called welfare. Outdoor relief consisted of public aid—food, fuel, small amounts of cash—given to needy people outside of institutions. Administered by towns, counties, or parishes, it was one of the earliest responsibilities of American local governments. Dreary, often depressing, outdoor relief remains the least-studied facet of America's welfare history. Nevertheless, in various guises—home relief, General Assistance, AFDC, and now Temporary Assistance for Needy Families (TANF)—outdoor relief has proved to be the bedrock of American welfare. Its persistence shows the crucial need for a government role in the care of needy people throughout America's past and undermines the claim that voluntarism and private charity suffice to meet the needs of people unable to survive on their own.[2]

By the late-eighteenth and early-nineteenth centuries, outdoor relief had surfaced as a major concern of public policy. Immigration, urbanization, and the spread of wage labor increased the number of people unable to care for themselves, especially in cities and large towns. As local and state authorities complained of rising expenses for poor relief, they faced issues familiar in current debates about poverty and welfare. The first enduring question was how to distinguish between those who would receive help and those who would not. Because neither public nor private resources have ever been adequate to relieve all need, government and charities struggle to identify who merits help. Until the second and third decades of the nineteenth century, most commentators talked about drawing a line between the able-bodied and the impotent poor—those who could work and those who could not. In practice, no one could draw such a line with any precision. By the mid-nineteenth century, this old dichotomy had been moralized into the deserving and undeserving, or the worthy and unworthy, poor, and "behavior," in addition to physical condition, had become a criterion for relief.

The second enduring issue was the impact relief might have on work incentives and family life. Critics worried that relief sapped the will to work. Generous relief policies, they believed, lessened the supply of cheap labor and encouraged the formation of a permanent pauper class. The adverse consequences spilled over into family life; the demoralized poor failed to properly train or supervise their children, families disintegrated, and pauperism perpetuated itself across generations. Added to this concern was a third issue: the limits of social obligation. What should communities provide even the deserving poor? What do citizens owe each other? These matters remain as contentious today as they were two hundred years ago.

In the late-colonial period and the early republic, the "settlement" issue complicated definitions of social obligation. Then, the responsibility of a community extended only to its members. Those who belonged to the community—who had a settlement—were entitled to public assistance; others were "warned" out or forcibly driven or transported outside town or county boundaries. Advancing welfare policy beyond the narrow confines of family and community required a moral and theoretical leap—in Michael Ignatieff's phrase, the extension of kindness to strangers. Succeeding generations made this leap reluctantly and imperfectly, and an unwillingness to help those who seem different, alien, or outside a narrow definition of community poses as great an obstacle today to generous social welfare policy as in the days of the old settlement laws.[3]

The poor law reforms of the early-nineteenth century attempted to address many of these problems. The first major initiative was the construction of poorhouses (indoor relief) by state governments. By forcing everyone who wanted relief into poorhouses, they hoped to deter people from applying in the first place. If fewer applied, dependence would be less of a problem, relief would not undermine labor supply, and the costs of assistance would drop.

Poorhouses did not accomplish their purposes. Indeed, they proved much more expensive than outdoor relief, and the number of people seeking relief continued to rise. For decades, poorhouses served many relatively young and able-bodied men as temporary refuges during times of slack work or while they looked for employment. Initially, they also served as orphanages for children and hospitals for the mentally ill. They housed helpless and sick old men, some old women (though women more often lived with their children), and, on occasion, young unmarried pregnant women. They were terrible places—dirty, disorderly, full of disease, with miserable food and accommodation. As the nineteenth century progressed, state governments removed more and more inmates from poorhouses into separate institutions or onto the streets: children, able-bodied men, the mentally ill, the sick. By the early-twentieth century, poorhouses had essentially become public old-age homes.[4]

Moreover, despite the construction of poorhouses and a barrage of criticism from politicians, public officials, and reformers, many more people still received outdoor than indoor relief. And many reformers looked for ways to end or reduce it. The most notable nineteenth-century war on outdoor relief began in Brooklyn, New York, in 1878, when Mayor Seth Lowe persuaded the city council to abolish it. Brooklyn was one of ten of the nation's forty largest cities that did away with public outdoor relief between the late 1870s and the early 1890s; others reduced the amounts provided. But their expectation that private charity could meet the legitimate needs of the worthy poor proved illusory, and they found they could not do without public outdoor relief for long. By the second decade of the twentieth century, even former opponents of outdoor relief recognized it as a necessity, and debate shifted away from its justification to its administration. Whether relief was public or private mattered less than honesty, efficiency, and professional management.

In 1911, another form of outdoor relief arrived when Illinois and Missouri became the first states to offer mothers' pensions, which were small payments to widows. Championed by reformers since the late-nineteenth century, mothers' pensions for the first time made outdoor relief a state as well as local responsibility. By 1919, mothers' pensions existed in thirty-nine states and the territories of Alaska and Hawaii. In 1931, they supported 200,000 children, in every state except Georgia and South Carolina. Even so, their low benefits covered only a fraction of potential recipients, and they required longtime state residence and good behavior as a condition of eligibility. However, despite their limitations, they helped prevent the breakup of many families and represented the first halting step on the road from charity to entitlement.

During the New Deal era, women reformers in the newly created Children's Bureau urged the federalization of mothers' pensions in order to permit deserving women—still mainly widows—to remain at home with their young children rather than work for wages. The Aid to Dependent

Children provision of the Economic Security Act of 1935 resulted from their efforts. At the time, President Franklin Roosevelt did not realize that in ADC his administration had set in motion a major new federal public assistance program, and no one predicted its growth and transformation into what AFDC became.[5]

The New Deal was the first time that the federal government provided outdoor relief. The Federal Emergency Relief Administration (1933) and the Civil Works Administration (1934) were the two major agencies founded for this purpose. At its peak, the Civil Works Administration employed 4.26 million workers, or 22.2 percent of the potential workforce. Combining work with welfare, it was the greatest public works experiment in American history. But President Franklin Roosevelt had authorized federal relief only as an emergency measure to avoid mass starvation and save bankrupt state and local governments; he shared the conventional view that relief eroded the will to work and bred dependence. As soon as he could, he returned the responsibility for outdoor relief to the states. The end of federal relief brought great hardship; many people were left with no money for food, fuel, housing, and—despite a new federal work program, the Works Progress Administration—no job.[6]

While FDR is remembered as the founder of the welfare state, the boldest attempt to transform welfare was proposed by, surprisingly, President Richard Nixon in 1969. His Family Assistance Plan would have introduced a "negative income tax"—a guaranteed minimum income for all. It would have eliminated specific disincentives to work and made unnecessary a welfare bureaucracy to determine eligibility and monitor compliance. It met defeat in Congress, however, where a later reform of outdoor relief similar to Nixon's promoted by President Jimmy Carter was also turned down. After that, the idea of a negative income tax faded as a potential public policy solution despite the fact that dissatisfaction with "welfare" was shared by everyone—conservatives, liberals, and recipients alike.

Even after two centuries of attack on the problem of dependency, in the late 1980s probably a higher proportion of Americans received outdoor relief than at any time other than during the Great Depression. With their goal of reforming outdoor relief—now packaged as AFDC—champions of the Family Support Act confronted a challenge that earlier generations of reformers had consistently failed to meet.[7]

Work Relief

By the early 1980s, an insistence on work as a precondition of benefits joined the concern with dependence to form the core of a "new consensus" about welfare. "People on welfare ought to work, work, work," declaimed Senator William L. Armstrong of Colorado, "because it is good for the soul, because it is fair to the taxpayers, because it rankles people who are paying taxes to support these programs to see people who are recipients not get out and work." This message was reinforced in Lawrence Mead's *Beyond Entitlement,* which argued that permissive government had increased welfare dependence by giving people benefits without requiring them to work. Richard Nathan, a social policy analyst and former federal official, summed up the new consensus in the label "new style workfare": "The operative concept is *mutual obligation,* which combines an obligation on the part of the state to provide services and on the part of recipients to participate in these services." The emphasis on work and the preoccupation with dependence pointed to the same solution: the goal, said Senator Daniel Patrick Moynihan, the Senate's leading expert on poverty and welfare, was to convert welfare from "a permanent or even extended circumstance" to "a transition to employment."[8]

Outside policy circles, however, critics blasted "new style workfare." At best, workfare "would provide opportunities for a handful of welfare recipients," observed political scientist Frances Fox Piven and social critic Barbara Ehrenreich. At worst, it would introduce a "new form of mass peonage that would ultimately be as damaging to society as to the women and children it purports to help." Although without question, "well-funded voluntary programs offering high-quality child care and job training would help," they doubted that the proposed programs would offer either.

The historic record of attempts to join welfare to work also called into doubt the prospects of workfare. Indeed, for two centuries, seemingly intractable contradictions had undermined efforts to use work as a deterrent to relief, to force paupers to contribute to their own support, or to move dependent individuals from public assistance to regular jobs.[9]

In the eighteenth and nineteenth centuries, outdoor relief generally carried no work requirement because it supported mainly women with young children or the elderly and infirm. Nonetheless, the American equation of work with virtue permeated early welfare reform, especially plans for poorhouses, which called for inmates to work—as a deterrent and a test of motivation as well as to build character and defray costs. But most poorhouse superintendents failed to find useful work for inmates, and "idleness," in the language of the day, remained a "great evil." Private charities, meanwhile, often applied work tests to men and teenage boys who asked for relief. When they could, they directed them to jobs, which they expected them to take as a condition of further aid. Women presented a dilemma because they were expected to stay at home with their children. Still, the Charity Organization Societies employed some women in laundries and encouraged others to sew at home or take jobs as housekeepers, which meant cleaning and supervising the tenements in which they lived in exchange for free rent.[10]

It was not until the depression of 1893 that work became a form of public assistance rather than a condition of relief. Faced with unprecedented suffering, cities for the first time developed public works projects—street sweeping, sewer construction, street paving, building construction—as forms of relief, and private associations turned over the money they collected to city governments to spend on creating jobs. Neither the states nor the federal government provided any funds for work relief. And these projects had other limits, too: none outlasted the economic crisis; they reached a minority of those who needed help; and they paid very little. Even so, they met with angry criticism from advocates of scientific charity, who believed such jobs would demoralize the poor, and from businessmen, who objected to government meddling in the labor market.

Thus, a hundred years ago, work relief already confronted a vexing and persisting problem: how to avoid interfering with the private labor market. Used indiscriminately, work relief could steal jobs from employed workers, and low wages could undercut their pay. High work relief wages, on the other hand, could swell the rolls of public assistance and drive up costs by making it too attractive. Wages were only one of the problems that undercut work relief over the years. Others became especially evident in the New Deal's unprecedented and massive work programs, which flourished until World War II briefly eliminated unemployment.[11]

In addition to its early public assistance programs, the New Deal provided federal work relief through the Civilian Conservation Corps and the National Youth Administration as well as the Works Progress Administration, which within a year had put more than 3 million people to work. But despite their many achievements, none of these programs met its goals. The WPA, for instance, reached only a fraction—by one estimate, one-quarter—of the eligible unemployed. Wages paid for work relief failed to lift workers out of poverty or even to provide them with enough money for subsistence. Because the federal government had no employment and training infrastructure in place, at times of crisis it was faced with a choice between developing programs slowly and carefully or responding quickly with inadequately considered improvisations. Moreover, the inconsistent goals of public works programs proved impossible to reconcile. To be useful and efficient, programs needed qualified workers, incentives for good work, and the power to dismiss the incompetent or lazy. But they were also supposed to maximize employment, which meant hiring unskilled workers, offering few incentives, and rarely firing anybody. Workers, for their part, found themselves expected to show gratitude for public generosity by toiling hard while forgoing normal workers' rights, such as collective bargaining or strikes. The question of eligibility further complicated matters. Who needed help most? Every criterion discriminated against somebody. The WPA tried to solve the problem by choosing workers only from relief rolls and limiting employment to one job per family, but its rules hurt the recently unemployed, women, and large families.[12]

For a brief moment during World War II, economic and welfare policy seemed ready to merge in a federal commitment to full employment. As historian Alan Brinkley writes, the work of the National Resources Planning Board, appointed by President Roosevelt to plan for the postwar era, "represented an effort to link the commitment to full employment with the commitment to a generous welfare state." However, conservatives, appalled by its vision of central planning and a generous welfare state, quickly scuttled the NRPB report and forced the board out of existence. To some liberals the Employment Act of 1946, which declared full employment a national goal, appeared to be a second chance to realize the NRPB's objective, but the bill's vague language and subsequent dilution only reinforced the separation of economic goals from welfare policy.[13]

During the 1960s, the federal government tried to link economic growth and welfare reform by experimenting with labor market policy. Officials in the Department of Labor stressed the importance of job training to macroeconomic policy; members of Congress argued for the creation of public jobs to supplement work available in the private labor market; Willard Wirtz, secretary of labor, wanted to include "subemployment" among the nation's official employment problems; and President Johnson tried to involve the private sector in public job training. Nonetheless, concluded political scientist Margaret Weir, all this activity "left a surprisingly meager legacy." One reason was that the War on Poverty took precedence over effective training policy and subsumed labor market programs. By the late 1960s, observed Weir, "labor market policies," associated increasingly with African Americans, "had become politically identified as income maintenance policies not much different from welfare."[14]

In 1967, with the Work Incentive Program (WIN)—now known as workfare—the federal government revived work as a precondition of relief. WIN required welfare officials to refer employable AFDC clients to jobs and used incentives—welfare recipients were allowed to keep some of their earnings, for example—to encourage employment. It did not try to reshape labor markets by creating jobs, and it did not train welfare recipients for employment that would help them escape poverty. Like earlier programs, WIN failed. In the program's first twenty months, only 10 percent of the 1.6 million cases referred for work were considered employable. Conservatives criticized WIN for not reducing welfare dependency; liberals objected that it did not lift families out of poverty— only 24 percent of men and 18 percent of women who participated in WIN training found a job when the program ended, and those who did find work earned low wages. Furthermore, WIN did not stop the rapid growth of the AFDC rolls.[15]

In the 1970s, Democrats trying to focus their party position seized on public employment as a cure for joblessness. The result was a new 1973 public-service job creation program, the Comprehensive Employment and Training Act (CETA), which subsumed earlier programs. It emphasized short-term job creation, often for unskilled and semiskilled positions like clerks, typists, guards, and road crews, along with jobs in maintenance, repair, and warehouse work. It did not provide any training, and its critics accused it of favoring individuals capable of finding jobs for themselves rather than those in need of skills. Critics also contended that local governments used CETA funds to pay for existing jobs rather than to create new ones. Administered locally, CETA "bore the earmarks of pork barrel politics."[16] In retrospect, CETA's accomplishments have received less attention than its failures, and yet, especially after Congress revised the program in 1976, its achievements were substantial. For instance, CETA funded community-based organizations like the Opportunities Industrialization Centers; Jobs for Progress/Service, Employment, and Redevelopment; and the National Urban League. It supported many projects for youth, such as experimental programs in the Job Corps (originally part of the Economic Opportunity Act of 1964) and projects designed to rehabilitate young offenders. Most of these projects, which would not have been implemented without CETA's resources, provided useful public services while employing participants from mostly disadvantaged backgrounds, who performed their jobs as well as regular employees. Nonetheless, CETA did not transcend the historic tensions that crippled work relief and public works programs, and it was not part of a comprehensive policy designed to increase economic growth by creating human capital and permanent jobs.[17]

After 1980, the newly ascendant Republicans, responding to supporters who believed that job training programs distorted labor markets and inflated wages, cut the programs to the bone. Not simply "an incremental shift in policy," noted Weir, this decimation signaled a "rejection of the notion that the government could—and should—directly intervene in the economy to ensure adequate employment for its citizens." Federal spending on labor market programs plummeted from $15.6 billion in 1980 to $5 billion in 1985. In 1982, the Reagan administration replaced CETA with the much less costly Job Training Partnership Act, an example of the increasing reliance on the private sector to administer public programs. The JTPA offered more help to employers in search of low-cost labor than it did to potential workers looking for good jobs, and it served women worse than CETA had. Furthermore, its record of job placement was not impressive. From April to June 1987, for example, 45 percent of women and 39 percent of men left the program without finding a job. In Milwaukee, a study found that 51 percent of those who did find employment no longer held the same job three months later.[18] Thus the history of putting welfare recipients to work, which would be a primary objective of the Family Support Act, was far from encouraging.

Child Support

The Family Support Act also emerged partly as a response to the frustration of public officials unable to force absent fathers to support their children. In one way or another, the problem of child support has hovered around questions of relief and welfare throughout American history. No one could cast young children among the undeserving poor, but how to help them without rewarding their dissolute parents or encouraging adult dependence has been an enduring dilemma.

When most women with young children who applied for relief were widows, or when, as was often the case in the nineteenth and early-twentieth centuries, their husbands had been incapacitated by illness or industrial accident, the problem of enforcing support by absent fathers was moot. Women bearing children out of wedlock appear to have been more likely to give them up for adoption than to seek public assistance. Many sought shelter in a maternity home or, if desperate, a poorhouse. A large if indeterminate number placed their children in foundling homes, or "baby farms," where the infants often died.[19]

The great nineteenth-century question about child support revolved around the capacity of poor families to care for and raise their children. From early in the century, some observers connected an alleged rise in juvenile crime and immoral behavior to deficient parenting. Their relentless rhetorical attack on the family life of the urban poor conjured fears that vast numbers of unsocialized youngsters—often with immigrant parents—would overrun American cities. Public schools offered one answer, and public school systems were promoted partly as antidotes to crime, poverty, ignorance, and cultural difference.

But public schools parted children from their parents for only a few hours a day. In many instances, when parents required public assistance or private charity, when they drank too much or let their children run unsupervised in the streets, permanent separation appeared necessary. Parents lost custody of children who were committed to reform schools and became wards of the state. When reformers finally won a long battle to remove children from poorhouses, the result was often to separate them from their parents by moving them into other institutions, like orphanages. In the 1850s, the New York Children's Aid Society became the most famous of the several agencies that shipped children to farm families in the West, even though most of them still had a living parent. In the 1870s, Societies for the Prevention of Cruelty to Children gained quasi-public power to police poor families and separate children from parents they considered neglectful or abusive. And Charity Organization Societies often urged widowed or deserted mothers to place their children in institutions.[20]

In the 1890s, reformers who considered themselves "child savers" began to advocate for the preservation of families. Their efforts to reverse the family separation strategy that dominated public policy and private charity culminated in the first White House Conference on Children in 1909, which endorsed their views. Family preservation carried a high price, however: adequate support for mothers and supervision of families in their homes. Mothers' pensions were one response to the problem of support; juvenile courts and the emergence of social services addressed the need for supervision. Kindergartens and other educational reforms enhanced the public role in socialization. Although the number of children in institutions continued to grow during the early-twentieth century, progressive policy now considered institutions poor alternatives to families, not prime instruments of policy.

As the meaning of "child support" changed, policy debate focused less on the moral and financial capacity of poor families to raise their children and more on capturing financial support from absent parents. This shift reflected demographic and cultural transformations. By the late-nineteenth and early-twentieth centuries, desertion had emerged as a significant problem that impoverished many women. Men often abandoned and then returned to their families; wives, undoubtedly desperate for support, abetted their husbands in this process by taking them back. In New York, when wives wanted to extract support from absent husbands, they could sue them in magistrate's courts, but even when they won, enforcement was difficult. "Between 1890 and 1915, every state in the union," writes historian Michael Willrich, "enacted new laws that made a husband's desertion or failure to support his wife or children a crime, punishable in many locales by imprisonment at hard labor." To enforce the new statues, in the 1910s and early 1920s cities throughout the country introduced "the 'socialized' family court," often called Domestic Relations Courts. After midcentury, other factors added to the problems caused by desertion. Starting in the 1960s, marital separation and divorce rose steeply, and the number of out-of-wedlock births escalated. Meanwhile, the stigma attached to out-of-wedlock births, which had once led women to give up their children, faded. A great many mothers and children were now poor because their husbands and fathers refused to support them, not because these men were incapacitated by illness or dead.[21]

The politics of child support also shifted after midcentury. Until the mid-1970s, the federal government took only a minor role in enforcing child support, which remained the responsibility of state and local governments. In 1950, Winfield Denton, an Indiana congressman, proposed a "runaway pappy" law that proved too harsh for Congress, which instead passed a bill requiring AFDC officials to tell local law enforcement officers of deserting parents among families receiving public assistance. Prosecutors, however, rarely pursued absent fathers. And liberals suspected that such child support legislation harmed single mothers more than it helped them because it gave local authorities the right to deny aid to mothers who allegedly failed to cooperate in the pursuit of absent fathers. Thus, liberals successfully opposed the notification requirements in the courts. Nancy Duff Campbell, a former legal services lawyer, told historian Jonah Edelman, "Although welfare mothers at the time made the argument that they did want this kind of support, there wasn't a lot of sympathy for this paternity and support issue" among welfare rights advocates.[22]

Liberal opposition, however, eventually crumbled, in part because of changes in family demographics. Between 1970 and 1985, the proportion of families headed by women nearly doubled. As a result, nearly a quarter of children under the age of eighteen lived in single-parent families, but only a minority of them received support from absent parents. Clearly, the problem was becoming too widespread and serious to ignore. One Senate aide pointed to another reason that the politics of child support had changed—"because the women's groups latched onto it." Women's organizations viewed child support as a way of helping all women, not just those receiving public assistance. The growing number of women in Congress felt the same way, and child support won favor with politicians from both parties. As Edelman observes, "Liberals [liked it] because stricter child support enforcement would make mothers financially better off; conservatives because financially better-off mothers would be less dependent on welfare; both sides but especially conservatives because unlike every other social program, child support, on balance, brought more money into government coffers than it spent and helped defray welfare costs as a result." Both sides also agreed on principle that absent fathers should support their children.[23]

Nonetheless, variable state standards left awards to judicial discretion, resulting in payments that were far too low to meet children's needs, and only a fraction of noncustodial parents paid anything—an evasion reinforced by the inability of state governments to pursue them across state lines. Congress responded, first, in 1974, with the landmark Child Support Act, which created a federal Office of Child Support Enforcement and required states to open comparable offices. The new legislation also extended federal funding to pay for three-fourths of state expenses for enforcement. In 1980, Congress again strengthened child support provisions and in 1984 added the Child Support Amendments, which required every state to set fixed numerical guidelines for child support awards and to withhold payments from the wages of delinquent parents. Despite the conflicts between constitutional rights, civil liberties, and the mandatory provisions of the law pointed out by liberal critics, the 1984 Child Support Amendments passed with no resistance: 422 to 0 in the House and 94 to 0 in the Senate.[24]

As a result of the 1984 amendments, the amount of child support awards started to increase, although only one-third of single parents received any child support payments, and payments remained too low to make a dent in women's poverty or their dependence on public assistance. Thus, improved child support became a logical, irresistible, and urgent component of welfare reform—one of the main objectives of the Family Support Act and one that helped win its passage.[25]

Women who left welfare for work needed child support of another sort—subsidized care for their children. Even with income supplemented from children's fathers, these women's low wages could rarely pay the going rate for child care. And public officials who wanted to push mothers from welfare to work were unwilling to provide them with the support necessary to remain independent. In America, the history of child welfare is shot through with similar contradictions between rhetorical concern for children and the refusal to fund their welfare. (One of the best historical accounts of public programs for children is aptly titled *Broken Promises*.)[26]

Child care has found itself entangled with welfare policy since the nineteenth century. The first day nurseries, which originated to help poor mothers who needed to go to work, met with hostility from women and men who believed mothers belonged in the home. This ambivalence about the legitimacy of working mothers hobbled the development of child care, which remained unable to shed its association with poverty and welfare. In the early-twentieth century, sponsors of family preservation and mothers' pensions wanted to help poor women to stay out of full-time work; the women who ran the federal government's Children's Bureau were by and large hostile to mothers' employment; and with Aid to Dependent Children, the drafters of the New Deal's Economic Security Act also hoped to help mothers stay at home. The only major break in this attitude toward working mothers before the 1970s came during World War II, when the demands of war required full-time employment from women as well as men.[27]

When massive numbers of married women entered the labor force in the 1970s, pressure built to move mothers from welfare to work. Congress responded in 1974 and 1976 by designating federal money to raise public day-care standards and bring more low-income women into child care jobs. These new child care subsidies were restricted to needy families. However, even this modest start on federal child care support stalled and reversed in the 1980s, when the Reagan administration cut funding. The 1981 budget legislation began to transfer responsibility for child care to the states by bundling funds, which had been cut by 20 percent, into block grants and eliminating requirements for state matching funds.[28]

Other Reagan administration policies made use of the tax system to subsidize child care, which increased the advantages only for middle-class women. Federal legislation allowed individuals to exclude the value of employer-provided child care from their gross income and to shelter pretax income in "flexible spending plans." Employers and proprietors also received tax breaks for providing child care and building facilities. This pattern of support through the tax system bifurcated child care along class lines: only women with taxable incomes benefited from tax breaks, which moved child care into the private market.[29]

Responding to government incentives and increased demand, employer-sponsored child care programs mushroomed, and for-profit firms entered the field. In 1977, 41 percent of child care centers were profit making, mostly small independent operations—but child care soon became a big business as chains and franchises moved into the industry: By 1985, Kinder-Care's 1,040 centers served 100,000 children, and Children's World ran 240 centers in thirteen states. Nonprofit centers expanded as well, while in-home care by relatives declined. During the 1980s, as Sonya Michel observed, a new class-based child care system could be divided into four groups: "Publicly funded centers or family caregivers struggling, with declining resources, to provide child care for poor and low-income children; family child care with a primarily working-class and lower-middle-class clientele; voluntary or proprietary centers for middle-class families; and in-home caregiving by nonrelatives, supplemented by nursery schools, for the well-to-do."[30] For the poor, access to child care was governed by the war on dependence. Only the drive to move mothers from welfare to work justified increasing funds for child care. To this day, child care retains its class structure: it remains an adjunct of welfare reform, not a universal right.[31]

The Family Support Act

Despite widespread disgust with AFDC, welfare reform stalled in the early 1980s, a victim of partisan disagreement and historical inertia. Then, in 1986, a combination of events bumped welfare reform up to a higher priority on the national agenda. First, President Reagan called for reform in his State of the Union message: "In the welfare culture, the breakdown of the family, the most basic support system, has reached crisis proportions—in female and child poverty, child abandonment, horrible crimes, and deteriorating schools. . . . And we must now escape the spider's web of dependency." Reagan charged the White House Domestic Council to present him with a strategy "to meet the financial, educational, social, and safety concerns of poor families" by December 1, 1986. Second, the Democratic capture of the Senate placed Daniel Patrick Moynihan in the chair of the crucial Senate subcommittee in charge of the legislation. And lastly, the cuts in federal funds for public assistance that had increased states' fiscal burdens—as well as unmistakable public antiwelfare sentiment—stimulated governors to form a bipartisan commission on welfare reform headed by Governors Bill Clinton of Arkansas and Mike Castle of Delaware.[32]

However, until the results of new welfare-to-work demonstration programs became available, no one had solid evidence that welfare reform—defined as moving AFDC recipients into jobs—could succeed. The Omnibus Budget and Reconciliation Act of 1981 had allowed states more latitude to design such programs, and a number of states had seized the opportunity. None of these programs offered very much job training. Instead, they stressed job search—a cheap way of moving people quickly off the rolls and into jobs, but one whose long-term benefits were uncertain.[33]

The Manpower Demonstration Research Corporation (MDRC), a nonprofit organization, evaluated these new programs in eleven states to "test what works for disadvantaged welfare families." Summarized in a book by MDRC's president, Judith Gueron, *Reforming Welfare with Work* (1987), the results influenced the design and passage of the Family Support Act. "A major shift in the nation's social policy," later wrote a social scientist who had interviewed the key players in federal welfare reform, "seems to have been shaped largely by research and analysis."[34]

The MDRC studies showed that even programs that offered only modest help with job searches led to gains in employment and income among women (but not men) on AFDC and that the most disadvantaged participants gained most. Cost-benefit analyses argued that programs' gains slightly outweighed their expense. And, according to surveys, most participants did not object to mandatory work requirements. Nonetheless, individual gains were small. Most women earned $150 to $600 a year over their former welfare grants, not counting increased work-related expenses, which left most of the women close to the poverty line; most of the increased earnings came from longer work hours, not higher wages. Although the demonstration programs helped some women leave AFDC, Gueron admitted that they "do not appear to move a large percentage of the welfare caseload out of poverty," and many returned to the welfare rolls. A 1987 General Accounting Office analysis drew a similar conclusion: "Evaluations of the work programs have shown modest positive effects on the earnings and employment of participants. But wages were often insufficient to boost participants off welfare. Thus, programs should not be expected to produce massive reductions in the welfare rolls." And the carrots dangled by workfare proponents—child care, education, medical benefits—remained limited and "vastly underfunded."[35]

Despite the modest results of these demonstration programs, state governors and congressional welfare reformers hailed them as the elusive answer to the dilemma of work relief. For the first time in American history, they proclaimed, welfare recipients had been put to work in the regular labor market. The specific welfare proposals before Congress, however, were hardly supported by the MDRC studies. MDRC had not examined the effect of work requirements on mothers with children between the ages of three and six, a group targeted by the proposed legislation, and the studies had focused on short- rather than long-term recipients, the group whose dependence so alarmed welfare reformers. Skeptics could have just as easily used the MDRC data to argue fairly that the proposed welfare legislation would fail.

Nonetheless, the MDRC results buoyed hopes for welfare reform and helped break the legislative logjam in Congress. Viewed by many in Congress as hard, impartial data, the reports appeared to show that work reduced welfare at a reasonable cost, and they reinforced the idea that "citizens who accepted public money owed a mutual obligation." An official of the National Governors Association claimed, "For the first time, we could characterize reform as an investment." A Senate staff member observed, "It was unique. In all the years I worked on welfare reform, we never had a body of data that showed what worked. Now we had it. And those findings were never contested at any level." MDRC, as a *New York Times* editorial noted, "created the data base that convinced Republicans and Democrats that welfare recipients are willing and capable of working." The MDRC results, widely publicized, did not by themselves recommend specific policies. Rather, according to one reporter, they gave "very solid support to the directions people wanted to go in," and in 1988 they convinced undecided House and Senate members to vote for the Family Support Act.[36]

The first major welfare legislation in decades, the 1988 Family Support Act commanded strong bipartisan support, passing the House 347 to 53 and the Senate 96 to 1. Nonetheless, sharp divisions had separated the contending proposals for welfare reform, and the final bill reflected compromise as much as consensus. Republicans and Democrats reached agreement most easily on enhanced enforcement of child support. More controversy surrounded the new state employment and training program (called JOBS) intended to move AFDC clients from welfare to work. "Created as an alternative to mandatory work," observed one analyst, "JOBS became a new (if only partially funded) entitlement to education and training grafted onto an existing entitlement to cash assistance." Although the bill allowed states to design their own programs, it required all of them to offer education, job skills training, and job placement, and it called for 55 percent of JOBS funds to be spent on clients who were already, or were likely to become, long-term AFDC recipients. One of the bill's most contested provisions required clients with children under three years old to participate in JOBS. The bill attempted to facilitate the transition to work through active case management and by extending one year of Medicaid and child care benefits to families who left AFDC for employment.[37]

Congressional conservatives contested the legislation's mandatory extension of AFDC Unemployed Parents (AFDC-UP) to all states. Introduced in 1961 and made permanent but not mandatory in 1962, the program had allowed states to offer AFDC to two-parent families when the "principal earner" was unemployed. By 1988, only a minority of states participated in the program. As their price for making federal public assistance universal, conservatives exacted a stricter work requirement for unemployed than for single parents. They also prevented the adoption of a national standard for AFDC, whose benefits continued to vary greatly from state to state.[38]

The national press hailed the FSA's passage. "Striving to break a cycle of dependency," proclaimed the *New York Times*, "the Senate today approved the first major revision of the welfare laws since their enactment in 1935." The *Washington Post* praised the FSA as a "landmark overhaul of the welfare system"; the *Los Angeles Times* called it the "most sweeping revision of the nation's principal welfare program—Aid to Families with Dependent Children—since it was created in 1935."[39]

In reality, the FSA offered little hope of reforming welfare, at least in the short run. As two early critics pointed out, it rested on unrealistic assumptions about the availability of good jobs for welfare clients. Most jobs open to low-skilled workers with limited education, a group that included a large share of AFDC clients, did not pay enough to lift a family out of poverty, were frequently insecure, and offered few fringe benefits or opportunities for upward mobility. With the flight of industry from cities, the suburbanization of work, the increase of subcontracting, and the impact of foreign competition and automation, good, long-lasting jobs had become scarce. Nor did workfare—working off welfare payments through employment—open a path to unsubsidized jobs and independence. Employers usually offered only minimal training and support to employees hired through workfare, which itself carried a stigma that made jobs in the regular labor market harder to find. The Family Support Act, predicted another knowledgeable critic, would shuffle people into dead-end jobs in shrinking sectors of the labor market. "Requiring people to work without preparing them for long-term employment will, in the long run, fulfill the worst expectations of welfare reform."[40]

The Family Support Act did enhance child support. It forced women to identify the fathers of their children as a condition of receiving public assistance, set legislative guidelines for awards, and required employers to withhold child support payments from the paychecks of absent fathers. However, the rise in out-of-wedlock births outstripped the increase in the number of awards against unmarried fathers. Although the 1997 share of single mothers receiving support, 31 percent, had risen only slightly in two decades, this overall statistic masked an important change. Among never-married mothers support increased more than four times, from 4 percent to 18 percent, while among previously married mothers it rose from 36 percent to 42 percent. Because state implementation of child support policies varied from state to state, the likelihood that a mother would receive child support still depended very much on where she lived.[41]

. . . .

It is a mistake to judge the intent of social policy solely by the rhetoric of reformers, legislators, or public officials—the real priorities and goals emerge from the study and comparison of budgets. Where, then, have government and private philanthropy been willing to put their resources? For the most part, not in innovative social policies and institutions. For all the talk in praise of work, Congress has never funded work programs adequately. CETA received funds sufficient to employ only about one in twenty of the unemployed, or one in ten of the working poor, and Congress provided its successor program with 70 percent less money. By 1988, funding for WIN, or workfare, had dropped to less than one-third its 1980 level.[42]

The FSA—severely underfunded by Congress—was no exception, although it could claim some accomplishments: improved mechanisms for collecting child support, the extension of AFDC to two-parent families in a number of states, the movement of a small number of clients off AFDC, and the encouragement of state demonstrations of "welfare reform." Nonetheless, doubts that it could meet its goals proved accurate. In contrast to the federal fanfare, states gave the Family Support Act a low-key reception. More progressive states used it to reinforce initiatives already under way. Others proceeded more slowly and reluctantly. By and large, states followed the letter rather than the spirit of the law. They did not, for example, strengthen "mutual obligations" by forcing welfare recipients to work. Mandatory participation, the source of so much public controversy during the bill's passage, proved moot in practice: with state programs reaching only a small fraction of AFDC clients, most participants remained volunteers. The failures of the FSA did not surprise badly paid state social workers, who experienced firsthand the problems caused by too little money for education and training, too few job opportunities, and caseloads that were too high. Rarely could they offer the personalized case management called for by the law.[43]

Money aside, the FSA foundered on the historic separation of welfare from the labor market in American social policy. Sponsors of the FSA assumed that jobs would be available to AFDC clients. They did not want to create jobs, and they permitted state welfare departments to design programs without serious analyses of local labor markets or consultation with labor departments. At a time of declining real wages and fringe benefits, they asserted that after one year, former welfare clients would support themselves—and pay for child care and health insurance—through work. The research with which they justified their claims supported none of these assumptions.

By 1995, the federal and state governments, reported economist Norton Grubb, operated a "bewildering array" of job training programs that cost more than $20 billion each year. What was the result? Grubb put it this way: "The gains in employment and earnings are quite small from a practical standpoint: they are insufficient to move individuals out of poverty or off welfare; their effects very often decay over time, so that even the small benefits are short lived; and, as they are currently constructed, they do not give individuals a chance at middle class occupations or incomes."[44]

The Family Support Act did not improve on this history or revolutionize AFDC. What undermined it, ultimately, was a shift in the welfare debate. By every indication, public sentiment had turned harsher and more punitive. The point was to cut benefits, not extend them. Women should be chased off AFDC with sanctions, not lured away with incentives and new supports. The new benefits, moreover, reflected an out-of-date paternalism, a failed liberal reliance on big government, rather than on the market principles already being applied in state and city government, the nonprofit sector, and the private welfare state.

The FSA strengthened the federal role at the moment when state governments had begun to clamor for more independence and authority. In 1986, an official of the Reagan administration, Charles Hobbs, had proposed to reform AFDC through block grants to the states. Although his recommendations were rejected, he had seen the future. By the 1990s, the initiative in welfare reform had shifted to the states. On the day it was passed, the FSA was already an anachronism.[45]

GOVERNORS AS WELFARE REFORMERS

In the 1990s, state governors proved to be the most aggressive welfare reformers. It was pressure from the governors, in fact, that had broken the congressional welfare logjam in 1988 and paved the way for passage of the Family Support Act. When the FSA failed to transform welfare, states took it upon themselves to cut benefits, change regulations, and experiment with new programs. The governors radically restructured AFDC and Medicaid, trimmed or abolished state assistance programs, and implemented welfare-to-work programs. Although these actions were part of the larger movement to reduce dependence and adopt market models in the welfare state, more than anything else they ushered in a new era in public policy characterized by the devolution of authority from the federal government. The primary leaders within the states were two Republican governors, John Engler of Michigan and Tommy Thompson of Wisconsin.

The Centralization of Social Welfare

The governors claimed they wanted to restore public assistance to its historic and constitutional place in America's federal system. They drew, first, on the Tenth Amendment to the United States Constitution, which reserves powers not granted to the federal government to the states; second, on the tradition of public assistance as a state responsibility throughout the nation's past; and third, on the reputation of states as the pioneering laboratories for innovation during the formative years of American social policy.[1]

Throughout American history the authority over welfare policy had thrust upward toward higher levels of government. The governors proposed to redirect this history of public assistance. From the colonial era until well into the twentieth century, public assistance remained profoundly local. Counties, parishes, towns, and cities developed their own policies toward outdoor relief with increasing but never complete regulation by state governments. As a result, hundreds of local governments administered outdoor relief with a huge variety of rules and benefits.

During the nineteenth century state governments, as we have seen, worked to increase their control of public assistance by curbing the costs of poor relief, revising outmoded settlement laws, and building poorhouses. In New York, the legislature eased some of the burden on local governments by labeling individuals without a settlement (including many immigrants) state paupers and funding their care in poorhouses directly. State governments also opened new institutions to care for the dependent poor: mental hospitals, reform schools, general hospitals, and penitentiaries.[2]

By the close of the Civil War, state governments found themselves supporting a wide array of public and private institutions, which were run with no oversight and accountable to no one. With the dislocation of war, the explosive growth of industry during the Gilded Age, and widespread unemployment resulting from unsteady work and periodic downturns in the economy, the cost of relieving dependence mounted, and the demands for help by institutions and private charities escalated. State governments responded by creating state boards of charities (or bodies with similar names) to collect data and recommend policy. Massachusetts was first in 1863, followed by New York and Ohio in 1867, Illinois in 1869, Pennsylvania in 1870, and other states soon after. Advisory only, sometimes in conflict with local government, these boards lacked executive authority; in 1872, the New York board defined its role as "the moral eye of the State and its adviser in relation to the management of all its eleemosynary institutions."[3]

In the early years of the twentieth century, state governments cautiously innovated in social welfare. They introduced workers' compensation, mothers' pensions, and, in some cases, unemployment insurance, and began to professionalize the administration of public assistance by replacing state boards of charities with departments of public welfare. Expanded and modernized state governments increased their spending in the 1920s. Between 1922 and 1929, per capita state spending, in constant dollars, financed mainly by debt, increased 60 percent. In the same years, cities, starting with Kansas City in 1913, began to create their own public welfare departments and to modernize their administrative procedures.[4]

Any hope that public welfare—or the provision of economic security to all Americans—could remain primarily a state and local function collapsed during the Great Depression of the 1930s. State and local governments facing bankruptcy, unable to turn to private charity, which also was overwhelmed, surrounded by misery, and confronted by militant demands for relief appealed to the federal government for help.[5]

Although President Franklin Roosevelt, as discussed, initially responded with emergency relief—the first federal outdoor relief in American history—followed by a massive program of work relief, it was his Economic Security Act that gave the federal government permanent and unprecedented responsibility for the economic security of the elderly, the unemployed, and dependent children.[6]

The New Deal changed the relationship between the federal government and the states. Under the Constitution, the federal government could not order states to participate in its old age assistance or mothers' aid programs. Instead, it needed to lure state governments with new money. Grants-in-aid, widely used by the federal government for the first time during the 1930s, circumvented the constitutional issue. The federal government did not impose its will on the states; rather, it offered them money they could not afford to refuse, and attached conditions to it. In the process, the New Deal redesigned American federalism. Instead of the constitutional allocation of government functions by level, federalism became a system in which major functions were shared among local, state, and national governments. It is this profound and enduring shift in the nature of federalism that governors in the 1990s tried to modify or reverse.[7]

In the 1930s, the laboratories of policy innovation also moved decisively from the states to the federal government. "The American state is finished," one authority on state government announced. "I do not predict that the states will go, but affirm that they have gone." More accurately, states were the drag retarding progress in public policy. Southern states, intent on preserving cheap labor and a racial caste system, exacted as their price for support of the Economic Security Act the exclusion of agricultural and domestic workers, meaning most blacks, from Social Security. Other states failed to modernize or adequately fund and staff their operations. Even in the early 1960s, state governments still earned the scorn of public policy scholars and professionals who called them the "weak sisters," "fallen arches," and "weakest links" of the federal system.[8]

Thus in the 1960s, the federal government, by necessity, initiated the next great burst of social policy innovations. A private agency, New York City's Mobilization for Youth, funded with Ford Foundation money, and, then, on a larger scale, the President's Committee on Juvenile Delinquency, not state governments, served as laboratories for ideas underpinning the War on Poverty. The poverty war's Community Action Program initially tried to bypass both state and city governments to deliver money directly to new local agencies. Medicare, like Social Security, remained a federally funded and administered program. Meanwhile, Medicaid, a branch of public assistance, followed the AFDC model requiring state matching funds and state administration under federal guidelines. The federal government also directed the most important housing programs, and, of course, it passed the Civil Rights and Voting Rights Acts and enforced desegregation. Progressive changes in social policy, most analysts assumed, could and would issue only from Washington.

Nevertheless, at the height of federal power, state activity in social welfare was still extensive and crucial. States administered and set benefit levels for AFDC and Medicaid, oversaw most federal grant-in-aid programs, and often ran their own General Assistance programs. With major responsibility for public health, even today states outspend federal and local government, operating three times as many hospitals and disbursing two-and-a-half times as much as the federal government on "civilian services" (education, roads, welfare, public health, hospitals, police, sanitation). They contribute 49.8 percent of the cost of elementary and secondary education, compared to 43.8 percent from local and 6.5 percent from the federal government.[9]

A cursory look at a state budget hammers home the magnitude of the contribution. In the late 1990s, the Pennsylvania Department of Public Welfare spent about $5.4 billion out of a total state budget of approximately $17 billion; only spending on education, $6.7 billion, was higher. The department supported about thirty-five services and grant programs, including the county assistance offices, cash grants, county child welfare (which cost nearly $400 million), and homeless assistance. Other departments spent money for social welfare purposes, too. The Department of Education budget included funds for the education of migrant children, the education of indigent children, school-to-work opportunities, and tuition for orphans and children placed in private homes. The Department of Community and Economic Development spent money on housing and redevelopment assistance and on community revitalization. The $200 million budget of the Department of Health included expenditures for maternal and child health, state health care centers, and other programs for low-income families. The Department of Labor and Industry paid for workers' compensation, programs for dislocated workers, and employment services; the Department of Aging funded a variety of social services.[10] Clearly, American welfare remained a state, as much as a national, affair.

The Origins and Early History of Devolution

The history of devolution from the federal to state governments started in the administration of President Richard Nixon. By the time Nixon assumed office, the Great Society's proliferation of new federal grant-in-aid programs had created a maze that state and local officials found difficult to navigate. In succeeding years, the situation only grew worse. The number of grants-in-aid exploded from 160 programs in 1962 to more than 600 in 1981. From 1970 to 1980, their cost increased from $24 billion to $82.9 billion. State and local officials decried these categorical grants-in-aid for "their red tape, rigidity, insensitivity, and contradictions." In the mid-1980s, for instance, 230 programs administered by ten different federal agencies dealt with health care. Not only did goals conflict, but programs often bypassed governors, legislators, and mayors by directly funding public and private agencies.

Nixon's hostility to government bureaucracy along with his goal of returning power to elected public officials and state governments shaped his response to the profusion of government programs. As the key to his New Federalism, Nixon introduced General Revenue Sharing—federal funds sent directly to states to use as they saw fit—and new block grant programs that greatly increased state and local government authority over the allocation of funds. Nixon's New Federalism, however, did not decrease federal spending, and his influence on the balance of federal-state power proved inconsistent.[11]

In the 1980s, devolution signaled an ideological position on American federalism as much as a practical policy, and President Ronald Reagan's commitment to state power reflected the intent of a newly ascendant conservative politics to reduce the size and scope of the federal government. Reagan's policies gave state and local governments more authority and less money as budget cuts fell with special severity on AFDC and on programs that assisted the working poor. Ironically, his cuts in social welfare spending actually increased federal power; that is, he trimmed AFDC costs by increasing federal control over eligibility requirements and benefit calculations. Although he had opposed an increased federal role in AFDC when he was governor, in 1982 Reagan suggested a hastily conceived and inadequately detailed "swap and turnback" plan: the federal government would completely take over the funding of Medicaid but turn AFDC and food stamps over to the states. At the time, governors objected; they called for "a federal takeover of AFDC rather than a pullout."[12] A little more than a decade later, they would sing a very different tune.

In the first five years of the Reagan presidency, federal aid to states and localities plummeted 23 percent in real terms. Both liberals and conservatives predicted that states would pass along cuts in federal aid by reducing services and trimming social programs. Actual responses, however, generally confounded expectations as state and local governments frequently found creative ways to replace federal funding.[13] The expected "race to the bottom" failed to occur. Federal retrenchment did result in a massive withdrawal of benefits in one area, however: AFDC. Because of changes in the eligibility rules for AFDC, state governments were able to drop many people from the public assistance rolls. Despite a recession, some states reported lower expenses, while others compensated for reduced caseloads by raising benefits. (In other recessions, both caseloads and expenditures have risen.) Cutbacks hit low-income working parents hardest. In an attempt to restrict aid to the "truly needy," the Reagan administration rescinded the rule that permitted recipients to keep some earned income without losing benefits, which made the working poor ineligible. Cuts in federal subsidies for school lunches and food stamps also targeted the working poor, who found their incomes further reduced when the rent for subsidized public housing was increased.[14]

Several other factors also hastened the transfer of power to the states. Originally, the restrictive conditions placed on federal grants-in-aid reflected distrust that state government could, or would, meet national goals and standards. By the mid-1980s, this "lack of confidence and respect" appeared ill founded because the administrative capacity of state governments had improved, often dramatically. In 1985, a comprehensive study reported a transformation "in almost every facet" of state government "structure and operations." Between 1960 and 1974, for instance, professional staffing of state legislatures increased 130 percent, executive branches were reorganized, and the National Governors Association reemerged as a lively forum for policy debate and the vigorous advocacy of state interests.[15]

In *Baker v. Carr* (1962), the Supreme Court facilitated legislative reform and the modernization of state government by reapportioning congressional districts, which gave greater representation to urban areas and broke the dominance of rural interests. The Supreme Court's 1954 rejection of racial segregation, the Civil Rights Act of 1964, and other civil rights legislation further stimulated the resurgence of state government by ending what political scientist Martha Derthick calls "southern exceptionalism." Integration and the civil rights revolution meant that "the case for the states" at last could be "discussed on its merits," unhindered by racial apartheid. In addition, as a result of civil and voting rights legislation, younger and better educated representatives, as well as increased numbers of blacks and women, were being elected to state legislatures.[16]

The strong recovery of the nation's economy from the 1981–82 recession also reinvigorated state government in the 1980s. State treasuries began to fill up just as Reagan's cuts in federal aid started to take effect, and the states found themselves able "to spend more and do more" in those areas where the federal government had started to retrench. Not only did their revenue increase; their responsibilities—education, manpower development, planning—gained more importance in a restructured economy.[17]

Despite the powerful combination of trends reviving state government, devolution remained limited until the 1990s. By cutting back federal funds, the Reagan presidency had forced state governments to innovate, but it had devolved only power over capital and operating authority. Entitlements, which accounted for two-thirds of federal grants-in-aid, remained under federal control. By the 1990s, in contrast to the early 1980s, governors began to clamor for control over entitlement programs. More conservative governors committed to the Tenth Amendment had taken office, and all of them faced escalating costs for public assistance and Medicaid. Governors wanted to implement their own policies, which they believed would work better than Washington's, and they felt that the federal government stood in their way.

Among the new Republican governors, John Engler of Michigan and Tommy Thompson of Wisconsin, along with William Weld of Massachusetts, stood out for their bold "risk-taking style," "ideological crispness," and public policy innovations. "A dozen new Republican governors all seem to have the same battle plan," observed one commentator who dubbed them the "captains of conservatism." At the core of this "New Republicanism" another observer found "free-market purism," or the belief that "economics rules all and everything has a price tag. Government has no business interfering with market transactions—i.e., just about everything. Moreover, government is wasteful and can't do anything as well as the free market."[18] Ironically, in the name of free-market reform Engler and Thompson increased welfare bureaucracies and intruded further into the lives of citizens.

John Engler: From the Abolition of General Assistance to Welfare Reform in Michigan

In a 1990 electoral upset, John Engler ousted two-term Democratic governor of Michigan James Blanchard by 17,600 votes. The eldest of seven siblings, Engler, born in 1948, had grown up on his family's farm near a small town in central Michigan. When he defeated a seven-term incumbent to win his first election to office at the age of twenty-two, Engler became the youngest state representative in Michigan's history. Later, he served in the state senate and as senate majority leader. His 1990 election as governor capped nine straight election victories.[19]

A disciple and friend of conservative philosopher Russell Kirk, Engler found at the center of Kirk's "first principles" the "apprehension that order, justice, and freedom are mutually dependent on one another. . . . So that it is not just freedom, but ordered freedom that we must strive to preserve." Ordered freedom, he mused, quoting another conservative philosopher, Edmund Burke, flourished in small communities—"the little platoons we belong to in society," which "enrich our lives and humanize our relations with one another." However, these little platoons were being torn apart by the "centrifugal forces of modern times." Engler drew on a bowdlerized version of history to place the blame for accelerating social disintegration on the Great Society, a "horrendous, $5 trillion experiment in centralized authority." At the heart of the Great Society, "there evolved more than 300 welfare programs, a number of which rewarded ignorance, idleness, and illegitimacy—the absolute antithesis of the qualities you want a free citizenry to possess. These programs have worked untold mischief on the American republic." It was their legacy Engler set out to transform.[20]

Engler heaped scorn on the federal government, especially its role in welfare. "I am not an advocate of pruning federal programs," he said, "because those of you who are gardeners know that pruning just makes things grow faster than ever. What I advocate is getting a firm grip on the system as we know it, and pulling it up by the roots." Uprooting these programs was "the crucial first step in the long process of returning authority and responsibility where they ultimately belong—to the 'little platoons' of civil society—to our families and neighborhoods, churches and charitable organizations." Citing the Tenth Amendment to the Constitution, he stressed the separation of powers—no one at the Constitutional Convention of 1787, he argued, "called for giving the federal government a role in alleviating poverty."[21] When he spoke to the libertarian Cato Institute, Engler stressed the intrusiveness of big government and the virtues of free markets. Government is "not just too big in size. It intrudes where it shouldn't and interferes with our lives."[22] Washington not only barged in where it had no business; it blocked "free-market reforms."

Engler's vision of government also drew on Catholic social philosophy. In his keynote address to the Catholic Campaign for America's First National Convention, Engler described an embattled America threatened by corrupting cultural change "along a front that is both broad and deep." But "despite the scale of the war," he reassured his audience, "we have tremendous moral and spiritual armament upon which to draw. Our fortress is the Catholic Church; and the parapet on which we stand is its teachings. Our commander-in-chief is the Lord; and his able lieutenant—whose talents perfectly match the needs of our day—is the Holy Father." His interpretation of Catholic teaching led Engler to oppose abortion and the assisted suicides staged in Michigan by Dr. Jack Kevorkian; it also conveniently supported his plans for welfare reform. He believed the principle "the best welfare program in the world is a job" was "consistent with the teachings of the Catholic Church" and that "returning power and authority to the states" was "perfectly consistent with the Catholic principle of subsidiarity." (Engler did not comment on the ways in which his policies contradicted the pro–welfare state position of the United States Catholic bishops in their 1986 pastoral letter, *Economic Justice for All.*) Above all, Engler found in Catholic teaching, as well as the writings of Russell Kirk and the words of his mentor, former Michigan governor George Romney, an admonition to passion and courage in public life. Reflecting on his own political career, Engler urged his listeners, "Be bold and do the right thing. . . . If you have courage and if you are guided by sound principles, you will not only usher in an era of significant reform; you'll live to tell about it."[23]

Engler won his campaign against Blanchard on promises to lower property taxes, increase funding for education, get tough on crime, and cut government spending—especially welfare. He was helped by Blanchard's accumulation of a deficit of more than $1 billion, which forced him to cut spending by 9 percent in the closing days of his administration, and the perception in Detroit that his programs favored well-to-do suburbanites at the expense of the city. Engler also appealed to Reagan Democrats hurt by rising taxes exacerbated by a recession—Michigan had the fourth highest property taxes in the nation. Engler took office at a time when Michigan's unemployment rate, 7.6 percent (and expected to grow to 8 percent), exceeded the national average, and when personal income had declined 7 percent in less than a decade. At the same time state taxes brought in less revenue, expenses for the criminal justice system had swollen from 2.8 percent to 7.2 percent of the state's budget, or $688 million, during the decade. Although Michigan ranked sixth in the nation for major crimes in 1990, it expected to incarcerate a larger proportion of its population than any other state. Meanwhile, education's share of the state budget had declined from 37 percent to 30 percent.[24]

Despite high unemployment, Engler persisted with his plans to slash the state's budget, which he accomplished by persuading the Senate to approve Democratic spending proposals so that he could excise them from the budget with his line-item veto. In February 1991, shortly after assuming office, he vetoed a Democratic supplemental appropriation bill, causing deep cuts in social programs, and he closed several large state-run psychiatric hospitals and ended state funding for the arts. He decreased AFDC benefits by 17 percent and aid to foster parents by 22 percent, and planned to reduce payments to physicians and other health care providers in the Medicaid program by 18 percent. His actions risked the loss of all the state's AFDC and Medicaid funds because spending threatened to fall below federal minimums.[25]

Michigan was only one of several states to sharply reduce spending on AFDC and other poverty-related programs during the recession year 1991. In contrast to Ronald Reagan's cuts in 1981, which focused on the working poor, these cuts "concentrated on the poorest of the poor," slashing programs to their lowest levels in at least a decade. Forty states reduced or froze benefits for AFDC. The harshest states cut cash assistance and medical assistance while, at the same time, they reduced aid to the homeless.

Cuts in General Assistance surpassed even the reductions in AFDC. As social policy expert Robert Greenstein observed, General Assistance was "the program of last resort," providing money for individuals who were ineligible for federal cash benefits.[26] In 1982, Pennsylvania, under Republican governor Dick Thornburgh, began the modern war on outdoor relief by drastically reducing General Assistance benefits. "Thornfare," as the policy was called, was supposed to concentrate assistance on the truly needy while forcing others into the workforce. The policy assumed that most General Assistance recipients were healthy young adults who could find work. Contrary to official predictions, very few of the thousands of persons who lost their General Assistance found jobs. At the end of the year, most were out of work, and those lucky enough to find employment earned wages too low to lift them out of poverty. The health of many deteriorated; homelessness increased among them; and shelter placements in Philadelphia more than doubled during the first year of Thornfare. Although research had invalidated the premises on which Thornfare rested, twelve years later, a Democratic governor, Robert Casey, cut state General Assistance benefits even further.[27]

On taking office in Michigan, Engler almost immediately proposed the virtual elimination of the state's $250 million General Assistance program. In October 1991 he succeeded; more than 80,000 individuals lost their benefits. General Assistance had provided a maximum cash benefit of $160 a month and access to Medicaid; recipients also remained eligible for food stamps. When the legislature abolished General Assistance, it created a new disability program with less stringent eligibility requirements than Supplemental Security Income, the federal disability program. It also dropped but eventually reinstated its medical program—shifts that left former recipients confused about their medical insurance.

Although Engler hoped to use the savings from General Assistance to balance the state's budget, the program had long been a target of conservatives for reasons other than its cost. Engler, his spokesmen said, "hoped to end 'welfare dependency' by forcing 'thousands of able-bodied people to find work.' The jobs are out there. . . . They may be minimum wage but most people will be able to find one. And if they work full time at just minimum wage they could make twice as much as they did on G.A." State Representative David Jaye, a Republican from Shelby County, announced, "The most important thing is we took $300 million out of welfare for single, healthy employable adults and said, 'Get a job or hit the road, Jack.' We can't afford it anymore. These people are going to have to go cold turkey." In fact 40 percent of the "employable" adults who lost benefits were more than forty years old. Nearly half lived in Detroit and lacked transportation to suburban jobs. And 61 percent—many newly widowed or divorced women who had been supported by their husbands' wages—had never worked.[28]

Engler's abolition of General Assistance raised a howl of protest. Demonstrators pitched a tent city dubbed "Englerville" on the capitol lawn; Jesse Jackson led three thousand people in a protest march in Lansing; a coalition of thirty community organizations held a pre–Mother's Day mock trial of Engler; United Auto Workers president Owen Bieber and vice president Ernest Lofton called the General Assistance cuts "inhumane and senseless." An Ingham County Circuit Court judge, James Giddings, ruled that the abolition of General Assistance violated the Michigan constitution and ordered the restoration of the program, but the Michigan Court of Appeals overturned Judge Giddings's decision and unanimously refused to restore it.[29]

"We are the number one reform administration in America," proclaimed Engler. "The nation is watching Michigan to see what we have accomplished." Indeed, other states, for example Ohio, followed Michigan's lead by also eliminating General Assistance. Of thirty-eight states with General Assistance programs in 1989, twenty-seven restricted eligibility during the next decade. Hardest hit were "able-bodied adults without dependent children": the number of states offering them General Assistance dropped from twenty-five to thirteen in 1998; of these, only four states provided cash benefits. States also reduced General Assistance for disabled, elderly, and unemployed persons, notably those with a "temporary disability."[30]

General Assistance, Engler contended, had "subsidized people who had simply chosen not to work." But abolishing it along with cutting other programs and services shifted "incalculable costs . . . to local hospitals, jails, and other facilities where homeless people might land." Less than six months after the cuts were implemented, the Salvation Army estimated that homelessness had increased by 30 percent. Shelter capacity in Detroit doubled after General Assistance ended, and the demand greatly exceeded the available beds. Engler responded to the expected rise in homelessness by paying the Salvation Army ten dollars a night to shelter each homeless person. By 1995, the Salvation Army had received $38 million in state contracts. Engler's roots in Catholic social thought and belief in the free market underpinned his preference for contracting out government services to faith-based agencies. "Much of our success," he told a conservative Heritage Foundation audience, "is due to the fact that we contract out to private agencies, many of them church-run, because they provide an important element in the battle against poverty."

Taxpayers across the nation, not just in Michigan, also paid some of the bills for Engler's elimination of General Assistance, reduction of AFDC benefits, and cuts in other programs. In 1992, one federal agency increased Michigan's funds for coping with homelessness by 194 percent, even while cutting funds nationally by 8 percent. Former GA recipients began to apply for Supplemental Security Income, a federal program, and SSI payments in Michigan rose faster than elsewhere in the nation.[31]

As with Thornfare, Michigan's former General Assistance recipients fared poorly. Most did not find jobs. Although three-quarters had some previous work experience, only 38 percent found any formal employment during the two years following the loss of General Assistance; at their last interview, only one in five was working. Excluding those with assistance from a disability program, only about one-third fared as well as they had under General Assistance, and only 26 percent of the nondisabled earned a steady income comparable to their previous benefits. Indeed, without some form of public help, most former recipients could not survive; only 5 percent reported "resources comparable to or above GA through private means alone." Nor were they healthy. Half reported a deterioration in their health in one of the two years following the loss of their benefits, and 60 percent (three-quarters of those over forty) reported a chronic health problem. Similarly, in Ohio (as in Pennsylvania a decade earlier), six months after aid ended the proportion of former clients working rose only 2 percent, and among those who lost benefits homelessness rose 17 percent.[32]

All along, General Assistance had served a purpose different from what Engler and other critics alleged. It did not foster dependence and an unwillingness to work. Forty-three percent of General Assistance recipients in 1991 had received no help from any state program two years before and 44 percent received none two years after General Assistance ended. "This confirms," observed the two authors of the most authoritative study of General Assistance recipients, that "GA itself did not hamper incentives to work. Rather, it provided a legitimate safety net for those times when people were unable to be self-supporting."[33]

At first, Engler's budget cuts eroded his popularity. Before he abolished General Assistance, his assault on money for "social services and mental health, arts and cultural programs, environmental protection, job training and foster care" even prompted an unsuccessful attempt to recall him from office. Shortly after the legislature ended General Assistance, a poll showed Engler's popularity slipping badly, but his declining approval rating proved temporary and was not a result of his abolition of General Assistance, which 61 percent of residents approved. He won reelection with the largest Republican majority since 1928; in May 1995 his popularity stood at 70 percent. Although advisers had warned him that abolishing General Assistance was "political suicide," in 1994 not one of his Democratic challengers called for reviving it. If his experience during his first term proved anything, said Engler, "it's that you survive by doing what is right and making the tough decisions."[34]

A revived Michigan economy eased Engler's second term considerably. By 1996, as the Midwest led the national rebound from the 1991 recession, Michigan's unemployment rate had dropped to 4.6 percent, its lowest level in a quarter century and a point lower than the national average. Personal income had risen more than 25 percent. The state had added 450,000 new jobs. The automobile industry had recovered. An increased revenue base helped Engler fulfill his promise to cut taxes and balance the budget. He claimed that by 1998 his tax cuts would total $8.6 billion. He also addressed fears of crime by adding more state troopers and building more prisons, and he tried to stimulate economic growth through the creation of the Michigan Growth Authority, which assisted new businesses.[35]

Education remained a priority of Engler's throughout his administration. In 1991 he increased education funding as he cut spending on social services, public assistance, and other programs. In 1994, he broke a historic logjam over property tax relief and inequities in school funding: when Democrats in the state legislature tried to embarrass him by voting to abolish property taxes, he signed the legislation and sponsored a referendum that shifted school finance away from the local to the state level, where it was supported by a combination of an increased sales tax and other measures. Property taxes throughout the state plummeted; inequities between rich and poor school districts lessened. Under a complex formula, affluent districts were still allowed to spend more—only

Detroit and the other large cities did not fare well because the new formula favored poor rural districts. Voters liked the change in tax policy; a "Democratic poll reported that 56 percent of residents thought Michigan was going in the right direction."[36]

Aggressive welfare reform remained central to Engler's strategy, but real innovation required permission from the federal government—which Engler, like other governors, both resented and pursued relentlessly. A "zealous lobbyist for welfare overhaul," he turned up twenty-one times in Washington in 1995. "Mr. Clinton's system," complained Engler, "makes America's governors trek to Washington, hat in hand, begging beltway bureaucrats for permission to change." Engler was objecting to the waiver process, which had become the vehicle through which state governments—in the absence of federal legislation—were transforming public assistance. In 1962 Congress had authorized waivers of AFDC requirements to allow states to experiment with improved ways of administering and delivering services. At the time, Congress did not intend the use of waivers to curtail benefits or limit entitlements.[37]

With encouragement from the federal government, in the late 1980s state governments began to use waivers as vehicles for welfare reform. A Reagan administration working group argued, "the federal government should create the proper climate for innovation by giving states the broadest latitude to design and implement experiments in welfare policy." Despite the invitation, states responded slowly with waiver requests, even though President George Bush extended the offer: "Often, state reform requires waiving certain federal regulations. I will act to make that process easier and quicker for every state that asks for help." In 1992, as several states appointed welfare reform commissions, the Clinton administration also answered demands for increased state flexibility by encouraging waiver requests, which increased rapidly.[38] No philosophy or vision guided the award of waivers; the Department of Health and Human Services did not evaluate requests on their merits. The Clinton administration required only that waivers be constitutional, "cost neutral," and include "rigorous evaluation" of their results. "We are not in the business of turning down waiver requests," observed Mary Jo Bane, the assistant secretary of Health and Human Services for welfare. "We are in the business of helping states do what they want to do." Thus, waivers cut in different directions, opening the door to the neglect and punishment of the poor as well as to more flexible and constructive policies.

In the summer of 1995, Clinton boasted that his administration had approved welfare experiments affecting half the nation's 14 million AFDC recipients in thirty-two states—"more than all previous Administrations combined," he observed. By the time the 1996 federal welfare legislation was passed, the number of states with approved waivers had reached forty-three. Frustrated by Congress, responsive to the governors, Clinton attempted to implement welfare reform by executive order. In July 1995, he told the governors that he had directed the Health and Human Services Department to reduce the approval process for waivers from 120 days to 30 days. He also announced approval of new state welfare experiments and changes in regulations sought by the states.[39]

During the 1990s, waiver requests led to a wide array of changes. Some of these, as in Michigan— especially during the recession of 1991— aimed at saving money by manipulating benefit levels. Others tried to promote incentives for self-sufficiency by correcting problems in the way the welfare system treated work, family, and marriage. For example, by the summer of 1995, roughly thirty states allowed AFDC families to retain assets over the federal limit—$1,000, excluding a home and automobile—and about twenty provided transitional benefits—child care and Medicaid—to women who moved from AFDC to jobs. Other states implemented new programs to move AFDC clients into jobs by setting time limits on receiving benefits, imposing work requirements, or subsidizing wages paid by private employers. (Most of these initiatives sought to undo the impact of the Reagan administration's 1981 AFDC actions, which effectively ended benefits for the working poor.) A third round of waiver requests, collectively dubbed the "new paternalism" by some observers, proposed to reward or punish behavior. Wisconsin's Learnfare, which tied sanctions to children's nonattendance at school, and New Jersey's "family cap," which denied benefits to children of mothers already receiving AFDC, were leading examples. Many states required teenage parents to live at home with their own parents or another responsible adult in order to receive benefits; others required parents on AFDC to immunize their children.[40]

In 1992, federal waivers allowed Engler to implement a plan called To Strengthen Michigan's Families. The waivers increased the amount of money AFDC recipients could earn and the number of hours they could work without forfeiting benefits. They encouraged parents to remain together by eliminating "marriage penalties," provided some transitional child care and medical coverage when cash assistance ended, and enhanced child support enforcement tools. Additional waivers in 1994, part of a mandatory social contract, allowed the state to reduce and eventually end grants and food stamps for recipients who did not cooperate

with employment and training requirements. Waivers in April 1996
allowed Engler to implement Project Zero, an ambitious attempt to eliminate unemployment among AFDC recipients in six cities and put in
place child support reforms.[41] The state signaled the new emphasis in its
public assistance program by renaming the Department of Social Services the Family Independence Agency.

Engler and his colleagues claimed stunning success for their welfare
reforms. "In the three years since implementation of our welfare reform
initiative, To Strengthen Michigan's Families, the results have been truly
remarkable," claimed the Michigan Family Independence Agency. More
clients were working and the number reporting earnings had reached an
all-time high of nearly 30 percent, rising to almost 50 percent for families
headed by two parents. The state had closed over 70,000 AFDC cases
since 1992 as a result of earned income, and almost three-quarters of
recipients were participating in the Social Contract, which called for
twenty hours of "productive activity" each week. In contrast to the
national trend, the number of children removed from their families on
account of abuse and neglect had decreased 7.6 percent from its all-time
high in May 1992. By May 1997, 38 percent of "targeted" cases (those
required to work) statewide and 61 percent in the six Project Zero sites
reported earned income. Overall, the public assistance caseload had
decreased for thirty-eight consecutive months and reached its lowest
level since August 1971.[42]

Engler's welfare reform had its critics. Some worried about the impact
of recession. Economic growth, they argued, not welfare reform, had
increased jobs among former public assistance clients. What would happen when jobs dried up and tax revenues went down? A study by Abt
Associates suggested Engler's successes were overstated. Abt compared
people in Engler's program with a control group. After two years,
Engler's program increased adult employment over the control group by
only 2.4 percent. Without enough education or skills, the long-term job
prospects of Michigan's former public assistance clients were not bright,
especially because the new program shifted them out of educational programs and into low-wage jobs as quickly as possible. The goal of Michigan's welfare reform seemed to be to move people off the rolls, not to lift
them out of poverty. This was confirmed when two University of Michigan researchers, Sheldon Danziger and Jeffrey Lehman, asked how
many women would be able to earn more than poverty wages once they
left public assistance. The answer, they found, was very few; these
women were simply too ill equipped for the labor market. Only 8 percent, for instance, of black never-married women between eighteen and

twenty-five years old without a high school diploma who had young children could expect to earn higher than poverty wages.[43]

By 1996, welfare reform had not dented child poverty. In Detroit, 60 percent of children under five lived in poverty, the highest rate among the twelve largest cities in the nation. Statewide, 27.7 percent of children lived in poverty, compared to 25 percent nationally, even though most of them lived in working families.[44] Michigan's experience underlined something welfare reformers preferred not to address: cutting public assistance rolls and reducing poverty were not synonymous.

Tommy Thompson and the Abolition of Welfare

Together with John Engler, Wisconsin's governor Tommy Thompson led the campaign to devolve public assistance to the states. "Engler and Thompson are calling the shots," claimed Richard Nathan, an authority on state government, "and deserve the credit or blame—choose your descriptor—for the new 1995-style federalism."[45]

Tommy Thompson, wrote one commentator in 1994, "is a man of subtle contradictions. He's a conservative who considers himself a populist; a Republican who is compared to long-departed Democrats; a masterly politician who at almost every step of his 28-year political career has been underestimated." Like Engler, Thompson grew up in rural and small-town America. Born in Elroy, Wisconsin (pop. 1,642), in 1942, he worked in his father's grocery store. Elroy remains his touchstone—and it appears in virtually every speech he makes. "Everyone has his or her own common sense," asserted Thompson. "Mine is rooted in the values I learned growing up in the small Wisconsin community of Elroy."[46]

At age seventeen, Thompson entered the University of Wisconsin, where in 1963 he organized Barry Goldwater's presidential campaign on the liberal Madison campus. His first extended encounter with Washington was an internship on Capitol Hill during his senior year, where the person who impressed him most was Jimmy Hoffa. He returned to the University of Wisconsin for law school; in his third year there, 1966, he decided to challenge the sixteen-year incumbent state representative from his home district. To everyone's surprise, he won. Thompson practiced law and served in Wisconsin's part-time legislature—where he became minority leader in the state assembly—until his upset election as governor in 1986.[47]

Thompson ran a low-cost, grass-roots campaign; his platform stressed "cutting taxes, controlling spending, reforming welfare, and creating an economic climate of opportunity for business and individuals." He attributed his success to listening to the problems of voters and asking for their solutions. "And I really listened to each and every suggestion I received. We took all of these ideas and came up with policy proposals that I believed could really turn our state around."[48] Despite Democratic victories in the Senate and in gubernatorial races in neighboring Minnesota, Michigan, and Ohio, Thompson found himself at age forty-four the Republican governor of Wisconsin. Reelected in 1990 and 1994, he became the longest-serving governor in Wisconsin's history. He carried the state in 1994 with 67 percent of the vote, including about 30 percent of the African American vote, and became the first Republican in fifty years to win the usually Democratic city of Milwaukee.

Thompson took office at a fortunate moment. The state's economic recovery from the recession of the early 1980s had already begun, making it an opportune time to attempt to move people from welfare to work. Between 1983 and 1989, employment in manufacturing had risen 16 percent in Wisconsin, compared to 6 percent elsewhere. The relative absence of defense-industry jobs spared Wisconsin the worst of the downturn in employment between 1989 and 1994. In those years its manufacturing employment rose 2 percent, while nationally it dipped by 10 percent. As a consequence of greater job growth, total unemployment in Wisconsin remained below national levels.[49] Wisconsin's demography also favored welfare reform. The state experienced slow population growth, and its minority composition (5.1 percent black in 1990) was small. Migration into the state, despite its relatively generous welfare policies, had not been large.

Upon gaining office, Thompson inherited another advantage to Wisconsin welfare reform: his predecessor, Governor Anthony Earl, had initiated a promising welfare-to-work program that resembled the Family Support Act. It gave Wisconsin's state government experience with such programs, strengthened administrative capacity, and provided Thompson with a foundation on which to build.

Thompson also negotiated a stunning financial deal with the federal government. In 1986, President Ronald Reagan had appointed a Low-Income Opportunity Working Group to recommend ways to reduce welfare dependency. In February 1987, when the governors met to discuss Reagan's encouragement of welfare reform and the report of the working group, they developed a proposal of their own, with only one dissent—from Tommy Thompson. The governors' plan stressed state employment and training programs, and it influenced the passage of the 1988 Family Support Act. Thompson, however, chose a different direction. He did not take his plan to the White House and Congress. Instead, he went directly to the U.S. Department of Health and Human Services and proposed a package of welfare experiments similar to the experiments called for by the Low-Income Opportunity Working Group, except they carried no additional cost to the federal government.[50] By cutting benefits, Thompson and the legislature saved the federal government money, and thanks to Thompson's deal, the savings were effectively returned to Wisconsin. This is how he funded his welfare experiments without additional federal dollars.[51]

Thompson's first five major welfare reform policies, proposed in early 1987, required waivers from the federal government. Three of them focused on improving incentives for recipients to graduate from public assistance and on extending medical assistance. A fourth was intended to extend work requirements to mothers of preschool children. The fifth was Learnfare—the "centerpiece of the first round of Wisconsin initiatives."[52]

Under Learnfare, teenagers in AFDC families who failed to attend school would not be counted in determining the size of their family's benefit. This meant a large income loss for their families—between 15 and 43 percent of their monthly AFDC benefit. In Milwaukee, the monthly AFDC income of teen parents living with one child dropped by $190, about half the money needed to support two persons above the poverty line; in a family of four, the AFDC reduction amounted to about $100, reducing income to about two-thirds of the poverty level. These sanctions affected many families. From September 1988 through December 1989, in Milwaukee County alone, the state "sanctioned" 6,612 teenagers.[53]

Learnfare, of course, proved controversial. A report found that a high proportion of teenagers sanctioned in Milwaukee came from families with indications of child abuse or neglect. Critics argued the program was unfair because some parents did not want their children to walk through dangerous neighborhoods; homeless families might be "preoccupied with survival"; rebellious teenagers often disregarded parents' orders; schools could not notify parents who lacked telephones of their children's absence; and children would gain "undue power over their parents, allowing them to use threats of skipping school as a form of blackmail." Most of all, critics doubted that Learnfare would work—that it would boost school attendance. Early studies appeared to prove them correct. Despite arguments over research methodology, no one—including the nonpartisan state research agency—could produce data that showed that Learnfare had increased the school attendance of Wisconsin's teenagers.[54] Nonetheless, other states copied Learnfare, and variations surfaced in state legislatures across the country. By February 1996, thirty-four states had received permission to link welfare benefits to school performance. A Connecticut proposal focused on the parents of truants; others concentrated on teen parents or dropouts. An Ohio variant, LEAP, which relied on incentives by rewarding teenage parents with cash for staying in school, appeared modestly successful. But, overall, Learnfare failed to meet its goals.[55]

Learnfare reflected a new emphasis on "personal responsibility"—a mantra in the larger war on dependence—in public policy. In 1989, Democratic pollster Mark Mellman's survey of Americans on family values concluded that "the single most widely shared value in this country is that people ought to be responsible for their actions." The national crackdown on "deadbeat dads," a Los Angeles policy of holding parents responsible for the gang activities of their children, and "family caps" on public assistance benefits are examples of other 1990s public policies enforcing personal responsibility. There is of course an irony, if not a contradiction, in the use of paternalist big government—with its heavy-handed intrusion into the lives of individuals and families—by governors who champion the free market and rail at Washington. "Paternalistic reform is popular and effective," observed Lawrence Mead, "but it means continued big government, not an escape from it. Thompson attacks bureaucracy in Washington, but at home his reform is government-led."[56]

With a second round of demonstration programs well under way, Thompson dubbed his policies a resounding success. In the eight years following December 1986, the AFDC caseload dropped a stunning 22.5 percent. Although Thompson assigned all the credit to his policies, three-quarters of the decline occurred in his first term, before his policies had time to take effect. In fact, there were a number of other influences at work. One was tighter eligibility standards. Another was the favorable economy. Indeed, the labor market proved crucial to welfare's decline. When unemployment increased in the recession of 1991, the caseload crept upward; it began to fall again when the state's unemployment rate resumed its decline. A third influence was the federal JOBS program, whose principles, rooted in the approach of the Family Support Act, Thompson, ironically, had opposed. Because of its head start with a similar program, Wisconsin had developed the administrative capacity to implement JOBS far more effectively than had other states. But the success came at a cost: the administrative expense of Wisconsin's program exceeded the national average by 14 percent. Thompson had discovered that effective welfare-to-work programs are expensive. "Those individuals who have not been in welfare reform," Thompson told the Senate Finance Committee, "think that you can just change the system from one based on dependency and you receive a check once a month to one in which you require people to go to work. They are going to be sadly mistaken when they start the program because there is an upfront investment. You can save money on the back end, but the upfront capital investment is more and we have done that."[57]

When President Bill Clinton visited the annual meeting of the National Governors Association in February 1993, he reiterated his pledge to "end welfare as we know it" and promised the states new flexibility to experiment. "I returned home to test that promise," recalled Thompson. He and his aides designed the first time-limited public assistance program in the nation—Work Not Welfare. The program would require each individual applying for AFDC to sign a contract pledging to work in return for benefits and to start a job or begin training for one in the private or public sector within thirty days. Within twelve months all participants would be at work; the state would provide child care for those who needed it; and after twenty-four months, cash benefits would end, although transitional benefits—child care and health care—would continue for another year. The state would also guarantee access to job training and education and other help from a team of employment specialists.

Despite dissent among his advisers, Thompson decided on strict time limits. "This reform had to be about changing the fundamental culture of welfare. To do that, there had to be a ticking clock." Thompson was confident about the state's ability to find jobs for everyone who wanted to work, although he could not prove it. "I was certain that if we did not have a time limit, we would never know if it could be done." Thompson also rejected proposals to guarantee a government-funded job at the end of the two-year limit. "To my thinking, this would have eviscerated the experiment. With a guaranteed job at the end of the road, the urgency of preparing for and finding a job would be lost"[58] Fear, more than an anticipated escape from poverty, underpinned the incentives used in the tough new world of welfare reform.

With only waivers from the federal Department of Health and Human Services—and not legislative approval—Thompson implemented a test of the program, called Work First, in two counties. According to Thompson, it was an unqualified success, and throughout 1995, the state expanded Work First to forty-eight counties. In January 1996, now under the name Self-Sufficiency First, it extended the program to the entire state.[59] After fifteen months, the caseload in Fond du Lac, one of the demonstration counties, dropped 55 percent, compared to 10 percent in Milwaukee, 20–25 percent in the state overall, and 33 percent in two comparison counties. Nonetheless, the Fond du Lac experience could not be easily extrapolated as a statewide or national model. The county was small and primarily rural, and it received a massive infusion of funds unlikely to be repeated elsewhere. Although the state spent generously on the program itself, it did not allot enough resources to evaluation. As a result, researchers could not say for certain whether a similar Work Not Welfare model could "succeed" as well in other contexts.[60]

Critics assailed Work Not Welfare "as heading for a precipice, going too far too fast, offering no guarantees for jobs and virtually eliminating the proverbial safety net." The *New York Times* warned that the Wisconsin plan "might make some progress in moving some welfare recipients off the rolls and into productivity. But there are virtually guaranteed to be some ugly outcomes." Others predicted a rise in poverty.[61]

Thompson did not discuss poverty; he talked about moving people off the welfare rolls, and he took advantage of a wave of bipartisan anti-welfare sentiment to prematurely end Work Not Welfare and replace it with an even more comprehensive program. The Democrats, fearing their thunder had been stolen on the welfare issue, tried to embarrass Thompson by attaching a condition to the Work Not Welfare bill when it passed the state legislature: they ordered the state's Department of Health and Human Services to draw up a plan to end AFDC by December 31, 1998. Thompson did not veto the legislation, as expected. Instead, he seized the opportunity handed him by the Democrats. Using his line-item veto to modify the requirement, Thompson agreed to submit a plan to replace AFDC sometime in 1995. A conservative think tank from Indianapolis, the Hudson Institute, opened an office in Madison to provide technical assistance to the governor's task force on welfare reform, and it solicited money from other foundations, notably the Annie E. Casey Foundation of Baltimore, to support its work in Wisconsin. In early spring 1995 the Wisconsin Department of Health and Human Services and the Hudson Institute completed their plan, known as Wisconsin Works, or W-2.[62]

As he articulated his goals for W-2, Thompson wrapped criticism of dependence in the language of the market: "AFDC has been easy to get on, too easy to stay on, and harmful. For so many it's been a trap." Its replacement will "be less about welfare, dependency and assistance, and more about opportunity, responsibility, and incentives."[63] "Under W-2," announced the program's official "fact sheet," "there will be no entitlement to assistance, but there will be a place for everyone who is willing to work to their ability." W-2 held great importance for states and the nation. It was the first fully developed example of what a state welfare system might look like in the era of block grants that followed the 1996 federal welfare legislation, and it raised great moral questions. By ending entitlements, Wisconsin deliberately shredded the safety net that guaranteed protection to its neediest citizens.[64]

W-2, observed Michael Wiseman, who has studied it carefully, "justifiably can be said to end welfare as we know it, if the welfare we know is a system of means-tested income support, based on family size, to which persons are entitled on the basis of income, assets, and the presence of children in the household." The new program rejected entitlements and family size as a basis of support. It rested instead on the principles identified in Wisconsin's demonstration programs as essential for successful reform: "For those who can work, only work should pay." "All parents are capable of working." "Recipients are best served by programs that replicate the working world." "Education and training models in welfare programs are best built on the premise that the best training is actual work experience." *Work* was the key word, and the state signified its new orientation by renaming the Department of Health and Human Services the Department of Workforce Development.[65]

W-2 participants met with a Financial and Employment Planner—a new position—to find their place on a four-level employment ladder. Total time on any step of the ladder was limited to twenty-four months; the maximum time on the ladder was five years, with some room for extension in exceptional cases. From the emphasis on work flowed a number of W-2's key policies: mandatory work requirements, benefit time limits, quick job placement, and minimal training. Other key policies were maximum child support and the full use of the Earned Income Tax Credit and food stamps. The emphasis on supports—child care, health care, and transportation assistance must be available in sufficient quantities to facilitate employment—committed the state government to intensive case management and to spending heavily on the program. The goal of strengthening family and community, which included reducing "skyrocketing" out-of-wedlock births, translated into requiring teenage parents to live with their parents or in a "structured government supervised setting"; establishing Children's Services Networks in the counties; and continuing food stamps and Medicaid for children whose parents exhausted their time limits for cash assistance. The desire for local program administration led to contracting out services to government, nonprofit, and for-profit firms on a competitive basis and integrating employment and training programs in One-Stop Job Centers.

On April 25, 1996, Thompson signed the legislation creating W-2. On May 30 he delivered to the federal government a request for the forty-eight waivers necessary for its implementation, and in the early summer, he railed at President Clinton's failure to accept welfare legislation that would allow him to move ahead with his plans. When Congress finally passed the Personal Responsibility and Work Opportunity Reconciliation Act in August 1996, Thompson received his mandate. Under the new federal block grant provisions, he could implement most of W-2. Only his plans to charge Medicaid recipients for their insurance needed a federal waiver, which the Clinton administration eventually denied. Wisconsin, Thompson pointed out with pride, was the first state to submit a complete block grant proposal to the federal government. It won quick approval.[66]

Many observers wondered if W-2 could perform as promised and what its impact would be. Milwaukee, in particular, posed a challenge that the earlier welfare reform measures had not surmounted. With the only sizable "inner city" area in the state, its AFDC rolls had declined much less than elsewhere. In fact, between 1990 and 1994 they rose slightly (0.4 percent) despite a continued drop (13.6 percent) in the rest of the state. As a result, Milwaukee's share of the caseload had increased. Under pressure to reduce it, Milwaukee officials stressed "severe sanctioning," strictly enforced work requirements, and lowered benefits. It was not a coincidence, according to local social service professionals, that in 1996 the city witnessed an increase in poverty and homelessness.[67]

W-2 also threatened the well-being of children by lowering the quality and raising the cost of child care. Although state spending on child care would increase overall, pointed out one critic, "the amount spent for each child will go way down." Families earning more than 165 percent of the poverty level would lose all child care support. Families with lower incomes would remain eligible but their copayments would rise significantly—for a single mother with two children and a monthly income of $1,600, for example, copayments would increase from $62 to $910. At these rates, most poor families could not afford licensed child care. To meet their needs, the state created a category of "provisionally certified workers"—expected to receive about half the amount paid to licensed child care centers—who were not required to undergo any training. Unfortunately, research suggested that low pay produced high turnover and undermined the quality of child care.[68]

Critics of W-2 worried, too, about the absence of any guarantee of jobs and about time limits. What would happen to clients if the state failed to deliver on its promises to place them in work and provide them with services? The plan contained no fallback for program failure; the clients bore all the risk. When time limits ran out clients could find themselves with no work and no aid from the state, which would have no responsibility whatsoever for their well-being. Nor would they necessarily be trained for success in the labor market—indeed, with the insistent emphasis on mandatory work requirements, they could be diverted from, say, intensive literacy classes. Nor had the state planned for a recession. During the recession earlier in the decade, poverty in Wisconsin had increased at a higher rate than elsewhere in the nation. Even without a recession, many families, pointed out Mark Greenberg of the Center for Law and Social Policy, "working every available hour under program rules will be poorer than they are under current law."[69]

There were a variety of other potential problems with W-2. Because it allowed employers to fill vacancies with its low-wage clients, the availability of jobs at regular wages for ordinary workers might decrease. W-2 workers also lacked all normal protections concerning working conditions, and they might be used to displace existing workers. And like much previous Wisconsin work-based welfare reform, W-2, according to organized labor, could become a tool with which to bust unions. Moreover, the high cost of W-2 tempted the state government to use financial tricks to pay the program's bills, and some legislators complained that the Thompson administration was diverting funds from other pools of money to pay for it. Regrettably, whether W-2 would work as promised would be difficult to know: unlike earlier programs, the legislation authorizing W-2 did not mandate evaluation.[70]

Even without evaluation, it should have been obvious that Wisconsin was not a realistic model for other states to emulate. Before Thompson's innovations, its economic growth and low unemployment had helped initiate the decline in AFDC; tightened eligibility and lower benefits kept many people from the rolls in the first place and, according to some estimates, may have worsened poverty; its favorable deal with the federal government allowed it to spend heavily on welfare-to-work and related programs; and it had only one real, problematic inner city. Nonetheless, Wisconsin became a national beacon for welfare reform.

As in Wisconsin, welfare reform elsewhere responded to a widespread hostility to public assistance that cut across conventional party lines. Harsh action in Massachusetts, usually a liberal state, reflected the deep antiwelfare sentiment around the country. There, Governor William Weld led the charge. Unlike Thompson and Engler, Weld, a U.S. attorney, had family money and spent $1.1 million of his own funds on his Republican primary campaign. Elected with support from "women and baby boomers" in a close 50 percent to 47 percent contest in 1990, Weld "cut spending, privatized services, slashed public payrolls" and set in motion nine tax cuts in four years. At the same time, he outspokenly supported choice in abortion and gay civil rights and reversed his earlier opposition to gun control. In 1994, responding both to the state's economic recovery and to Weld's blend of fiscal conservatism and social liberalism, Massachusetts voters reelected him with the same overwhelming support—71 percent of the vote—given in Michigan and Wisconsin to Engler and Thompson in their second campaigns for governor.[71]

Weld's assault on welfare also combined the same themes as Engler's and Thompson's. He sought freedom from federal regulation, tried to use welfare reform to reduce the dependence associated with out-of-wedlock births, and stressed the reduction of entitlements inherent in market-driven social policy. Anticipating congressional action on a welfare bill that would allow states greater flexibility, Weld became the first governor in the nation to propose cutting cash assistance to unwed mothers under eighteen. "Any welfare reform that doesn't attack illegitimate births is not going to get the job done," he said. "Every American is entitled to certain things that can never be taken away. Public education is one, free speech is another, but we do not see welfare in the same terms. Welfare should not be permanent. It is not a right, and it should not be an entitlement."[72]

On February 10, 1995, Weld approved legislation "establishing one of the most restrictive welfare systems in the nation." Along with Michigan and Wisconsin, Massachusetts became a beacon for welfare reform in other states and in the federal government. As he signed the legislation, Weld remarked, "We are obliterating, today, the mistakes of welfare as it has existed for decades." The new law reduced welfare benefits by 2.75 percent and limited them to two years. It also required teen parents to live with their parents or in an approved setting and complete high school. Meanwhile, "able-bodied welfare recipients with school age children" would receive only sixty days of benefits, after which the law required them to get a job or perform community service. As in Michigan and Wisconsin, to symbolize the change in philosophy the new law renamed the Department of Welfare the Department of Transitional Assistance.[73]

Almost immediately the Massachusetts measure influenced Virginia, which used it as the model for a tough new welfare law passed in a racially divided vote. In the 140-member General Assembly, only two white members failed to vote for the measure, while all thirteen black members opposed it. "Welfare," said David G. Brickley, a Democrat and cosponsor of the bill, "originally was designed to give people a lift while they were in an emergency. Now, families stay on for generations. We want to make it more profitable to work than to receive welfare." Like many of its counterparts around the nation, the Virginia approach did not increase the profitability of work by raising wages or improving benefits; rather, it made welfare more restrictive by cutting off benefits after two years, forcing recipients to work, and denying aid for children born to mothers already receiving AFDC.[74]

Parallels in the Virginia, Massachusetts, and Michigan stories reveal the emergence of a national bipartisan consensus about welfare reform. As soon as Tommy Thompson announced his plans for W-2, President Bill Clinton praised them—although he later qualified his approval. John Engler's plans for welfare reform in Michigan also drew praise from leading Democrats.[75] The new consensus, tougher and more punitive than the understanding that led to the Family Support Act in 1988, rested on a dislike of welfare, hostility to its recipients, and faith in mandatory work as the key to its reform. It emphasized the stick, rather than the carrot, and it wanted to use government not just to reduce costs, but to change people's behavior. With reduced caseloads the sole measure of success, governors and state legislators talked very little about poverty. In fact, they remained perfectly willing to risk innovations likely to increase poverty for significant numbers of families.

By seizing the initiative, state governments had precipitated a historic transformation of American social welfare. For more than 150 years control of social welfare had lurched toward the center. Until the 1990s most discussions of welfare reform assumed the leadership of the federal government, and most welfare reformers advocated the continued expansion of the federal role, especially the creation of a national benefit standard for AFDC analogous to that of Social Security. Aggressive governors and state legislatures challenged these assumptions. By refusing to wait for congressional action on welfare reform or to accept restrictive and counterproductive regulations, the states began to redefine the structure of America's welfare state—and the nature of American federalism itself.

URBAN SOCIAL WELFARE IN AN AGE OF AUSTERITY

In the 1980s and 1990s, cities—unlike the states—could not displace misery onto other levels of government; the devolution of responsibility ended in their streets. Poverty, homelessness, AIDS, and the consequences of drug use strained their welfare, human services, and public health systems. In addition, crime, decaying infrastructure, and rising municipal payrolls confronted city governments squeezed by a declining tax base and the withdrawal of federal aid. Caught between fewer resources and escalating costs, cities scoured the landscape for new sources of revenue and ways to cut expenses. As they developed an array of cost-cutting strategies, mayors in the 1980s turned first to the usual sources: the federal and state governments. But federal aid dried up, the Family Support Act offered no real help, and state governments provided little new money—and in fact, by cutting back on General Assistance and other forms of "welfare," they threatened to increase the poverty and homelessness that undermined the fiscal and social health of the cities.

In the 1990s, a new cohort of mayors, both Democrats and Republicans, realized that the rules of the game had changed; they could no longer expect mass infusions of money to bail them out. Their solution was to trim labor expenses, cut services, tighten management, privatize city responsibilities—to assimilate city government to the market. They asked the federal government to lift unfunded mandates and redirect, not increase, spending in ways that would create incentives for inner-city investment. The likely casualties of the new urban agenda were social welfare services, inner-city neighborhoods, and the poor. But mayors claimed that fiscally sound cities, which created work, would eventually help poor people and their neighborhoods more than conventional social programs would.

Under the Reagan and Bush administrations, the flow of federal funds to cities slowed, diminishing the federal role in the economic and physical development of cities and heightening the difficulties confronted by the urban poor. Although the Clinton administration revived urban policy with new initiatives, federal urban policy did not return to the government spending/social-action template of the Great Society era. Rather, its major innovation—empowerment zones—was created with the intent to revive cities by creating markets in spaces that markets had abandoned. Despite the many differences between Republican and Democratic administrations, strategies for urban and housing policies shared key priorities and reflected the great forces—dependence, devolution, and markets—that were redefining America's welfare state.

The Fiscal Crisis of Urban Social Welfare

America's cities, towns, and counties have always been the last resort of men, women, and children in need of help. For most of American history, as we have seen, poor relief remained a local responsibility, funded and administered primarily through local taxes. Cities and counties also maintained dispensaries and hospitals for the poor; buried paupers; and coped with cholera, tuberculosis, and other public health crises that ravaged the impoverished. They gave milk to needy children; placed orphans in institutions; financed courts to resolve the domestic disputes of the poor; employed truant officers and school nurses; allowed the homeless to sleep in their police stations and opened municipal lodging houses to shelter them.[1]

Poverty cost cities and counties huge sums of money, and until the 1930s, they were by and large on their own financially. In 1902, when the number was first calculated, local governments accounted for about 50 percent of all government spending. With the exception of the World War I years, local nonschool employees outnumbered federal government workers. Only in 1940 did federal spending begin to outpace state and local governments' expenditures.[2]

During the twentieth century, state and federal governments have shared more and more of the burden of caring for the urban poor. Besides funding public assistance and housing, the federal government helped cities by providing their residents with social insurance and, especially after the public welfare amendments of 1962, social services. The social insurances removed large numbers of the urban elderly from poverty, supported the urban unemployed and disabled, and provided medical care to urban residents unable to afford it by themselves. Welfare pumped enormous amounts of money into cities and supported neighborhood businesses as well as families and individuals. For example, in the mid-1990s, Philadelphia residents received about $1 billion each year through AFDC, Supplemental Security Income, and food stamps; adding the state's contribution to various programs brought the total to $3.2 billion, a huge amount in a city with a $24 billion wage tax base.[3] Often funneled through state governments, federal aid lifted a share—but by no means all—of the fiscal burden of dependence from cities, which still paid a disproportionate share of the bill for the nation's poverty—disproportionate because poverty arose from great national and global forces beyond the control of individual cities. In 1985, direct poverty-related expenses in Philadelphia were $302 million; of that the city paid $83 million, or 6.71 percent of its budget. By 1995, the total figure soared to $713 million and the city's share had grown to $134 million, or 7.6 percent of its budget.[4]

Three observations about these figures are in order: first, their size underlines the fiscal burden of urban poverty, no matter who pays the bill. Second, they highlight the massive rise in poverty and poverty-related conditions in the latter half of the 1980s. And third, they illustrate the growing share of poverty-related expenses borne by cities.

Growing expenses for poverty hit cities hard. First, their tax bases began to decline. In older cities, the slide in population and manufacturing began as early as the 1970s, and the resulting fiscal distress hit cities with populations over 300,000 with special force. In 1987–88, according to a National League of Cities survey, 3 percent of them had declining revenues; by the next year the proportion had increased to 21 percent.[5]

As their taxable resources eroded in the 1980s, cities also lost the federal dollars that had partly compensated for the exit of population and jobs. Largely on account of increased Medicaid payments, the aggregate dollars received from the federal government between 1980 and 1990 for social welfare assisting individuals increased (in 1990 dollars) by 18 percent, but funds to governments, meanwhile, plummeted by 46 percent. Public service jobs and job training programs lost 69 percent, community development block grants 54 percent, and social services block grants 37 percent. The average share of big-city expenses covered by federal aid slid from 22 percent to 6 percent. In the same years, state aid, as a share of city revenues, held steady at 16 percent.[6]

National statistics mask a great variety among cities in their social welfare expenditures and dependence on federal funds, as these 1986 figures of total per capita spending for six major areas of social welfare show:

New York City	$1,670
San Francisco	$1,633
Vicksburg, Mississippi	$562
Dallas, Texas	$502

The federal share of this welfare spending ranged widely, too:[7]

Jackson, Mississippi	91 %
New York City	67 %
Core Grande, Arizona	57 %
Caro, Michigan	57 %

Thus, the consequences to poor people of federal fiscal withdrawal varied by city. Wealthy cities with lots of taxable resources and few poor people could choose to retain existing service levels without raising taxes very much. But cities with few taxable resources and many poor people could not turn to local taxes to compensate for lost federal revenue. Not only were states mandating balanced budgets, but cities feared tax increases would accelerate the exodus of high-income families and businesses. Given these problems, cities, not surprisingly, ratcheted down services and, with the exception of medical coverage, virtually froze the level of social benefits.[8]

Under any circumstances, the combination of lost tax revenue and declining federal funds would have strained cities' capacity to pay for social welfare. But in the 1980s and 1990s four developments intensified the gulf between needs and resources: heightened poverty, increased homelessness, the emergence of AIDS, and the rising human and fiscal costs associated with drug use, especially of crack cocaine.

From the 1970s to the 1990s, the number of ghetto neighborhoods, census tracts with a poverty rate of at least 40 percent, in major U.S. metropolitan areas grew from 1,177 to 2,726; their population rose from 4.1 million to 8 million; the number of blacks within them nearly doubled in number to 4.2 million, while the number of Hispanic residents soared from 729 thousand to 2 million. In 1990, 79 percent of the children in these poor districts lived in families whose income fell below the poverty line.[9]

AIDS and drug use, meanwhile, were spreading rapidly. "Cities' fiscal needs," reported *U.S. News and World Report* in 1989, "are immense." Analysts expected the cost of treating AIDS to rise to $12 billion nationally by 1992. In New York City, officials predicted expenses for AIDS to increase from $230 million in 1989 to $740 million in 1992 and for the "hidden costs" of drugs and AIDS, notably foster care and child abuse, to double by 1993. In 1994 alone, New York City's public welfare programs spent almost $1.1 billion on city residents who abused drugs and alcohol.[10]

Homelessness also devastated city social welfare budgets. Philadelphia officials projected an increase in the costs of human services in the 1980s from $79 million to $187.5 million; they expected services to adults, which included expenses for the homeless, to skyrocket from $5.7 million in 1980 to a peak of $40 million in 1989. That same year, Terry Goddard, mayor of Phoenix, Arizona, and president of the National League of Cities, identified the "no. 1 problem of the cities" as "housing to try to stem the plight of homelessness." The recession of 1990–91 only intensified the strain on city resources. Between 1992 and 1995, the public cost of serving the homeless in Philadelphia rose from $44 million to $66 million. New York City, which provided more care for the homeless than did any other city, spent about $500 million each year.[11] In some places, such as Connecticut, municipal officials found their welfare budgets "woefully inadequate"; at one early 1991 meeting of thirty-six municipal social service directors, only two thought they could reach the end of the year without extra money.[12]

Pushed to the brink of bankruptcy, many cities were being pressed further by a decayed infrastructure and the wages and benefits of city employees. A 1988 report found 42 percent of the nation's bridges unsound and 60 percent of its roads in need of rehabilitation. The estimated cost of necessary infrastructure repairs by the century's end was $100 billion a year, twice the level of current government spending. In the same period, city payrolls bulged and increasing municipal wages and benefits took ever-larger chunks out of shrinking city resources.[13]

In the 1980s, mayors responded to their fiscal crises with techniques pioneered in New York City during its near bankruptcy in the mid-1970s. New York City paid for its rescue with a program of austerity whose cornerstone was a financial control board that removed effective power over funding government operations from local officials and vested it for the most part in financial and corporate leaders. The austerity program decimated services throughout the city and helped persuade unions to accept lower wages. It also richly rewarded city bondholders and freed capital by reducing wage and tax expenses.[14] In the late 1980s, other cities also slashed services and laid off employees. As Philadelphia appeared about to go bankrupt, the state government appointed a financial oversight board roughly analogous to the Municipal Acceptance Corporation in New York City to reassure investors and the financial markets.

As they struggled to cope with fiscal crises, mayors and their advocates railed at federal cuts in urban aid, asked for more money, and demanded relief from unfunded mandates. At a news conference a reporter asked Alan Beals, executive director of the National League of Cities, "For the last seven or eight years, you all have been asking the federal government for money. The federal government keeps saying no. Why do you continue to ask them?" Beals equivocated, but in the 1990s a new cohort of mayors took the question seriously, realizing they were on their own. Rudolph Giuliani of New York, Dennis Archer of Detroit, Ed Rendell of Philadelphia, Richard Riordin of Los Angeles, Bret Schundler of Jersey City, Stephen Goldsmith of Indianapolis, Michael White of Cleveland, and John Norquist of Milwaukee all looked primarily to their own resources to rescue their cities. They downsized government, privatized city services, and faced down city unions. *Time* praised this "new breed of activist mayors" for its "pragmatism" and "flexible, post-ideological approach" to politics. "As parties become less important and as Republicans and Democrats search for ways to set themselves apart," observed a *New York Times* article, "mayors are setting the course for post-ideological, pragmatic politics."[15]

Wrote Stephen Goldsmith, mayor of Indianapolis, in *The Twenty-First Century City*:

A new breed of mayors now occupies city halls across America. With a deep understanding of the need for smaller government, and determined to attain a better life for citizens in tough urban neighborhoods, these new mayors have blurred the lines between Republican and Democrat, conservative and liberal. They do not want bigger checks from Washington; they want freedom to solve their cities' problems in their own way. In many respects, they have more in common with each other than they do with some of their respective parties' national leadership.[16]

Consulting regularly, borrowing each other's ideas, these Republican and Democratic mayors formed an informal network. In "a radical break with their predecessors," they concentrated on "managing city government efficiently in the public interest rather than using it as a mechanism for arbitrating competing group interests." Although the press called them pragmatic, they shared the belief "that cities can dramatically alleviate seemingly endemic urban afflictions without a massive redistribution of wealth, that the way to achieve this is by using competition to make city services radically more efficient, and that cities must tolerate diverse identities without celebrating them to the detriment of a shared sense of public interest." Harvard Business School professor Michael Porter provided a theoretical basis for the new urban strategy in his influential 1995 article "The Competitive Advantage of the Inner City." "A sustainable economic base can be created in the city," claimed Porter, "but only as it has been created elsewhere: through private, for-profit initiatives and investment based on economic self-interest and genuine competitive advantage."[17]

The disseminator of this new market-based urban policy was the conservative Manhattan Institute and its magazine, *City Journal*, financed with about $6 million a year from conservative foundations and corporations. New York mayor Rudolph Giuliani called the Manhattan Institute "the only institutional voice that has challenged the thinking that led to decline in this city. To the extent that the city is moving in a new direction . . . the Manhattan Institute should take a great deal of the credit for that." Like the governors, mayors saw themselves leading, not following, the federal government. Giuliani told the National Press Club that "in many, many ways our cities are ahead of the federal government. Many of the things that are being debated in Washington now are things that we're doing."[18]

Ed Rendell: "America's Mayor"

With his April 1994 "new urban agenda," Philadelphia's Ed Rendell, dubbed by Vice President Al Gore "America's Mayor," emerged as the leader of these activist mayors.[19] Elected in 1992, Rendell, a former district attorney, inherited a city on the verge of bankruptcy: its debt was huge, its services inefficient, its residents cynical and demoralized.[20] In the previous decade, Philadelphia's tax base had eroded by $2.1 billion; a national survey had ranked Philadelphia last in fiscal soundness among America's fifty largest cities. But within eighteen months, Rendell had turned a projected $450 million deficit into a $3 million surplus, and within two years, he had balanced the city's budget without raising taxes. His tactics included management reforms, privatizing several city services (he preferred to call it "competitive contracting"), freezing municipal wages, trimming benefits, and changing work rules. His twenty-one privatization initiatives officially saved the city $32 million a year and allowed him to reduce the city's workforce by 1,200 without any layoffs. When municipal unions struck his administration, Rendell did not budge, and the strike was over in sixteen hours.[21]

The city's five-year financial plan for 1995–99 proudly reported the Rendell administration's achievements. As a new convention center opened and services improved, for the first time in many years Philadelphians felt cautiously optimistic about their city's future, and Rendell's popularity soared, especially among business leaders. He won reelection with nearly 80 percent of the vote. *American City and County* named Rendell "Municipal Leader of the Year" in 1996. "Rendell has spearheaded one of the most dramatic turnarounds in the history of urban America," observed the magazine as it explained its award.[22]

"Early on," wrote national urban affairs commentator Neil Peirce, Rendell "distanced himself from many of his big-city colleagues by insisting that mayors had to stop 'whining' for a return of the federal aid of the '60s and '70s." Rendell told a conference of mayors to "forget help from Washington." Nonetheless, the city could not ignore the federal government. City officials, for instance, wanted the federal government to consult with them on the impact of its proposed policies, such as welfare reform. Although Rendell had moved Philadelphia toward solvency without outside help, he believed the city could not solve its most intractable problems without federal assistance, and in his "new urban agenda" he tried to reformulate the relation between cities and the federal government.[23]

Instead of asking "Washington for a 'handout' in the form of revenue sharing or massive amounts of aid to city government," said Rendell, he would ask the federal government to redirect its existing spending in ways that would better serve cities by creating incentives for investment. "The federal government has to level the playing field for cities, especially in terms of offering tax incentives," Rendell contended. Fifteen percent of all federal purchases, he argued, should be placed with companies in inner-city "empowerment zones." When the federal government shut down or moved facilities, it should insist on urban impact assessments similar to environmental ones, and its decisions should favor distressed urban areas. Rendell called for Congress to restore tax incentives repealed under the Tax Reform Act of 1986 that would make investment in cities more attractive, and he wanted the federal government to introduce new tax incentives for city-suburban cooperation. Rendell, like other mayors, also wanted the federal government to reverse policies, such as unfunded mandates, that placed unwarranted burdens on cities. A recent study, he commented, had discovered that the number of federal mandates had grown from two in 1960 to sixty-one in 1990 and sixty-six in 1993.[24]

Rendell preferred to label his strategy "a new economic agenda" because it did not directly address social welfare and public health issues. "This is not an attempt to deal with and address all of the problems of the cities. It doesn't deal with education, it doesn't deal with housing, it doesn't deal with crime, other than the fact that if we could create new jobs in American cities, reverse what is in most cities a quarter-of-a-century slide, where the tax base and job base has been eroded . . . if we could reverse that trend and start to build back jobs, obviously it would have a dramatic effect on everything—crime, drugs, housing, all of the ills of the cities."[25]

Rendell's urban strategy, like that of other new mayors, reflected faith in the discipline of the market. In his praise of recently elected Republican mayors, one conservative commentator observed, "If the GOP's new urban guerrillas can show that market-oriented solutions are the best way to save America's cities, then pulling the voting lever for Republicans may cease to be such an alien experience for urbanites." Nonetheless, he could not distinguish Republicans' policies from those of Democrats like Rendell, who expected that competition generated by privatizing city services would lower costs and improve quality, and whose willingness to dismantle the public sector helped convince municipal unions to accept his demands for a wage freeze, benefit concessions, and changes in work rules.[26]

In January 1994, with city finances stabilized, Rendell launched an Economic Stimulus Program to revive troubled neighborhoods, attract and retain businesses, implement defense industry conversion, and support the development of the hospitality and tourist industry on which he pinned much of the city's future prosperity. (Rendell also promoted riverboat gambling as a source of economic development.) The $2.2 billion for the program would consist of $866 million from city-controlled resources; $640 million in federal, state, and Delaware River Port Authority Funds; and $700 million in private investment.[27]

For all his successes, however, Rendell and his programs were not enough to overcome the serious obstacles confronting a deeply troubled city. In August 1996, its financial position, reported Rendell's chief of staff, David Cohen, was still "incredibly precarious," and some of the problems facing the city had worsened during Rendell's administration. For one thing, the exodus of jobs and people continued. From 1990 to 1996, the city lost 107,575 residents, about 1,800 residents a month, or 425 every week, the largest population loss among the nation's ten largest cities. Almost 100,000 jobs had disappeared since 1988. From 1992 to 1994, outmigration cost the city $1.6 billion in income. In March 1997, the U.S. Bureau of Labor Statistics finally reported that the city had at last experienced a year without losing jobs. Whether it could sustain this progress, nobody knew.[28]

Nor, in the short run, did Rendell's fiscal and management reforms reduce poverty. Although economic improvement since the 1991 recession had brought the poverty rate down from its peak, in 1997 about 40 percent of Philadelphia's children still received support from federal public assistance, and between 23 percent and 31 percent of the entire population lived below the poverty line. Rendell and others worried that the time-limited welfare bill passed in 1996 would push this number to disastrous levels.[29] In addition, the economic revival had barely touched the city's many ailing neighborhoods. John Kromer, head of the city's Office of Housing and Community Development, described the losses suffered by city neighborhoods in the previous thirty years as "unprecedented and irreversible" and of "catastrophic proportions." "Beyond the tightly controlled curtain of the downtown," observed Buzz Bissinger in his history of Rendell's first term, "a city once known for its neighborhoods was increasingly becoming a patchwork of vacant lots. In a radical shift of policy caused by population loss and acceptance of the hard fact that there was no longer any point in trying to save or rehabilitate blighted housing, acre after acre of the city was being leveled."[30]

At the same time, public housing remained a quagmire, and the city faced a crisis of housing for low-income residents. In September 1997, 16,000 families crowded the waiting list for subsidized housing; the Philadelphia Housing Authority had accepted no new applications since 1990; 84,000 low-income families paid more than half their income in rent.[31]

Homelessness proved to be an especially crippling problem. On top of the financial burden, homelessness threatened to tarnish the shiny new image Philadelphia worked so hard to project and to interfere with the corporate transformation of downtown. Across the nation, ordinary citizens, tired of being approached by beggars and fearful of crime, increasingly lost sympathy with the homeless men and women they encountered on city streets, and public campaigns against begging told them they were right to refuse to give them money or food. City officials viewed the homeless as impediments, scaring away employers, shoppers, and tourists. Occasionally, homeless shelters or encampments occupied land that cities wanted for redevelopment. The mayors' new market-based strategy of urban redevelopment demanded clearing the streets and redefining urban space.

Consequently, many city councils passed ordinances restricting panhandling and loitering, and public architecture was built to discourage sleeping or sitting. With these measures cities tried to drive the homeless away from central business districts or to concentrate them in new, out-of-the-way skid rows shielded from public view.[32] Philadelphia moved the homeless out of a subway concourse where many slept. In New York City, "the most visible clusters of homeless people in the most trafficked parts of the city have been cleared away," said an article in the *New York Times*. Many had moved to the city's margins, living on piers, in nooks and crannies under bridges and highways, or in other locations where the police would leave them alone. The new "geography of Manhattan's homeless population" complemented Giuliani's crackdown on "quality-of-life" crimes, which included begging and loitering. In January 1997, Los Angeles's top elected officials also launched a new attack on these crimes that would give the city "the most aggressive ordinance of its kind in the nation." Although most homeless people do not beg, reported the *Philadelphia Inquirer*, cities like Los Angeles "tried to make [their] familiar haunts inhospitable." To contain its large homeless population, Los Angeles created a "sleeping zone" in which it funded single-room-occupancy hotels—"a key to getting people off the streets." Not all zone residents slept in hotels, however: "Every night on the edge of downtown a couple of dozen men and women hustle cardboard boxes from the trash and arrange them, like a row of coffins, behind a red line painted on the sidewalk." Even this new skid row did not prove secure: by 1997 the city had started to eye it for redevelopment and as the site of a major sports arena and a downtown Catholic cathedral.[33]

In July 1996 Philadelphia began to turn "able-bodied" single men and women and some families away from its homeless shelters because the city had exceeded its budget for homeless services by $4 million. Rendell argued that only through saving money in the summer could the city meet the projected need for shelter in the winter. The city found it "extremely hurtful and painful . . . to take this kind of action," said Rendell's chief of staff, David Cohen, "but we are at the end of our rope." Philadelphia funded about fifty-two shelters managed by private operators. In the summer they housed 2,600 individuals, 300 more than expected, and the city predicted a population of 3,900 during the winter. Philadelphia had pumped significant resources into its shelters—in 1995, $18 million of its own funds, which was an increase of $4.3 million since 1993. Federal and state funds brought total spending on the homeless in the city to about $66 million. Under pressure from homeless advocates, Rendell eased admission criteria to shelters a bit in August, and in September unexpected federal grants helped alleviate the crisis. Nonetheless, Philadelphia remained far from able to cope with its homelessness problem. In January 1997, explaining his new budget, Rendell told City Council that "this budget does not include enough money for shelter [for the homeless] next winter."[34]

In particular, he and his colleagues blamed federal and state governments for cutting back on funds at the very time their policies increased homelessness. State funding cuts even threatened to force the city to close two of its community health centers. "We're left with a Hobson's choice," Rendell reflected. "Either we're letting our needs go unmet, creating havoc, with crime, homelessness and people living in the streets. Or we meet them dollar for dollar, forcing us to raise taxes and continue a horrible vicious cycle of losing our tax base, which gives us less revenue for our programs." By the winter of 1996–97 Rendell had backed away from his independent stand; faced with enormous social needs, which were likely to worsen, he started to ask the federal government for more money.

Stephen Goldsmith: "Prince of Privatization"

In Indianapolis, Mayor Stephen Goldsmith, the former Republican prosecutor for Marion County from 1979 to 1990, faced less daunting problems than those confronting Ed Rendell in Philadelphia. When he assumed office in January 1992, Indianapolis boasted one of the lowest rates of violent crime among the nation's fifty largest cities; public education appeared better than in Chicago, Milwaukee, and other major cities; during the previous quarter century, annexation had increased the city's population by about one-fourth; the city had recently lured a $1 billion United Airlines maintenance facility; and its remarkably cohesive corporate community, led by the Eli Lilly Company, a Fortune 500 pharmaceutical business headquartered in the city, helped leverage unusually large amounts of private support for economic development and public facilities. Shortly after taking office, Goldsmith appointed a commission of nine business leaders to conduct an ongoing study of the city government's efficiency: how well it used its assets, the quality of services it provided, and the competitiveness of its costs. The chair of the Service, Efficiency, and Lower Taxes for Indianapolis Commission was Mitch Daniels, vice president of corporate affairs at Eli Lilly.[35]

Goldsmith, who considered himself the equivalent of a CEO, tried to model city government after an efficient private corporation. By the end of his third year in office, he had privatized more than fifty city services; cut the city's budget by $10 million; increased the number of police officers on the streets; and invested $500 million in infrastructure improvements. He also allowed private businesses to compete with city departments for service contracts. When faced with outside competition, the city streets department reduced the cost of fixing potholes by 25 percent; the city's garage mechanics outbid three large national firms for the job of servicing the city's cars and trucks. Private companies, meanwhile, ran the public golf courses and waste-water treatment plant and handled the city's photocopying, microfilming, sewer billing, and messenger services. Indianapolis, Goldsmith claimed, had added 15,000 jobs in three years, and unemployment had plunged to 3.9 percent. Two years later, in 1997, unemployment had dropped to 2.6 percent and the city faced a labor shortage.[36]

Although some called him "the prince of privatization," Goldsmith preferred a different name for his strategy. Indeed, "in our office," he told a group of bankers, "my staff has banished the word privatization. Rather, they focus exclusively on competition." Although "privatization," he reasoned, "seemed like a useful piece of shorthand for what we wanted to do, it was actually misleading and threw us off track. The key issue . . . was not whether tasks were performed by public or private institutions. . . . Without the spur of competition, the difference in what we could expect in price and quality would be distinctly unrevolutionary."[37]

Governments, observed Goldsmith, "are inefficient because they are monopolies, and I hoped that a good dose of free-market competition would allow the city to provide better services for less money, freeing up precious resources." Goldsmith's reliance on competition reflected his faith in the market. "The basic concept is the market produces competition, competition produces value," he argued. The "way to create wealth," he told a Senate committee, "is through the marketplace, not through government spending." The "key" to successful urban governance, Goldsmith maintained, rested in creating "a marketplace for municipal services." Everything, Goldsmith told columnist George F. Will, "can be sold or submitted to competition except police and fire services." Goldsmith described his approach as "marketization." "For us, marketization meant creating a market where none previously existed. Today, throughout city government, we are trying to create a true market, a place where competition continually generates lower costs, better service, and new ideas for helping citizens."[38]

For Goldsmith the marketization of city government served moral as well as economic ends. He told the Republican National Convention in Indianapolis, "We're working with churches to discourage teenage pregnancy and encourage responsible fatherhood and we're paying welfare providers by how many people they get back into the workforce." Goldsmith even proposed discouraging teenage births by reintroducing "a stigma surrounding unwed pregnancy." His proposals included "segregating teen fathers and mothers in schools and limiting their extracurricular activities."[39]

Inner cities, however, posed intractable obstacles. "The free market," Goldsmith asserted, "does not exist in the inner cities of America, period. Any attempt to revitalize our cities must begin with this understanding, or it is destined to fail." As evidence he cited welfare "that pays more than work," public schools that "graduate kids who can't read," crack use that placed criminals beyond "traditional sanctions," and "high taxes and crumbling infrastructure" that kept businesses away. Also part of the problem were federal public housing policies and giant programs, which stifled innovation and encouraged "decay" with perverse incentives.[40]

One traditional solution—raising taxes—was a dead end or, worse, a sure route to disaster. Goldsmith agreed with Ed Rendell about the need to lower taxes. "If we do not [lower taxes]," he quoted from Rendell's

1997 budget presentation, "our hopes of growing our economy will disappear, and future mayors and councils will constantly be arguing how to divide a shrinking pie among competing demands that far exceed the size of the pie." When cities increase taxes even to fund crucial programs, continued Goldsmith, elaborating on Rendell's argument, "the result is a faster flight of wealth to the suburbs and more pockets of poverty."[41]

Without the money to "solve the problems afflicting" America's "inner cores," Goldsmith countered, federal, state, and local governments should concentrate on creating "wealth through the marketplace, not through government spending." The key to successful urban policy, he told the Senate Banking Committee, lay in tax policy rather than in federal programs. Tax incentives, he predicted, would reduce the size of the federal government and "apply a tourniquet to the flow of businesses and jobs out of cities." Goldsmith wanted Congress to bundle all the federal money spent on affordable housing, community economic development, and the salaries of program administrators into block grants, to repeal all laws and regulations that applied to public housing, and to have all its building deeded to communities or local agencies, with tenants given "family-based vouchers" based on fair market rents.[42]

He thought the way to start rebuilding "free markets" in inner cities was by "reforming" welfare. "There are all sorts of awful side effects of the welfare system as it currently operates," Goldsmith argued. Welfare recipients acted "rationally in the best interests of their families"; they earned so much in benefits that they would lose money by entering the workforce. "Our local efforts to create markets cannot succeed as long as this is the case," he proclaimed. Instead, he wanted to introduce health and child care that would "taper off gradually" as recipients gained work experience. Welfare recipients should be started "on the road to employment from day one," not trapped for two years "and then cut adrift." The administration of welfare also needed market-based reorganization: "Break up the monopoly and create a system of 'charter' welfare offices with competitively awarded, performance-based contracts that reward caseworkers for getting people out of the welfare system, not keeping them in it."[43]

Market-based welfare reform topped Goldsmith's second-term agenda. He wanted to replace AFDC with "a system of performance-based contracts with companies that put welfare recipients to work." Indiana, he said, "needs a competitive, performance-based system with many different providers. Non-profits, private agencies and even religious institutions should be allowed to compete for contracts to help the needy." Never modest, he called his plan the "best designed" in the nation.

Although the Indiana House narrowly defeated his bill to transfer Marion County's welfare operations to the Private Industry Council, Goldsmith did manage in Indianapolis to contract with a private firm, America Works, to place one hundred welfare recipients in jobs, and he tried to "engage the religious community in welfare reform." Like the governors, Goldsmith relied on the Tenth Amendment to the Constitution to argue for the devolution of welfare by the federal government. Unlike the governors, though, he thought that cities, not states, should assume leadership of welfare reform. Authority should flow from Washington "through the state governments and continue down to the local level." Merely substituting "bloated, unresponsive state bureaucracies" for federal ones would "not do much to help the poor." Instead, "strategies must be designed at the local level to be effective."[44]

Although Goldsmith won a second term with 58 percent of the vote, his critics chipped away at his record by pointing to the darker side of privatization. Three city Democrats called the mayor's privatization initiative "the worst sham that has been visited upon a citizenry that one can possibly imagine." Goldsmith, they claimed, had increased spending 63 percent above that of his predecessor. Although the annual city budget had decreased, its deficit had soared because Goldsmith financed privatization and construction with bonds. "What he can't pay for in cash," argued another critic, "he puts on his credit card. . . . But they're going to take away that credit card and then what is he going to do?" Nor had he adhered to the principle of competition in privatization. Instead, he had assigned important contracts without competitive bidding. In other cities, argued an unsuccessful Democratic candidate for municipal office, independent committees oversaw the budget and verified the "actual costs and savings" from privatization. That public oversight did not exist in Indianapolis, and therefore "accountability is extremely difficult and it's hard to know how much the city is really saving because all the numbers come from the administration." Democratic councilwoman Susan Williams called Goldsmith's 40 percent cut in the city's payroll "a shell game": He had "shifted the money into the pockets of paid consultants." Some critics said that consultants had used city offices and equipment for political business on Goldsmith's behalf. At times, his campaign received "contributions from contract winners within days after the business was let." Williams called Goldsmith's tactics "pinstripe patronage." Rather than competitive bidding, she claimed, "It's more a case of 'take care of your buddies who take care of you, or find new buddies.' "[45]

Goldsmith could offer a plausible defense. The city's long-term debt represented an investment in facilities whose return would eventually far exceed their cost. A few instances of corruption or impropriety reflected individual wrongdoing, not weaknesses in the privatization strategy. And regardless of the criticisms, Democratic as well as Republican officials came from all over the nation to study Indianapolis's achievements, and the national press continued to lavish praise on Goldsmith.

Proof that Goldsmith's strategies worked could come only in the long run. For the present, Indianapolis still had plenty of poverty, urban decay, and racial tension. In 1998, one advocacy group estimated that 20,000 households representing 44,000 people were "threatened with homelessness because they earn sub-poverty level incomes and spend more than half of their income on rent." Another estimated that 39 percent of Indianapolis families would need to pay more than the recommended 30 percent of their income to afford a two-bedroom apartment. The city's family shelter workers found themselves "forced to turn away homeless families because their shelters' beds" were already occupied. Shelter providers estimated that more than 7,000 Indianapolis residents "lapsed into homelessness" in 1997. Despite efforts to improve policing, the introduction of crack cocaine fueled the escalation of crime, and homicides broke city records in 1994, 1996, and 1997. Schools remained troubled; 82 percent of sixth graders failed basic skills tests. Taxes also rose because Indianapolis's metropolitan government permitted authorities other than the city to levy taxes: between 1990 and 1998 the school board raised its tax rate 33 percent.[46]

Indianapolis's stubborn problems reflected, one observer noted, "what mayors can't do." A buoyant economy had generated revenues that permitted the city, if not other local taxing authorities, to cut taxes. What would happen during a recession? How deep into the social structure would prosperity trickle? Indianapolis represented a best-case test of the new urban policy. If the combination of devolution, markets, and the war on dependence could not bring permanently improved government and widespread prosperity there, it was unlikely to succeed anywhere else.[47]

By 1998 cities' limited capacity to revitalize themselves without substantial federal assistance was calling into question the new urban agenda. Without renewed federal aid, the "supermayors" had reached the limits of their achievements. Not only Goldsmith proved unable to solve all his city's problems. In John Norquist's Milwaukee crime continued to rise; in Rudolph Giuliani's New York unemployment far exceeded the national average; in Rendell's Philadelphia more residents fled to the suburbs than in other big cities. To make matters worse, the 1996 "welfare reform" threatened to overwhelm their resources for shelter and relief by throwing thousands of residents off the public assistance rolls. "A mayor can make a difference, but the expectations of what we can achieve are just ludicrous," Goldsmith told a reporter. In Indianapolis and other cities, more money—much more money—remained essential to hire police officers, pay for summer schools for low-achieving students, demolish abandoned houses, clean polluted industrial sites, fund treatment programs for drug addicts, and staff truancy courts, among other needs. With subsidies to suburban housing and highway construction, the federal government had helped destroy the viability of American cities. It did not seem too much to ask assistance in repairing the damage. By itself, federal money could not overcome problems of fragmented government authority, concentrated and persistent poverty, or industrial flight. But it could help, and without it, all would likely grow worse.[48]

The Federal Government and the Marketization of Urban Policy

Like big-city mayors, Reagan, Bush, and Clinton drew on markets as models for urban policy. Despite the differences between Republican and Democratic administrations, three strategies linked urban and housing policies from the 1980s through the 1990s: replacing housing construction with certificates and vouchers; promoting homeownership among low-income families; and re-creating markets in depressed urban cores. All three administrations also confronted one major unanticipated problem: the emergence of homelessness in the early 1980s.

Until the 1930s, state and local governments approached the issue of housing timidly. Reluctant to interfere with markets, they had tried to improve housing conditions by regulating builders and landlords, while philanthropists sponsored the construction of model housing designed to show that developers could build low-income housing at a profit. Neither approach significantly influenced the supply and condition of housing for the poor. Faced with a catastrophic housing crisis in the Great Depression of the 1930s, the federal government helped homeowners by insuring mortgages and restructuring mortgage lending, and it aided low-income renters with the first federal public housing. In the years since the passage of the 1937 public housing legislation, the federal government has used housing assistance as a major form of social welfare for poor families. In 1996, 5.1 million households received rental subsidies from the federal government; together, all federal housing assistance programs cost $26 billion.[49]

There is one important way in which housing assistance has always differed from other forms of public assistance. Unlike AFDC, food stamps, or Supplemental Security Income, housing never became an entitlement. The federal government, alone or in partnership with state and local governments, never could afford to provide housing, either directly or through rental subsidies, to all who qualified. Although 15 million households qualify for housing assistance, only about a third of them receive it. Of those, roughly one-third live in public projects and the rest receive rent subsidies.[50]

A 1982 presidential commission on housing articulated the goals of the Reagan administration's housing policy. It recommended a shift away from construction and toward direct subsidies to tenants; greater reliance on the private sector; the encouragement of free and deregulated housing markets; and the promotion of "enlightened federalism."[51] In one area the report remained largely silent: racial segregation. Although it acknowledged that blacks fared worse than whites in housing and credit markets, it nowhere called attention to the intense and growing racial segregation that marked America's cities and their housing.

The commission diagnosed America's housing problem as a crisis of affordability, not supply. What low-income Americans needed was access to the housing that already existed, that is, "income supplements" that would allow them to live in "decent housing." According to the commission, construction programs cost more than "consumer-oriented" programs, served fewer households, and burdened the government with long-term subsidies. Income supplements, however, were not to be new entitlements: "The nation cannot afford yet another system of entitlements expanding endlessly out of effective control."[52] The Reagan administration translated the commission's Housing Payments into a proposal for vouchers. With vouchers, tenants could rent any apartment that met minimum quality standards. If the rent exceeded their income-based subsidy, they would pay the remainder; if it was less, they could keep the difference. In 1983, the administration proposed transferring 120,000 families from the existing rent subsidy program to vouchers and adding 45,000 new families. Congress, skeptical, initially authorized only 15,000 vouchers as part of a demonstration project. In 1987, it made them permanent.[53]

Reliance on the private sector meant moving the hand of government off the controls of the housing and home-finance markets and public housing. The federal government "should increasingly complement, rather than compete with, the private market," and it should reduce excessive regulation because the "marketplace" was "a better mechanism" than government "for determining what should be built and where." Instead of burdening the financial and credit markets with regulations, the federal government, argued the commission, should help stabilize and expand them by deregulating thrift institutions, savings and loan associations, and mutual savings banks. (The Reagan administration followed this advice to deregulate the thrifts—with disastrous consequences only too well known.) The federal government should also, the commission contended, devolve authority over public housing to local governments and private markets because the "rigidity of Federal rules" restricted the "ability of local authorities to solve their own problems."[54]

"Owning one's own home," rhapsodized President Reagan, "means far more than merely having shelter. It is a concept deeply rooted in the hearts of our people, for it carries with it a whole constellation of values—family, neighborhood, community, independence, self-reliance, citizenship, faith in our country and its future." The commission echoed this sentiment: "For many Americans" homeownership represented "the most important factor in . . . overall economic well-being." But, despite its faith in homeownership as the foundation of American virtue and stability, the commission, afraid of inflation, moved cautiously, proposing only minor tax-based incentives. However, the commission did recommend one new policy direction that, it felt, held the key to inner-city revitalization: the use of enterprise zones to create markets. This idea, in modified form, would not be put into practice by the federal government until the Clinton administration.[55]

In fact, the Reagan years proved more notable for reducing funding for cities than for launching any urban policy initiatives. Reagan's cuts in funds for public housing and aid to cities hurt families and decreased the supply of affordable housing. He raised the housing costs of poor families by increasing the rent for public housing from 25 percent of income to 30 percent, and he excluded many poor families by lowering the income threshold for renters of subsidized housing from 50 to 45 percent of the poverty line. The number of new families who received housing assistance fell from 325,000 in 1979 to 177,000 in 1981 and 89,000 in 1984, and new subsidized housing construction plummeted more than 80 percent from 1982 to 1986.[56] As with Reagan's changes to AFDC, these cuts in benefits affected the near or working poor most severely.

One other initiative—the sale of public housing—illustrated the Reagan administration's preference for privatization. Influenced by Margaret Thatcher's sale of "council" housing in Britain, Congressman Jack Kemp, backed by the Reagan administration, proposed legislation encouraging the sale of public housing to tenants, and HUD began an experimental tenant purchase program. Privatization meant not only selling public housing but using private agents for tasks previously reserved to government: private realtors to sell public properties, private agencies to hold funds in escrow, private lenders to co-insure mortgages and loans. When Kemp became HUD secretary under Bush, he predicted that a million public housing tenants would become homeowners and advocated increased tenant-management, a goal built into the 1990 Housing Act. But with public housing filled with low-income and elderly tenants, Kemp's plans proved wildly optimistic. An assistant secretary of HUD estimated the number of potential sales to tenants at only 20,000 to 30,000 of the 1.2 million public housing units.[57] In the end, during Kemp's four years as secretary, HUD sold only 135 units to tenants.[58] In Britain, the sale of public housing had proved more successful because many of its tenants had relatively much higher incomes than those in the United States.

Meanwhile, operational responsibility for remaining HUD programs shifted to political, rather than civil service, appointees, and HUD became a scandal-ridden, often ineffective agency, incapable of formulating or directing effective urban and housing policy. Between 1981 and 1988, HUD's share of the total U.S. budget dropped from 4.59 percent to 1.31 percent; in 1989, HUD officials reported that at least twenty-eight of the department's forty-eight programs and activities had " 'significant problems' attributable to fraud, mismanagement, and favoritism."[59] The result, said HUD secretary Jack Kemp, "gives capitalism a bad name."[60]

The Reagan and Bush administrations left America's cities with deeper problems than they found them. Concentrated poverty, racial segregation, homelessness, and economic stagnation all increased during the 1980s. With justice, critics remember the era for its reduction in social benefits and federal withdrawal from the cities, and they contrast it with the revival of urban policy under Clinton. But the story is more complicated. The Clinton administration's more vigorous urban policy did not reject the strategic directions of the Reagan/Bush era. Rather, with renewed optimism about the future of cities, it tried to implement them more effectively. The "new consensus" that many commentators discerned in welfare policy underpinned much of urban and housing policy as well.[61]

The Revival of Urban Policy

President Bill Clinton signaled his seriousness about reviving urban policy by appointing Henry Cisneros secretary of HUD. Cisneros, a highly successful four-term former mayor of San Antonio, Texas, held bachelor's and master's degrees in urban planning, and a master's and a doctorate in public administration. Sociologist and urbanist Douglas Massey called Cisneros "the best secretary of HUD the nation's ever had." The "first secretary to pursue avidly the goal of integrating the poor into mainstream society," Cisneros assumed office with an "ambitious plan to eliminate homelessness, rebuild America's decaying cities," and transform public housing. Within two years, the election of a Republican majority in Congress had combined with presidential indifference to frustrate his intentions. When Cisneros stepped down in January 1997, he left behind "an agency in deep financial chaos—despised by Congress and ignored by the White House." Whoever took his job, said urban scholar Anthony Downs, "needs a mental examination." Cisneros's successor, HUD assistant secretary for community planning and development Andrew Cuomo, took office in early 1997. The son of former New York governor Mario Cuomo, he had founded a nonprofit housing group in New York, which became the nation's largest provider of homeless services, and Genesis, a nonprofit that developed innovative approaches to urban development.[62]

Despite what they considered the Reagan and Bush administrations' "decades of decline," Cisneros and Cuomo remained optimistic about the possibility for urban revitalization. They rejected the view that technology had rendered the need for face-to-face contact obsolete, and they drew on a new urban economics to argue for the increased importance of cities as the core of metropolitan regions competing in a global economy. With metropolitan areas as "the building blocks of the national economy," competition between cities and suburbs had become an anachronism that hindered the advancement of both, explained a HUD report. "Today, Detroit's real competition is not its suburbs, but the metropolitan regions of Baden-Wurtemburg in Germany and Kyushu in Japan."[63]

Although unacknowledged, Clinton's new urban policy, "the urban empowerment agenda," reflected the same emphasis on rent vouchers, homeownership, and the re-creation of markets in inner cities that had underpinned policy in the Reagan/Bush years. For instance, HUD proposed "to transform its low-rent housing programs so that they provide subsidies to people rather than projects," but policy, in fact, had been moving in this direction for two decades, as is revealed by a look at the share of federal rent subsidies that went to help tenants rent existing housing rather than fund new housing projects:[64]

1980	Carter	27%
1985	Reagan	67%
1990	Bush	72%
1994	Clinton	69%

Unlike the Reagan and Bush administrations, though, Clinton's experimented with innovative approaches, including a demonstration program to test the effect of residential mobility on poverty. As a result of a Supreme Court decision, 7,100 black Chicago public housing residents moved to racially desegregated suburbs. Researchers who followed the families discovered improvements in their employment, earnings, and education. What started as a means of reducing segregation turned out to be an antipoverty strategy as well. Impressed by the Gautreaux studies, as the Chicago experience was known, in 1992 Congress created a demonstration program known as Moving to Opportunity for Fair Housing, which set out to test the program's findings in five major cities with a larger number of families. (Although early results proved promising, definitive findings will come only with tracking families in the experimental and control groups over a number of years.)[65]

For all its rhetoric, however, the Clinton administration's appropriations for housing assistance rose only modestly. In current dollars, appropriations administered by HUD under Clinton rose to $13 billion in 1995—more than its low of $9 billion in 1988 and 1989 but much less than its high of $32 billion in 1978. Also, almost all the increase reflected the cost of renewing rent subsidies paid to landlords. And despite Clinton's call for "a full attack on homelessness," funding for homeless programs reversed direction and declined after 1995. Between 1995 and 1997 HUD's budget was slashed 25 percent, funds for public housing dropped 20 percent, and homeless funding decreased nearly as much. More recently, signs of a turnaround have finally appeared. In the budget for fiscal year 2000, the allocation for homelessness rose from $975 million to $1.02 billion; money for the public housing capital fund increased; and a variety of other programs received modestly higher funding as well. Despite the growth of HUD's budget to $26 billion in 2000 and Clinton's request for $32.1 billion for 2001, HUD funding was still below levels in the late 1970s.[66]

Even with reduced funds in the 1990s, HUD took a series of "small but real steps" to increase the amount of money available to finance private housing and small business development in neglected areas of the nation's cities. HUD persuaded federal agencies to put a larger percentage of the mortgages they insured in underserved areas, and it matched union pension fund investments in housing and loans for community development corporations. It also created a network of community development banks and an investment fund that used government money to attract private capital to support their work. At the same time, Clinton also ordered an overhaul of the regulations governing the Community Reinvestment Act (1977), which required federal regulators to take a bank's loan-making record in low-income areas into account when deciding on applications for mergers, acquisitions, or new branches. The CRA, according to one estimate, each year pumped between $4 billion and $6 billion of additional credit into low-income neighborhoods.[67]

Homeownership also played a key role in Clinton's urban and housing policy. Here Clinton moved much more aggressively than his predecessors had to advance beyond rhetoric to real programs. "Homeowners," claimed the president's first report on urban policy, "have both a financial and emotional stake in the future of their communities, which encourages them to maintain their housing, collaborate with their neighbors, participate in community organizations, and promote the security and vitality of their neighborhoods." Often homeownership proved "the most effective antidote to the many problems that ail a city." Clinton proposed pushing homeownership to an all-time high by the year 2000. Helped by HUD's Urban Homesteading Initiative, in June 1997 the goal seemed within reach because over the previous three years homeownership had experienced its largest expansion in three decades. In 1998 Congress allowed housing authorities to use vouchers to help tenants buy homes and raised the limit on federally insured mortgages to help more middle-class home buyers qualify for FHA-backed loans.[68]

At the heart of Clinton's urban policy lay the re-creation of markets in inner cities through empowerment zones. His 1993 empowerment zone initiative expanded the enterprise zone concept popular, but not implemented, during the two previous Republican administrations. In enterprise zones, government relaxed controls, reduced taxes, and modified regulations and other "inhibitions on business investment." British urban planner Peter Hall first proposed free trade zones, or "freeports," in cities in 1977; Margaret Thatcher's chancellor of the exchequer, Sir Geoffrey Howe, designated eleven sites in Britain as enterprise zones, the first of which formally opened in 1981. The conservative Heritage Foundation imported the idea into the United States, where Congressman Jack Kemp became its major advocate. Enterprise zones, according to economists Barry Bluestone and Bennett Harrison, were Reagan's "only positive (albeit rather lukewarm) proposal for new urban economic development." But presidential endorsement was not enough to persuade Congress to pass a "full fledged enterprise zone proposal," although thirty-seven states and the District of Columbia did create enterprise zones "offering a grab bag of small incentives."[69]

The Clinton plan, by contrast, targeted $2.5 billion in tax incentives and $1.3 billion in flexible grants at 105 severely distressed areas over ten years. The Urban Empowerment Zones each received $100 million in flexible block grants for activities ranging from social services to building physical infrastructure. Businesses located in the zones received a

$3,000 annual tax credit for each employee, as well as other tax credits for investment and tax-exempt bond financing. Another set of localities, designated Enterprise Communities, each received $2.95 million in flexible block grant funds and tax exemptions. A new President's Empowerment Board removed red tape and regulatory barriers inhibiting the flexible use of federal funds. In 1997, Congress authorized fifteen new urban empowerment zones.[70]

Empowerment zones expanded the earlier enterprise zone concept to include improving social services, infrastructure development, and active community participation. They required "unprecedented levels of private sector involvement and investment" and brought "all stakeholders in a community—residents, nonprofits, business and government—to the table to develop a locally fashioned and locally controlled, comprehensive revitalization strategy," noted one social scientist. The administration expected government action only to jump-start the recreation of private markets, which held the key to community regeneration. Empowerment zones made "the private sector the driver of economic growth, with the government acting as a partner."[71] By February 1998, the Clinton administration announced that more than $4 billion in new investments from the private and public sectors had been committed to urban empowerment zones, which the administration claimed had "made significant strides" in using their federal dollars and tax incentives "to attract private sector investments, generate job growth, stimulate business openings and expansion, construct new housing, expand homeownership opportunities, and stabilize deteriorating neighborhoods."

Outside the administration, empowerment zones received a less favorable evaluation. "In city after city," reported the *Los Angeles Times*, "programs have been dogged by mismanagement, misinformation, infighting, and ineffectiveness that have cast shadows over even touted victories." The U.S. Office of the Inspector General discovered problems in Atlanta, Chicago, Philadelphia, and Detroit, which were the only four empowerment zones it audited. In Philadelphia, systems set up "to further grassroots leadership have instead produced a cumbersome organization that has discouraged business and slowed projects of all sorts to a crawl." In June 1999 the Philadelphia empowerment zone reported that it had helped businesses create four hundred jobs, but it could not say whether those jobs already existed or were projected for the future. Most of the money set aside for tutoring teenagers and crime prevention and public safety had not even been spent. Two supermarkets that were promised in the application had not been built, while in nearby areas, grocery markets "initiated by churches, private business and traditional public development agencies" had already opened or were under construction. To be sure, empowerment zones could point to some successes, like the location of a Chrysler engine plant and related industries in Detroit and of CitySort, a mail-sorting business, in Philadelphia. But the record did not match the expectations with which the Clinton administration had launched its flagship urban initiative.[72]

Critics focused on the assumptions underlying empowerment zones as well as on the political and administrative problems that inhibited their success. Empowerment zones were "place-based" urban strategies—an approach to policy, claimed one authority on urban economics, that misdiagnosed the source of urban problems as the decline of population and employment in central cities. In fact, poverty concentration and discrimination were the real culprits. Together, they increased housing prices for minorities, imposed high social services costs on cities, limited employment opportunities, and "ensured a steady expansion of slum housing, an erosion of adequate housing in the central city, and a deterioration of urban neighborhoods." Empowerment zones mistakenly imposed "inefficient incentives for housing or industrial investment" in hopelessly dormant sections of cities. Rather than try to revive these areas, policies should directly address poverty and discrimination with housing, income, and transportation subsidies, he argued. Instead of limiting "the locations chosen by households or firms," policy should try to maximize mobility. If the critics of place-based policy were right, empowerment zones—in contrast to Moving to Opportunity—were marching urban policy in exactly the wrong direction.

Whether or not Clinton's initiatives pointed in the wrong direction, they did not cost a great deal of money. By the standards of the Great Society era, Clinton's initiatives remained modest programs, and they rested on a vision of government's role much different from the one underlying the social programs of the 1960s and 1970s—closer to Ronald Reagan than to the Great Society. "Federal agencies cannot possibly know what is best for each of America's diverse regions and communities," asserted Clinton's first report on national urban policy. "They cannot design a 'one size fits all' strategy for reconnecting poor city residents to opportunity or for reenergizing the economic potential of inner-city communities."

By the summer of 1999, all the components of Clinton's urban strategy were clear. It focused on the revitalization of places through the recreation of markets. Its principal tools were tax incentives and the mobilization of private capital. The federal government provided neither massive funds nor direct services. Instead, it served as catalyst and impresario. All these elements came together in Clinton's New Markets initiative. In July Clinton traveled to seven poor rural and urban communities he called "untapped areas for potential investment." Inner-city neighborhoods, explained HUD, are "undiscovered territories for many businesses." Clinton hoped to use federal tax credits and loan guarantees "to inspire private companies to build plants and stores" in areas "that the economic boom has largely passed by." He hoped new and existing programs would leverage $15 billion in private funds during the next five years, and he proposed to establish America's Private Investment Companies to leverage the kind of domestic investment that the Overseas Private Investment Corporation raises for emerging markets elsewhere. "There's real money to be made in these markets," said one banker. Gene Sperling, the White House chief economic adviser, pointed out, "The goal is not to ask people to make charitable contributions, but to make companies take a second look in our own backyard where there could be profitable business opportunities while also helping rebuild communities that have been left behind." In November, on a second "poverty tour" designed to spotlight and encourage corporate investors, Clinton told a high school audience in Newark, New Jersey, "Now is the time to say the rest of America should be part of our prosperity, and they're our next great economic opportunity—the new markets of the 21st century. . . . We're focusing not only on where to find potential, but how to turn that potential in our inner cities and our rural areas into long-term economic partnerships."[73] Clinton's upbeat rhetoric simply elided the weaknesses in place-based programs and the mixed record of empowerment zones—there was still no evidence that reliance on markets and private investment would reduce poverty and turn around depressed inner cities or rural areas. Nonetheless, late in 2000, both Republicans and Democrats in Congress appeared ready to turn a version of Clinton's proposals into law.[74]

The Problem of Affordable Housing: Public Housing, Section 8, and Homelessness

Clinton wanted to transform public housing "so that it is no longer a dead end but, instead, a platform to self-sufficiency." He hoped to rally "those who have been mired in dependency and despair to the traditional values of self-motivation, personal responsibility, and self-sufficiency." Like Reagan's 1982 President's Commission on Housing, Clinton's plans called for deregulation, the devolution of authority, more businesslike practices, and strict oversight and enforcement.[75]

In several ways, Clinton's diagnosis of public housing's ills did not differ very much from that of the Republicans. Although Clinton and other Democrats would demur at Senator Bob Dole's attack on public housing as the "last bastion of socialism," they would concur with a number of the charges leveled by Ronald D. Utt, a housing specialist at the conservative Heritage Foundation. According to him, public housing was much more expensive than rent vouchers; high-rise housing projects segregated the poor and minorities in crime-ridden and "hopeless communities with little chance of escape"; local authorities managed public housing badly; and HUD lacked the capacity to oversee the thousands of local agencies. As government-supported monopolies, many public housing authorities found "little incentive to provide quality services at reasonable costs," and "generous taxpayer subsidies" sustained some of America's "worst housing and most dangerous neighborhoods." Utt, along with HUD secretary Cisneros, wanted to force public housing authorities to compete for residents by turning all funds over to tenants in the form of vouchers. Utt also wanted to introduce competition into the management of public housing by allowing bids from private property-management companies.[76]

There was, however, another way to look at public housing—a view that found more potential in existing projects and in government's capacity to run effective programs. Conservative critics of public housing, argued Nicholas Lemann, national correspondent for the *Atlantic Monthly*, overlooked its successful early history before the late 1940s, when it served "not the very poor but people with jobs one notch higher on the economic ladder." Lemann contended that public housing began its decline when new rules restricted the working poor from occupancy. Even so, troubled public housing projects represented only a small fraction of the total; many others provided decent and safe homes for people with no other alternatives.[77] Public housing needed reform, not abandonment to the marketplace.

Public housing was a huge responsibility that government could not easily shed. In 1996, HUD supervised about 3,400 local housing agencies that managed 13,200 developments with 1.4 million housing units providing shelter for 4.3 million tenants. (America's commitment to public housing has remained far lower than that of European countries, however. About 3 percent of Americans live in public housing, compared to over a fifth in many European nations, which, unlike American public housing, does not serve only the poor.) The Clinton administration proposed to reform this huge, unwieldy system with block grants, vouchers, tenant purchase and management plans, a greater income mix among residents, tough and vigorous anticrime and antidrug policies for housing complexes, the demolition of the nation's worst high-rise projects, and new social services aimed at moving tenants from public assistance to self-support.[78]

Republicans responded by proposing to repeal the 1937 Public Housing Act, the charter of public housing, and increase the share of higher-income tenants in public housing even more than Clinton recommended. They also wanted to require eight hours of community service each month from unemployed able-bodied public housing residents. Some Democrats objected that corporations and others receiving government subsidies faced no requirement that they perform a similar service. As the disagreements over public housing dragged on without resolution, the Clinton administration seemed less enthusiastic about the need for new legislation. HUD officials said they could " 'come very close' to revamping public housing without changing any laws." By 1997, even without enabling legislation, HUD claimed great progress, and Clinton's 1999 budget proposal cut operating and capital funds for traditional public housing.[79]

Aside from the perennial problem of public housing, in 1997 one enormous cloud—Section 8 renewals—loomed over the hope that the federal government together with the new mayors could move cities along the road to revitalization. Section 8 subsidizes tenants in private rental housing. Tenants pay approximately 30 percent of their income, and the federal government makes up the difference. For families, argued the Clinton administration, Section 8 "is more than a contract or subsidy; it is often the foundation from which they can build lifelong self-sufficiency. Renewing these contracts, then, becomes a fulfillment of a social contract between government and a vulnerable family." Congress, however, was threatening not to renew them.

Rental assistance contracts on 1.8 million housing units that sheltered 4.4 million persons were coming due in 1998; by 2002, contracts for another 2.7 million units, or 6.4 million people, were scheduled to expire. What would happen if the federal government did not renew these contracts? Over 90 percent of the households subsidized were elderly, disabled persons, or families with children. These people "could risk losing their homes—either through evictions or unbearably sharp increases," stated a government report. Not only would individuals and families be hurt, but whole communities would suffer.[80]

As it was, the nation was approaching "a crisis in affordable housing," according to HUD secretary Henry Cisneros. Over 5 million families lived in "substandard or over-crowded conditions" or were "spending more than half their incomes for rent." The number of low-income households in serious need of decent, affordable housing had reached "an all-time high" and continued its growth "through both economic recession and recovery." The national shortage of affordable housing stood at 4.7 million units, the largest gap since 1970. The families who needed housing were mostly "America's working poor." Congress, Cisneros argued, had responded to the affordable housing crisis "in the worst way possible," by threatening "to end the 20 year bipartisan record of increasing the number of new rental vouchers for America's poor and working poor families." Congress had cut additional housing vouchers for three straight years. "In President Reagan's worst budget, he included 40,000 new vouchers. We proposed 50,000 new vouchers. Congress, for three years now, has responded with zero additional vouchers," and, despite a growing demand, private housing markets had failed to respond "to the acute needs of the lowest income renters by producing units affordable to them."[81]

"The sad truth," HUD secretary Andrew W. Cuomo commented, "is that more and more people working at low-wage jobs, as well as older Americans living on fixed incomes, are being priced out of the housing market as rents rise." In New York City the wait for either public housing or rental-assistance vouchers was eight years. In just two years, the waiting lists of forty big-city housing authorities had increased 25 percent. And the situation continued to worsen. In 1997, 5 percent of households, one-sixth of all renters, "paid more than half their income for housing or lived in severely inadequate housing," reported HUD. Many were "merely a paycheck or unexpected medical bill away from homelessness."[82]

At the last minute, Congress and the Clinton administration reached a compromise. Congress funded existing Section 8 contracts but refused to fund new Section 8 certificates or vouchers. With welfare reform on the horizon, "the lack of new housing assistance will be more devastating than ever," warned the National Low-Income Housing Coalition. Congress also refused to fund Bridges to Work, a proposed HUD program designed to help with the transition from welfare to work. In other ways, too, claimed the coalition, Congress worsened "the housing crisis for low-income Americans," especially the homeless.[83] With criticism mounting—and an unmistakable, looming catastrophe—in October 1998 Congress surprised observers by authorizing far more new Section 8 vouchers—90,000—than expected, and in his budget proposal for 2001, Clinton requested funds for 120,000 "new vouchers to help America's hard-pressed working families."[84]

Congress not only increased the amount of housing assistance for low-income families; it broadened the income mix among public housing tenants by allowing public housing authorities to offer apartments to families with higher incomes than before, though most were still reserved for families with well-below-average incomes. Despite official reassurance, low-income housing advocates worried that proposed reforms would reduce the number of housing units available for poor families. On the other hand, supporters claimed the new law would remove disincentives to work and marry by disregarding increases in tenants' incomes for twelve months in setting rents. "It will value work and reward work, and it won't raise your rent if you work," asserted HUD secretary Andrew Cuomo. Congress also imposed a community service requirement of eight hours a month on most public housing residents, and allowed resident management corporations to operate public housing projects.[85] If projects seemed hopeless, the law permitted their demolition.

The federal government had finally taken an important first step along the difficult road to revitalizing the worst public housing projects and expanding housing assistance to the working poor. It also modestly improved the acute shortage of low-cost housing. But the approach remained for the most part after the fact. Federal programs responded to housing emergencies; they did little to address the reasons why so many Americans remained unable to afford decent housing in the first place, or why so many remained homeless.

During the 1970s and 1980s, homelessness emerged as the most visible statement of the crisis in affordable housing, the growth and transformation of urban poverty, and the holes in America's safety net. Nonetheless, the Reagan administration proved reluctant to admit that homelessness constituted a public problem. When forced to respond, it treated homelessness as a temporary emergency. Legislation in March 1983 gave the Federal Emergency Management Agency responsibility for administering a $100 million emergency food and shelter program. In the same year the Defense Department allocated funds for the renovation and repair of military facilities to house the homeless. The Reagan administration, writes Joel Blau in his book on homelessness, "did everything possible to prevent a coordinated set of policies and programs from taking hold within the federal government."[86]

Major legislation to address homelessness—the Stewart B. McKinney Act—finally passed in 1987. Although it allocated more money for the homeless, it remained seriously underfunded, and, by dividing money among several different agencies in the same state and refusing to pay for some crucial services, it failed to counteract the fragmentation of federal policy. State social services for the homeless remained a patchwork of programs, with most federal funds directed to shelters that offered emergency housing. Very little went to transitional or permanent housing, medical care and education, or programs to encourage independence. To make matters worse, legislation intended as an emergency response to a pressing public problem remained mired in red tape, and the Interagency Council on the Homeless created by the act to facilitate the application process remained "timid and ineffective in its role."[87]

The Clinton administration, recognizing the weaknesses in prior homelessness policy, promised to move vigorously to correct them. Five months after taking office, Clinton signed an executive order instructing the Interagency Council on the Homeless to develop one coordinated federal plan for "breaking the cycle of homelessness and preventing future homelessness." The new plan, called Continuum of Care, streamlined application processes, devolved significant initiative and authority to cities and locally based nonprofits, and bundled existing activities into four new programs. With a shift in emphasis from individual projects to "community-wide strategies for addressing the problem of homelessness," HUD encouraged local groups to plan collectively, submit joint applications, and partner with local private sector institutions. HUD also required applicants to identify nonfederal funds they could leverage to support their programs.[88]

Between 1993 and 1995, the money that Continuum of Care pumped into homeless programs increased the number of persons assisted. Although all programs benefited, HUD transferred its emphasis from emergency shelters to transitional and permanent housing. The value of leveraged funds skyrocketed an astonishing 3,000 percent from $38 million to $1.1 billion. At the least, transitional and permanent housing programs served four times as many persons at any one time in 1995 as they had three years earlier, and HUD expected an increase of 843 percent in the number of disabled persons assisted in special programs.[89]

Despite some remarkable accomplishments in its first two years, Continuum of Care spent relatively little money on the prevention of homelessness, which, by all accounts, continued to increase. HUD's innovative policies under Clinton still mainly addressed the already homeless rather than the source of their condition. Not surprisingly, persistent poverty combined with housing shortages to undermine the signs of precarious progress. From Boston: "Some of the more serious underlying causes of homelessness continue unhampered. . . . The extremely high cost of rental housing in Greater Boston and the resulting disincentive for developers to increase the stock of low and middle-income housing, will continue to keep a growing number of families and individuals 'on the edge of homelessness.' " From Denver: "The ultimate goal of the introduction of the Continuum of Care for both the individual and community, is to end homelessness. When asked what kinds of impacts the Continuum of Care has had in this regard, most respondents said that they did not see an obvious improvement." From Detroit: "The size of the homeless population is about double the city's available shelter."[90]

The public increasingly, if incorrectly, associated the homeless with beggars cluttering the streets—that is, with the undeserving poor.[91] In New York City, Mayor Rudolph Giuliani wanted to force all able-bodied homeless people to work for their shelter and to put the children of mothers ejected from shelters into foster care.[92] The homeless themselves lacked political power or influential advocates, and at century's end, the long-term prospects for reducing homelessness and moving its casualties to self-support appeared dim. As market-based urban policies failed to prevent homelessness, all levels of government floundered, incapable of devising programs that worked on different principles. The intractable persistence of homelessness underlined the limits of the market as a universal solution to public problems.

By several measures, the condition of most major cities improved after the recession of 1990–91. From one angle, the mayors' new, tough, market-based strategies had seemed to work. Cities had used conservative revenue estimates to trim costs. When the economy improved, revenues exceeded expectations. At the same time, by containing wages and benefits and increasing productivity, cities kept spending growth to 0.50 percent in 1993, compared to 3 percent in the late 1980s and 2 to 2.5 percent in the early 1990s. By early 1995, cities across the country had made "stunning comebacks from the hard times of the recession" and were "even running surpluses for the first time in years." President Clinton's 1997 report on the cities pointed to the income generated by the federal government's deficit cutting; the response of cities to economic restructuring; and the decline in unemployment in the fifty largest cities from 9.2 percent in January 1993 to 6.5 percent in January 1997: "Cities have retooled themselves, to some degree, from the previous two decades of decline as the U.S. economy moved away from manufacturing toward information-based and service industries." When the National League of Cities asked mayors to compare conditions in their cities in January 1997 with conditions a year earlier, most reported improvements in every area from crime to the economy. In June 2000, the mayors assembled at the annual meeting of the U.S. Conference of Mayors complained of the problems of prosperity: "too many high-skill jobs, and not enough people to fill them; too many well-off people moving back to the city, and not enough houses for all of them, driving up prices for everyone else; and too much demand for parks and serenity, and not enough open space to offer the new city dwellers appalled by sprawl."[93]

Nonetheless, cities remained fragile. The disparity between cities and suburbs continued to grow. Unemployment remained higher in cities; suburbs attracted the lion's share of jobs. Poverty increasingly concentrated in cities, isolating the poor, heightening segregation, and burdening services. As population declined and middle-class jobs continued to leave, the proportion of low-income families increased, and the need for affordable housing threatened to turn into a crisis. Anything could provide the trigger: an economic slowdown or proposed congressional funding cuts could suddenly undermine urban fiscal progress; unions, impatient after years of wage freezes, might agitate for raises. Whether empowerment zones would generate enough jobs and capital to have a significant impact on urban unemployment and inner-city decay remained unclear and hotly debated. The record of enterprise zones in Britain or of those funded by state and local governments did not inspire confidence. Nor did poverty, the needs of the homeless, the expenses associated with AIDS, or the consequences of drugs decline significantly. By decimating social services, some experts argued, cities had balanced their budgets on the backs of the poor. Cities had "pulled back, in most cases, from thinking that they can solve the problems of poverty and social ills" and tended to focus "on day-to-day services," noted one authority.[94]

A cynical observer might conclude that the new mayors, indifferent to the growing inequality in America, had written off poor neighborhoods and accepted the emergence of "dual cities" serving the affluent far better than the poor. The new urban policies, in this view, were much more than strategies designed to revitalize cities; they signaled a new form of class war that was of a piece with the latest trends in "welfare reform." A more charitable observer would argue—as, surely, would the mayors themselves, supported by the Clinton administration—that, as in the formerly communist countries of eastern and central Europe, only tough medicine would induce recovery. The cold bath of the market, painful (even fatal) to many in the short run, with all its aggravation of inequalities, eventually would produce a solid and lasting prosperity that would diffuse work and good wages among the entire population. This was not class war but necessary discipline, and in this view the new urban strategies offered the urban poor their only long-range hope. At the close of the twentieth century, both views, the cynical and the optimistic, remained untested but plausible. With the stakes so high, the consequences for America's welfare state, as well as for its cities and their residents, remained enormous.

THE INDEPENDENT SECTOR,

THE MARKET, AND THE STATE

Throughout U.S. history, state, local, and federal governments have paid private agencies and institutions to carry out public tasks, whether caring for orphans, healing the sick, or delivering social services. Because governments have relied so heavily on private institutions and agencies, the history of nonprofits has defied theories that predicted their decline in the face of the growth of the state. To the contrary, the state and nonprofits have expanded together, for the most part collaborators rather than rivals. The result is America's distinctive mixed economy of social welfare, with its blurred boundaries between public and private. At the same time, in the way they earn their incomes and manage their businesses, nonprofits have grown closer to the world of commerce; they have watched, too, as for-profit firms, also sustained by public funds, have invaded their domains and found new ways to make money from human and social services. By imbricating nonprofits in the marketplace, the recent commercialization of private social welfare has smudged the line between nonprofit and for-profit agencies and facilitated the redefinition of America's welfare state.

Themes in the History of Charity

The history of American charity remains shrouded in myth: in the old days Americans helped their needy neighbors voluntarily and without money from government. With no prodding from elected officials, the women and men who formed voluntary associations to provide services today performed by government made sure that the deserving poor remained neither hungry nor homeless. With compassion born of religious faith, they solved problems that, in our time, render government impotent.

This simple and inspiring tale remains more fiction than history. But it matters because conservatives have seized it to justify dismantling the public welfare state. Once upon a time, they argue, families were strong, out-of-wedlock births minimal, violent crime unusual, drug abuse rare—and public welfare almost nonexistent. If welfare were moved out of the hands of bureaucrats and governments and back to volunteers and private charity, America could move forward by retreating into its Golden Age.[1]

Contrary to conservative myth, however, private charity never proved an adequate response to dependence in America's past. Nor did compassion permeate responses to poverty. Destitute women and men "warned out" of eighteenth-century towns where they lacked a "settlement" (roughly, legal residence) or shunted into foul nineteenth-century poorhouses found little sympathy in their moments of need. Indeed, many sources, both published and archival, tell of horrifying deprivation and misery. Despite the proliferation of voluntary associations in the nineteenth century, charities faced a constant shortfall of money and volunteers. Only an ill-informed or deranged homeless adult, orphaned child, or charity worker would choose to time-travel back to the end of the nineteenth century, despite the appeal of such a journey to one prominent conservative writer.[2] Nor was social welfare solely the responsibility of private charity. Government, despite the claims of conservatives, always played a crucial role in America's response to dependence. The history of American social welfare from the earliest times reflected a mixed economy, with public and private sectors joined in an intimate, ever-changing, and intricate dance.

Between the early Republic and the Gilded Age (roughly 1800–1870), charity arose from several sources. Emergencies, such as fires or epidemics, provoked some of the first responses to poverty and need. When calamities struck, groups of leading citizens organized associations to help the poor. Before 1840, under the influence of the Second Great Awakening, evangelical Protestantism became another powerful force: as revivals spurred the organization of missionary societies to spread God's word to the poor, missionaries, armed with tracts and Bibles, toured the slums, where they encountered deep poverty. Over time, they began to distribute more temporal goods, and some missionary societies evolved into associations for relief. Catholics also organized to relieve misery. They responded both to the poverty of their poor Irish immigrant congregants and to the evangelical proselytizing of Protestants by creating their own orphan asylums, hospitals, and homes for young women. Their principal relief association was the St. Vincent de Paul Society, founded in France and imported to the United States in 1846. The Catholic Church almost certainly spent a larger proportion of its resources on charity in this era than did Protestant denominations.[3] In the same years, virtually all immigrant groups formed societies for social and fraternal purposes and to help new arrivals. They supplied members with insurance (including, importantly, burial insurance) and emergency assistance. Occupational groups—indeed, almost every trade—also organized to help members and their families in similar ways.

In the nineteenth and early-twentieth centuries, many charities and social reformers wanted to improve poor people—to change their behavior—not just to supply their material needs. The personal and spiritual transformation of the poor underlay the goals of evangelical Protestant missionaries to the poor, who founded Sunday schools all over the country. Huge numbers of children attended. In 1825, the American Sunday School Union estimated that about one-third of the six- to fifteen-year-olds in Philadelphia attended Sunday school; in New York City in 1829 a survey put the proportion at 41 percent. Beside religion, Sunday schools instructed the children of the poor in both reading and moral and social values, including deference and discipline.[4]

In the course of the nineteenth century, large new Protestant organizations replaced the early missionary and benevolent societies. They limited their charitable goals, bureaucratized their operations, and replaced volunteers with paid full-time staff. The great example was the New York Association for Improving the Condition of the Poor (1843). Professionalization altered the gender relations of charity. Until then, women had composed the shock troops of voluntarism. In most cities and towns, a Female Charitable Society or Ladies Benevolent Society dedicated to helping widows constituted one of the first charitable associations. Women also usually ran early orphan asylums. These institutions offered women from the middling classes an outlet for their energy and talent as well as a means of putting their evangelical faith into practice. However, by the Civil War, men had sometimes edged women out of authority by assuming control of institutions, starting rival associations, and relegating women to less public roles. The emergent harsh, moralistic, bureaucratic, male, protoprofessional charitable style, which aimed more at the behavior of the poor than at their souls, pointed the way toward the "scientific charity" that would flourish in the Gilded Age.

In these years, it is crucial to remember, private charity did not compose the only response to dependence and destitution. Everywhere, as we have seen, local public authorities gave outdoor relief to large numbers of people. Across the nation, county and city governments opened poorhouses, which overflowed with the destitute. State governments built mental hospitals for the indigent insane; local governments constructed city hospitals for the sick poor; and public authorities paid for children in orphanages and gave money to an array of other institutions that served the needy. Both conservative welfare history and mainstream historiography obscure this activist role of local government in the first three-quarters of the nineteenth century.[5]

This history of the public response to dependence intersects the story of charity in two places. First, it refutes the fantasy that private charity ever cared for all or most of America's needy. Although thorough quantification is impossible, the existing data suggest that even in the nineteenth century, especially in cities and large towns, public funds assisted far more dependent people than private charity did. Second, this record underscores the mixed economy of social welfare in the American past. Very early in their histories, state and local governments used private institutions to accomplish public purposes. Many institutions supported by public funds remained technically private but sustained themselves partly with public money. The New York Free School Society, for instance, later renamed the Public School Society, was a private corporation that used state funds to educate all willing poor children in New York City until the 1850s. Reform schools, hospitals, orphanages, and mental institutions were often funded in similar ways.[6]

Although charity reorganized during the Gilded Age (the 1870s and 1880s), it proved unable to cope by itself with the casualties of America's emergent urban-industrial transformation. The depression of the 1890s exposed both the inherent limits of private charities and the bankruptcy of their major strategy: scientific charity. Scientific charity emerged out of several concerns: fear of radicalism, violence, and labor unions; disgust with the corrupt administration of municipal public assistance; concern over the rising cost of relief; and determination to apply modern scientific methods to age-old problems. Charity Organization Societies, a British innovation imported first to Buffalo, New York, in 1877, became the primary instruments of scientific charity. They were supposed to maintain centralized, citywide registers of applicants for relief; investigate applicants for other agencies; supervise the poor through "friendly visiting"; collect data on pauperism, relief, and related subjects; and encourage the replacement of public outdoor relief with private charity.[7]

Scientific charity influenced public policy and private action briefly but powerfully. Charity Organization Societies sprang up everywhere, although nowhere could they follow the ideal blueprint laid down by reformers. Under the influence of scientific charity, ten of the nation's forty largest cities abolished public outdoor relief in the late 1870s and 1880s; many others reduced the amount they gave. In 1878, Brooklyn, New York, became the first, and most famous, city to do away with public outdoor relief. Civic leaders argued that they had destroyed a corrupt system and saved money without hurting the poor. Private charity, they contended, had continued to help the truly needy, while many whom public assistance previously had aided supported themselves through work or with the help of families. Champions of scientific charity elsewhere uncritically accepted Brooklyn's claims; even in the 1990s conservatives still used them as evidence for the feasibility of replacing public assistance with charity.[8] Unfortunately for them, Brooklyn's official line misrepresented what had happened. Abundant evidence points to great hardship in the city. Many who lacked support apparently left; others turned to hospitals for help; and, in time, outdoor relief found its way back to Brooklyn and other cities.

The case for scientific charity lost its remaining credibility in the massive depression of the 1890s, when private charity proved unable to cope with the misery on the streets. Theories that held individuals responsible for their own poverty rang hollow, and public officials slowly began to reintroduce outdoor relief. Reformers, meanwhile, argued vigorously for increased public action. "Child savers" organized around children's issues; "social gospelers" pointed to the imperative of social action in Christian theology; tenement house reformers pressed for the regulation of unsanitary housing; public health advocates advocated improved sanitation and free milk and vaccinations for children; and idealistic young reformers moved into the new settlement houses in inner cities. All these activists championed an increased role for government in preventing or alleviating poverty and its consequences.

The results of reform intensified the public/private mix in American social welfare. Whereas scientific charity had tried to divide public and private sharply by carving out a separate sphere of action for each—indeed, even in the early-twentieth century in the Northeast, Charity Organization Societies opposed public mothers' pensions—the new generation of reformers usually advocated an expanded role for the state and stressed cooperative rather than competitive relations between public and private. The women and men working in private organizations realized that the massive problems they confronted required public resources. Private charities served as pioneers, identifying and publicizing social needs and then pressing for government action to address them.

Three other developments that shaped the history of America's independent sector before the 1980s deserve special mention: first, the organization of local charities into federations or "community chests"—precursors of the United Way. The first community chest started in Cleveland in 1913. However, few cities followed its lead until after World War I; by 1929, community chests existed in 329 cities. A new class of experts, professional fund-raisers, made community chests possible. They encouraged large-scale corporate giving, broadened the base of support outward from the wealthy to a larger cross section of the population, professionalized administration, and reduced the role of volunteers. In the process, charity became philanthropy. As they bureaucratized charity, community chests blurred the line between public and private and, by their control of resources, pushed small, innovative, or dissident organizations outside the bounds of respectability, where, struggling to survive, they have remained ever since.

The Great Depression of the 1930s was the second development. Not only did the crisis overwhelm charities' resources, but New Dealers used federal programs to assert the primacy of government in the field of social welfare. Most of the New Deal initiatives—from the Federal Emergency Relief Administration to Social Security—required public agencies to distribute funds directly, not to funnel them through private charities. As important as private charity remained, it would exist thereafter in the shadow of government.

The third major shift in the role of private charities and social services came in the 1960s and early 1970s. The Public Welfare Amendments of 1962 and Title XX of the Social Security Amendments of 1974 injected massive amounts of federal money into the social services. As the federal government began to buy many more social services from private sources, social agency budgets depended increasingly on government funds, and social agencies metamorphosed into government contractors.

This transformation of charity exposes a final note of fantasy in the calls by conservatives to return public welfare to the world of voluntarism. Only occasionally or in small towns does charity consist of bands of women and men helping their needy neighbors. In the metropolitan regions where most Americans live, most charities, social agencies, and philanthropies are themselves bureaucracies staffed by full-time professionals sometimes assisted by volunteers. The independent sector may exist between government and the market, but in its own way it is big business. In 1998 the heads of America's largest philanthropic foundations earned an average of $363,000 a year.[9]

The Assimilation of Social Welfare to the Market and the State

"Independent sector" is often used interchangeably with "third," "voluntary," or "nonprofit sector." It is the self-definition selected by the more than eight hundred corporate, foundation, and voluntary organizations joined together in the Independent Sector, an organization that embraces a dazzling and diverse array of institutions whose activities often have little or nothing in common: churches, private colleges and schools, hospitals, foundations, day-care services, arts organizations, advocacy groups, social service agencies, and many more. Together they compose "a distinctive sector" because, as one authority puts it, "they engage people in collective purposes outside of the market and the state and are independently organized and self-governing." In 1994, the total budget of the independent sector amounted to $568 billion; it included 1.03 million institutions, generated 6.3 percent of national income, and employed 15.1 million people—9.7 million full- or part-time and 5.5 million full-time-equivalent volunteers. Nationally, it has grown at an astounding rate: the number of nonprofits rose from 309,000 in 1967 to over 1 million thirty years later. In Minnesota, to take one example, from 1987 to 1997 the nonprofit sector grew at a rate of 5 percent a year.[10]

Most nonprofits are small and have few assets. A handful of giants control most of the nonprofit wealth. Excluding religious congregations and very small organizations, the 3.8 percent of nonprofits (6,751 organizations) with expenses exceeding $10 million held 76 percent of the assets. Three sources—private contributions, government grants, and private payments (dues, fees, and charges)—provided 89 percent of the independent sector's income. During the nearly two decades from 1977 to 1994, the share of each income source shifted: private contributions declined from 26 to 18 percent; government contributions rose from 27 to 31 percent; and private payments increased from 38 to 39 percent. The sources of independent sector funding also differ dramatically by category of activity. In 1992, social, legal, and health services depended most heavily on government funds, and arts and culture, the least.[11]

Within the independent sector, the boundaries between public and private remain much less rigid in practice than in theory. By 1980, about 40 percent of the money spent by governments on a broad spectrum of human services was paid to private nonprofits; about 20 percent went to for-profit agencies; and only 40 percent was spent directly by government. The independent sector, in other words, delivered most of the human services in America.[12]

Nonprofits produce as well as consume resources. In 1996 Baltimore's 2,142 nonprofits pumped $3.1 billion into the city. They generated an additional $2.3 billion in economic activity for other city businesses. This total included $2.1 billion in wages and salaries for city residents. The nonprofits offered the full-time equivalent of 56,000 jobs for employees who both lived and worked in the city; this number exceeded all the jobs in durable goods manufacturing for the entire Baltimore metropolitan area. Nonprofits also generated 24,000 full-time-equivalent jobs for city residents working in other businesses. Jobs for 26 percent of the city's workforce originated with the spending of nonprofits, their employees, and their visitors. Taxes on the earnings of their employees amounted to $41 million.[13] Clearly, the activities of the independent sector constitute a huge share of America's economy.

Classifying the components of the independent sector proves very difficult. One cut divides them into public charities and private foundations. Charities provide services; foundations usually provide funds. Charities consist further of two major types, identified by their number in the tax code: 501[c](3) and 501[c](4). Both are exempt from federal taxes and local property taxes. Only the former can receive tax-deductible contributions. As a condition, they cannot lobby for social and economic legislation.[14] In 1992, about 546,000 organizations enjoyed 501[c](3) status, but only about one in three of them engaged in human services, which is to say that only a minority constitute a part of the welfare state.[15]

In the modern history of the independent sector, the first great story is simply growth. The operating expenses of private nonprofit organizations jumped from $18.4 billion in 1960 to $499.1 billion in 1993, or in constant 1987 dollars, from $126 billion to $375.5 billion. This growth represented more than a doubling of their share of gross domestic product, from 3.6 percent in 1960 to 7.9 percent in 1993. The combined growth of the private welfare state's two branches—the social services and charities as well as employee benefits—was even more explosive: between 1972 and 1992, the private share of social welfare funding (health and medical care, welfare and other services, education, and income maintenance) climbed from 8 percent of GDP to 13.7 percent, while public spending rose more modestly, from 16.6 percent to 20.5 percent.[16]

A great deal of the private spending reflected increased government funding of private agencies. Indeed, the massive increase in federal funding since the 1960s is the next great story. By the 1980s, private agencies received at least 30 percent of their $500 billion annual income from governments—more than came from donations. Medicare and Medicaid made government a major source of income for private health care providers, and private agencies increasingly served as contractors or service providers for government—indeed, most of the money spent by private social services came from government sources. In Massachusetts, for example, the state government's purchase of services multiplied more than thirty times between 1971 and 1988—from $25 million to $850 million. Governments not only provided more of the funds for nonprofits; they began to shape the provision of services by contracting for entire programs and even creating "providers where they otherwise did not exist."[17]

This growth in government social welfare spending before the 1990s took place in two periods. From the Great Society era through the first Carter administration (1965–77) spending rose 149 percent in constant dollars; from Carter's last years as president through the Reagan/Bush presidencies, spending grew much more slowly: 36 percent in constant dollars from 1977 to 1989. These figures, however, mask real differences in growth between sectors. Driven by prior commitments, government spending on health and housing grew while spending on social services and income maintenance declined. In 1990 dollars, the federal Social Services Block Grant plunged from $44.4 billion in 1980 to $2.6 billion in 1991. Between 1982 and 1997, social services lost $35.1 billion in federal funding. In 1997, federal support for social services was 79 percent of its level in 1982.[18]

One analysis claimed that between 1982 and 1994, nonprofits lost over $38 billion they would have received if the federal government had continued to spend at prior levels. In 1981 and 1986, federal tax acts added to nonprofits' fiscal problems by reducing incentives for charitable giving. Health care remained the massive exception. Of all government support for nonprofits, more than three-quarters went to hospitals and other health care providers—a reflection of the size and growth of Medicare and Medicaid. Between 1982 and 1997, federal support for health rose 185 percent, to $664.9 billion. Yet, nonprofits faced the same issues of homelessness, AIDS, crack cocaine, and heightened poverty that were overwhelming city and state resources.

In the mid-1990s, Congress threatened nonprofits with another round of cutbacks. The Republican Congress elected in 1994 reduced spending on discretionary programs by 12 percent from 1995 to 1996. Cutbacks proved severe in fields that served the poor: 17 percent in the Social Services Block Grant, 20 percent in postsecondary student assistance, 24 percent in disadvantaged housing, 26 percent in community service, 32 percent for the Legal Services Corporation, and 34 percent for low-income energy assistance. Cumulative cuts projected for the period from 1997 to 2002 would cost nonprofits $50.2 billion of their federal revenues and leave annual spending 9 percent below 1995 levels. Independent sector authority Lester Salamon called these cuts the fiscal crisis of the nonprofit sector.[19]

Indeed, in December 1995 the impact of these cuts appeared grim. A meals-on-wheels program lost a New York City grant that paid for nursing visits to the homebound elderly; a social service program no longer had the money to pay a social worker to visit day-care centers to look for signs of child abuse and neglect; a rent assistance program whose federal financing expired could help only those who faced eviction in seventy-two hours. Tales abounded. City officials in New York and elsewhere documented sharp increases in demand for social services as public funds diminished. City charities retrenched. In December 1995, one authoritative calculation projected federal funding cuts would translate into 137,055 fewer meals for the elderly poor provided by Los Angeles's Jewish Family Service during the next seven years; a reduction of 349 families served by the child-abuse program in San Antonio; a drop of one-third in the 750 dinners a night served by the Coalition for the Homeless in New York City. About half the Detroit area's social service nonprofits lost federal and state government funds. Catholic Charities USA, which depended on federal, state, and local governments for 63 percent of its $1.9 billion budget, predicted a doubling of need during this time of federal spending cuts.[20]

Surprisingly, these cuts did not diminish the growth in the number of nonprofits or overall independent sector revenues. To the contrary, in the 1980s, paid employment in nonprofits grew by 41 percent in the United States, which was more than double the growth of national employment.[21] From 1979 to 1989, revenues, adjusted for inflation, rose an astonishing 79 percent. Where did the money come from?

In part, it came from state and local governments. From 1980 to 1988, state and local spending on social welfare services rose from $4.8 billion to $7.3 billion as federal social welfare expenses dropped from 64.6 percent to 52.4 percent of the total. State governments took over many services that federal grants had initiated in the 1970s—for instance, drug and alcohol treatment—and they provided them by purchasing services from nonprofits.[22]

Private contributions also made up some of the difference, but not the major share. Private donations rose 53 percent between 1979 and 1989, or about 4 percent a year, adding 15 percent to the growth of income. In 1964, private contributions composed 54 percent of current operating funds; in 1993, 24 percent. The reason was increased government support for health care, hospitals, education, and human services. At the same time, annual giving dropped from an average 1.81 percent of individual income in the 1970s to 1.76 percent from 1983 to 1992; in 1998 it reached 1.9 percent for the first time since 1973. While total charitable giving increased a remarkable 9.1 percent in 1999, giving by foundations—influenced by a federal law requiring them to give away at least 5 percent of their assets each year—rose at almost twice the rate as giving by individuals. The tax laws that reduced incentives for charitable giving impacted the contributions from the wealthiest individuals the most: between 1983 and 1993, the average charitable deduction taken by all taxpayers increased 30 percent, but it declined 55 percent for taxpayers with adjusted gross incomes of $500,000 to $1 million. With so much more wealth now composed of investments, however, income represented a less useful measure of charitable effort than it had two or three decades earlier. Indeed, the rise in charitable giving in 1998 did not come close to matching the 27 percent increase in the Standard and Poors stock index. Economist Edward N. Wolff estimated that giving amounted to 0.69 percent of the nation's wealth in 1999, compared to 0.71 percent in 1998. "The very top group could be giving 10 times more than they do and not impair their wealth at all," observed an investment adviser who had set up a nonprofit group to encourage giving by the wealthy.[23]

Between 1991 and 1997, donations to social service charities dropped while contributions to health and hospitals, education, and religion increased:

Social Services	−5%
Health and hospitals	+25%
Education	+21%
Religion	+12%

Although in 1998 and 1999 the buoyant economy and surging stock market boosted charitable giving in all areas, great disparities remained. In 1999, for instance, religious charities received nearly $82 billion and human services $17.6 billion. As one United Way official observed, "People who work for the big companies in the cities are not giving to the inner city charities."[24] Instead, religious institutions receive around half of all private giving, although the figure fluctuates from year to year. Even more striking, religious institutions receive a majority of total household contributions:

Religion	60%
Human services	9%
Health	5%

In 1995, to put the figures another way, Americans gave the following amounts:

Religious institutions	$63 billion
Educational organizations	$18 billion
Health organizations	$13 billion
Human services organizations	$12 billion

To put these numbers in perspective, the federal government spent about $1.5 trillion on social insurance and public assistance.[25]

Americans contributed a significant amount of time as well as money. In 1993, about 47.7 percent of adults volunteered an average of 4.2 hours each week. They gave a total of 19.5 billion hours—15 billion in formal volunteering and 4.5 billion informally helping neighbors or organizations on an ad hoc basis. One estimate puts the monetary value of their time at $183 billion. Again, religious organizations received the greatest share of volunteer effort, nearly 29 percent, more than twice the 14 percent devoted to human services. By some measures, however, voluntarism has declined. Although Americans reporting some volunteer activity in 1998 increased their contribution by 1 percent more than in 1989, they donated 400 million fewer hours. Sara Melendez, president of the Independent Sector, observed, "People are volunteering, but when they do, it's more of a one-shot deal—half a day one Saturday, instead of once a week for x number of weeks."[26]

Three facts about these trends stand out: private giving cannot substitute for public funds, and charity cannot take over the financial role of government; when it comes to any purpose other than religion, Americans are not very generous with their money; and private contributions did not account for very much of the startling rise in nonprofit sector income during the 1980s.

With declining government funds and stagnant private contributions, the independent sector survived by entering the marketplace. This was a "shift in the basic structure of the American social welfare system," wrote Lester Salamon, that was more important than even the Reagan-era spending cuts. The "marketization of welfare" combined the penetration of marketlike relations and activities into social welfare practice with "a striking expansion of commercial activity on the part of nonprofit firms, blurring the distinction between nonprofit and for-profit providers and raising serious questions about who will serve those in need."[27]

Marketlike incentives permeated the world of charity and social service through government-funded vouchers, which turn clients into customers. No longer restricted to housing, vouchers penetrated other corners of the welfare state and threatened to invade public education as well. Between 1981 and 1986, the share of federal assistance received by nonprofits through voucher payments to individuals rose from 53 percent to 70 percent. Contracting out government services also reflected the penetration of the market into the welfare state—with the ironic result that the involvement of governments in the affairs of nonprofits rose to unprecedented levels. Winning and managing government contracts shifted the attention of nonprofits to managerial concerns and heightened the "role of market norms of efficiency" in social services.[28]

Nonprofits entered the commercial market in other ways as well, including fees charged for service and the sale of products, activities that spread from health and education to other areas of human services. From 1982 to 1992, fees and service charges accounted for 52 percent of the growth of the nonprofit sector, while private giving accounted for only 8 percent—well below its share at the start of the period. In the 1990s, fees, dues, and other charges constituted 40 percent of the revenues of charities, double their receipts from private giving and one-third more than supplied by government. Nonprofits' income grew most from health-related services, which covered everyone, thereby shifting resources away from areas that served the poor. Even the social services, long dominated by nonprofits, followed the same trend, as fee income expanded from 11 percent of their revenues to 20 percent. By 2000, some nonprofits even had aggressively entered the world of e-commerce. Burton A. Weisbrod, a national authority on the independent sector, observed, "Seemingly isolated events touching the lives of virtually everyone are, in fact, parts of a pattern that is little recognized but has enormous impact: the commercialization of nonprofit organizations."[29]

Some agencies responded to cuts in federal funding by switching to state-funded contracts or other federal programs. Medicaid, an entitlement, proved a very attractive funding source for nonprofits, used especially by mental health and family service programs for counseling and therapy. Fee income for these agencies increased substantially during the 1980s. Other agencies simply shifted their focus to acquire federal dollars. For instance, one Massachusetts agency replaced cut funds by reorienting itself and picking up the federal cheese-and-butter distribution and fuel assistance programs.[30]

The recent history of the Red Cross illustrates the commercialization process at work in nonprofits. When she became president of the Red Cross, Elizabeth Dole, wife of then senator Robert Dole, inherited an organization troubled by a deteriorating financial condition and a weak bureaucracy. For years the Red Cross had violated safety regulations by shipping blood infected with hepatitis B and the AIDS virus. In 1993, the Federal Food and Drug Administration, armed with a Justice Department consent decree, began to monitor the Red Cross in the "most extensive enforcement action" in FDA history. The cost of compliance drove the Red Cross into a deficit. Until the late 1980s, blood had generated a profit. With the increased costs of collection and tests, it began to lose money—a trend exacerbated by the demand of hard-pressed hospitals for lower-cost blood. In fiscal 1994, the blood division lost $50 million and in 1995, $113 million. Elizabeth Dole responded, observed the *New York Times*, by creating a "marketing arm" and with "other tactics more associated with business than with charity." As a result, "today's Red Cross is more like a big business than the voluntary relief agency founded by Clara Barton in 1881."[31]

Under Dole, the Red Cross started to compete aggressively with community blood banks for a larger share of the blood market by undercutting the prices local blood banks charged hospitals. Its strategy relied in part "on exploiting the Red Cross' national presence by collecting blood in low-cost markets where supplies are plentiful, like the Midwest, and selling it in high-priced urban areas where blood is scarcer," said the *Times* article. One Red Cross official commented, "If you want to stay efficient and effective in a declining or flat market, you have to get a bigger share of the pie. . . . We're not forcing hospitals to take products from us." Dole negotiated a deal with Federal Express for exclusive rights to conduct blood drives among its 24,000 Memphis employees; at the same time, the Red Cross signed an agreement to ship its blood exclusively with Federal Express. A Federal Express vice president denied a connection between the two events. When a local blood supplier complained, Federal Express backed down and agreed to let both organizations collect blood from its employees in the following year. The Red Cross also bid for exclusive rights to collect blood at military bases, but the Pentagon eventually refused.[32]

The commercial activities of the Red Cross and other nonprofits troubled small businesses that felt unable to compete with the giant organizations that began to invade their markets. A former investment banker who advises nonprofits on mergers, acquisitions, and money raising told a group of nonprofit executives, "We believe the days of the small, local nonprofit are coming to an end." "Small business," wrote one critic of the trend toward large businesslike nonprofits, "is raising hell as it discovers that some of America's largest nonprofit charities unfairly earn millions of dollars by 'hocking their halo.' " He pointed to the American Cancer Society, American Heart Association, American Lung Association, Arthritis Foundation, and others that had entered the "business world" by selling "everything from vacation packages to mutual funds. Small businesses complain they can't match the deals offered by their tax-exempt business rivals." They called the nonprofits' practices "unfair competition" and complained that they sometimes copied their products and stole their customers by "trading on the charity's good reputation." The proof was everywhere: Duke University's nonprofit Medical Center was starting a business unit to compete with private companies running drug and medical-device trials; "nonprofit food banks established to feed the poor are building food-dehydrating plants that compete with private firms"; churches conduct tours that compete with private travel agencies. The most "notorious example" of a nonprofit that has used its good name to sell hundreds of millions of dollars worth of products annually is the American Association of Retired Persons. Businesses have wondered why AARP should remain "exempt from taxes when virtually identical companies not affiliated with the nonprofit giant must pay taxes to provide the same services."[33]

The line between nonprofit and for-profit blurred more when nonprofits spun off profit-making branches or, in health care, sloughed off their charitable skin altogether. Charities often operated their for-profit arms with considerable secrecy. Minnesota Public Radio reported to its contributors that its president earned about $74,000 a year; the organization did not tell contributors that he also earned a $380,000 salary from its affiliated for-profit corporation. William Armony, who was then the president of United Way of America, redirected thousands of dollars to a for-profit subsidy "to pay for an apartment, personal trips and gifts for his mistress."[34]

In the same year, for-profit firms increasingly drew the human services even closer to the marketplace. Originally attracted by the prospect of government funds, for-profit firms might have backed out of the social services when government funds were reduced in the 1980s. Government support, however, did not decrease evenly across all types of services, and for-profit firms positioned themselves to profit from the growth that did occur. They "enjoyed certain advantages in going after the resulting 'business,' " claimed Salamon, and as a consequence, for-profits expanded their market share in "virtually every field of social welfare."[35]

Consider the example of health care. By 1977 over half of all the income of nonprofit health care organizations derived from commercial fees and charges, largely paid by third-party insurance. The huge resources pumped into health care by the combination of private insurance, Medicare, and Medicaid attracted for-profit firms. By the 1980s, although the total number of hospitals had declined, the number of for-profit hospitals rose 28 percent and their share of beds grew 41 percent. For-profit providers proved able to respond more quickly to market shifts, especially the demand for short-term specialty care. Although the trend toward for-profit expansion slowed in the late 1980s and early 1990s, by mid-decade it had "resumed with a vengeance." Rather than build new hospitals, commercial interests began to take over nonprofit institutions and convert them to for-profit status. In 1994, 31 nonprofit hospitals shifted to for-profit status, usually after they had been bought by for-profit chains; in 1995 the number increased to 59; in 1996, Salamon estimated, another 200 reported being in "active discussion" with for-profit firms. At the same time, nonprofit Blue Cross and Blue Shield organizations across the nation began to convert to for-profit status. As an article in the *New England Journal of Medicine* concluded, "Nonprofit health plans are a byproduct of the past."[36]

Similar tends marked home health care and outpatient clinics. Between 1975 and 1988, adjusting for inflation, outpatient spending increased 208 percent and home health care 450 percent. For-profit institutions accounted for almost 85 percent of the new clinics and related health services. By 1992, they virtually had displaced nonprofit providers. For-profits accounted for all the growth in home health care establishments and 74 percent of the growth in employment. For-profits, only 36 percent of social service agencies in 1977, were 48 percent of all the new ones created between 1977 and 1987. Between 1977 and 1992, for-profit firms took over most day care, with 80 percent of the growth in facilities and 70 percent in employees.[37]

For-profits gained ground in other social services with the federal welfare reform bill of 1996. The bill allowed states to contract out the administration of public assistance to for-profit firms and religious organizations. The "ink was hardly dry," recounts Salamon, before giant firms like Lockheed Martin and Andersen Consulting began to bid on the process of moving millions of clients from welfare to work. Nina Bernstein at the *New York Times* was first to report on the movement of large American corporations into welfare administration. Lockheed Martin, "the $30 billion giant of the weapons industry," she reported, was bidding against Electronic Data Systems (the $12.4 billion information technology company founded by Ross Perot) and Andersen Consulting to run the $563 million welfare program in Texas. Lockheed, which had hired two experienced federal welfare officials and a senior welfare official from Texas, planned "to market even more comprehensive welfare contracts to states and counties in what is potentially a new multibillion-dollar industry to overhaul and run welfare programs." Three smaller companies—Maximus, Curtis and Associates, and America Works—had preceded the giant corporations in the welfare-to-work business. Previously, they had competed primarily with Goodwill Industries and churches. Whether they would fill a niche or whether Lockheed, EDS, and Andersen would swallow them remained unclear. The Clinton administration dealt privatization in Texas and elsewhere a setback when it refused to allow the state to combine eligibility for all federal programs (food stamps and Medicaid as well as public assistance) in one privatized system. Texas governor George W. Bush promised to find ways to work around the law. Meanwhile, reports of privatization fiascoes under Lockheed surfaced in California, Connecticut, and elsewhere, while accusations of shady dealings dogged Maximus.[38]

Even before 1996, state welfare reform had blurred the already fuzzy boundaries between nonprofit and the state. In Michigan, Governor John Engler turned over the homeless shelter business to the Salvation Army. Between 1991 and 1995, the state paid the Salvation Army $38.5 million, which the organization parceled out at the rate of $10 per person per night to shelter operators, who also often received private contributions. In Mississippi, Governor Kirk Fordice established a Faith and Families project intended to make state social-service nonprofits, many with religious roots, the agencies of choice for delivering state programs. Maryland lawmakers planned "to solicit charities and religious groups to provide a wide assortment of services for the poor." By November 1997, New York City had contracted with nonprofit companies to run thirty-three of its forty shelters for homeless single adults.[39]

The privatization of public assistance administration highlighted the ironies in America's mixed economy of social welfare. Take Lockheed: the federal government had bailed Lockheed out in the 1970s and 1980s; the corporation's backlog of government contracts exceeded $50 billion; and it lobbied for $1.6 billion in public subsidies for mergers with two former competitors. By moving into public assistance administration, Lockheed furthered its dependence on government funds. It could no more sustain itself without them than could a single mother on welfare.

The assimilation of social welfare to the market and the state provoked unease across the political spectrum. Would Michigan's reliance on the Salvation Army to administer funds for the homeless, one observer asked, help the agency serve more people in need or, instead, "dilute—or pollute—their ability to exert the moral and spiritual influence that makes them uniquely successful?" Events in Michigan did not leave her sanguine because the state limited its contract to emergency services only—a "myopic view," according to one Salvation Army official. "Not only does government waste public funds on ineffective programs," argued another critic, it "changes charities' incentives" by "giving them reason to keep caseloads up instead of getting them down by turning around people's lives." The National Commission on Philanthropy and Civic Renewal also deplored the influence of government on charity. "Some of us who devote our days to working in poor communities know first hand that the rigid bureaucracy of government welfare programs has also eroded the independence and authority of many service organizations that have themselves become dependent on government support and subservient to its rules and procedures."[40]

A symbiotic relationship between nonprofits and government, charged social critic Theresa Funiciello, breeds corruption as well as independence, while it turns charity workers into "agents for the status quo." John McKnight, a writer and advocate of community-based social change, also saw only danger in the emergence of the powerful new "service economy and its pervasive service institutions," which "have commodified the care of community and called that care a service." Do welfare workers "need the welfare clients more than the clients need their services?" asked McKnight. Like Funiciello, the answer, he said, "is clear. The recipient is much more valuable in her dependency; she is a national resource." As they entered profitable markets, nonprofits began to encounter "massive competition" from for-profit firms. In order to compete, the nonprofits squeezed their "profit margins severely, undermining" their original mission, such as charity or research. Other critics warned that in the flood of commercial firms into the human service business the drive for profit inevitably would work against the interests of the people served. "No company can be expected to protect the interests of the needy at the expense of its bottom line, least of all a publicly traded corporation with a fiduciary duty to maximize shareholder profits," argued Henry A. Freedman, executive director of the Center on Social Welfare Policy and Law, a research and advocacy law office.[41]

Charities and social services confronted the emergent world of marketized social welfare uncertain about their future support. Reduced funding for public services, feared many in the independent sector, would swamp charities with "unprecedented numbers" of the disadvantaged. "There is very little capacity in the voluntary sector to absorb the responsibilities of the federal government," said W. Mark Clark, president of the Travelers Aid International. "People can't send us the problems without sending us the funds for dealing with them." In November 1997, representatives of fifty of the nation's largest nonprofits—the National Assembly of National Voluntary Health and Social Welfare Organizations—warned "that voluntary health and human service organizations can't single-handedly maintain the 'social safety net' supporting the needy." The assembly's executive director, Gordon Raley, claimed, "As a nation, we have been too intent on ending welfare instead of solving the human needs which necessitated its use in the first place. . . . Health and human service organizations are being forced to take over the 'social safety net' while facing unprecedented difficulties as government becomes less involved in meeting human needs." The president and

CEO of Second Harvest, Christine Vladimiroff, explained that her organization would have to increase its capacity by 425 percent in the next five years to compensate for cuts in the food stamp program. "Is that likely? No."[42]

Unlike many human service agencies and other nonprofits, charities could not respond with market-based strategies to the human misery they saw on the horizon. Poor women and children or the homeless could not pay fees. Only giant corporations with contracts to administer public assistance would profit from their poverty. Nor could charities turn for more help to state and city governments. To the contrary, responding to their own fiscal crises, state and city governments threatened to worsen the nonprofits' dilemma by attempting—but so far not succeeding—to withdraw their tax exemptions.[43]

City governments also threatened the future of charities by trying to curb their growth. In 1996, Hartford, Connecticut, attracted national attention when the city imposed two consecutive moratoriums on the opening of any new sites for services and on the expansion of existing ones. The growth of soup kitchens, shelters, and other social agencies, according to supporters of the moratoriums, was "ruining the climate for urban revitalization, hurting businesses, shrinking the tax base and scaring away the middle class." At least thirty other cities also used zoning laws to limit social service agencies. "What we're seeing is two trends on a collision course and most likely headed for disaster," warned Maria Foscarinis, executive director of the National Law Center on Homelessness and Poverty. Hartford city officials justified their actions by arguing that the city's abundant social services housed a disproportionate number of the state's needy people. Arthur Feltman, the council member who drafted the ordinances, associated Hartford's action with the national war on dependence: "There's a paternalistic view in the social-services community that the poor will always be poor, the needy will always be needy, and that if not for us do-gooders, everyone is going to die. I think we have to have some confidence that, given the right opportunity, people can do more for themselves and take more responsibility."[44]

Faith, Charity, and Inner Cities

Much of the misery predicted by nonprofits would land on the steps of churches and other faith-based providers, who, along with city governments and secular charities, offered Americans in need their last resort. Religious congregations have always served this purpose. The work of the early-nineteenth-century Protestant missions, the Catholic institutions of the Jacksonian period, and the Progressive Era social gospel was continued in the work of countless congregations and religious groups in the twentieth century. Religious (or, as it is now often called, faith-based) charity and social service remain a crucial part of today's private welfare state.

An irony underlies this history, however. By the last decades of the nineteenth century, advocates of scientific charity (the era's version of welfare reform) wanted to reduce the role of congregations in relief (what we today would call welfare). They believed that church members, often duped by the undeserving poor, engaged in indiscriminate charity that only heightened claims for relief and reinforced individual dependency. Decades later, at the dawn of the American welfare state in the New Deal, religious institutions played a very minor role in federal planning for economic security. By contrast, the last several years have witnessed a resurgence of faith-based responses to poverty fueled in part by the policies of the federal government and supported by political liberals as well as conservatives.

Faith-based agencies have not escaped the great forces redefining the welfare state. They are instruments of the devolution of public social welfare activity, and their advocates find in them a unique weapon in the war on dependency. Their relation to the market remains less consistent. They rest on the motivating power of faith, not profit. But their activities often draw them into the commercial arena—whose principles they must adopt to survive—while dependence on public money at the same time draws them close to the state.

Faith-based responses to poverty remain impossible to count with anything like precision. They vary from small soup kitchens to the enormous Catholic Charities USA. They encompass efforts rooted in congregations and ones that cross denominations. Some of them are very large: Bread of the World is approaching a membership of 50,000; Habitat for Humanity, a product of an evangelical founder, is the seventeenth-largest home builder in America; the Pacific Institute for Community Organizing and the Industrial Areas Foundation are large community organizing networks that usually work through churches. In 1995, Catholic Charities USA spent $1.93 billion.[45]

More than half—57 percent—of congregations contribute toward social service activities. These congregations include 75 percent of people who attend religious services. A third support or participate in food programs, 18 percent have shelter programs, and 11 percent provide clothing. Fewer than 10 percent offer programs that deal with health, education, domestic violence, tutoring or mentoring, substance abuse, or work issues. Only about 12 percent of congregations actually run food programs by themselves—for the most part they support activities of

other organizations. Indeed, congregational involvement in social service activities remains small. Only 12 percent have a staff person who
devotes at least a quarter of his or her time to social service projects, and
social service activities amount to only between 2 and 4 percent of the
average congregation's total budget. Although in half of congregations
volunteers participate in social service work, in one year 80 percent of
congregations managed to mobilize fewer than thirty people—indeed,
the average congregation mobilized just ten.[46]

Although it is impossible to quantify, all observers agree that faith-
based charity and social service has grown in size and importance during
the last several years. The first reason is simply demand. All the problems forcing new responses from nonprofits and the public sector press
on faith-based providers as well. Between 1981 and 1995, the annual
number of clients served by Catholic Charities USA more than tripled,
from 3.1 million to 10.8 million. In 1981, "emergency needs—food, shelter, light and water bills, domestic violence"—consumed 23 percent of
CCUSA's budget; in 1995, they took two-thirds of its money. By the late
1990s, CCUSA was providing social, hospice, and other services to
almost 20,000 AIDS patients.[47]

By encouraging states to engage faith-based organizations as
providers of federally funded welfare services, the "charitable choice"
provision of the 1996 welfare bill accelerated the devolution of the welfare state. In 1998, Congress extended the charitable choice provisions
to Head Start, community service block grants, and low-income housing
assistance. In 2000, a number of bills before Congress proposed to
broaden it even further.[48]

Reliance on faith-based organizations fits well with the conservative
agenda. By justifying reduced state activity, it serves conservatives' hostility to government while it promotes the role of religion in public life.
"The odd thing," pointed out two scholars from Cornell, "is that many
prominent conservatives who . . . suggest that government ruins everything it touches are ardent advocates of a partnership between government and churches."[49]

Politically, faith-based charity and social service finds active promoters among liberals as well as conservatives. The Democratic and Republican nominees for president in 2000, Al Gore and George W. Bush,
championed the federal government's increased reliance on faith-based
agencies to provide social and human services. "The left would do well
to think beyond this year's presidential posturing and consider the long-
term politics of social services," advised political scientist Dennis R.
Hoover in the *Nation*. "A strong and diverse FBO community, more
engaged than ever in public-private partnerships that serve the poor,

may be a strong ally in defending federal funding when the good economic times stop rolling."[50]

As secretary of HUD in the Clinton administration's first term, Henry Cisneros established the Religious Organizations Initiative in the Special Actions Office. Its "mission" combined "extensive outreach to the faith community" with the engagement of "religious institutions as partners" in reaching HUD's priorities. Among all institutions, only "faith-communities," as Cisneros called them, combined four features that give them "a special role" in inner cities. First, they "are still there." Unlike most businesses and clubs, they have not deserted inner cities. Second, "community is central to their mission." Meeting physical as well as spiritual needs always has animated not only the ministry of Jesus in Christianity but other religions as well, such as *zakat* in Islam or *tzedakah* in Judaism. Third, "faith communities have unique resources." Their "inherent strengths" as institutions derive from their "linkages to the world outside" and the "rare . . . organizational skill" of their leaders, who "think actively about the problems of their communities and have the ability to conceive solutions, mobilize support, and provide follow-through." Fourth, "faith communities touch the soul." Problems of inner-city neighborhoods extend "far beyond simple lack of material wealth." Youths require "values and moral structure to hang on to . . . reasons to believe that there are things worth living for." Other than the faith community, "few institutions . . . can provide youth with this kind of support."[51]

To many observers such as Cisneros, local faith communities increasingly appeared the best hope for responding to the poverty and social crises within African American inner-city neighborhoods. They have been crucial weapons in the struggle to reduce violence, promote responsible parenthood among young men, and reduce the dependency associated with out-of-wedlock births and single-parent families. The historic role of black churches compounded the strength of Cisneros's case for the unique effectiveness of religion-based responses. Everywhere in inner cities, black clergy and their congregations engaged in innovative, often successful work, especially with young people. Cisneros highlighted a Denver study that showed 60 to 75 percent of the city's eighty African American churches providing "at least one community service." The study identified 333 programs; 148 assisted adults and families, commonly with food and clothing. Another 106 programs reached children with "youth activities, tutoring services, scholarship assistance, drug and alcohol education, and before-school and after-school programs." The 59 community development activities included "church-sponsored voter registration drives and candidate forums, as well as the operation of credit unions and housing development."[52]

Boston's Reverend Eugene Rivers III, founder of Asuza Christian Community in an inner-city African American neighborhood, gained national prominence for his successes in fighting drugs and violence, turning around hard-to-reach youth, and persuading adult men to serve as mentors. He pioneered the "Ten Point Coalition, a growing faith-based network of religious entities in Boston (and more recently, nationally) committed to reclaiming the inner city." Rivers found faith the missing element in secular policy. "With faith, one can see beyond discrimination and poverty to a future that has meaning," he said. "Secular agencies don't explain to you why human life is meaningful, why there is a moral difference between spitting on the ground and killing another black person." Rivers did not ignore the material side of poverty or discount the importance of public money. Indeed, he lobbied against the 1996 welfare legislation. But, like others committed to the role of black churches in social action, he viewed poverty, dependence, and violence as moral and spiritual crises—not solely material issues.[53]

Narratives of success should not overshadow the difficulties confronting inner-city black churches or arouse greater expectations than they can fulfill. Black America, wrote Andres Tapia, associate editor of Pacific News Service, in *Christianity Today* (1996), "is under siege, and its casualties are falling at the church's door." Gayroud Wilmore, retired church history professor from Atlanta, Georgia, observed, "At stake is whether the black church will remain a viable institution in the African-American community in the twenty-first century or whether it will become irrelevant." According to him, the mainstream black church, which for four hundred years had served as "the social glue and center in black communities," had lost its "dynamic." A Howard University School of Divinity professor warned of a "meaningless religiosity" in black churches that "lets people off the hook and is seen by many as the 'priest of the status quo.'" Others complained that black churches had "imitated the excesses of the white church" by jettisoning "the gospel of the uplifting of the downtrodden." Only one generation ago, 80 percent of blacks went to church; by the mid-1990s the number had dropped by half, to 40 percent.[54]

Alongside the story of the declining influence of mainstream black churches emerged a more hopeful one: "the story of the prophetic black churches that have recaptured the traditional place of the church in the community while using cutting-edge, sophisticated methods of ministry." This "rising class" of African American churches had begun to energize "whole communities through economic empowerment projects, effective work at getting kids off drugs, keeping them out of jail, and sending them to college." Church attendance had become the most effective indicator of whether urban black men would become criminals, and innovative churches began to attract men traditionally hard to reach and to increase overall attendance.[55]

Evaluating the effectiveness of black churches, or other faith-based agencies, in their inner-city work remained very difficult, however. By the late 1990s, when governments increasingly turned to them for assistance, no one really knew what they had accomplished or could be expected to achieve. For all the praise, evidence of their successes rested mainly on anecdotes, and research remained thin and preliminary. "One theory . . . popularly advanced on behalf of parochial schools and faith-based community development," pointed out Isaac Kramnick and R. Laurence Moore of Cornell University, "holds that teachers and social workers who see their labors as part of a divine calling perform better than people who merely work for a salary, especially when that salary is paid by government." However, no "systematic evidence" supported this argument, "only anecdotes marshaled with partisan intent," and both history and current events proved "patently untrue" the assertion that "only a sense of religious mission" could inspire a commitment to alleviating the deepest problems of inner cities. As counterevidence, one could point to the American settlement house movement at the turn of the century; Teach for America; or, on a smaller scale, in Boston, close to Reverend Rivers's Asuza Christian Community, the secular Dudley Street Initiative, led by "worldly liberals," which was "rejuvenating a once moribund inner-city neighborhood."[56]

A record of accomplishment did emerge clearly in church housing initiatives. Cisneros highlighted several projects: the rehabilitation of 177 apartments and 120 town houses in Chicago by the Antioch Missionary Baptist Church in collaboration with HUD; the redevelopment of a forty-block area and the rebuilding of 40 housing units and 22 duplexes by a coalition of ten churches in Brooklyn, New York; and housing developments built in part by the Allen Baptist Church in Oakland, California. In 1997, 400 ministries in America, an increase of 200 in just two years, participated in the Chicago-based Christian Community Development Association.[57]

Economic development complemented housing on the agenda of many churches. "Coinciding with society's recent collective push for welfare reform," observed two commentators, "more churches are purposefully shouldering the burden of moving the chronically unemployed into the workforce." No one denied the importance of jobs, but whether churches could create and train people for them remained debatable. Bob Lupton, a member of an organization of urban ministries in Atlanta, called "the vision of Christians providing massive economic development as human service providers or urban missionaries . . . a 'romantic' notion." Still, promising examples existed: the Jobs Partnership of Raleigh, North Carolina; New Community Corporation in Newark, New Jersey (whose enterprises employed 2,000 people); and the Christian Economic Coalition in Boston.

Faith-based housing and economic development seemed to succeed best when it used good business practices. Housing management in inner cities demanded "integrating social and business functions," pointed out the Committee on Economic Development. As an example, take the community development corporation founded by the St. Nicholas Roman Catholic Church in Brooklyn, which manages 1,150 housing units. "St. Nick's takes seriously the business aspects of housing management. The organization has a reputation for vigilant tenant selection and for not being afraid to evict residents who repeatedly cause problems or fail to pay their rent." Whether religion could incorporate a market model without losing the spiritual qualities that supplied its special power remained an unanswered, and very important, question. Some observers of Habitat for Humanity, who found local executives sent as volunteers "debating the wisdom of dispensing with volunteers, if that were the more cost-effective way to build houses," warned of "the dangers to a common citizenship not just from an over-regulatory state, but also from an untrammeled appeal to market metaphors."[58]

Two other dilemmas confront faith-based agencies as well. One is constitutional. How can government support them without violating the separation of church and state required by the Constitution? In *Bowen v. Kendrick* (1988), the Supreme Court enumerated criteria that are supposed to adequately protect the Constitution's establishment clause. The decision did not satisfy all religious groups. Many complained about meeting "state-mandated fair employment practices and a host of other regulations." In 1998, Congress exempted faith-based providers from the fair employment practices included in the Civil Rights Act and prohibited government from requiring them to change their internal governance practices or to remove "religious art, icons, scriptures, or other symbols" as a condition of eligibility for federal funds. Federal law no longer requires the availability of a secular provider as an alternative, and it does not prohibit federally funded faith-based providers from discriminating against beneficiaries on account of their religion.[59] Although the site for major church-state battles remains schooling rather than social service, debates in education inevitably will bear on the future of government support for faith-based charities and social agencies. At the same time, the administration of public assistance and other benefits by faith-based providers almost certainly will push the issue into the courts if, for instance, the only local "welfare" office is run by a religious organization or an agency denies someone benefits because of their religious beliefs.

The growing insularity of churches, despite their myriad service activities, posed another dilemma. The "most significant trend in American religious life," the Commission on Philanthropy and Civic Renewal pointed out, was the "growth of the very large church." Only 12 percent of churches, some with more than ten thousand members, absorbed more than half of church attendance. Within their walls these enormous churches contained all the institutions of community. Large churches, in the words of one Dallas businessman who headed a network of churches, were "shopping malls," with entertainment and services all under one roof. The danger, thought the commission, was the transformation of these giant congregations into "the sectarian equivalent of gated communities, enclaves in which members can shut themselves away from the urgent problems of nearby communities." For instance, while some of the eighteen largest churches in Dallas made significant contributions to "benevolent activities," others, including some that were very wealthy, spent "next to nothing for activities that benefit nonmembers." In 1994, Mississippi's governor, Kirk Fordice, asked each congregation in the state to adopt a needy family. Of the state's 5,500 churches, 267 signed up. Of these, most failed to follow through, and by September 1996 only 15 churches were matched with families.[60] Whatever one thinks of Fordice's proposal, the Mississippi experience, like the policies of the inward-turning Dallas churches, highlights the limits of transforming voluntary, faith-based organizations into the nation's primary safety net.

The Apotheosis of Voluntarism

President Bill Clinton's 1997 summit on community service underlined the limits as well as the potential of voluntarism. Clinton, like President George Bush before him, hoped to mobilize Americans' readiness to volunteer. In his 1988 acceptance speech at the Republican National Convention, Bush compared the nation to a network of charitable organizations that shone "like a thousand points of light in a broad and peaceful sky," and two years later a group of his friends and supporters established the private Points of Light Foundation. Although Bush's thousand points of light exerted little practical impact on the troubles of

America's inner cities, in January 1997, with Bush at his side, Clinton announced a national community service summit in Philadelphia in April directed toward helping poor children and adolescents. The summit was to blend Bush's emphasis on voluntarism with Clinton's own AmeriCorps program of community service.[61] In addition to Bush, former presidents Gerald Ford and Jimmy Carter promised to attend, as did Ladybird Johnson and Nancy Reagan. Clinton named the enormously popular former chairman of the Joint Chiefs of Staff, retired general Colin Powell, to chair the summit; outgoing HUD secretary Henry Cisneros was to serve as vice chair.

Clinton directed his call for voluntarism to corporations and nonprofit organizations as well as to individuals. He wanted them to commit to providing goods and services to impoverished communities and to expand their philanthropic work. Rather than issue a general call for voluntarism, the summit organizers listed five specific ways that volunteers could help young people in need: mentoring, after-school programs, health care, job training, and "service by the needy themselves" or "an opportunity to give back through community service." To build on the summit's momentum, organizers promised a new organization, America's Promise—the Alliance for Youth, which would seek more commitments and monitor their implementation.[62]

Two concepts of voluntarism coexisted uneasily among the summit's sponsors. Conservatives, pointed out Rutgers professor Benjamin Barber, viewed voluntarism as "replacing a government that 'doesn't work,' rather than being a road to better government." They stressed the private, apolitical side of voluntarism and the transfer of responsibility from the public to the private sector. Progressives, on the other hand, saw voluntarism as "a strengthening of democracy, a devolution of power not to individuals and private corporations but to local democratic institutions and self-governing communities." Voluntarism offered a way to pull down rather than erect walls between government and citizens by strengthening the mediating structures between the market and the state that theorists refer to as civil society. An active civil society invigorates government through the creation of dense networks of individual relationships, which in turn create the bonds essential for civic engagement and effective democratic governance.[63]

To skeptics and critics, the president's summit reflected the conservative more than the progressive view of voluntarism. They called it cynicism when two administrations, those of Bush and Clinton, that had slashed funding for public benefits asked for voluntary contributions to compensate for a tattered safety net. They viewed the summit less as a call to a new form of citizenship than as a rationalization for sloughing off government responsibility for poverty, homelessness, and related national problems. They remained underwhelmed by corporate donations that, it could be argued, served to polish corporate images and, in any event, were in large part paid for by ordinary taxpayers in the form of tax deductions. Nor, said critics, did summit promoters appreciate the complexity of deploying volunteer labor or the organizational weaknesses and lack of coordination in the nonprofit sector that left a great many agencies incapable of managing a massive influx of voluntary help. Clinton and other summit supporters denied any intent to assert the irrelevance of government; instead, they said, they viewed voluntarism and government as partners, not substitutes. Still, the aura of moral and practical superiority that hovered around voluntarism left critics suspicious.[64]

Was the summit a success? Its supporters answer with an unequivocal yes. An amazing array of political and corporate leaders gathered in Philadelphia for the three-day event. Corporate donations poured in. The city of Philadelphia had decided to focus volunteer efforts for the day of the summit on painting over graffiti on Germantown Avenue in North Philadelphia, and places for volunteers were oversubscribed. The weather cooperated, and thousands turned out to rallies while disappointing numbers showed up at the concurrent protests. President Clinton and other distinguished guests joined the volunteers painting over graffiti; they also met in invitation-only seminars. The event ended with a spectacular fireworks display.[65]

But the event also illustrated the limits of voluntarism. Logistical problems prevented volunteers from completing the work of graffiti removal. Lacking training, they worked far less efficiently than the city's paid Anti-Graffiti Task Force, and some of the work was very sloppy. Five months after the summit, agencies around the nation had not been flooded with offers of volunteers. Indeed, there was "little evidence as yet of masses coming forward nationwide." America's Promise, the organization designed to encourage and monitor the effort, went through two directors, experienced other administrative delays, and lacked any way of verifying information from corporations about their compliance with their pledges. On the other hand, about a dozen major firms had made large new commitments of time, products, and money without informing the organizers of America's Promise. A year later, a Philadelphia-area offshoot of the summit reported that employers had increased their commitment to volunteer work and generally honored their promises; in April 1998, volunteer coordinators for companies reported that enthusiasm among volunteers was "building." Although the Philadelphia gathering apparently had led to about 150 "mini-summits" at the state and local levels, the initial response to the summit was "not over-whelming," according to Anne Kaplan, research director of Giving USA, which monitors contributions to nonprofits. In July, a survey of 580 nonprofit organizations discovered that only a "small number had experienced an increase in the number of inquiries about volunteering" after the summit. Even where volunteering had increased, Paul Clolery, editor of *NonProfit Times*, reported that "the challenge is enabling gifts and volunteers to get into the hands of nonprofits. The delivery systems are simply not in place." A year after the summit, a writer for the *Philadelphia Inquirer* summed up the mixed evidence of its results: "More people are volunteering in the region, and the need for volunteers has not diminished. Whether half full or half empty, the volunteering glass is not overflowing yet. But more people surely understand that there's a glass that needs to be filled. . . . But quantifying the difference in regionwide volunteerism one year later is like juggling Jell-O." By October 1999, the future of America's Promise did not shine brightly. Critics found evidence that it had inflated its results and claimed "credit for corporate contributions and activities in which it had little involvement." It refused to divulge the salaries of its top executives and conceded it would need to "operate well beyond its original deadline to meet its goals." Whether America's Promise should continue had become an open question. The president's summit was ending not with a bang but with a whimper.[66]

The summit on voluntarism underlined the collapse of partisan difference on social policy and the consensus between centrist Democrats and Republicans on a sharply reduced role for government. It did not seem accidental that the summit followed on the heels of federal legislation that destroyed the entitlement of needy Americans to public assistance. In an era of diminished expectations, the summit was one response of downsized, reinvented government to the crises of youth in inner cities, which it had done so little to alleviate.

The summit also made clear that voluntarism touches deep and abiding themes in the national culture. It has always seemed an unequivocal good in an American political culture that distrusts government and exalts the individual. A note of national pride and self-congratulation always accompanies the statistics that show the high proportion of Americans who volunteer. But there is less readiness to dwell on the reluctance of Americans to spend their volunteer time or their money on people unlike themselves, on institutions to which they do not belong, or on causes outside their neighborhoods. The volunteer summit did little to reverse these patterns on a national scale; instead, it highlighted both a commitment to voluntarism that was long on rhetoric and short on action and a pattern of generosity that in most instances did not stray very far from home.

Community Development Corporations and the Limits of Nonprofits

Community development corporations tested the capacity of nonprofits to substitute for the state. As the federal government abandoned new housing construction, CDCs tried to fill the gap. Their experience underlined the inability of even the most effective nonprofits to solve great public problems.

In cities across the nation, thousands of community development corporations work at the task of revitalizing communities and building affordable housing. CDCs stress the importance of citizen control of economic development and the role of local institutions in the revival of low- and moderate-income neighborhoods. For the most part, they work on a small scale; their efforts focus intensively on a single, bounded community.[67] In 1994, between 2,000 and 2,200 fully established CDCs were at work with perhaps another 300 or 400 in a fledgling state. Two-thirds had been formed after the mid-1970s, mostly in the 1980s; nearly two-thirds, 63 percent, served urban areas; and almost all their housing production and other services targeted low-income people and communities—more than 90 percent of the housing produced by CDCs went to people with incomes below 80 percent of the median. They produced about 30,000 to 40,000 units of affordable housing each year. Collectively, during their history they had produced 400,000 units, developed 23 million square feet of commercial or industrial space, lent $200 million to business enterprises, and created 67,461 full-time jobs or equivalent positions, excluding jobs due to construction activities. Relative to the national need for affordable housing, this output seems small, but it has more than tripled the average level of new federally funded public housing.[68]

CDCs emerged in the 1960s out of a confluence of forces: the War on Poverty and its Model Cities program; the emphasis of the civil rights movement on fair and affordable housing legislation and reformed banking practices; the growth of community organizing; the example of international aid projects that emphasized local initiatives; and the emergence of local empowerment as an antipoverty strategy within major foundations. In 1966, a walk through the poor African American section of Bedford Stuyvesant in Brooklyn made Senator Robert Kennedy determined to press for a more comprehensive response to poverty than current Office of Economic Opportunity programs offered. Together with Congressman James Scheur, also from New York, and Senator Jacob Javits he sponsored an amendment to the Economic Opportunity Act (the charter of the War on Poverty) that created the Special Impact Program (SIP), which was designed to spur economic development in poor neighborhoods. SIP funds financed a demonstration program that in 1969 awarded $11 million in grants to local agencies, which became CDCs. Early favorable results impressed even the Nixon administration, and in 1972, Title VII of the Economic Opportunity Act institutionalized community-based economic development. From 1977 to 1982, Title VII supplied between $46 million and $48 million annually to CDCs, while other federal agencies also funded them. During the 1970s, hundreds of smaller CDCs also formed as a result of both advocacy efforts—such as struggles against highway construction, urban renewal, and redlining—and the activities of local groups using housing and social services to revitalize communities.[69]

The creation of national advocacy and technical assistance organizations also supported the growth of CDCs. Two of the most prominent were the Center for Community Economic Development, in Cambridge, Massachusetts, and the National Housing and Economic Development Law Project, affiliated with the University of California at Berkeley's Bolt Hall Law School. Foundations provided the other great source of early support. The Ford Foundation helped fund community economic development work in Bedford Stuyvesant and several organizations in other poor black neighborhoods that later became CDCs, such as the Woodlawn Organization in Chicago. In 1979, the Ford Foundation took the lead in financing the creation of the Local Initiatives Support Corporation (LISC), the major national intermediary for loans, grants, and equity investments to CDCs. By early 1989, LISC had raised $250 million from 515 corporations and foundations; this money, in turn, leveraged more than $1 billion in direct investment for 525 CDCs. The Enterprise Foundation, funded by developer James W. Rouse in 1982, also became a major national intermediary. By 1989, it had developed a network of job placement centers and a social investment corporation that developed funding sources for low-income housing.[70]

The 1975 Community Reinvestment Act, discussed earlier, opened another funding stream for CDCs. The CRA forced merging banks to prove they were serving the needs of poor as well as of affluent neighborhoods. By applying the CRA vigorously, housing advocates turned increased bank mergers in the 1980s into a source of money for CDCs. In fact, CRA funds facilitated the transformation of many advocacy groups into CDCs. By the end of the 1980s the act had pumped more than $5 billion in new credit into low-income neighborhoods.[71]

By the end of Carter's presidency, an estimated $2.6 billion flowed annually from the federal government to community-based initiatives;

by 1988, the Reagan administration had cut that amount in half. Nonetheless, the number of CDCs increased remarkably during the decade, and over 90 percent of those funded by Title VII survived. Despite the Reagan-era cuts, federal dollars still supported most CDCs; without them, CDCs would be nearly out of business. However, virtually no CDC relied exclusively on federal funds. Instead, they packaged income from a variety of sources—partnering with private sector players, such as banks, corporations, and churches, and with state and city governments, who began to seek cooperation with CDCs as the federal ax fell on funds to build and rehabilitate low-income housing. In 1986, a change in federal tax law, the low-income housing tax credit, allowed investors in qualifying housing projects generous write-offs against tax liabilities. National intermediaries used these credits to generate millions of dollars of investments in CDCs. Under pressure from the CRA, the role of banks in funding CDC activities also increased throughout the decade, while in the 1990s new programs for affordable housing, the homeless, and the elderly once again made more federal funds available.[72]

New funding sources tilted the emphasis of CDCs away from comprehensive economic development and toward housing. In 1994, 90 percent of CDCs reported housing production, and only 23 percent reported business development. Two-thirds, however, reported some form of advocacy and other community-based activity, such as job training and placement, senior citizen programs, emergency food assistance, and youth programs.[73] Still, these activities remained subordinate to the main task of CDCs: building and rehabilitating affordable housing.

CDCs had originated as responses to the failures of both the market and the state. Government had failed to build nearly enough affordable housing, and federal funding for the construction of low-income housing in the 1980s virtually ended. For-profit developers did not fill the void left by the state because they could not build or rent profitably in inner cities. In these circumstances, nonprofits inherited the field. Dedicated and unencumbered by the drive for profit, they wanted to revitalize neighborhoods—not to move residents out of them—and they remained committed to the idea that individuals should participate in the decisions affecting their lives. CDCs emerged from this blend of idealism and practical action.[74]

Early CDC organizers often challenged city governments that had destroyed neighborhoods through urban renewal and then neglected the devastation that remained; they also opposed the market-driven philosophy that elevated profit over community. Eventually, the search for income pushed them away from advocacy or militance and into partnerships with the market and state they originally had opposed.[75]

CDCs stood at the nexus of both public/private and for-profit/nonprofit interests. Survival required a constant scramble for funds from an eclectic collection of potential donors with different motives and goals. One result of this need to serve many masters was that by the end of the 1980s, it had become obvious that CDCs had shed their early confrontational style.[76] Where earlier they had clashed angrily with city hall, they now partnered with urban government to build affordable housing and shelter the homeless; where in the early 1970s they had led protests against redlining and corporate disinvestment in inner cities, they now channeled Community Reinvestment Act funds and tax-exempt dollars from banks and corporations into sound investments. The imperatives of survival had drawn CDCs closer to the market and the state.

By the mid-1990s, observers within the CDC movement began to raise uncomfortable questions about both the consequences of market-driven practices and the effectiveness of CDCs at meeting their initial mission of improving economic well-being in inner-city neighborhoods. Jeremy Nowak, executive director of the enormously successful Philadelphia-based Delaware Valley Community Reinvestment Fund, underscored the limits of a locality-based strategy in a regional economy. For a decade, he pointed out, his fund had invested millions of dollars in the low-income neighborhoods of metropolitan Philadelphia. Nowak and his colleagues assumed that, like similar efforts in other cities, investments in places "increasingly isolated from the mainstream economy" would reverse the "outflow of jobs, capital, and people from the inner city." They assumed, as well, that the appropriate agencies of revitalization were local. However, what had the investments guided by these assumptions accomplished? Although every major city harbored dozens of community development corporations and related agencies, "the persistence and acceleration of poverty" marked "the very areas where so much community development activity" had occurred, noted Nowak. This coincidence of CDC activity with growing poverty highlighted "limitations of the approach: limitations of *scale and perspective*." CDCs, according to Nowak, remained too small to undertake the massive redevelopment needed to "restore the ordinary mechanisms of the marketplace" to vast stretches of big cities or to make them places "in which anyone with choice" would care to live. Most community development also ignored the "requirements of social mobility." In other words, it had paid "far too little attention" to "household poverty defined by access to good jobs and the accumulation of wealth." Nowak observed that the interpretation of poverty as a problem of place in public policy confused the links between neighborhood revitalization and "poverty alleviation." "Neighborhood development strategies," he concluded, could "reinforce the segregation of the poor by building housing in the worst employment markets." Rather than abandon community economic development, Nowak wanted to reorient it toward "poverty alleviation," which, in turn, required linking inner cities to regional economies through strategies that promoted opportunities and helped families build assets.[77]

In the 1990s, a new emphasis on economic development and social welfare represented "a return to the original, comprehensive intent of community development" and a realization that "housing alone" remained unable to "reshape distressed communities."[78] Partnerships among local CDCs, brokered by the Ford Foundation and other intermediaries, in tandem with new "comprehensive community initiatives," opened one route to increasing the scope of community development. Nonetheless, critics continued to worry that CDCs had "become another developer following a supply-side free market approach to redevelopment rather than fighting for the social change necessary to support sustainable development."[79]

Their differences notwithstanding, few observers of CDCs would deny two facts about the history of community development. First, the demands of funding and survival had transformed the politics, management, and orientation of CDCs. Dependent on federal, state, and local governments as well as on foundations, banks, and corporations, CDCs, like other nonprofits, had become a part of the market and the state. Second, CDCs remained incapable of meeting the nation's need for affordable housing or for reducing poverty. "As the 1980s drew to a close," noted a critic, community development more closely resembled "a guerrilla war against poverty than a large-scale invasion." More than any other variety of nonprofit, CDCs had attempted to fill the void created by public abandonment. Although they accomplished a great deal, they only scratched the surface of need, and their experience underscored the inability of the nonprofit world to substitute for the state.[80]

THE PRIVATE WELFARE STATE
AND THE END OF PATERNALISM

In America a vast system of work-related benefits complements the social welfare delivered by public authorities, private charities, and social services. Largely a product of the years since World War II, the private welfare state has given many American workers and their families unprecedented security during illness and old age. However, because its benefits are not universal, the private welfare state has intensified inequalities among workers and dampened demands for the expansion of public social benefits. Always a privilege, never a right, the benefits of the private welfare state have proved more fragile and, even, reversible than many had supposed. Faced with the need to cut costs and increase flexibility in order to compete in a global market, employers have redesigned work and reduced the price of labor by extracting concessions on wages, work rules, and benefits. Just as welfare reform was an attempt to increase individual responsibility by reducing dependence on the state, the emerging benefits strategy has pushed workers toward greater self-reliance by weaning them from dependence on employers. The decline of manufacturing employment, lower benefits, reduced union strength, massive layoffs, and increased part-time jobs have left more workers vulnerable, unprotected, and have forced them to turn to whatever help they can find—private charity or the public welfare state.

Origins of the Private Welfare State

The private welfare state originated with the small pensions offered by a few nineteenth-century firms. In the United States, American Express first offered pensions in 1875; in 1882, Alfred Dolge, builder of pianos and organs, introduced them in manufacturing. Initially, few workers earned pensions, which required continuous work in the same firm for many years. Nor were pensions entitlements. Instead, employers considered them gratuities, to be offered and withdrawn at will, and sometimes used them to control behavior, including requiring retired workers to act as strikebreakers or prohibiting them from filing compensation claims for injury. Employers also hoped pensions would reduce labor turnover, which was extraordinarily high, and prune older and less productive employees from the workforce. In the early decades of the twentieth century, large employers—especially in heavy industry—used pensions as one tactic in their counterattack against the threat of unions. Pensions also promoted efficiency. "By the 1920s," writes Steven A. Sass, in his major history of private pensions, "astute business people knew that pensions reduced neither strikes nor turnover. But the instrument helped structure the flow of human resources through corporations from recruitment to retirement." Labor spokesmen understood these motives and until the 1930s generally opposed corporate pension plans—preferring, instead, to keep them under the control of unions.[1]

Labor identified the weaknesses of early company pension plans accurately. Between 1910 and 1920, only about 21 large firms a year started pension plans; in the 1920s, the number rose to about 45. By 1925, over 200 firms, led by the railroads, which dominated the expansion of private pensions, offered them. But neither small nor medium-sized businesses had instituted pensions. And even in firms with pensions, only a small share of workers would stay employed long enough to collect retirement benefits. In 1929 fewer than 4 percent of men employed in industry and fewer than 3 percent of women had worked long enough at a single firm to qualify. The benefits themselves remained insecure, subject to reduction or elimination and unprotected from inflation.[2]

Pensions spread more quickly in the public sector as city governments tried to clear urban workforces of older, allegedly incompetent members. At the same time, pensions promised to alleviate the worries of teachers, firemen, and policemen who had not earned enough to save for their old age. Chicago introduced the first teachers' pensions in 1895; no other cities followed for fifteen years; then, between 1911 and 1915 the number multiplied rapidly. By the late 1920s, retirement funds for policemen, teachers, and firemen had become nearly universal. Nonetheless, as of 1932, only about 15 percent of American workers were eligible for them.

The national government, for its part, promoted the spread of pensions with tax incentives. In 1921 it gave employers tax exemptions for contributions to trust funds designed to accumulate and distribute capital for fringe benefits. Treasury rulings in 1914 and 1921 allowed businesses to deduct pension expenses from the recently enacted income tax. The 1926 Revenue Act wrote these administrative rulings into law. These tax incentives show that well before the New Deal the federal government had begun to subsidize social welfare, and they highlight the interweaving of public and private—the mixed economy of America's welfare state—operating at the national level even in the early-twentieth century.[3]

A number of employers in the early decades of the twentieth century experimented with programs, in addition to pensions, known first as welfare work, later as welfare capitalism, that subsequently became the foundation of the public welfare state. Welfare capitalism largely replaced the paternalism embodied in failed attempts to create controlled industrial villages, such as Pullman, Illinois, built by railroad magnate George Pullman between 1881 and 1884. Employers turned to welfare work to reduce labor turnover, boost production, defeat attempts to unionize workers, and sidetrack the movement for public social insurance. Their industrial welfare strategies included improved plant working and safety conditions, along with plans to help workers buy property, save at high interest rates, earn bonuses, and purchase stock. They also introduced insurance against accidents, illness, old age, and death. Many of them also offered medical services, classes and sports programs, land for gardening, and assistance with a variety of personal problems.[4]

Before the 1920s, conventional gender relations governed the organization of work-related benefits, and women made up more than half the beneficiaries. Distinctive programs for men and women rested on expectations of their different economic and social roles. Programs for men were designed to reinforce their status as household heads and principal earners. "Long and loyal labor 'earned' male workers a good pension, a financial bonus, even a home," as historian Andrea Tone noted, privileges that solidified their position as family providers. Programs for women "defined femininity through chastity, physical vulnerability, domesticity, and marriageability." They included rest periods to protect women from hard industrial labor and homemaking classes designed to promote their fitness as "mothers and wives of tomorrow." Employers emphasized welfare programs for women because they thought women better suited for them than men. They also hoped to reduce the high turnover of female employees and to deflect the call for legislation designed to protect women workers.[5]

In the early-twentieth century, "welfare work" became a national movement. The National Civic Federation created a Welfare Department in 1904; large corporations began to appoint welfare secretaries; and universities started to train students in welfare work. With fears of radicalism enhanced after World War I, the introduction of welfare measures into work accelerated during the 1920s, and welfare capitalism shifted away from social, educational, and athletic programs and toward programs with financial incentives, such as insurance and pensions, that male breadwinners "earned." In the process, men replaced women as the majority of the beneficiaries of welfare capitalism. "By the end of the 1920s," noted Tone, "welfare benefits had become almost exclusively a male preserve." Welfare plans, however, never covered more than a minority of workers, and they varied greatly from company to company. They also did not address the issues of unemployment or wages that failed to keep pace with productivity. But industrial welfare plans did transform the management of labor through the professionalization of employee relations and the creation of personnel management as a specialty. The National Association of Employment Managers, formed in 1918, attracted more than two thousand people to its 1919 convention and more than five thousand in 1920.[6]

Workers responded to welfare capitalism with ambivalence. Organized labor in the 1920s clearly loathed private welfare work, which it correctly perceived to be in large part an effort to win worker loyalty away from unions. But welfare work fostered a complex, fragile "negotiated loyalty" to employers and a sense of benefits as entitlements rather than privileges. When their employers abandoned welfare plans during the depression of the 1930s, workers often felt betrayed. Belief in a "moral capitalism," argued historian Lizabeth Cohen, promoted support for New Deal programs by encouraging workers to look to unions and government as replacements for the failed welfare benefits of the private sector.[7]

Although the Depression appeared to kill welfare capitalism, it "did not die," contends historian Sanford Jacoby, "but instead went underground—out of the public eye and beyond academic scrutiny—where it would reshape itself." With company unions outlawed, collective bargaining required by public policy, and the rudiments of a federal welfare state in place, welfare capitalism reconstituted itself as a system of employee benefits that supplemented Social Security. By the late 1940s, America's distinctive public/private welfare state had emerged, now supported by organized labor and large employers.[8]

Instead of driving out the nascent private welfare state, the new public social insurance introduced by the New Deal reinvigorated it; in the provision of employee benefits, public and private sectors became partners, not rivals. Indeed, the number of firms offering pensions and health or accident insurance climbed surprisingly in the early years of the Depression and then multiplied by the mid-1940s. One reason lay in the remarkable fiscal stability of the insurance industry, which managed to honor its pension liabilities even during the Depression. Between 1929 and 1935, the proportion of firms with 250 or more employees offering pensions increased from 2 percent to 13 percent, and offering health/accident insurance from 16 percent to 34 percent. In the next decade, pensions rose to 48 percent and health/accident insurance to 67 percent. Although the proportions were lower, the number of smaller firms offering such benefits increased during this period as well.[9]

The early New Deal encouraged employers to establish secure pension and health plans. It tightened regulation of banks and insurance companies, prohibited employers from mandating participation in company unions, and, with the National Industrial Recovery Act of 1932, entirely banned the company unions that had been the vehicles for discretionary and uninsured pension plans. Also in the early 1930s, increased corporate taxes made tax deductions for insured pensions even more attractive. In 1954, Congress encouraged employer-paid health benefits by exempting them from taxation as employee income.

Private firms, helped by the development of a sophisticated insurance industry, found in both public programs and labor relations a number of new incentives to offer benefits. The low benefits paid under the Social Security Act (1935) accelerated firms' initiation of supplementary private insurance, which became a fairly inexpensive way to earn worker loyalty and, even more, to reward key personnel and draw them into career relationships. As firms designed plans to dovetail with public social insurance, they also faced new demands from organized labor, especially the CIO, which had exchanged its hostility to employer-sponsored insurance for active bargaining over employee benefits. The Wagner Act (1935) emboldened labor to challenge employers' refusal to bargain over benefits in the courts, and the low level of public benefits—pensions too small to live on and no health insurance—encouraged labor to focus on private firms.[10]

In part, the catalytic rise of private pensions and insurance in the 1940s grew out of the 1943 wage freeze during the Second World War. Prohibited from raising wages, employers could increase benefits. However, the great rise in benefits began before the freeze took effect and continued after it ended. It reflected a conjuncture of interests among labor, business, and the state. Unions, increasingly convinced of the impossibility of winning adequate security from government, focused on improving private benefits. Congress failed to pass health insurance, and in real dollars, Social Security benefits as a percentage of income declined dramatically between 1939 and 1946. The passage of the Taft-Hartley Act in 1947 was another motivating factor. It was a setback for organized labor, leaving unions less able to force employer recognition, maintain internal solidarity, or mount successful strikes. In this climate, campaigns for fringe benefits wanted by the rank and file offered unions a chance to reassert their effectiveness.

As proof, in 1946, the number of strikes over fringe benefits rose. At their peak, 55 percent of strikes in 1949 and 70 percent in 1950 focused on health and welfare issues in labor contracts. In 1949, in a dispute between Inland Steel and the United Steelworkers, the National Labor Relations Board ruled that the Wagner Act required firms to bargain over employee benefits. The federal government—which wanted to dampen the labor unrest disrupting the economy—had weighed in decisively in favor of the union position, and employer resistance to bargaining over benefits effectively crumbled.[11] Nonetheless, the union victory remained less than complete. The law required employers only to *bargain*, not to provide any set level of benefits, or even any at all. (Employers fought to preserve this distinction—for example, when President Clinton proposed employer mandates in his unsuccessful universal health care proposal.)

Private pensions also remained voluntary—totally discretionary on the part of firms. Few firms funded their pensions in advance, and the same plans covered both white- and blue-collar employees. Most plans that required a contribution from employees did not pay interest. In noncontributory plans, the right to a pension depended on both length of service and behavior, such as loyalty.[12] Employers had agreed to only a limited and contingent private welfare state.

The federal government tried to bring some order and security to pensions with 1942 legislation that for the first time imposed funding requirements on pension plans, which received tax exemptions, and established new rules concerning the taxation of past contributions. The reorganization of the pension industry, however, thwarted government rationalization. Firms sponsoring pensions turned away from the large insurance companies that had dominated the industry. Looking for lower costs and greater flexibility, they began to insure their own risks and to make their own design and investment decisions. In the process, they turned increasingly to new firms that offered professional benefits management. The results left pension funds financially vulnerable—insufficiently funded, tied to the prosperity and persistence of individual firms, and open to abuse, manipulation, and, sometimes, corruption. To take a vivid example of workers' vulnerability, when Studebaker failed in 1964, it terminated its pension plan and left seven thousand former employees with little or nothing in return for their years of work at the firm.[13]

In the 1950s and 1960s, federal officials would have accepted a trade-off: lower private pensions for higher Social Security. Unions, however, balked at this alternative and cut their own deals with business for higher pensions. In fact, the slow rise in Social Security benefits during these decades reflected the growth in private pensions. After major unions had "carved out a . . . private welfare state for their own members," pointed out historian Nelson Lichtenstein, they "no longer saw an increase in federal welfare expenditures as an urgent task." The creation of a private welfare state divided "the American working class into a unionized segment, which until recently enjoyed an almost West European level of social welfare protection, and a growing group—predominantly young, minority, and female—who were left out in the cold." "After World War II," argued Charles Noble in his history of welfare, "the best organized industrial workers all but gave up the struggle for universal public provisions to wrestle with employers over private benefits. . . . Organized labor's determined pursuit of the mixed-benefit strategy made it impossible to mount an effort to win universal public benefits or redistributional taxes."[14]

The private welfare state not only dampened organized labor's drive for expanded public benefits and divided the working class; it fueled blue-collar resentment toward people supported by state welfare or public assistance. In the postwar era, the unionized working class experienced "double taxation." They "pay to support two welfare systems: their own, funded by a 'tax' on their total pay . . . and that of the state and federal government, paid for by a tax system that grew increasingly regressive with the passing of time." Organized labor's response to the War on Poverty reflected the gulf that divided it from the poor: unions preferred economic stimulation, a raised minimum wage, and improved Social Security and demanded narrowly targeted job creation programs restricted to the public sector—the only strategy, it believed, that could constrain antipoverty programs' potential disruption of private labor markets and the wages of organized workers.[15]

The private welfare state fostered conservatism in other ways as well. It constricted the agenda of national politics by lifting a major set of welfare issues out of the political arena and placing them within the labor market, where they received less public debate or scrutiny and where they remained less subject to public control. It also shifted public loyalty away from government and toward the corporation, and it reinforced the idea that the private sector offers a viable alternative to public programs.[16] Nonetheless, for nearly four decades the private welfare state provided a majority of American workers and their families with unprecedented security undreamed of by earlier generations. It gave to a generation of steadily employed workers a freedom from pauperization in sickness and old age unimaginable to most of their parents and grandparents. Few understood its foundation in employer self-interest rather than worker entitlement or foresaw its fragility—or how evanescent the moment of security would seem.

The Scale of the Private Welfare State

The private welfare state is vast. It provides most Americans with their health care, a large share of their retirement income, and much of their life insurance. Employers offer a wide array of benefits; in 1997, benefits, beside pensions and insurance, offered by more than 40 percent of employers included time off for dependent care, child care services, employee assistance programs, tuition reimbursement, on-site cafeterias, and health promotion initiatives. There are many more offered by a smaller proportion of firms.[17]

The sheer size of the private welfare state has transformed worker compensation and economic security in the years since World War II. In 1948, employer contributions to private pension and welfare funds constituted about 1 percent of GDP; by 1992 they had multiplied to more than 5 percent. Although American workers have always financed a large share of their own security, the balance shifted between 1960 and 1980. In the 1960s, individual workers contributed more to their benefits than employers did; by 1980 the situation had reversed, and employers contributed by far the largest share. As a percentage of total compensation, employee benefits grew from 8 percent in 1960 to 18 percent in 1993. In 1994, employers spent $746.5 billion on major voluntary and mandatory employee benefit programs; about 47 percent of the total went to retirement benefits, 41 percent to health care, and the rest to other programs. Individuals contributed $306 billion toward their pensions and health benefits, a sum well under half that spent by employers. As a result of this massive infusion of money into retirement accounts, pension funds have an enormous influence on the national economy. In just the decade between 1985 and 1995, their assets doubled from about $1.3 to $2.7 trillion; from 1950 to 1994, they increased their holdings from about 1 percent to 25 percent of all equities in the U.S. market. According to one estimate, pension plans hold about one-quarter of national wealth. About three-quarters of this wealth remains in private pension plans, with the rest held by plans in the public sector.[18]

In the United States, employee benefits emerge from a partnership among businesses, government, and individuals. Firms provide them voluntarily, encouraged by federal tax incentives or as a result of collective bargaining. The federal government requires businesses to contribute to other benefits: Social Security, unemployment insurance, workers' compensation, and family and medical leave. And individuals contribute some for themselves, encouraged by a tax code that promotes individual saving through life insurance contracts and death benefits as well as individual retirement accounts. The result is a private welfare state heavily regulated by government. The major legislation shaping the framework for private pensions is the 1974 Employment Retirement Income Security Act (ERISA), which superseded state law, set the standards to which private pensions plans must adhere in order to retain their favored tax status, and created a new government agency to insure benefits in case employers went out of business. ERISA also added pension incentives for individuals through individual retirement accounts and pensions for the self-employed (called Keoghs), and legalized employee stock-ownership plans.[19]

Four years later influential new legislation established deferred compensation plans called 401(k)s that excluded from taxation a portion of pay that individuals chose to put aside for a later date, usually retirement. By allowing individuals and firms to deduct pension and insurance contributions, the federal government heavily subsidized retirement, health care, and economic security. In 1996, pension contribution deductions cost the government $69.6 billion in forgone revenue, an amount much larger than the income lost through the deductibility of home mortgage interest. Between the 1960s and the late 1990s, tax expenditures for employer pensions, adjusted for inflation, grew at an annual rate of 6 percent. The deductibility of medical, life, and disability insurance and employee stock-ownership plans further increased the cost of forgone taxes to the federal government by more than half.[20]

Despite the web of regulations surrounding it, the private welfare state remains decentralized, complex, and sometimes chaotic. Employers offer private benefits at their discretion, and they cling ferociously to the voluntary basis of the private welfare state. Because benefits vary from firm to firm, the private welfare state consists of "a patchwork of variegated and often less-than-fully portable benefit programs." Employers can escape government regulation by self-insuring their health benefits, and they can avoid the rigors of ERISA by terminating their pension plans and purchasing annuities for employees from private insurance carriers. No central structure of regulations governs benefits; instead, regulators respond to problems on a piecemeal basis. ERISA divided responsibility for pension oversight among the Departments of Labor and Treasury and the new Pension Benefits Guarantee Corporation. The IRS Code devotes more than one thousand pages to employer pensions. A new benefits industry of experts, counselors, and consultants has emerged "to lobby and interface with government regulators and lawmakers."[21]

Trends in the Private Welfare State

Employee benefits have historically responded to the shape of labor markets. In the late-nineteenth and early-twentieth centuries, employers promoted retirement partly as a way to ease older and less-productive workers out of the labor force. Progressive employers practiced welfare capitalism to increase worker loyalty and decrease labor turnover. They developed pension systems tied to individual firms and requiring long periods of employment for vesting. ("Vesting" was perhaps the major issue delaying the passage of ERISA, which finally reached a partial resolution of the issue.) Pensions were not very portable; layoffs put them at risk. They were designed for employers who wanted to hold the same workers for many years and for employees who built long-term careers with the same firms. This system made less sense in the new global economy. In an ironic twist of history, many employers now looked to benefits to facilitate short-term employment. They wanted flexible workforces capable of contracting or expanding rapidly in response to competitive pressure and shifting global demands, and they began to redesign employee benefits around the assumption of mobility. Trade unions had long tried to protect their members by organizing their own benefit plans. Multiemployer plans covered unionized workers in the same industry, whether or not they changed employers, and they protected the benefits of workers against layoffs or the failure of individual firms.[22] But as union membership declined, the new labor market became an increasingly powerful force reshaping the economic security of American workers.

The design of benefit plans also responded to corporate culture. Firms organized along "functional, hierarchical lines" stressed long-term employment and security, and high benefits rewarded employee perseverance. They were much more likely than other kinds of firms to offer conventional pensions, medical insurance fully paid by employers, and medical benefits for retirees over the age of sixty-five. On the other hand, where flexibility reigned, less generous benefits that required employee contributions ruled, with the assumption that most employees would not spend their careers in the same organization. Organizations with network cultures—"highly flexible, innovative, and transitory" companies that partnered with other firms for specific purposes—offered the least and most flexible benefits and oriented them, according to the *Hay's Benefit Report*, "to the short term, consistent with the short-term focus of each venture."[23]

In recent years, the inequalities built into the employee benefit structure have widened. From 1979 to 1993, health insurance coverage for adult private sector workers declined from 71 percent to 64 percent. (In 1995, employment-based health insurance covered 63.8 percent of the nonelderly population.) Private sector pension coverage declined less—from 48 percent to 45 percent in the same years.[24]

These general trends mask a number of differences. First, the rate of coverage varied by the size of firms and between public and private employers. Although the percentage of both large and small firms providing benefits declined, at all times larger firms offered health insurance and pensions more often than did small ones. Workers in the public sector more often had coverage than did those employed by private firms. Wide variations separated types of industry as well; for instance, in 1995, health insurance covered 86 percent of workers in manufacturing, 67 percent in retail, and 58 percent in personal services. Of employers in durable manufacturing in 1993, 77 percent sponsored pension plans compared to 42 percent in retail trade and 30 percent in business, personal, and entertainment services. Higher-income workers more often had health insurance and pensions. Not only did lower-income workers earn benefits less often, the decline in coverage hit them hardest: three times more of the poorest than of the top fifth of full-time workers lost health benefits and almost twice as many lost pensions. In the same years, pension coverage for workers without high school degrees dropped 17 percent—far more than among other employees.[25]

Full-time workers of course fared much better than part-time: in 1995, the difference in health insurance coverage was 88 percent compared to 21 percent. Neither gender nor race, however, made a great deal of difference. Women who worked had health insurance a little more often than men and they earned pensions about as often. Similarly, white and black workers earned pensions at the same rate. However, more whites than blacks had health insurance. Much more important than demography was union membership, which greatly increased the likelihood that workers would receive both health insurance and pensions. In 1993, 88 percent of union-covered firms sponsored pension plans, compared to 57 percent of those not covered by unions. In 1995, together, benefits and wages amounted to a "union premium" of $6.14 an hour, or 37.8 percent.[26]

Employee benefits generally followed the fault lines of American society. Reduced coverage spread insecurity across all its divisions, but it hit those with the fewest resources to begin with hardest. Poorly paid, nonunionized, part-time workers in retail and service jobs fared worst.

Although employee benefits had once compensated for some of the differences in pay that separated workers, by the 1990s they reinforced and accentuated the growing wage inequality that marked the social structure of the new global economy.[27] Indeed, the forces reshaping the national and world economy joined with demographic trends to drive changes in the private welfare state.

The decline in benefits mirrored the erosion of the manufacturing industries in which they had been most common. When firms downsized or closed, workers often lost their pensions and health care as well as their jobs. At the same time, jobs moved dramatically toward small firms and the service industry, which offered lower pay and fewer employee benefits. Part-time employment, which frequently offered no benefits, also increased about 10 percent from 1973 to 1995. Just under half of part-time employees worked for employers who offered health insurance plans. Union membership, the best guarantee of benefits, declined from about 30 percent of the workforce in 1950 to just under a quarter in 1973 and 14.5 percent in 1996. Some experts also attributed the slow formation of new pension plans to recent federal legislation and regulations that imposed high administrative costs and complex rules on employers.[28]

Where workers once had bargained over wages and improved benefits, in the 1980s and 1990s they increasingly negotiated over the rollback of the private welfare state—concessions in wages, benefits, and work rules. (Some employers tried to lessen workers' hostility to concessions with two-tiered benefits, which preserved benefits for current employees and gave lower benefits to those newly hired.) With unions weak, many employers took advantage of their freedom to redesign pensions and health care benefits at will. Public sector employers, like big-city mayors, brandished the threat of privatization to frighten workers into accepting concessions. In the private sector, employers could threaten to close their firm or find less expensive labor in another region or country. Not surprisingly, concessions occurred most often in poorly performing firms and ones paying high base wages and less often in large firms and ones with high rates of union coverage. "Welcome to the increasingly Darwinian world of reduced expectations," J. P. Morgan's retired global benefits director observed. "I am less than optimistic that most baby boomers will retire in relative financial comfort given the substitution of relatively less generous" pension plans, "reduced job tenure, increasing life expectancy, and high retiree medical and long-term care costs."[29]

In the late 1990s an emerging labor shortage dealt unions a more powerful bargaining hand and offered the possibility of reversing the downward trend in pension benefits. Indeed, by the mid-1990s, unions had begun to shift their primary interest from wages and health benefits—the key issues of the previous decade—to pensions. In 1996, Ford Motor Company and the United Automobile Workers for the first time agreed that retirees would receive an inflation-indexed adjustment to their pension benefits. Also in 1996, workers at Wheeling-Pittsburgh Steel mounted a successful ten-month strike to win a traditional defined-benefit pension plan of $1,200 per month. In August 1997 drivers prevented United Parcel Service from taking over their pensions from the Teamsters. UPS drivers won another contested issue—the right to remain in a Teamster, rather than a company, health plan. Whether the Wheeling-Pittsburgh and UPS strikes were aberrations or harbingers was unclear. Despite labor's successes, a 1996 survey found many employers planning to offer only modest wage increases and two-fifths planning to demand new or expanded health-care cost sharing.[30]

Escalating health costs prodded employers to look for ways to reduce the expense of insurance. The cost of health benefits to employers jumped from $3.4 billion in 1960 to $266.5 billion in 1980 and $305.1 billion in 1994. Even discounted for inflation, these constituted enormous increases. By 1994, the average cost of an employee in a group health plan had reached $3,741. (In 1997, employers also worried about the potential costs generated by recent federal legislation prohibiting group health plans from imposing lower limits on mental health than on other medical benefits.)[31]

In the same years, the aging of the population, the growth of single-parent families, and mothers' entrance into the workforce also affected the demand, provision, and cost of benefits in both the public and private welfare states. Single-parent families and working mothers heightened the need for more child care and maternity leave; older workers earned higher wages, their health care cost more, and their potential nursing home costs could be high. Demographers projected the proportion of the population age sixty-five or over to increase from about 13 percent in the 1990s to roughly 20 percent by 2040. Still, the projected old age dependency rate for the United States remained significantly below the expected rate for Canada, Japan, and western European countries. Because of its potential impact on retirement costs, increased life expectancy posed a financial problem compounded by huge numbers of older men leaving the workforce. Between 1965 and 1985, the proportion of men from ages fifty-five to sixty-four in the labor force plummeted from 85 percent to 66 percent.[32] With these trends, retirement benefits loomed as an increasingly sensitive and important issue for both the private and public welfare states.

The End of Paternalism

"The world of work is changing," observed Dallas Salisbury, president of the Employee Benefit Research Institute. "Employers have increasingly moved away from a philosophy of paternalistically looking after employees." Reduced and redesigned benefits reflected more than economic and demographic pressure; they rested on a philosophic shift in the relation between employers and employees. Employers, said Salisbury on another occasion, were teaching workers about "the need to take individual responsibility and not to depend exclusively on company-provided pension plans." They "are schooling employees in the end of paternalism and an end to the entitlement mentality. This pattern will not reverse."[33]

As they constructed smaller, more flexible workforces, employers redesigned benefits to suit mobile workers likely to change jobs several times during the course of their careers. To save money and enforce individual responsibility, they also shifted some of the costs of benefits to workers.

The shift from *defined benefit* to *defined contribution* pensions reflected these changes. Defined benefit plans calculate benefits according to rules based on pay and length of service; they pay benefits as a life annuity; usually they are noncontributory—that is, employers pay all costs and assume all risks. (This is the usual, not universal, case; in the public welfare state, Social Security, a defined benefit program, is a massive exception.) Under a defined contribution plan, contributions flow to a participant's individual retirement account; sometimes only employers make contributions, but more often employees contribute as well, especially to the popular 401(k) plans. Employees often can choose among a number of investment options for the money in their accounts. Because benefits paid at retirement derive from the money accumulated in individual accounts, they reflect both the amount of contributions and investment performance.[34]

The shift to defined contribution pensions was a result, partly, of employers reacting to the increasing financial difficulties of defined benefit, pay-as-you-go plans threatened by the coming retirement of the baby-boom generation. Even more, though, they reflected the competitive global economy, "where products and services typically have short shelf lives and companies must innovate constantly," as Christopher Conte, a pension expert, observed. In this new setting, employers emphasized controlling costs and "maintaining 'flexibility' in managing their workforces." Defined contribution plans met these objectives better than did defined benefit plans, with their "associated entitlement fostering mentality," noted the retired global pension manager from J. P. Morgan. Defined benefit plans, moreover, proved "dysfunctional" because as employees' salaries rose, their value to the company declined after long years of service. Defined contributions also suited "corporate mergers, acquisitions, and divestitures" better than did conventional pensions.[35]

Beginning in the mid-1970s, the number of defined contribution pension plans exploded. In the private sector, the number of qualified plans grew from 208,000 to 619,000 between 1975 and 1993, and by 1997, 99 percent of employers offered them, with 44 million workers covered—an increase of 32 million in just eighteen years. Most of the growth occurred in smaller firms, for which defined contribution plans offer advantages of simplicity as well as lower costs. In the same years, the number of defined benefit plans dropped from 103,000 to 84,000—with the estimate for 1997 falling to 53,000 providing them. Although the proportion of employers offering defined benefits dropped from 92 percent to 64 percent, between 33 and 40 million workers remained covered by them, despite the decrease in their number.

The termination of defined benefit plans did not leave thousands of workers without pension coverage, as the numbers at first suggest. Most of the plans terminated were very small; that is, 56,000 of 86,000 covered only two to nine employees and another 13,000 covered ten to twenty-four, which explains why the number of employees covered by defined benefit plans remained relatively stable despite the decline in their numbers. Many small plans also apparently served as tax shelters, a practice virtually ended by federal tax legislation in 1982 and 1986.[36]

Although defined benefit plans remained more common in the public sector, there, too, defined contribution plans increased—in the federal government from none in 1981 to 20 percent of plans and 30 percent of participants by 1995; they appear to be growing more common among state and local governments as well. By the late 1990s, a number of employers also had developed hybrids, with features of both defined benefit and contribution plans. One form of hybrid popular with younger employees was the "cash balance" system, by 1998 adopted by about 10 percent of companies with 5,000 or more employees.[37]

In theory, defined contribution plans benefit both employers and workers. They release employers from managing and funding their own pension plans, and they increase the portability of pensions for workers who change jobs. Whether workers will end up with as much or more retirement income will not be known for some years, until a very large number have retired. (How much retirement income workers receive also will depend on what happens to public plans, notably Social Security, whose support could soften with higher returns on private investments.) Unions, objecting to cost-shifting onto employees and worried about the potential hardship from poor investment decisions, vigorously oppose defined contribution plans. Employees often prefer defined benefit plans because they guarantee a check for life. Investment choices under defined contribution plans could leave them broke, and many amateur investors fear the results of a falling stock market. Bill Patterson, chief of pension policy for the AFL-CIO, observed, "The bull stock market makes it easier for companies to promote defined-contribution plans because right now it looks like everyone who is in the stock market can get rich, but that won't last and the danger is that there will be losses and there won't be enough money at the end of the road."[38]

According to a study by the Employee Benefit Research Institute, the investment decisions made by workers in three large corporations (AT&T, IBM, and New York Life Insurance Company) proved union anxiety justified. Many workers remained ill informed about pension plan details. Only 59 percent knew the maximum they were allowed to contribute, for instance, and only 41 percent contributed the maximum allowed. A significant number of young workers did diversify into equities, but many held no equities in their accounts, which put them at risk of insufficient retirement assets. Lower-paid workers made the most conservative choices; relatively few of them invested heavily in equities. Different investment decisions thus promised to heighten the already steep and growing income inequality among employees.[39] By forcing workers to partially fund their own old-age security and invest the money in their own retirement accounts, defined contribution plans have subjected workers to the uncertainties of the market from which pensions had been designed in part to shield them. Like any market-based strategy, defined contribution plans have heightened both the potential risks and rewards.

Employers have shifted the cost of health care as well as pensions to their employees. In 1979, employers in large- and medium-sized firms paid the full cost of health insurance for 73 percent of employees participating in health plans; by 1993, the proportion had dropped by 37 percent. Health plans required workers to pay higher deductibles and out-of-pocket maximums. Employers also increasingly turned to utilization review programs to monitor employee health care on a case-by-case basis, and most have used one or another form of managed care to reduce rising health care costs. From 1980 to 1994, the number enrolled in health maintenance organizations jumped from 9.1 million to 43.4 million. (Health maintenance organizations did not become a major alternative to traditional fee-for-service medicine until the HMO Act of 1973, which encouraged their growth.) Between 1992 and 1995, the percentage of insured Americans enrolled in fee-for-service plans sank from 58.9 percent to 35 percent. Most of the managed care enrollment occurred in preferred provider organizations (PPOs), which consist of networks of physicians, rather than in conventional HMOs, which employ their own staffs. In only a few years, employers had accelerated the movement of Americans into managed care. One survey showed that 61 percent of employers offered traditional fee-for-service plans in 1992; by 1996 the percentage had dropped by half, to 30 percent. In 1997, the Hay Group predicted that fee-for-service plans would become a "rarity" as the primary form of health insurance offered by employers.[40]

Between 1988 and 1993, the number of nonelderly Americans covered by employers' health plans decreased. This reduction in employee health benefits—which spilled over onto a wider group because many plans covered employees' dependents—was one reason for the rising share of nonelderly Americans with no health insurance. Other reasons were that more people worked part-time, employment shifted from manufacturing to service industries, and an indeterminate, though large, number of employees refused health insurance because of the rising share of their costs.[41]

Retired workers over the age of sixty-five also faced rising Medicare premiums with less help from their former employers, who balked as the average annual cost of health benefits per retiree grew from $2,548 in 1992 to $3,182 in 1996. Former employees were retiring earlier and living longer, and insurance companies were raising premiums. Some of the minority of firms that offered retiree health coverage responded by dropping it or requiring retirees to pay a greater share of premiums. From just 1993 to 1996, the proportion of large employers providing coverage to retirees over the age of sixty-five declined from 40 percent to 33 percent, and the share of insurance premiums paid by retirees rose from 38 percent to 60 percent. Smaller firms were even less generous.[42]

In 1998, a federal appeals court heightened the tension between business and labor over retirement health benefits. Ten years earlier, when General Motors had cut health care benefits for retired workers despite promising them lifetime coverage, 84,000 retirees brought a class action suit against the company. A decade after the suit had been filed, the Fifth U.S. Circuit Court of Appeals in Cincinnati ruled in favor of GM. "If the ruling stands," worried an attorney for the retirees, "it could open the way for U.S. corporations to slash health coverage and other retirement benefits." The plaintiffs appealed the decision to the U.S. Supreme Court. Horace Deets, executive director of the Association of American Retired Persons, warned that if the lower court decision stood, "no retiree will ever be certain of his or her health benefits and . . . no employer will ever have to fear the consequences of breaking faith with his retirees on health care." In June 1998, the Supreme Court refused to consider the appeal of the circuit court's decision. An attorney for the AARP commented, "This has been the case people have been watching, and it sends a signal to employers that they can go ahead and change their retirees' health benefits."[43]

Employers might also reduce retirement costs by persuading workers to retire later. But even with redesigned benefits, delaying retirement likely would prove a hard sell. One survey found that half of those retired had left the workforce earlier than they had planned; 46 percent of current workers planned to retire before age sixty-five, but 72 percent *wanted* to retire before then, and 72 percent opposed raising the Social Security retirement age to seventy.[44]

Increasingly, employers swept away the remaining vestiges of paternalism by outsourcing the administration of employee benefits and corporate "human relations." A 1996 survey found that "HR departments have now been whacked down and reengineered dramatically at 58 percent of large U.S. corporations." Because traditional benefits departments often found themselves unprepared to fulfill new roles, many employers looked "outside the company to consultant insurance companies and mutual funds for assistance in administering benefits." Another 1996 survey of 231 employers nationwide found that nearly half had contracted out part of their human resource or employee benefit functions. Of these, 56 percent planned to farm out additional activities, and 15 percent of employers not outsourcing at the time of the survey planned to start the practice in the future. Sixty percent of outsourcing employers wanted "technical and regulatory expertise"; 59 percent hoped for "more value for their dollars spent"; and about half looked for improved "customer service."[45]

Outsourcing proved attractive because it promised to both redefine relations between employers and employees and reduce costs and administrative headaches. At the same time, it responded to the pressures experienced by firms competing in a world market—increasing investment in internal departments could cost a firm its competitive advantage. Its advocates argued that outsourcing gave competitors access to the best human relations services in the world, who could do a better job more quickly and inexpensively than in-house departments. Thus, outsourcing allowed companies to concentrate on their "core business" and to speed up shifts in employee benefit design and administration to match the accelerating pace of business change. If done well, outsourcing also reduced costs through increasing efficiency and transforming a fixed into a variable cost, by purchasing only those services needed rather than employing a full benefits and human relations staff. Firms, however, could not justify outsourcing as a way to cut the costs of compensation because federal law prohibited employers from firing workers to reduce benefits.

The most important change in employee benefit administration, said one writer, was the "shift in employers' attitudes . . . from a 'paternalistic' approach to one in which employees are required to assume responsibility for making appropriate choices." Now employees would be provided "access to the tools necessary to process and follow up on their benefit transactions." Some employers, unable to shake a lingering paternalism, worried that outsourcing would sever their ties with employees by cutting off communication. Not to worry, explained one cheerful consultant; outsourcing did not end direct contact with employees, but began "a new era of strategic employee communication that transcends simple employee benefit design features."[46] Workers found their concerns over health, disability, and old age transmuted into problems of communication.

The term *outsourcing* covers a wide array of practices, including handing off administrative and processing functions and creating internal markets by consolidating functions in an in-house department that sells services to line managers.[47] (These responses parallel mayors' introduction of competition in city services, described in chapter 5. Mayors not only outsourced or privatized; they often allowed city employees to bid on service provision.) However, the great variety of practices subsumed under the outsourcing label cannot mask its significance. Outsourcing constricts the relation between employer and employee to narrow interactions around jobs; it reduces the dependence inherent in paternalism and devolves responsibility to outside specialists; and it redesigns the administration of employee benefits and human resources on a market model.

The End of Paternalism in Action

An excellent example of the transformation in employee benefits is SBC. SBC (formerly Southwestern Bell) experienced great changes following its 1984 split from AT&T.[48] In ten years it downsized from 91,000 to 59,000 employees. At the same time, it managed to increase efficiency: in 1985, it deployed 60.48 employees for every 10,000 telephone access lines; by 1995, the number had decreased to 34.08. In the same years, the share of business provided through its telephone company declined as mobile telephone systems grew at an astonishing pace. A small start-up company with 236 employees in 1985, a decade later Southwestern Bell Mobile Systems employed 5,400 people in 70 national and international markets.

As part of a telephone monopoly, the company enjoyed certainty and security before 1984. The company's transition to a competitive environment in the new world where computers, telephones, television, and entertainment converged upset the old operating assumptions and demanded new forms of organization, skills, and relations with employees. Management viewed its mission as transforming "our company from a monopoly to a competitive, lean organization."

Employment security became one casualty of this transformation. AT&T "had developed a very paternalistic, parent to child relationship with employees." Now Southwestern Bell focused on building "a more adult relationship to the benefit of each party." In the words of its midwives, the brave new competitive world could make everyone who played by its rules a winner; there were no zero-sum games.

The company's history of employee relations divided into three phases. In the years before 1984, AT&T operated as an integrated company in a regulated monopoly environment. It designed benefits to attract and hold a stable workforce. As a result, it tied many benefits to age and years of service. Its generous benefits ranked in the top quartile in comparative surveys. Employees could expect security in case of illness, disability, retirement, and death. They received noncontributory pensions and health insurance for themselves and their dependents as well as extensive benefits during short- and long-term disability. Pensions were adjusted for inflation, and medical coverage for workers and their dependents during retirement remained generous. AT&T applied benefits uniformly across all its business units. Not surprisingly, employees and retirees considered their benefits entitlements.

In its first ten years of independence Southwestern Bell formed multiple business units that operated on a relatively decentralized basis. Most employees still received noncontributory health coverage and defined benefit pensions. However, starting in 1987, the company introduced cost containment features into its medical coverage, including the adoption of managed care, a cap on Medicare Part B premium reimbursement, and other measures. In 1989, it changed its corporate employee savings plan by increasing the company's matching contributions to employee saving and investing all the money in corporate shares. Management intended this variant of employee stock ownership to heighten employee commitment to the success of the corporation. The company also started an information program designed to emphasize the need for retirement planning and introduced long-term care and supplemental medical plans paid for by employees themselves. Nonetheless, because of the decentralized nature of the company, business units varied in the benefits they offered or negotiated with unions. Units across the company offered four medical plans, three dental plans, four vision plans, and a variety of retirement options. Some subsidiary companies introduced employee health care premiums or dropped defined benefit pensions and retiree medical coverage.

Southwestern Bell changed its name to SBC in 1995 and began to realign its operations, which meant recentralizing some of its operations and practices. It moved toward "market based pay for performance," and scrutinized all aspects of its benefits. It asked whether current programs would attract, retain, and motivate its workforce, and "whether employee benefits should remain as significant a portion of the total compensation package as today." The company moved to defined contribution pensions that allowed employees "to directly manage their retirement savings" and changed its life insurance plan "to enhance employee self-direction." In 1995, it also was considering outsourcing parts of its benefits and human relations administration. At SBC, the paternalism of AT&T remained only a memory.

DuPont offered an even more radical example of the end of paternalism in employee benefits. Founded in Delaware in 1802 to manufacture black powder for guns, the DuPont Company had become a global chemical and energy giant with about 100,000 employees (60 percent living in the United States) by the late-twentieth century. In the nineteenth century, manufacturing gunpowder proved a dangerous business, and explosions sometimes killed workers. DuPont responded by looking after their survivors, and echoes of the "caring nature" of its benefits policy lingered into the early 1980s, for example in the company-paid survivor benefits in its pension plan.[49] Employees could count on job stability—the company usually recalled those laid off temporarily during bad times—and DuPont offered the best pay and benefits in the area: "The culture was filled with paternalism, security and entitlement. It was not overt, and usually not even felt. It was just the way things were."

DuPont's corporate culture changed during the 1980s with acquisitions and divestitures. In 1985, during its first major downsizing, 10,000 employees left voluntarily: "This signaled a change from lifetime employment." Other "voluntary" retirements followed, provoked by a 1991 study that found the company needed to cut $1 billion in costs to remain competitive. Retirees now more frequently were around fifty years old.

Downsizing and other changes raised a key question: "What is DuPont's employment contract?" Clearly, it had ceased to be lifetime employment. Indeed, the company redefined long-term employment as a consequence of profits, not a right. "While there is value for a long-term employment relationship, it is the product or result of a successful interdependency, not a right or a promise. Business success is the key." A group within the company trying to predict the shape of employment in the year 2020 thought that employees "might be more like the 'stringers' in the news media. People may truly be associates, meaning they have some relationship with the company." This scenario called for a major redesign of benefits.

Historically, the company had "done too much of the planning" for its employees. Now it provided "flexible benefits with a financial planning program as an option for employees." At the same time, it was examining "variable pay for a broader segment of the workforce. This has the potential to reinforce the link between personal success and business success, but it also provides an opportunity for failure." As in any market-based transaction, risk had entered the new employment relation. Not surprisingly, the company was also reconsidering its defined benefit plan, which reflected "too many elements of the old culture." The point of these changes was to force pay and benefits to "follow, align and support the business plan."

DuPont found an analogy that helped it rethink the new relationship between the company and its employees. Like running water, the constant flow of employees renewed the company and assured its health: "We see the new employment relationship like a river. The organization is dynamic, not static, with some people thriving on the fast pace, some keeping up with the flow, and some not able to keep up and being left behind. There is stability within the entity, but it is not stagnant; it is dynamic." In the revived social Darwinism at the heart of the American corporation, employees who could not hack the pace became the new undeserving poor.

Mead, a 150-year-old firm, proved that even stable, healthy companies redefined their responsibilities toward employees. Mead manufactures paper and paperboard and distributes school and office products. Its annual sales totaled about $5 billion, and it employed 16,000 people, mostly in the United States. About half the workforce belonged to unions. Mead began to take stock of its corporate direction in the spring of 1992, when a new CEO assumed office. Although the company's staff seemed competent, its facilities excellent, and its balance sheet strong, it did not earn above-average return on its capital, and shareholders were "not very happy."[50]

The new CEO began by trying to define "a new vision in values" or "organizational philosophy," which emphasized decentralized operations. The company's central administration "made a very specific compact with the divisions in terms of what they had to deliver. . . . You put together a business contract and you are going to be held accountable for that." The company also completely reorganized its corporate human relations along a market model to better serve the divisions. "The interesting thing that . . . they created was a real focus on who exactly was the customer." At the same time it downsized, or, in a euphemism it preferred, "rightsized." The process "took out about 20 percent of corporate staff and about 10 percent of the overall throughout the entire Mead Corporation."

These elements of corporate redesign took place from 1992 to 1994. The results paralleled those at Southwestern Bell and DuPont. "Paternalism was gone. We created an adult to adult relationship that focused on expectations, accountability, raising the bar, very specific in terms of what was expected of each of us as an organization and each of us as individuals." The process "obviously" heightened job insecurity, and management did not "try to sugarcoat that. We said, 'Yes, that's true and it's really driven by a competitive environment.' " Management summarized the new employment relationship with the concept of "mutual obligation" among adults. "If it's an adult relationship, we bring things to the party, the employee brings things to the party."

As the company explored its operations, management discovered widespread dissatisfaction with benefits administration among both the divisions and employees. Task forces appointed to recommend changes reported several alternatives, and the company decided on the total outsourcing of all benefits—"401(k), defined benefit, health and welfare, everything. We're going to get it out because that wasn't our business." (In 1995, Mead contracted with Fidelity to take over benefits administration in stages.) The point was not to save money: "The whole reason we're going forward is because of its effectiveness. It is consistent with the message we were telling people about you're going to take charge of the way we run the business. We also said you're going to take charge of the way benefits are run." Management told employees that it needed to outsource benefits to improve benefit administration and "to give you enough information that you can make savvy benefit decisions." As with Southwestern Bell and DuPont, at Mead the needs of the corporation meshed neatly and conveniently with the best interests of its employees. The end of paternalism, and the virtual lifelong employment and economic security that accompanied it, liberated employees to enter the marketplace; it transformed them from dependent children into adults responsible for their own decisions.

The transformation of employee benefits paralleled welfare reform. Governors like Tommy Thompson, John Engler, and William Weld shared a common enemy with corporate leaders. Governors labeled the enemy dependence and corporate leaders called it paternalism, but both terms referred to the same essential characteristics: paternalism reinforced the idea that benefits were entitlements, undermined individual initiative and responsibility, and drove costs to unacceptable levels. Governors, by time-limiting welfare, and corporate leaders, by redesigning benefits, proposed to force individuals to take charge of their lives—which meant treating them as adults, not children, and binding them with mutual obligations. New obligations reflected a market model: state governments and businesses tried to narrow the scope of their relations with clients or employees by outsourcing the administration of benefits; wherever possible they turned to managed care or internal competition to increase efficiency and cut costs. This translation of welfare and employee benefits into commodities involved no inherent conflicts or contradictions. Although the new social contract rested on the power of one party to coerce the participation of the other, in a happy coincidence it served the best interests of both sides to the bargain.

By the mid-1990s, governors-as-welfare-reformers had reversed the trajectory of federal-state relations and employers had redirected the history of the private welfare state. Governors had seized the initiative in welfare reform and used waivers of federal law to redesign state public assistance. Employers had cut back the employee benefits that had expanded in the years after World War II and remodeled those that remained. They also had undertaken the vigorous reeducation of American workers to depend more on themselves and the market than on the paternalism of their employers. The end of paternalism helped employers design flexible new strategies for competition in the global marketplace; it also left employees increasingly vulnerable to the insecurities of unemployment, sickness, and old age.

INCREASED RISKS FOR
THE INJURED, DISABLED,
AND UNEMPLOYED

Markets enhance risk, which is the other side of responsibility. In the new social Darwinism that informs social policy, not much sympathy cushions the losers in the competitive global marketplace. Rather, they bear responsibility for their condition, and their uselessness merits only the smallest support. American social programs label those individuals they treat meanly or exclude as morally suspect or unworthy: the undeserving poor, the malingerer, the cheat, the lazy shirker, even, recently, the deceptive child and her dishonest parent. The dynamic of American social policy over and over again re-creates the "other" as a standard against which to define those whose misfortunes public safety nets should cushion.

In America, federal, state, and local governments patch together public safety nets from social insurance and public assistance programs. Social insurance is intended to protect against common risks, but as a result of its recent history, risks experienced by all Americans during their lives have increased.[1] Whether they are injured at work, disabled by disease, sick, laid off from work, or simply old, Americans still face a world with few assurances.

Social insurance originated in Germany. Bismarck introduced sickness insurance in 1883, workers' compensation in 1884, and old age insurance in 1889. Germany's first unemployment insurance began in 1927. As a conservative, Bismarck intended social insurance to bind workers to the state and preserve social order. In England, social insurance started a little later: workers' compensation in 1897, old age in 1908, and sickness and unemployment in 1911. In the United States, some state governments pioneered social insurance in the years between 1911 and the 1930s; Veterans' Pensions was the only federal program. But in contrast to Europe after World War II, where national social insurance programs developed into a relatively universal and unified system, America's social insurance structure remained rickety, incomplete, and poorly coordinated; it was part national and part state, and it left whole categories of individuals without guaranteed protection, dependent on private or public charity.

In both America and Europe, worries about the impact of social insurance—as well as of relief, charity, and "welfare"—on labor markets have always retarded the development of public programs to reduce risks and relieve poverty. The question asked again and again has been, Do they erode the will to work? The disincentives thought to result from social insurance and relief are what economists label "moral hazard."

The term originated with Hazard, a very old game of dice played in England. Early insurers, with the help of mathematical theory, applied the idea of odds to the risk involved in insurance, and nineteenth-century commentators added the "moral." In insurance, moral hazard, according to legal scholar Tom Baker, identified people "unusually susceptible" to the temptations created by insurance. It was also used to describe the situations that heightened the temptation. Modern economists have tried to strip the judgmental component from moral hazard by replacing "temptation" with "incentive." In economic theory, moral hazard now "refers to the tendency for insurance against loss to reduce incentives to prevent or minimize the cost of loss." Economists have not been able to draw strict boundaries around the term, however, and others in the policy world continue to use the concept of moral hazard to identify the allegedly perverse consequences of social insurance and public assistance: workers' compensation benefits produce more workplace injury; disability insurance encourages malingering; unemployment insurance tempts people to leave their jobs; "welfare" creates dependence. As an idea, moral hazard, writes Baker, supports efforts to reduce the "public and private benefits available to the sick, the injured, and the poor because it 'proves' the harmful results of helping people." Its economics "legitimate the abandonment of redistributive policies" not as an exercise of power, but as the result of scientific research.[2]

Moral hazard provides a powerful weapon in the struggle against social insurance entitlements and the welfare state. It is, after all, in no one's best interest to perpetuate policies that worsen the conditions they are intended to alleviate. If valid, moral hazard would offer the strongest theoretical criticism of redistributive social policy. But moral hazard is not a technical, value-free concept. Faulty assumptions limit its usefulness and undercut its capacity to guide social policy. Just why moral hazard provides an inadequate justification for dismantling the welfare state will emerge more clearly after a look at the features and recent history of major social insurance programs.[3]

A master narrative of policy reform links the idea of disincentives embedded in moral hazard to the recent histories of workers' compensation, disability insurance, and unemployment as well as to Social Security and public assistance. Its features are the discovery of a crisis of numbers and cost (rising rolls); the assignment of blame to morally suspect persons (the undeserving); the reduction of program size through controlling eligibility more than reducing benefits (reform); the measurement of achievement by fewer beneficiaries (success); and the failure to track the fate of those denied help (willful ignorance). This American story begins with the oldest of the social insurances—workers' compensation.

Workers' Compensation and the New Conflict Between Business and Labor

Workers' compensation occupies a space between the public and private welfare states. Mandated and regulated by state law, workers' compensation resembles employee benefits because it is paid for directly by employers, either through insurance premiums or self-insurance. Benefit levels, however, are set by state governments, and conflicts are litigated in state courts and industrial commissions, where struggles over workers' compensation turn into conflicts between capital and labor. In most states, private insurers provide workers' compensation; a few insure through state-owned and -managed funds, while the federal government insures its own employees and pays for most benefits in cases of "black lung" disease contracted by miners. The insurance premiums paid by employers vary with the risk involved in the job, the industry's industrial classification, and sometimes with the employer's record—which is supposed to give employers an incentive to promote safe workplaces. Despite the variations from state to state, one principle underlies all workers' compensation laws: employers should assume the costs of occupational injury and illness without regard to fault. In return, workers give up the right to sue. The "no fault" system, observed law professor Emily Spieler, former secretary of Occupational Health and Safety in West Virginia, may have expanded the number of workers eligible for benefits, but it also "served to shield employers from any legal obligation to eliminate workplace hazards and from any psychological sense of fault."[4]

Workers' compensation benefits, which soared in the 1980s, reached nearly $43 billion in 1993. In states across the country, escalating costs triggered the master narrative of policy. As in other corners of America's welfare state, "reform" meant not only attacking fraud and abuse and introducing market-based management strategies, but cutting benefits. Like welfare mothers, malingering workers became the objects of reform designed to replace incentives for dependence with a quick push into a job.[5] Declining claims and costs signified the success of worker-compensation reform just as shrinking numbers on the rolls signified the success of welfare reform. Worker-compensation reformers did not measure improvements in the health, safety, and economic condition of workers, just as welfare reformers neglected to ask whether those who had left the rolls also had escaped poverty.

From its beginning, workers' compensation served the interests of labor, big business, and insurance companies. Its appeal to these usually competing interests explained its early acceptance in public policy. The first government social insurance program in the United States, workers' compensation spread across the nation between 1909 and 1920, when forty-three states required employers to compensate their employees for injuries sustained at work.[6]

Labor wanted protection for American workers, who experienced the highest rates of accidents in the industrialized world. Between 1900 and 1906, American miners' annual mortality rate averaged 33.5 per 1,000, compared to 9.1 in France, 10.3 in Belgium, 12.9 in Great Britain, and 20.6 in Prussia. American railroads also killed and injured many times more workers than their European counterparts did. Accidents happened more often in the United States than Europe, said one observer, "partly because of the higher pressure under which our work is carried on and partly because of the rapid introduction of a new element of labor unfamiliar with our methods of mechanical production, but largely because of our general attitude of indifference toward human life itself."[7]

Even workers injured so badly they could never work again found it difficult to collect compensation, and families of workers killed on the job received at best token settlements. Although workers could sue their employers, when they went to court they encountered obstacles in the common law: fellow-servant precedents excused employers who could prove that injuries occurred as a result of the negligence of another employee. Nor could workers collect if their own negligence contributed to their injuries or if they had agreed to work in conditions they knew to be dangerous. In the late-nineteenth century, state courts began to modify all these long-standing common law doctrines. As a result, injured workers more often sued, and they usually won. One study found that juries sided with employers in only 98 of 1,043 cases; another study, of Cleveland, found juries in state courts siding with workers in virtually all instances, and the amount awarded workers soared.[8] Nonetheless, litigation was slow, and employers could usually find ways to delay paying awards.

Employers, for their part, found the cost of litigated workers' accident claims an unpredictable and growing burden. They wanted to stabilize expenses and take decisions out of the hands of juries, who invariably showed more sympathy to workers than to their bosses. Employers tried to protect themselves by purchasing liability insurance, but although the value of liability policies escalated from $200,000 to $35 million between 1887 and 1912, it did not solve the problem. Both employers and labor representatives criticized insurance companies, whose large premiums seemed to pay more for profits and overhead than for benefits to injured workers. And insurance companies remained dissatisfied because they could not predict the size of claims or awards.

Legislation that transformed workers' compensation from an adversarial process to an administrative procedure promised to resolve the issues confronting these competing interests. Injured workers and their families would receive prompt and adequate compensation without the delay and expense of court proceedings. Employers, also free of costly litigation and unsympathetic juries, would know the cost of compensation. Insurance companies would cut their legal expenses, predict costs more accurately, and improve public relations.

Workers' compensation held still another benefit, which appealed to the academic advocates of social insurance: accident prevention. With the threat of higher premiums, employers would pay more attention to safety, argued social insurance experts. This incentive would lead public officials and employers to join together to figure out ways of preventing accidents. Discussions of safety intertwined with the workers' compensation movement, and one result was the 1913 establishment of the National Council for Industrial Safety.

Despite the congruence of interests, agreement on the desirability of workers' compensation legislation did not occur quickly. Labor at first proved a reluctant partner. Samuel Gompers and the AFL initially preferred liberalized liability laws and came to accept legislation only in the second decade of the century. Business support mounted slowly, too, led by the National Civic Federation, which argued that workers' compensation would improve relations between capital and the conservative wing of the labor movement, discourage labor from entering politics, and deflect the threat of socialism.

Even if the parties agreed in principle, working out the details of legislation in the various states proved difficult—workers' compensation poses notoriously intricate and contentious issues about how to determine disability, appropriate reimbursement, and determine someone's capacity for work, and it leaves open other questions that still animate debates nearly a century later. Some states originally left the administration of workers' compensation to state courts, with disastrous results. Others created industrial commissions to administer the laws, but here too there were disappointments. Litigation failed to disappear, costs remained high, and injured workers received inadequate compensation.

For the most part, legislatures passed "no fault" workers' compensation laws that favored business interests. Workers gave up the right to sue in exchange for an entitlement to compensation benefits fixed by state regulation, and many workers—notably farm help, domestics, casual workers, and employees of small firms—were still not covered by the new laws. In addition, coverage remained voluntary for employers, and benefit rates very low. Through labor's influence, some states pegged rates at more than half a worker's customary wages, but most had low ceilings, usually ten dollars a week or less, and limited duration, generally three hundred or four hundred weeks for total disability or death. Although most injuries were of short duration and employees returned to work, inadequate compensation left most injured workers and their families with a crippling loss of income. Employers gave up very little by accepting workers' compensation because they passed its costs on to employees, especially those not in unions, in the form of lower wages.[9]

Despite the inadequacies of workers' compensation, its principal features have endured. "Workers' compensation laws today retain the same fundamental structure as they had when first enacted," points out Spieler. But because each state designs and runs its own program with almost no federal influence, benefits and regulations still vary widely. In 1994, for instance, nearly all states pegged compensation at around two-thirds of wages. But the maximum weekly payment varied from $243.75 in Mississippi to $817.00 in Iowa. Alabama mandated a $3,000 burial allowance, compared to $7,500 in Minnesota. The loss of an arm at the shoulder was worth $31,200 in Colorado and $86,542.50 in Delaware. Loss of a great toe earned $3,420 in Rhode Island and $12,852 in New Hampshire.[10]

Workers' compensation benefits and coverage changed relatively little until the 1970s. By then, criticism of the system—especially its low benefits and restricted coverage—had mounted from all sides, and the Occupational Safety and Health Act of 1970 (OSHA) mandated the National Commission on State Workmen's Compensation to study state laws. The commission, which reported in 1972, recommended universal compulsory coverage; it also urged substantial increases in the amount of benefits, expanded medical and rehabilitative care, employee choice of physician, more active encouragement of safety, and improved administration.[11]

By the early 1990s, states on the average had adopted two-thirds of the commission's nineteen essential recommendations, and courts increasingly handed down decisions that liberalized workers' compensation. As a result, the total cost of workers' compensation benefits skyrocketed. It increased during the 1970s from $3 billion to $13 billion. By 1990, it had reached $38 billion, and it peaked at $45 billion in 1992. Looked at another way, from 1940 to 1970 workers' compensation benefits declined slightly from 1.19 to 1.11 percent of covered payroll; during the next two decades, they more than doubled, to 2.31 percent. Nor had no-fault legislation eliminated, or even severely curtailed, litigation, which, as at the turn of the century, mounted in frequency and cost. In Florida, for example, attorneys' fees for workers' compensation increased from $69 million to $137 million between 1988 and 1991. A 1991 survey found that three of four employers believed that in five years workers' compensation costs "would be somewhat or completely out of control." In January 1994 the National Council of State Legislatures reported that by the mid-1980s, "the nation's oldest insurance program had become outrageously expensive, adversarial, and . . . out of control."[12]

A major part of the expense was soaring medical costs. In 1980, they accounted for one-third of annual workers' compensation claims; by 1993, the proportion had risen to 50 percent. In 1990 they totaled more than $15 billion, compared to $435 million in 1960. Rising costs did not mean more money was paid to injured workers. The share of benefits (although not necessarily the amount) paid to workers declined as the amount paid to other parties ("including medical providers, lawyers, rehabilitation specialists, third party claims administrators") increased.[13]

Inflation was only one factor that drove up medical costs. Another cause was a dramatic rise in repetitive motion injuries, including carpal tunnel syndrome, which fueled injury claims in the 1990s. In 1982–83, employers did not see enough cases of carpal tunnel syndrome injuries to report them to a major survey; by 1997, repetitive motion or cumulative trauma injuries struck about 100,000 workers each year and accounted for one of every three dollars spent on workers' compensation. Between 1981 and 1991, repetitive trauma, still "vastly underreported," increased from 18 percent to 61 percent of reported occupational illness cases. Medical costs rose as well because of the structure of workers' compensation. Workers' compensation insurance generally covered the entire cost of employment-related injuries while, increasingly, ordinary employment-based health insurance required copayments. The absence of any copayment gave employees an incentive to define illnesses and injuries as work related, which drove up the medical costs of workers' compensation. Finally, rising costs reflected the aging of the workforce and the deregulation of the insurance market, which permitted insurance companies to raise premiums for employers designated "high risk."[14]

Some observers argued that increased benefits constituted a moral hazard that induced more workers to file claims, but very little hard evidence supported this assertion. An equally credible explanation was that workers filed more claims in part because they felt more secure in their jobs. New common-law protections for injured workers, workplace antidiscrimination laws, and security against employer retaliation in state statutes encouraged workers to claim their rights.[15]

Allegations of fraud and abuse also fueled the debate on workers' compensation costs during the 1980s. But no compelling evidence linked fraud to increases in worker compensation costs, either. In California, where accusations of fraud played a large role in gutting workers' compensation in the early 1990s, insurance companies reported fewer than 1 percent of claims as suspicious in the three years following the legislative crackdown. In any case, most fraud did not reflect dishonesty among workers. Rather, it was perpetrated by medical and legal "mills" that milked the program of large amounts of money, often without giving much, if any, help to injured workers. "High profile campaigns that focus primarily on worker fraud," concluded a review of the research literature, "are actually public relations campaigns to convince the public and legislatures of the demonstrably false assertion that the workers' compensation system is rife with worker fraud." These campaigns helped persuade the public and government officials to accept reforms that reduced benefits to disabled workers, and they cast a stigma on injured workers that left many reluctant to file legitimate claims. Put another way, "Attacks on benefit levels or eligibility criteria for social programs are easier to countenance if the people who are excluded . . . are perceived to be malingerers and cheats."[16]

Ideas based on moral hazard—for instance, that generous benefits easily obtained encouraged workers to feign injuries and lie—also wrongly assumed that money compensated for all loss—in the case of workers' compensation, that workers would be tempted to risk their health, indeed, their lives, because they could claim compensation if they lost. Moral hazard also wrongly assumed that workers controlled their workplaces and could reduce risks to their own safety by themselves. The "beneficiaries of workers' compensation," writes Baker, "use equipment that they did not make and work in places that they did not design and do not control." The "economics of moral hazard," he concluded, "have been used systematically to favor the interests of manufacturers and employers over the sick and injured."[17]

Despite rising costs, workers' compensation did not cover all the needs of injured workers or relieve them from long delays in receiving benefits. In most states, waiting periods for benefits ranged from seven to twenty-three days. With disputed claims, the time could be much longer. In California, most minor claims took three or more years to resolve, and workers received slightly less than 40 percent of their lost wages.[18]

The struggle by employers and state governments to reverse the meteoric rise in workers' compensation started in the 1980s, and more than thirty states passed significant workers' compensation reforms between 1992 and 1997. The number of employers reporting cost control initiatives, one survey found, had grown dramatically in just the two years between 1991 and 1993. By the mid-1990s, costs appeared headed downward. Between 1990 and 1995, workers' compensation premiums fell more than 10 percent; in 1996, they declined another 5.2 percent. Both costs and benefits continued to fall, and by 1998 benefits had declined by 35 percent and employer costs by 38 percent of payroll since 1992.[19]

The methods used to drive down the price of workers' compensation included "reforms" that directly controlled medical costs and put limits on the duration and amount of indemnity payments, especially those for temporary disability—in other words, benefit cuts. Some states, for example, reduced benefit payments from 66.67 to 60 percent of workers' gross wages. Other "reforms" tried to eliminate structural inefficiencies by limiting attorneys' fees, discouraging litigation, redesigning administrative procedures, and, where allowed by law, using managed care. In 1997, Florida became the first state to require managed care for all workers' compensation cases. (In many states, laws that allowed injured workers to choose their primary care physician blocked managed care for a time.) Unions objected to managed care in workers' compensation because they feared modern versions of the old company doctors who took the side of management. "Twenty-four-hour health insurance," which allowed employers to provide medical insurance for both occupationally related and ordinary health conditions under one policy, found many advocates, although opponents argued that it shifted costs to injured workers through copayments and deductibles not required under workers' compensation medical plans.[20]

As in other areas of the welfare state, a market model underlay many of the "reforms" designed to reduce the cost of worker's compensation. In 1997, wrote two analysts, "experimentation [in cost reduction] has shifted to private, market-driven initiatives." The key (as in welfare reform) was a quick return to work. Many workers' compensation insurers created "programs that encourage employers to take a more active role in bringing injured workers back to the workplace, either by making changes in their former job until they are able to resume their usual work activities or retraining them for more suitable work."[21]

At the century's end, as at its beginning, safety still remained a major problem in American industry. In 1990 alone, injury rates rose 6 percent and occupational illnesses 17 percent. Today, over 10,000 workers are killed and more than 6 million injured on the job each year, and more than 100,000 others "die from occupational exposure to toxic chemicals." Improved workplace safety, concluded one expert, constitutes "the only lasting solution to controlling workers' compensation costs." In the 1990s, the rhetoric of safety spread through workers' compensation debates, and workplace safety campaigns seemed to be having an effect: work-related injuries fell 25 percent between 1992 and 1998. This startling decline included all types of injuries, including a 30 percent drop for carpal tunnel syndrome. While the cause of the decline remained "something of a mystery," according to economic analyst Alan B. Kruger, "many managers recognized that occupational injuries had a significant effect on the bottom line. Instead of viewing injury costs as unavoidable, they developed safety programs to cut risks. The 1990s' investment boom in new, and safer, plants and equipment probably abetted this effort."[22]

As all parties—insurers, state agencies, workers' compensation administrators, academic researchers, employer organizations—began to beat the "safety drum," state legislatures began to make safety, something about which all parties could agree, a principal feature of workers' compensation reform. New state laws required a wide variety of measures from accident prevention services and safety committees to oversight by a government agency, for example. Workers might find themselves safer on the job, but they also would find themselves less well taken care of when they were injured—if, in fact, they could prove their claim to compensation at all. In 1997, four years after a major workers' compensation reform, one of five workers' compensation cases in California ended up in litigation with both worker and employer represented by an attorney.[23]

Despite the new emphasis on safety, a paradox ran through the recent history of workers' compensation. Although all the evidence shows the economic value of deterring workplace injuries, employers by and large were slow to adopt proven methods of prevention. Instead, they preferred to blame workers for their carelessness and lawyers, physicians, and politicians for their greed. They were more ready to run and ask the state legislature for a benefits cut than to review their safety practices. Their actions did have a logic, however: with all risks insured and employers immune from being sued, the system encouraged them to neglect the influence of their own activities on workers' compensation claims and costs. For this reason costs rather than injury rates continue to drive the political debate over workers' compensation.[24]

Insurance companies, as well as employers, retained a major stake in workers' compensation costs. When costs turned around in the 1990s, insurance companies, which had been losing money on workers' compensation, began to earn a profit once more. Indeed, between 1991 and 1996, they reduced their losses by $3.6 billion. Whether costs would stay level remained an open question. An econometric analysis attributed declining costs to the economic slump of the early 1990s and predicted increases from inexperienced new workers, speedups, and overtime as the economy heated up.[25]

No two states reduced the cost of workers' compensation in the same way. Oregon pioneered in cutting costs by combining cost controls with safety measures—on the one hand, limits on medical costs, tight eligibility requirements, and the aggressive denial of claims, and on the other, "market-driven" safety initiatives by private employers, mandated joint labor-management safety and health councils, and increased health and safety enforcement by the Oregon unit of OSHA. These reforms not only saved money, they improved the situation for injured workers through faster resolution of claims and payment of benefits. Nonetheless, a nagging question remained: had Oregon cut costs at the expense of injured workers? Massachusetts, another state with above-average claims and costs in the 1980s, first cut benefits without improving workplace safety. It also reined in medical costs with treatment guidelines and a new "impartial physician" process designed to reduce the expense and conflict arising from the opinions of multiple and partisan physicians. Injured workers, of course, lost a medical advocate. As a result of administrative reform, workers had their cases heard and received payment more quickly, but fewer of them received benefits at all, while those who pressed their claims successfully found themselves with less money than they had received before.[26]

In 1997, a major conflict over workers' compensation reform in Ohio pitted business interests and the governor against organized labor in a high-stakes battle with consequences that stretched far beyond the state's borders. The conflict exposed the interests underlying the technical details of workers' compensation laws and the contested meaning of "reform." It also underscored the revived power of the labor movement to mobilize a constituency broader than its membership around issues that seemed to threaten all workers.

The story is straightforward. As in other states, in Ohio the escalating cost of workers' compensation had spurred a movement for reform. In the 1990s, the legislature passed a number of bills that streamlined the system, gave increased control to the governor, and moved injured workers into managed care. As a result, costs and premiums began to decline. In 1997, the Republican legislature, backed by business interests, wanted to complete the work of reform and, on a partisan vote, passed another workers' compensation bill, which the governor signed. Union representatives objected vigorously to most of its provisions, which, they argued, would both cut benefits and make them more difficult to claim. Opponents of the new law gathered enough signatures to place a referendum on the November ballot. After a bitter campaign, in which supporters of the law heavily outspent opponents, voters overwhelmingly rejected the workers' compensation bill.[27]

Even a cursory look at the bill's provisions reveals why labor opposed it, although it did meet a few of labor's objections to the current system. The bill reduced the number of weeks of benefits for temporarily disabled workers from 200 to 26, even if they could not find jobs. To move injured workers back into the workforce as quickly as possible, the Ohio Bureau of Workers' Compensation now could require anyone claiming benefits to be evaluated as a suitable candidate for vocational rehabilitation. Only those considered nonemployable qualified for benefits, but the definition of "nonemployable" became more restrictive because it excluded factors such as education or age; only medical condition counted. Because "few claimants are declared permanently and totally disabled based on their medical conditions alone," explained Lex Larson, a workers' compensation expert, the elimination of nonmedical grounds for disability would decimate the number of injured workers eligible for permanent benefits.[28]

The bill also redefined repetitive motion disabilities as occupational illnesses rather than injuries and forced workers to prove that they had developed the condition as a result of the job—something very difficult to do with a disease such as carpal tunnel syndrome, which might also occur as a result of sports or common household activities. By increasing the difficulty of claiming compensation for repetitive motion injury, the bill attacked the major source of medical claims—one-fourth of all serious occupational injuries. The bill also reduced or eliminated claims for the aggravation of preexisting diseases, unless the job had worsened them substantially, and with only a few exceptions, it reduced the time for filing a claim from ten to five years. Although five years sounds like plenty of time, one critic pointed to the case of a worker not diagnosed for a decade, partly because his employer withheld information. The bill further attempted to lessen the involvement of attorneys by lowering their fees and reducing the number of litigated claims. (Allegedly unscrupulous attorneys became whipping posts for the proponents of reform. In fact, only 12 or 13 percent of claims involved attorneys at all.) The bill also required the use of the American Medical Association's guidelines for evaluating impairment in cases of permanent partial disability, tough standards that the AMA said were not appropriate for workers' compensation cases. At the same time, the bill lessened workplace safety, partly by reducing employers' incentives. It made the records of the State Division of Safety and Hygiene, which included reports of accident investigations, closed to workers, the media, and the public. In this way, the bill prevented workers from protecting themselves or putting pressure on employers.[29]

The bill did increase benefits for funeral expenses—"and we know what you have to do to get that," said one labor spokesman. Labor claimed that workers' compensation reform constituted nothing more than a smokescreen to reduce employers' costs and lower their insurance premiums. An independent analysis found that the new regulations would cut benefits by $100 million a year and save employers 7.5 percent annually on their insurance premiums.[30]

Business representatives argued that the bill served the interests of workers as well as employers and fought hard to sustain it in the November referendum. Employers evading the law or failing to obtain coverage were now guilty of a felony, they pointed out. The "entire unfortunate effort" to defeat the bill, claimed Roger R. Geiger, state director of the National Federation of Independent Business, "must be laid directly at the doorstep of the same trial lawyers and labor leaders who for years have opposed every attempt to streamline our workers' compensation system."[31]

The coalition working to sustain the bill, Keep Ohio Working, argued that high workers' compensation costs were driving jobs from the state. But to the contrary, for the three years prior to 1996, Ohio ranked as the top state in the nation for business expansion; in 1996, it ranked second only to North Carolina. The coalition had been formed on July 23 by the Ohio Chamber of Commerce, the National Federation of Independent Business, the Ohio Farm Bureau, and the Ohio Manufacturers' Association. The Manufacturers' Association spent almost $500,000; the Ohio Chamber of Commerce added $350,000; other large contributors included the Ohio Contractors Association, General Motors, Honda, Ford, Timken Steel, LTV Steel, Chrysler, Goodyear, B. F. Goodrich,

Nationwide Insurance, The Limited, American Financial, AK Steel, Mead Corporation, BP, and Wolfe Associates. In all, Keep Ohio Working raised nearly $4.8 million, and it received support from the state's major newspapers as well. An editorial in the *Cleveland Plain Dealer* observed, "It is repulsive that the needs of the injured and the wallets of taxpayers are being ignored in this attempt to squash critically needed reforms."[32]

Proponents presented the reforms as technical measures designed to enhance the efficiency of the system. But, as legal scholar Martha McCluskey explained, the idea of efficiency in workers' compensation, as in other welfare state programs, masked the political and moral choices embedded in every policy decision—"conventional economic efficiency goals distort policy making through a false appearance of impartial rigor." It leaves "certain alternatives outside the political debate" as fixed constraints and avoids the central question, "Who should benefit and who should lose from the efforts to reduce the costs of work accidents?"[33] In Ohio, as elsewhere, workers' compensation reform was not a neutral method of increasing efficiency; it was a means of redistributing resources and power away from workers.

Opponents of the new bill, organized in the Coalition for Workplace Safety, raised much less than their opponents—$2.1 million. The largest share, nearly $533,000, came from the Ohio AFL-CIO; the UAW added about $125,000; and the Service Employees International Union and the Ohio Civil Service Employees Union also contributed, as did the Ohio Academy of Trial Lawyers. "By seeking to overturn existing law—something not tried in nearly 60 years," pointed out one commentator, labor was "waging a high-stakes battle. Victory would be a potent sign that Ohio labor still has political juice, and it could embolden unions in other states to deploy the same strategy. A defeat could further undermine union clout in the state, broadcasting the image of a shrunken giant that poses little threat at the ballot box." The outcome of the struggle would have national implications. A victory for the Ohio labor coalition, argued Robert Weissman, editor of the *Multinational Monitor,* could "stop in its tracks the unending series of workers' comp 'reforms' [throughout the nation] and perhaps herald a reversal. If the pro-worker coalition fails, the nationwide corporate crusade to eviscerate workers' comp will continue unabated."[34]

In the November referendum voters in seventy-three of Ohio's eighty-eight counties rejected the workers' compensation bill. With 57 percent of the vote, it was a stunning victory. The referendum proved a massive defeat for Governor George Voinovich, who had championed the bill, as well as for the business interests, which had "underestimated the potency of an issue that matters more than almost any other to voters: economic security." Voinovich and the state Republican legislators did not understand the emotional force of workers' compensation for the people who depended on it: "It is one thing for legislators in Columbus to draft changes citing abstract notions like efficiency and fairness. It is another thing to persuade people that it is in their interest to approve a law that could reduce the money they collect if they lose their jobs."[35]

The Ohio referendum exposed workers' compensation as a key site in the conflict between business and labor. Whether labor could build on its victory in Ohio to roll back or prevent attacks on workers' compensation in other states remained uncertain. The Ohio victory—following as it did the Teamsters' win on benefit issues in the United Parcel Service strike— underscored the resurgent power of labor. At the least, labor's victories signaled that as long as the economy remained strong and the labor market tight, further assaults on economic security would confront real resistance.

Disability Insurance and the New Undeserving Poor

Disabled Americans also found themselves less secure. Although the Reagan administration had been so aggressive in attacking eligibility requirements that public opinion forced a retreat, the war on dependence could not pass up such a large target for very long, and in 1996 the 104th Congress took aim at some of the most vulnerable Americans. As with other social insurances and public assistance, the attack focused more on erecting new barriers to public support than on lowering the benefits of those still admitted. Growing disability rolls and increased costs gave Congress the occasion to claim a crisis that demanded tough action. Newly constructed categories of the undeserving disabled justified the assault.

In America, persons disabled or injured confront a confusing array of programs. While workers injured on the job in theory can claim workers' compensation, men and women with a history of employment in jobs covered by insurance but unable to work because of some disabling condition (not a work injury) can apply for Disability Insurance (DI), which is a federal program added to Social Security in 1956. Supplemental Security Income (SSI) serves only the poor. It is the main federal program that benefits injured and disabled men and women without work histories in the regular labor market; it is also the program that provides cash benefits to needy disabled children. A national program formed in 1972 by combining aid to the blind, disabled, and elderly not eligible for Social Security, SSI replaced separate public assistance or state-federal welfare programs that previously had served these groups.

Disability is not an unambiguous idea. Throughout the history of social insurance, employers, the state, and labor have all contested its meaning. Public policy, not objective standards, defines disability, and its definition is always in flux. Political scientist Deborah A. Stone points out that "the very notion of disability is fundamental to the architecture of the welfare state; it is something like a keystone that allows the other supporting structures of the welfare system and, in some sense, the economy at large to remain in place." The idea of disability permits societies to resolve the tension between work and need by identifying morally faultless individuals unable to support themselves. "Disability" thus solves the problem of moral hazard with a justification for public support that does not undermine work. The problem has always been validation. In practice, what criteria identified incapacity and who applied them? There were, Stone notes, a number of historic methods of validation. Authorities questioned acquaintances; designed "elaborate forms of social inquiry directed at applicants for relief"; devised experiments to force "the deceiver" to expose himself; constructed situations in which applicants' behavior (such as willingness to enter a horrible poorhouse) would constitute a "revelatory sign"; and forced them to undergo an "adversarial test" (for instance, to sue their employer) to prove the legitimacy of their claim. Modern welfare programs replaced these historic means of validation with "clinical judgment."[36]

The burden of proving disability fell on medicine, which is supposed to render a clear, objective, and scientifically based decision. Physicians realized the subjectivity underlying determinations of disability and only reluctantly accepted the role of gatekeeper to the welfare state. Like nineteenth-century public officials who found it impossible in practice to draw the line between the able-bodied and the impotent poor, modern medicine often cannot say with certainty whose impairment unfits them for any work. What role to assign mental and emotional states, such as "stress" or addiction to alcohol or narcotics, is not a medical decision. Neither is capacity for work when measured by medical criteria that do not take age, education, and the labor market into account.

Beside the ancient tension between work and need, another contradiction undercuts disability policy, points out Edward D. Berkowitz, the major historian of modern American disability policy. Advocates of benefits for disabled and injured workers "fight to keep people on the disability rolls and out of the labor force." At the same time, advocates of disability rights struggle to gain access to public facilities and jobs for the disabled and handicapped. In 1990, their campaign culminated in the Americans with Disability Act. The "efforts to open up the labor force to the handicapped and the efforts to protect the rights of the handicapped to retire proceed in parallel, never touching one another."[37]

Disability remains not only a constructed category undermined by contradictions; it also has acquired three distinct meanings, as Berkowitz points out. In courts or workers' compensation programs, "disability means the damages that one person collects from another as a result of an insult or injury." For Social Security Disability Insurance, it signifies "a condition that links ill health and unemployment." And in civil rights laws, disability connotes "handicap." The confusion extends to the terms used in the disability debates, as policy analysts parse the distinctions between "functional limitations, impairment, disability, and handicap." The multiple meanings of *disability* and the lack of consistent uses of key terms also block more rational policies toward injury and impairment.[38]

In the 1970s and again from the late 1980s through the early 1990s, a language of crisis surrounded discussions of disability policy. A "need-based system," notes Stone, "will be labeled as 'in crisis' at precisely those moments when the *restrictiveness* of a category is felt to be too loose or ineffective."[39] Workers' compensation, Disability Insurance, and SSI all seemed out of control, growing too fast, serving clients poorly, wasting money through inefficiency and fraud—egregious examples of moral hazard. The symptom was the growth in the numbers of people claiming disability, which followed a different pattern in each program but marked all of them at one moment or another in recent times. This "crisis" of rising costs discovered by political conservatives prompted Congress and the Social Security Administration to tighten boundaries by toughening eligibility requirements, defining the most vulnerable among the disabled as dishonest or undeserving, and purging them from the rolls. The war on disability revealed how power shapes the definitions of "injury" and "disability" and determines the application of "moral hazard."

At first, the Disability Insurance story appears to be one of steady growth—a 27 percent rise in the rolls between 1980 and 1994 and an increase in benefits from $19 billion to $41 billion. Translated into incidence rates—the number of benefit awards per 1,000 workers—the trends appear quite different. Incidence rates fluctuated: they reached an all-time high of 7.2 in 1975 and an all-time low of 2.9 in 1982. They peaked again in the last half of the 1980s, then rose and flattened out in the first half of the 1990s. Supplemental Security Income, the bottom of the public safety net, appeared to follow a more straightforward upward path. Its rolls grew from 4 million to 6.5 million, but its growth masked compositional changes. Women, now a much larger proportion of workers, composed a disproportionate share of new DI beneficiaries—a rise of 44 percent, compared to 15 percent for men. With SSI, the number of old people, now supported almost entirely by Social Security, declined while the number of children under eighteen awarded benefits because of a disability increased from 373,000 in 1991 to 906,000 in 1995. The reasons had little to do with changes in the condition of children.[40]

The same factors underpinned changes in the size of both DI and SSI for adults. To begin with, more people joined the disability rolls than left. Men and women exit Disability Insurance because they die (the death rate did not change very much in the 1980s or 1990s) or because they reach retirement age, return to work, or are found to be medically recovered. In the late 1980s and early 1990s, none of these events outpaced the growth of programs. Instead, revised medical criteria and advances in treatment influenced the composition and swelled the size of disability rolls. The proportion on the rolls because of cardiovascular conditions declined steeply as medical treatment made them far less disabling than in the past. By contrast, the recognition of depression as an impairment (the National Institute of Mental Health launched its Depression: Awareness, Recognition, and Treatment campaign in 1985) and new criteria for evaluating mental disorders issued in the mid-1980s, prompted in part by the courts, fueled the growth of the rolls. Mental disorders rose from 10 percent of the reasons for disability in 1981 to 25 percent in 1995.[41]

Disability rolls also usually increase during recessions, when they act as a disguised form of unemployment insurance. Although the recession of the early 1980s proved an exception because of the policies of the Reagan administration, disability programs did indeed grow during the downturn of 1990–91. Disability also helped ease redundant workers out of employment much as early retirement programs moved white-collar workers out from middle-management positions. Besides recessions and labor market displacement, cuts in public aid programs also moved people onto the disability rolls. Men and women bounced from state General Assistance programs sometimes found their way to Supplemental Security Income. So did some of those denied workers' compensation. The same may happen when the time limits in the 1996 welfare bill cut families off. Because it is difficult to apply for DI or SSI, many people prefer to try other, easier programs first and turn to disability only when alternatives fail.[42]

Public policy fueled the growth of SSI as well. Federal disability programs allow states to shift costs by off-loading them onto the federal government. Closing mental hospitals and moving patients out of other institutions into communities increased disability programs because SSI provides essential life support for the severely disabled living on their own. Cost pressures on hospitals also drove up the rolls. With tightening controls on Medicare and lower payments from private insurance, hospitals, required to treat the uninsured poor, helped indigent patients qualify for Medicaid, which also increased their eligibility for SSI. In 1989, Congress appropriated funds for outreach to increase the enrollment of eligible persons in SSI, and outreach became a priority of the Social Security Administration. At the same time, Social Security Administration staff, which had been reduced by 25 percent, could not monitor state actions as effectively, especially when applications increased rapidly during the recession of 1990–91. As a result, the rate of benefit awards grew.[43]

Explanations of the growth in disability rolls often overlook the powerful interests that support program expansion. A strong case exists, Stone argues, for the fact that "the state, employers, legislators, disability program agencies, and rehabilitation agencies all benefit from having a disability category they can manipulate." The state, for example, finds in disability a convenient way to disguise and manage high unemployment (disability rolls in all countries appear to rise during periods of high unemployment); employers can shift older or unproductive workers to disability programs, for which they do not pay direct premiums; legislators can use flexible standards to help constituents; agencies can receive continued funding by showing their services are needed.[44]

Nonetheless, a suspicion of malingering and fraud always hovers around the growth of the disability rolls. As the boundaries between work and need seem to dissolve, the undeserving poor appear to be raiding the public treasury, driving up taxes, undermining morals, and threatening labor markets. The suspicion becomes most acute in periods when government itself is suspect and when many think the object of policy should be to reduce dependence and inject market discipline into public affairs and private behavior. Two episodes show this dynamic at work in the years since 1980. One was the attempt by the Reagan administration to toss people off the disability rolls. The other was the effort in the mid-1990s to reduce the number of SSI recipients, especially children, by redefining disability.

The Reagan administration had promised to reduce the size and cost of government partly by applying restrictive eligibility criteria to disability awards, which had soared in recent years. From 1970 to 1975, for example, the number of awards grew at an annual rate of 11.1 percent, and the awards per 100,000 insured workers at 8 percent each year. The growth in numbers resulted from the passage of laws liberalizing Disability Insurance at a time of high unemployment, increased awareness of the program, and tax administration. Although required by law to review continuing benefits, the Social Security Administration's procedures remained haphazard, and the agency reviewed or terminated few cases. To many recipients, benefits increasingly became a permanent entitlement. Many members of Congress objected to the alleged moral hazard of disability insurance, which, they argued, discouraged a return to work by paying benefits higher than the wages that most recipients could earn in a job. Thus, in 1975, Congress imposed tighter standards on the state agencies that evaluated claims. As a result, initial awards began to fall— by 5.7 percent a year between 1975 and 1980.[45]

In 1980, as Reagan took office, new legislation tried to further rein in disability costs by mandating three-year reviews of every case, capping family benefits, and changing the method of computing benefits. Previously, to end benefits the SSA needed to prove that a person's medical condition had improved; now, it only needed to show medical evidence that the person seemed able to work. This new and much looser standard gave SSA the tool it needed to pry people from the rolls. With support from the administration, SSA compensated for its former haphazard procedures by reviewing massive numbers of cases (more than it could handle with any degree of care) and ordering the end of benefits for nearly half of them. "What had been conceived by Congress in 1980," observes political scientist Martha Derthick, "was deliberate invigoration of a review procedure that had been too feeble to have much effect. What was set in motion in 1981 was more like a purge." Periodic reviews began as a bipartisan attempt to reduce costs; they quickly became a political football, as Democrats charged the Reagan administration with a heartless attempt to reduce the deficit on the backs of the disabled. The president of a local union of Social Security employees claimed, "We are witnessing a savage purge of the rolls, with mean applications of self-serving rules, and without heart or mind to the consequences." Jack Weinstein, a New York District Court judge, argued that the SSA was following the dictates of "a zealous administration that believed it had congressional sanction to cut costs at the expense of what some believed was an impotent constituency." (Republicans liked to remind Democrats that tightened eligibility standards and reviews had begun under President Jimmy Carter.)

Between March 1981 and November 1983, state agencies, under federal pressure, carried out over a million disability reviews and concluded that the benefits of 470,000 persons should end. The SSA did not deny a larger share of initial applications or terminate a higher proportion of cases—rather, it vastly increased the number of cases it reviewed, from 83,651 in 1978 to 436,498 in 1983.[46]

Benefits for many persons did not stop when the SSA decided against them, however. Instead, a great many appealed their cases, primarily to administrative law judges, who usually found in favor of the disabled. In 1982, administrative law judges restored benefits to two-thirds of those the SSA had wanted to drop from the rolls. Increasingly, too, appeals of SSA decisions ended up in federal district courts. The rate at which these courts reversed SSA benefit denials rose from 19 percent in 1980 to 60 percent in 1984.[47] With the rate of success in court high, the proportion appealing their cases increased from 70 percent to 90 percent. The Reagan administration had promised to cut 500,000 from the disability rolls. In the end, after appeals, the number was 83,360—a small figure in light of the expense of litigation and the suffering of the disabled who had to fight their way through the courts to win back their benefits.[48]

A constitutional crisis nearly erupted as the actions of administrative law judges overruled the Social Security Administration, which refused to accept the judges' opinions as binding precedents.[49] Public opinion shifted decisively to the courts and the cause of the disabled. Even state governments revolted. By February 1984, thirty-eight states refused to process disability reviews. The media (which publicized heartrending cases and instances of suicide among disabled persons cut off from benefits), advocates for the disabled, and even Congress eventually turned the tide against the review process into an irresistible torrent. The SSA finally suspended reviews for eighteen months, and in 1984 Congress passed the Disability Reform Act (402 to 0 in the House and 99 to 0 in the Senate), which returned the criterion for continuing benefits to the earlier "medical improvement standard" but left a number of issues unclear or unresolved, a certain sign of future trouble.

After a hard fight, the first round in the disability wars of the 1980s had gone to the disabled, but as their legal advocates knew, they remained vulnerable, subject to a renewed war on eligibility.[50] When it came a decade later, the target had shifted to the two most helpless categories among the disabled: children and men and women addicted to alcohol or drugs.

Disability surfaced as an issue again in the 1990s as part of the conservative assault on the welfare state. "Do disability cash benefits provide a strong disincentive for people to work?" asked a National Academy of Social Insurance panel. It answered with a resounding and unambiguous "no." The panel found that the programs' "strict and frugal design," the characteristics of their beneficiaries, and a comparison of U.S. disability spending with that of other countries all supported the conclusion. SSI and DI imposed the "strictest" disability test of any program in the

United States, "public or private." DI beneficiaries were poorer than retirees, had pensions or savings less often, and held "vastly smaller" assets. Average incomes of the disabled in 1996 were about 70 percent of the poverty line. Nor was the United States generous by international standards. Its combined DI and SSI spending amounted to 0.7 percent of the gross domestic product, which was less than half of the share in the United Kingdom or Germany and a fourth of Sweden's.[51]

As in other corners of the welfare state, a concern with work drove attempts to reform disability programs. With the issue of benefit adequacy swept off the table, the significant question that remained was how to move people back into a job. The panel responded with two new programs designed on market models. To put incentives and personal choice at the heart of the system, the panel recommended giving beneficiaries a return-to-work (RTW) ticket, very like a voucher, that "they could use to shop among providers of rehabilitation or RTW services in either the public or private sector." The Social Security Administration would pay providers only after the beneficiary returned to work and left the disability rolls. The panel also proposed a "disabled worker tax credit," modeled after the Earned Income Tax Credit, that would be paid as a wage subsidy to low-income disabled persons who worked; "it would reward work for low earners with disabilities without increasing reliance on disability benefit programs that are designed primarily for persons who are unable to work."[52]

Conservative congressional critics of disability did not follow the recommendations of the National Academy panel. They struck hardest at adults disabled due to drug or alcohol addiction and disabled children. In March 1996, the 104th Congress declared people disabled because of drug or alcohol addiction ineligible for both Disability Insurance and SSI Disability. Losing their disability benefit also would sever their link to Medicare and Medicaid. The new law applied to both new applicants and those already receiving disability benefits, whose cases would face review. The benefits of those found ineligible would end on January 1, 1997, although people who lost benefits could appeal or reapply on the basis of some other impairment. Congress argued that providing benefits to substance abusers "fails to serve the interests of addicts and alcoholics, many of whom use their disability checks to purchase drugs or alcohol." In *Investor's Business Daily*, a writer complained that "people can gain disability status with acts many think of as vice, or even illegal activities. . . . These include smoking or alcohol or drug abuse." The National Alliance of the Mentally Ill, however, pointed out that many individuals were dually diagnosed with severe mental illness and substance abuse disorders—

among young people with severe mental illness, the number of addicts exceeded 50 percent, and it reached even higher among the homeless and severely mentally ill. What would happen to them when their disability benefits ended? worried the Alliance. In June 1996, the Social Security Administration notified over 200,000 people that they would lose benefits under the new law unless they successfully appealed. By February 1997, the SSA had terminated the benefits of 141,000, and the number continued to grow. The first research tracking former SSI recipients supported the worst fears of mental health advocates. Unemployed, sometimes homeless, substance abusers often could not afford to continue with rehabilitation programs.

Critics of SSI also found ammunition in the number of children on the rolls. Writing in the *Wall Street Journal* in January 1995, Heather Mac-Donald, a contributing editor to the conservative Manhattan Institute's *City Journal*, warned that the "explosive growth" in SSI "increasingly supports people whose main problem is not a traditional medical impairment that makes working impossible, but a host of social handicaps that no doctor could cure—drug abuse, a chaotic upbringing, and a lack of education and work ethic." "The group of claimants that has stretched the concept of disability the farthest," asserted MacDonald, was not addicts, "but children with behavioral problems. . . . It is debatable whether disability payments are even appropriate for children, since they are intended to replace lost earnings. Children not only are not required to work; they are legally prohibited from doing so. Moreover, Medicaid picks up most of the medical expenses of poor disabled children."[53]

Contrary to MacDonald's assertions, by enrolling the children of the poor, SSI had served the purposes for which it had been designed. The different standards that applied to adults and children were appropriate and important, pointed out the National Academy panel. The disabilities of low-income children "pose additional costs to their families and, if they do not have appropriate developmental supports when they are young, they are at high risk of relying on public support when they become adults." Without SSI, argued the panel, poor disabled children would stand a "much greater risk of losing both a secure home environment and the best opportunity for integration into community life, including the world of work." The panel found no evidence to support another common allegation of critics, that parents coached their children to misbehave or perform poorly in school to qualify for benefits.[54]

Conservatives did correctly identify one source of the rising number of children receiving SSI. In 1990, the Social Security Administration expanded the number of children eligible by updating its listing of childhood mental disorders (the approximately one hundred specific mental or physical conditions described in regulations) to reflect the same conceptual framework as the adult listings developed in 1985 as a result of court decisions and federal legislation. That year, the U.S. Supreme Court in *Sullivan v. Zebley* also increased eligibility. Before *Zebley*, disability determination for children used only medical criteria. Adults whose conditions failed this stringent test retained one alternative: an individual assessment of their "residual functional capacity." *Zebley* extended individual assessments (called "individual functional assessments," or IFAs) to children. At the same time, the Social Security Administration reinstated and paid back benefits to 141,000 children found to have been illegally denied benefits.[55]

The campaign to purge children from the disability rolls did not rest on statistical evidence. It began when an insurance representative and Arkansas state legislator, Pat Flanagan, thought one of his constituents was defrauding the government by claiming her children were disabled. Flanagan went to the *Arkansas Democrat-Gazette*, which ran a story about fraud and abuse in the child disability program based solely on a few anecdotes and an informal study done by a part-time student for a term paper. In Louisiana, a midlevel disability examiner, Wayne Parker, whose wife, a schoolteacher, suspected children of cheating the system, went to his congressman, Jim McCrery (Republican). McCrery took the issue to Congress, and national newspapers—including the *Washington Post* and the *Wall Street Journal*— ran major articles based, again, solely on anecdotal evidence. An ABC *Prime Time Live* special, "Crazy Checks," fueled the controversy with evidence from a Harrisburg, Pennsylvania, pediatrician who had not reviewed the medical records or examined the children she claimed had defrauded the program. She claimed she had been fired as a contractor for the Social Security Administration because she insisted on disqualifying children whom other examiners found to have legitimate disabilities.[56]

However, four major studies of the SSI program found no evidence of widespread fraud or abuse. Congress's Disability Policy Panel, which produced one of the reports, was not asked to testify by the House committee that voted to cut the program, even though it had been appointed by its congressional parent. Despite all the evidence to the contrary, Representative McCrery, who led the campaign to tighten eligibility requirements for children on SSI, argued, "Frankly, the SSI children's program has grown out of control and well beyond helping truly needy children." He claimed that parents placed some children on medication for mental disorders that did not exist and that others remained untreated for fear of losing disability benefits. Current SSI disability rules, argued Philadelphia psychiatrist Kenneth Carroll, created a classic case of moral hazard by rewarding bad parenting. Many of the problems of children receiving SSI originated with the neglect or abuse by their parents: "Behavioral and emotional problems, or conduct disorders that are directly attributable to inadequate parenting, are being called disabilities, and the parents are receiving a cash award for having achieved the problem."[57]

Amid the frenzy of anecdotal allegations of fraud, waste, and abuse, Congress set up a national hotline for teachers and other school personnel to report suspected cases of parents coaching children. In 1994–95, the hotline received only about 230 reports, out of the 1 million children receiving benefits, and the Social Security Administration considered only 83 worth investigating. However, Jane Ross, director of Income Security Issues in the federal government, reported that SSI remained a program at "high risk" because of its exposure to "fraud, waste, and abuse" through its reliance on individuals' own reports of their incomes and resources and other administrative weaknesses.[58]

The 1996 welfare bill responded to critics of SSI by tightening the definition of child disability for both new applicants and existing beneficiaries, whose cases would be reviewed. The law also eliminated the individual functional assessments required in 1990. It targeted "less severely disabled children" and tried to restrict SSI to children with "significant disabilities." In practice, less severe disabilities meant primarily behavioral problems.[59]

The Congressional Budget Office estimated that from 1996 to 2002, 22 percent of previously eligible children would become ineligible: 15 percent of children would lose benefits they already received, and 30 percent of new applicants who met former guidelines would fail to receive benefits. The new standards of eligibility would save $8 billion, or 14 percent of the amount to be saved by the new welfare bill. One estimate predicted that 185,000 children would lose their SSI checks by July 1997.[60] (This number proved high.)

Losing SSI benefits promised hardship for low-income families. Parents needed SSI to replace earnings when they had to remain at home with sick or disabled children who required intensive, specialized care. In the 1990–91 recession, outreach by the Social Security Administration coupled with the expansion of beneficiaries that resulted from the *Zebley* decision allowed many parents impoverished by lost jobs to turn to SSI to support their disabled children.[61]

Families receiving SSI had a median income of $14,000, of which 30 percent came from SSI benefits. Over half were single parents who faced special difficulties trying to replace lost federal income with work. SSI paid each eligible disabled child up to $484 a month in cash assistance, and some states supplemented the amount. In most states, children receiving SSI automatically became eligible for Medicaid. In all cases, they lived with families with incomes below the poverty line and met eligibility standards for disability. The "bottom line," wrote one expert, "is a loss of federal dollars supporting the general safety net for low-income families."[62]

Children's advocates tried to persuade the Social Security Administration to use the discretion allowed it by law in implementing the new standards. Depending on how the SSA interpreted the law, as many as 200,000 or as few as 100,000 children could lose their benefits, advocates said. "There is a distinct risk of overkill, putting in jeopardy children even the vocal critics would not want to be 'terminated' from the program," claimed Jonathan Stein, a Philadelphia Legal Services attorney who had argued the *Zebley* case in 1990 and played an important role in the disability review litigation in the 1980s. "The administration," said Stein, "should be looking for a way that harms the least children."[63]

Although top Social Security Administration officials admitted the difficulty of devising a new standard, the outcome was harsh. On February 11, 1997, the Social Security Administration announced that it would review 260,000 cases and probably end benefits for 135,000 children. By September 6, 1997, the agency had reviewed the eligibility of 246,211 children and found 52.6 percent, or 129,541, ineligible. Social Security Administration officials were also discouraging families from appealing the decisions. One claims representative, referring to benefits already paid, warned the guardian of a disabled child in Philadelphia against exercising her right to appeal: "You will have to pay it back. The government will hound you until you pay it back."[64]

Parents and guardians were not the only ones warned not to exercise their rights; the Social Security Administration "told its administrative law judges, who rule on claims for benefits, that they might face remedial training and 'disciplinary action' if they did not follow the agency's policies or if their productivity [that is, number of children terminated] was considered too low," reported the *New York Times*. The SSA advised its judges to follow agency policy even when it conflicted with precedents in federal law. When the agency disagreed with a court's interpretation of the law, the new policy decreed, "Social Security Administration decision makers will continue to be bound by SSA's nationwide policy rather than the court's holdings." Not surprisingly, not all federal courts agreed with the agency. Judge Roger L. Wollman, writing for the U.S. Court of Appeals for the Eighth Circuit in St. Louis, warned the Clinton administration that whether or not the commissioner of Social Security agreed with court decisions, she was "still bound by the law of this circuit and does not have discretion to decide whether to adhere to it. . . . The regulations of the Social Security Administration are not the supreme law of the land."[65]

As the Social Security Administration ended the cash benefits of over 100,000 disabled children, members of Congress as well as judges and advocates began to object. They argued that the government was applying stricter standards than the 1996 law required, that federal officials were discouraging families from appealing benefit terminations, and that the results of benefit review varied greatly around the country. Children lost benefits in more than 75 percent of reviews in Iowa, Kansas, Louisiana, Mississippi, and Texas, but in fewer than 35 percent of reviews in Hawaii, Michigan, Minnesota, and Nevada. In fact, the range extended from 82 percent in Mississippi to 34 percent in Nevada. Others defended the Social Security Administration. A trade group for disability examiners "praised the new standards as necessary to regain control of the $27 billion program, which has exploded in growth in recent years." Representative McCrery explained, "If you look at the cessations, you will see that not one of them indicates that a child whose benefits were ceased has what any reasonable person would conclude would be severe disabilities," and the Social Security Administration "sent Congress a compendium of case studies designed to show that although many marginal cases" had been terminated, "the neediest children have not been cut off."[66]

Faced with criticism of his agency, Kenneth Apfel, Clinton's nominee to head the Social Security Administration, promised a quick, "top-to-bottom" review of cases where the agency had ended benefits. By November, Social Security officials had "found evidence that the Government improperly terminated disability benefits for many poor children, misinformed parents of their legal rights and actively discouraged some parents from appealing" its decisions. The agency planned to change its policy by helping parents find lawyers and sending notices to thousands of them to give them a new chance to appeal. Families that appealed stood a good chance of success: they had prevailed in 57 percent of the 10,508 cases already decided. The agency expected to review 60,000 cases: 45,000 where existing benefits had been ended and 15,000 where new benefits had been denied. "I believe these families deserve a second chance," said Apfel. In the end, Apfel predicted that 100,000 rather than 135,000 children would lose SSI cash assistance.[67]

Thirty-five thousand children is not a trivial number, and saving their benefits is not insignificant. But in the larger context it represents a small victory. Children's advocates found themselves forced to settle for limiting the damage to another piece of the nation's tattered safety net.

Uninsuring the Unemployed

In America, to be out of work is not necessarily to be considered unemployed, because "unemployment" requires a recent history of work at a regular job. The consequences of this distinction are immense. The officially unemployed qualify for benefits under a social insurance program; those simply out of work can call on only public assistance. With state General Assistance reduced or abolished, men and women out of work, unless injured or disabled, can turn only to the remaining public assistance programs: food stamps and Temporary Assistance for Needy Families (TANF)—the 1996 replacement for AFDC. However, to qualify for these stigmatized and means-tested programs, which were designed to serve only the very poor, families need to meet asset rules, which demand stripping off most possessions and savings acquired during years of employment. In any event, the combination of food stamps and AFDC or TANF will not boost them above the poverty line. Despite its limited duration (usually twenty-six weeks) and low benefits (about 36 percent of the average wage), unemployment insurance remains the public income support program of choice for men and women too young for Social Security. However, even the officially unemployed often find difficulty claiming unemployment insurance, which pays benefits only to a decreasing minority of them.[68]

As an entitlement contingent on work, not poverty, unemployment insurance in America has two purposes: the temporary and partial replacement of lost wages to involuntarily unemployed individuals with a prior attachment to the labor force, and the stabilization of the economy during recessions. In recent years, the definition of an acceptable work history has become narrower and harder to meet, and state governments have further qualified it by adding criteria based on behavior that also make unemployment insurance more difficult to keep. Nonetheless, it is one of America's largest and most important social insurance programs. In 1996, state unemployment insurance programs paid about $23 billion to 9 million people.[69]

In European countries, the idea of social obligation underpins unemployment insurance. In the United States a belief in individual responsibility shapes the design of the program. In Europe, when unemployment insurance expires, it is succeeded by unemployment assistance, a means-tested program with lower benefits but a guarantee of at least some income for an indefinite period; the United States has no counterpart to unemployment assistance. In the last analysis, American workers must look out for themselves—government's responsibility remains limited and partial. On every financial measure, the United States contributes less to unemployment insurance than do major western European countries. A fear of moral hazard has restrained American spending and influenced the design of unemployment insurance to avoid creating dependence.[70] In the world of unemployment insurance, the worker who leaves a job voluntarily, is fired for misconduct, or refuses an offer of work assumes the mantle worn by the malingerer in workers' compensation or the unmarried young mother in public assistance—the unworthy other against whom the deserving are defined.

The distinction that is made between unemployment and lack of a job seems less odd when we recall that unemployment as an idea is not much more than a century old. Unemployment assumed its modern meaning at the end of the nineteenth century with the maturation and expansion of industrial economies. By the early-twentieth century, social scientists and social insurance advocates had abandoned the old idea of personal responsibility for unemployment. Great Britain passed the first unemployment legislation in 1911 and, between 1919 and 1930, ten countries followed.[71]

In America, the idea of personal responsibility softened more slowly; resistance to government intrusion in the labor market remained stronger; and unions feared state intervention. Early hopes for addressing the problem of unemployment centered on labor exchanges—voluntary agencies for matching unemployed workers with jobs. In theory, unemployment reflected the lack of information—knowing where the jobs were—in a poorly integrated labor market. Britain implemented the first labor exchanges around 1910, and several American states and cities followed in the same years. None of them met their goals. Economists also tried to persuade businesses to stabilize their demands for labor by staggering production more evenly throughout the year and creating their own internal reserve funds that would tide workers over during slow times. Between 1916 and 1934, a small number of companies started such funds. In the peak year, 1931, they covered about 50,000 workers. All these funds collapsed during the Great Depression, which also proved that even the most well run firms could not stabilize production and employment during economic crises. Nor did the idea of compulsory public unemployment insurance receive much support from organized labor prior to the Great Depression. Samuel Gompers, president of the AFL, had opposed it consistently. He distrusted government and wanted to restrict its role to public works programs. Unions, he thought, should support their members in times of need. However, as the Great Depression emptied the few existing union unemployment funds, the AFL changed its position and at its 1932 convention overwhelmingly endorsed unemployment insurance. That same year Wisconsin passed the first state unemployment law. Only four other states followed before the first federal legislation in 1935.

Two approaches competed in the design of early unemployment programs. The "Wisconsin" approach, known as the American plan, favored prevention and advocated compulsory unemployment insurance paid by employers into individual reserve accounts for each firm. Because employers' tax rates would reflect claims against them, the plan would give them an incentive to prevent unemployment. The "Ohio plan"—sponsored by social insurance advocates from that state—doubted the capacity of individual firms to stabilize employment and objected to individual reserves. Insurance remained most effective, it argued, when it covered the largest number of people at risk. As a consequence, the Ohio plan advocated funds from all employers deposited in a common pool.

The Unemployment Insurance program established by the Economic Security Act of 1935 followed the American plan. It was a joint federal-state system with states creating their own unemployment insurance regulations, financed with taxes that reflected the success of individual employers in preventing unemployment. The federal architects of unemployment insurance, however, faced a constitutional issue. How could the federal government compel states to create unemployment insurance programs, and how could it influence their design? The Supreme Court had recently found the centerpiece of the early New Deal, the National Recovery Act, unconstitutional. There was every reason to worry that it might invalidate unemployment insurance as well. The answer was an elaborate tax scheme (the Federal Unemployment Tax Act of July 1937). The federal government taxed employers for unemployment insurance, and then returned all but a small portion of the tax to employers in states that created their own unemployment programs, as long as the programs met certain minimal standards. With the money it retained, the federal government paid for the administration of the program and kept money in reserve to bail out states that exhausted their trust funds. With this federal incentive, all states soon had in place unemployment insurance programs that survived constitutional challenge. Wisconsin paid the first unemployment insurance benefits in July 1936; more than twenty states paid benefits in January 1938; and by that year, all states collected unemployment insurance taxes.[72]

The first unemployment insurance did not cover all workers, however. It applied only to employers in industry and commerce who had eight or more workers for at least twenty weeks of the year. This restriction excluded most workers in small firms, agriculture, domestic service, the public and nonprofit sector, and seasonal workers, which is to say, among others, most African Americans and women.[73] The committee that had recommended the design of the unemployment insurance program expected the exclusions to be temporary and justified them on administrative grounds—the difficulty of assessing taxes on small employers. Undoubtedly, the political difficulty of passing a broader program played a role in its thinking as well. The original legislation built the framework of the unemployment system that persists to this day, even though the character of the labor market has changed radically. Unemployment insurance, as designed in the 1930s, rested on a model of an industrial economy dominated by full-time male workers who experienced relatively short spells of cyclical unemployment before they were rehired by their former employers. The model did not accurately reflect circumstances at the time of its design; it has since become even more of an anachronism.[74]

The limits of this early system became clear when, in the recession of 1973–74, states exhausted their trust funds, and the federal government had to lend them money at no interest. As state governments began to rebuild their funds, they faced three alternatives for avoiding a similar crisis in the future: raise taxes on employers, cut benefits, or reduce the number of people on unemployment insurance. Worried about the impact of taxes on their ability to compete for businesses with other states, they chose the low-tax route and began to tighten eligibility standards. The decline in the rate at which the unemployed successfully claimed insurance benefits accelerated in the 1980s with the actions of the Reagan administration. In 1981 federal legislation made it almost impossible for states to qualify for extended benefits, which provided funds for those unemployed longer than twenty-six weeks, and the federal government began to charge interest on loans to the states. As a result, far fewer of the unemployed received extended benefits during the recession of the early 1980s than in the mid-1970s. In this changed political and fiscal climate, state governments ratcheted up their eligibility standards even higher and found new ways to end the benefits of workers already receiving unemployment insurance. Then, in 1986, the Reagan administration made unemployment benefits taxable as income, which effectively lowered their value.[75]

Between 1981 and 1987, forty-four states raised work and earnings requirements for unemployment insurance and added criteria for disqualification. Three reasons disqualified a person from unemployment insurance: voluntarily quitting a job without good reason; refusing "suitable work"; and losing a job through misconduct. New rules narrowed the meaning of "involuntary" job loss, loosened criteria for serious misconduct, and expanded the definition of "suitable work." In 1993, the state of Washington, for instance, defined disqualifying misconduct loosely as "an employee's act or failure to act in willful disregard of the employer's interest, where the effect of the act or failure to act is to harm the employer's business." In 1995, Connecticut law clarified acceptable grounds for voluntarily leaving a job: "Good cause for voluntarily leaving employment will be restricted to that attributable to the employer; good cause does not include good personal cause." Many states disqualified workers who refused to take a drug or alcohol test, or who tested positive, regardless of any indication that they failed to do their work adequately. (Attorneys for employees responded by "fashioning new liability theories under state privacy law to prevent drug tests and the termination of employees who refuse to submit to tests or who flunk the tests.") All states disqualified workers who participated in labor disputes, although the definition of "labor dispute" remained murky. The key distinction separated strikes from lockouts; most states did not disqualify workers locked out by their employers. In practice, strikes and lockouts are often hard to distinguish from each other, and labor disputes remain an area full of conflict in unemployment law. States not only have found more reasons to disqualify workers from unemployment insurance; they have disqualified them for longer periods of time. Most states used to suspend benefits for a period of weeks; now most suspend them for the duration of the unemployment spell. In 1971, twenty-eight states suspended benefits for the entire duration of unemployment; in 1990, all fifty states had adopted the practice.[76] As in other parts of the welfare state, policy became more punitive—its instrument for shaping behavior the stick, not the carrot.

The percentage of the unemployed receiving benefits dropped from a peak of 75 percent in 1975 to a low of 32 percent in 1987 and 1988; in 1994, it was 37 percent. This is the great story in the recent history of unemployment insurance. Besides state policy, the shift of population to southern and mountain states, with historically lower unemployment/insurance ratios, and the drop in manufacturing employment also hastened the decline in the number of unemployed who received insurance during the 1980s. However, to leave the analysis with demographic and economic trends begs the question: why were ratios lower in Sunbelt regions and service industries? Part of the answer lies with the role of unions, which are still the most powerful voices supporting more liberal unemployment insurance policies. Declining union membership has weakened labor's resistance to the barriers to unemployment insurance erected by state governments. Only where unions retain political power have state legislatures even minimally resisted pressures from business interests to lower the number of workers awarded benefits.[77]

Unions, of course, are weakest in the southern and mountain states, and they remain stronger in manufacturing than in other kinds of work. Southern states, in fact, want to lower unemployment taxes even further. In 1997, seven of twelve southern states proposed cutting their unemployment taxes by hundreds of millions of dollars. With unemployment low, governors gambled that "the U.S. economy has moved beyond the boom-and-bust cycles of the past." In December 1995, North Carolina passed a one-year moratorium on taxes for businesses that had paid more money into the system than they had withdrawn from it. This exempted 80 percent of the state's businesses and reduced the trust fund from $1.7 billion to $1.37 billion. In North Carolina and Florida, funds at their current levels would last only nine months during a severe recession. Florida's governor nonetheless proposed a $151 million cut in the state's unemployment taxes, even though the state currently could support 458,000 fewer claimants than it had in the recession of 1990–91.[78]

Unemployment insurance also still disadvantages women, African Americans, and part-time and low-wage workers. In an age of increasing part-time and contingent work, its benefits assume steady, long-term attachment to the same job. While periods of unemployment are lengthening, its ordinary twenty-six-week maximum is designed to serve the short-term unemployed. With wages declining, it bases eligibility on money earned rather than simply time worked. It penalizes reentrants to the workforce, who disproportionately are women, and allows little flexibility for family-centered reasons for irregular work histories. For the same reasons, the labor market works against the interests of African Americans, points out political scientist Robert C. Lieberman. African Americans find themselves more often unemployed or employed irregularly. Although they need unemployment benefits more often than whites, their labor market history leaves them less eligible. They also often remain unemployed longer than whites, in danger of exhausting the benefits they receive.[79]

Unemployment insurance differs from other social insurance programs because the demand for benefits fluctuates unpredictably. Demand reflects economic cycles; it is highest during downturns, when government revenues are lowest. With the length of unemployment spells increasing, even in good economic times, workers often exhaust their twenty-six weeks of benefits. (Most, however, do not qualify for twenty-six weeks in the first place.) These unpredictable and fluctuating demands underscore the importance of reserve funds; they also show why states frequently cannot cope with unemployment without help from the federal government.

For many years, the federal government passed temporary benefit extensions; in 1970 it legislated a permanent program, triggered by the unemployment rate, that extends benefits for thirteen weeks past the usual twenty-six.[80] This "second tier" program, however, still does not adequately match demand during serious recessions. As a result, since 1972, the government periodically has passed emergency benefits. Despite the regular recurrence of emergencies and the arbitrary and inadequate twenty-six-week standard, neither federal nor state governments, primarily interested in lowering taxes, have shown much interest in revising benefits to match the labor market at the end of the twentieth century. State governments and businesses also assume that "under reasonably good economic conditions workers should be able to find reemployment reasonably quickly," and they worry about moral hazard—"that workers offered benefits of unlimited duration would extend their spells of unemployment to unacceptable lengths."[81]

As with workers' compensation, disability insurance, and welfare, in the 1990s quick reinsertion of workers into the labor force emerged as a key goal of unemployment policy. In addition to cash benefits, the unemployment insurance system is supposed to help workers find new jobs, and the historic responsibility for reemployment rests primarily with the Employment Service, which delivers services in over 1,700 local offices. For the most part, it has failed badly. One 1989 survey found that only 1.4 percent of persons about to exhaust their unemployment benefits had participated in on-the-job or occupational training programs. Only 6 percent had participated in job search assistance classes, job clubs, or job counseling, and the placement rate of the Employment Service declined significantly in the twenty years following the mid-1970s. With this record of failure in mind, the Employment Service experimented with new programs, some of which seemed marginally successful, but together touched only a very small fraction of the unemployed.[82]

In the 1990s, advocates of federal devolution mounted a campaign against the national government's role in unemployment insurance that echoed the call for devolution in public assistance. Mark Wilson of the conservative Heritage Foundation identified the problems with federal domination as "unnecessarily high payroll taxes, the buildup of billions of dollars in seldom-used federal trust funds, hundreds of millions of dollars in needless paperwork costs, a lack of flexibility for states to operate efficient programs designed to meet the needs of their own workers and employers, and an erosion of state program integrity that has led to longer spells of unemployment and lower tax collections."[83] (Critics exaggerated federal control because state laws vary greatly.)[84]

Although public statements by advocates of devolution stressed the inefficiencies and inequities in the current program, supporters of a strong federal role suspected them of using devolution to capture and gut the system. The AFL-CIO's specialist on unemployment insurance, Marc Baldwin, called the proposal for devolution a "Trojan Horse" hiding plans to lower taxes on employers by eroding unemployment benefits even further. The Advisory Council on Unemployment Insurance also championed a strong federal role in the administration of unemployment insurance and the stimulation of the labor market with macroeconomic policy, although it wanted to limit federal involvement to areas where "an essential national interest exists" and where state and national interests might diverge. Without federal oversight, the Advisory Council worried, the escalating competition among states to attract business would undermine the purpose of unemployment insurance by instituting excessively tight eligibility requirements and inadequate benefits. Stabilizing the economy during recessions also demanded a "unified national strategy."[85]

Employers found another way to keep their taxes from rising—and it required no help or permission from government. Increasingly, they outsourced the administration of unemployment insurance to firms that not only relieved them of paperwork but successfully fought the claims of their former employees. Their motive extended beyond efficiency; specialists helped them contest the claims to insurance filed by former workers. Because the insurance rates that firms pay reflect the number of claims filed against them, it is in their interest to prove that workers left of their own accord or were fired for good reason. The firms that specialize in the administration of unemployment insurance join the ranks of a new and growing American profession: specialists in the certification of the undeserving poor.

An article in the business journal *Solutions* explained the trend to outsourcing. Because "the laws are open to liberal interpretation, many people who are not actually eligible for benefits file unemployment claims and collect." (The article cited no evidence for wrongful collection of unemployment.) Many companies, it continued, had "abandoned aggressive policies of challenging unwarranted unemployment claims" because they had little success or because they found the rules and regulations too complex to master. To help companies "minimize their UC costs," some payroll service bureau companies took over the management of unemployment compensation for private firms. The Sports Authority, Inc., offers a good example of this trend. A fast-growing sports merchandise firm with eighty stores in twenty states, the Sports Authority faced a growing number of unemployment compensation claims in 1993. Its employee relations manager, Jim Scott, thought that half the claims paid in 1991 "should never have been allowed in the first place." The Sports Authority turned to Automatic Data Processing (ADP) of Roseland, New Jersey, which already handled its payroll and represented 350,000 corporate clients—and had an entire division devoted to handling and contesting unemployment claims. ADP saved the Sports Authority "potentially millions of dollars at a fraction of the cost they would have incurred doing it in house," and the savings were cumulative because a firm's state unemployment taxes are based on the number of claims filed against it. In 1993, 504 unemployment claims were filed against the Sports Authority. The company contested 394 of them and won in 266 cases, for a success rate of 68 percent. "There's no way we could have done that on our own," observed Scott.[86]

In Illinois, appeals of unemployment claims by companies increased 50 percent between 1986 and 1995, apparently also partly a result of companies' "increasing use of outside personnel firms to fight their unemployment insurance battles," according to a report in the *Chicago Sun-Times*. Employee advocates worried that firms like ADP threatened workers entitled to benefits. Tim Huizenga, who supervised employment law for the Legal Assistance Foundation of Chicago, claimed, "It's tougher to win cases today. Employers are doing a better job of knowing employment law. Claimants almost never do."[87]

Labor supporters offered alternative recommendations for improving the unemployment insurance program without radically redesigning it. These included basing eligibility on time worked, not wages; introducing a "movable base period" that would credit recent work history (something important for reentrants to the workforce and part-time workers); and fully funding trust funds in advance of recessions. These changes would extend benefits to some workers now excluded and assure the system's financial stability. But they would work at the margins. They would not reverse the decline in the number of workers receiving unemployment benefits, repeal the "durational" suspensions of benefits, or promote less-punitive definitions of misconduct.[88]

Incremental reforms could not dissolve the pervasive fear of moral hazard and the lingering blame that hovered around the unemployed or overcome the historic reluctance of American governments to interfere with labor markets. Even the gentlest reforms bumped up against an opposite trend promoted by state governments concerned with keeping and attracting businesses and by employers honing their edge for the new global economy through ever lower costs. In the late 1990s, it was by no means clear that even the modest and inadequate system that existed could be defended and preserved. The major hope for those who wanted to reverse the trends of the last two decades lay in the labor movement and the vigorous efforts of the AFL-CIO to protect and improve unemployment insurance. The odds were formidable. In the man or woman who left work "voluntarily," refused the offer of a suitable job, or violated a standard of misconduct—at a time when "voluntary," "suitable," and "misconduct" were redefined sometimes annually by state governments—unemployment insurance found its own version of the undeserving poor, and state policies treated them accordingly.

NEW MODELS FOR SOCIAL SECURITY

A rhetoric of crisis distorts the past and probable future of Social Security. Contrary to popular opinion, the program does not face an imminent catastrophe that demands fundamental structural change. Nor is the debate over Social Security's future strictly a technical matter. In truth, the technical details are mind-numbingly complex. Understanding the impact and predicting the future effects of a program that covers all older Americans demands equations that simultaneously model dozens of variables based on estimates in which no one has very much confidence. But the real question lurks beneath the technical details. What is clear is that older Americans can reasonably expect to receive benefits through a public program probably called Social Security into the indefinite future. The issue is the model that underlies it. A determined and powerful coalition wants to move Social Security away from social insurance and toward a market-based model. At stake is not just Social Security, but the design of all programs that protect Americans against risk and disaster. Just as workers' compensation and unemployment insurance are key sites of the new class war, Social Security is the site for the struggle over the core of the welfare state, and, even, the nature of political community in America.

The Origins of Social Security

Fear of an impoverished old age has haunted men and women for centuries. In nineteenth-century America, elderly people faced four alternatives: live on savings, move in with children, subsist on the crumbs of private and public charity, or keep on working—the alternative many chose before retirement became a common expectation. Very few working people—that is to say, the vast majority of the population—could save anything in their lifetimes, although a lucky minority had bought a house. Worthy widows could turn to a few benevolent societies for help, but not men, who, it was thought, should have looked out for themselves. Outdoor relief also kept some old people from starving or freezing. Many elderly women and fewer men lived with their children. Otherwise, the most realistic option remained the dreaded poorhouse. More than any other factor, the absence of a family distinguished the old people who ended their lives in institutions.[1]

From the late-nineteenth through the early-twentieth century, one large exception to this pattern brought economic security to some fortunate men and women. The federal government operated a massive pension program for Civil War veterans. Congress granted the first Civil War pensions to veterans in 1862; in 1890 it expanded pension eligibility to any veteran who had served at least ninety days, regardless of combat experience or injury, or to his dependents. The qualifying condition, instead, was the inability to perform manual labor, usually defined by age. A 1906 amendment labeled age sixty-two the commencement of "permanent specific disability"; other legislation increased benefits. As a result, at least one of every two elderly, native-born Northern white men and many of their widows received pensions from the federal government. Veterans' pensions, justified partly as a means of soaking up an excessive federal surplus, became the largest item in the federal budget after the national debt. Because of veterans' pensions, the United States spent more on its elderly than did Britain, which already had a national old-age pension scheme in place.[2]

Pressure for a new form of old-age assistance surfaced after about 1910, as Civil War veterans and their dependents began to die. Although veterans' pensions had supported a large fraction of the elderly, they gave noncontributory pensions a bad odor because they were mired in graft and corruption. Veterans' pensions, from one point of view, constituted a very large barrel of political pork. When social insurance advocates began to design new pensions at the state level and, in the 1930s, at the federal level, they used veterans' pensions as a precedent they did not want their new programs to emulate.[3]

The demise of Civil War pensions was not the only development that pushed support for the elderly to the top of the public policy agenda in the early-twentieth century. Another was the steep rise in the proportion of the population over the age of sixty, especially among immigrants, who, along with African Americans, had the fewest resources with which to support themselves in old age. At the same time, for various reasons the share of old people living with their children also began to decline steeply. The transformation of poorhouses into old-age homes represented one response to this demographic and family change; another was a burst of new private institutions for the aged. Of roughly twelve hundred charitable homes for the aged operating in 1939, nearly two-thirds had been founded between 1875 and 1919. By the 1920s, in fact, a revolt had begun against institutional care of the elderly.[4]

The elderly also found themselves increasingly unwanted in the workplace. Industrialists facing both harsh competitive pressures and organized labor's demands for a shorter workday turned to new technology to increase production. They believed older workers could not keep pace, and immigration from southern and eastern Europe brought a constant supply of younger workers. In these circumstances, public and private pensions developed in part as a response to the drive to push older employees out of the workforce.[5]

The Great Depression hit many of the elderly very hard. They faced even more difficulty than before finding work; their children struggled to support their own families; and state and local governments and private charities ran out of money for relief. The hardships of older Americans ran up and down the social ladder, hurting the middle class as well as the perennial poor. But older Americans constituted an articulate, impatient lobby with a great deal of political influence. Many of them supported the proposal of Dr. Francis Townsend for a universal federal government pension of $200 a month that would require recipients to stop working and spend the entire monthly stipend. The Townsend movement, which swept the country and found supporters in Congress, frightened the Roosevelt administration, which thought it would bankrupt the nation. Without an alternative federal policy, however, it seemed possible that the Townsend plan or some equally extreme scheme would find its way into law. Under pressure from the elderly, old-age policy moved near the top of the policy agenda.[6]

A new public assistance program for the elderly, Old Age Assistance, was, as we have seen, the immediate response; Social Security—a contributory, non-means-tested pension for the elderly—was the long-term solution. Social Security, along with other important programs, originated with the Economic Security Act of 1935. The Committee on Economic Security, charged with designing the legislation, proposed a partially self-funding system that resembled private insurance. FDR was adamant that the system, like private insurance, be wholly funded through contributions. "I believe that the funds necessary to provide this [old-age and unemployment] insurance," FDR advised, "should be raised by contribution rather than by an increase in general taxation." The CES staff knew that Social Security's reserve fund would run dry in a few decades, and they recommended eventually supplementing it with taxes, but FDR refused to take to Congress and the public a scheme that could not fund itself perpetually through advance contributions (collected as payroll taxes), and he forced the staff to close the projected gap between reserves and liabilities. This tension between a pay-as-you-go system, funded by the taxes of current workers, and one financed through reserves based on contributions accumulated in advance has persisted throughout Social Security's history and continues to haunt debates about its future.[7]

Although the original Social Security legislation scheduled its first payments for 1942—after the first insured cohort had worked long enough to earn benefits—for political reasons the date was pushed back to 1940. This is why the Economic Security Act also offered matching grants to the states for means-tested old age assistance to meet the immediate emergency. At first, Social Security paid very low benefits, and it excluded whole categories of workers, notably, those who worked in agriculture and as domestics, which meant many women and most African Americans, as well as employees in nonprofit, voluntary organizations. Because of constitutional concerns, always a sword that New Deal architects, with good reason, saw pointed at their innovations, it also excluded most public employees. (In 1937 the Supreme Court found Social Security constitutional.) Initially, Social Security covered only about 53 percent of the workforce. Until 1951, more people received Old Age Assistance than either Social Security or Aid to Dependent Children, the other public assistance program founded by the act.[8]

Social Security benefits expanded in 1939 with amendments that added insurance for survivors. The amendments also shifted it from a system financed primarily through reserves to one based on current contributions—"pay as you go." Worry about the size of Social Security's reserves partially motivated the change. With veterans' pensions still in mind, it was easy to imagine Social Security's reserves turning into a giant slush fund. (Social Security moved back to a funded system after 1983.) The 1939 amendments had another crucial consequence: they extended the social protections offered by Social Security from individual workers to families. With protection for nuclear two-parent families now the center of policy, Social Security, pointed out Michael K. Brown, "drew an arbitrary distinction between married and unmarried women, legitimate and illegitimate families," and it "reinforced the notion that women's place was in the home, not in the work force." Other expansions occurred with a major benefit increase and extension of coverage in 1950; the creation of disability insurance in 1956; and the indexing of benefits in 1972. In between these milestones, the program grew in incremental fashion, guided by the Social Security Board and friends in Congress.[9]

Social Security and Social Insurance

Expanded Social Security coverage and the benefit increases did not dislodge the social insurance principles on which the program rested. Historian Jerry Cates calls the principles—which also underlie unemployment insurance—the "conservative social insurance ideology": risk selection, contribution, and unequal benefits. Risk selection means that insurance covers only certain targeted contingencies (old age, unemployment, and disability, for instance), not the economic needs of all. Contribution is the principle that individuals should contribute to their own support. Unequal benefits implies that benefits should reflect wage-based contributions. Social Security, however, has two other goals, not part of the conservative social insurance model. One is modest redistribution: Social Security replaces a higher proportion of the income of lower-paid workers. The other is adequacy: benefits should keep people out of poverty.[10]

Social Security is a *social* insurance program, which is to say that it differs in important ways from both private insurance and public assistance. It is compulsory, sponsored and regulated by government, financed through earnings-based contributions, redistributive—and its benefits are prescribed by law. It exists as a separate account within the federal budget, and its financing represents projected revenues into the future (seventy-five years for Social Security).[11] Public assistance shares none of these features, except redistribution, which it accomplishes with tax money, however, not with earnings-based contributions. Private insurance, meanwhile, must earn a profit. Except for automobile insurance, it is not compulsory, and its benefits, which are not prescribed by law, are tied closely to premiums rated by the risk to the company, not by income, as with Social Security.

Social Security forms only one pillar, although it is the largest one, of America's retirement policy. The others are employer-sponsored pensions, private savings, and a safety-net program (SSI) for the most impoverished elderly, blind, and disabled persons. Nonetheless, Social Security provides all the retirement income for about half of elderly Americans. Three of ten elderly Americans derive 90 percent or more of their income from Social Security, and two of three receive more than half. Social Security is now nearly universal: 92 percent of persons age sixty-five or over receive benefits; another 3 percent will receive them when they retire.[12]

Without doubt, Social Security has reduced poverty among the elderly. In 1966, 28.5 percent of the elderly, a figure nearly three times the rate for the whole population, lived in poverty. In 1993 the proportion was 12.2 percent; in 1999, it was about 10.5 percent, a figure lower than for the population as a whole. Without Social Security, by one estimate, 56 percent of the elderly would have lived in poverty by 1992. Yet Social Security has not drained the public treasury. To the contrary, pointed out Robert Ball, a leading expert on Social Security, it "has been self-supporting; it has not added one cent to the deficit"; and it has passed all but a tiny percentage of the money it has collected on to beneficiaries: its administrative costs amount to less than 1 percent of its income. Social Security has never missed a payment. "No program has ever done more to prevent and alleviate poverty or to protect income against erosion," argued one group of advocates of maintaining Social Security's current structure. "None has done more to protect children against impoverishment when a wage-earning parent dies or becomes disabled. And no social program has ever enjoyed greater public support."[13]

With these great accomplishments to its credit, what is the problem with Social Security? For one, many analysts believe it will run out of money. The retirement of the baby-boom generation in the twenty-first century, they say, will deplete the Trust Fund and leave Social Security unable to pay its promised benefits unless the federal government raises taxes to unacceptable levels. Aside from its fiscal liabilities, Social Security's problems, to many of its critics, also arise from the principles on which it rests. They argue that it does not give contributors their money's worth. Its benefits are unfair and inadequate, and it reflects outmoded models that violate the logic and ignore the potential of the market. A separate line of complaint attacks Social Security for its historic and current gender bias.

There is no question that Social Security, like unemployment insurance, originally favored men. As feminist critics like historian Linda Gordon argue, both programs rested on conventional ideas of family and gender relations. In addition to excluding occupations that employed many women, they covered only wage labor, not the non-waged work of maintaining a family and household, and embedded into policy an invidious distinction between two-parent nuclear families and single individuals, and between "legitimate" and "illegitimate" children. Their eligibility requirements still favor long-term, full-time employment, which disadvantages women, who move in and out of paid work and who, more often than men, work part-time. The computation of benefits, moreover, works against the interest of widows in various ways. As a result, poverty rates remain unacceptably high among elderly women.[14]

The alternative view of Social Security's history, argued by historians

Edward Berkowitz and Blanche Coll, for instance, contends that the Economic Security Act, which represented the best political bargain possible at the time of its passage, launched the federal government on an unprecedented course toward improving the economic security of the great majority of Americans and set the foundation for the measures that in time lifted most of the elderly out of poverty and provided them with previously unaffordable health care. Social Security advanced in incremental fashion, gradually overcoming some, if not all, the gender biases built into its origins. Today, Social Security benefits more women than men and has transformed the experience of most elderly American women for the better. In 1992, 20.55 million women and 14.96 million men received Social Security, and 2.84 million women and 1.57 men benefited from Supplemental Security Income. In 1997, 58 percent of Social Security's retirement and survivor benefits flowed to women, who paid 38 percent of the program's payroll taxes. Without Social Security, 53 percent of women and 41 percent of men would have found themselves living in poverty. Social Security assists women in other ways, too. With benefits fully indexed, it protects against inflation, a feature important for women, who usually live longer than men. Social Security also affords special help to widows with a history of below-average earnings—often the result of working at low-paying jobs or taking time out to care for children or other family members—by replacing a higher proportion of lower wages. Despite lingering inequities that need correction, improvements in the last half century eliminated or reduced the worst gender biases, and Social Security now provides women with a degree of security and independence unparalleled in history.[15]

Social Security's financing is the most contentious issue. The program has never paid benefits with interest drawn from its Trust Fund. The contributions of the working generation have always supported the retired. This arrangement leaves Social Security dependent on the size of the active workforce and on the growth in its wages. Since 1983, contributions have built up an enormous surplus in the Trust Fund, which will start funding a portion of Social Security payments in the early twenty-first century until they are exhausted around 2037—unless new sources of funds are added or the official projections of economic growth prove overly pessimistic. Social Security Trust Fund moneys do not sit like cash in a bank teller's drawer. They are invested in federal government securities and counted as income in the federal budget. The Trust Fund holds government IOUs. "When the time comes to make good on them," pointed out political scientist Edward A. Patashnik, "the government must do what it ordinarily does to finance other programs—raise taxes, reduce other spending, or increase public borrowing." There is nothing sinister about this. The money could not just sit uninvested, and government bonds are the safest investment. "The government bonds that the trust funds hold have value as secure as the dollar bills that every citizen holds—and they are secure for the same reason," argued Max J. Skidmore, a political scientist and strong supporter of Social Security.[16]

Social Security's current fiscal troubles date from the early 1970s. Prior to the 1970s, Congress had legislated each increase in benefits, including two large ones in the 1960s. Because each benefit increase resulted from complicated negotiations, Social Security was mired in congressional politics. In 1972, when Congress decided to end the politicized practice of legislating ad hoc benefits by indexing future benefits to inflation, the timing could not have been worse. The economic downturn following the 1973 oil crisis fueled inflation, and prices rose faster than wages. As a result, the cost of Social Security increased more than the wage-based taxes that paid for it. Legislation in 1977 failed to correct the problem, partly because the economic situation continued to deteriorate. In 1980, for example, benefits automatically rose 14.3 percent, compared to a rise of only 9 percent for wages. The size of the Social Security Trust Fund dropped from its peak of $37.8 billion in 1973 to $19.7 billion in 1983. For a moment in 1983, it seemed possible that for the first time in its history, Social Security would not be able to send checks to beneficiaries.[17]

Alarmists prophesying bankruptcy exaggerated the threat to Social Security's future. They left the public "with a heavy and uncomfortable feeling in the pit of its stomach. Images of fiscal crisis, instability, unaffordability, waste, and political deadlock began to spoil the sense of security the system was intended to provide. Indeed, an air of gloom came to surround almost any mention of Social Security," said political scientists Theodore Marmor, Jerry Mashaw, and Philip Harvey.[18]

On December 16, 1981, President Reagan responded to the threatened bankruptcy of the Social Security Trust Fund by appointing a bipartisan commission chaired by Alan Greenspan. The National Commission on Social Security Reform decisively rejected proposals to restructure Social Security: "The members of the National Commission believe that the Congress, in its deliberations on financing proposals, should not alter the fundamental structure of the Social Security program or undermine its fundamental principles."[19] Instead, the commission proposed a series of measures, adopted by Congress with only minor modifications, that stabilized Social Security without altering its principles or structure. The congressional agreement made one-half of benefits taxable income, expanded coverage to new federal employees, delayed the cost-of-living adjustment for six months (a real reduction in benefits for current retirees because it lowered the base for the calculation of future benefits), raised the normal retirement age to sixty-seven, beginning in 2003, and increased payroll taxes slightly. As a result of the commission's recommendations, the Trust Fund for the first time found itself with a growing surplus, and Social Security moved "away from pay-as-you-go and more in the direction of partial reserve funding." According to the best estimates at the time, the trust fund would peak at $2.9 billion in 2018.[20]

The certainty with which the National Commission accepted the underlying principles and structure of Social Security would not last. Its achievement was to give the program a reprieve, not an enduring new foundation. In the late 1980s, critics discovered new crises, which they used to attack the premises on which Social Security rested. In only a little more than a decade, the discord among the members of another bipartisan national commission reflected the distance the debate over Social Security had traveled.

In 1988, when the editors of the *New York Times* warned of a coming "crisis of trillions . . . in slow motion," they echoed the language of crisis that by the late 1980s again enveloped Social Security and extended, internationally, to the whole welfare state. A 1995 report of the Bipartisan Commission on Entitlement and Tax Reform heightened this anxious atmosphere around Social Security. The commission predicted that, left unchecked, federal spending on entitlement programs would "lead to excessively high deficit and debt levels, unfairly burdening America's children and stifling standards of living for this and future generations of Americans." By 2030, the projected cost of Medicare, Medicaid, Social Security, and federal employee retirement programs alone would devour all federal tax revenues. Only immediate long-term planning—which would mean real benefit cuts—could solve the looming disaster, concluded a majority of the commissioners, even though they could not agree on a set of specific policies.[21]

The idea of crisis blended two issues—"generational equity" and finance. Critics argued that America spent too large a share of its resources on the elderly at the expense of the young, who would end up with a much lower rate of return on their Social Security contributions than had earlier generations, or even with no benefits at all. For the present and immediate future, therefore, the expense of Social Security meant the nation could not afford other needed programs for groups like children and working Americans. (In the late 1980s, critics blamed the Trust Fund surpluses, not the deficit, for robbing the young.) "Forty years from now," wrote Henry Fairlie in the *New Republic* in 1988, "if the present array of programs and benefits is maintained, almost two-thirds of the budget will go to supporting and cosseting the old. Something is wrong with a society that is willing to drain itself to foster such an unproductive section of its population, one that does not even promise (as children do) one day to be productive."[22]

In 1984, Senator David Durenberger (Republican, Minnesota) founded AGE, Americans for Generational Equity, an influential organization that escalated the conflict between young and old. Former commerce secretary and investment banker Peter Peterson, a prominent spokesman on public issues, and political analyst Neil Howe further fueled concerns about generational equity with their alarmist 1988 criticism of the welfare state in *On Borrowed Time: How the Growth of Entitlements Threatens America's Future.* In 1996, Peterson added to the sense of crisis around Social Security with *Will America Grow Up Before It Grows Old? How the Coming Social Security Crisis Threatens You, Your Family, and Your Country.* When AGE folded in the 1990s, Peterson helped found the Concord Coalition, which "reiterates the conservative position that government spending favors older, more affluent Americans at the expense of a younger generation that is already under financial distress." In his proposal to the Bipartisan Commission, of which he was a member, Peterson warned, "Our current entitlement system is based on a huge generational injustice. On average, today's retired Americans will receive windfalls that far exceed the value of their prior contributions. On average, Baby Boomers will be lucky to break even— and even that will only be possible by condemning still younger generations to unthinkable tax hikes."[23]

Why generational equity suddenly surfaced as a major public issue in the 1980s remains less than clear. Certainly falling wages, job insecurity, and the impact of reduced government spending set the scene for critics of the welfare state to play on anxieties about the future by creating a wedge between generations. "Greedy geezers" became the analogue of the undeserving poor in public assistance, the malingerer in workers' compensation, or the shirker in unemployment insurance. With the transmutation of a public policy issue into a crisis and the identification of an enemy, the master narrative of social policy reform began to unfold in Social Security.

Future generations, argue Social Security's critics, will receive less of their contributions back in benefits than earlier ones did. The main reason is that fewer active workers will have to support more retirees. In 1960, 5 workers were available to support each Social Security beneficiary; today the number is 3.3; by 2040, estimates put it at 2. While literally accurate, the implication that this decline portends economic crisis is misleading. For one thing, the ratio has declined more steeply in the past—from 8.6 in 1955 to 3.3 today—with no economic disaster. "To say that Social Security will go broke because of the declining number of workers per retiree," write economists Dean Baker and Mark Weisbrot in their important book *Social Security: The Phony Crisis*, "is like saying that we should be very hungry right now because the percentage of the workforce in agriculture has declined from 5.1 to 1.1 over the last 40 years. The problem is that simple dependency ratios do not take into account productivity increases."[24]

The generation that retired in the 1960s received a return of 12 percent on its contributions; those retiring in the 1980s received about 6 percent; future retirees will receive much less. Declining rates of return, however, are not "sinister," point out Baker and Weisbrot. To have avoided them, in 1935 Congress would have had to postpone initial Social Security payments for "generations until a collective pension fund could have been built up, with payments based on a return from these assets." With massive poverty among senior citizens, this was not an "attractive option" during the Great Depression. Instead, the nation chose "a pact between generations, and this accord has been maintained." Although some people may find it unfair that earlier generations received a higher return on contributions, how many of them "would trade their grandparents' return on Social Security taxes *and also* their lifetime income for their own?" To focus on falling rates of return, moreover, is to misunderstand the purpose of Social Security, which never was intended to give the highest possible return on investments. Rather, Social Security exists to insure an adequate living standard for elderly Americans. Its purpose, point out Henry Aaron and Robert Reischauer, policy experts with the Brookings Institution (Reischauer is former director of the Congressional Budget Office), is "*to assure basic income during retirement, disability, and survivorship.*" Social Security, former American Economics Association president Robert Eisner emphasized, "was not meant to be a get-rich scheme or a competitor to go-go investment funds. It is social insurance. It is meant to provide at least a minimum standard of support for all, regardless of initial station or life's vicissitudes."[25]

In other words, benefits reflect wages only to a point; they replace more of the wages of low-paid employees because the payback on the first few thousand dollars of average earnings is larger than on higher wages. For workers who earn 45 percent of the average earnings the replacement rate is 56 percent, compared to 25 percent for the maximum taxable earnings.[26] Moreover, we do not demand return on investment from property, casualty, term life, or automobile insurance. If we are lucky, we draw benefits that amount to much less than the premiums we have paid or, better, no benefits at all. We evaluate the insurance according to the apparent fairness of premiums and the promptness and adequacy of compensation when we experience an accident or disaster. Looked at as insurance, Social Security is a bargain. Recall that Social Security pays not only retirement benefits; 38 percent of Social Security benefits flow to disabled workers and their families and to survivors of workers who have died. "The disability insurance in Social Security," claimed Eisner, "has been estimated to be equivalent to a $207,000 policy in the private sector. And a comparable dependent and survivor policy for a twenty-seven year old, average-wage worker with two small children would cost $307,000." Because Social Security redistributes benefits across the life cycle as well as among individuals, it is better thought of as a program that smoothes income during an individual's life and during disability than as one that spends on the old at the expense of the young.[27] The question for the future is not primarily generational equity, but whether Social Security will be able to deliver adequate benefits at a reasonable cost.

The argument that spending on Social Security diverts money from other, more socially important purposes also rests on questionable premises. All the money for Social Security derives from special payroll taxes. (Some also comes from income taxes paid on Social Security benefits.) Whether taxpayers would accept higher levies for other purposes if they did not have to pay Social Security taxes remains unknowable. Certainly, the turn away from social spending in the 1980s and 1990s and local "tax revolts" cast doubt on the idea that a lower Social Security tax would have resulted in more money spent, for instance, on education.

The most effective misinformation campaign, however, has convinced many Americans that Social Security will go bankrupt in the twenty-first century. Although Social Security enjoys great public support, it does not enjoy great confidence. In 1997, when asked, "Do you believe you will receive any Social Security benefits after you reach retirement age?" 52 percent of respondents under age thirty-four answered no.[28] But the belief that Social Security will run out of money rests on an "intermediate" scenario of the Social Security trustees. The "low" forecast projects a much more frightening situation; the "high" forecast keeps Social Security solvent for at least another seventy-five years. Virtually every past forecast about Social Security's future has proved wrong because projections rest on predictions about mortality, retirement age, and economic growth, none of which is certain. The reason does not lie in any lack of intelligence among planners. Rather, it reflects the impossibility of predicting the variables that together compose the size of Social Security's obligations and the capacity of its resources. These variables include mortality, immigration, wages, inflation, productivity, GDP, and labor force participation, to name the most important. Eisner chided skeptics who predicted Social Security's disappearance: "Projections three decades and more ahead are, to use a gentle word, dubious. Even relatively short-term forecasts can be notoriously inaccurate." When he commented on the projected fifteen-year budget surplus on which President Bill Clinton's 1999 Social Security proposal was based, Federal Reserve Board chairman Alan Greenspan observed that "budget forecasts have been notoriously unreliable in the past and are likely to remain so in the future." Recall, for instance, that unanticipated inflation left Social Security without the income to pay for the expansion of benefits legislated in 1972 and nearly bankrupted the program.[29] The moral is clear: all predictions are soft. Inevitably, most will be wrong. The idea that one can legislate a permanent fix for Social Security based on a forecast of the future is an illusion.

What is known is that the number of working-age adults for each retired worker will probably continue to fall. Because Social Security pays benefits with the taxes collected from current workers, fewer workers will have to support more retirees. At the same time, people will live longer, though just how much longer remains uncertain, increasing the cost of supporting the elderly. The demographic situation, however, is not as certain as it seems. Adding the population under age twenty to the population over age sixty-five shows that in 1965 workers supported more "dependents" than they do now—or will do through the year 2075. It is also possible that fertility will not fall as far as predicted and that more immigrant workers will enter the labor force. Labor-force participation and productivity growth, moreover, could almost wipe out the shortfall anticipated from the decline in the ratio of workers to retirees. From 1940 to the mid-1990s, the proportion of men ages fifty to sixty-five in the paid labor force plummeted from 77 percent to 36 percent as more and more men chose early retirement. If men older than fifty-five could be persuaded to work at the same rate they did in 1970, they would add 2.9 million wage earners and increase the total projected labor force growth by one-fifth. As for productivity, in the twelve months that ended on June 30, 2000, it rose an astonishing 5.2 percent, which was the largest one-year increase since 1983. Unlike 1983, however, when the economy was emerging from recession, this productivity increase—part of a steady upward trend since 1996—followed a decade of economic growth and tight labor markets.[30]

An increase in wealth, productivity, or output per worker would also reduce the problem of supporting an aging population. A 1 percent increase in productivity per year, modest by historical standards, claimed Eisner, would raise output per worker more than 40 percent by

2030. "This would increase income per capita by more than a third, ample to improve vastly the lot of all—the elderly, the young, and those in their working prime." The Social Security trustees' intermediate estimate of the future rests on a conservative projection of economic growth lower than the rate enjoyed in the late 1990s. A rate that is not improbably higher, argued former labor secretary Robert Reich, would wipe out Social Security's projected deficit. The trustees project a growth in GDP of 1.4 percent for the next seventy-five years, compared to the 3.3 percent of the last seventy-five years. This estimate implies a per capita growth in GDP, pointed out economist Doug Henwood, of 1 percent per capita (1.4 percent minus 0.4 percent population growth). Compared to the 1.7 percent rate for western Europe this decade, widely considered "the stuff of crisis," this official projection for the United States appeared unrealistically pessimistic. Rerunning the projections with more reasonable although still conservative estimates, Henwood found that the crisis "largely or fully disappears. If the employment-population ratio for those aged 20–64 remains constant, a third of the projected shortfall for 2020 disappears; if it rises, because the share of women employed approaches that of men, then two-thirds of the projected shortfall disappears. . . . If the economy grows at a modest 2.5% rate, red ink will turn into black."[31]

Even with no changes, Social Security, by conservative estimates, would be able to meet 75 percent of its expenses from current income in 2037. The shortfall would be 25 percent or, looked at another way, 2.2 percent of payroll. Finding a way to fill this gap does not present an insurmountable problem or one that threatens major reductions in the benefits of future retirees. The components of sensible reform are well known; various plans combine them in different ways.[32] Social Security requires prompt adjustments; every year of delay increases the expense. But it is not in danger of collapse, and it is not a system in crisis.

Models of Social Security's Future

The most radical idea for recasting Social Security—promoted by the libertarian Cato Institute—proposed to redesign Social Security on a market model through privatization. In 1995, the media treated the Cato Institute's new report advocating the privatization of Social Security as a fringe proposal favoring an idea beyond the pale. Within less than two years, it had moved to the respectable center of the debate. "Two years ago," commented a *New York Times* reporter in April 1998, "Social Security privatization probably had no more support in Washington than the legalization of marijuana." Now it had "become a very real possibility."[33]

The Cato Institute called Social Security an "unfunded pay-as-you-go system, fundamentally flawed and analogous in design to illegal pyramid schemes." No reforms to its existing model could disguise the fact that Social Security provided "an increasingly bad deal for today's young workers." The Cato Institute wanted to abolish government paternalism, end labor conflict, and facilitate the hegemony of free market ideas. "The government paternalism inherent in any forced savings plan violates the foundational principle that your life belongs to you. . . . Once paternalism is accepted as a valid function of government, there is no limit to the actions that it may take in controlling our lives and restricting liberty." The Cato Institute thought Social Security should consist of individual retirement accounts funded with a combination of mandatory and voluntary contributions, instead of taxes paid to a government fund. The ensuing dissolution of paternalism by privatization would transform American workers into capitalists. The "social and political effect would be to sharply increase support for free market economic policies" and reduce the demand for "unnecessary tax burdens and regulations" that harm "business performance." Worker-capitalists also would be less likely to strike or place unreasonable demands on their employers. "General labor strife and antagonism between labor and management would be replaced by cooperation" because workers would not want to damage the prosperity of the firms in which their investments gave them a stake. The Cato Institute called for a program guided by "personal risk preference. . . . Individuals should be free to choose their own retirement age. Government intervention and regulation should be minimized."[34]

As proof that privatization could work, the Cato Institute pointed to Chile, where the government had implemented a plan with many (though not all) of the features it advocated. The Chilean model, however, was much less successful and attractive than its American champions admitted. Although returns to individual investments were at first high, in 1995 they were a negative 2.5 percent; administrative costs were enormous; and a large percentage of Chileans did not participate. An excellent analysis by Joseph Collins and John Lear concluded, "There is a very strong possibility that a very large percentage of Chileans (especially women and temporary seasonal workers) will either be excluded completely from the benefits of the private system or condemned to receive the government-subsidized minimum (and minimal) retirement benefits."[35]

The economic crisis that spread from Asia to Latin America in the summer of 1998 qualified enthusiasm for Chile's privatized pension plan even further, reported the *New York Times*. Between August 1997 and August 1998, the value of Chile's stock market dropped 25 percent, frightening pensioners and workers. "Simply put, privatization has proven no panacea for the insecurities people feel when thinking about retirement." As the Chilean pension funds dumped Chilean stocks to stem their losses, they "effectively helped drive down the same stock market they once drove up. And the market swings have prompted some workers to put off retirement."[36]

Cato Institute spokesmen Peter J. Ferrara and Michael Tanner pointed not only to Chile but to other nations in Europe and Latin America that have adopted one or another version of privatization. The trend, they argue, clearly "is away from pay-as-you-go systems toward systems based on individual accounts and private investments. . . . The Chilean model is being increasingly copied by other countries—from Latin America to Eastern Europe." Those countries' experience "provides overwhelming evidence that privatizing Social Security is both desirable and possible." They said that in Britain, which introduced a "two-tier" pension system, a basic grant of roughly $100 a week paid to all retirees coupled with private or company-sponsored individual investment accounts offers one model of success. As in Chile, however, events qualified this rosy portrait. In the early 1990s, "high pressure sales of individual pensions programs and other financial services" led to "heavy losses for many people and cast a shadow over the entire process," pointed out a *New York Times* article. "In Great Britain," reported Max J. Skidmore, "huge numbers of citizens who opted into a privatized system have been shattered financially." Rather than acting as a model of success, the British experience raised "warning flags for the United States about the perils of transforming guaranteed government pension programs into investment-oriented plans that force people to make their own financial decisions."[37]

The libertarian advocacy of privatization exaggerated the fiscal crisis facing Social Security, misrepresented the program's purpose, deployed false analogies to call its integrity into question, and distorted and underestimated its value. As a practical plan, it was riddled with flaws. The transition costs—the need to pay for existing obligations during the switch to the new system—would prove enormous. Variable investment returns would mean inadequate pensions for some retirees and large variations in pensions among former workers whose contributions had been similar. Also, inflation could eat away at the pensions of long-lived retirees, and, argue Aaron and Reischauer, "political support for the crucial antipoverty role that Social Security has played for over a half-century could atrophy."

Aaron and Reischauer raise two other problems with privatization: "administrative costs and individual ignorance about financial markets." As a national system, Social Security enjoys huge economies of scale that private plans could not match. Individual accounts would result in higher costs that would eat away at investment results. The great winner in a system of privatized individual accounts would be the financial services industry, whose annual revenue from managing the funds, even with an average cost of 1 percent, could easily reach $14 billion in ten years. (The potential windfall from privatization undoubtedly constitutes the reason why financial interests have spent generously to advance its political fortunes.) Aaron and Reischauer also fear that individuals would begin to consider their funds personal property and bring political pressure on government to allow early withdrawals, as happened with IRAs. In addition, both ends of the process—investment decisions and choices about how to annuitize or withdraw funds—would confront individuals with complex alternatives and risks they "are poorly equipped to handle."[38]

As the debate over privatization and other alternatives for reform heightened in the 1990s, a federal government Advisory Council on Social Security explored the alternatives. Unlike the 1983 commission on Social Security, the Advisory Council could not reach consensus. Disagreements among its members reflected the new debate about the principles and structure of Social Security that had surfaced in the last decade. Instead of one set of recommendations, the council presented three. One defended the existing structure of Social Security, which it proposed to shore up with moderate reforms. A second proposed to move toward a privatization of the system with individual accounts. A third suggested splitting the difference but managed to satisfy neither camp. Because Social Security remains a defined-benefit program at a time of rapid movement toward defined-contribution pensions, the debate among Advisory Council members over its future echoed the controversies surrounding the end of paternalism in the private welfare state. Not surprisingly, the three labor union representatives on the Advisory Council favored retaining the current defined-benefit approach, while representatives of business and industry advocated moving toward defined contributions, which meant taking a major step toward the privatization of Social Security.

The Advisory Council did agree on one controversial issue: the dangers of means testing. Some proponents of Social Security reform, like Peter Peterson, advocated the progressive elimination of benefits for wealthier individuals. The "affluence test" would target public dollars where they were most needed and would save an enormous amount of money, claimed Peterson. The Advisory Council disagreed. The absence of a means test encouraged savings and made "it feasible for employers and employees to establish supplementary pension plans." A means test, moreover, "would send the wrong signal to young people and wage earners generally." It would tell them that if they saved and built up enough income to supplement Social Security, they would face a penalty by having their Social Security benefits reduced. "This message is both unfair to those who work and save and creates the wrong incentives."[39]

Government reports usually mask disagreements among members with the language of consensus and technical details. The Advisory Council report was unusual not only because it listed three options for policy, but, as well, for the passion that occasionally seeped through the recommendations of each of the three camps. Proponents of the "maintain benefits" plan wrapped their proposal in praise of Social Security's historic accomplishments. Had the United States arrived at a point when its retirement system was "failing" and required "fundamental change? We say no. We believe that the system has been and continues to be a major success, and that with relatively minor modifications it can provide a sound basis for planning for the future." They worried that public discussion of the future of Social Security reflected "misinformation about its financing. *Social Security is not facing a crisis.*" The other plans, they feared, "would undermine rather than strengthen Social Security's unique role in providing multi-generational family protection." "Putting it bluntly," they argued, "this Advisory Council report does not offer three acceptable plans from which to choose. We believe that two of the plans are inherently and fundamentally flawed. . . . In abandoning Social Security, we would be shifting from a time-tested national strategy of protecting against individual risk to a scheme involving increased exposure to risk. . . . Above all, we would be substituting a plan based on an extraordinarily high degree of go-it-alone individualism for our most successful expression of community. . . . It undermines the commitment to each other that is at the heart of the Social Security program."[40]

Very different priorities underpinned the personal security account model, with its emphasis on individual accounts. Proponents of the PSA plan responded not only to the fiscal imbalance of Social Security, "the growing lack of confidence about the future of Social Security, but also to the growing concerns about the value of Social Security to younger workers; the increasing interest in private alternatives to Social Security, including reforms being undertaken in many countries throughout the world, plus our own sense of the growing interest in these approaches at home; and, more generally, the growing concerns about the impact of Social Security on the federal budget." They predicted that "reform would turn the vast majority of Social Security taxpayers into investors and, in the next decade alone, would release literally hundreds of billions of dollars of payroll taxes for investment in the private sector" while the "tier-one benefit"—a guaranteed minimum benefit—"would serve as a back stop to the PSA accumulations." Undeniably, there would be risk, but in the long run workers would learn to make intelligent investment decisions and would fare better under their system than under either of the others. They objected to characterizations of their plan as "radical." Every aspect of the current Social Security system, they pointed out, had been considered radical at one time or another. Personal security accounts already were in place in countries around the world. Progress on reform required moving beyond "politically charged words," and they did "not believe that decrying the plans as 'radical' or as 'fundamentally changing the nature of social security' " promoted "an open or informative exchange of ideas."[41]

Proponents of individual accounts, however, the remaining alternative, recognized that the other plans represented "two starkly different visions for Social Security" and found both of them inadequate. They worried (as did PSA advocates) about the disruptive impact and politics of a massive injection of government capital into the market to increase returns on the Trust Fund, as the "maintain benefits" scheme recommended. They predicted that other plans would not adequately promote national savings, and they disliked the high transition costs of the personal security accounts. Their plan promised to preserve adequate basic benefits, keep administrative costs low, and minimize risk by preventing unwise investment decisions by workers and the newly retired. "The IA plan," they claimed, "seems clearly the most sensible way of compromising among the many retirement saving objectives now facing the nation."[42]

These differences among options should not mask some reasonable conclusions about Social Security. Social Security was solvent for more than thirty years; even with no change, Social Security would be able to pay benefits indefinitely at a minimum of 75 percent of the current level; and relatively small changes could assure continued benefits at close to the same level and with only a minor additional cost for another three-quarters of a century. There was no impending catastrophe that demanded a radical change of course. There was, however, as the debate within the Advisory Council made clear, a sharp disagreement about whether the social insurance model on which Social Security was based should be jettisoned for one designed to imitate the private market.

Crisis Resolved: The Magical Surplus

Social Security confronted President Bill Clinton, as it had Presidents Ronald Reagan and George Bush, with a hot political problem. Clinton wanted to secure the program's future at a reasonable cost. But there were minefields along every path. Organized labor opposed raising the retirement age. Banking interests wanted to move toward privatization. Organizations representing the elderly resisted reductions in benefits. Nobody wanted to raise taxes. Yet fear about Social Security's future remained widespread, especially among young workers. A consensus among members of the Advisory Council could have helped Clinton resolve the dilemma, just as the agreement within the 1983 commission had given Reagan a clear mandate for action. But Clinton was not so lucky. Still in search of broad agreement, Clinton asked two organizations with widely differing views on social insurance programs—the Concord Coalition and the American Association of Retired Persons—to organize forums around the country, at which he dutifully listened to the anxieties of citizens and to advocates of alternative positions, with which he was undoubtedly already familiar.[43]

Just when it seemed as though Social Security reform had reached a political impasse, the economy came to Clinton's rescue. Economic recovery turned the deficit into a surplus—a gigantic one projected far into the future. It even promised to wipe out the national debt. The first inkling of good news came when new budget projections pushed back from 2032 to 2037 the date at which the Trust Fund under current projections no longer would be able to pay for all the program's obligations. But the news just got better and better. No longer was the question whether the nation could afford Social Security. Suddenly it was awash in money. The question became how to spend it wisely and in a way that secured the future of Social Security and Medicare.[44]

By January 1999 in his State of the Union message Clinton could offer a plan that used the surplus to secure Social Security's future painlessly. He proposed to put $2.7 trillion, or 62 percent, of the projected $4.4 trillion surplus over the next fifteen years into Social Security's cash reserves. Two trillion dollars would be used to reduce the national debt to its lowest level as a percentage of GDP since 1917. The remaining $700 billion would flow into the stock market. A new board, insulated from politics, would handle investment decisions. Clinton also proposed to allow workers ages sixty-five to sixty-nine to continue to work while they received full benefits, and he promised to improve benefits for widows. On the sticky question of raising the retirement age, he punted. He left the decision, along with other structural changes (such as adjusting the cost-of-living index, raising the wage base for payroll taxes, including new state and local employees in Social Security, and extending the period used to calculate average earnings) to be decided later. Clinton met the advocates of privatization partway with a plan to use $500 billion from the surplus to create "universal savings accounts." The federal government would give low- and middle-income Americans the initial cash to set up their own accounts in financial markets; it then would match their contributions on a sliding scale based on income.[45]

His plan, Clinton believed, offered great advantages. The money invested in the stock market would earn substantially more than the return on government bonds. The added return, the White House said, based on historic averages, would extend the life of the Trust Fund by five years while paying off $2 trillion in public debt during the next fifteen years. By crediting the interest on the $2 trillion in additional bonds to the Social Security Trust Fund, the Treasury Department would increase the money available to pay retirement benefits. This, in turn, "should strengthen the economy by lowering interest rates and opening the way for more productive private investments," summarized a *New York Times* article. "A stronger economy would increase the number of people working and the size of their paychecks and make it less painful for workers to pay the taxes needed to support Social Security."[46]

The politics of Clinton's plan proved hard to label. One *New York Times* reporter, Richard W. Stevenson, placed it on the political left, "an opening move not from the center, as many Republicans had hoped, but from the left. The Clinton plan set out . . . precisely what liberal Democrats have been advocating." On the other hand, another *Times* reporter, Michael M. Weinstein, found Clinton once again stealing Republicans' thunder: "President Clinton's proposal to shore up the financially shaky Social Security system leans heavily on a leading Republican plan" by investing some of the surplus in the stock market. Neither Republicans nor Democrats wanted to raise taxes or cut retirement benefits or to question whether the projected budget surplus extending so far beyond the horizon was a realistic expectation or the pot of gold at the end of the rainbow. But L. Randall Wray, senior scholar at the Jerome Levy Economics Institute, warned, "Our nation has never—let me repeat, *never*—run budget surplus for such a period. Indeed, every time we had significant surpluses, the economy quickly collapsed into a depression that created budget deficits. Our federal government *will not* run surpluses for the next 25 years or the next 15 years."[47]

Republicans, meanwhile, agreed that the surplus should be locked away to guarantee the future of Social Security, except they wanted more of it to go for a massive tax cut. They also liked the idea of paying down the national debt. Their objections to Clinton's plan centered on the government's investment in the stock market. They did not believe the government capable of making independent investment decisions unbiased by politics. With administration estimates that the government would own 4 or 5 percent of the value of the stock market, they worried about the distorting influence of massive amounts of government money on both the market and individual firms. "I do not believe that it is politically feasible to insulate such huge funds from government direction," warned Federal Reserve Board chairman Alan Greenspan. Representative Jim Kolbe of Arizona tarred Clinton's plan with the familiar red brush. "It amounts to nationalization of American industry." Clinton's supporters pointed to the successful investment practices of state and municipal governments and of the Federal Retirement Thrift Investment Board, which Congress created in 1986 to invest pension money for federal employees. Aaron and Reischauer proposed "a board that would turn the Social Security money over to private managers of widely diversified mutual funds. No government official would have any say over actual purchase decisions."[48]

Clinton had put the Republicans in a tough position. He had stopped short of accepting individual retirement accounts privately invested as part of Social Security. But he had offered a plan with components Republicans favored: no new taxes, debt reduction, and investment in the stock market. While he had excluded the individual investment of Social Security's own funds, he had proposed a new program of government supports for individual retirement accounts. Republicans generally favored allowing workers ages sixty-five to sixty-nine to keep their Social Security benefits, and no one publicly could oppose increasing benefits for widows, especially when it involved no redistribution or new taxes. Republicans could dig in their heels and defeat Clinton's plan because of its reliance on government investment in the stock market. But the strategy carried a high potential political price: the consequences of obstructing a reasonable and painless reform of America's premier domestic program.

Republicans needed an alternate plan, and they floundered looking for one. Their first proposals stressed the need to safeguard the surplus even more than Clinton had proposed by walling off Social Security— that is, by removing it from the federal budget. In May 1999, two Republican leaders, Representatives Bill Archer of Texas, chairman of the House Ways and Means Committee, and E. Clay Shaw, Jr., of Florida, chairman of the Social Security Subcommittee, left members of their own party "flabbergasted" with a proposal that "would strictly limit private investments, pay the same benefits to retirees no matter where they invested their money and leave nothing at retirees' death that could be willed to the next generation." The Archer-Shaw proposal earned only scorn from conservatives at the Heritage Foundation and Cato Institute, as well as from Congress. Conservative Ohio congressman John Kasich said, "I could never support anything like that."[49] Without a plan of their own, Republicans ceded the Social Security issue to the president.

Meanwhile, in a *New York Times* op-ed article, former Congressional Budget Office director Robert Reischauer outlined recommendations for assuring Social Security's solvency for the next seventy-five years that were endorsed by leading Social Security experts Henry J. Aaron, Robert M. Ball, Peter Diamond, Robert Greenstein, and Alicia H. Munnell. A moderate approach, the experts' recommendations could serve as the basis of a bipartisan compromise, if Republicans chose not to resist a reform initiated by the president they had impeached. The Social Security experts endorsed Clinton's proposal to allocate most of the projected surplus to Social Security reserves. In addition, they recommended raising the Social Security tax ceiling to include 90 percent of total earnings, rather than the current 86 percent. They also advocated investing a portion of the reserves in bonds issued by federal agencies—an action permitted under current law. Guaranteed by the federal government and completely safe, the bonds would pay higher interest than the Treasury securities that comprised the Trust Fund's current portfolio. They suggested that the Trust Fund also invest some of its reserves in high-grade corporate bonds.

The experts suggested a middle ground—a way to increase returns to the reserves without incurring the political risks of investing them in securities. They did not mention Clinton's proposal for individual retirement accounts outside the Social Security program. They also encouraged Congress to explore a number of other, and more controversial, reforms, including raising the age at which full benefits are paid and adjusting the calculation of cost-of-living increases. But, they urged, "the President and Congress should not permit possible disagreements about these additional reforms to stand in the way of the immediate priority: to close completely the projected long-term deficit in Social Security." Anxious to break the deadlock, Clinton backed away from his proposal to invest some of the Trust Fund in the stock market.[50] With this reasonable plan on the table, Republicans had to decide whether to hand the Democrats a victory or an election-year issue.

Despite the legislative impasse, in April 2000 Congress did reach agreement on one hugely popular Social Security reform: it lifted the limitation on earnings that applied to Social Security recipients under the age of seventy. As a result, they now could earn any amount of money without having their benefits reduced. (Under earlier rules, Social Security benefits fell steeply when a recipient earned more than $17,000 a year.) This was about as far as most observers expected Congress to take the explosive Social Security issue in an election year. The great budget surplus had arrived just in time to allow Clinton and moderate reformers to elide most of the disagreement over social philosophy and to stave off extreme privatization.[51]

To everyone's surprise, Governor George W. Bush, the Republican presidential nominee, reinjected the issue of Social Security into the presidential campaign. He probably touched this "third rail" of American politics to attract younger voters worried that Social Security would be bankrupt by the time they retired and attracted by the prospect of high returns in the stock market. Bush proposed a variant of "privatization"—allowing a portion of current payroll taxes to be invested in individual retirement accounts. Although he did not give the details of his plan, most observers expected the amount to be about 2 percent, or roughly one-sixth of the current tax. Bush also promised not to raise Social Security taxes, lower benefits for anyone nearing retirement, or invest the Trust Fund money in the stock market. When a team of leading experts analyzed Bush's plan, they concluded that younger workers would lose a large amount of benefits: for single wage earners age thirty in 2002, total retirement benefits would be, conservatively, 20 percent lower than under current law, while risks would be greater.[52]

Vice President Al Gore, the Democratic presidential nominee, not only criticized Bush's proposal; he offered his own alternative—a complex plan to use the portion of the budget surplus derived from excess Social Security payroll revenues to pay off the $3.5 billion national debt held by the public and to use the savings—the amount that would have been spent on interest—to pay for future benefits. Gore responded to the interest in personally controlled investments by picking up President Clinton's proposal for new individual accounts outside the Social Security system in which the government would match contributions from lower- and middle-income workers. Gore also proposed improved benefits for parents who left the workforce to raise their children and for widows. Gore's plan would extend the solvency of Social Security until at least 2050 with no benefit cuts. But it would obligate the government to pay a portion of future benefits out of general revenue, a return to the pay-as-you-go system that had been replaced in the 1980s.[53]

Whatever the merits of his plan, Bush had forced a crucial issue of principle to the forefront of the campaign. His debate with Gore revived one of the key questions about the future of the American welfare state:

individual risk versus collective risk and responsibility.[54] Subsumed under the bland and positive concept of "choice" or the more controversial label "privatization," the resolution of the question—perhaps to be postponed once again with no clear mandate emerging from the 2000 presidential and congressional election—promised to define not only the way the American welfare state delivered future benefits, but its core principles as well.

THE ASSIMILATION OF HEALTH
CARE TO THE MARKET

Worries about costs drove debates over the future of health care just as they did Social Security. But health care carried other burdens beyond a potentially bankrupted trust fund: the elderly who needed expensive long-term care in nursing homes and prescription drugs; the indigent and working poor unable to afford insurance; the high price of new technology; and a payment system that fueled inflation. Access was the other great issue: the number of Americans without health insurance not only remained stubbornly high; it continued to rise, and America remained the only developed country that did not consider health care a right offered to all citizens through some form of national insurance. In the growing ranks of the uninsured, America reaped the consequences of linking its welfare state to employment.

The earliest American proposals for health insurance focused on the link between sickness and poverty. When the agents employed by Charity Organization Societies set out to investigate applicants for relief in the latter decades of the nineteenth century, they found illness implicated over and over again in destitution. In cities, poor families often found free medical care in dispensaries or hospitals supported by private and public charity (the quality of care was another matter), but they lost the income from sick or injured family wage earners. Whether from accidents at work, poor sanitation, or inadequate diets, illness cut off the limited incomes of working poor families and undermined their fragile independence. This link between poverty and sickness is the reason why early American health insurance proposals focused on assuring some income during periods of illness, what today we would call disability insurance.[1]

Health insurance held an important place in the reforms championed by social insurance advocates in the late-nineteenth and early-twentieth centuries. In the years before World War I, even the medical profession showed sympathy toward compulsory health insurance. However, despite the support of some progressive business leaders, business interests, buttressed by the insurance industry, remained generally hostile. To the great disappointment of social insurance advocates, labor, led by Samuel Gompers, also opposed compulsory public insurance, because it feared it would undermine union autonomy.[2]

World War I and the Russian Revolution reversed the fortunes of the nascent compulsory health insurance movement. Opponents emphasized the "foreign" associations of health insurance, while business and insurance interests escalated their opposition. Crucial to defeat, however, was the new hostility of the American Medical Association. By the 1920s, advances in science had increased medicine's ability to treat diseases, while changes in the organization of health care had transformed hospitals from last resorts of the poor to institutions that also routinely served the middle classes. The organized medical profession's enhanced stature increased its ability to influence legislation and public opinion, and through the AMA it flexed its new muscles by announcing its implacable opposition to health insurance. Looking to the experience of their colleagues in Britain, physicians had come to fear a loss of both autonomy and income. Combined with the power of business interests, they overwhelmed social insurance promoters, despite new support from labor. Supporters of health insurance, organized into the privately funded Committee on the Costs of Medical Care, also undermined their own goals because they could not agree on a single set of recommendations.

In the 1930s, the architects of the New Deal knew to treat health insurance gingerly. During the Great Depression, the cost of health care as well as the loss of income from illness became a major issue; money to pay doctors and hospitals dried up; and charities could not meet the massive needs for free care. As a result, federal relief programs for the first time paid some of the medical costs of the indigent, and hospitals turned to public authorities to subsidize treatment of patients on relief—a practice that has remained a part of medical financing in one form or another to the present. Although the Committee on Economic Security appointed by President Roosevelt supported health insurance, political realities forced it to treat the issue only in general terms. FDR asked the CES for a separate report on health insurance, which he did not publish because he feared that it would doom his plans for Social Security legislation.

Every president from FDR to Jimmy Carter wanted to institute or extend health insurance. (Before his death, FDR indicated that he would press for health insurance when the war ended.) In Congress, Senator Robert Wagner from New York proved the most constant champion of insurance. With colleagues, he repeatedly and unsuccessfully introduced the Wagner-Murray-Dingell Bill that at least kept the issue alive for debate. Health insurance received strong support from President Harry Truman, who, nonetheless, proved unable to translate his advocacy into legislation (although he did live to attend the signing of the Medicare bill in 1965). With the advent of the cold war in the 1940s, opponents tarred health insurance with the label of socialized medicine, which further weakened its legitimacy, and business and insurance interests kept up their attack on the issue.

Despite the opposition's success in blocking a public and compulsory plan, forms of health insurance with enduring significance developed in the 1930s and 1940s. In 1929, Baylor University Hospital in Dallas pioneered the first form of prepaid hospital insurance. With the support of the American Hospital Association, Blue Cross—private, nonprofit plans approved and regulated by state governments—spread across the country.[3] The American Medical Association, although opposed at first, found the plan could work to its advantage and soon approved physician-controlled insurance plans known as Blue Shield. In practice, despite differences of ideology and control, Blue Cross and Blue Shield worked together and often shared a common administration. Private insurance carriers also developed group health plans that they sold to employers.

Although it failed to achieve national health insurance, the federal government spent heavily on medical research and education and on the infrastructure of health care by funding the National Institute of Health, the National Science Foundation, and Public Health Service research grants and training fellowships. In addition, the Hill-Burton Act of 1946 paid for the construction of hospitals and medical equipment throughout the nation, primarily in rural areas and smaller towns.[4] As a result of the work of congressional liberals, hospitals that received Hill-Burton funds were required to offer "a reasonable volume of hospital services to persons unable to pay." For the next two decades, however, "reasonable volume" went undefined by regulations, and many hospitals in the South refused to treat blacks until the Supreme Court ruled the practice unconstitutional in 1963.

By the 1950s, America had a nascent system of health insurance that—uniquely among industrialized nations—tied benefits to employment. Insurance covered individuals with jobs that offered benefits or who could afford to pay the premiums on their own. Among Blue Cross's early subscribers, lower-income families remained very underrepresented. By default, public policy had rejected the idea of medical care as a right of citizenship. Instead, it remained a consequence of income and class. Unless they were married to an insured worker, women were far more often uninsured than men. As in other areas of the welfare state, agricultural and household workers were generally left out, as were the elderly who did not have a pension that included health benefits. Nonetheless, progress under private insurance had been swift and stunning. Between 1940 and 1966, the share of the population covered by hospital insurance had grown from 9 percent to 81 percent.[5]

Despite hostility to universal health care, support developed for subsidizing the medical care of very poor people. Congress responded, first, to the medical plight of the elderly poor in 1960 with the Kerr-Mills Bill, which gave matching grants to states for the medical care of the medically indigent. (The program served relatively few people beyond the states of California, New York, and Pennsylvania.) Although President John Kennedy and, after his assassination, President Lyndon Johnson wanted to move forward with a national health insurance plan, Republicans and southern conservatives in Congress had enough votes to block legislation. The situation changed with the massive Democratic victory in 1964 and was reinforced by the conversion of the powerful House Ways and Means Committee chairman, Wilbur Mills, from opponent to supporter of health insurance legislation.[6]

The result, approved by Congress in 1965, was Medicare and Medicaid. These new programs did not give America comprehensive national health insurance. Instead, they enshrined the distinction between social insurance and public assistance into medicine, where it remains firmly anchored. Medicare provided benefits only for individuals age sixty-five and over. Part A covered hospital costs; Part B paid doctor bills. Only Part A, financed primarily with payroll taxes paid to the Federal Hospital Insurance Trust Fund, was compulsory; Part B was funded with general revenues and individual premiums. Premiums, which did not vary with income, were a much greater burden for the low-income elderly than for the affluent. Neither Parts A nor B covered all costs, and many people purchased additional private and often expensive "medigap" insurance. Since the late 1980s, Medicaid has subsidized the expenses of those too poor to afford medigap coverage by paying Medicare deductibles and Part B premiums. Physicians and hospitals did very well under Medicare. To prevent their opposition, the program reimbursed hospitals for reasonable costs and physicians for prevailing charges.[7] This open-ended funding arrangement built into Medicare unleashed the inflation of medical costs, which began to soar.

In contrast to Medicare, Medicaid, an extension of Kerr-Mills, served the indigent, primarily those on federal public assistance. Like AFDC, it was a joint federal-state program financed with matching grants. States retained broad authority to determine eligibility and benefits, which varied greatly, required a means test, and were less generous than those offered under Medicare. Physicians and hospitals were also paid much less by the program.[8]

Medicare and Medicaid left the nation with an uncoordinated health care system divided between private insurance for the employed and well off, social insurance for the elderly, and public charity for the poor. The system invited cost inflation while it excluded millions of Americans. It is the most expensive in the world; has the largest share of uninsured individuals among advanced nations; and allows a rate of infant mortality in poor neighborhoods that rivals or exceeds that of the Third World.

"When Medicare and Medicaid made the indigent eligible for subsidized care in private institutions," points out sociologist and medical historian Paul Starr, "they undermined the rationale for municipal, veterans', and other government hospital services."[9] Instead of producing medical care and related services itself, the government chose—as it usually did in America—to rely on the market. The programs developed in the 1960s followed and strengthened this historic pattern. Government production of medical care diminished as government funding increased and health care was outsourced to private providers.

Still, the limits built into the design of Medicare and Medicaid should not obscure their swift accomplishments in extending and improving medical care for the elderly and poor—just as the shortcomings of Social Security cannot mask its role in reducing poverty. A very large share of the elderly enrolled and used services. By May 31, 1966, 17.6 million out of 19 million eligible individuals had enrolled in the optional Part B. Medicare resulted in a very large increase in the use of medical care by the elderly: in its first three years, 100,000 participants entered hospitals each week. Hospital discharges of the elderly increased from 190 per 1,000 in 1964 to 350 per 1,000 in 1973. Between 1963 and 1970, the proportion of Americans using the services of a physician increased from 68 percent to 76 percent, and the proportion who had never been examined by a doctor dropped from one-fifth to 8 percent as poor people began to visit doctors at the same rate as everyone else. The number of prenatal visits to doctors by poor women rose dramatically between 1965 and 1972, while infant mortality among blacks dropped by half, and the difference in life expectancy between whites and blacks shrank from about eight to five years.[10]

The War on Costs

In the 1970s, concern with both the expense and the number of uninsured Americans returned national health care to the agenda of federal politics. President Richard Nixon said in a 1969 press conference, "Unless action is taken within the next two or three years . . . we will have a breakdown in our medical system." A 1970 *Business Week* story warned of the "$60 billion crisis" in health care.[11] In the same year, Senator Edward Kennedy of Massachusetts and Representative Martha W. Griffiths of Michigan introduced a bill calling for a comprehensive system of free health insurance; Kennedy held hearings on health care across the country; and the National Governors' Conference endorsed national health care. President Nixon countered with his own proposal. As opposition to national health insurance "melted," Kennedy brokered a compromise, which was rejected by labor and liberal organizations, who anticipated a legislative sweep after Watergate. "If the name on the administration's plan had not been Nixon and had the time not been the year of Watergate," speculates Starr, "the United States might have had national health insurance in 1974. . . . This was the last moment in the 1970s when any such program had a serious chance of adoption."[12] (In 1976, presidential candidate Jimmy Carter pledged to enact comprehensive national health insurance, but the combination of budget pressures and inflation prevented any legislation.)

Instead, containing costs became the overriding goal for federal health care policy. Government spending on health rose from $10.8 billion in 1965 to $27.8 billion in 1970. Of course, after 1965, costs were supposed to rise because Medicare and Medicaid benefits were extended massively. Even though Medicare and Medicaid added large costs to government budgets, in their first decade the annual increase in the amount the programs reimbursed hospitals and physicians for each patient generally did not outstrip inflation. After 1975, however, costs rose faster than recipients and outpaced prices in the rest of the economy. From 1975 to 1984, for instance, enrollment in hospital insurance grew at an annual rate of 2.4 percent, while patient costs rose at an annual rate of 15.8 percent. In less than two decades after its creation, Medicare had become the second largest and the fastest-growing domestic program in the federal budget. From 1972 to 1994, the Medicaid population increased from about 18 to 35 million. In the same years, the cost of the program (not adjusted for inflation) soared from $8 billion to $144 billion. By 1997, it had reached $185 billion, of which the states paid $80 billion. By 1980, Medicaid often was the largest program in state budgets, and by the 1990s it cost governors six times as much as AFDC.[13]

Increased costs came from various sources. The most important were Medicare's virtually open-ended arrangements for reimbursing hospitals and physicians, the rising price of medical technology and of hospital operating costs, and "third-party payer" domination of medicine, in which the patient usually sees only a fraction of the cost of care, and physicians are insulated from the consequences of their recommendations. This availability of payment through insurance companies constituted a moral hazard that raised the cost of care by encouraging patients and providers to spend more liberally.[14]

The extension of benefits to new populations also raised costs. In 1972, the federal government extended Medicare to the disabled and to patients with end-stage renal disease. Between the late 1980s and early 1990s, pregnant women and poor children under the age of nineteen were added to Medicaid. They accounted for 45 percent of the increase in enrollment, but only 9 percent of the growth in costs, while long-term care for the disabled, blind, and elderly added fewer people but drove up costs disproportionately. Formerly providing benefits almost exclusively to women and children on public assistance, Medicaid broadened into a program that assisted a wider array of people with low incomes and provided long-term institutional care. The proportion of Medicaid recipients that qualified because they were on public assistance dropped from about 84 percent in 1984 to 60 percent in 1992.[15]

The other great influence on costs was the increased number of the elderly. As with Social Security, their numbers and longevity increased spending on Medicare, while their need for long-term nursing home care fueled the rise in Medicaid expense. Between 1990 and 1993, the number of elderly people supported by Medicaid in nursing homes rose from 601,000 to 1.6 million. In 1994, the 27 percent of Medicaid recipients who were aged and disabled received 70 percent of the dollars spent on the program. By contrast, AFDC children and adults, 71 percent of recipients, received 29 percent.[16]

In the 1970s, the federal government began trying to rein in health costs with regulations and planning. One tactic was to encourage the growth of health maintenance organizations (HMOs). Pioneered in California by Kaiser Permanente, HMOs offered prepaid health care. With income per patient fixed, HMOs had incentives both to keep patients healthy and to hold costs down. In 1970, the Nixon White House approved HMOs as a means of containing costs, and in 1973, legislation required businesses with more than twenty-five employees to offer at least one HMO as an alternative to conventional insurance. Despite the Nixon administration's predictions, HMOs grew very slowly during the 1970s and early 1980s and did not significantly affect the delivery of medical care until the 1990s. Some states during the 1970s tried to use Professional Standards Review Organizations, composed of physicians, to oversee Medicaid utilization, but they failed to contain costs as predicted. And in 1974, a new health planning law—the "climax of regulatory legislation"—created two hundred Health Systems Agencies, run by boards with consumer majorities, but the agencies lacked authority or power.[17] In the end, the experience of the 1970s showed the futility of trying to contain costs through planning and regulation.

In 1981, the new Reagan administration began to approach health care costs more directly. Its Omnibus Budget Reconciliation Act lowered the federal matching rate for AFDC and restricted eligibility, which also reduced the number eligible for Medicaid. It also allowed states to design alternative systems for delivering Medicaid less expensively.[18] As a result, the growth of Medicaid costs slowed dramatically until Congress expanded eligibility later in the decade.

Although the Reagan administration and Congress also limited hospital reimbursement rates for Medicare in 1981 and 1982, they launched the major attack on Medicare costs in 1985, with the introduction of the Prospective Payment System and its Diagnosis-Related Groups. Supported by both political parties, Prospective Payment radically restructured the way in which the government reimbursed hospitals. Medicare now paid hospitals a fixed sum according to a patient's diagnosis on admission. The goal was to give hospitals the incentive to cut costs by eliminating unnecessary tests and treatments or unneeded days of hospitalization; the danger was that hospitals would cut corners in the quality of care and discharge patients too soon. This new form of payment accomplished its goals: hospital admissions and the average length of stay declined.[19] As in the familiar master narrative of policy reform, policy makers judged their success by the lower numbers and paid little attention to the consequences for patients or clients.

Prospective Payment, as political scientist James Morone argued, proved one of the few effective methods for lowering medical costs because it took the problem out of politics. Instead of a political decision, it appeared a scientific, rule-driven, narrowly targeted program—regulation by bureaucracy, too arcane for public interest or understanding. Other similar and highly technical measures also helped lower costs. Congress began to limit physician payments in 1984, and in 1989 it authorized a Medicare Fee Schedule, developed by experts, to be phased in between 1991 and 1996. It cut other areas of Medicare by reducing benefits, increasing cost sharing, and raising deductibles and premiums. The Congressional Budget Office estimated that changes during the 1980s reduced the growth of Medicare by 20 percent over what it would have been. In the process, Congress pushed back the date of the expected depletion of Medicare's Trust Fund.[20]

Ironically, Prospective Payment, Reagan's principal health care policy, undermined his own principles. Reagan had ridden to office partly on a wave of antiregulatory sentiment shared by Republicans and Democrats alike. Even before he took office, writes health policy expert Theodore Marmor, "the time was ripe for celebrating 'competition' in medicine, getting government off the industry's back, and letting the fresh air of deregulation solve the problems of access, quality, and cost." When policy goals conflicted, however, the need to cut costs trumped ideology, and the Reagan administration supported more federal regulation, which, in other areas, it had worked to reduce or eliminate. Prospective Payment, observes historian Rosemary Stevens, "significantly increased the federal role in hospitals in the 1980s," despite the administration's advocacy of decreased influence for the federal government.[21]

In the 1980s, the failure of another Medicare reform illustrated the class politics of Medicare. The short unhappy life of the Medicare Catastrophic Care Act (MCCA) proved the oddest episode in the recent history of health care. Passed in June 1988, the MCCA was designed to lessen the impact of extended or "catastrophic" illness on the elderly. Low-income elderly persons benefited most from the MCCA because it authorized Medicaid to pay Medicare deductibles and coinsurance for the poorest among the elderly, and it reduced out-of-pocket expenses for most others with low incomes. However, the supplemental tax raised the cost of Medicare substantially for the middle-income elderly, and the act's complexity obscured its potential benefits. Despite support from the AARP, a protest among the elderly—nurtured by the Pharmaceutical Manufacturers Association, which objected to the inclusion of prescription benefits—and the National Committee to Protect Social Security led in October 1989 to a repeal of all but the act's Medicaid benefits. Even minimal changes, the episode showed, are expensive, and the elderly, when they are asked to pay for them directly, object, especially if benefits are slanted toward the poor and away from the middle class. The MCCA may have lived a very brief life, but it forced the problems of Medicare onto the public agenda and launched the debate over its future.[22]

While the federal government struggled to balance competing interests and contain costs, business interests were reorganizing medical practice into a "medical-industrial complex." Corporations, Paul Starr observes, began "to integrate a hitherto decentralized hospital system, enter a variety of other health care businesses, and consolidate ownership and control in what may eventually become an industry dominated by huge health care conglomerates."[23] As Medicare, Medicaid, and HMOs helped make health care a field ripe for corporate investment, medicine followed a path unfamiliar in health care but common in other industries. As a result, by 1991, one in four nonfederal acute-care hospitals were owned by investors, and the number was expected to increase dramatically. At the same time, an emphasis on efficiency and businesslike management invited corporate methods, including mergers, acquisitions, and diversification. For-profit hospitals also offered physicians incentives—such as joint ownership—and expensive equipment, and they purchased group practices, which aligned physicians' interests with the hospitals' search for profits.[24]

The corporate makeover of medicine did not immediately curb costs or increase the number of Americans with access to health care. On the contrary, employer plans, which became less comprehensive and more expensive, covered a smaller share of employees. Between 1970 and 1987, the proportion of the population covered by private health insurance dropped from 86 percent to 74 percent. Part of this decline reflected the increased role of Medicare and Medicaid, but part of it resulted from an increase in the number of people with no insurance at all. The results accentuated the class differences in medical care. Medicaid covered only about half the poor, and low-income elderly people paid an extraordinary proportion of their income for health insurance. In 1987, persons over sixty-five spent more than 20 percent of their median income on health care, while workers displaced from jobs—as so many were—lost health insurance for themselves and their families.[25] These problems—rising costs, declining coverage, increasing inequality in health care—confronted the administration of President Bill Clinton.

The Failure of National Health Care, Once Again

President Bill Clinton proposed to reorganize health care in America. With public sentiment in favor of sweeping reform, Clinton appeared poised to achieve national health insurance—an innovation that would be comparable to the achievements of the New Deal. Only Medicare could approach it in importance, and Medicare did not embrace the entire population.

Despite the early favorable signs, in less than a year Clinton's proposal had died a public and ignominious death. Its failure pushed national health insurance off the public agenda and helped bring about the Republicans' landslide victory in the 1994 congressional elections. The odds always were against Clinton's plan because it trod on powerful interests and because historical circumstances demanded that it resolve two problems—coverage and costs—whose solutions pulled policy in different directions. In the end, Clinton's plan failed for many reasons, including his own strategic errors as well as the massive and underhanded campaign against it launched by the health care industry, business interests, and political conservatives. [26]

Three circumstances catapulted health care to the top of Clinton's early agenda: the escalating costs of medical care, the growing number of uninsured Americans, and the surprising victory of Harris Wofford in a special Senate election in Pennsylvania. James J. Mongan, who spent twenty-five years as a congressional staffer and worked on health care under Presidents Nixon, Carter, and Clinton, observed that the "key lesson" he had learned is that in Congress the health care reform debate "is not now, and never has been, primarily about health care—it is about the *financing* of health care. It is about who pays." Rising middle-class health premiums, not the plight of the uninsured, drove the debate. In its concern with costs, Congress reflected public opinion. A 1993 Gallup Poll, pointed out pollster Daniel Yankelovich, found 74 percent identified "rising costs" as the "main problem facing health care in the US today," compared to only 8 percent who cited access and 4 percent who chose quality. "Without reform," warned *The President's Health Security Plan*, "spending on health care will reach 19 percent of GDP by the year 2000. If we do nothing, almost one in every five dollars spent by Americans will go to health care by the end of the decade, robbing workers of wages, straining state budgets and adding billions of dollars to the national debt."[27]

The deficit compounded the problem of costs. The Reagan administration had run up a huge deficit partly to justify slashing social programs. Faced with pressure to reduce the deficit, Clinton had to find a way to slow the rising cost of medical care without putting the government further in debt. Even more, as a "New Democrat," he had promised to reduce, not enlarge, the size of government, which, polls showed, had lost public trust. How could he restructure the vast and complicated American health care system and universalize coverage without expanding the role of government and raising taxes?[28] To restructure health insurance, Clinton had to assert a strong role for government at a time when public trust in government had dropped to near historic lows. He had to pay for universal access while concern with the deficit drove national politics, and antitax sentiment reigned across the nation.

In the private welfare state, health insurance premiums absorbed more than half the increased cost of compensation for full-time employees and contributed to the decline in real wages. Businesses shifted some of the expenses of medical care to employees in the form of deductibles and copayments and by turning to managed care. But workers with employment-based insurance were still the lucky ones. As firms down-sized and trimmed costs, the number of Americans without health insurance escalated. Most of the adults among the approximately 37 million Americans without insurance worked, often for small employers who did not carry insurance. Many of those with insurance worried about what would happen to them if they lost their jobs, and the recession of 1989 to 1991 only heightened their fears. As a result, in the two years between October 1989 and November 1991 the proportion of Americans agreeing that health reform should "rebuild totally" doubled from a little over 20 percent to 42 percent. "Millions of Americans," said President Clinton, "are just a pink slip away from losing their health coverage, one serious illness away from losing their savings. Millions more are locked into jobs for fear of losing their benefits. And small business owners throughout the nation want to provide health care for their employees and families but can't get it or can't afford it."[29]

In the spring of 1991 Pennsylvania Republican Senator John Heinz died in a tragic helicopter accident. The state's Democratic governor appointed Harris Wofford, his secretary of labor and industry, a JFK civil rights staffer, and a founder of the Peace Corps and former president of Bryn Mawr College, to Heinz's Senate seat. Former governor and attorney general Richard Thornburgh opposed Wofford in a special fall election to replace Heinz. Wofford, with little name recognition and running against a popular former governor, appeared to have a minimal chance of winning, and he trailed badly in the polls. But in September, a television spot featured Wofford standing in a hospital emergency room saying, "If criminals have the right to a lawyer, I think working Americans should have the right to a doctor. . . . I'm Harris Wofford, and I believe there is nothing more fundamental than the right to see a doctor when you're sick." National health insurance turned Wofford's campaign around: He won with 55 percent of the votes, a stunning victory, even in regions of the state and among groups of voters that normally voted Republican. Politicians around the country heard the message, and in 1992 candidate Bill Clinton inserted health insurance as a central plank in his campaign: "I pledge to the American people that in the first year of a Clinton Administration we will present a plan to Congress and the American people to provide affordable, quality health care for all Americans."[30]

Clinton assigned the job of formulating what he later called his Health Security Plan to a special task force headed by his wife, Hillary Rodham Clinton, and Ira Magaziner, a former Rhodes scholar friend of Clinton at Oxford and a successful business and public policy consultant with a strong interest in social issues.[31] The task force grew to more than 634 people divided into eight "cluster teams" and thirty-four "working groups." Fearing premature leaks. Clinton directed the group to work mainly in secret. In their compelling narrative history of the Clinton health plan, *The System*, journalists Haynes Johnson and David Broder argue that these arrangements virtually doomed the prospect for health care reform. By taking the development of the plan out of the normal policy process in government departments, such as Health and Human Services and Labor, Clinton weakened commitment to it within his own administration; by assigning it to the First Lady he muted criticisms that might have avoided mistakes; and by keeping the process relatively secret he fostered suspicions and handed opponents a potent criticism.

When the Task Force began its work, three models of health care reform (aside from a "tax credit" model directed only toward increasing private insurance and favored by Republicans) competed for attention. The "single-player" plan, often identified with Canada, proposed to break the link between health insurance and employment. The national government would use payroll taxes to pay for medical care provided by private practitioners. Consumers would be free to choose their physicians. The plan promised universal coverage coupled with lower expenses because the huge administrative cost of private insurance, about one-third of premiums, would be eliminated and the government could mandate maximum costs. A number of studies showed that in health insurance financing, the public sector was more effective than the private. The second proposal, called "play-or-pay," gave employers a choice between paying for insurance for their employees or paying a tax that would support coverage for the uninsured. Play-or-pay would not cut the costs of insurance or medical inflation, and it did not necessarily imply universal coverage. The "managed competition" option represented a compromise between the two other plans that promised to curb costs, universalize coverage, and retain the link between employment and insurance. It was a market-based scheme through which private health plans would compete under terms set and supervised by government. Businesses and individuals would benefit through the collective purchase of insurance at prices negotiated by government, which would subsidize coverage for those unable to afford it. Two groups—the "Jackson Hole" group led by Dr. Paul Ellwood of Minnesota and Stanford economist Alain Enthoven and one led by California insurance commissioner John Garamendi—advocated variants of "managed competition."[32]

From the start, the task force adopted "managed competition." Although a single-payer approach was simpler and would reduce costs more effectively, it appeared politically unfeasible, despite support from a surprising number of Democrats in Congress and labor unions. Insurance and business interests decried single-payer as a potential source of increased taxes, a powerful new national government agency, and "socialized medicine." Indeed, powerful interest groups mounted a media campaign against single-payer insurance by vilifying and grossly distorting the Canadian experience. In fact, Canada spends much less than the United States on health costs; its citizens live longer; and they report a much higher degree of satisfaction with their health care system than do Americans.[33]

Managed competition fit with the market-oriented approach to public policy favored by the Clinton administration. "The Health Security Act," claimed the official explanation of the president's plan, "seeks to build on what works best in the American economy and fix what is broken. What works best is a competitive market that provides products and services to Americans at the highest quality and lowest price." Its adherents argued that the plan avoided the stigma of big government; extended coverage to all citizens; guaranteed choice; and assured insurance to workers who lost or changed jobs. It accomplished these goals while retaining the familiar link between employment and health insurance and restraining costs. Clinton believed managed competition responded to the new labor markets and employment relations based on labor mobility rather than on permanent jobs. As he proposed to restructure insurance to facilitate flexible careers, Clinton echoed the strategies of businessmen who redesigned employee benefits to match the end of paternalism in the new economic order.[34]

Clinton's 1,324-page national health insurance bill proposed an intricate and complicated plan that a great many Americans, including those well-disposed toward fundamental reform, found hard to grasp. It required all employers to provide group health insurance and to finance 80 percent of the cost, with the remaining share paid for by employees. Unemployed and self-employed individuals would purchase their own private insurance, and all individuals would receive guaranteed health benefits with one of three different levels of patient cost-sharing arrangements. States would be required to create one or more regional health alliances, which would use their market power to negotiate lower-cost coverage for the public from private insurance companies. In part, savings on insurance premiums would finance the expense of the proposed new health care system: lower costs negotiated by alliances would free up money from employer premiums to pay for expanded benefits; savings in Medicare and Medicaid would allow the federal government to extend coverage to the uninsured and assist small employers. Despite its promises, Clinton's plan did not resolve the tension between cost and coverage, the two pressures driving health care reform. Making health care universal was expensive; restraining costs meant reducing benefits. Most Americans would pay more for their coverage; the elderly and the poor on Medicaid might receive lower benefits. Some restriction on access to expensive technology almost inevitably would follow the imposition of a national health budget.[35]

Opponents of Clinton's plan exploited its ambiguities. Because few people could understand it, attacks on the plan dramatically undercut its public support. Indeed, opposition came from every side. Private insurers and the private health care industry mounted a vicious, expensive, and effective campaign of misinformation against it. In fact, the attempt to defeat national health insurance had started a few years earlier as public sentiment in its favor appeared to mount. Between 1989 and 1991, there was a stunning correlation between rising public support for fundamental health care reform and increased contributions from the health care industry to both Republican and Democratic members of Congress. A vote for health reform, argues Nicholas Laham, could cost a member of Congress the funds essential for reelection. Consequently, he contends, members appeared to support health care reform in public while they worked to make sure bills would never emerge from committee.[36]

Meanwhile, physicians were divided about the Clinton Health Security Plan, with the American Medical Association in opposition. On September 8, 1993, the Health Insurance Association of America (HIAA) launched its infamous Harry and Louise television advertisements, which portrayed a middle-class couple fearful that Clinton's plan would destroy their choice of physician and the quality of their care. HIAA also established the Coalition for Health Insurance Choices (CHIC) to mobilize grass-roots opposition. CHIC's television spots provided a toll-free telephone number for viewers to call to register their protest. In only a few months it enrolled twenty thousand members. HIAA's advertising, which misrepresented the Health Security Plan, harped on two themes: the Clinton plan would take away individual choice of physician and initiate severe rationing of health care. Neither was accurate. The HIAA adopted Clinton's emphasis on markets and competition, except that it twisted them into an argument that transmuted the Health Security Act into the source of a big government, anti-market, anticompetitive monopoly.[37]

Small businesses, fearful of the cost of "employer mandates" to provide health insurance, united in opposition to Clinton's health plan as well. Opponents convinced owners of small businesses that the Clinton plan would shut them down by driving up costs. They raised the specter of massive job losses. In fact, research showed that the impact on jobs would be trivial. Business interests disliked mandates, and they feared that the generous benefits required under the Clinton plan would be too expensive. Initially, some large businesses, led by the automobile industry, favored it because they saw in the Clinton plan a way to reduce cost-shifting, which dumped the cost of care for the uninsured employees of small businesses into their premiums. By February 1994, however, most large businesses had lined up with small firms to oppose Clinton's plan. Three major business organizations worked to defeat Clinton's plan: the National Federation of Independent Business, the Business Roundtable, and the Chamber of Commerce.[38]

Not surprisingly, Republicans in Congress opposed the Health Security Act. They were in a delicate position, however. With public support for health care reform strong, they did not want to appear obstructionist. Instead, they argued against the model of reform in Clinton's plan and proposed their own alternative. Although they raised the possibility of compromise, Republicans had no intention of handing Clinton a victory, which is what any health care bill would appear to be. With his eye on the 1994 election, Congressman Newt Gingrich, the minority leader in the House, privately determined to keep Republicans from cooperating with Clinton and to prevent the passage of any health care legislation.[39] Republican proposals or hints of compromise constituted little more than smoke screens disguising a political strategy to win back Congress and, then, the presidency.

While Republicans opposed his plan, Democrats, divided among themselves, supplied a weak base of support. Some still favored a single-payer plan; others looked toward more conservative and politically salable alternatives. Senator George Mitchell tried but failed to craft a compromise that would achieve something less than universal coverage without an employer mandate, unless coverage did not reach 95 percent. In the end, Republican opposition and Democratic division left Clinton with almost no congressional support for his plan, which never reached the floor of the House or Senate. To make matters worse, at critical moments when health care demanded his full attention, events distracted Clinton: the killing of U.S. Marines in Somalia and the Haitian crisis, the Whitewater scandal, and the revelation of Hillary Clinton's dealings in the futures market, which tarnished her image and fanned the ferocious, often slanderous attack on her mounted by right-wing forces and on talk radio.[40]

The failure of the Health Security Act cannot be blamed solely on its opponents, historical contingencies, or the lukewarm support from congressional Democrats. Clinton and his team made mistakes from the beginning. Political scientist Jacob Hacker faults "the conception of politics on which their reform strategy was based"—a "remarkably crude" political logic that mistook politics for a problem of policy analysis and assumed that incorporating "all the critical provisions that each side wanted" would insure "a policy package that all sides would support." The Clinton health care team focused so intensively on the proposal that it "never truly grasped that the opportunities for reform were slipping away."[41]

With supporters unable to offer a clear and reassuring explanation and opponents frightening the public, support began to erode. By the summer of 1994, the Clinton plan had collapsed. Popular enthusiasm for health care reform had always been weaker than it appeared on the surface. The public, write Haynes Johnson and David Broder, "came to see the Clinton reform as threatening the security of the middle class, not benefiting it. In the battle for the American mind, failure to win this point would be disastrous." Most people did not care very deeply about extending protection to the uninsured. Rather, they cared mostly about the prospect of losing their own insurance and about rising costs. When they thought that Clinton's plan threatened their own unrestricted access to care or raised their expenses, they easily gave up support of universal coverage in the belief that they were preserving their own autonomy. They were mistaken—the failure of the Clinton Health Security Act actually reduced their choices and increased their costs.[42]

Redefining Health Care Reform

Clinton knew that national health insurance would solve a variety of problems. It would make moot the Medicare and Medicaid crises by subsuming the programs into a national system. It would reverse declining coverage by making insurance universal, and it would contain costs through planning and competition. It also would unlock the door to the reform of AFDC by allowing women with children to take jobs without fear of losing their medical insurance. The failure of Clinton's Health Security Plan stalled progress on all these fronts, and it left the twin problems of cost and coverage unmodified by the national government.

In the private welfare state, market forces worked to curb costs for employers at the expense of their employees. But the market did not alleviate the problem of coverage. "The stimulus for market change," pointed out an Urban Institute report, was "buyers' demands for less expensive health coverage and care." In fact, market change worsened coverage, as the number of Americans lacking health insurance continued to grow. "Americans—patients and physicians—have been running frightened from a phantom of nationalized medicine," observed Quentin

Young, president of the Health Policy Research Group, "when they're going to be gobbled up instead by corporate medicine." The issue, as Theodore Marmor explained, was not just about market share: "What is clear is that there has been a massive shift in the *character* of American medicine"—invasion by the ethos of the corporate world. The big story was the assimilation of American medicine to the market.[43]

Republicans capitalized on the failure of Clinton's health plan to win a sweeping victory in the 1994 congressional election. Although the reform of Medicare and Medicaid played virtually no role in their conservative design for public policy—"Contract with America"—Republicans moved quickly to bring them within the framework of limited government, increased markets, and reduced entitlements. They wanted to transform Medicare by allowing participants to choose from an array of options, with the expectation that most would pick a form of managed care, and to allow individuals to opt out of Medicare by buying only catastrophic insurance coverage and setting up Medical Savings Accounts rather like Individual Retirement Accounts (IRAs). For some time, writes sociologist Theda Skocpol, "conservatives . . . have been highly critical of Medicare, holding that it wastefully encourages older people to go to the doctor too often and not 'take responsibility' for their own health and financial planning."[44]

Republicans also wanted to raise premiums. By shifting costs to consumers and encouraging competition, they expected to slice $270 billion from the program over several years. They planned to eliminate $170 billion from Medicaid by capping expenses, giving block grants to the states, and ending the program's status as an entitlement. They thought states would save money by requiring Medicaid participants to enroll in managed care programs. At the same time, they tried to eliminate federal standards for nursing homes and turn their regulation over to the states, "whose lax oversight," one critic noted, "created the need for them in the first place."[45]

Critics worried that the Republican plan would destroy Medicare by siphoning off the healthiest elderly into low-cost plans and leaving the public program with the sickest. By increasing Medicare's deficit, this result would lead to lower payments to physicians and hospitals, who would leave the program. State governments, critics contended, would respond to Medicaid cuts by reducing the size of the program's rolls and leaving many more people uninsured. Others pointed out that the Republican program offered a huge windfall to the medical-industrial complex. "Embedded in the vast legislation to overhaul Medicare and Medicaid," wrote *New York Times* reporters Martin Gottlieb and Robert Pear, "are a series of narrowly focused, widely overlooked provisions that would relax Federal regulation of doctors and their laboratories,

reimburse private hospitals for some local taxes and grant benefits potentially worth hundreds of millions of dollars to manufacturers of prescription drugs and medical devices."[46]

Democrats accused Republicans of wanting to destroy Medicare.
Republicans objected that they really wanted to save it. Members on
each side exaggerated or distorted the other's position in the increasingly
partisan debate. In the end, the legislation passed each branch of Congress on a partisan vote, but Republicans could not override President
Clinton's December 1995 veto. In a welfare bill, which Clinton also
vetoed, Republicans further proposed to sever the link between Medicaid and cash assistance and to impede the ability of states to expand
Medicaid as some wanted to do.[47]

Governors did not wait for Congress to act on health care. State governments, for instance, moved before the federal government did to
extend health insurance to children. Many states had modest programs
aimed at providing insurance for children whose parents did not qualify
for Medicaid, while Massachusetts and Minnesota initiated comprehensive programs for all uninsured children. On May 1 the National Governors' Association released a study arguing that states already covered
800,000 of the nation's 10 million uninsured children.[48] Facing Medicaid costs that were six times larger than the cost of AFDC, states also
implemented their own plans, which stressed moving all program participants into managed care. The federal Balanced Budget Act of 1997 rati-
fied state actions by eliminating the need for states to obtain waivers for
this purpose. A number of state governments—for instance, Tennessee,
Oregon, Arizona, and Hawaii—used versions of managed care to stabilize costs as well as to extend coverage, and Medicaid managed care grew
dramatically, with mixed results.[49]

"We can allow well-to-do people to have free choice of doctors, and
middle-income and lower-income people to lose that free choice,"
lamented Princeton economist Uwe E. Reinhardt. "We no longer trouble either the entrepreneur or anyone else over the issue of social equity
and over the people who fall through the cracks." A 1998 Urban Institute
report concluded, "It is perhaps a testament to a near-blind faith in managed care that it has grown so rapidly with little convincing evidence as
to its ability to provide states with more value for their expenditures."
The spread of managed care also threatened to undermine the capacity
of providers, notably hospitals, "to continue to provide care to the uninsured." In the past, private insurers overpaid hospitals, which used the
surplus to finance care for those without insurance. With managed care
aggressively negotiating contracts, hospitals lost the revenues that
financed uncompensated care.[50]

State efforts, however, paled beside the influence of the corporate restructuring of medical care. In the private welfare state, employers had joined with managed care providers to stabilize prices and shift costs to employees. "A restructuring of America's health care system is now occurring in the marketplace without any significant government intervention," wrote two policy analysts in 1996. "Market-driven health system reform is occurring faster than federal legislation and regulators can measure, much less control," observed Stanford health economist Alain Enthoven. "Washington is right now a sideshow in health care," observed *Fortune* in 1994. "In the main tent, and much more worth watching, is a boisterous, cost-reducing, free-market affair." In April 1996, Aetna Life and Casualty Company, a major health insurer, bought U.S. Health Care, one of the largest national HMOs, for $8.9 billion. A few days before, Columbia/HCA, a large for-profit hospital chain, bid on a portion of Ohio Blue Cross and Blue Shield. More than fifty of the historically nonprofit Blues had started for-profit units, and others were considering converting to for-profit status. In 1991, Blue Cross and Blue Shield plans operated more than two hundred subsidiary companies. A 1993 survey of Blue Cross and Blue Shield chief executive officers found that 73 percent thought their national association should drop its nonprofit license standard. Hospitals, insurance companies, and medical group practices were joining together in regional health networks, with revenues exceeding $1 billion in 1996. Health care had become a trillion-dollar-a-year industry, with its income divided as follows: hospitals, including the big and fast-growing chains ($410 billion); physicians ($200 billion); insurance companies ($65 billion); and others ("dentists, optometrists, physical therapists and pharmacists") (over $100 billion). Battles in health care revolved as much around profits as around the quality and extent of care. Joseph Califano, secretary of health, education, and welfare in the Carter administration, said of the 1995 congressional fight over health care, "Think of health-care reform as throwing a trillion-dollar pot of gold up for grabs. . . . It's a bare-fisted brawl over who gives to and gets from the rich business of health."[51]

The corporate reorganization of health care created casualties. Cities lost funds to care for the indigent, and public hospitals were squeezed for money. "The medical industry," observed Katherine Dowling, a family physician at the University of Southern California Medical School, "is divesting itself of the registered nurse." In New York City, a number of older private hospitals serving neighborhoods faced a financial crisis that forced them to lay off large numbers of their staff. In 1996, two research groups predicted that in the next three years managed care would force the closure of at least fifteen of the city's seventy-eight hospitals, with a loss of 12,000 hospital beds and 80,000 jobs. In Philadelphia, profits at city hospitals tumbled to almost nothing in 1996, and several suffered huge declines in revenue. Mark Pauly, an economist at the Wharton School, observed that "survival of the fittest seems to be well underway," and he and other economists predicted even greater difficulties ahead "as area hospitals struggle to contain expenses and private and government payers drive down prices in a competitive market with excess hospital beds." Pauly predicted that the "weeding is going to continue. You have to take the capacity out of the system, and the Darwinian process will take out the weakest links." The subsequent collapse of Philadelphia's Allegheny Health System and the financial troubles confronting other area hospitals, including the University of Pennsylvania's, proved Pauly correct.[52]

The Darwinian process also threatened many community health centers. These centers originated in 1965 as a means of bringing high-quality medical care to poor people in inner cities. Medicaid and other government subsidies constituted their primary source of funds. They treated about 10 million patients each year, three-quarters of them minorities. With Medicaid patients siphoned off into HMOs, the centers lost their source of government funds at a time when uninsured patients, ineligible for Medicaid—whose numbers rose from 2.9 million to 3.2 million between 1994 and 1996—increased demands on them for care.[53]

For-profit hospitals, meanwhile, did not lower costs; they increased them. They decreased the care available for the indigent and uninsured, and they often tried to avoid Medicaid patients. This trend toward corporate behavior, observes Dave Lindorff in *Marketplace Medicine*, "led to an increase in 'dumping' of poor patients onto publicly owned hospitals and, in turn, has created a budget crisis at the nation's public hospitals." When public hospitals faced bankruptcy, corporate chains arrived to either manage or buy them "at fire-sale prices, at which point they ceased to be hospitals for the poor." The example of corporate hospitals had a powerful influence on nonprofits. "Even in jurisdictions with no for-profit hospital, most independent and not-for-profit hospitals," notes Lindorff, "responded to real or perceived threats from for-profits by imitating their behavior: bringing in professional managers and marketing experts, embarking on expensive remodeling or rebuilding programs, tightening up on providing charity care to indigents."[54]

Just as it seemed poised to triumph, corporate medicine overreached and provoked a furious backlash. It encountered trouble, all of its own making, on three fronts: disgruntled patients, the exposure of fraud and corruption, and a reversal of financial fortune. Americans did not like medicine guided by the bottom line. "Voters in every state," observed a *New York Times* editorial, "are demanding more regulation of an industry they perceive to be driven by profits rather than concerns for patients' health." Patients and physicians alike began to protest the gag rules preventing physicians from telling patients about alternative treatments, the denial of specialized services, the substitution of medications based solely on cost, and a host of other problems related in story after story from coast to coast. Physicians across the country complained that HMOs "limited their ability to talk freely with patients about costly treatment options or HMO payment policies, including the financial incentives for doctors to withhold care." The Kaiser Permanente HMO in Ohio even forbade its doctors to give patients information about proposed treatments before obtaining permission from Health Risk Management, an outside firm hired to review requests. Another HMO contract stipulated that the HMO "and provider shall portray each other in a positive light to enrollees and the public." Another contained the clause: "Provider shall use its best efforts to insure that no employee of the provider or subcontractor of the provider makes any derogatory remarks regarding [the HMO] to any member."[55]

The backlash forced HMOs to abandon many of the cost-cutting measures that rewarded doctors and hospitals for limiting care, although insurers continued to tighten rules and reduce the fees they paid doctors. From early 1995 to the middle of 1996, according to the *New York Times*, thirty-four states "outlawed or curtailed methods that many health maintenance organizations have used to shorten some types of hospital stays, discipline physicians or keep patients in the dark about the incentives and ground rules of managed care." In the first five months of 1996, four hundred bills that affected managed-care practices were introduced in state legislatures, and in succeeding years others followed.[56] In the summer of 1999, hostility toward managed care even invaded national politics with a partisan fight over a bill protecting patients' rights.

Dissatisfaction with managed care drove some physicians to consider unionizing. Labor experts predicted the number of doctors in unions would grow 15 percent a year. By early 1999, about 35,000, or 5 percent of the nation's total, had joined unions. Unionization, however, received a setback in May 1999, when the regional director for the National Labor Relations Board ruled that hundreds of physicians from southern New Jersey could not bargain collectively with AmeriHealth HMO because they were independent contractors, not employees. The union promised to appeal. The regional NLRB ruling did not kill the union drive among doctors. In June 1999, the American Medical Association, which represented 34 percent of the nation's physicians, reversed its long-standing opposition to unions. It announced plans to try to unionize doctors who were salaried employees and medical residents, about one-third of all doctors, and to persuade Congress to grant the other physicians the right to collective bargaining. In June 2000, the House passed legislation exempting physicians from antitrust laws, and supporters turned to the Senate, where success was more doubtful. Whatever the outcome in Congress, collective bargaining among physicians seemed likely to grow.[57]

Accusations of fraud also damaged the reputation of some insurance companies and large health care corporations. The saga of Empire Blue Cross in New York revealed the underside of even the not-for-profit insurance industry, but the most dramatic story was the fall of Columbia/HCA. Under the leadership of its aggressive president, Richard L. Scott, Columbia Health Systems expanded in less than a decade from two small hospitals in El Paso, Texas, to the world's largest health care system—a $20 billion a year giant with 350 hospitals, 550 home health care offices, and scores of other medical care businesses in other states. Along the way it merged with another large health system, Health Corporation of America (HCA). Columbia/HCA was noted for its aggressive tactics—including a willingness to destroy local institutions that refused to cooperate—as it moved into communities and gobbled up hospitals and medical practices. Its most controversial practice proved to be selling shares in its hospitals to physicians who profited handsomely, despite the appearance of possible conflicts of interest. In March 1997 the *New York Times* ran a series of articles based on its own analysis of Columbia/HCA's billing practices. The health care giant, it appeared, had been defrauding the government by overbilling for Medicare, ordering unnecessary tests, and shifting costs. As federal investigators swarmed over the corporation's facilities, more than a dozen federal whistleblower suits were filed, charging Columbia/HCA with a variety of schemes to defraud national health programs like Medicare. Scott was forced to resign as president, but a nearly $10 million golden parachute and stock options eased his fall from power. Then his successor, Dr. Thomas F. Frist, former president of HCA, earned such a huge profit on HCA stock options that the IRS questioned it as excessive compensation. Frist promised to cooperate with the investigation, reorganize the company, and stop selling shares in hospitals to physicians. With the cost of restructuring and lawsuits mounting, Columbia/HCA announced that it would cut its network by about one-third. Its profits dropped in both the third and fourth quarters of 1997, and its stock fell by 45.7 percent in the first year of the investigation. In July 1999 a federal jury convicted two Columbia/HCA Health Corporation executives of defrauding Medicare and other insurers of almost $3 million.[58]

Managed care and large networks of hospitals and physicians expanded too fast. By 1997, the industry had started to lose money as profits plummeted. "The managed-care industry," reported a *New York Times* article, "once widely seen as a panacea for the nation's health care woes, is now entering a troublesome new phase: struggling with the consequences of its extraordinary expansion this decade, forced in many cases to raise premiums, lay off doctors and close clinics." Oxford Health Plans—one of the largest managed care systems in the Northeast—lost $291.3 million in 1997; its doctors complained of delinquent payments. A sharp drop in the price of its shares cost the state of Connecticut's retirement fund $404,200 on shares originally worth $646,250. In the second quarter of 1998, Oxford lost $507.6 million. (Oxford finally broke a twenty-one-month string of consecutive losses in the third quarter of 1999.) In Kansas City, Blue Cross and Blue Shield closed eleven of their HMO's twenty-two clinics, laid off thirty of sixty-five primary care physicians, and reduced the salaries of the rest. In 1998, the HMO industry lost $490 million—an improvement over the $768 million loss in 1997. Across the nation, health systems responded to excess capacity through consolidation. In May 1998, one of the largest insurers, United Healthcare Corporation, agreed to buy Humana, Incorporated, for $5.5 billion. Combined, the two health plans enrolled 10 million members. In July 1998 the for-profit company Vanguard Health Systems signed a letter of intent to buy nine Philadelphia-area hospitals owned by the bankrupt Allegheny Health, Education, and Research Foundations. Financially troubled medical centers that had expanded too rapidly called in the Hunter Group, a consulting firm that advised them on how to cut costs. After the Hunter Group's visit, the University of Pennsylvania Medical Center announced it would lay off 20 percent of its staff.[59]

As some HMOs struggled to raise profits, they also began to pull out of Medicaid and Medicare, often leaving patients forced to change physicians or, even worse, leaving them stranded for health care altogether. In September 1999, the Clinton administration warned that health maintenance organizations would no longer provide free drug coverage to Medicare beneficiaries and that copayments would rise substantially. A *New York Times* article reported in July 1998 that over the previous year, eight health plans had dropped Medicaid programs in New York State. Aetna, the second largest HMO in Connecticut, closed its program there. And the third largest HMO in California dropped out of Medicaid in that state. The reason for their withdrawal lay in falling government reimbursement rates, which, in some states, had dropped since the mid-1990s by up to 20 percent. For similar reasons, HMOs dropped 407,000 Medicare patients in 1998 and another 327,000 in 1999. The federal government estimated that 10 percent of all the beneficiaries of Medicare enrolled in HMOs had been or would be dropped in 1999 or 2000. In July 2000, it put the number at 900,000.[60]

Despite its difficulties, managed care did help slow the growth of medical costs in the public as well as the private medical system. Although health spending exceeded $1 trillion for the first time in 1996, the rate of growth was the lowest in thirty-six years. Employers and providers felt the benefits of slower growth more directly than consumers did. Employers shifted more of the cost of health care to their employees; insurance companies raised premiums for medigap insurance, which paid the deductibles and coinsurance required by Medicare; Medicare Part B premiums increased; and public assistance rules disqualified more people from Medicaid.

Although growth in health care spending had matched the pace of the economy for four years and had held steady at about 13.5 percent of GDP, officials warned that spending could start rising again because of pent-up demand among insurers, who had held premium increases below medical costs. Their predictions proved accurate. A Department of Health and Human Services report in September 1998 predicted that the share of the GDP consumed by health care would grow to 16.6 percent by 2007, with faster growth in the private sector than in the public. In 1999, employers expected health care costs to rise 9 percent as a result of the aging of the baby-boom population and the use of new medical technology. Already, premiums charged individuals by employers' group policies had started to climb; the increase for 1999 was expected to range from 8 percent to 20 percent. Despite the increased costs of private health insurance plans, Medicare spending startled even well-informed observers by dropping 1 percent in the fiscal year that ended in September 1999. The decline—which reflected a variety of causes, including the cuts in reimbursement to doctors, hospitals, and nursing homes enacted by Congress in 1997, low inflation, and efforts to curb fraud—probably would prove temporary. Unlike private plans, Medicare did not cover prescription drugs, which were consuming an ever-larger share of health costs. Nonetheless, former Congressional Budget Office director Robert D. Reischauer called it a "phenomenal development" in light of "the increase in the number of beneficiaries and the resurgence of rapid growth in health costs in the private sector."[61]

With insurance premiums up and fewer people eligible for medical assistance, the number of the uninsured continued to rise. A 1996 Harvard School of Public Health study found an extraordinary 31 percent of Americans without health insurance or with difficulty obtaining or paying for medical care at some point during the year. Thirty-seven million adults reported that they were uninsured at the time of the survey or at some point during 1995.[62] In May 1999 the bipartisan National Coalition on Health Care, headed by former presidents George Bush, Jimmy Carter, and Gerald Ford, offered a chilling prediction:

> In 1997, 43.4 million Americans, 16 percent of the population, had no health insurance. Over a three-year period, about 30 percent of the population—81 million people—can expect to experience a gap in their coverage lasting at least one month. And 44 percent of workers who lose their jobs can expect to experience a gap in health insurance coverage lasting a month or longer. Even if the rosy economic conditions prevalent since 1992 prevail for another decade, a projected 52 to 54 million non-elderly Americans—one in five—will be uninsured in 2009. If an economic downturn occurs, we project as many as 61.4 million non-elderly Americans—one in four—could be uninsured in 2009.

The decline in coverage, the commission reported, hit some groups harder than others: low- and middle-income families, young adults ages eighteen to twenty-four, the near elderly (ages fifty-five to sixty-four), minority and immigrant populations, and people who work in small businesses or are self-employed or have alternative work arrangements such as day-labor, temporary, or part-time jobs. In 1998, according to the Census Bureau, 16.3 percent of the population, or 44.3 million people, an increase of 1 million since 1997, lacked health insurance.[63]

Much of the rise in the number of uninsured adults reflected the loss of health benefits by employees laid off from their jobs. Benefits were not portable from job to job, and the health plans offered by new employers could refuse to insure employees because of preexisting conditions. The Kennedy-Kassenbaum Act (named for its two sponsors, Democratic senator Edward Kennedy and Republican senator Nancy Kassenbaum) allowed workers to keep their health insurance if they changed or lost their jobs and barred insurance companies from refusing them coverage based on preexisting medical conditions. But state governments and insurance companies found ways to circumvent the new law. A March 1998 survey found that thirteen states "discouraged individuals from applying for the coverage or charged them rates 140 to 600 percent of the standard premium." As a response, in July President Clinton promised to punish insurers who denied individuals coverage under the law by excluding them from participating in the market for insuring federal employees.[64]

The Kennedy-Kassenbaum Act was the first of the incremental measures that chipped away at the problems of coverage and cost that continued to characterize health care in America. Like the others, it arose as a response to a specific issue, not as part of a systematic plan for reform. Another was the Mental Health Parity Act of 1996, which forbade group health insurance plans from imposing lower limits on mental health benefits than on benefits for other medical conditions. As an example to employers that found ways to get around the law, President Clinton drafted model standards for mental health coverage benefits for federal employees.[65]

Clinton also proposed extending Medicare to adults ages fifty-five to sixty-four by allowing them to buy into the program, and he proposed a patient "bill of rights" that responded to the complaints of patient mistreatment, especially in managed care. At the same time, he used his executive authority to introduce new consumer protections for Medicaid patients in HMOs while judges across the nation reversed years of precedents by allowing patients to sue health maintenance organizations. In a national class-action suit, patient rights advocates won a victory in August 1998 when a federal appeals court in San Francisco ruled in favor of HMO Medicare patients' entitlement to immediate hearings and explanations when denied benefits. By early in 2000, lawyers had filed at least sixteen class-action suits, and new state laws opened the possibility of still more suits against the managed care industry. At issue most often was whether financial incentives to physicians, and the secrecy that surrounded them, worked against the best interests of patients. In the summer of 2000, however, two federal court decisions—one by the Supreme Court and one by a federal appeals court in Philadelphia—upheld core cost-cutting practices of HMOs, reversing the legal momentum of managed care's critics.[66]

Congress finally took up the issue of HMO patient rights in the summer of 1999 as Republicans and Democrats each offered their own bills. The parties differed on who should be covered and on whether patients denied treatment should be allowed to sue HMOs. With the stakes very high, the health care industry and the American Medical Association poured money into lobbying against the Democrats' bill. The Senate, on a straight party-line vote, approved the Republican plan. As action shifted to the House of Representatives, President Clinton promised to veto the Republican plan, which he called "an empty promise to the American people." Indeed, the Republican plan provided most HMO patients no tangible benefits. With popular pressures mounting, many House Republicans abandoned their leadership to vote for a bill supported by President Clinton that gave patients wide new rights, including the right to sue health insurance plans that denied them care or provided substandard treatment. As the bill went to a conference committee to iron out differences with the restrictive Senate version, HMO representatives, worried about the possibility of lawsuits, urged a compromise that would allow patients the right to take grievances to an independent panel of medical experts. Meanwhile, in November 1999, United Health Group, one of the nation's largest managed care companies, stunned the industry—it responded to criticism by announcing that a patient's doctor now could decide on hospitalization or other treatment without prior review or permission. Other managed care companies followed United's lead and announced changes designed to appeal to customers. Nonetheless, despite public pressure and mounting bipartisan consensus, Congress remained unable to agree on a patients' bill of rights, which, not surprisingly, became a partisan issue in the 2000 election. With Congress deadlocked, Clinton promised to act administratively by issuing new federal rules that would apply to claims under employee health benefit plans—an action permitted by the 1974 Employee Retirement Income Security Act. The new rules would include many of the protections sought by proponents of patients' rights legislation, although not the right to sue.[67]

With the federal government stalled and legal action blocked, initiative passed to the states, which moved faster on patient rights and other health care issues than the federal government had. California, the leader, expanded the rights of HMO patients and mandated staffing ratios in nursing homes. In some states, most notably Massachusetts, citizen coalitions worked to place a health care referendum on the ballot for the fall 2000 election. In Maine, the state legislature voted to put price controls on prescription drugs sold in the state. With popular pressure for action mounting, in 1999 states passed 1,400 health care bills—the largest number on any topic. Early in 2000, there were 16,000 health care bills on the table in forty-four states—once again, more than on any other issue. "It's a populist issue. It's not a Republican or Democratic issue. It's state legislators and legislatures trying to address the needs of their constituents," observed Lee Dixon, director of the health policy tracking services of the National Conference of State Legislators.[68]

Among some employers, hostility toward managed care provoked another reaction. A number of them considered getting out of their role as middlemen in health insurance altogether and, as with pensions, letting employees make their own decisions about benefits—and carry more of the responsibility. One idea was to turn health care into a "defined contribution" benefit—that is, to give each employee the cash with which to buy insurance. The proposal, which faced many obstacles, resembled the voucher-style plan long used by federal workers and advocated in the 2000 presidential campaign by former senator Bill Bradley.[69]

One important incremental addition to the health care system emerged from the balanced budget compromise in the summer of 1997. Congress set aside $24 billion for children's health care coverage in the next five years. The money would flow through states, which would have wide latitude in designing plans for spending it. This new money, which would add to the programs for children already under way in most states, was intended to insure half of the 10 million uninsured children, although critics argued that it would cover far fewer because many employers would drop family coverage. Although Congress authorized enough money to cover 6 million children, only about 2.9 million children met the program's criteria. Thus, as a result of its design, the Children's Health Insurance Program (CHIP) would reach only 30 percent to 40 percent of uninsured children.[70]

Concerned that too few children had enrolled in either CHIP or Medicaid, President Clinton set up a toll-free telephone line that automatically connected callers with the Medicaid agency or health care department in the state from which they were calling. Still, by May 1999 states were using less than 20 percent of the money Congress had authorized for CHIP. Too few children lived in income-eligible families to absorb the available funds, and Congress had drawn the legislation so narrowly that states could not apply unused funds to other uninsured children. Many states, too, such as Texas, had proved less than prompt in setting up programs and reaching out to eligible children. In August 1999, Clinton announced he would send federal officials to all states to find out if they had improperly excluded children from CHIP and Medicaid; in October he ordered federal officials to visit schools to enroll uninsured children. In January 2000 he proposed a $2.7 billion initiative to sign up more children.[71]

The 1997 budget bill also changed Medicare along the lines proposed by Republicans in 1995, although less drastically. The bill targeted $116.4 billion in Medicare savings over the next five years. It promised to save a great deal of money by scaling back payments to providers and increasing premiums for beneficiaries. By opening up choices to senior citizens, it threatened to fragment the program by undermining the universal social insurance principles on which it was founded. With costs rising at a slower rate, the pressure for a quick financial fix had lessened, but the long-range financial viability of Medicare remained unresolved in the legislation, which called for a Bipartisan Commission on the Future of Medicare.[72]

The legislation reduced Medicare spending faster and more sharply than its sponsors expected. They predicted that the rate of increase in spending would slow down; instead, in the six months ending in March

1999, it was less than for the same period in the previous year. As a result, the budget office revised projected Medicare spending downward for the next four years. The president of the Association of American Medical Colleges observed, "There was a gross underestimate of the savings from the Balanced Budget Act," while Kenneth E. Raske, president of the Greater New York Hospital Association, said, "Congress really overshot the runway when it passed the law." With cuts deeper than Congress had intended, "health care providers of all types" were "furiously lobbying Congress to restore money cut from their payments"; Congress responded with plans for restoring some, although by no means most, of the funding.[73]

Under the new rules, Medicare participants could choose one of several options. Of these, Medical Savings Accounts were the most controversial. Like Individual Retirement Accounts, Medical Savings Accounts allowed individuals to prepay health care expenses. They cost less than other plans and offered much lower benefits. Insurers proved very slow to offer Medical Savings Accounts, which appeared much less attractive to them or to beneficiaries than their market-oriented advocates had expected. The whole package of options, Medicare Plus Choice, was set to begin in 1999, when seniors would have to choose among plans. The options confused and frightened many people. Relatively few understood the choices; many feared they would lose valuable benefits. "Scrambling to explain choices that barely exist," wrote *New York Times* health affairs columnist Milt Freudenheim, "government officials will mail bulletins or handbooks early next month [November 1998] to millions of people who, not surprisingly, often have little understanding of the thicket of rules that already govern Medicare." A health care researcher at George Washington University predicted "mass confusion. . . . Is this choice or chaos?"[74]

In another area—home health care, the fastest growing part of Medicare—Congress attacked costs directly. Still paid by the visit, the current home health care program encouraged unnecessary visits and scams by providers. (The number of home health care visits increased from 69,500 in 1990 to 300,000 in 1997.) Congress capped home health care at just below 1993–94 levels and required providers to post bonds to do business—a policy that threatened to drive legitimate providers out of business. It also changed the basis of payment: the law limited the amount for each beneficiary; it no longer reimbursed for every visit. The result squeezed providers and encouraged them to cut the number of visits and the time spent with clients and to focus on clients with short-term, acute problems rather than ones in need of long-term care. In just two years, Medicare spending on home health care plummeted 45 percent. In August 1998 the National Association for Home Care reported that 752 agencies had closed since January. By December another report put the number at 1,300. The new rules also enforced eligibility standards that attempted to deny home health care to anyone with even minimal independence—a policy that occasioned hardship for many elderly persons. The reaction paralleled the termination of disability benefits under the Reagan administration because the courts apparently agreed that home health benefits had been denied unfairly. Thirty-nine percent of those who appealed the denial of benefits won at the first level of review, and 81 percent prevailed on appeal. By 2000, even some Republicans admitted that the cutbacks in home health care had been more extensive than Congress had intended, and support for a modest reversal was building.[75]

The 1997 budget deal also responded to governors' complaints about the inflexibility and rising costs of Medicaid by freeing them to cut payments to nursing homes for the long-term care of the elderly. In 1996, nursing homes accounted for 20 percent of Medicaid expenses, and 70 percent of nursing home residents depended on Medicaid. By cutting nursing home rates, Congress expected the states to compensate for a $15 billion reduction in federal Medicaid contributions. Nursing home representatives feared the cuts would raise the cost for paying patients to unbearable levels and reduce the quality of care for both those who paid and those supported by Medicaid alike. There were good reasons to fear for the quality of nursing home care. The Balanced Budget Act not only reduced payments; it repealed a 1980 law tying Medicaid reimbursement to minimum federal and state quality-of-care standards. The legislation pitted state Medicaid officials against the nursing home industry, whose largely private providers argued that reimbursement rates, already too low, threatened quality. Providers themselves, however, came under sharp attack for cutting corners at the expense of patients. Even with standards, the quality of care, compromised by profit-hungry providers, often was appalling. In "The Shame of Our Nursing Homes: Millions for Investors, Misery for the Elderly," Eric Bates contrasted the huge revenues in national nursing home "empires" with the miserable care many of them provided. While the executives and shareholders of Beverly, the largest chain, "profited from the company's rapid growth during the eighties," claimed Bates, "many patients suffered. Across the nation, health officials filed reports on Beverly nursing homes documenting filthy living conditions, infected bedsores and painful deaths." Nursing homes also raided the public treasury through setting up subsidiaries from which they purchased supplies and by submitting improper claims—more than $3 billion worth in 1996 and 1997.[76]

Nursing homes and home health care were not the only medical issues troubling the elderly. A 1998 study found that 2 million elderly persons who lived at or below the poverty line spent more than 50 percent of their income on medical expenses not reimbursed by Medicare; for the average Medicare recipient the amount of annual income spent was 19 percent, or $2,149. Prescription drugs constituted the most worrying of these expenses. In his 1999 State of the Union message, President Clinton claimed that Medicare should cover "the greatest growing need of seniors: affordable prescription drugs." Standard copayments, even for patients with insurance, were often doubling, and drugs not on insurers' approved lists experienced even larger increases—as much as 300 percent or more. For Medicare beneficiaries, the median out-of-pocket expense for prescription drugs was only $200, but 29 percent spent more than $500, 14 percent more than $1,000, and 4 percent topped $2,000. Rising drug costs also hurt insurance companies, which, in New York, began to pay as much for prescription drugs as for hospitalization, a startling shift in the allocation of the region's health expenses. In June 1999, when Clinton announced his Medicare prescription drug plan, many Democrats said they had been "stunned at the power of the issue in recent months." With great fanfare Clinton proposed a plan that remained a good deal less than the sum of its rhetoric. While Clinton's plan would reduce the cost of prescription drugs for all the elderly, it would still leave them with large, and in many cases crippling, costs, and experts doubted its effectiveness. At the same time, Congress had also begun a battle over the duration of a company's exclusive rights to drug patents. Under pressure from the drug industry—one company increased its 1998 lobbying expenses to $4.3 million, up from $1.9 million two years earlier—legislation extending such patents remained a real possibility. The stakes were high: for instance, a three-year extension of the patent on Claritin, a popular antiallergy drug, would cost consumers $7 billion.[77]

As the contest over prescription benefits escalated, drug makers and insurance companies fought each other, and the White House admitted that its plan would cost 35 percent more than it had estimated only seven months earlier. Nonetheless, popular pressure continued to mount, and, early in 2000, a broadly acceptable plan seemed a possibility when drug makers suddenly and unexpectedly dropped their opposition. The industry had been shaken by comments from Clinton administration officials that price controls would result from its continued intransigence in the face of public demands for Medicare drug coverage. Two industry officials "said they were tired of being excoriated by the White House and wanted to set a constructive, pragmatic and positive tone for the coming debate on Medicare drug benefits."[78]

Clinton's proposed drug benefit was one element in his plan to "modernize and strengthen Medicare for the 21st century," which he offered as a substitute for proposals by Senator John Breaux, chair of the National Bipartisan Commission on the Future of Medicare. Clinton rejected Breaux's plan, which fell one vote short of commanding a majority on the commission, because it failed to include an adequate and affordable prescription benefit and did not earmark 15 percent of future federal budget surpluses for Medicare. Breaux had proposed opening Medicare to competition with private health plans. Rather than paying individually for each service, the government would give each beneficiary money to buy insurance from a plan supervised by and negotiated with a new Medicare Board. Higher-income beneficiaries would pay higher premiums; beneficiaries would pay 10 percent of the cost of home health visits (currently without copayment); and the age of eligibility for Medicare would rise from sixty-five to sixty-seven during the years between 2003 and 2027. Although Breaux objected to descriptions of his proposal as a voucher plan, like vouchers it rested on faith in market principles—competition and choice—to rein in the costs of Medicare without beneficiaries' sacrificing essential benefits.[79]

Like Breaux, Clinton intended to use the power of the market to improve Medicare's efficiency by injecting competition in purchasing and pricing, incentives for physicians to keep costs reasonable, and inducements to beneficiaries to choose lower-cost plans. He promised to smooth out some of the inequities that resulted from the Balanced Budget Act of 1997, eliminate cost sharing for all preventive benefits, reform medigap plans, and allow Americans younger than sixty-five to buy into Medicare in certain instances. About half the savings in Medicare over ten years, he predicted, would result from "innovative proposals to adopt successful private sector tools and competition"; another $45.5 billion would derive from allocating a portion of the expected federal budget surplus to Medicare. Once again, the fortuitous surplus rescued Clinton from the hardest choices. The plan, commented one observer, represented "another Clintonian compromise, this time between the ardent defenders of traditional Medicare and the true believers in the marketplace." But it also reflected a "realistic appraisal" of the ideas that had led to the health insurance fiasco in 1993. Then, many of the administration's "health planners saw managed care and a well-organized marketplace as nothing short of wondrous in their ability to control costs and improve quality." In 1999, following "a private sector revolution that pushed most working Americans into managed care with mixed results," the euphoria had dissipated. Clinton's Medicare plan faced a rough ride in Congress. Drug makers opposed the prescription benefit plan as a precursor of price controls and unleashed a critical series of television commercials and newspaper advertisements; the Congressional Budget Office concluded that Clinton had grossly underestimated the plan's cost; and Republicans, reluctant to give him a victory, resisted it. With his original Medicare plan stalled, Clinton floated a scheme for moving Medicare patients into networks of preferred providers that charged the program lower rates. But this idea, too, met a hostile reception that killed it, at least for the existing Congress. Congress did approve the extension of Medicare and Medicaid to allow individuals with disabilities to return to work without losing their health insurance—an expansion of coverage affecting hundreds of thousands of people. Nonetheless, real Medicare reform hung as much on the power of wealthy lobbies and political calculations as on the merits of competing ideas. And it remained urgent. A panel of Medicare experts convened by the National Academy of Social Insurance concluded "that none of the plans currently being considered would produce savings sufficient to sustain a program similar to what Medicare now provides." With no changes to its benefits or structure, taxpayers would have to pay twice as much for Medicare in the year 2030.[80]

With politicians at last responding to the working poor unable to afford health insurance and to the indefensible situation of millions of uninsured children, health care promised to be a major issue in the 2000 presidential campaign. In January 2000, in fact, Clinton announced a major new health initiative designed to reduce the number of uninsured adults, assist low- and moderate-income families with the costs of medical insurance, accelerate the enrollment of children in federal-state insurance programs, extend insurance to individuals "facing unique barriers to coverage," and pump more money into programs that provide health care directly to the uninsured. Whether in an election year Clinton could persuade Congress remained uncertain, but his willingness to propose the "largest investment in health coverage since the establishment of Medicare in 1965" pointed to Democrats' identification of health care "as the most potent issue" in their drive to recapture the House of Representatives and retain the White House.[81]

Both presidential candidates—Vice President Al Gore and Texas governor George W. Bush—promised prescription drug benefits and Medicare reforms. But their proposals differed sharply—not only in details, but also in the principles on which they were based. Gore defended a strong, guiding role for government; Bush wanted to outsource the provision of more health benefits to the private market. All the political positioning over drugs revolved around the same point. As Drew Altman, president of the Kaiser Family Foundation, which specializes in health policy, observed: "There is an underlying philosophical difference, with the Democrats preferring to expand a public program and the Republicans wanting to go with private insurers and the market-place." The Republican drug plan proposed using federal subsidies to persuade insurance companies to sell prescription drug policies to the elderly. Promising every beneficiary a choice between at least two plans, the proposal, said Republican representative James C. Greenwood of Pennsylvania, "reflects our faith in the marketplace versus our faith in government." House Democrats, by contrast, wanted to add standard-ized prescription drug benefits to the existing Medicare program. While the program would be voluntary, it would be guaranteed to every benefi-ciary. Similarly, Gore's plan proposed to pay all prescription drug costs for the 13 million Medicare recipients without insurance, as long as their incomes were below 135 percent of the poverty line. For those with higher incomes, there would be a sliding scale of benefits, and no one would pay more than $4,000 of their own money in any one year.[82]

Partisan differences over health care extended to the Medicare pro-gram as a whole—"the pace of any Medicare restructuring, how much the traditional fee-for-service program should be protected in any new competitive marketplace, what kind of oversight and regulation should exist, and what kind of financial incentives should be used to encourage older Americans to consider managed care plans." Democrats, stung by the record of managed care, started to doubt the "virtues of the private market," claimed *New York Times* reporter Robin Toner. Gore, cam-paigning on the party's record as Medicare's "guardian," promised to assure Medicare's solvency by dedicating $400 million of the budget sur-plus to it—putting the money in a "lock box" that would protect it from spending on tax cuts or other programs. Besides adding a prescription drug benefit to the program, Gore supported the "modernization" pro-posals advocated by the Clinton administration, and he also proposed moving toward universal health insurance "step-by-step instead of trying to cover everybody in one fell swoop." The first task, he said, was expanding the Children's Health Insurance Program and Medicaid to cover all children by 2005. Although the details of Bush's plan for Medicare were not specific, he supported building on Senator Breaux's proposal, which would preserve the traditional fee-for-service program but force it to compete with other plans. Ideally, private plans would compete for the business of beneficiaries, who would annually decide how to allocate their government-provided premiums. Beneficiaries could also add their own money to buy more extensive benefits.[83]

The politics of Medicare reform in the 2000 election reflected the public anger at health insurers and managed care. Powerful corporate forces had restructured the American health care system by aggressively taking authority away from providers, limiting the choice of individuals, and reorganizing hospitals, insurers, and physicians into vast regional systems that controlled markets for health care. Although Americans disliked managed care, it had become nearly universal in the private welfare state. The corporate players restructuring health care, however, had overreached, and a strong public backlash against secretive, restrictive, medically questionable, and profit-driven HMO practices surfaced around the country. At the same time, the national government faced consumers worried about losing coverage, senior citizens stretched to the limit by rising insurance premiums and out-of-pocket expenses, millions of uninsured children, state governments strapped by rising Medicaid costs, angry physicians, a looming funding crisis in Medicare, a Republican Congress pushing its own market-based health proposals, and a loosely regulated and out-of-control medical-industrial complex built in part on piles of financial sand. The Clinton administration had responded with incremental changes—modest measures addressing one or another problem—but federal policy appeared reactive and incoherent. This was the politically explosive context in which Gore and Bush formulated their plans for health care reform—certainly, the most complicated issue for domestic policy. The election could determine whose proposals stood the most realistic chance of implementation. Not only did the well-being of millions of Americans hang on the outcome, so did the future model of the welfare state. Instead, the close election results left the resolution of the health care issue ambiguous and less likely to be resolved soon—a situation that, with rising costs and an angry public, could prove dangerous and explosive.

FIGHTING POVERTY
1990S STYLE

Health care linked the problems of the working poor to those of mothers on AFDC. Without health insurance, the working poor lacked security; without a guarantee that health benefits would continue, mothers would be foolish to trade AFDC for a low-paying job that offered no benefits. Health care seemed the logical starting point for policies directed toward improving the condition of the working poor and reducing welfare dependence. Because he understood the primacy of health care reform, President Bill Clinton assigned it priority early in his administration. The political risk was very high, and when his ambitious health plan failed, everything else became more difficult.

Clinton, however, had other plans for addressing poverty and improving the condition of workers who earned low wages. He hoped to jump-start the economy, create jobs, and repair crumbling infrastructure all at once through an ambitious economic stimulus plan, which died in Congress even before his health insurance plan did. With the massive Republican victory in the 1994 congressional elections, the expansion of the safety net became moot; Clinton had to struggle just to prevent it from tearing completely apart. His success proved only partial: he helped preserve the federal entitlement to food stamps, Medicaid, and Supplemental Security Income and the existence of federal legal services, but at the price of restricting eligibility for each program.

Clinton did have one real antipoverty plan in his policy arsenal: expanding the Earned Income Tax Credit. Before the election of the 104th Congress, he moved a massive expansion through Congress. Even a conservative Republican majority proved unable to turn it back. Coupled with more tax credits for child care, new health insurance for low-income children, a higher minimum wage, and other programs, the expanded Earned Income Tax Credit lifted large numbers of working families above the poverty line.

At century's end, the only politically viable antipoverty strategies either attached benefits to employment, like the Earned Income Tax Credit, or worked indirectly through markets, like the program Clinton announced in the summer of 1999 to attack poverty by harnessing the power of the market to regenerate depressed cities and rural areas. The few Great Society programs that remained suffered in the competition for funds, and the idea of a massive frontal war on poverty led by the federal government seemed a fading memory, an anachronism inappropriate to an era skeptical of federal capacity, hostile to dependency, and entranced by the power of the market. With government a less willing provider, nonworking poor people often turned elsewhere for the resources essential for survival. They found some of them in a privatized safety net that combined very old strategies with ones that put market products to unexpected uses.

Earned Income Tax Credit: A Real Antipoverty Program

In 1996, full-time, year-round work at the minimum wage earned 70 percent of the poverty line for a family of three and 55 percent for a family of four. Between 1978 and 1994, poverty grew 42 percent among families with children where the head of the household worked. Three of every five poor children lived in a household with a working member. The proportion of workers who were poor had increased from 5.9 percent in 1977 to 7.4 percent in 1993. Most of them were of "prime working age," that is, ages twenty-five to sixty-four. This was the problem of the working poor. "Working poverty" was not an oxymoron; it was a contradiction. Working poverty violated the idea that in America anyone who "worked hard and played by the rules" should not be poor, and it undercut efforts to move people away from dependence.

Working poverty was the anomaly that the Earned Income Tax Credit was designed to prevent. The EITC is the federal government's fastest-growing entitlement program and its most effective means of lifting children out of poverty. It won broad political support because it promised to eliminate the embarrassment of the working poor with minimal cost to employers and only a modest increase in the minimum wage. It also hastened the redefinition of the American welfare state by attaching social benefits even more closely to employment.[1]

In fact, the EITC, which dates from 1975, is specifically designed to provide incentives to work. Only those employed in the regular labor market receive benefits, which increase with income until they reach a ceiling. Although originally very small, its subsequent expansions transformed the EITC into a major cash income supplement for the working poor. Between 1975 and 1978, the number of families served by the EITC tripled from a little more than 6 million to 18 million and its cost rose even faster—from $2.5 billion to $27 billion. The EITC survived the Reagan administration's attack on social spending and grew during the recessions of the 1980s and early 1990s, despite concerns with inflation and deficits. In 1993, a major expansion of the program by President Clinton raised benefits significantly and for the first time extended some aid to childless workers.[2] (Clinton proposed another major expansion in 2000). Like AFDC, the real value of EITC benefits declined between 1975 and 1985, but unlike AFDC, Congress indexed them for inflation, and their real value increased even before their 1993 expansion. The EITC also reaches a very high proportion, about 80–86 percent, of those eligible for its benefits.[3]

Above all, it is popular. It even survived the victory of the conservative Republicans in the congressional elections of 1994. Until the welfare debates of 1995, almost no one objected to its expansion; even then, criticism remained muted. Indeed, its bipartisan support shielded the EITC from serious assault when Republicans attacked "welfare" in 1995 and 1996.[4] With the exception of the most conservative public policy commentators, critics for the most part limited objections to technical and administrative matters that did not challenge the program's underlying principles. In 1999, when the Republican leadership tried to save money by delaying EITC payments, a howl of protest—even from other Republicans—quickly ended the idea. This broad bipartisan support for an expanded and more expensive EITC shows that the debate over "welfare" concerned much more than money.[5]

The EITC succeeded in part because it met the needs of the working poor. Indeed, after the 1980s, both Republicans and Democrats competed aggressively for the votes of the working poor—a "swing constituency" comprising about 20 percent of the electorate. "By expanding the refundable Earned Income Tax Credit," asserted President Bill Clinton, "we will reward the work of millions of working poor Americans by realizing the principle that if you work 40 hours a week and you've got a child in the house, you will no longer be in poverty."[6] For the Clinton administration, changes to the EITC had four goals: making work pay, eliminating poverty among full-time year-round workers, targeting benefits to individuals with the greatest needs, and improving the verification of eligibility and the ease of claiming benefits. Most criticism of the EITC focused on verification. Both anecdotal evidence and official studies showed a very high rate of error—as high as 21 percent—in the awarding of EITC benefits. Some errors resulted from fraud; a lot stemmed from honest mistakes because of the complexity of the formulas. The Clinton administration responded with legislative and administrative action expected to reduce the errors drastically.[7]

The most conservative critics argued that the EITC was just another government handout that, at best, should be restricted to the very poor and not given to working families. Even then, the program should just eliminate the Social Security tax liability of the poorest taxpayers, not supplement their income. The "plain fact," wrote former speech writer for Vice President Dan Quayle, Linda Schiffren, "is that the EITC is not a refund of taxes paid, but merely a transfer program for people who are too successful to qualify for welfare." Conservatives were outraged that in 1996 a family with two children and an income of $28,495 could receive a tax credit. They also argued that the EITC discouraged marriage by levying a penalty on married couples. (In theory they were accurate about the potential marriage penalty; in practice, though, its impact was minor.) Other conservative critics complained that the EITC introduced a new moral hazard through incentives to reduce time spent at work—complaints that distorted the research that found its overall impact on work to be modestly positive.[8]

The impact of the EITC on poverty signaled the program's success. It lifted more children out of poverty than had any other safety net program. In 1998, it raised 4.3 million individuals, of whom more than half were children, above the poverty line—a result of the fact that it targeted most benefits on families near the poverty line. In constant dollars, in 1993, a working parent with two children who earned the minimum wage and received the EITC had an income of $10,569, well below the poverty line. In 1998, with the expanded EITC and higher minimum wage, her income had increased 27 percent—to $13,268, hardly affluent but out of official poverty.[9]

The EITC won wide support because it resolved the contradiction between the virtue of work and falling wages by partially socializing the cost of labor. Work remained the ultimate goal of welfare reform; from work flowed independence, personal responsibility, and citizenship. Work policed the border between the deserving and undeserving poor. In America, work had always marked the approved channel, if not to riches, then at least to comfort. Although this story bordered on myth, its influence heightened the sense of promises betrayed, the anxiety of downward mobility, and the fearful prospect of dependence aroused by falling wages.[10] For social policy, falling wages threatened more than an already overburdened welfare system; they destroyed incentives to good behavior. What would be the point of leaving welfare if work did not guarantee a ladder out of poverty? What would be the point of working hard at an unpleasant job that offered few rewards?

As a rallying cry, "Make work pay" bridged the partisan divide. The question was, how? One route was to raise the minimum wage, which had declined in real value—between 1979 and 1996 (in 1996 dollars) the minimum wage had fallen $3,800 to its lowest level since 1955, when it was 75¢ an hour. The minimum wage remained a very contentious path, followed by Clinton with modest success in both his first and second terms. The result, however, did not lift a working poor family out of poverty or restore the minimum wage to anything like its earlier value.[11]

Another way to "make work pay" was for employers to pay higher wages. But after spending nearly two decades cutting wages and wringing concessions from employees, they remained unwilling or unable to raise wages very much. In these circumstances, socializing the cost across all taxpayers became the most direct route to higher incomes—that is, subsidizing employers as well as wage earners. The EITC, delivered impersonally through the tax system, lacked the stigma of public assistance, "welfare," or charity. Like the deduction of home mortgage interest, it became an earned benefit for employed citizens, neither public assistance nor social insurance.[12]

The expansion of the EITC hastened the redefinition of the American welfare state by tightening the link between social benefits and employment. Since the 1940s, as we have seen, the benefits offered by the welfare state through social insurance—unemployment insurance, workers' compensation, Social Security—in one way or another depended on a history of employment. Only the very poor received health care—albeit second-class care—as a right. With the EITC, cash assistance also attached itself more closely to paid work. The EITC, observes political scientist Christopher Howard, "may be touted as an antipoverty policy, but it cannot touch the truly disadvantaged."[13] Indeed, the rights of citizens depended increasingly on their participation in the regular labor market. "The Clinton-Gore focus on poverty reduction," emphasized Gene B. Spirling, a top Clinton economic adviser, "has been very much grounded in a vision of rewarding work for poor families." Social policy, commented David T. Ellwood, a leading expert on poverty and welfare at Harvard's Kennedy School, "has been transformed—with support withdrawn from lone parents who are home with children and expanded for those who go to work."[14] This was fighting poverty 1990s style.

In the best of times, the link between benefits and employment left the millions of individuals outside the labor market without cash assistance. A tight labor market masked the dangers of linking benefits to employment and obscured the history of past recessions. No mechanisms were in place for coping with the consequences of a labor market flooded with excess workers.[15] In a time of high unemployment, a job-based strategy of income support would collapse, and the burden would fall on the tattered safety net and the remnants of the Great Society.

Food Stamps, Legal Services, and the Safety Net

The EITC is a supplement to wages, not a part of the safety net. It supplements earnings, but it is of no help to anyone unable for one reason or another to work. They must turn instead to the nation's safety net. At best, the safety net assures survival to those unable to work; it does not—and it is not intended to—lift people out of poverty. At the close of the twentieth century, for anyone on the losing end of one of life's common risks, the safety net appeared increasingly thin and tattered. Food stamps, in many ways the heart of the safety net, survived a major struggle and retained their status as an entitlement, although one reduced in scope and adequacy. The Legal Services Corporation, which helped individuals claim benefits from the safety net or other welfare state programs, also survived a major threat to its existence, but at a high cost.

FOOD STAMPS

Food lies at the heart of the safety net: nothing is more important or basic. A number of federal programs provide food to the needy either by supplying it directly, subsidizing its purchase, or funding nonprofits who distribute it. These programs include school breakfasts and lunches; supplemental nutrition for women, infants, and children; nutrition for the elderly; emergency food assistance; surplus food distribution; and, the largest, food stamps, which consumes 65 percent of the U.S. Department of Agriculture's food-assistance budget. In 1996, these programs served about one of six Americans at a cost of $38 billion. Together, they provided a "nutritional safety net for people in need."[16]

Like the Earned Income Tax Credit, the idea of food stamps enjoys bipartisan support. Just as the EITC helps resolve the contradiction between the importance of work and low wages, the food stamps program responds to the absurdity of hunger in a land of excess food. Although a means-tested program and a form of public assistance, food stamps are not what most people have in mind when they talk about "welfare," and almost no one proposes to abolish public spending on food for the deserving poor. Food stamps escape the taint of welfare because, first, their benefits extend to the working poor and the elderly. Although it is not universal, it is targeted less narrowly than

AFDC or TANF. Second, its benefits are paid in kind, not in cash. Food stamps constitute a special form of currency deemed appropriate for the poor.

As in other areas of the welfare state, in the mid-1990s the forces of "reform" reduced benefits in the food stamps program, tightened eligibility requirements, and strengthened the program's links to employment. Like the "welfare" rolls, the food stamp rolls declined precipitously— even though evidence from various sources showed that hunger remained at unacceptable levels and may have been growing. Nonprofits and city governments feared that people denied food stamps would turn to them for help and strain their resources beyond endurance. Urged by governors, mayors, and President Clinton, Congress restored some though by no means all lost benefits, and a minority of states used their own funds to buy food for the needy.

The federal government distributed surplus food for the first time in the 1930s. It thought of food distribution more as a way to support agriculture than to improve nutrition or alleviate hunger. From 1939 to 1943, the federal government also operated a food stamp program under a complex scheme with two colors of stamps. The program ended with the full employment during World War II. In the 1940s and 1950s, federal food policy consisted only of the distribution of commodities. The size of federal purchases varied with the size of farm surpluses rather than with food needs, while the politics of agriculture—competition between commodities for government purchase, for instance—dominated the program. As a presidential candidate, John F. Kennedy saw the prevalence of hunger in rural America and mining regions and promised to put food programs high on his domestic agenda. In 1961, his first executive order set up eight pilot food stamp projects, which expanded to forty-three by 1964. Southern agricultural interests, however, blocked the expansion of food stamps into a national program until 1964, when a congressional compromise promised them continued support in return for a more ambitious food stamp program. Food programs, nonetheless, remained small and inadequate and still charged for stamps even as evidence mounted that hunger was a severe national problem. By the late 1960s, a number of events helped bump hunger higher on the national agenda, starting in 1967, when a Senate subcommittee traveled to the Mississippi Delta, and Senators Joseph Clark and Robert F. Kennedy confronted rural hunger and poverty firsthand. The committee publicized its findings and petitioned President Johnson to expand the size of the food stamp program. In 1968, Hunger USA, a nonprofit group, released a study that CBS turned into a television program. In the same year, a new Senate Select Committee on Nutrition and Human Need, chaired by Senator George McGovern, made hunger into an issue in the presidential election.[17]

In May 1969, President Nixon announced that the time had arrived "to put an end to hunger in America itself for all time." A combination of administrative and legislative actions in 1969 and 1970 doubled the average food stamp benefits, and legislation in 1973 required all counties to offer them by July 1974; in 1977 they became free. By the time Ronald Reagan took office, nearly one of ten Americans received food stamps, which served a much broader slice of the population than did any other means-tested program. Without doubt, food stamps, along with other food and nutrition programs, reduced hunger and significantly increased the incomes of recipients. By the early 1990s, food stamps provided one-quarter of the average AFDC family's total purchasing power; in states where AFDC benefits were low, the share reached 50 percent or more.[18]

In 1981, President Ronald Reagan cut spending on food stamps as he did on other welfare state programs, but with food stamps his assault lasted only until 1985, when Congress reauthorized the program and liberalized its eligibility requirements and rules. Legislation in subsequent years continued its expansion. As a result, spending on the food stamp program grew from about $12 billion to $14 billion during the Reagan administration, and then jumped to $25 billion by the end of the Bush presidency. In 1995, the program cost about $27 billion.[19] Food stamps, which had grown larger than AFDC or the Earned Income Tax Credit, were the nation's largest public assistance program.

Food stamps appears at first a relatively uncomplicated program. Eligible individuals receive stamps that they exchange for food at approved stores. The simplicity of its underlying idea, however, masks complex issues in the program's design. Who is eligible? How much should recipients get? What income or assets should a family be allowed to deduct when calculating its eligibility for food stamps? What kind of goods should recipients be allowed to purchase? Should they be compelled to work for their benefits? How should the program police and prevent fraud and abuse? Should benefits be distributed electronically rather than with stamps? These are the principal questions in the design and administration of food stamps, and they have received different answers over time.

All public assistance recipients are automatically eligible for food stamps. Food stamps, however, serve a more diverse population than cash assistance, thus casting a safety net wider than any other social program except Medicaid, with which it overlaps in clientele. In 1994, Medicaid served about 31 million persons and food stamps about 28 million. In general, food stamp recipients must have incomes that do not exceed

130 percent of the federal poverty line. Because individuals can exclude some of their assets and expenditures, eligibility extends modestly into the ranks of the working poor. The program excludes certain categories of people (strikers, illegal aliens, most postsecondary students, people in institutions) and, unless they are exempted, requires recipients to register for work, accept a suitable job, or fulfill work and training requirements. The federal government funds 100 percent of food stamp benefits and, for the most part, half the cost of state administration of the program. Benefits are based on the assumption that a family should spend 30 percent of its income on food. The amount of the benefits also depends on family size. In 1995, monthly benefits averaged $71 a person and $175 a household.[20] Although food stamps is an essential program, it is not a very generous one.[21]

Sociologist Viviana A. Zelizer points out that food stamps constitute a special form of currency. As in-kind relief, they echo the centuries-old suspicion in welfare history that poor people are incompetent to manage cash. Both public officials and the agents of charity have always preferred to give the poor redeemable orders for groceries, fuel, rent money, clothes, or medical care—but not cash, which is too easily fungible or wasted. Cash might be spent on drink or unjustified luxuries or just frittered away. The search for alternative forms of currency more narrowly targeted and less subject to abuse runs through the design and administration of public assistance and private charity from the early days of public relief until the present. Alternative currencies serve the interests of control as well as charity, for they define the needs of the poor in terms set by those who command the resources.

The use of in-kind currency escalated after the 1960s: "restricted in-kind assistance to the poor—primarily food, housing, and medical care—increased dramatically, while cash payments fell," points out Zelizer. In the 1980s, "only three out of every ten welfare dollars were being transferred as cash." The food stamp program is a case in point. In 1993, it served 26.6 million people, twice as many as AFDC and more than 10 percent of the population, and all of them bought food with coupons. "But not any food: Under U.S. Department of Agriculture regulations, Food Stamps cannot buy, among other things, alcoholic beverages and tobacco, hot foods ready to eat, lunch-counter items, vitamins or medicines, pet food, or any nonfood items. Neither can Food Stamps be traded for cash." Public authorities, she observes, "have worked hard to preserve or create separate, identifiable, controllable currencies for the poor, either coining new monies, such as Food Stamps, or regulating the uses of legal tender, as with protective payments." Critics have urged replacing coupons with cash, but the Food and Nutrition Service, which administers food stamps, objects, fearing the erosion of public and political support for food stamps through an equation with welfare.[22]

Still, coupons have drawbacks. They must be printed and then picked up in person or mailed. They can be traded illegally for cash. They often embarrass recipients, who sense that other customers think less of them when they pay with stamps. In the 1990s, the use of electronic benefits transfer (EBT) began to address these issues. With EBT, recipients receive a plastic card just like an ATM card. When it is swiped at the supermarket checkout, the amount of the purchase is deducted from the recipient's balance. Despite the worries of some advocates for the poor, recipients feel far less stigma; the program is easier to administer; and merchants receive payment instantly without the need to tally and submit stamps.[23] The Food and Nutrition Service emphasizes that EBT does not transform food stamps from an in-kind to a cash program. The EBT card can be used only at approved stores and for approved items.

Its advocates also expected electronic transfers to reduce the fraud that has bedeviled the food stamp program and caused more concern in Congress than benefit levels or eligibility rules. Fraud has been easy: recipients could sell coupons for a fraction of their face value and do what they wanted with the money. In 1995, Representative Pat Roberts of Kansas, chair of the House Agriculture Committee, claimed that fraud over the last six years had cost $1.8 billion. A 1995 Food and Consumer Service study estimated that retailers illegally exchanged up to $815 million, or 4 percent of food stamps, for cash. The problem did not lie with supermarkets, where the rate was very low, but mainly with small retailers. Two years later, a General Accounting Office official reported that EBT, along with other measures, had helped curtail fraud, which, nonetheless, remained a serious concern.[24]

The Contract with America called for consolidating all nutrition programs into block grants, and in 1995, the conservative 104th Congress initially set out to follow its recommendation. As with Medicaid, this action would have ended the entitlement to food stamps and curbed the growth of the program by capping expenses and giving the states more flexibility in designing their own programs. Clinton opposed block grants. "While food and nutrition programs must be made more flexible and easier for states to administer," argued Ellen Haas, Undersecretary for Food, Nutrition, and Consumer Services, "Federal standards are the reason that the programs work." Many Republicans, including governors and members of Congress, also remained queasy about ending the entitlement to food stamps, even though they supported abolishing AFDC. For them as well as for Democrats, food stamps were the "ultimate national safety net." They agreed that the growth of spending on food stamps should be slowed by keeping the rate of increase below inflation; they wanted stricter work regulations attached to food stamps; and they intended to give states much more flexibility in administering the program. In the 1996 welfare bill, they got some of what they wanted.[25]

In the 1996 welfare bill, Republicans won $27.7 billion worth of cutbacks in food stamps. Benefits were expected to fall almost 20 percent by the year 2002 and to drop from an average of 80¢ to 66¢ per person for each meal. Over six years, about two-thirds of the cuts would come from reduced benefits for families with children. Two groups would lose benefits completely: legal immigrants, except those who had worked in the United States more than ten years, and those associated with the military. In addition, able-bodied childless individuals between ages eighteen and fifty would receive benefits for only three months in any thirty-six-month period, unless they worked at least twenty hours per week or participated in an acceptable employment and training program. The Center on Budget and Policy Priorities warned of the "proscriptive rules" the new law imposed on the "kinds of work programs states can operate for people reaching the time limits." Few current state employment and training programs would qualify participants for food stamps. The Congressional Budget Office estimated that time limits, when fully implemented, would deny food stamps to a monthly average of half a million people willing to work if offered a job.[26]

As well as tying benefits more closely to work, the new regulations greatly expanded the role of the states, mostly by allowing them to operate "simplified" programs that applied the same rules to cash assistance and food stamps. Congress did leave some modest loopholes. In areas of high unemployment, states could ask for waivers from the time limits, and most states did in fact receive waivers that exempted 35 to 40 percent of those with benefits scheduled to expire. States could also exempt up to 15 percent of the people whose benefits were slated to end for whatever reason they chose. State governments did not use this privilege very aggressively, nor did they seem interested in using the money that Congress made available—about $200 million—for training and work programs. Although in the late 1980s and early 1990s, one state after another had withdrawn most General Assistance, at least able-bodied adults without children had remained eligible for food stamps. Now, for many, even this very small benefit disappeared.[27]

By December 1997, the new rules had also cut about 770,000 immigrants from the food stamp rolls across the nation. Immigrants, however, won a minor reprieve. In June 1997, Congress responded to complaints from governors, advocates, and the Clinton administration by allowing states to use their own money to buy food stamps for legal immigrants. (Store owners in immigrant areas also complained about the impact of the cuts on their businesses.) Within a short time, thirteen governors in states with large immigrant populations took advantage of the new rules to buy food stamps for immigrants. At the same time, Clinton continued to press Congress to rescind the prohibition against food stamps for immigrants, and he included more food stamp money for them in his budget. In the spring of 1998, Congress finally restored some food stamp assistance to legal immigrants, although not as much as Clinton had requested.[28]

The new eligibility restrictions helped to lower the food stamp rolls. From a peak of 28 million in March 1994, they dropped to 20 million in December 1997, a stunning 29 percent decline. The food stamp program has always reflected the economy, and the robust job market fueled some of the decline. But a large, if indeterminate, portion of it happened because so many immigrants and nonelderly adults lost their eligibility. Indeed, the largest decrease, 3.5 million persons, occurred in 1997. Local officials also contributed to the decline by discouraging people from applying for food stamps. Some states and cities, aggressively pruning public assistance rolls, required applicants to search for a job for more than a month before receiving benefits. New York City required a second visit to a welfare office, a practice that violated federal law. Also, many beneficiaries believed incorrectly that the end of "old style" welfare meant that they lost all government benefits. As a result, some states, prompted by the federal government, began to advertise the availability of food stamps. Maryland planned to mail brochures about food stamps and Medicaid to the 2,500 single mothers who left cash assistance each month; South Dakota sent out hundreds of letters for the same purpose; Wisconsin placed food stamps and Medicaid workers in some hospitals. In July 1999, alarmed by the drop in food stamp rolls, Clinton announced a major national effort to sign up eligible people. Nonetheless, nearly a year later, Nina Bernstein reported in the *New York Times* that "food-stamp applications in most states have become so onerous that they are deterring needy people from applying for the subsidies." In twenty-nine states, people applying for food stamps were asked if they owned a burial plot; two states wanted to know if applicants had sold their blood; another state asked for garage-sale receipts, another for bingo winnings, and still another if anyone in the household had a paper route. Department of Agriculture figures showed that applications took an average of five hours and two visits—for a benefit that averaged only $73 a month per person. As a result, 12 million eligible people who needed the benefits were not receiving them.[29]

The great decline in the food stamp rolls did not signify a correspondingly massive reduction in hunger. In 1995, the first national federal analysis of hunger found 88.1 percent of American households "food secure" during the whole year. About 4.1 percent, or 4.2 million households, were "food insecure with hunger." Although the number of food insecure households dropped 12 percent in the next few years, in 1999, 31 million Americans, or 10.1 percent of households, were food insecure, meaning, according to a U.S. Department of Agriculture study, that "they were uncertain of having, or unable to acquire, adequate food sufficient to meet basic needs at all times due to inadequate household resources for food." Food insecurity, of course, was concentrated among poor households. At some point in 1995 more than three of every ten black, Hispanic, and female-headed families with young children worried about having enough to eat. Nonetheless, hunger has gone down over time—partly as a result of federal food programs and, even more, as a result of economic growth and rising real wages. At any time before World War II, the idea that 88 of every 100 Americans could pass through a year without worrying about having enough to eat would have seemed utopian. Still, despite the roughly $36 billion a year in federal funds devoted to food assistance, hunger remained a serious problem in America.[30] With tightened eligibility and reduced food stamp benefits, it was likely to grow more severe.

Critics of the 1996 cuts in food stamps predicted that soup kitchens and food banks would be flooded with demands for help. Although the initial need appeared lower than expected, pressure on private food providers swelled in the winter of 1997–98. In November 1997 directors of food pantries and social service agencies in New York City reported "a significant increase in hunger," and the Coalition Against Hunger said that demand for food had risen 23 percent. Mayor Rudoph Giuliani spent $26 million in city funds to purchase food stamps for immigrants. Demand for food increased across the country, in less urbanized areas as well as in cities. In Idaho, after five months of the state's new welfare law, the number on welfare had plummeted but lines waiting at soup kitchens stretched into the streets. In December 1997, the U.S. Conference of Mayors reported a 16 percent rise in requests for emergency food, which was the largest increase since 1992. In June 1999, a Philadelphia non-profit's survey found that requests for emergency food in the city and suburbs had increased 18 percent in the past year.[31]

According to a study by Second Harvest, the largest private hunger-relief agency in the country, 26 million people asked for assistance in 1997 at soup kitchens, food pantries, and shelters; "an additional 700,000 were turned away because of a shortage of more than 115 million pounds of food." The people who asked charities for food fit the profile of food stamp recipients: over half lived in rural areas or cities with fewer than 100,000 residents, and in 39 percent of families one adult worked. The "dominant faces of hunger in America," observed Second Harvest, "are young, white and female, and they are turning up more in rural areas." J. Larry Brown, director of the Center on Hunger, Poverty and Nutrition Policy at Tufts University, commented, "The data run counter to nearly every stereotype we have of who needs assistance. . . . It's mainly families that are playing by the rules."[32] For individuals dropped from food stamps the safety net had shrunk to almost nothing. With no political power, they could turn to only one source for help in claiming what few benefits might be theirs: the Legal Services Corporation, which itself reeled from conservative attack.

LEGAL SERVICES

The struggle over the Legal Services Corporation was partly about power. Legal Services helped individuals in disputes involving family law, housing, and social benefits. It also represented the collective interests of low-income people by challenging landlords, employers, and governments and by using the law as a tool to pry rights from public authorities and build protections for disadvantaged individuals. Its stunning successes threatened entrenched interests everywhere, and they responded without mercy. From the early 1980s, conservatives waged an intense campaign against the Legal Services Corporation. Until the 1980s, they won only a reduction in funding, which curbed but did not cripple its activities. But the 104th Congress renewed the fight with great intensity. No one argued against helping poor people with legal expenses. The argument was about which legal needs should be met with public funds, what the role was of pro bono assistance, whether advocacy was legitimate, and whether a legal services or legal aid model should shape assistance to poor people. Conservatives wanted to transform legal services into charity. Although they failed to abolish the Legal Services Corporation, they forced it to accept compromises that threatened to erode its effectiveness and reduce its income. The stronger local branches of legal services responded with creative strategies for raising funds from new sources and re-forming themselves into organizations capable of continued advocacy. By the end of the century, the battle between supporters and opponents of the Legal Services Corporation had settled into a kind of trench warfare whose outcome remained far from certain as Legal Services adapted to an environment ruled by devolution and markets.

Free legal help for the poor began with the New York Legal Aid Society in 1876. By 1919, 40 agencies offered free legal assistance, and their number grew slowly to 249 by 1963. Although the Economic Opportunity Act did not specify legal services as part of the War on Poverty, Sargent Shriver, the Office of Economic Opportunity director, had decided to include it. By the end of 1960, OEO had allocated over $20 million to 130 legal services projects, and demonstration projects were developed during the 1960s with Ford Foundation funds in New Haven, New York, Boston, and Washington, D.C. The result was that by 1965 a unique American model of legal services had taken shape. It relied on staff attorneys working for nonprofit agencies rather than on private attorneys funded through "judicare" programs. In addition to helping individual clients with everyday problems, legal services advocates wanted to parallel the use of law in the civil rights and civil liberties movements "as an instrument for orderly and constructive social change," points out Alan W. Houseman, director of the Center for Law and Social Policy and a leading figure in legal services. Clint Bamberger, one of its founders, claimed legal services would deploy "the forces of law and the power of lawyers in the War on Poverty to defeat the causes and effects of poverty."[33]

Supporters of legal services believed that only an independent agency could argue aggressively on behalf of poor people. In the early 1970s, they began to advocate for a nonprofit corporation funded by Congress but outside of government control. Although a presidential commission also argued that legal services should be moved outside the executive branch, Nixon twice vetoed bills that would have created an independent Legal Services Corporation, and in 1973 he systematically began to dismantle the OEO, including legal services. Legal service proponents compromised; they agreed to allow the president to appoint all eleven board members to the new corporation, subject to Senate confirmation. With this compromise in hand, in August 1974, shortly before his resignation, Nixon signed the legislation creating the Legal Services Corporation as a "private, nonprofit corporation funded by Congress and established in the District of Columbia to provide financial support for programs of legal assistance in noncriminal proceedings or matters to persons financially unable to afford legal help." It would be governed by an independent, nonpartisan board with no more than six members from the same political party and with no federal employees.

The American model of Legal Services, with its locally based "full service providers," supplied "high quality legal assistance before courts and public agencies and in private negotiations." In theory, Legal Services assured everyone full access to the legal system, regardless of income. Legal Services also developed a "unique infrastructure" consisting of national and state supports, training programs, and a national clearinghouse that backed up local offices and offered leadership on key issues. State and national offices also litigated poverty-related issues and represented clients before state and federal courts and administrative agencies.[34]

The Legal Services Corporation started with restrictions on its activities: it could not participate in desegregation or Selective Service cases. Its attorneys were not allowed to participate in political activities or take most abortion cases; its federal money "could not be used for research unrelated to specific cases." Despite these limits, Legal Services attorneys helped welfare clients organize to claim benefits, and they argued the major Supreme Court cases that expanded welfare rights. By compelling public bureaucracies to adhere to "rules and laws and to treat the poor equitably and in a manner sensitive to their needs," Legal Services attorneys fundamentally changed the way public and private agencies dealt with the poor.[35]

Nonetheless, the "vast majority" of its cases, reported Legal Services Corporation president Alexander D. Forger in 1995, are "individual matters growing out of the everyday legal problems of the poor. The most common categories of cases are family, housing, income maintenance, consumer, and employment." Typical cases included "evictions, foreclosures, divorces, child custody, child support, spousal abuse or neglect, bankruptcy, debt collection, and unemployment, disability, veterans, and other benefit claims." In 1995, the Legal Services Corporation expected to close about 1.7 million cases directly benefiting 5 million people. About 80 percent of cases benefited children living in poverty.[36]

In the late 1970s, neither the Ford nor Carter administrations tried to interfere with the Legal Services Corporation, and they appointed board members, including Hillary Rodham Clinton, who supported an independent program. Still, critics who kept up their attacks saw successful advocacy on behalf of the poor as evidence of inappropriate and illegal activity. Attacks on legal services, observed *New York Times* editorialist Anthony Lewis, reflected "resentment by those who have power in this country when, occasionally, they are held legally accountable for injuries to the weak." Conservatives had always disliked the Legal Services Corporation. "Perhaps no other program stands like such a Rorschach test in the American political system," pointed out a reporter in the *Wash-

ington Post. "What liberals see as evening the scales of justice for the poor is seen by others as outrageous taxpayer subsidies of left-wing causes."[37]

The Legal Services Corporation's funding reflected its contentious history. In its first year, Congress appropriated $71.5 million; by 1981, the amount had reached $321 million. The Reagan administration began to cut the budget immediately. Between 1981 and 1996, funding decreased 13.5 percent, while the cost of living rose 72.6 percent. Although conservatives complained about its budget, by international standards the United States always had funded legal services meanly. England paid about $1 billion for legal assistance to a population one-fifth the size of the United States. The province of Ontario spent $11.40 per person on civil legal aid in 1993, a figure that in America would have added up to a total budget of $2.85 billion. Among industrialized Western nations, only Italy ranked lower in public legal assistance.[38]

Ronald Reagan repeatedly zeroed the Legal Services Corporation out of the federal budget, but not because it cost too much. The real reason, argued two Legal Services executives, was the administration's opposition to "independent, publicly funded legal assistance for poor people." The idea that the federal government should insure access to the legal system for all Americans resonated widely with the public, however. Moderate Republicans also supported the Legal Services Corporation, and Congress consistently restored the funds eliminated by the administration. Near the end of his final term, even Reagan rejected the recommendations of his conservative Legal Services Corporation appointees to radically restructure the organization. Nonetheless, the conservative board succeeded in making it more difficult for the poor and elderly to qualify for assistance from Legal Services. And new regulations prohibited it from using federal funds in congressional redistricting litigation or for lobbying.[39]

With the conservative victory in the 1994 congressional elections, the Legal Services Corporation faced renewed attack. Since the 1980s, conservatives had wanted to move Legal Services toward a market model by requiring clients to pay for services according to a sliding income scale. They also wanted to devolve more funds from the Legal Services Corporation to local offices and to transform legal services into conventional legal aid by drawing primarily on private rather than staff attorneys. Republican Representative Robert Dornan urged his colleagues to "defund the left" by abolishing the program. In a report for the Heritage Foundation, "Why the Legal Services Corporation Must Be Abolished," Kenneth F. Boehm, a former Legal Services Corporation official, and Peter T. Flaherty claimed that legal groups funded by the Legal Services Corporation engaged in "political, lobbyist, and cause-advocacy activities, often at the expense of providing real legal services needed by poor people." Legal Services suffered from an "institutionalized ideological bias," which was revealed in its attorneys' promotion of "racial preferences and illegal immigration," while politicized grantees involved themselves in "congressional redistricting, litigation, and . . . ballot referendum questions." For three decades, they said, the Legal Services Corporation had served as "the legal pillar of the welfare state," and its actions had added millions of people to the welfare rolls and cost billions of dollars. Further, it even litigated "to prevent the eviction of drug dealers from public housing"; its advocacy of children's rights weakened families; and its protection of "aggressive panhandling" and "the right to camp in city parks and streets" eroded public order. A review of the Legal Services Corporation cases revealed that it had "never filed a major case opposed to the goals of the homosexual, feminist, or environmental movements or designed to help poor clients preserve the right to home schooling, defend the right to own firearms, stop the establishment of substance abuse facilities in their neighborhoods, or challenge any type of gender or ethnic quota." Another critic argued that in its efforts to win more funds from Congress, the Legal Services Corporation underreported its income from other sources and in other ways falsified its data. Because the Legal Services Corporation's structure rendered it immune from accountability and congressional control, reform had proved impossible, and local grantees had "all but ignored" the attempt of the Legal Services Corporation board to exercise oversight. To Boehm and Flaherty the only effective reform was abolition.[40] Conservative critics wanted to reduce the Legal Services Corporation to fit a legal aid model—and to make legal assistance a charity rather than an entitlement.

Not surprisingly, advocates of the existing model argued vigorously to leave the program as it was. Legal Services Corporation president Alexander Forger pointed out that it already fit the principles guiding the "reinvention" of government: "local control, public-private partnership, promotion of volunteerism, accountability to the taxpayers, elimination of layers of bureaucracy and unnecessary paperwork, and an emphasis on efficiency and effectiveness." All but 3 percent of the Legal Services Corporation's budget went directly to local programs providing legal assistance to the poor. Only one case in ten went to court, and most of those involved issues of family law that must be decided there. The staff attorney model embodied the virtues of specialization: most private attorneys were not nearly as familiar with the details of housing, welfare, and family law, and the central resources of the Legal Services Corporation provided essential support to the lawyers in the many small Legal Services offices throughout the country.[41]

Nevertheless, in September 1995, the House Judiciary Committee voted along party lines for the abolition of the Legal Services Corporation. After a hard fight, Congress compromised. The Legal Services Corporation would still exist, but with a reduced budget, new operating instructions, and a restrictive wall around its activities. The budget dropped by one-third, and the state and national institutions that supported legal services and supplied their infrastructure lost all their Legal Services Corporation funds—now to be awarded on a competitive basis. Its attorneys had to record how they spent their time, and they no longer could assist prisoners, undocumented immigrants, or people evicted from public housing for alleged drug dealing. They could not accept class-action suits or cases related to legislative redistricting, lobbying, abortion, or ones that challenged the legality of state or federal welfare laws. The restrictions applied not only to federal funds but also to the use of money raised from private and state sources.[42]

Congress's draconian conditions split the Legal Services community. "Last year," reported David Cole, law professor at Georgetown University Law Center, "the Legal Services Corp. board chose to put the organization's budget above the Constitution, and agreed to a set of unconstitutional restrictions on legal assistance to the poor, ostensibly to save the corporation from a worse fate—no funding at all." Alan Houseman, meanwhile, defended the compromise, arguing that Legal Services programs still could address the problems of low-income persons in "virtually all substantive areas." More than "95 percent of the work done in legal services in 1995 can continue in 1997," he said, "and over 98% of the cases brought to court in 1995 could be brought in 1997." Some legal services attorneys filed suits against the new congressionally mandated restrictions, while advocates of the compromise feared that challenging Congress would provoke a backlash. Although in New York the opponents of the compromise won initial victories in state courts, the issue dragged on, unresolved, a divisive influence among legal service staff and supporters. In New York in 1999, the United States Court of Appeals for the Second Circuit struck down the restriction that prohibited Legal Services attorneys from any "effort to amend or otherwise challenge existing law" in cases relating to welfare. The regulation, wrote Judge Pierre N. Leval, was "viewpoint discrimination" that "clearly seeks to discourage challenges to the status quo." In October 2000, the case reached the Supreme Court on appeal, where sharp questions from justices indicated that the Court might find Congress had exceeded its authority. Justice David Souter told the federal government's deputy solicitor general, who was arguing in favor of the restriction, "You're getting just about to the molten core of the First Amendment. . . . There's something very risky going on here."[43]

Even before the congressional budget cut was put fully into effect, local legal service offices throughout the country had begun to lay off attorneys. One-third of the seventeen attorneys at the Legal Aid Society of Orange County, California, resigned with severance packages rather than face the anticipated layoffs. The office also stopped accepting "lengthy cases, such as contested divorces and other family law issues." And it became "much harder for clients to get through the door," reported the supervising attorney for the senior citizen program. "They're going to receive much less services than they did in the past." John F. O'Toole, a veteran poverty lawyer and director of the National Center for Youth Law, a specialized center that would lose all its federal funding under the compromise, reflected, "It's probably the most fundamental shift in how government deals with disadvantaged people at any time since the Great Depression. At the time when our clients need us most, the government is cutting back on the amount of work we can do for them." In 1996, Georgia Legal Services employed 80 lawyers and 37 paralegals. Within a year the numbers dropped to 60 lawyers and 24 paralegals with more cuts expected. The formerly busy legal service office in Wayneboro, Georgia, had closed; a video rental store occupied its former space. A "circuit-riding" Legal Services attorney based in the Augusta office, which covered thirteen counties, visited a few times a month. "They hand out pamphlets. There is a hot line to call. There is a lot of bitterness, too."[44]

As the first "era of legal services" ended, its context changed dramatically, pointed out Houseman. To survive, Legal Services had to adapt not only to reduced funding, new restrictions, and the unrelenting hostility of its opponents; it also needed to adjust to the devolution of public policy. As a result of the 1996 welfare bill, a great deal of the law on which advocates had relied no longer was available for use. Instead, Legal Services attorneys would have to base their cases "on fact specific situations" as they tried to persuade "agency officials or caseworkers" that clients deserved assistance. At the same time, advocates needed to shift their attention to state rather than federal government. "How civil legal services for low-income Americans are provided will be dependent as much on actions taken at the State as on the national level," noted Houseman. Some states flexed their new muscles by passing legislation that set the initial benefits for newcomers at the level of benefits in their former home state— a practice that appeared to violate *Shapiro v. Thompson* (1969), one of the Supreme Court's famous welfare rights decisions. Legal Services attorneys played a leading role in successfully arguing against these "durational residency" rules in state courts and, eventually, in 1999, the Supreme Court.[45]

Some of the larger Legal Services offices with access to nonfederal funds responded creatively to the new requirements by dividing into two organizations. One used Legal Services Corporation funds to serve the everyday needs of clients, and the other, with no federal funding, carried on the work of advocacy and the representation of clients who otherwise would have been excluded. Critics charged that the division was an artificial dodge to avoid the law because, in practice, both organizations occupied the same building and shared resources. In most areas, including virtually all of the South, the point was moot because local Legal Services offices could not afford to divide their functions. In all of Pennsylvania, Philadelphia's was the only office that split off a separate branch to continue advocacy and related work.[46]

With fewer federal funds, Legal Services had to rely on a mix of state and private funds, including support from state and local bar associations. Particularly important were the funds known as Interest on Lawyers' Trust Accounts, or IOLTA. Most states required lawyers to give the interest generated from their clients' trust accounts to Legal Services programs. In Philadelphia, for instance, the funds allowed Legal Services to continue operating at the same level as before the cuts. With new sources of money and a redesigned structure, the larger Legal Services offices appeared to have weathered the conservative attack. But a conservative challenge to IOLTA reached the Supreme Court, which in a five-to-four decision found that the interest on the trust accounts was the property of the clients. The Court did not rule on whether Legal Services' use of the interest amounted to an unconstitutional "taking" of private property. Lower federal courts would address that issue, which, eventually, promised to wend its way back to the Supreme Court. Although not a definitive ruling on the issue, the decision threw the use of IOLTA funds—a crucial support for legal services—into question.[47]

Conservatives found even more ammunition in their battle against Legal Services in a 1999 General Accounting Office report that the agency overreported its cases by tens of thousands. However, whether or not it overreported its cases, Legal Services had never met more than a fraction of the legal needs of the nation's poor, even in its heydey. Every study of legal needs concluded that the current system met at most one-fifth of the legal needs of the population it was intended to serve. And, at the same time, law firms were cutting back on free services for the poor. Many of the nation's largest legal firms, reported the *New York Times* in August 2000, "have cut back on pro bono work so sharply that they fall far below professional guidelines for representing people who cannot afford to pay." Only a massive increase in funding and less restrictive operating rules would permit legal services to meet the needs of low-income Americans.[48]

The struggle over Legal Services turned as much on power as on money. When fundamental changes occurred, they resulted from conservative attack, not the ambitions of Legal Services advocates to expand the program's scope. Congress allowed the Legal Services Corporation to live but tried to defang it as an effective political force on behalf of the poor. Although the conservative attack had forced Legal Services to restrict and narrow its activities, opponents continued their relentless scrutiny, hoping to weaken legal services even more and to redefine legal help for the poor as a charity, not a right.

PRIVATIZING THE SAFETY NET

When the public safety net gives way, a private one cushions the fall. There is nothing new in this. But the private safety net reflects its context in time and place. In late-twentieth-century America, it combined variants of very old survival strategies with ones that used market products in some unexpected ways.

Before the industrial era a great deal of poverty was seasonal. When workers found themselves out of a job in the winter or during cyclical downturns of the economy, they moved back to family farms—a coping strategy largely impossible anymore by the third quarter of the nineteenth century. In towns and cities, impoverished families of course reduced expenses. They moved to cheaper housing, ate less, and sometimes kept their children out of school for lack of food and clothing. Parents who hit rock bottom often found themselves forced to give up their children to orphanages or agencies that placed them with families on farms or in distant towns. Everywhere, when poverty struck, people turned for help first to families and friends. Old folks moved in with children, younger families with parents or siblings. Friends and neighbors often gave them food, clothes, or small amounts of money. Expectations of reciprocity bound poor people in loose networks; they gave when they could in the expectation that when their time of need came, someone would do the same for them. Unfortunately, the families and friends of people in need usually could help only a little. They might prevent starvation or freezing to death on a city street, but they, too, were poor and lived always on the verge of destitution.[49]

With help from family and friends insufficient, destitute families turned to their children, who were sent out to scavenge coal, rags, or bits of clothing. They went to work selling newspapers, running errands, or doing odd jobs. They stayed home to take care of younger brothers and sisters when their mothers found work. When poor families periodically ran out of the cash they needed for rent or food, they sometimes begged on the street or went to one of the myriad charities or to the public authorities for outdoor relief. There they found an uncertain reception—with luck a little help and few questions asked; at other times intense investigation and intrusive supervision; sometimes they were simply turned away. Three alternatives to homelessness or starvation were left: the poorhouse; petty crime, mostly prostitution or theft; or credit. Landlords and local grocers were the primary creditors of the poor. They carried them from month to month, cajoling and threatening but not charging interest. Sometimes, of course, landlords evicted them and grocers cut them off, but without the credit from local merchants, poor people could not have survived. Along with help from relatives, it was the sturdiest thread in the private safety net.

Current-day survival strategies are not so very different. Family help, which declined after World War II, rebounded in the 1980s and 1990s. When Kathryn Edin and Laura Lein found that none of the mothers they interviewed could survive on public assistance, they classified the ways these mothers made ends meet. They found 46 percent of mothers engaged in "work-based strategies"—mostly unreported work that would have lowered their public benefits. Even more, 77 percent, used "network-based strategies"—help from family and friends or cash from boyfriends and absent fathers. Fewer, 31 percent, turned to "agency-based strategies"—looking for help from private charities and services.[50]

Credit also remained crucial to the late-twentieth-century private safety net. Undoubtedly, informal credit from family, friends, and merchants still was common, if impossible to quantify. But a new form of credit gained more attention as people in economic trouble transformed credit cards and bankruptcy—market tools—into a part of the private safety net. Credit card use among the poor increased dramatically. Between 1983 and 1995, the share of poor households with at least one credit card more than doubled from 17 percent to 36 percent, while, in 1995 dollars, their average balance rose from $778 to $1,380. The combination of easy access—credit card companies seeking out new markets—with declining real wages fueled the use of credit to sustain even a modest standard of living. Overall, debt as a percentage of after-tax income rose from under 40 percent in 1952 to more than 90 percent in 1997. U.S. households spend about 17 percent of their after-tax income on debt service. Rising household debt, points out economics writer Doug Henwood, was linked with the growing concentration of wealth. As a result "of the decline in real hourly wages, and the stagnation in household incomes, the middle and lower classes have borrowed more to stay in place; they've borrowed from the very rich who have gotten richer. The rich need a place to earn interest on their surplus funds, and the rest of the population makes a juicy lending target."[51]

When people could not pay their debts, they turned to bankruptcy, which, while not pleasant, was not especially difficult. In 1975, roughly one of every 1,000 Americans filed for bankruptcy; by 1995, the number had multiplied five times. In 1998, about 1.4 million Americans filed for personal bankruptcy—about triple the number twelve years earlier. Bankruptcy was not a route chosen by the most destitute, who had not been able to amass either debts or possessions. It remained much more common among the near and newly poor. Single mothers, the working poor, workers laid off from jobs: all found their way to bankruptcy court. Rather than personal extravagance, it was more often the price of survival in late-twentieth-century America—for example, huge medical bills—that pushed average citizens into bankruptcy. With the demand for aid increasing and the supply of benefits contracting, bankruptcy had become the ultimate safety net of the late-twentieth century. Like the rest of the safety net, however, it appeared about to shrink. The banking and credit card industries, whose aggressive marketing tactics bear some of the responsibility for the rise in bankruptcy, wanted Congress to make it harder for individuals to avoid paying their debts by declaring bankruptcy. In early 2000, Congress appeared ready to comply.[52]

. . . .

To individuals, fighting poverty 1990s style often meant maxing-out credit cards and declaring bankruptcy. To the federal government it meant linking some benefits more closely to employment and delivering others through the market. The Earned Income Tax Credit was the most direct antipoverty strategy. Not welfare, but a credit delivered impersonally through the tax code, the EITC moved many people over the poverty line, but only if they had worked. Clinton's "New Markets" policy, along with empowerment zones, as we have seen, attacked poverty indirectly. They proposed tax breaks and other incentives to lure businesses to depressed areas where they would re-create markets, which, in turn, would mean jobs and income—the best antidotes for poverty. In the 1990s, poverty had become a problem of market failure. With attention focused on antipoverty strategies linked to work and markets, older programs inherited from the New Deal or Great Society struggled, out of favor even when tolerated as inescapable. Food stamps stumbled along, buffeted by political winds, with its coverage and benefits reduced. Legal Services barely weathered assaults to survive in a downsized, attenuated form while the entitlement to public assistance succumbed completely as Congress and the president engineered the end of welfare.

THE END OF WELFARE

In 1996 conservative Republicans helped President Bill Clinton honor his campaign pledge to "end welfare as we know it." After many months of political skirmishing, Clinton agreed to sign legislation that withdrew the entitlement of the poorest Americans to federal cash benefits and turned over much of the authority for public assistance to the states. Three years after "the end of welfare," the public assistance rolls had declined dramatically, far more than almost anyone had anticipated, leaving states awash in federal cash. Although they spent some of their windfall on improved welfare-related services, a great deal of federal money remained untouched, and no one could say whether the brave new world of public assistance would deliver on its promise to move most recipients to independence and work, or whether it would consign them to jobs that paid poverty wages and to periodic dependence.

The End of Welfare

AFDC enjoyed no real support. Liberals had pointed out its inadequacies for decades. Conservatives thought its benefits overly generous and its incentives perverse. Recipients found it mean and stigmatizing. With their massive congressional victory Republicans finally had both a popular mandate and the political power to end welfare, and liberals found themselves in the ironic position of defending a program they despised.[1]

The case for the end of welfare rested in part on a manufactured crisis of cost. A Heritage Foundation report by Robert Rector and William F. Lauber, *America's Failed $5.4 Trillion War on Poverty*, argued that from 1965 through 1994 "welfare spending . . . cost the taxpayers $5.4 trillion in constant 1993 dollars." Not only was this spending ineffective, they contended, it worsened the very problems—dependency and out-of-wedlock births—it was supposed to solve. In 1996 congressional Republicans repeatedly used Rector's numbers to support their version of "welfare reform." Only Representative Chakah Fattah of Philadelphia refused to play a part in his colleagues' charade. The bill, he said, "is built on the biggest lie that has ever been told to the American people . . .

that we are spending too much as a country to help poor people." No "legitimate analysis of a federal budget would tell us that we spent $5 trillion on the War on Poverty. It is all made up out of whole cloth."[2]

Representative Fattah was right. The $5.4 trillion war on poverty was a fiction. For one thing, a very large share of the money spent by the programs included in the calculations did not flow to recipients of federal public assistance. For instance, in 1994, only 16 percent of the largest means-tested entitlement program, Medicaid, was spent on AFDC beneficiaries; 46 percent went to low-income elderly and disabled persons. Little of the Earned Income Tax Credit went to AFDC recipients, either, unless they worked; most of it, instead, helped the working poor. Nor was public assistance "designed to foster self-sufficiency or help families work their way out of poverty." Its purpose, rather, was to help poor people survive. Rector and Lauber also were inaccurate when they argued that the poverty rate had remained "virtually unchanged" since the onset of the War on Poverty. When economic growth, higher wages, and more generous antipoverty programs coincided, poverty rates went down. Between 1964 and 1973 the poverty rate plummeted from 19 percent to 11 percent, while the number of poor people declined by more than 13 million. Moreover, the statistics of income poverty are not a full or accurate measure of the beneficial impact of many of the programs they derided. Because food stamps, housing, and Medicaid, for example, do not deliver benefits in cash, their influence does not show up in statistics of income poverty.[3]

Contrary to conservative myth, AFDC was not expensive. In 1993, AFDC supported nearly 14 million people, of whom 9 million were children. Monthly benefits varied greatly by state, for example, from $607 in California to $120 in Mississippi. These differences cannot be explained by the cost of living. The cost of AFDC benefits, annually about $22 billion, constituted only about 1 percent of the federal budget and 2 percent of federal entitlement spending. AFDC cost less than one-tenth as much as Social Security, and, unlike Social Security, the value of AFDC benefits had declined—between 1970 and 1996, the decline in the median benefit was a stunning 51 percent.[4] The real secret of AFDC's persistence lay in its cheapness. It is hard to imagine a less expensive way to keep millions of nonworking people alive.

Rising alarm shared by both Republicans and Democrats at out-of-wedlock births and the consequences of dependency provoked the 1990s assault on AFDC. The numbers were alarmingly high: in 1995, 56 percent of black children lived in single-parent families, compared with 33 percent of Hispanics and 21 percent of whites. In 1994, 70 percent of black children were born outside marriage. This large number of single-parent families kept poverty rates high because about half of them were poor.[5] The "new politics of poverty," observed political scientist Lawrence Mead, was about dependence, not money. Welfare experts Mary Jo Bane and David Ellwood wrote, "It is hard to miss the profound shift in emphasis and tone in poverty discussions over the past ten to fifteen years. A decade or two ago, the academic debate and to a large degree the popular debate were often focused on matters of adequacy, labor supply responses, tax rate, and opportunity. Now 'dependency' is the current preoccupation."

In the 1980s, Charles Murray's book *Losing Ground* proved the most influential conservative attack on AFDC. Murray argued that the well-meaning but misguided extension of social benefits during the Great Society years had fueled the rise of single-parent families, out-of-wedlock births, and dependence. Although social scientists thoroughly discredited Murray's book by exposing its shoddy statistics and fallacious arguments, their writing did little, if anything, to dislodge it as a respected source among conservatives or to lessen its use by politicians. In the 1990s, Rector played something of the same role as Murray, although without a major book. Rector, along with Lauber, argued that "the welfare system has paid for non-work and non-marriage and has achieved massive increases in both. By undermining the work ethic and rewarding illegitimacy, the welfare system insidiously generates its own clientele. . . . Welfare bribes individuals into courses of behavior which in the long run are self-defeating to the individual, harmful to children, and increasingly a threat to society." Welfare's worst result was "its corrosive effect on family structure, driving up illegitimacy, which in turn is a powerful factor contributing to other social problems." It also fueled "long-term inter-generational dependence," thereby "trapping many families in a repeating cycle of debilitating and self-destructive behavior." [6]

Not jobs, wages, or globalization, but the collapse of family threatened America's future, and its major source was welfare. The answer lay in the total reconstruction of welfare policy to enforce morals, support marriage, and push women into the labor force. The stakes were very high. The future of America hung on the ability of social policy to turn around the behavior of young black and Hispanic women. Pennsylvania's Senator Rick Santorum, who helped design the Republican position on welfare, said most Republicans believed welfare "is the number-one societal problem, that it's at the root of the disintegration of families in the inner city, the social decay we have seen in the last 20 years. What we have to stop doing is guaranteeing people failure. These programs have done nothing but keep people poor."[7]

The links between welfare and family structure begin to crumble on close examination. Like Murray, Rector and Lauber do not explain why AFDC rolls climbed as benefits declined. If young women responded to incentives, the rolls should have grown smaller. They also ignore the falling fertility of black women—the steady reduction in the number of children in an average AFDC family, from 4 in 1969 to 2.8 in 1993. And other than the inducement of "welfare" benefits, they offer no explanation for declining marriage rates and rising out-of-wedlock births among black women—low wages and the poor job prospects of African American men, for instance, play no role in conservative explanations.[8]

Indeed, the timing of demographic trends undermined the attempt to pin the blame for these trends on AFDC. Unmarried mothers often needed public assistance to survive, and the increase in their numbers drove up the AFDC rolls. However, the availability of AFDC is not the reason why the number of out-of-wedlock births and single-parent families increased. In fact, after the recession of the early 1990s began to ease, AFDC rolls started to decline. Among blacks, births to unmarried women, the number of one-parent families with a never-married mother, and the number of children living with one parent all also moved downward from their peak. Other parts of the conservative criticism likewise disintegrated under close analysis. Studies found that surprisingly small numbers of women who grew up in welfare-dependent families were themselves dependent, and three of four supported by public assistance had not received it as children. Although daughters (but not sons) growing up in AFDC-dependent households were somewhat more likely than others to turn to AFDC themselves, by itself the correlation proved nothing about causation. Many other factors, such as parents' education, poverty, the quality of schools, and the impact of neighborhood could have influenced the outcome. In the welfare debates of the 1990s, conservative accounts of research simply misrepresented the evidence. James Q. Wilson, professor of management and public policy at the University of California, Los Angeles, dismissed the argument that abolishing AFDC would reduce out-of-wedlock births as "in large measure based on untested assumptions, ideological posturing and perverse priorities. . . . It is, at best, an informed guess."[9]

Very large numbers who left the AFDC rolls were poor in the following year—a result of low wages. Not surprisingly, within two years, more than half the women who had left AFDC to take a job were back on the rolls. This "churning" of the AFDC rolls—the frequent movement on and off—showed that poor families try to find ways to help themselves. By and large, they did not want to remain dependent on government, and their personal histories described an intermittently successful search for an elusive independence. Many, of course, did not leave; they composed the core of long-term recipients—the majority of women on AFDC at any one time—incorrectly believed typical of women assisted by AFDC. For them, AFDC indeed had become a way of life.[10]

The program's own structure, in fact, undermined independence and self-support more than the bad example set by parents or the generosity of AFDC's benefits. Eligibility rules defeated attempts to save modest amounts of money or keep a reliable car to drive to work. The rules allowing recipients to keep some of their earnings, virtually eliminated during the Reagan years, removed incentives to supplement AFDC with work. The threatened loss of medical insurance built risk into the exchange of AFDC for a low-wage job, and without subsidies for child care, employment often was impossible. These structural impediments in AFDC increasingly appeared irrational to both conservatives and liberals, and state waivers focused on modifying many of them. Indeed, governors, tired of asking Washington for waivers, demanded further devolution and chafed at persisting federal controls—at the need, as governors put it, to beg Washington to ask permission to experiment. Representative Gerald Solomon of New York told the House, "We have heard testimony on this floor from State after State that [in] the waiver process . . . thoughtful and experimental governors must troop to Washington DC, hat in hand, and request permission to reform low-income programs at home. The waiver request is then subject to endless debate by bureaucrats and subject to negotiation and even change by the Federal departments involved."[11]

. . . .

Many ordinary Americans objected to welfare for other reasons. As they worked harder for less pay, many resented what they believed was the free ride offered by welfare, and many working mothers, now the majority, found it hard to understand why "welfare mothers" should not be compelled to juggle the same burden of work and child care as they did every day. The most important component in Americans' intense dislike of welfare, reports political scientist Martin Gilens, was the "widespread belief that most welfare recipients would rather sit home and collect benefits than work hard to support themselves." Representative John Kasich of Ohio reminded his colleagues in the House of the "cynicism" felt about AFDC by "the folks who get up and go to work every day for a living. . . . Those mothers and fathers who have had to struggle for an entire lifetime to make ends meet, they have never asked for Food

Stamps, they have never asked for welfare, they have never asked for housing, and they are struggling. . . . These people were becoming cynical, they were being poisoned in regard to this system, and they were demanding change."[12]

To many, "welfare" became a code word for race, and the "welfare problem" signified the rising number of young, unmarried black or Hispanic mothers on the rolls. In 1994, people of color composed a majority, 63 percent, of AFDC recipients—a number that had increased solidly during the past decade. The proportion was much higher in conservative, "antiwelfare" southern states. The share of black AFDC recipients was 75 percent in Alabama, 74 percent in Georgia, and 83 percent in Mississippi. In older cities, it was very high as well—for instance, 97 percent in Washington, D.C.[13] The color of welfare intensified the gulf between its clients and the white working poor and reinforced the conservative attack on AFDC. By placing responsibility for out-of-wedlock births and single-parent families on AFDC, conservatives helped discredit government policy and reinforced the belief that government is the source of social problems, not their solution. By offering up a convenient scapegoat for widespread anxieties about economic insecurity and fears of downward mobility, they helped construct an image of the undeserving poor that fractured the potential for political unity among low-income Americans.

Capitalizing on the antiwelfare sentiment that cut across political divisions, Bill Clinton ran for president in 1992 partly with the promise to "end welfare as we know it." Clinton's plan, points out one of his principal policy advisers, David Ellwood, rested on a strategy with four key elements: "make work pay"; "two years and you work"; "child support enforcement"; and "fight teen pregnancy." Despite a plan ready to roll, Clinton postponed welfare reform in favor of national health insurance, which at the time seemed a logical first step.[14]

Clinton did not introduce his own welfare reform plan until the summer of 1994. By then, attention had shifted to the forthcoming congressional election and the proposals in the Republicans' Contract with America. The Contract criticized Clinton's proposals to reform AFDC—which were attacked as too harsh by Democrats to the left of the president—as tepid and inadequate. Instead, conservative Republicans proposed much tougher changes, including the abolition of AFDC. Clinton objected to the more extreme measures, like orphanages, the threat to federally mandated free lunches for poor schoolchildren, and the abolition of AFDC, but he remained virtually silent about the details of the "welfare reform" legislation working its way through the House and Senate, where the debate on welfare turned harsher, nastier, and more punitive. On the floor of the House of Representatives, John L. Mica, a Republican from Florida, hoisted a sign that read, "Don't Feed the Alligators." He explained: "We post these warnings because unnatural feeding and artificial care create dependency." Representative Barbara Cubin of Wyoming offered a similar analogy from her state: "The Federal Government introduced wolves into the State of Wyoming, and they put them in pens, and they brought in elk and venison to them every day. . . . This is what I call the wolf welfare program."[15]

On March 24, 1995, the House, led by Speaker Newt Gingrich, passed a draconian welfare bill. The Senate's slightly more moderate version also relied on block grants and time limits to end the status of AFDC as an entitlement. An authoritative analysis of the bill concluded that it would push more than 1 million children into poverty. On September 19 Clinton signaled that he would sign the Senate's bill anyway.[16] Throughout the fall, the House and Senate worked to reconcile their differences, and for a time, it seemed possible that they would indeed produce a bill that Clinton would sign. As he tried to define a nonideological middle ground and also claim some of the credit, Clinton, to the dismay of more liberal Democrats, inched toward the Republican position. The conference bill, which moved closer to the House version, proposed enormous cuts in programs that aided the poor. The Office of Management and Budget concluded that it would push 1.5 million children into poverty and worsen the poverty of large numbers of children already poor. "Reductions of this magnitude in programs for the poor," observed the Center on Budget and Policy Priorities, "are unprecedented in U.S. history." Aside from transforming AFDC, the bill would have ended the entitlement to Medicaid and food stamps and reduced nutritional supplements to children by turning these supports into block grants, which proved more than Clinton was willing to accept, and in January 1996 he vetoed the bill.[17]

Despite their disagreements, both Clinton and the Republicans, worried about the November elections, wanted a welfare reform bill. Clinton seemed vulnerable because he had already vetoed two welfare bills, while Republicans had not yet managed to turn their decisive 1994 congressional victory into legislative success. Compromise, however, remained elusive, and throughout the early summer another Clinton veto seemed possible. On July 18, 1996, the House passed another welfare bill by a vote of 256 to 170, and the Senate passed a slightly different version five days later by 74 to 24. The bills' core provisions commanded a consensus among Republicans and most Democrats. While Clinton accepted the end of the federal guarantee of public assistance for women and children and the transformation of AFDC into time-limited block grants to the states, he proposed four amendments: benefits for legal immigrants, food and commodity vouchers for children whose mothers' benefits had expired, Medicaid continuation after the AFDC time clock ran out, and a federal guarantee of food stamps. Although the House-Senate conference committee accepted only the last two of his amendments, on July 31, 1996, Clinton announced he would sign the bill—the Personal Responsibility and Work Opportunity Reconciliation Act, which passed the House and Senate within two days and received Clinton's signature on August 22, 1996.[18] Clinton admitted the law was far from perfect, and he promised that with subsequent legislation he would fix its worst features.

Congress and the president together had ended the nation's sixty-one-year-old federal guarantee of cash assistance—and the public supported them. In one poll, 82 percent approved of the final welfare reform legislation. "With this legislation," said Representative Mike Castle of Delaware, "we have finally begun the process by which America's underclass problem can be solved, and break a generational cycle and culture of dependency and poverty." To Representative Deborah Pryce of Ohio the law replaced "a welfare system debilitated by Federal control with a system based on innovation and flexibility at the State and local level."[19] Under the new law, state authority increased exponentially, with one interesting exception. While states gained authority in public assistance and child care, the federal government tightened its control over child support, which it tried to forge into a more national system. Given the obvious drawbacks of a decentralized system that allowed delinquent parents to evade their obligations by moving out of state, governors in this instance ceded authority to the federal government without much complaint.

As a result of the bill, market models now pervaded the goals, administration, and philosophy of welfare. The new law reoriented public assistance around the transition to work. A job in the regular labor market was the overriding goal. The "key word" in the new public assistance program, pointed out Representative Solomon, "is temporary. After being taken care of on a limited basis, these people are going to have to go to work. . . . We should emphasize welfare as a temporary boost from despair to the sense of self-worth inherent in work." States were now free to encourage work by turning to the private market—to contract out the administration of public assistance to private providers, whether non-profit, faith-based, or for-profit, either directly or through vouchers.

The market logic also was reflected clearly in the largely gratuitous abolition of the entitlement to public assistance, which was not necessary to accomplish the purposes of the new legislation. Rather, entitlement fell because it contradicted the market imperative that drove welfare reform. Once a term that signified the solidarity of an expansive welfare state that extended the rights and meaning of citizenship, in the 1990s "entitlement" became a term almost as negative as "welfare." "We have generation after generation," proclaimed Representative Don Manzullo of Illinois, "locked in a seemingly endless cycle of destitution and poverty. They are the lost forgotten statistics, dependent on the Federal entitlement trap."[20] To critics, entitlements posed several problems. First was cost: as instruments of social policy, entitlements, such as Social Security, Medicare, or food stamps, threatened to escalate out of control because they were open-ended commitments.[21] They also created moral hazards: entitlements encouraged dependency by providing economic support independent of work, while some entitlements, like AFDC, rewarded the undeserving poor, whose bad behavior had earned them public benefits in the first place. Finally, entitlements suppressed personal responsibility, detached rewards from work and merit, and promoted the stagnant paternalism of big government rather than the dynamism of competitive markets.

President Clinton had a more sophisticated understanding of entitlements, and he refrained from attacking them on principle. Why he agreed to end the entitlement to public assistance remains something of a mystery. Certainly, he probably saw it as the price he had to pay for a politically necessary bill. But, as former Clinton administration official Peter Edelman points out, he may just have not considered it a very important issue:

> Perhaps he did not see the entitlement as being quite so meaningful as others did. It is important to remember that he is not only a former governor but the former governor of Arkansas. AFDC benefits in Arkansas were so low that he might not have seen the entitlement as meaning what it does in higher-benefit states. He might have thought that as governor of Arkansas he would have been able to design a better program if he had received the federal money in the form of a block grant, without the restrictions, limited as they were, that were imposed by the federal AFDC program.[22]

The new welfare law replaced the entitlement to cash assistance under AFDC, which it abolished, with two new block grants to the states intended "to help families escape welfare." One provided "cash and other benefits to help needy families support their children while simultaneously requiring families to make verifiable efforts to leave welfare for work and to avoid births outside marriage." The name of the new program—Temporary Assistance for Needy Families (TANF)—reflected its purpose. The second block grant combined four major child care programs for low-income families.[23]

The new legislation also expressly tried to promote two-parent families. The bill was full of "findings" about the adverse effects of out-of-wedlock pregnancy. Congress gave states cash incentives to bring down the rate of teenage births and ordered them to try. At the same time, the bill implicitly recognized that families had changed. Like it or not, to exchange dependence for a job, young unmarried women needed help with child care, health insurance, job training, and perhaps transportation. The 1996 law made a modest start at providing these supports. Much would depend on how states used their new authority and how Congress would respond to further requests for money. Whether the two policy directives—reversing out-of-wedlock births and supporting single mothers in their transition to work—would coexist or collide no one yet knew, or had asked.

Public assistance under TANF is temporary in more than name. It limits the total lifetime benefit period to five years, although states may exempt 20 percent of their caseload or, as some states have done, set even shorter time limits. In addition, within two years—sooner if a state wants—all able-bodied recipients had to participate in an acceptable work activity designed to help them become self-supporting. When the law is fully implemented, states must place half their recipients in work programs at least thirty hours a week. Education by and large does not count as acceptable work; instead, the program emphasizes quick entrance to the labor force. The new law ended AFDC-related child care programs, including the guarantee of subsidized child care for parents at work or in educational programs. It replaced them with the child care block grant. To protect workers, it prohibited employers from using workfare to fill jobs open because of layoffs.

Block grants equaled the amount states had received for public assistance and child care programs in fiscal 1994 or 1995. To receive full grants, states also needed to spend their own money—at least 75 percent of what they spent in 1994; if a state failed to meet its work participation quota, its proportion rose to 80 percent. There was a $1 billion cash bonus for states that succeeded in meeting program goals. Despite these federal requirements, the law allowed states latitude in how they used their TANF grant. They could shift up to 30 percent of it into child care or social services block grants, use it for employment placement programs, or contract out the administration of welfare services. They could deny additional aid to mothers who gave birth while on TANF, and limit or deny all cash benefits to unmarried teen parents. Unwed teen parents were required to live at home or with a responsible adult and attend school to receive benefits.[24] With Medicaid, however, states did not gain the flexibility they wanted because Medicaid remained an entitlement that states must provide for a year to low-income families that lose TANF eligibility on account of work or child support.

Some of the more than fifty changes to current child support laws in the 1996 bill focused on locating and tracking parents; the law required employers to report information on newly hired employees to a state registry within twenty days and to share it with other state agencies. The Federal Parent Locator Service—a vast new national database on individuals—matched information from state registries and federal agencies. The law also tightened procedures for establishing paternity, and for the first time, it permitted federal foster care payments to for-profit institutions.[25]

Legal immigrants lost benefits under the law, which denied them Supplemental Security Income and food stamps; barred them from most means-tested programs during their first five years here; and, with immigrants who arrived after August 22, 1996, allowed states to deny them assistance under almost any means-tested program. In 1997 and 1998, Congress, prodded by the president, reinstated Medicaid, SSI, and food stamps for some, but by no means all, legal immigrants. Clinton's chief domestic-policy adviser, Bruce Reed, exaggerated when he claimed the president had "kept both promises he made when he signed the welfare law, to reform the nation's welfare system and to restore benefits that never should have been cut in the first place."[26]

Republicans delighted in the new welfare bill and tried to take all the credit. Senator Slade Gorton of Washington labeled it "a magnificent new experiment. . . . It would be difficult to do worse than we've been doing over the course of the last several decades. We have a marvelous opportunity to do far better." Representative E. Clay Shaw, Jr., the primary author of the bill, proclaimed it "a revolutionary way to attack poverty." Congress had launched a "rescue mission to save millions of children from poverty and lives of dependence on welfare." Republican governors also greeted "welfare reform" warmly. Not only did it embody principles they championed; it gave them the flexibility they wanted.[27]

Others predicted disaster. The Senate's leading welfare expert, Senator Daniel Patrick Moynihan, termed the bill "the most brutal act of social policy since Reconstruction." The administration had refused to allow the Congressional Budget Office to comply with a congressional request for an estimate of how many children would be thrown into poverty by the pending welfare legislation. In effect, Moynihan admonished, the administration had said, "We will not tell the Senate what it is doing. If it knows what it is doing, it wouldn't do it." David Ellwood, a leading welfare and poverty researcher and former Clinton administration official, warned that the new legislation was "more dangerous than most people realize. No bill that is likely to push more than a million additional children into poverty—many in working families—is real reform." Opponents of the bill included the National Conference of Catholic Bishops, the Union of American Hebrew Congregations, the Children's Defense Fund, the National Urban League, labor unions, civil rights groups, and many big-city mayors. Mayors predicted calamity; the welfare bill "would profoundly increase the nation's homeless population, leaving local governments ill-equipped to contend with a growing demand for services." Increased costs for crime, job training, and lost purchasing power, they said, would quickly eat up the modest annual $9 billion savings from the bill.[28] With private charity already stretched thin, the result, worried political scientist Margaret Weir, "could be a new class of invisible poor" shunted hungry and homeless from program to program.[29]

Former Clinton administration official Peter Edelman, who resigned over the welfare bill, called it "the worst thing Bill Clinton has done." Neither the food stamp cuts nor the denial of benefits to immigrants, Edelman emphasized, had "anything to do with welfare reform." Many of the bill's provisions were just mean. No longer could people "thrown off the rolls without justification" go to court for a hearing. Although states found themselves initially with more money, the cap on block grants would leave them with less in six years, when they would face choices between spending on benefits and job-related activities. Nor was there more than a small contingency fund for recessions. In five years, when the first time limits were reached, many people would "fall into the abyss all at once," warned Edelman. The Congressional Budget Office estimated that the bill was underfunded by $12 billion, which was necessary for states to meet work requirements, and "even the highly advertised increased child care funding" remained "more than $1 billion short."[30]

Were Edelman and other critics correct? Was the new welfare bill driving American social policy toward disaster? Or would it move massive numbers of people from dependence to self-support? Would the law unleash the creative energy to transform an intractable and failed welfare system? Would Clinton, as he promised, be able to fix the law's worst features? The early evidence proved ambiguous.

After the End of Welfare

Nobody knew what would happen after the end of welfare. Predictions ranged from apocalyptic visions of hungry children and homeless men and women roaming city streets to optimistic scenes of an energized and self-supporting citizenry assuming personal responsibility and building strong families. As the new system took effect, though, the great story became the astonishing decline in the public assistance rolls.

The 1996 legislation more or less had ended the great ideological battles over welfare. Whatever one thought about the issue, the entitlement to public assistance was over. Congress and the president had settled the argument over whether work should be mandatory. The issue became how to run the new system most effectively and efficiently, or, from the advocates' view, with the least harm to those who remained vulnerable.[31]

Many state and local officials across the country began by working to change the culture of welfare administration. Consider a report from the state of Washington as an example:

> "Welfare" has clearly changed, and, to reinforce the new message at every possible turn, offices across the state are rearranging their lobbies, hanging new banners, and changing the way they greet clients. . . . A fresh coat of paint and some creative rearranging help ensure that the WorkFirst message gets through, as does a prominent position for job listings, but the changes at play are more than cosmetic. DSHS offices across the state are incorporating computer centers into their offices to allow clients to search for work on the Internet and scroll through job listings on-line.

In Philadelphia, caseworkers substituted employment assistance for the routine questions used to certify eligibility in the past. "Caseworkers across the region and the country are asking their clients pointed questions and making serious demands," observed a reporter for the *Philadelphia Inquirer*. "They're prodding them to finish school, coaching them on interviewing skills, exhorting them to find jobs."[32]

The ability of welfare recipients to find jobs depended, in part, on the willingness of businesses to hire them. In February 1997, in his State of the Union Address, President Clinton singled out five large corporations for their success in hiring former welfare recipients, and he urged other employers to follow their example. "I'd like to say to every employer in this country who has ever criticized the old welfare system, 'You cannot blame the old system anymore.' We have torn it down. Now do your part. Give someone on welfare a chance to work." In November, on a trip to Wichita, Kansas, he again called on business leaders to open jobs to welfare recipients. "This has to be an American crusade," said the president. He praised the private, nonprofit Welfare-to-Work Partnership, created in the spring, that had signed up 2,500 companies pledged to hire welfare recipients. Still, the five companies he praised in February had hired only a few hundred former welfare recipients to join the ranks of their more than 700,000 employees, and despite the pledges of the 2,500 companies, more than 10 million people remained on public assistance. The pace accelerated, however, and by March 1999, 10,000 companies in the Welfare-to-Work Partnership had hired 410,000 welfare recipients. Clinton used more than the bully pulpit: he ordered federal agencies to hire welfare recipients. In April he announced that federal agencies would hire 10,000 welfare recipients during the next four years, a goal exceeded ahead of schedule, by March 1999. (To put this number into perspective, in 1997, the federal government, excluding the postal service, employed about 1.8 million people.) In July 1999, Clinton claimed that the proportion of welfare recipients at work had multiplied four times since he took office.[33]

Moving welfare recipients into jobs was expensive and difficult. The combination of training, job search, subsidized child care, and health insurance added up to a costly package of supports. Indeed, welfare-to-work programs confronted serious obstacles in the availability and cost of child care and in the "spatial mismatch" between the location of jobs and the residence of potential workers. Congress responded with a $3 billion Welfare-to-Work Program as part of the Balanced Budget Act of 1997. Administered by the Department of Labor and local Private Industry Councils, WtW stressed moving individuals into jobs with a potential for upward mobility and providing them with services; it focused on long-term, hard-to-employ recipients. Its eligibility requirements, however, undermined WtW's potential success. States had difficulty finding clients who met the strict criteria. As a result, in its first eighteen months, WtW spent only about 8 percent of its first year's money. After one year, Philadelphia's WtW program, Greater Philadelphia Works, enrolled only 7,995 of the 15,000 welfare recipients it had targeted. Just over half, 3,800, were placed in jobs, and half of those quit or were fired. Compared to other projects across the nation, however, the Philadelphia program succeeded: its 3,800 job placements were one-fifth of the national total.[34]

Only time would show whether state and local governments would find creative ways to move people from welfare to work or whether they would take the low road to "welfare reform" by emphasizing tough sanctions instead of employment-related support. State governments now could shift responsibility for administering TANF to counties and cities. Some states, such as California, seized the opportunity to devolve public assistance responsibility downward, and local governments responded with a variety of plans. The profusion of plans made it hard to draw any systematic picture of welfare reform at the local level, although early state efforts surprised advocates. A child care expert at the Children's Defense

Fund commented, "States are doing more than I expected. The question is will it continue?" States had not responded to their new relative autonomy with the "race to the bottom" that some critics had predicted. But they were flush with money. Wendell Primus, a former federal official who resigned in protest at the 1996 law, predicted, "The time when a race to the bottom will happen is when a recession hits."[35]

States carved out remarkably different TANF plans, which varied in every detail from asset limits to family caps. Similar "policy variation" marked the response of cities to welfare reform. Those states with the largest declines in welfare caseloads usually spent a lot of their own money on job training and placement. "Operating on the assumption that work requires support," reported Jason DeParle in the *New York Times*, "many states are investing in work-related services. Near-record increases for child care head the list, but states are also spending more on transportation, job placement, and programs that let working recipients keep more of their benefits even while earning paychecks." Illinois, for one, added $100 million in state money for child care to its federal grant, which meant it could offer a child care subsidy to families earning up to $22,000 a year. Alabama increased the maximum amount of assets allowed a family while receiving TANF and disregarded the value of a car. For TANF recipients who found employment, it did not count the first three months of earnings in calculating the amount of benefits. At the same time, the state imposed stricter work requirements and sanctions.[36]

In fact, before they exhausted their time on the rolls, tens of thousands of people lost benefits because they violated new rules; others were discouraged from applying in the first place. A study by the *Washington Post* found that 38 percent of former recipients had left the rolls because of state sanctions "ordered for infractions from missing appointments with caseworkers to refusing to look for work." Sometimes clients refused to cooperate; sometimes they were "so hampered by serious problems that they are unable to comply with the new requirements." In 1997, more than half the 14,428 cases closed in Indiana in a three-month period resulted from sanctions, not from people taking jobs. Florida officials reported 27 percent of 148,000 cases closed in the last six months of 1997 because of sanctions. State policies on sanctions differed. In New York, for example, caseworkers could not terminate the entire amount of a client's check for failure to work; by contrast, Georgia banned families from assistance for life who received two sanctions. In Alabama, clients who failed to appear for a single appointment without good cause could lose their benefits, but they could reapply in a month. State officials saw in the high sanction rates proof of the new welfare law's effectiveness. In their view, sanctions increased because officials discovered people with unreported jobs and because they impressed "upon recipients that they can no longer receive aid indefinitely without preparing themselves for work." Advocates for the poor interpreted sanction rates differently, warning "that many states are imposing severe measures that end people's benefits with no assurances that their children will be fed or their houses heated." In their rush to impose sanctions, states also made mistakes. A former welfare administrator in Utah pointed out that in a pilot program, half the sanctions were imposed in error. On top of sanctions, by November 1997, thirty states were also practicing "diversionary strategies"; that is, they diverted people from applying for benefits by requiring them to pursue other possibilities first. Diversion was not a new strategy. In the late-nineteenth and early-twentieth centuries, for instance, charity officials required men to break stones or chop wood before giving them help for their families. At the end of the twentieth century, diversion included, instead, "one-time lump sum payments, pursuing alternative resources (e.g., child support), and requiring that applicants search for employment before qualifying them for benefits." Clearly, then, the decline in welfare rolls resulted from fewer applicants and sanctions as well as from work. No one, however, could disaggregate the proportions.[37]

Even states willing to invest heavily in the transition from welfare to work confronted administrative problems as they implemented new systems. For instance, despite Wisconsin's investment in day care and case managers, in Milwaukee an average of 4,200 families a month lost income because they violated rules, but later investigations found 36 percent of these penalties had been levied incorrectly. Another early dispute concerned whether states could use their own money for purposes prohibited by federal law, such as aiding legal immigrants. And a year later, the American Public Welfare Association and National Governors' Association objected to proposed administrative regulations for TANF, which, they claimed, would unwisely circumscribe state autonomy.[38]

State and local governments also collided with federal authorities over the issue of wages. State programs proposed to send large numbers of welfare recipients into "workfare," that is, mandatory community service jobs, as well as private employment. The issue was whether workfare counted as a real job that entitled them to the wages and protections found in regular employment. State and local governments usually argued that they could not afford to pay the same for workfare as for other employment, while unions feared that a flood of low-paid workers would displace their members in much public employment. A study by economists reinforced that prediction, and in New York, union fears proved justified. The city's Work Experience program (that is, workfare) employed 34,100 people at city jobs, many of which previously had been held by some of the 20,000 workers cut by Mayor Rudolph Giuliani when he trimmed the city's payroll by 10 percent.[39]

In response, the AFL-CIO leadership decided to try to unionize workfare in February 1997. A workfare participant employed in park maintenance in Brooklyn observed, "Believe me, we are workers. We do the same work as regular park workers, but we earn one-third or one-fifth what they do. Other workers get vacation. We work 52 weeks a year." Union organizers wanted to improve working conditions and to force state and city governments to provide permanent jobs. Andrew L. Stern, president of the Service Employees International Union, said, "If the Government can give tax subsidies to employers who hire welfare recipients, why can't we pay these recipients more for the work they do?" "One of the things we'll seek," pointed out Gerald W. McEntee, president of the State, County, and Municipal Employees Union, "is to make sure that workfare jobs lead to permanent jobs." The union enjoyed its first success organizing three hundred workfare participants in Alaska. It met resistance in New York City and other communities, where state and local governments denied that workfare participants were employees. Despite this opposition, the budget agreement reached in July 1997 extended the minimum wage and other labor laws to workfare participants. Governor John Engler of Michigan called it a "payback" by the Clinton administration for organized labor's support in the 1996 elections. "It's going to be terrible for everybody including welfare recipients," said Florida Representative E. Clay Shaw, Jr. "The states are simply not going to be able to afford to produce as many of the jobs that are needed."[40] However, the experience of the next few years contradicted Shaw's pessimistic predictions.

As important as they were, all the other results of "welfare reform" remained sideshows to the main event: the great decline in the welfare rolls. The downward slide had started in 1994, before the new legislation, but it accelerated after 1996. In July 1997, President Clinton pointed out that welfare caseloads had fallen by 3.1 million people since he assumed office; between August 1996, when he signed the new welfare legislation, and April 1997, 1.2 million had left the rolls. "This is the largest decrease in the welfare rolls in history, giving us the lowest percentage of our population on welfare since 1970," he observed. Some individual states were reporting even more dramatic declines than the national average. By January 1998, across the nation, the number on welfare rolls had dipped below 10 million for the first time in twenty-five years. In September 1998, 8 million people remained on TANF rolls, a stunning 44 percent decline from the 14.3 million on the AFDC rolls in

1994. In the next three months, 340,000 more left as the exodus began to slow.[41]

TANF rolls, however, did not decline uniformly in all places. In fact, welfare reform has mapped new inequalities onto the nation's already unequal social geography and altered the demography of public assistance. Whites left the rolls faster than blacks and Hispanics, who now outnumber them among recipients 2 to 1. At the same time, the rolls went down much more slowly than elsewhere in the nation's largest cities. As a result, state TANF caseloads concentrated in urban areas. Between 1994 and 1998 in the urban counties with the thirty largest cities, caseloads declined 35 percent, compared to 44 percent in their home states. Among cities, caseload declines varied from a low of 18.1 percent in Los Angeles to a high of 71.6 percent in Milwaukee—in part, a reflection of overall state differences: California saw its caseload drop 21 percent and Wisconsin 83.9 percent.[42]

Declining welfare rolls raised many questions. What caused the decline? Who left the rolls? Why? What happened to them? What was the prognosis for the future? In the first few years after the passage of the 1996 bill, no conclusive answers to these questions emerged—indeed, it was too soon to expect any. The rolls could decline because people left sooner or because they did not apply in the first place. It was, moreover, difficult to get a fix on the welfare population because people often returned to the rolls after they had left; a stable population of 10 million at one point in time meant that between 13 and 14 million were on them at some point during the year.[43] Undoubtedly, some combination of factors added up to the decline, but no one had yet quantified the proportions.[44]

Rebecca Blank, a welfare expert on President Clinton's Council of Economic Advisors, attributed the caseload decline to four factors: the outstanding national economy, notable especially for low unemployment, low inflation, and, after a long period of stagnation, rising wages; the surprisingly vigorous and creative actions of state governments; the impact of federal policy, especially the Earned Income Tax Credit and increased minimum wage; and the stunning increase in labor force participation. Certainly, new money from the federal government also helped.[45]

With the decline in the rolls, states found themselves with "more money for child care, more money for job training, more to help people make the transition from welfare to work," pointed out Representative Shaw. Between 1994 and 1996, on a national basis, the money available for each family on the rolls increased an average of 41 percent. In Wyoming, Wisconsin, Tennessee, Oregon, and Louisiana, it rose more than 80 percent. Flush with cash, states used their own money as well as funds from the Child Care Block Grant to pump more money into child care. Federal funds for child care, which increased 80 percent during the first six years of Clinton's administration, helped parents pay for care for about 1.25 million of the 10 million eligible children; Clinton proposed to expand care to another 1.15 million children during the next five years.[46]

According to *New York Times* welfare specialist Jason DeParle, the "flood of federal dollars" to the states created a "rare, perhaps even unprecedented, moment of opportunity in programs for the poor. And it is almost wholly an unintended one—a rich new financing stream for anti-poverty efforts created by the most conservative Congress in a generation." With federal funding pegged to 1994 and 1995, states found themselves with $6 billion more than they would have had under the old law. States used some of the windfall for new services, but they left much of the money—nearly one-quarter—unspent. Federal subsidies increased 64 percent for each family, while actual state spending rose only 28 percent. Despite their spending on child care, DeParle observed, "few states" were "investing in the intensive services their more troubled clients will need, like drug treatment and mental-health counseling," and few were "setting aside rainy-day money for a slower economy," although almost everyone believed the good economic weather could not continue indefinitely. States slowest to spend the money—for instance, New Mexico, Mississippi, and Louisiana—were among the neediest. Most reluctant to spend the money were the Mountain states, bastions of conservatism: Wyoming spent only 9 percent of its funds and Idaho 24 percent. Many congressional Republicans, not surprisingly, wanted to take back the unspent money, but they met stiff resistance from a coalition of Republican and Democratic governors supported by the president.[47]

The decline in TANF caseloads stunned everyone. Even optimists had not predicted such a fast and dramatic turnaround. No one could recall when another major trend had reversed so speedily. This was not the way social change was supposed to happen. The conjunction of a strong economy—an economy that could not be more favorable for moving people from welfare to work—with federal and state policy were the influences that officials preferred to discuss. Others pointed to the high rate of sanctions that removed clients from the rolls for often minor violations of the rules and the diversionary activities that kept others from applying. Sanctions and diversions raised the questions usually elided by celebrants of caseload decline. What would happen when the economy weakened? What impact had the caseload decline had on poverty? What had happened to the people who left the rolls? No one had good answers.

Neither the federal government nor the states at first tracked recipients who left the welfare rolls. "Eighteen months after federal lawmakers dramatically changed the nation's welfare program," wrote two reporters for the *Washington Post*, "it is becoming clear that the mass of data the government requires states to collect is in such disarray that it is impossible to determine whether the law is working." Wisconsin's governor Tommy Thompson said he did not need a study to know how former recipients were faring: "We know the vast majority of them have jobs and are working, which is how it ought to be. They're doing better and they like it." Pressed for his evidence, Thompson "acknowledged it was unscientific. 'It's anecdotal evidence,' he said." In May 1999 the Senate rejected Senator Paul Wellstone's proposal for a national study to track the well-being of former TANF recipients.[48]

The Senate's refusal, Thompson's remarks, and the initial failure of states to follow the people who left welfare rolls highlight the master narrative of social policy reform at work in public assistance. A false crisis of cost—Robert Rector's spurious failed $5 trillion War on Poverty—along with the politics of dependence helped channel the perennial dislike of AFDC into a movement for legislative change. Blame settled on the behavior of young unmarried mothers, mainly women of color, rather than on the economic and political sources of their poverty. "Reform" took the shape of an attack on eligibility—time limits and sanctions—rather than on the size of benefits. After the passage of the 1996 law, as public assistance rolls plummeted, champions of "reform" claimed victory. By failing to ask what happened to those no longer on the rolls, they replicated the willful ignorance found in other corners of America's welfare state.

But willful ignorance proved troubling, and both independent organizations and state governments gradually undertook tracking studies. The Urban Institute's Assessing the New Federalism project and research by the Manpower Demonstration Research Corporation were the two largest independent studies. By early 1998 every state at least had begun to think about the question, though, according to the National Governors' Association, twelve remained in the planning stage, and only ten had reported any data. How useful the state studies would prove was another issue. Different definitions and methods would leave their results incomparable.[49]

The most thorough canvas of the first eighteen months under the new system came from *New York Times* reporter Jason DeParle. There were some surprises. It had proved easier to reduce welfare rolls than almost anyone had imagined, but only about half of those who left the rolls had jobs—for example, in Massachusetts 50 percent of former recipients reported jobs. In Idaho the number was 52 percent, in New Mexico 56 percent, in Maryland 49 percent. This percentage did not improve much on the past; the most authoritative study in the 1980s had found 46 percent with jobs after they had left the rolls. "Experts and advocates for the poor" claimed that the research "provided the strongest evidence yet that people were being knocked off the welfare rolls by a host of new sanctions and rules even though they have no prospect of legitimate employment." Subsequent studies proved more encouraging. In eleven states surveyed, at least 50 percent of former welfare recipients were working—in fact, the majority reported that between 65 and 80 percent of former welfare recipients were working. However, the different methods used for calculating employment made comparisons difficult.[50] In 1999, a safe estimate seemed to be that between a half and two-thirds had found work.

Yet, "even under optimal circumstances," reported DeParle, "the new laws are claiming casualties." Big-city mayors did not need social scientists to tell them that welfare recipients had more difficulty finding jobs in cities than in suburbs or that poverty was concentrating on their turf, and they were not sanguine about what would happen when people in their cities bumped up against the new time limits in public assistance. Even the existence of jobs did not guarantee former welfare recipients a straightforward path to employment. In Philadelphia, for example, the 21st Century League described the bureaucratic nightmare that confronted the women who tried to find the road to independence—the byzantine labyrinth they had to navigate to move from welfare to work. In November 1997, Philadelphia's mayor, Ed Rendell, went to Washington to present a report from the U.S. Conference of Mayors that painted "a bleak picture for Philadelphia and other cities in their effort to move residents off welfare and into a job." The mayors wanted between $8 billion and $9 billion in federal money "to help ease the burden of welfare reform."[51]

Finding a job did not end the problems of many former welfare recipients. Their wages were usually low and job loss frequent. As a result, many of those who left the welfare rolls remained in poverty. In Tennessee, for instance, a survey found three-quarters of former recipients working after three months. Of these, 48 percent worked full-time at an average of $5.82 an hour. Their projected annual income of $9,987 remained well below the $12,500 poverty level for a family of three. In Maryland, those working earned on the average a poverty-level annual wage of $8,300. The Earned Income Tax Credit and food stamps increased wages, but usually not enough to lift these families out of poverty. In New York City, only 32.7 percent of families that left the rolls between July and September of 1996 showed earnings of at least $100 in the next quarter; for those who left between January and March 1997, the number dropped to 22.1 percent. Statewide, the numbers improved to about a third. In Virginia, according to a November 1997 report, "most of the first 40 families . . . pushed off welfare into jobs seem destined to fall back into poverty when special benefits received during the transition run out next year." Although across the country former welfare recipients generally earned above the minimum wage, it was not usually enough to reach the federal poverty level.[52]

Wisconsin, with its early and aggressive "welfare reform" and booming economy, provided a best-case test of what happened to former welfare recipients. In January 1998 state officials publicized results that looked promising: 83 percent of former welfare recipients had found work; 62 percent were still employed at the time of the interview; and most earned more than the minimum wage. But other results were less positive. In 1997, 24 percent of Milwaukee's children remained in poverty. Although almost half of families surveyed had more money than when they were on welfare, almost three of ten were "just barely making do." A third could not afford child care, compared to 22 percent while on welfare. In Milwaukee County only 28 percent projected yearly incomes of $10,000 or more for two consecutive quarters, and only 16 percent earned more than the federal poverty standard of $16,000 for a family of four. Three-quarters of those who had located jobs had lost them within nine months.[53]

The most encouraging results came from a Minnesota pilot program that had begun in 1994. The program combined financial incentives to work with generously increased supports for working families. It did not include time limits. In four years, the program increased family income and reduced poverty. For two-parent families it also reduced the pressure for both parents to work and increased the stability of marriages. However, the program's gains came at a high cost: between $1,900 and $3,800 more per year than AFDC for each family. It was doubtful that other states would follow Minnesota's lead, or even that Minnesota would retain the program's most generous features in the new era of welfare reform.[54]

. . . .

Another way to look at the results of welfare reform was to track the income of the poorest families. Between 1995 and 1997, the poorest 20 percent of female-headed families with children suffered a $580 drop in income—even counting food stamps, housing subsidies, and the Earned Income Tax Credit. Their incomes remained below three-quarters of the poverty line. The poorest 10 percent fared even worse; they lost

$810, or an average of one-seventh of their incomes. "More than three-quarters of the income loss among both the poorest tenth and the poorest fifth of female-headed families with children resulted from declines in assistance provided through means-tested programs, primarily cash and food stamp aid," reported the Center on Budget and Policy Priorities. This immiseration of the poorest Americans was the underside of welfare reform.[55]

"The whole point of this is to eliminate poverty in the United States, not just to get people off of welfare," lamented Donna Shalala, secretary of the Department of Health and Human Services in the Clinton administration. The author of the 1996 welfare bill, Representative E. Clay Shaw, Jr., saw the issue differently. "You're going to have some who are just not going to be able to make it. Welfare reform didn't just present an opportunity. It also presented a certain amount of pain for not being able to take control of your life."[56] For all their promises of how the new system would help recipients, its architects slipped easily into Darwinian metaphors. "Personal responsibility" and "work opportunity" meant exactly what they said. States might provide more supports, but ultimately the individual was cut loose, left to seize or reject opportunities and to succeed or fail on his or her own.

Before long, reports of hardship related to welfare reform surfaced around the nation. From the Grow Clinic at the Boston Medical Center, the National Center for Children in Poverty at Columbia University, and Second Harvest, the nation's largest hunger charity, came troubling reports of hunger and malnutrition among children. In Detroit during the prosperous year 1997–98, the number of clients served by a sample of food pantries and soup kitchens increased from 49,000 to 71,000. In New York State, declining public assistance rolls resulted in a financial crisis for homeless shelters because a state law tied their funding to the number of people eligible for welfare. In 1999, a study based on the experience of adults who had left welfare rolls in thirteen states found "evidence of lives made harder by the loss of cash assistance." Many families fell behind on rent and utility bills, and a small number reported worse problems: "Some were going without food, losing their housing or putting their children in the care of others." Yet despite reported increases in homelessness, most of the families who left the rolls did not wind up on the streets. They proved surprisingly resourceful, drawing on families, boyfriends, relatives, private charity, and under-the-table jobs. Mothers and grandmothers continued to carry most of the burdens. Indeed, reports of burdens on relatives, especially grandmothers raising children, became common. And a study by researchers from the University of California at Berkeley and Yale University found many of the children of mothers moving from welfare to work in low-quality child care and behind their peers in language and social development. Dr. Bruce Fuller, one of the researchers, observed that "this study did find early warning signals of a child-care problem that's going to get worse as the work requirements of the welfare law ramps up from 30 percent to 50 percent of the women getting assistance."[57]

In July 1999 Peter Edelman once again summed up the criticisms of "welfare reform." All over the country people were "being pushed off the rolls," often for minor infractions, and between 30 and 50 percent of those who left the rolls failed to find jobs. "Many people who lose jobs can't get welfare"; welfare officials subjected them to "diversion"—that is, when they came for help, they were told to first look for a job and they were not told they could claim food stamps and Medicaid immediately. Even those who found a job were not guaranteed escape from poverty: unemployment among them was high and many jobs paid poorly. "The bottom line," argued Edelman, is that "the poor are not better off." The number of the "extreme poor," with incomes less than half the poverty line, had increased from 13.9 million to 14.6 million people between 1995 and 1997, and, despite a slight decline, one out of five children was still poor—contrasted to one of seven in the 1970s.[58]

The news, however, was not all gloomy. As businesses, churches, and nonprofits increased their participation in welfare programs, media portraits of welfare recipients started to soften. Less often depicted as lazy, ineffective, and demoralized, welfare recipients increasingly appeared as unfortunate but plucky moms willing to work long and hard to support their children. "That shift, seeing recipients as workers, as fellow citizens, is enormously important," stressed Olivia Golden, who oversaw federal programs for women and children as assistant secretary for the Department of Health and Human Services.[59] If Golden was right, the refurbished image of welfare mothers would stand as one of the great achievements of welfare reform. But had welfare reform really transformed the historic language of poverty by transmuting the undeserving poor into "fellow citizens"? How pervasive was this new image? What of those who failed for whatever reason to work? What were the consequences of tying citizenship to work in the regular labor market? After the end of welfare, who, really, was a citizen?

WORK, DEMOCRACY, AND CITIZENSHIP

Ancient questions lie at the heart of modern debates about the welfare state. What distinguishes those who merit help? What is the impact of welfare on personality, families, and labor markets? What are the limits of social obligation—what do we owe one another? Who provides in times of need—families, charities, employers, or the state? These remain questions without definitive answers because they are not objective and cannot be subjected to empirical resolution. They are, instead, questions of political and moral philosophy. Hard evidence can be brought to bear on each of them, but in the end, even the best research must be filtered through interpretive screens that determine its meaning. Our answers to welfare's enduring questions reveal as much about our views of public and private responsibility, national community, the role of government, and the meaning of citizenship as they do about the results of social science. In light of its recent history as told in this book, what can be said about current answers to the core issues underlying America's welfare state?

Consider, first, the question of who merits help. No community or state can meet all its members' wants or needs. It must draw lines between those who merit help and those who do not. The oldest line attempted to separate the "able-bodied" from the "impotent" poor. In the nineteenth century, discussions of welfare, or relief as it then was called, added a moral layer to dependence and transmuted the older, competence-based categories into the distinction between the deserving and undeserving poor. Needless to say, these refurbished categories proved no more precise than the ones they supplanted. Nonetheless, the category "undeserving poor" has echoed across two centuries; it persists, today, as vividly as a century and a half ago. Only its content has changed over time.

The "undeserving" poor include two groups: imposters—those who supposedly fake dependence—and those who are dependent because of their own bad behavior or moral failing. The identification of fakers and frauds constitutes a perennial quest in the history of welfare reform. Frauds included beggars on nineteenth-century streets who allegedly pretended blindness, children forced to beg and feign poverty by their able-bodied parents, professional mendicants milking charities with phony stories of hardship, and "welfare queens" with Cadillacs parked outside their public housing apartments. Identifying frauds served a useful purpose: it placed them unambiguously among the undeserving poor and justified refusing assistance.

The same dynamic is at work in the late-twentieth century. But the matter is no more simple or objective now than in the past. One person's "greedy geezer" is another's parent trying to survive old age with some comfort and dignity. What one administrator refuses to consider a legitimate disability appears to merit public support on appeal to a judge. The childhood conditions that Congress declines to consider disabilities impoverish parents. An illegitimate work-related injury to one employer is crippling carpal tunnel syndrome contracted through hours at a keyboard to an employee. Hidden income to a welfare official is a needed supplement to declining benefits to a single mother. Rather than an objective standard, fraud remains an uncertain and conflict-ridden border erected to contain the costs of the welfare state. Of course, there is real fraud, although most studies find less of it than critics suppose exists, and providers, not beneficiaries or clients, usually commit the most expensive acts designed to cheat the public.[1] The point is not that fraud should be condoned but that it is a less clear-cut matter than often assumed, and its exaggeration serves political ends that work to discredit social welfare programs rather than to improve them.

In the nineteenth century, shirkers and alcoholics filled out the other category of undeserving poor—those poor on account of their own lazy, feckless, or immoral behavior. Today, in the public view, they consist mostly of unmarried black and Hispanic mothers. The late-twentieth century has racialized the undeserving poor, who now carry the triple stigma of sexual licentiousness, willful poverty, and race.[2] As with fakers, assigning someone to the undeserving poor on account of bad behavior serves nicely to justify low benefits, or no benefits at all. It is the easiest way to police the boundaries and the expense of the welfare state.

The category "undeserving poor" has always included many out-of-work and destitute men. In America's nineteenth-century land of opportunity, any man unable to support himself became suspect. The Gilded Age defined wandering unemployed men, casualties of the first great industrial age, as tramps and responded to them with punitive local laws instead of relief. In Buffalo, New York, at the end of the nineteenth century, several charities supplied the needs of old women; none helped old men. Even today, workers who descend into poverty because they are on strike find themselves among the undeserving poor, ineligible for unemployment compensation or food stamps. Men—now especially young black men—remain the least sympathetic or deserving population. Aside from the pittance sometimes available through General Relief and, in some instances, food stamps or Supplemental Security Income for the disabled, no public programs assist out-of-work men before they turn sixty-five. When their dependence crosses the line from poverty to menace, as it often seems to do, they finally find support in prison. America has responded to the chronic joblessness among inner-city minorities not with public work or support but with a new and hideously expensive form of public assistance: mass incarceration.[3]

Fear of undermining work incentives and families marches through the history of relief and welfare. It is as lively an issue today as it was in debates over subsidized wages in eighteenth-century Britain or in eighteenth- and nineteenth-century attempts in the United States to assure that no one could live as comfortably on relief as at work. In current debates, concern with work incentives motivates the preoccupation with moral hazard in discussions of social insurance and public assistance, while critics of recent welfare reform worry that time-limited public assistance and workfare will flood low-skilled labor markets and erode wages. Employers justify trends in the private welfare state by arguing that "paternalistic" labor relations and employee benefits reinforce labor market rigidities and undermine the flexibility they need to compete in the global marketplace. At the same time, worry about the impact of welfare on families underpins the hostility of the religious right to the welfare state. Indeed, as we have seen, conservatives often argue that welfare's perverse incentives have destroyed families by inducing unmarried women to have children and discouraging them from marrying.

The question of what we owe each other—the limits of social obligation—divides into two parts: What do we owe fellow citizens? Who is entitled to that help? In his classic book *Citizenship and Social Class* (1950), which still dominates writing about citizenship, British social theorist T. H. Marshall argued for a link between the answers to these two questions. Citizenship, Marshall argued, had expanded in three stages during the last two centuries. Civil/legal citizenship emerged first in the eighteenth century as early capitalist systems developed institutions for the protection of property, equality before the law, and civil liberties. Political citizenship followed in the nineteenth century with the franchise granted first to the middle and later to the working classes. By the late 1940s Marshall saw a third stage—social citizenship—that guaranteed everything "from the right to a modicum of economic welfare and security to the right to share to the full in the social heritage and to live the life of a civilised being according to the standards prevailing in the society."[4] Social citizenship took shape as the welfare state.

Within the welfare state, ideas about citizenship vacillate between two concepts—citizenship as a preexisting and as an achieved status. As a preexisting status, citizenship does not depend on individual virtue, good behavior, or contribution to society. It is a set of rights that derive solely from birth or nationalization. As an achieved status, citizenship deemphasizes rights in favor of obligations or merit; it is earned through contributions to society. It is true that men and women do not lose formal citizenship because they lack work or do not pay taxes, but a definition of citizenship that rests on obligation and contribution marginalizes those who do not work at regular jobs and creates second-class citizens.[5]

For Marshall citizenship was a status, a product of birth or nationality, not a privilege earned by work or good behavior. This idea of citizenship as a status reversed the old and still prevailing idea that the welfare of some people mattered much less than the welfare of others. Citizenship's commitment to social inclusion redefined assumptions about who belonged as full members of the national community.[6]

The idea of social citizenship remains the starting point, and the whipping post, for most discussions of citizenship. Marshall's definition, many commentators point out, rests on English history, which his book describes in a remarkably unilinear and whiggish fashion. It obscures the overlap among struggles to achieve the varieties of citizenship; pays insufficient attention to conflict; and applies poorly to women, who achieved political citizenship long after men and gained less than the full rights of social citizenship. It fails, as well, to provide a guide through the thicket of new conceptual difficulties posed by the attempt to work out definitions of citizenship that can be applied in an era of massive international migration and the creation of new international entities, notably the European Union.[7] Nonetheless, despite a half century of criticism, the concept of social citizenship endures as shorthand for the goals of the welfare state.

Marshall stressed the conflict between civil and social citizenship at the heart of the welfare state. Civil citizenship "gave to each man, as part of his individual status, the power to engage as an independent unit in the economic struggle and made it possible to deny to him social protection on the ground that he was equipped with the means to protect himself." Social citizenship, to the contrary, created "a universal right to real income which is not proportionate to the market value of the claimant." The goal of social rights was "class abatement." Thus, civil and social rights conflicted. "Social rights in their modern form imply an invasion of contract by status, the subordination of market price to social justice, the replacement of the free bargain by the declaration of rights."[8]

This book has traced the tension between ideas of citizenship and the welfare state—between market price and social justice—in late-twentieth-century America. By showing how markets have eroded the idea of social citizenship, it has suggested that rights are contingent—they may be withdrawn as well as extended, contracted as well as expanded.[9]

Citizenship defines the rights and duties that accompany membership in a unit of society, especially a nation. How to delimit this membership—how to draw the boundaries of citizenship—is a question with a turbulent history.[10] Because citizenship is about boundaries, it is defined by exclusion as well as inclusion. Through citizenship a community defines who does and who does not belong. As such, it serves as a criterion for denying people the benefits of the welfare state as much as it does for awarding them.

Who, then, enjoys full membership in a nation and entitlement to all its benefits? The question has always proved enormously complex—more so in the United States than in many other nations because of both massive and continuous immigration and the nature of federalism. The United States has allowed immigrants to earn citizenship more readily than European nations that tie nationality to blood. In one sense, American history in the twentieth century can be read as the extension of civil and political citizenship to previously excluded groups—women, African Americans, Asians—as formerly legal exclusions fell before legislation or court challenges.

Nonetheless, the history of American citizenship diverged from Marshall's scheme. In recent decades, immigrants admitted as resident aliens received social citizenship—access to the full benefits of the welfare state—before they qualified for political citizenship, a situation seriously modified by the 1996 federal welfare legislation. Earlier in the nation's history, civil and political citizenship spread unevenly, with African Americans in the South, for instance, excluded from civil citizenship by segregation and from the exercise of the political citizenship to which they held legal claim long after white males and, much later, white women, had gained both. In his brilliant history of American citizenship, political scientist Rogers Smith terms the ruling American tradition, based on clear civic hierarchies, "ascriptive Americanism." He points out that "when restrictions on voting rights, naturalization, and immigration are taken into account, it turns out that for over 80 percent of U.S. history, American laws declared most people in the world legally ineligible to become full U.S. citizens solely because of their race, original nationality, or gender. For at least two-thirds of American history, the majority of the domestic adult population was also ineligible for full citizenship for the same reasons."[11]

Indeed, contests over citizenship lie at the core of American history. In the Revolution, Americans exchanged the status of subject for the new mantle of citizen, which they deployed to justify separation. The Revolution, however, left Americans with the problem of drawing the boundaries of citizenship. Who was in and who was out proved an urgent question when courts and legislatures had to deal with the civil and political standing of former Tories who had sided with Great Britain. Massive immigration posed other problems: America needed the labor of newcomers, but many of them seemed strange, with alien ways and no experience of self-government. Race confronted Americans with the most difficult questions. How were they to draw the boundaries of citizenship in a way that excluded black slaves and Native Americans? How were they to define and defend an idea of citizenship restricted to white men when every state could construct its own laws? Conflicts over citizenship were part of the great controversies over race and nationality that wracked antebellum America: the Missouri Compromise, the Kansas-Nebraska Act, the Dred Scott decision, and the Civil War. Later, the issue would arise again, not only for former slaves and Native Americans, but in the successful campaigns late in the century to restrict suffrage, in the battles over immigration restriction, and in debates about extending the vote to women. American history, or for that matter any national history, can be said to "prove" few things, but one of them is the contentious, contested, and shifting meaning of citizenship.

In America, federalism further complicated citizenship because of the routine assumption during much of American history that individuals held both state and national citizenship. In fact, for nearly the first two-thirds of the nineteenth century the federal government showed little active interest in citizenship; the last significant national legislation of the nineteenth century governing naturalization passed Congress in 1802. Only after the Civil War, with the Fourteenth and Fifteenth Amendments to the Constitution, did the national government assert clear primacy over the states in the determination of citizenship. Even then, states retained control over significant components of citizenship, especially qualifications for voting.[12] The great civil rights cases and the battles over states rights in the 1950s and 1960s reflected the legacy of divided authority over citizenship and the federal government's continuing effort to establish its authority.

Even as social citizenship expanded, whole categories of people remained outside its benefits. The exclusion of domestic and agricultural labor from the original Social Security legislation constitutes the most notable example, for it denied many women and African Americans the benefits more widely available to white male citizens. Unemployment insurance still privileges white men over women and African Americans because of their more irregular work histories. The situation with Aid to Dependent Children proved even worse. Especially in the South, state governments, which remained at liberty to set regulations and benefit levels, found ways to keep African American women off the rolls and to pay them less. Unlike the situation with Social Security, African American women did not automatically benefit from the passage of national legislation.[13]

For yet another reason many women remain less than full citizens of the welfare state: they are assigned tasks outside the world of paid work. With the "real citizen" understood "as taxpayer," women in the early decades of the welfare state found themselves second-class citizens, pushed outside the circle of first-class benefits. The private work of caring for children, the elderly, and the ill, historically and still very much today the work of women, fails to qualify as employment. Although the rapid entrance of women into paid employment has improved their standing as citizens and beneficiaries of the welfare state, everywhere in the developed world, a 1996 OECD study found, both their obligations as caregivers and their exclusion from the full benefits of social citizenship continued.[14]

While the legacy of T. H. Marshall still influences discussions of the links between welfare states and citizenship, the legacy of William Beveridge, architect of the British welfare state, remains visible in the politics of welfare policy. For Beveridge, the rights of citizenship grew out of a contract centered on work. Only full employment could underwrite an expensive system of social protections, and, he argued, benefits should follow an insurance model, using contributions made during paid work to support workers during periodic unemployment or hardship.[15]

Work has proved even more important to American than to British or European ideas of the welfare state, which have made benefits less contingent on employment. As political scientist Judith Shklar observed, work holds a special place in ideas of American citizenship: "The individual American citizen is . . . a member of two interlocking public orders, one egalitarian, the other entirely unequal. To be a recognized and active citizen at all he must be an equal member of the polity, a voter, but he must also be independent, which has all along meant that he must be an 'earner,' a free remunerated worker, one who is rewarded for the actual work he has done, neither more nor less." In recent decades, this book has shown, the links joining welfare to employment and citizenship have tightened. As a result, only those Americans with real jobs are real citizens.[16] Where real citizens should receive their benefits, however, remains far from clear. After all, in America's mixed, multitrack economy of social welfare, many possibilities exist. This book has described a number of the historic and current permutations and the debates that surround them. It has told the story of the collapse of the Progressive–New Deal–Great Society nexus and the adoption of policies that echo older attempts to sharpen the often fictive line between public and private. This reliance on updated Gilded Age answers finds support not so much in social Darwinism, as it did in the late-nineteenth century, as in sociobiology and a sophisticated neoclassical economics more reminiscent of classic liberalism than of the Keynesianism that influenced public policy in the postwar decades. More than at any time since the New Deal, the answer to the question of where should Americans receive their benefits tilts toward the private sector.

In light of these current answers to old questions, how should we evaluate the great forces—dependence, devolution, and markets—redefining America's welfare state? First, consider the war on dependence. Who can oppose policies designed to help people reach independence? Who can deny that women and men will be happier and more satisfied with their lives if they can support themselves without turning to public or private charity? Were this the whole or real scope of the war on dependence, we might argue over strategies, but not over the idea itself. In fact, the war on dependence picks on the most vulnerable Americans and heightens their vulnerability by cutting away the guaranteed support they need to survive. It does little to lessen the sources of dependence rooted in the poverty and inequality of the new American city. It is a war in which government programs and individual behavior, not the production of want and insecurity, constitute the enemies. There is, as well, a disingenuous side to the war on dependence. Politicians and policy makers show little inclination to explore the various meanings of dependence, confront its multiple manifestations, or develop a theory that explains why some forms of dependence are acceptable while others are not. Why is it appropriate for farmers to depend on government subsidies, corporations on government contracts and tax concessions, and homeowners on tax-deductible mortgages—but not for single mothers to depend on public assistance?

The American answer almost surely would stress work—the new criterion of full citizenship. Because it is acceptable to subsidize those who "work hard and play by the rules" (whether this applies to all corporations or homeowners is another question), the future of work poses a great question for public policy. The first issue is mainly quantitative:

the number of jobs, their qualifications, pay, benefits, and prospects. Will everyone who "works hard and plays by the rules" find a job that pays a living wage?

Economists and pundits disagree about the future of work, and they have produced a complicated and contentious literature that offers sharply different scenarios. What does appear clear is that job trends will force American workers toward a greater reliance on the public and private welfare state. There is a contradiction between the trajectory of the welfare state—the increasing linkage between benefits and employment—and the trajectory of work, which is likely to leave more Americans without the work histories that entitle them to benefits, or at work in jobs that pay poorly and offer little if any insurance against sickness and old age.

The problem with work is not—and probably will not be—the number of jobs. Between 1992 and 1996, for example, the number of jobs increased by about 12 million. Joblessness increased only through the recession of 1990–92, and unemployment plummeted in the late 1990s. For many people, especially in inner cities, jobs are likely to remain selectively hard to find, not because of a weak economy but because of location, transportation, skill requirements, and racial preferences in hiring. Among African American men, high unemployment rates and chronic joblessness are likely to persist. The injection of millions of former public assistance recipients into the labor market as a result of time-limited welfare benefits probably will worsen competition for jobs and depress wages in low-skilled work within inner cities, and, despite some innovative programs, there exists little reason to expect a massive reduction of "spatial mismatch."[17]

The news about the types of jobs available is both encouraging and ominous. Most recent jobs are full-time, and there are many more of them. Between 1979 and 1998, employment rose from about 97 million to 132 million, while unemployment dropped from 5.8 percent to 4.2 percent. About 5 percent of work is part-time. Together with contract work, temporary jobs, which increased in the same years, form the category labeled "contingent work," which made up only 5 percent of all jobs in 1995. However, the explosive growth of firms that supply temporary workers underlines the importance and visibility of contingent work. Between 1991 and 1996, the industry group that grew fastest was personnel supply services, another term for "temporary help agencies." The revenue of publicly traded staffing firms averaged an annual increase of 24.5 percent between 1994 and 1996, and they composed thirty-four of *Inc. Magazine*'s five hundred fastest growing firms in 1996. A 1995 survey found that 64 percent of workers employed through temporary help firms and 61 percent of "on-call workers" wanted "other kinds of work." Economist Paul Osterman observed that the impact of contingent work extends "beyond the absolute numbers because regular employees are well aware of contingent employment within their organization and the implicit threat it entails."[18]

Despite a booming economy, "downsizing" also remains common. Between 1985 and 1989, 4.3 million workers were displaced. By January 1990 only 72 percent of them were reemployed, and 10 percent of these worked part-time. Of those who worked full-time, 40 percent earned lower wages. A 1994–96 survey showed that three years after job displacement, 43.3 percent experienced a decline in earnings of more than 20 percent, and another 10.3 percent a decline of 10–19 percent. Some data also point to growing job insecurity. Job tenure decreased for men of all ages and for women ages fifty-five to sixty-four; job turnover has increased; and the rate of job dislocation moved upward in the 1990s. Nor do unemployment statistics tell the whole story about those who seek work. Around 7 million Americans are officially unemployed. Another 6 million are too discouraged to actively seek work; roughly 4.5 million are involuntarily working part-time; 8 million hold temporary jobs; 2 million remain "on call"; and "many of the eight million independent contractors are downsized professionals." The result is a "large army of the partially employed."[19]

"Layoffs, and the dissolution of the bonds between employees and employers that these imply," argues Osterman, change workers' experiences, but they also point to something larger: "the rethinking and transformation of the employment relationship." Not only job tenure, but "the rules, procedures, expectations, and norms regarding work within organizations are changing." This is the story that underlies the turn away from paternalism in employee benefits and the decline in medical insurance and pension coverage that results. While "some firms are broadening jobs and devolving higher levels of responsibility to their workforce," says Osterman, they also "are reducing their commitment to the same workforce and increasingly treating them as expendable."[20] In the American welfare state, expendability can quickly translate into exclusion from benefits. This schizophrenic repatterning of labor relations not only increases material hardship; it demotes former employees to the status of second-class citizens.

New jobs have been most plentiful in lower-paid work in service industries. Robert Reich's forecast of a future full of "symbolic analysts" appears vastly exaggerated. In the U.S. Department of Labor's forecast of the thirty occupations with the greatest projected growth between 1994 and 2005, the first five were: "cashiers; janitors and cleaners; salespersons, retail; waiters and waitresses; registered nurses." Among the top thirty, those that match the definition of "symbolic analyst" accounted for 7 percent of current employment and 13 percent of projected growth. Projections of the need for skilled workers have confused numbers with percentages. Employment in computer science and engineering will grow by 100 percent, compared to 11 percent in food service. But food service is a vastly larger industry than computer science, which means that the smaller percentage yields a great many more jobs. Although managerial and professional occupations will need more workers, the quantities, points out Richard Rothstein, "pale compared with openings requiring less education. Employers will hire more than three times as many cashiers as engineers. They will need more than twice as many food-counter workers, waiters, and waitresses than all the systems analysts, computer engineers and database administrators combined." [21]

In addition, proponents of the "skills mismatch" thesis (the idea that America's shortage of highly skilled workers is the primary cause of increased income inequality) incorrectly assume that most jobs in high-tech industries require a lot of skill or education. Amazon.com, for instance, creates more jobs for warehouse workers than Website designers. Misunderstandings about the role of computers also feed inaccurate notions of the demand for skills. Computers sometimes reduce skill requirements—as in the case of cashiers who have to scan bar codes. In fact, computerization has not exerted a strong effect on the share of jobs held by low-skilled men, and the skill mix of jobs has held remarkably steady since 1983. Education is also a much more ambiguous factor than advocates of "skills mismatch" acknowledge. In the 1980s, about 20 percent of college graduates worked at jobs that did not require a college degree—a proportion that was expected to increase. Poverty among black and Hispanic college graduates actually rose from approximately 9 percent to 15 percent in the 1980s. Earnings inequality between *workers* of similar age, sex, and schooling accounted for a much greater share of income polarization during the last twenty years than did differences between *groups*.[22]

Economist Michael J. Handel shows that inequality growth concentrated during the recession years of the early 1980s before the emergence of the alleged imbalance between the supply and demand for workers with technological skills. In fact, as the imbalance supposedly widened, inequality stabilized. Compared to the 1970s, the skill requirements of occupations did not increase especially rapidly in the 1980s and 1990s, and the spread of computers did not seriously compromise the ability of the supply of trained workers to meet the growth in demand. What the recession of the early 1980s did coincide with was a dramatic decline in better-paid blue-collar jobs, notably in manufacturing. These trends, contends Handel, suggest that the causes of growing inequality lie in "macroeconomic forces and the decline of institutional protections for workers." In *Created Unequal*, economist James K. Galbraith further undermines the skills-mismatch idea. The timing and the association with productivity growth, he argues, are all wrong. For Galbraith the skills-mismatch idea masks the roots of income inequality in monopoly power rather than educational deficiency: "What the existing economy needs is a fairly small number of first-rate technical talents, combined with a small superclass of managers and financiers, on top of a vast substructure of nominally literate and politically apathetic working people."[23]

One result of these recent job trends is the spread of low-wage work and the decline in the share of employment and opportunities in the middle of the job ladder. The situation appears even worse when average wages across the workforce are broken down by age groups. Declining wages have hit young workers hardest. From 1979 to 1996, the median weekly earnings of twenty-five- to thirty-four-year-olds declined 23 percent for men and 4 percent for women. The ratio of their earnings to middle-aged workers also dropped. Low-wage workers—defined as full-time employees earning less than two-thirds of the median pay— compose a much higher proportion of the workforce in the United States than in other industrialized Western nations (approximately 25 percent in the United States compared with less than 20 percent in Britain and about 12 percent in France and Germany). Even skilled workers often fail to earn higher wages. In manufacturing as well as service employment, the trend has been toward jobs that require higher skills but pay lower wages. "Goods-producing industries with a high-wage, low-skill workforce," observes economist David Howell, "appear to have restructured in the 1980s by radically lowering wages and gradually raising skill requirements—in short, by moving in the direction of the typical service sector workplace." Downward pressure on the wages of low-skilled workers probably will increase as a result of three factors: competition from white-collar workers forced by lack of opportunity to compete for low-skill jobs; immigration of low-skilled workers; and the flow of large numbers of people from the public assistance rolls into jobs.[24]

Predictions are always hazardous. But recent jobs trends make it reasonable to expect that the future of work will leave millions of Americans vulnerable: they will be underemployed or subject to displacement. As the share of middle-income jobs continues to shrink, they will work in jobs that lack benefits and do not pay wages adequate to support a family. From time to time they will need support from a welfare state.

This scenario highlights a contradiction in public policy. Employers have heightened the insecurity of work deliberately because they want flexibility in their workforces; labor experts advise Americans to expect to change jobs and even careers more often; and the national government takes no action to slow the decline in employment security. As a result, workers will experience more periods of unemployment or underemployment; increasingly they will lack health insurance and pensions; and their incomes, even when they are employed, may fluctuate dramatically. Joblessness will remain high among men and women in inner cities, who will look for support in the underground and informal economies. At the same time, with the exception of children's health insurance, the national government encourages tightening the links between benefits and employment, which makes health insurance, retirement pay, or income support more difficult to claim outside of a regular job. Only the Earned Income Tax Credit and the Kennedy-Kassenbaum Act—which unsuccessfully tries to guarantee insurance portability—address this contradiction, and they do not match the magnitude of the problem, now or for the future.

There is another issue about work: its inherent importance in human experience. Whatever their politics, most people agree that engagement with work ranks high among life's satisfactions. Work shapes identity, status, and self-esteem, and the lack of steady, reasonably paid work—in America a sign of failure—means declining social position, insecurity, and shame. In *The Market Experience* social psychologist Robert Lane defends the centrality of "well-designed" work, which promotes "well-being . . . cognitive development, a sense of personal control, and self-esteem. . . . It helps people to learn about certain aspects of nature, to engage with other people more satisfactorily, and to cope with their environments with greater success."[25]

Unfortunately, not all work is "well-designed," and the qualities of modern work often undermine the benefits and satisfactions Lane describes. The idea that work—any paid employment no matter what its pay, conditions, prospects, or intrinsic rewards—trumps time spent at home with one's children supported by public assistance constitutes the key assumption underlying current welfare reform, with its time limits and quick labor-force attachment. The validity of this assumption is a question that has been unable to find much of a hearing on the agendas of public policy and social science. Yet, its consequences are profound. "What citizenship offers," explains social theorist Ralf Daharendorf, "does not depend on the readiness of people to pay a price in the private domain [of work]. Citizenship cannot be marketed." With citizenship turned into a commodity purchased with a job, nonwork pushes anyone out of employment to the margins of society, no longer to be a full citizen.[26]

The apotheosis of the marketplace not only commodifies the meaning of citizenship, it narrows the meaning of real work and reinforces the welfare state's gendered inequities by excluding socially important jobs—for instance, child rearing—that offer great human rewards. Some of the most satisfying and significant work exists outside the regular labor market, relegated disproportionately to women—taking care of old people, promoting the arts, building civic institutions, for example. "The welfare law puts us in a box if we believe that it forces us to equate work with monetary compensation," argues Edgar S. Cahn, president of Time Dollar Institute. "The market is governed by a pricing system that devalues precisely those activities most critically needed in communities: caring, learning, worshipping, associating, socializing, and helping."[27] There is something bizarre about a rich society that assigns so many of its important tasks to a voluntarism that is defined as different from work and that carries no entitlement to the social benefits of citizenship.

Like the case for the war on dependence, the argument for devolution appears on the surface straightforward and compelling. In recent years, commentators on the political left and right have written scathingly about the disfunctions of centralized bureaucracies, and vigorous grassroots movements have agitated for local control of public programs since the 1960s.[28] Devolution, moreover, seems consistent with American traditions of localism and innovative state government. The roots of America's welfare state, as we have seen, reach back beyond the New Deal into state houses, city halls, settlement houses, private charities, and the welfare activities of individual firms. Earlier in the century, private agencies pioneered programs and handed them off to government; state governments introduced new programs later taken up at the national level. Now the movement is in the other direction. What the national government devolves are not successful or promising programs, but whole functions, such as public assistance, while state governments turn other functions over to for-profit and not-for-profit firms and agencies. However, no guarantee exists that state and local governments will find new and promising ways to carry out the functions assigned them or that they will act in the best interests of their clients.

In the twentieth century, states have been sites of reaction as often as innovation. Both the federal government and advocacy organizations fought the civil rights struggle mainly against state laws and practices.

Where the national government has allowed states to set public benefit amounts, as in AFDC, outcomes have differed dramatically from state to state with the levels in some states appallingly low. As a result of these variations from state to state, families and individuals in need of public assistance, Medicaid, workers' compensation, or unemployment insurance find it much harder to survive in some places than in others. Public policy now holds that except for Social Security, Medicare, Supplemental Security Income, and food stamps, no minimum benefits exist to which all citizens may lay claim—that it is perfectly acceptable for citizens with identical situations to find life harsher because of an accident of geography. Americans seem willing to give up the idea of a nation of uniform laws and entitlements even as they support legislation protecting the flag. They show more concern over the symbols of nationality than with the shared experiences that unite a people.

As with devolution and independence, there is much to be said about the virtues of markets in social policy, but the discourse about them proceeds for the most part superficially. Politicians and commentators write unreflectively, as if all markets were the same. The policy literature contains few examinations of the relations of markets to power—how relations of exchange between unequal participants, which are neither free nor fair, may not serve all interests optimally, or how the interests of suppliers and customers for given policies shape the outcome of market processes. Nor is there sufficient discussion about where markets are appropriate and where they are not. The question extends beyond what many economists call market failure. Sometimes markets work perfectly well and serve the goals of their suppliers and customers—except they damage other, vulnerable parties without power to affect their outcomes. The great example, of course, is medicine, where managed care initially reduced costs, as business interests demanded, but at a mounting price to patients and physicians.

Markets are questions of political philosophy as well as economics. What functions should be left entirely to markets, and where does a public interest override efficiency and the lowest possible cost? In 1970 the British historian and theorist of social policy Richard Titmuss attempted to answer these questions in *The Gift Relationship*, which used blood donation as a case study in the impact of markets on social policy. Titmuss argued that embedding blood donations in the market, a practice even more common in the United States at the time he wrote than now, inherently corrupted the process and led to greater rates of impurity and infection than in Britain, where the blood supply had not been commercialized. In the 1990s in Britain, Will Hutton's *The State We're In* and in the United States, Robert Kuttner's *Everything for Sale* followed in the tradition of Titmuss by exposing the limits of market models in social policy and exploring the relation of markets to citizenship. In the last quarter-century, writes Kuttner, "a more complex view of society has given way to the claim that most issues boil down to material incentives, and most social problems are best resolved by constructing or enhancing markets. And, indeed, fewer people today enjoy protections against the uglier face of the market, or social income as a right of citizenship. More aspects of human life are on the auction block."[29]

One other point about markets needs emphasis. Markets can be radically individualizing. They can turn relations into commodities. They may erode notions of obligation based on citizenship or ties of common humanity. They are the opposite of the models to which we turn for examples of how to treat those we consider members of our own family or circle. We react uneasily to most attempts to commodify or marketize family relations (think of the hostility to the idea of wages for housework); we do not measure friendship by market standards, at least in theory. My point is this: market models do not constitute the only template for the execution of social obligations; if we look, we can find other paradigms, such as in the way we think about family, friends, and community. Market models seem appropriate to us when we deal with strangers—with the alien collectivity rather than the familiar individual. We make assistance for strangers conditional in ways we do not for family and friends. Only through work do strangers become members of the national family, citizens who merit our sympathy and help. And yet, as the definition of citizenship increasingly includes work, more Americans will find themselves, at least from time to time, strangers in their own country, outside the circle to which they thought they belonged.

Market arguments are also used to justify the limitations of the welfare state. Resources are not unlimited, and the demands of those in need often stretch them thin. But America's great productive capacity gives it a material abundance unparalleled in world history. The United States is a nation with the luxury, and the curse, of choices. Opponents of the welfare state often deploy the idea of scarcity as an excuse to draw the boundaries of exclusion more tightly, reduce public spending, and privatize public responsibilities.[30] In the name of fairness and economy, they promote the marketization of citizenship. In the process, they redefine not only the welfare state, but American democracy itself.

That is because market models recast democracy as consumer choice—a definition that accentuates inequalities and excludes the poor. The citizen of a democracy is free to choose her school, electricity provider, and retirement funds as well as her automobile, running shoes, and coffee. The more choices she has, the more perfectly is democracy realized. In one way or another, those who depend on public assistance are excluded from democratic participation—not only on account of their poverty, but also because they are subject to a host of regulations about work, family, and personal behavior that limit their capacity to exercise free choice. Thus, the freedom of anyone outside the regular labor market becomes moot because they are second-class citizens unable to participate in the democratic rituals of consumer choice.

The marketization of democracy also reduces what citizens may expect from their governments and what governments may expect from their citizens, for the practice of democracy depends on the wide diffusion of social citizenship. The "distinguishing mark of citizens," observes historian Linda Kerber, "is active engagement in civic life." Kuttner calls for the renewal and enlargement of "those spheres of community life where people are in the role of citizens rather than consumers. In the current era, the trend is largely in the opposite direction, as public institutions are privatized and the shopping mall becomes the new public square." Civic engagement, or the active practice of political citizenship, depends not only on a public sphere but also on freedom from want and the fear of impoverishment. "Unless everybody can live a life free of elementary fears," cautions Daharendorf, "constitutional rights can be empty promises and worse, a cynical pretence of liberties that in fact stabilize privilege." As its theorists have understood, a welfare state constitutes a precondition for modern democracy. Together, political, civil, and welfare rights, points out sociologist Anthony Giddens, fully integrate "the citizen into the wider social order."[31]

I have chosen to stress the limits rather than the virtues of markets because their champions speak with such a loud and triumphant voice.[32] I have tried to recognize and report that voice in the chapters of this book. In many instances, it is accurate. Markets can indeed bring needed efficiency and improvement to many areas of public life. But the marketization of everything proceeds with too little restraint or reflection. Unchecked it threatens to damage the individuals welfare states exist to help and to erode protection against misfortune even further. It also threatens to undermine the conditions of effective citizenship and the bonds that unite citizens in one nation. It is not multiculturalism or the languages of immigrants that threaten national cohesion, but the corrosive impact of the market's radical individualism, its processes of marginalization and exclusion, and its subversion of the public sphere.

In July 1999, President Bill Clinton's "New Markets" poverty tour highlighted the ironies of linking markets to citizenship. Clinton, as we have seen, argued that America's depressed rural areas, Indian reservations, and inner cities deserved private investment because they represent huge untapped markets. In America's great age of economic recovery, no potential worker or consumer should remain excluded from prosperity. The poor deserved help not because they are citizens entitled "to live the life of a civilised being according to the standards prevailing in the society," but because of their cash value. America could solve the problem of poverty by turning the poor into commodities and selling them, albeit with the price subsidized by government.

Clinton's market-based rhetoric viewed poor people as ready and willing to work hard at jobs and to spend their money intelligently at the mall. As he jettisoned the big-government strategies of the War on Poverty and Great Society era, Clinton also tossed overboard its language of deprivation, pathology, and culture of poverty. In the new markets era, poor people might have been passed by, but they were neither incapable of helping themselves nor victims. In the community action wing of the War on Poverty, poor people also were not victims, but their escape from poverty demanded not, as in Clinton's plan, their participation in newly created markets, but their capture of the agencies of local government and the independent sector. New social movements, not new markets, composed their goal. For Clinton, poor people were neither victims nor insurgents. They were folks, like everyone else, concerned about and, with a little help, capable of making a living. The image lacked the poignance of a Dorothea Lange photograph or the excitement of taking over a welfare office. But it at least exuded a faith in the competence of ordinary people to discharge the day-to-day responsibilities of citizens.

. . . .

However citizenship is defined in social policy, three features of the American welfare state call for immediate action. First, the links between public benefits and employment need to be loosened. They guarantee increased and unmerited hardship in a flexible labor market full of unstable and contingent work that encourages workers to move among jobs and careers. They also promise to reinforce the gendered inequities that limit the access of women to full social citizenship. Second, the denial of health care as an entitlement of citizenship not only leaves millions of Americans without medical insurance; it is also a national disgrace that signals this nation's capitulation to special interests that are held in check for the public's benefit in every other Western democracy. Third, the abolition of the poorest Americans' entitlement to public assistance represents more than a detail of "welfare reform" to be evaluated by the size of caseloads. Rather, it signifies a willingness to accept massive poverty and suffering if predictions of its success falter even a little; and it reveals a mean and truncated conception of social obligation and citizenship.

In one way or another, these three items call for expanding the meaning, boundaries, and prerogatives of citizenship. The welfare state is about a collection of specific benefits; but it is also about how we define America and what it means to be an American—and how we would like those questions answered not only now, but at the close of the twenty-first century.

NOTES

PROLOGUE: THE INVENTION OF WELFARE

1. See, for example, *Report of the Proceedings of the Third International Congress for the Welfare and Protection of Children* (London: P. S. King and Son, 1902); W. H. Slingerland, *Child Welfare Work in Pennsylvania: A Cooperative Study of Child-Helping Agencies and Institutions* (New York: Russell Sage Foundation; Concord, NH: Rumford Press, 1915); "Prologue," in Clarke A. Chambers and Esther Wattenberg, eds., *To Promote the General Welfare* (Minneapolis: University of Minnesota, Center for Urban and Regional Affairs, 1988), 2.

2. Pennsylvania Department of Welfare, *First Biennial Report of the Commissioner of Public Welfare for the Biennium Ending December 30, 1922, Public Welfare Report* (Harrisburg, PA: Bureau of Publications, 1925), 5; Pennsylvania Department of Welfare, *Second Biennial Report of the Secretary of Welfare for the Period Ending May 31, 1924, Public Welfare Report*, comp. John Montgomery Baldy (Harrisburg, PA: Bureau of Publications, 1925), 3; New York Department of Public Welfare, *Annual Report for 1920*, 7; New York Department of Public Welfare, *Annual Report for 1921*, 5; Illinois Department of Public Welfare, *General Information and Laws Effective July 1, 1917*, comp. Edward Brundage (Springfield: Schnepp and Barnes, State Printers, 1918), 7–8; "The Department of Public Welfare," *Institution Quarterly* 8, 3 (30 September 1917): 13. Clyde King, "Foreword"; J. L. Gillin, "The Public Welfare Movement and Democracy," *Annals of the American Academy of Political and Social Science* 105 (January 1923): 13–16.

3. Sophonsiba P. Breckinridge, *Public Welfare Administration in the U.S.—Select Documents*, 2d ed. (Chicago: University of Chicago Press, 1938), 601, 662.

4. For sources on "welfare work" in business, see chapter 7.

5. *Report to the President of the Committee on Economic Security* (Washington, DC: GPO, 1935), 45. A note on usage: ADC refers to Aid to Dependent Children only; A(F)DC refers to a characteristic of both programs that spans both its incarnations.

6. Brookings Institution, *Functions and Activities of the National Government in the Field of Social Welfare* (Washington, DC: GPO, 1949), 1; "Comprehensive Public Welfare Program," *Appendix to the Congressional Record*, 80th Cong., 1st sess., 1947, A2499; "The 'Poorhouse State' Is the Right Name for It," *Saturday Evening Post,* 19 November 1949, 10, 12. See also John J. Corson, " 'Need' Is an Anachronism," *Survey Midmonthly*, March 1950, 135.

7. There is a third track—taxation—that is much less discussed as a component of the public welfare state. See Christopher Howard, *The Hidden Welfare State: Tax Expenditures and Social Policy in the United States* (Princeton: Princeton University Press, 1997). I use "public" welfare state to differentiate these programs from

those in the private welfare state of employee benefits. Chapter 2 describes the tracks in the welfare state.

8. Daniel Nelson, *Unemployment Insurance: The American Experience, 1915–1935* (Madison: University of Wisconsin Press, 1969), 22–23, 105–6, 120; Roy Lubove, *The Struggle for Social Security, 1900–1935* (Cambridge: Harvard University Press, 1968), 171–72; Ohio Commission on Unemployment Insurance, *Report* (Columbus, 1932).

9. Blanche D. Coll, *Safety Net: Welfare and Social Security, 1929–1979* (New Brunswick, NJ: Rutgers University Press, 1995), 167; John D. Morris, "Government Aims on Relief Limited," *New York Times*, 1 March 1949; Coll, *Safety Net*, 157; William R. Conklin, "Woman in Mink," *New York Times*, 30 October 1947; "Mr. Truman Calls for the Dole," *U.S. News and World Report*, 18 March 1949, 19.

10. *Social Security Bulletin, Annual Statistical Supplement, 1976*, 200–201, tables 168 and 169.

11. Donald F. Howard, "Public Welfare on Page One," *Survey Midmonthly*, July 1947, 196.

12. Conklin, "Woman in Mink"; Rufus Jarman, "Detroit Cracks Down on Relief Chiselers," *Saturday Evening Post*, 10 December 1949, 17–19; Paul Molloy, "The Relief Chiselers Are Stealing Us Blind," *Saturday Evening Post*, 8 September 1951, 32–33; schoolteacher quoted in Joseph P. Ritz, *The Despised Poor: Newburgh's War on Welfare* (Boston: Beacon Press, 1966), 63.

13. Lucy Freeman, "Dewey Lists Gains in State Welfare," *New York Times*, 16 November 1949; John T. Flynn, "Welfare and the Welfare State," *Catholic World* 171 (April 1950): 100–101; "The 'Poorhouse State,' " 12; *Congressional Record*, 81st Cong., 2d Sess., 3 May 1950, 6294.

14. Harry S. Truman, "Labor Day Address at the Allegheny City Free Fair in Pittsburgh," *Public Papers of the Presidents of the United States* (Washington, DC: GPO, 1964), pp. 460–64; Truman, "Annual Budget Message to Congress, Fiscal Year 1949," *Public Papers*, 37.

15. Stanley Wencour and Michael Reisch, *From Charity to Enterprise: The Development of American Social Work in a Market Economy* (Urbana: University of Illinois Press, 1989), 260; James Leiby, *A History of Social Welfare and Social Work in the United States* (New York: Columbia University Press, 1978), 279, 282. See also Roy Lubove, *The Professional Altruist: The Emergence of Social Work as a Career, 1880–1930* (Cambridge: Harvard University Press, 1965).

16. M. Elaine Burgess and Daniel O. Price, *An American Dependency Challenge* (Chicago: American Public Welfare Association, 1963), 191; Coll, *Safety Net*, 173, table 7.1. An irony, as Michael K. Brown points out, is that in the 1960s, even as "welfare" increasingly signified African American, the most significant growth in AFDC occurred among whites. The average monthly caseload for white families rose 80 percent, compared to 2 percent for black families. Michael K. Brown, "Race in the American Welfare State: The Ambiguities of 'Univeralistic' Social Policy since the New Deal," in *With Friends Like These: The New "Liberalism" and the New Assault on Equality*, ed. Adolph Reed, Jr. (Boulder, CO: Westview Press, forthcoming); and Michael K. Brown, "The Ghetto in the Welfare State: Race, Gender and Class after the Great Society," paper presented at the Annual Meeting of the Social Science History Association, 16–19 October 1997. My great thanks to Professor Brown for sharing his unpublished work with me. Burgess and Price, *American Dependency Challenge*, 94.

17. Guida West, *The National Welfare Rights Movement: The Social Protest of Poor Women* (New York: Praeger, 1981); Charles Reich, "The New Property," *Yale Law Journal* 73 (April 1964): 733–87. See also William H. Simon, "The Invention and Reinvention of Welfare Rights," *Maryland Law Review* 44, 1 (1985): 1–37. On lawyers and welfare issues, see Martha Davis, *Brutal Need* (New Haven: Yale University Press, 1993). See also Rand E. Rosenblatt, "Legal Entitlement and Welfare Benefits," in *The Politics of Law: A Progressive Critique*, ed. David Kairys (New York: Pantheon, 1972), 262–78; Frances Fox Piven and Richard Cloward, *Poor People's Movements: Why They Succeed, How They Fail* (New York: Pantheon, 1977), 264–361; C. R. Winegarden, "The Welfare 'Explosion': Determinants of the Size and Recent Growth of the AFDC Population," *American Journal of Economic Sociology* 32 (1973): 244–56; R. Richard Ritti and Drew W. Hyman, "The Administration of Poverty: Lessons from the 'Welfare Explosion,' 1967–1973," *Social Problems* 25 (December 1977): 158–75; Gilbert Y. Steiner, "Reform Follows Reality: The Growth of Welfare," *Public Interest* 34 (1974): 47–65.

CHAPTER 1: THE AMERICAN WELFARE STATE

1. For a definition of welfare state, see Gosta Esping-Anderson, "Welfare States and the Economy," in *The Handbook of Economic Sociology*, ed. Neil J. Smelser and Richard Swedberg (Princeton: Princeton University Press; New York: Russell Sage Foundation, 1994), 714. Esping-Anderson credits Swedish social democracy with originating this concept of the welfare state.

2. For an instructive catalog of government subsidies to the wealthy, see Mark Zepezauer and Arthur Naiman, *Take the Rich off Welfare* (Tuscon, AZ: Odonian Press, 1996).

3. State governments run surprisingly large numbers of public assistance programs. Although in recent years state governments have reduced or eliminated the best known, General Assistance, they still run many others. In the early 1990s, Maryland residents, for instance, could draw on benefits from ninety-five means-tested programs. The largest were the federal or federal-state programs Medicaid (the most costly), food stamps, AFDC, and the Earned Income Tax Credit. Together, all means-tested programs cost $3.7 billion in 1991. The federal government paid 56 percent and the state 37 percent, with the rest funded through bonds. *Government Means-Tested Programs in Maryland* (University of Baltimore, Merrick School of Business, Jacob France Center, Regional Economic Studies Program, September 1993), 1–3. Thirteen of these provided cash and other financial assistance; twelve offered food and nutrition assistance; three, medical help; five, educational services; eighteen social services; five, job training and employment assistance; seventeen, housing subsidies or grants; twenty-one, low-income housing loans; and one, legal services. Thirty-two of the programs served families; eighteen, primarily children; and nine the elderly and disabled. The remaining were housing programs serving broad constituencies. U.S. House of Representatives, *1996 Green Book*, 305, 385, 386, table 8–1, 873, 1272, table, I–3.

4. *1996 Green Book*, 329, table 5–1, 1274, table 1–5.

5. *1996 Green Book*, 3–4, 133–134, 329, tables 3–1, 5–1, 1–5.

6. For details on these programs and references to their history and current status, see chapters 8–12.

7. Documentation for this paragraph is found in chapters 8 and 9.

8. The importance of taxation in the welfare state has been demonstrated recently with considerable force in Christopher Howard, *The Hidden Welfare State: Tax Expenditure and Social Policy in the United States* (Princeton: Princeton University Press, 1997). Not all benefits delivered through the tax code fit the definition of the *welfare state*; in this book I exclude measures designed primarily to benefit the middle class and affluent or to enhance the value of investments, such as the home mortgage tax deduction and investment tax credits. Zepezauer and Naiman (*Take the Rich off Welfare*) describe some of these programs. For the history of the home mortgage deduction, see Howard, *Hidden Welfare State*, 48–63. On the concept of tax expenditure, see the discussion in Mary E. O'Connell, "On the Fringe: Rethinking the Link between Wages and Benefits," *Tulane Law Review* 67 (May 1993): 1422–1529. See also Julian E. Zelizer, *Taxing America: Wilbur D. Mills, Congress, and the State, 1945–1975* (New York: Cambridge University Press, 1998), 283–89; *1996 Green Book*, 813–14, 819–20; Sherwood Ross, "Employers Are Due More Welfare Tax Credits Than They Collect," *Pittsburgh Post-Gazette*, 31 May 1998; Willem Adema and Marcel Einerhand, "The Growing Role of Private Social Benefits," *Labor Market and Social Policy, occasional papers no. 32*, (OECD, Directorate for Education, Employment, Labour, and Social Affairs, 17 April 1998), 33–34.

9. *1996 Green Book*, 807; see chapter 11 below for full references on the EITC.

10. Sources on the history and size of the independent sector are in chapter 6.

11. Adema and Einerhand, "Growing Role," 36. For the sources of these statistics and other references on the private welfare state, see chapter 8. Anyone interested in following its development should consult the excellent publications of the Employee Benefits Research Institute. Consult their Website for a list.

12. Alan Wolfe, *The Limits of Legitimacy: Political Contradictions of Contemporary Capitalism* (New York: Free Press, 1975), 108–75. See also Lester M. Salamon, "The Nonprofit Sector and Government: The American Experience in Theory and Practice," in *The Third Sector: Comparative Studies of Nonprofit Organizations*, ed. Helmut K. Anheier and Wolfgang Seibel (Berlin: Walter de Gruyter, 1990), 222–26. The issue is considered in comparative historical terms in Michael B. Katz and Christoph Sachsse, eds., *The Mixed Economy of Social Welfare: Public/Private Relations in England, Germany, and the United States, the 1870s to the 1930s* (Baden-Baden: Nomos Verlagsgellscaft, 1996).

13. The most useful typology of welfare states I have read is Gosta Esping-Anderson, *The Three Worlds of Welfare Capitalism* (Princeton: Princeton University Press, 1990). Anderson identifies three welfare state regimes: liberal, corporatist, and social democratic. The American exemplifies the liberal regime "in which means-tested assistance, modest universal transfers, or modest social-insurance plans predominate. Benefits cater mainly to a clientele of low-income, usually working-class, state dependent. In this model, the progress of social reform has been severely circumscribed by traditional, liberal work-ethic norms. . . . Entitlement rules are therefore strict and often associated with stigma; benefits are typically modest. In turn, the state encourages the market, either passively—by guaranteeing only a minimum—or actively—by subsidizing private welfare schemes" (26–27). In 1993, "voluntary private health benefits," which is to say health benefits provided through work, amounted to 5.15 percent of U.S. GDP, compared to 0.33 percent in the United Kingdom, 0.09 percent in Sweden, and 0.66 percent in Germany. Adema and Einerhand, "Growing Role," 22. I have told some of this story in various places. On poorhouses, Charity Organization Societies, and tramps, see esp. *In the Shadow of the Poorhouse: A Social History of Welfare in America*, 10th

anniversary ed. (New York: Basic Books, 1996), and *Poverty and Policy in American History* (New York: Academic Press, 1983); on the distinction between the deserving and the undeserving poor see *The Undeserving Poor* (New York: Pantheon, 1989). A solid recent account of mothers' pensions is Joanne L. Goodwin, *Gender and the Politics of Welfare Reform: Mothers' Pensions in Chicago, 1911–1929* (Chicago: University of Chicago Press, 1997).

14. Adema and Einerhand, "Growing Role," 28. According to a recent study, America was not always a welfare laggard. In the 1930s it ranked high among nations in the public provision of social welfare. See Edwin Amenta, *Bold Relief: Institutional Politics and the Origins of Modern American Social Policy* (Princeton: Princeton University Press, 1998); Gary Burtless, "Public Spending on the Poor: Historical Trends and Economic Limits," in *Confronting Poverty: Prescriptions for Change,* ed. Sheldon H. Danziger, Gary D. Sandefur, and Daniel H. Weinberg (Cambridge: Harvard University Press, 1994), 81, table 3.2. There is a great deal of useful comparative data and analysis in Katherine McFate, Roger Lawson, and William Julius Wilson, eds., *Poverty, Inequality, and the Future of Social Policy* (New York: Russell Sage Foundation, 1995).

15. Bruce Western and Katherine Beckett, "How Unregulated Is the U.S. Labor Market? The Penal System as a Labor Market Institution," *American Journal of Sociology* 104, 4 (January 1999): 1030.

16. Many sources describe the miseries of poverty in earlier times. For one discussion, see Michael B. Katz, "Surviving Poverty," Chap. 4 in *Improving Poor People: The Welfare State, the "Underclass," and Urban Schools as History* (Princeton: Princeton University Press, 1995), 144–72.

17. Some of the books that deal with the right turn in politics are: Godfrey Hodgson, *The World Turned Right Side Up: A History of the Conservative Ascendancy in America* (Boston: Houghton Mifflin, 1996); Thomas Byrne Edsall and Mary D. Edsall, *Chain Reaction: The Impact of Race, Rights, and Taxes on American Politics* (New York: Norton, 1991); Thomas Ferguson and Joel Rogers, *Right Turn: The Decline of the Democrats and the Future of American Politics* (New York: Hill and Wang, 1986); Sara Diamond, *Roads to Dominion: Right Wing Movements and Political Power in the United States* (New York: Guilford Press, 1995); Mary C. Brennan, *Turning Right in the Sixties: The Conservative Capture of the GOP* (Chapel Hill: University of North Carolina Press, 1995); William Berman, *America's Right Turn: From Nixon to Clinton,* 2d ed. (Baltimore: Johns Hopkins University Press, 1998); E. J. Dionne, *Why Americans Hate Politics* (New York: Simon and Schuster, 1991). There is some debate over the breadth and depth of the right turn in politics and culture. For instance, Ferguson and Rogers, in *Right Turn,* argued that American public opinion has not changed very much over a long period of time and did not cause the right turn in politics. Instead, they contend, the political shift resulted from "the disintegration of the New Deal system itself . . . killed off not by voters but by a dramatic realignment of major investors in the political system" (196). Opinion polls do show consistently high support for Social Security, for instance, but I think that events subsequent to their book's publication in 1986 point to a deeper shift within the voting public than they observed. For a discussion of the question of alternatives that might have been followed in the construction of America's welfare state, see Charles Noble, *Welfare as We Knew It: A Political History of the American Welfare State* (New York: Oxford University Press, 1997).

18. William Greider, *One World, Ready or Not: The Manic Logic of Global Capitalism*

(New York: Simon and Schuster, 1997), 15; Manuel Castells, *End of Millennium* (Malden, MA: Blackwell Publishers, 1998), 335–60; Barry Bluestone and Bennett Harrison, *The Deindustrialization of America: Plant Closings, Community Abandonment, and the Dismantling of Basic Industry* (New York: Basic Books, 1982); Ferguson and Rogers, *Right Turn*, 101–2.

19. Daniel Yergin and Joseph Stanislaw, *The Commanding Heights: The Battle between Government and the Marketplace That Is Remaking the Modern World* (New York: Simon and Schuster, 1998), 319–21.

20. Dionne, *Why Americans Hate Politics*, 81; Edsall and Edsall, *Chain Reaction*, 78–79.

21. Greider, *One World*. There is a large literature on the rightward movement of American blue-collar voters. Thomas Sugrue, *The Origins of the Urban Crisis: Race and Inequality in Postwar Detroit* (Princeton: Princeton University Press, 1996), argues that its origins lie in the 1950s, not, as usually claimed, in the 1960s. Sugrue is also excellent on race and housing. Another important work that deals with race and housing is Arnold Hirsch, *Making the Second Ghetto: Race and Housing in Chicago, 1940–1960* (New York: Cambridge University Press, 1983). See also Jonathan Rieder, *Canarsie: The Jews and Italians of Brooklyn against Liberalism* (Cambridge: Harvard University Press, 1995); and Dan T. Carter, *The Politics of Rage: George Wallace, the Origins of the New Conservatism, and the Transformation of American Politics* (Baton Rouge: Louisiana State University Press, 1995), 351–52. A moving and penetrating account of the economic stress experienced by blue-collar workers even at the time of their greatest prosperity is Lillian Rubin, *Worlds of Pain: Life in the Working-Class Family* (New York: Basic Books, 1976). See also her understanding of the relation of class to opposition to busing in *Busing and Backlash: White against White in a California School District* (Berkeley: University of California Press, 1972). The book that tells the story of blue-collar opposition to busing most vividly is J. Anthony Lukas, *Common Ground: A Turbulent Decade in the Lives of Three American Families* (New York: Knopf, 1985). Many scholars have documented the growing wage inequality of the period: see Bennett Harrison and Barry Bluestone, *The Great U-Turn: Corporate Restructuring and the Polarizing of America* (New York: Basic Books, 1988); Frank Levy, *Dollars and Dreams: The American Income Distribution* (New York: Russell Sage Foundation, 1987); Sheldon Danziger and Peter Gottschalk, *America Unequal* (New York: Russell Sage Foundation; Cambridge: Harvard University Press, 1995). Roger Lawson and William Julius Wilson, "Poverty, Social Rights, and the Quality of Citizenship," in McFate, Lawson, and Wilson, *Poverty, Inequality, and the Future of Social Policy*, 693–714, offers another important perspective on these issues.

22. Ferguson and Rogers, *Right Turn*, 290–92. "Sunbelt" is not a precise designation—its boundaries are disputed. In brief, I use it as a shorthand for the South and Southwest as well as southern parts of the far West.

23. Ferguson and Rogers, *Right Turn*, 99–100, 138, 140. There is an argument that Reagan increased the deficit in order to have an excuse for cutting social spending. Noble, *Welfare as We Knew It*, 123. Michael K. Brown, *Race, Money, and the American Welfare State* (Ithaca: Cornell University Press, 1999), argues convincingly that fiscal constraints have hobbled welfare state development since the 1930s.

24. I understand "evangelical" and the related although not identical term "fundamentalist" as defined in Albert J. Menendez, *Evangelicals at the Ballot Box* (Amherst, NY: Prometheus Books, 1996), 12–13: "The term evangelical will refer to those

Protestants who believe in a theological rebirth through faith in Jesus Christ and who accept the Bible as the only and the authoritative rule of faith and practice. The rebirth is generally said to have occurred at a particular time; hence, the phrase 'born again.' The Bible is also generally held to be in some ways inerrant, inspired, infallible, and trustworthy. Evangelicals also emphasize proselytism, evangelism, and missionary efforts to win others to their viewpoint. Fundamentalists are even stricter in their interpretations and their convictions are often accompanied with a degree of separatism and anti-intellectualism not found among evangelicals. Worship is often subjective and emotional, and less attention is given to historical forms of worship and belief such as sacraments and creeds." The story of the modern religious right is told very well in William Martin, *With God on Our Side: The Rise of the Religious Right in America* (New York: Broadway Books, 1996).

25. John H Garvey, "Fundamentalism and American Law," in *Fundamentalisms and the State: Remaking Polities, Economies, and Militance*, ed. Martin E. Marty and R. Scott Appleby (Chicago: University of Chicago Press, 1993), 31; Nancy T. Ammerman, "North American Fundamentalism," in *Fundamentalisms Observed*, ed. Martin E. Marty and R. Scott Appleby (Chicago: University of Chicago Press, 1991), 45.
26. Robert Wuthnow and Matthew P. Lawson, "Sources of Christian Fundamentalism in the United States," in *Accounting for Fundamentalism*, ed. Martin E. Marty and R. Scott Appleby (Chicago: University of Chicago Press, 1994), 31–32; Martin, *With God on Our Side*, 173.
27. Wuthnow and Lawson, "Sources of Christian Fundamentalism," 32.
28. Hodgson, *World Turned Right Side Up*, 175–84; Ammerman, "North American Protestant Fundamentalism," 43–44; Diamond, *Roads to Dominion*, 311.
29. Menendez, *Evangelicals at the Ballot Box*, 176–177.
30. Jerome L. Himmelstein, "The New Right," and Margaret Ann Latus, "Ideological PACs and Political Action," in *The New Christian Right: Mobilization and Legitimation*, ed. Robert C. Liebman and Robert Wuthnow (New York: Aldine Publishing Company, 1983), 28–29, 78; David Hammack, "Think Tanks and the Invention of Policy Studies," *Nonprofit and Voluntary Sector Quarterly* 24, 2 (Summer 1995): 173–81; Martin, *With God on Our Side*, 171; James A. Smith, *The Idea Brokers: Think Tanks and the Rise of the New Policy Elite* (New York: Free Press, 1991), 174–92 and the compilation of basic information on think tanks, 270–94; David M. Ricci, *The Transformation of American Politics* (New Haven: Yale University, Press, 1993), 152–73; Brennan, *Turning Right*, 1–5, 138–42.
31. Chuck Lane, "The Manhattan Project," *New Republic*, 25 March 1985, 14–15; Smith, *Idea Brokers*, 192; Hodgson, *The World Turned Right Side Up*, 282; Jean Stefancic and Richard Delgado, *No Mercy* (Philadelphia: Temple University Press, 1996), 89–90, app. tables 1, 2, 3; Vince Stehle, "Righting Philanthropy," *Nation*, 30 June 1997, 16.
32. Ricci, *The Transformation of American Politics*, 166; Smith, *Idea Brokers*, 194; Karen M. Paget, "Lessons of Right-Wing Philanthropy," *American Prospect* 40 (September–October 1998): 91; National Committee for a Responsive Philanthropy, "Moving a Public Policy Agenda: The Strategic Philanthropy of Conservative Foundations," July 1997; and "Conservative Foundations Prevail in Shaping Public Polices" [http:www.ncrp.org/reports/moving.htm].
33. Stefancic and Delgado, *No Mercy*, 140–46; Smith, *Idea Brokers*, 203.
34. Anderson quoted in Hodgson, *World Turned Right Side Up*, 8.

35. Hodgson, *World Turned Right Side Up*, xv. Two authors, Friedich Hayek and Russell Kirk, refracted the two poles between which modern conservatism has swung. Hayek located his work in the tradition of the great nineteenth-century liberals such as John Stuart Mill. Kirk, who abhorred the liberal tradition, placed himself in a conservative stream whose greatest spokesman was Edmund Burke.

36. Dionne, *Why Americans Hate Politics*, 157; Ricci, *Transformation of American Politics*, 74.

37. Hodgson, *World Turned Right Side Up*, 214.

38. Charles Murray, *Losing Ground: American Social Policy, 1950–1980* (New York: Basic Books, 1980); Lawrence Mead, *Beyond Entitlement: The Social Obligations of Citizenship* (New York: Free Press, 1986), 200, 6, 10, 87. There is an extensive literature of criticism on both Murray and Mead. Murray's empirical analysis has been effectively discredited by several leading social scientists, and his book is important for its ideology and influence, not for its substance, which is misleading. I have written in more detail about Murray and Mead. For example, see Michael B. Katz, *The Undeserving Poor: From the War on Poverty to the War on Welfare* (New York: Pantheon, 1989), 151–65.

39. Martin, *With God on Our Side*, 307–8; Thomas B. Edsall and Ceci Connolly, "A Gaping GOP Rift: Christian Right Increasingly Resentful," *Washington Post*, 27 March 1998. Hodgson also emphasizes the widening of old fissures within conservatism.

40. On this story more generally, see the excellent collection by Steven Fraser and Gary Gerstle, eds., *The Rise and Fall of the New Deal Order, 1930–1980* (Princeton: Princeton University Press, 1989).

41. Harry Braverman, *Labor and Monopoly Capital: The Degradation of Work in the Twentieth Century* (New York: Monthly Review Press, 1974), 279–80.

42. Dependence has at times referred to a social and legal status, "the lack of a separate legal or public identity"—for instance, in earlier centuries, the position of married women and indentured servants. Dependence also has meant "subjection to a ruling power," as with a colony or subordinate "caste of noncitizen residents." As an economic term it refers to the dependence of one person on "some other person(s) or institutions for subsistence," while the fourth meaning of dependence is more psychological or behavioral—"an individual character trait like lack of will power or excessive emotional neediness." Nancy Fraser and Linda Gordon, "A Genealogy of *Dependency*: Tracing a Keyword of the U.S. Welfare State," *Signs* 19, 2 (Winter 1994): 309, 311, 325–27.

43. Lawrence M. Mead, *The New Politics of Poverty: The Nonworking Poor in America* (New York: Basic Books, 1992), ix, 1, 15–16.

44. Michael B. Katz, Michelle Fine, and Elaine Simon, "Poking Around: Outsiders View Chicago School Reform," *Teachers College Record* 99, 1 (Fall 1997): 117–57; Yergin and Stanislaw, *Commanding Heights*, 372; Paul Osterman, *Securing Prosperity: The American Labor Market: How It Has Changed and What to Do about It* (Princeton: Princeton University Press, 1999).

45. Robert Kuttner, *Everything for Sale: The Virtues and Limits of Markets* (New York: Knopf, 1997), 11, 39.

46. Yergin and Stanislaw, *Commanding Heights*, 11–13, 374.

47. Economists define the market "as an abstract price making mechanism that is central to the allocation of resources in the economy." Exchange is "a process by which the buyers and sellers of a good interact to determine its price and quantity." Paul A. Samuelson and William D. Nordhaus, *Economics*, 12th ed. (New York:

McGraw-Hill, 1985), quoted in Robert Lane, *The Market Experience* (New York: Cambridge University Press, 1991), 11; Richard Swedberg, "Markets as Social Structures," in Smelser and Swedberg, *Handbook*, 255; Kuttner, *Everything for Sale*, 11, 40–41. "Liberal economic theory, originating with Adam Smith and culminating with modern neoclassical thought," points out Esping-Anderson, "promotes both a normative, prescriptive idea (the market ought to be autonomous from political interference) and an analytical statement (optimal market performance is conditional upon such autonomy)." "Welfare States," 713.

48. *Economic Report of the President, 1997*, transmitted to Congress [computer file]/ The Executive Office of the President, Council of Economic Advisors, 18–20, 191–92.

49. Lane, *Market Experience*, pp. 13–14.

50. Jeffrey R. Henig, *Rethinking School Choice: Limits of the Market Metaphor* (Princeton: Princeton University Press, 1994).

51. Polanyi et al. quoted in Neil J. Smelser and Richard Swedberg, "The Sociological Perspective on the Economy," in Smelser and Swedberg, *Handbook*, 15; Swedberg, "Markets," 271.

52. Yergin and Stanislaw, *Commanding Heights*, 368.

CHAPTER 2: POVERTY AND INEQUALITY IN THE
NEW AMERICAN CITY

1. Anthony M. Orum, *City-Building in America* (Boulder, CO: Westview Press, 1995), 110–111; Jon C. Teaford, *Cities of the Heartland: The Rise and Fall of the Industrial Midwest* (Bloomington: Indiana University Press, 1993), 164. See also Thomas J. Sugrue, "The Structures of Urban Poverty: The Reorganization of Space and Work in Three Periods of American History," in *The "Underclass" Debate: Views from History*, ed. Michael B. Katz (Princeton: Princeton University Press, 1993), 105; Barry Bluestone and Bennett Harrison, *The Deindustrialization of America: Plant Closings, Community Abandonment, and the Dismantling of Basic Industry* (New York: Basic Books, 1982), 32, table 2.2; Gregory D. Squires, Larry Bennet, Kathleen McCourt, and Philip Nyden, *Chicago: Race, Class, and the Response to Urban Decline* (Philadelphia: Temple University Press, 1987), 22.

2. For this typology I am indebted to John Hull Mollenkopf, *The Contested City* (Princeton: Princeton University Press, 1983).

3. Joel Schwartz, *The New York Approach: Robert Moses, Urban Liberals, and Redevelopment of the Inner City* (Columbus: Ohio State University Press, 1993), 238, 253.

4. U.S., Panel on Policies and Prospects for Metropolitan and Nonmetropolitan America, *Urban America in the Eighties* (Englewood Cliffs, NJ: Prentice-Hall, 1981), 4.

5. U.S. Department of Housing and Urban Development, *The State of the Cities, 1998* (Washington, DC: GPO, 1998), 4–6.

6. U.S. Department of Housing and Urban Development, *State of the Cities 1998*, 9.

7. Saskia Sassen, *Cities in a World Economy* (Thousand Oaks, CA: Pine Forge Press, 1994), xiii, 2, 12–14, 55, 66–67; see also Saskia Sassen, *Global City: New York, London, and Tokyo* (Princeton: Princeton University Press, 1991), 70–71, 127; William Greider, *One World, Ready or Not: The Manic Logic of World Capitalism* (New York: Simon and Schuster, 1997); Manuel Castells, *End of Millennium* (Malden, MA: Blackwell Publishers, 1998).

8. Emily Lounsberry, "Made (Poor) in America," *Philadelphia Inquirer*, 3 May 1998; Sassen, *Cities in a World Economy*, 105–6; Sassen, *The Global City*, 245–83; Carl

Husemoller Nightingale, "The Global Inner City: Toward a Historical Analysis," in *W.E.B. DuBois, Race, and the City: "The Philadelphia Negro" and Its Legacy*, ed. Michael B. Katz and Thomas J. Sugrue (Philadelphia: University of Pennsylvania Press, 1998), 217–58.

9. Sassen, *Cities in a World Economy*, 105–6; Sassen, *The Global City*, 245–83; Nightingale, "The Global Inner City," 217–58.

10. David Cay Johnston, "The Servant Class Is at the Counter," *New York Times*, 28 August 1995; Sassen, *Cities in a World Economy*, 114–15.

11. Mollenkopf, *The Contested City*, 13; Katherine Newman and Chauncy Lennon, "The Job Ghetto," *American Prospect* 22 (1995): 66–67. The point about the Harlem job market is included in Newman's important ethnography of the low-wage labor market in New York City. Katherine S. Newman, *No Shame in My Game: The Working Poor in the Inner City* (New York: Knopf; New York: Russell Sage Foundation, 1999); Cornell West, *Race Matters* (Boston: Beacon Press, 1993), 15–32; Carl Husemoller Nightingale, *On the Edge: A History of Poor Black Children and Their American Dreams* (New York: Basic Books, 1993); U.S. Department of Housing and Urban Development, *State of the Cities, 1998*, 14–28.

12. Alex Keyssar, *Out of Work: The First Century of Unemployment in Massachusetts* (New York: Cambridge University Press, 1986); William Julius Wilson, *The Truly Disadvantaged: The Inner City, the Underclass, and Public Policy* (Chicago: University of Chicago Press, 1987); William Julius Wilson, *When Work Disappears: The World of the New Urban Poor* (New York: Knopf, distributed by Random House, 1996); Lawrence M. Mead, *The New Politics of Poverty: The Nonworking Poor in America* (New York: Basic Books, 1992); Christopher Jencks, *Rethinking Social Policy: Race, Poverty, and the Underclass* (Cambridge: Harvard University Press, 1992), 154, 158–59; Paul A. Jargowsky, *Poverty and Place: Ghettos, Barrios, and the American City* (New York: Russell Sage Foundation, 1997), chap. 4, table 4.3. High-poverty census tracts have poverty levels of at least 40 percent. Sylvia Nasar and Kirsten B. Mitchell, "Booming Job Market Draws Young Black Men into Fold," *New York Times*, 23 May 1999; U.S. Department of Housing and Urban Development, *State of the Cities, 1998*, 20; Mark J. Stern, "Poverty and Family Composition since 1940," in Katz, *The "Underclass" Debate*, 220–53.

13. Sheldon Danziger and Peter Gottschalk, *America Unequal* (Cambridge: Harvard University Press, 1995), 49–50, 52; "Prosperity Breaks Out!" *Left Business Observer* 86 (14 November 1998). See also Sheldon Danziger and Daniel H. Weinberg, "The Historical Record: Trends in Family Income, Inequality, and Poverty," in *Confronting Poverty: Prescriptions for Change*, ed. Sheldon Danziger, Gary D. Sandefur, and Daniel H. Weinberg (Cambridge: Harvard University Press, 1995), 18–50; Edward N. Wolff, "How the Pie Is Sliced: America's Growing Concentration of Wealth," *American Prospect* 22 (Summer 1995): 58–64; Melvin L. Oliver and Thomas M. Shapiro, *Black Wealth/White Wealth: A New Perspective on Racial Inequality* (New York: Routledge, 1995), 25, 86. See also Dalton Conley, *Being Black Living in the Red: Race, Wealth, and Social Policy in America* (Berkeley and Los Angeles: University of California Press, 1999); and Erin Texeira, "Study Outlines Wealth Gap between Blacks and Whites," *Philadelphia Inquirer*, 31 July 1998.

14. Keith Bradshaw, "The Nation: Productivity Is All, But It Doesn't Pay Well," *New York Times* 25 June 1995; Lawrence Mishel, Jared Bernstein, and John Schmitt, "Finally, Real Wage Gains," Economic Policy Institute Issue Brief no. 127 (17 July 1998) [http://epinet.org/ib127.html]; Danziger and Gottschalk, *America Unequal*,

10; U S. Census Bureau, *Poverty: 1996 Highlights* [www.census.gov/hhs/poverty/
poverty96/pov96hi.html]; "Miscellany," *Left Business Observer*, 89 (27 April
1999): 8; U.S. House of Representatives Committee on Ways and Means, *1994
Green Book*, app. H; Danziger and Weinberg, "The Historical Record," 18. The
accuracy of the census count of children in poverty recently has been challenged by
Christopher Jencks and Susan Mayer, who find it too high. "Census Reports of
Children's Poverty Trends Misleading," *Center for Urban Affairs and Policy
Research News* 16, 1 (Summer 1995): 8. See also Richard W. Stevenson, "In a Time
of Plenty, the Poor Are Still Poor," *New York Times*, 23 January 2000.

15. Danziger and Weinberg, "The Historical Record," 35–37; Children's Defense
Fund, *1992 City Child Poverty Data* (Washington, DC: Children's Defense Fund,
1992); National Center for Children in Poverty, "Young Children in Poverty Fact
Sheet" (November 1997) [http://cpmcnet.columbia.edu/dept/nccp/ycpf.html];
"Young Child Poverty in the States—Wide Variation and Significant Change,"
Early Childhood Research Brief, no. 1 [http://cpmcnet.columbia.edu/dept/
nccp/cp1text.html]. See also Tamar Lewin, "Study Finds That Youngest U.S.
Children Are Poorest," *New York Times*, 15 March 1998; U.S. Department of
Housing and Urban Development, *State of the Cities, 1998*, 8; Lawrence Mishel,
Jared Bernstein, et al., *The State of Working America, 1998–1999* (Ithaca: Cornell
University Press, 1999), executive summary. See also "Rich Nation, Poor Chil-
dren," editorial, *New York Times*, 15 August 1995; Kathryn Porter and Wendell
Primus, "Recent Changes in the Impact of the Safety Net on Child Poverty"
(Washington, DC: Center on Budget and Policy Priorities, 1999).

16. James Grossman, *Land of Hope: Chicago, Black Southerners, and the Great Migration* (Chicago: University of Chicago Press, 1989).

17. Jacqueline Jones, "Southern Diaspora: Origins of the Northern 'Underclass,' " in
Katz, *The "Underclass" Debate*, 41; Howard P. Chudacoff and Judith E. Smith,
The Evolution of American Urban Society (Englewood Cliffs, NJ: Prentice-Hall,
1988), 262.

18. Chudacoff and Smith, *The Evolution of American Urban Society*, 264, table 8–1;
Squires et al., *Chicago: Race, Class, and the Response to Urban Decline*, 96; Arnold
R. Hirsch, *Making the Second Ghetto: Race and Housing in Chicago, 1940–1960*
(Cambridge: Cambridge University Press, 1983); Nicholas Lemann, *The Promised
Land: The Great Black Migration and How It Changed America* (New York:
Knopf, 1991). On return migration to the South, see Carol Stack, *Call to Home:
African Americans Reclaim the Rural South* (New York: Basic Books, 1996);
William O'Hare, Kelvin M. Pollard, Taynia L. Mann, and Mary M. Kent, "African
Americans in the 1990s," *Population Bulletin* 46, 1 (Washington, DC: Population
Reference Bureau, July 1991), 7–9.

19. Chudacoff and Smith, *The Evolution of American Urban Society*, 263; Stack, *Call
to Home*.

20. Paul E. Peterson, "The Changing Fiscal Place of Big Cities in the Federal System,"
in *Interwoven Destinies: Cities and the Nation*, ed. Henry G. Cisneros (New York:
Norton, 1993); 188–89; Chudacoff and Smith, *The Evolution of American Urban
Society*, 260; David R. Goldfield and Blaine A. Brownell, *Urban America: From
Downtown to No Town* (Boston: Houghton Mifflin, 1979), 369; Teaford, *Cities of
the Heartland*, 212, table 8; U.S. Department of Housing and Urban Development,
State of the Cities, 1998, 15. For figures on population change by city and region
from 1970 to 1995, see Elvin K. Wiley, Norman J. Glickman, and Micael L. Lahr,
"A Top 10 List of Things to Know about American Cities," *Cityscape* 3, 3 (1998):

12-14, exhibit 1; Camilo J. Vergara, *The New American Ghetto* (New Brunswick, NJ: Rutgers University Press, 1995).

21. Compiled from Reed Ueda, *Postwar Immigrant America: A Social History* (Boston: Bedford Books of St. Martin's Press, 1994), 156 table A-1; and Alejandro Portes and Ruben G. Rumbaut, *Immigrant America: A Portrait* (Berkeley and Los Angeles: University of California Press, 1990), 222.

22. Ueda, *Postwar Immigrant America*, 58.

23. Franklin K. James, Jeff A. Romine, and Peter E. Zwanzig, "The Effects of Immigration on Urban Communities," *Cityscape* 3, 3 (1998): 175 exhibit 3, 176; Portes and Rumbaut, *Immigrant America*, 41-42; Barry R. Chiswick and Teresa A. Sullivan, "The New Immigrants," *State of the Union: America in the 1990s*, ed. Reynolds Farley (New York: Russell Sage Foundation, 1995), 2: 227-28; Carl Abbott, *The New Urban America: Growth and Politics in Sunbelt Cities* (Chapel Hill: University of North Carolina Press, 1987), 20.

24. Kermit Daniel, "Fiscal and Political Implications of the Concentration of Immigration," Real Estate Center, Wharton School of the University of Pennsylvania Working Paper no. 186 (Philadelphia: Wharton Real Estate Center, 1994).

25. Neil Smith and Peter Williams, eds., *Gentrification of the City* (Boston: Allen and Unwin, 1986); M. Christine Boyer, "Cities for Sale: Merchandising History at South Street Seaport," in *Variations on a Theme Park: The New American City and the End of Public Space*, ed. Michael Sorkin (New York: Hill and Wang, Noonday Press, 1992), 183-84; Martha Irvine, "Survey Finds More Varieties, Acceptance of Family Living," *Philadelphia Inquirer*, 24 November 1999.

26. Extreme poverty areas are census tracts in which at least 40 percent of the people are poor. U.S. House of Representatives Committee on Ways and Means, *1994 Green Book,* apps. H, G, tables G-2, G-3, G-8; Sara McLanahan and Lynne Casper, "Growing Diversity and Inequality in the American Family," in Farley, *State of the Union,* 25; John D. Kasarda, "Cities as Places Where People Live and Work: Urban Change and Neighborhood Distress," in Cisneros, *Interwoven Destinies,* 101-4; Peter Passell, "Teenage Childbearing: The Cost Is Put at $8.9 Billion a Year," *New York Times,* 20 June 1996; U.S. House of Representatives, *1994 Green Book,* apps. H, G; Steven A. Holmes, "Economy Lifts Income of Single Black Women Who Head Households," *New York Times,* 18 August 1998. For a summary of literature on African American families see David T. Ellwood and Jonathan Crane, "Family Change among Black America: What Do We Know?" *Journal of Economic Perspective* 4, 1 (Fall 1990): 1-20.

27. Reynolds Farley, *The New American Reality: Who We Are, How We Got Here, Where We Are Going* (New York: Russell Sage Foundation, 1996), 226; O'Hare et al., "African Americans in the 1990s," 13; Colin McCord and Harold Freeman, "Excess Mortality in Harlem," *New England Journal of Medicine* 322 (1990): 173-77; Bob Herbert, "In America: Death at an Early Age," *New York Times,* 2 December 1996; Nightingale, *On the Edge,* 21; U.S. Department of Housing and Urban Development, *State of the Cities, 1998,* 12; Michael J. Sniffen, "Juvenile Violent Crime Falls Again, Justice Says," *Philadelphia Inquirer,* 24 November 1999.

28. Sorkin, *Variations on a Theme Park,* 11.

29. Chudacoff and Smith, *Evolution of American Urban Society,* 260; Herbert J. Gans, *Levittowners: Ways of Life and Politics in a New Suburban Community* (New York. Vintage Books, 1969); Kenneth T. Jackson, *Crabgrass Frontier: The Suburbanization of the United States* (New York: Oxford University Press, 1985),

190–218, 234–35; Paul Kantor and Stephen David, *The Dependent City: The Changing Political Economy of Urban America* (Glenview, IL: Scott, Foresman, Little-Brown College Division, 1988), 199–200; Goldfield and Brownell, *Urban America: From Downtown to No Town*, 343–45.

30. Goldfield and Brownell, *Urban America: From Downtown to No Town*, 296–97; Peter O. Muller, *Contemporary Suburban America* (Englewood Cliffs, NJ: Prentice-Hall, 1981), 132, 162–75; Squires et al., *Chicago*, 26; Edward W. Soja, "Poles Apart: Urban Restructuring in New York and Los Angeles," in *Dual City: Restructuring New York*, ed. John H. Mollenkopf and Manuel Castells (New York: Russell Sage Foundation, 1991), 371–72; Roger Friedland, *Power and Crisis in the City: Corporations, Unions, and Urban Policy* (New York: Shocken Books, 1983), 71; Lizabeth Cohen, "From Town Center to Shopping Center: The Reconfiguration of Community Marketplaces in Postwar America"; Thomas W. Hanchett, "U.S. Tax Policy and the Shopping-Center Boom of the 1950s and 1960s," and Kenneth P. Jackson, "All the World's a Mall: Reflections on the Social and Economic Consequences of the American Shopping Center," all in *American Historical Review* 101, 4 (October 1996); William W. Goldsmith and Edward J. Blakely, *Separate Societies: Poverty and Inequality in U.S. Cities* (Philadelphia: Temple University Press, 1992), 110–11; Joel Garreau, *Edge City: Life on the New Frontier* (New York: Doubleday, 1988).

31. Susan Snyder, "School District Says Disparities Are Growing," *Philadelphia Inquirer*, 20 August 1999.

32. David Rusk, *Cities without Suburbs* (Washington, DC: Woodrow Wilson Center Press, distributed by Johns Hopkins University Press, 1993). The importance of regional, or city-suburb cooperation, is the message of Cisneros, *Interwoven Destinies*. Another example is Theodore Hershberg, "Regional Cooperation: Strategies and Incentives for Global Competitiveness and Urban Reform," *National Civic League Review* 85, 2 (Spring–Summer 1996); U.S. Department of Housing and Urban Development, *State of the Cities, 1998*, 4, 6.

33. Abbott, *The New Urban America*, 1–2.

34. William K. Tabb, "Urban Development and Regional Restructuring: An Overview," 7; Kantor and David, *Dependent City*, 284–85.

35. Goldfield and Brownell, *Urban America: From Downtown to No Town*, 395.

36. Goldfield and Brownell, *Urban America: From Downtown to No Town*, 398–99.

37. Abbott, *The New Urban America*, 20–21.

38. Edward Shannon Lamonte, *Politics and Welfare in Birmingham, 1900–1975* (Tuscaloosa: University of Alabama Press, 1995); Kantor and David, *Dependent City*, 285–86; Paul A. Jargowsky, *Poverty and Place: Ghettos, Barrios, and the American City* (New York: Russell Sage Foundation, 1997), chap. 3, table 3.5. In the 1970s, the Rustbelt gained 636 ghetto census tracts, and the Sunbelt lost 46; in the 1980s, the number grew 536 in the Rustbelt, and in the Sunbelt 423. More than 10 percent of all city residents, twice the 1970 proportion, and more than one in four blacks and Hispanics live in high-poverty census tracts. U.S. Department of Housing and Urban Development, *State of the Cities, 1998*, 18–19.

39. Goldfield and Brownell, *Urban America: From Downtown to No Town*, 399; Kantor and David, *Dependent City*, 295; Abbott, *The New Urban America*, 183, 261.

40. Douglas Massey and Nancy Denton, *American Apartheid: Segregation and the Making of the Underclass*, 32–33. Also useful on the comparison between blacks and white immigrants are Stanley Lieberson, *Piece of the Pie: Blacks and White*

Immigrants since 1880 (Berkeley and Los Angeles: University of California Press, 1980); Theodore Hershberg, *Philadelphia: Work, Space, Family, and Group Experience in the Nineteenth Century: Essays Toward an Interdisciplinary History of the City* (New York: Oxford University Press, 1981).

41. Massey and Denton, *American Apartheid*, 31, 46–48, 64.

42. Massey and Denton, *American Apartheid*, 74, 85–87.

43. Philadelphia City Planning Commission, *North Philadelphia Plan* (November 1986).

44. Raymond A. Mohl, "Race and Space in the Modern City: Interstate-95 and the Black Community in Miami," in *Urban Policy in Twentieth-Century America*, ed. Arnold R. Hirsch and Raymond A. Mohl (New Brunswick, NJ: Rutgers University Press, 1993), 100–158. On the history of public housing and its relation to race, see Hirsch, *Making the Second Ghetto*; John F. Bauman, *Public Housing, Race, and Renewal: Urban Planning in Philadelphia, 1920–1974* (Philadelphia: Temple University Press, 1987); Thomas J. Sugrue, *The Origins of the Urban Crisis: Race and Inequality in Postwar Detroit* (Princeton: Princeton University Press, 1996), 57–88.

45. Paul Jargowsky, *Take the Money and Run: Economic Segregation in U.S. Metropolitan Areas* (7 August 1995) (photocopy).

46. For a magnificent account of slum clearance in late-nineteenth-century England, with relevance for the American situation, see Gareth Stedman Jones, *Outcast London: A Study in the Relationship between Classes in Victorian Society* (New York: Pantheon Books, 1984). See also Joel Schwartz, *The New York Approach: Robert Moses, Urban Liberals, and Redevelopment of the Inner City*; Katz and Sugrue, "Introduction: The Context of *The Philadelphia Negro*," in *W. E. B. DuBois, Race, and the City*, 11.

47. On changing images of downtown, see Alison E. Isenberg, "Downtown Democracy: Rebuilding Main Street Ideals in the Twentieth Century American City" (master's thesis, University of Pennsylvania, 1995). See also Mollenkopf, *The Contested City*, 6; Hirsch, *Making the Second Ghetto*, 100–170; Abbott, *The New Urban America*, 151–52; Schwartz, *New York Approach*, 204–28; Todd Swanstrom, *The Crisis of Growth Politics: Cleveland, Kucinich, and the Challenge of Urban Populism* (Philadelphia: Temple University Press, 1985).

48. Roy Lubove, *The Progressives and the Slums: Tenement House Reform in New York City, 1890–1917* (Pittsburgh: University of Pittsburgh Press, 1962).

49. R. Allen Hays, *The Federal Government and Urban Housing: Ideology and Change in Public Policy* (Albany: SUNY Press, 1985), 91–92. On the shift in federalism see Martha Derthick, *The Influence of Federal Grants: Public Assistance in Massachusetts* (Cambridge: Harvard University Press, 1970), 26; Joleen Kirschenman and Kathryn M. Neckerman, " 'We'd Love to Hire Them, But . . . ': The Meaning of Race for Employers," in *The Urban Underclass*, ed. Christopher Jencks and Paul E. Peterson (Washington, DC: Brookings Institution Press, 1991).

50. Chudacoff, *Evolution of American Urban Society*, 266; Hays, *Federal Government and Urban Housing*, 183–84; Schwartz, *The New York Approach*, 170–203; Robert A. Caro, *The Power Broker: Robert Moses and the Fall of New York* (New York, Knopf, 1974); Friedland, *Power and Crisis in the City*, 81; Mollenkopf, *The Contested City*, 79; James Q. Wilson, ed., *Urban Renewal: The Record and the Controversy* (Cambridge: MIT Press, 1966).

51. Mollenkopf, *The Contested City*, 116–19; Hays, *The Federal Government*, 223–32; Friedland, *Power and Crisis in the City*, 80, 85; Martin Anderson, *Federal Bull-*

dozer: A Critical Analysis of Urban Renewal, 1949–1962 (Cambridge: MIT Press, 1964); Goldfield and Brownell, *Urban America: From Downtown to No Town*, 352–53; Chudacoff, *Evolution of American Urban Society*, 271; Lee Rainwater, *Behind Ghetto Walls: Black Families in a Federal Slum* (Chicago: Aldine Publishing Co., 1970). For a qualified and convincing defense of public housing, especially in New York City, see William Kornblum and Terry Williams, "Saving Kids in the Projects: Islands of Hope in the City," *Nation*, 11 April 1994, 202–11.

52. Neil Smith and Peter Williams, "Alternatives to Orthodoxy: Invitation to a Debate," in *Gentrification and the City*, ed. Neil Smith and Peter Williams (Boston: Allen and Unwin, 1986), 1; Richard T. Legates and Chester Hartman, "The Anatomy of Displacement in the United States," in Smith and Williams, *Gentrification of the City*, 184.

53. Robert A. Beauregard, "The Chaos and Complexity of Gentrification"; Roman A. Cybriwsky, David Ley, and John Western, "The Political and Social Construction of Revitalized Neighborhoods: Society Hill, Philadelphia, and False Creek, Vancouver"; and Peter Williams and Neil Smith, "From 'Renaissance' to Restructuring: The Dynamics of Contemporary Urban Development," all in Smith and Williams, *Gentrification of the City*, 51–53, 99–117, 220.

54. David W. Bartelt, "Housing the 'Underclass,' " in Katz, *The "Underclass" Debate*, 118–57.

55. Peter Marcuse, "Abandonment, Gentrification, and Displacement: The Linkages in New York City," in Smith and Williams, *Gentrification of the City*, 153–54, 159, 163; Legates and Hartman, "The Anatomy of Displacement in the United States," 197.

56. Martha R. Burt, *The Growth of Homelessness in the 1980s* (New York: Russell Sage Foundation, 1992), 3; Dennis P. Culhane, Chang-Moo Lee, and Susan M. Wachter, "Where the Homeless Come From: A Study of the Prior Address Distribution of Families Admitted to Public Shelters in New York City and Philadelphia," *Housing Policy Debate* 7, 2 (1996).

57. The two laws were the Interstate and Defense Highway Act and the Highway Revenue Act. Kantor, *Dependent City*, 199; Mollenkopf, *The Contested City*, 110, 119–20; Mohl, "Shifting Patterns of Urban Policy," 17; Scott Greer, *Urban Renewal and American Cities: The Dilemma of Democratic Intervention* (Indianapolis, IN: Bobbs-Merrill, 1965); Sugrue, *The Origins of the Urban Crisis*.

58. Mollenkopf, *The Contested City*, 89.

59. Mike Davis, *City of Quartz: Excavating the Future in Los Angeles* (repr., New York: Vintage Books, 1992).

60. Jane Jacobs, *Death and Life of Great American Cities* (New York: Random House, 1961).

61. Roberta Brandes Gratz and Norman Mintz, *Cities Back from the Edge: New Life for Downtown* (New York: John Wiley and Sons, 1998).

CHAPTER 3: THE FAMILY SUPPORT ACT AND THE ILLUSION OF
WELFARE REFORM

1. Margaret Weir, *Politics and Jobs: The Boundaries of Employment Policy in the United States* (Princeton: Princeton University Press, 1992).

2. Unless otherwise noted, the accounts of the history of outdoor relief, work relief, and child support are based on my book *In the Shadow of the Poorhouse: A Social History of Welfare*, 10th anniversary ed. (New York: Basic Books, 1997).

3. Michael Ignatieff, *The Needs of Strangers* (New York: Viking, 1984). The old set-tlement laws made a comeback in Moscow in 1996. Overwhelmed with the poverty of recent immigrants to the city, officials began shipping them back to their com-munities of origin. Rachel Swarns, "Moscow Sends Homeless to Faraway Home-towns," *New York Times*, 15 October 1996.

4. Michael B. Katz and Christoph Sachsse, eds., *The Mixed Economy of Social Welfare: Public/Private Relations in England, Germany, and the United States, the 1870s to the 1930s* (Baden-Baden: Nomos, 1996).

5. Roy Lubove, *The Struggle for Social Security, 1900–1935* (Cambridge: Harvard Uni-versity Press, 1968), 91–112; Susan Tiffin, *In Whose Best Interest? Child Welfare Reform in the Progressive Era* (Westport, CT: Greenwood Press, 1982), 121–34; Molly Ladd-Taylor, *Mother-Work: Women, Child Welfare, and the State, 1890–1930* (Urbana: University of Illinois Press, 1994), 135–66; Theda Skocpol, *Protecting Sol-diers and Mothers: The Political Origins of Social Policy in the United States* (Cam-bridge: Harvard University Press, 1992), 424–79; Linda Gordon, *Pitied but Not Entitled: Single Mothers and the History of Welfare, 1890–1935* (New York: Free Press, 1994), 37–55; Joanne L. Goodwin, *Gender and the Politics of Welfare Reform: Mothers' Pensions in Chicago, 1911–1929* (Chicago: University of Chicago Press, 1997). On AFDC, see Lubove, *Struggle for Social Security*; Skocpol, *Protecting Sol-diers and Mothers*; Gordon, *Pitied but Not Entitled*; Edwin Amenta, *Bold Relief: Institutional Politics and the Origins of Modern American Social Policy* (Princeton: Princeton University Press, 1998), 100, 115–16, 141–49.

6. Amenta, *Bold Relief*, 80–161, Bonnie Fox Schwartz, *The Civil Works Administra-tion: The Business of Emergency Employment in the New Deal* (Princeton: Prince-ton University Press, 1984), 227–28; Josephine Chapin Brown, *Public Relief, 1929–1939* (New York: Henry Holt and Co., 1949), 165–66, 301–5.

7. The debate on AFDC and the social science literature surrounding it are discussed more fully and documented in chapter 12.

8. Quoted in Sarah K. Gideonese and William R. Meyers, "Why the Family Support Act Will Fail," *Challenge* 32, 5 (September–October 1989): 39; Lawrence M. Mead, *Beyond Entitlement: The Social Obligations of Citizenship* (New York: Free Press, 1986); Ron Haskins, "Congress Writes a Law: Research and Welfare Reform," *Journal of Policy Analysis* 10, 4 (Fall 1991): 619; Peter L. Szanton, "The Remarkable 'Quango': Knowledge, Politics, and Welfare Reform," *Journal of Pol-icy Analysis and Management* 10, 4 (Fall 1991): 590.

9. Frances Fox Piven and Barbara Ehrenreich, "Workfare Means New Mass Peon-age," *New York Times*, 30 May 1987.

10. Michael B. Katz, *Improving Poor People: The Welfare State, the "Underclass," and Urban Schools as History* (Princeton: Princeton University Press, 1995), 144–72.

11. On problems administering emergency employment in the 1960s and 1970s, see Howard Hallman, *Emergency Employment: A Study in Federalism* (Birmingham: University of Alabama Press, 1977). The new standard account of work relief dur-ing the New Deal is Amenta, *Bold Relief*.

12. On problems with the New Deal work programs, see the sympathetic yet sharp analysis in National Resources Planning Board, "Report of the Committee on Long-Range Work and Relief Policies," in *Security, Work, and Relief Policies* (Washington, DC: GPO, 1942), 462–69.

13. Alan Brinkley, *The End of Reform: New Deal Liberalism in Recession and War* (New York: Random House, 1995), 257; Weir, *Politics and Jobs*, 27–54; Gary

Mucciaroni, *The Political Failure of Employment Policy, 1945–1982* (Pittsburgh: University of Pittsburgh Press, 1990), 18–19, 25, 42–44.

14. Weir, *Politics and Jobs*, 62; Nancy E. Rose, *Workfare or Fair Work: Women, Welfare, and Government Work Programs* (New Brunswick, NJ: Rutgers University Press, 1995), 90–91; Mucciaroni, *The Political Failure of Employment Policy*, 59–62. Garth L. Mangum, *MDTA: Foundation of Federal Manpower Policy* (Baltimore, MD: Johns Hopkins University Press, 1968), calls MDTA's accomplishments "solid and demonstrable" (3). Desmond S. King, *Actively Seeking Work? The Politics of Unemployment and Welfare Policy in the United States and Great Britain* (Chicago: University of Chicago Press, 1995), 164; Weir, *Politics and Jobs*, 154, 245–61; W. Norton Grubb, *Learning to Work: The Case for Reintegrating Job Training and Education* (New York: Russell Sage Foundation, 1996), argues that job training programs remained disassociated from education programs, to the detriment of both (2).

15. Weir, *Politics and Jobs*, 95; Rose, *Workfare or Fair Work*, 92–95, 102–3.

16. Weir, *Politics and Jobs*, 99–100.

17. Grace A. Franklin and Randall B. Ripley, *CETA: Politics and Policy, 1973–1982* (Knoxville: University of Tennessee Press, 1984), 37; see also 189–200 for their evaluation of CETA, which includes a favorable analysis of its economic impact on participants. William Mirengoff et al., *CETA: Assessment of Public Service Employment Programs* (Washington, DC: National Academy of Sciences, 1980), 4–5; Weir, *Politics and Jobs*, 100. For an overview of work and training programs in the late 1970s, see U.S. Department of Labor and Department of Health, Education, and Welfare, *Employment and Training Report of the President, 1978* (Washington, DC: GPO, 1978).

18. Weir, *Politics and Jobs*, 3; Gary Burtless, "Public Spending on the Poor: Historical Trends and Economic Limits," in *Confronting Poverty: Prescriptions for Change*, ed. Sheldon H. Danziger, Gary D. Sandefur, and Daniel H. Weinberg (Cambridge: Harvard University Press, 1994), 57, table 3 1. See also King, *Actively Seeking Work*, 158; Grubb, *Learning to Work*, 10; Rose, *Workfare or Fair Work*, 141–48.

19. Jacob A. Riis, *How the Other Half Lives* (repr., New York: Hill and Wang, 1957).

20. Timothy J. Gilfoyle, *City of Eros: New York City, Prostitution, and the Commercialization of Sex, 1790–1920* (New York: Norton, 1992); George K. Behlmer, *Child Abuse and Moral Reform in England, 1870–1908* (Stanford, CA: Stanford University Press, 1982); Michael B. Katz, *The Irony of Early School Reform: Educational Innovation in Mid-Nineteenth Century Massachusetts* (Cambridge: Harvard University Press, 1968), 163–212; Katz, *Improving Poor People*, 144–72.

21. Reena Sigman Friedman, " 'Send Me My Husband Who Is in New York City': Husband Desertion in the American Jewish Immigrant Community, 1900–1926," *Jewish Social Studies* 44, 1 (1928): 1–18; Ari Lloyd Fridkis, "Desertion in the American Jewish Immigrant Family: The Work of the National Desertion Bureau in Cooperation with the Industrial Removal Office," *American Jewish History* 71, 2 (1981): 285–99; Michael Willrich, "Home Slackers: Men, the State, and Welfare in Modern America," *Journal of American History*, 87, 2 (September 2000): 460–89.

22. Jonah Edelman, "Passage of the Family Support Act of 1988 and the Politics of Welfare Reform in the United States" (Ph.D. diss., Oxford University, 1995), 85–86; Steven M. Fleece, "A Review of the Child Support Enforcement Programs," *Journal of Family Law* 20, 3 (1982): 492–93.

23. Edelman, "Passage of the Family Support Act," 88–89.

24. Robert G. Williams, "Implementation of the Child Support Guidelines Provision of the Family Support Act," paper presented at the Conference on Securing Our Children's Future: Welfare Reform and Child Support, Albany, NY, 19 May 1993; Maureen A. Pirog-Good, "Child Support Guidelines and the Economic Well-Being of Children in the United States," *Family Relations* 42 (October 1993): 453–62; Maureen A. Pirog-Good and Daniel R. Mullins, "—And Justice for All: Determining the Size of Child Support Payments," in the Proceedings of the National Association for Welfare Research and Statistics 34th Annual Workshop, 31 July–3 August 1994, 37–47; Irwin S. Garfinkel, Sara S. McLanahan, and Philip K. Robins, "Child Support and Child Well-Being: What Have We Learned?" in *Child Support and Child Well-Being*, ed. Irwin S. Garfinkel, Sara S. McLanahan, and Philip K. Robins (Washington, DC: Urban Institute Press, 1994), 2; Fleece, "Review of the Child Support Enforcement Programs," 497–500.

25. Studies showed that $20 or $30 billion more in child support could be raised each year by basing payments on new formulas and collecting them through employers, the way taxes are. By combining $2,000 a year in child support with measures to make work pay, predicted welfare policy expert David T. Ellwood, a part-time job would lift a woman off welfare and out of poverty. "Business Forum: Reforming Welfare," *New York Times*, 17 July 1988.

26. W. Norton Grubb and Marvin Lazerson, *Broken Promises: How Americans Fail Their Children* (New York: Basic Books, 1982).

27. Elizabeth Rose, *A Mother's Job: The History of Day Care, 1890–1960* (New York: Oxford University Press, 1999); Sonya Michel, *Children's Interests/Mother's Rights: The Shaping of America's Child Care Policy* (New Haven: Yale University Press, 1999).

28. Michel, *Children's Interests*, 251–55.

29. Michel, *Children's Interests*, 256.

30. Michel, *Children's Interests*, 259.

31. *Child Care* (Welfare Information Network, [2 September 1999]), http://www.welfareinfo.org/childcare.htm; April Kaplan, issue notes, *Financial Resources for Child Care* 2, 6 (Welfare Information Network, 1998), http://www.welfareinfo.org/Issuechild.htm; U.S. Department of Health and Human Services Child Care Bureau, *Child Care Bureau Programs* (17 February 1999), http://www.acf.dhhs.gov/programs/ccb/programs/.

32. Reagan quoted in Edelman, "Passage of the Family Support Act," 113.

33. Rose, *Workfare or Fair Work*, 131–39.

34. Richard P. Nathan, *Turning Promises into Performance: The Management Challenge of Implementing Workfare* (New York: Columbia University Press, 1993), 36; Szanton, "Remarkable 'Quango,' " 591.

35. Rebecca Blank, "The Employment Strategy: Public Policies to Increase Work and Earnings," in Danziger, Sandefur, and Weinberg, *Confronting Poverty*, 186; Nathan, *Turning Promises into Performance*, 37–38; "Data Back Welfare Overhaul," *New York Times*, 22 June 1988; U.S. General Accounting Office, *Work and Welfare: Current AFDC Work Programs and Implications for Federal Policy*, GAO/FHRD87-34 (Washington, DC: GPO, January 1987), 3; Joanna K. Weinberg, "Workfare—It Isn't Work, It Isn't Fair," *New York Times*, 19 August 1988.

36. Haskins, "Congress Writes a Law," 627; Mead, *Beyond Entitlement*. Quotations from Szanton, "Remarkable 'Quango,' " 597, 599.

37. Barbara Gamarekian, "Administration Is Uncertain on Welfare Compromise," *New York Times*, 18 June 1988. My interpretation of the politics of the FSA has

been influenced by an excellent master's thesis: Jonah M. Edelman, "The Politics of Welfare Reform and the Family Support Act of 1988" (Oxford University, 1994); and by his dissertation, "The Passage of the Family Support Act." Lynn A. Hogan, "Jobs, Not JOBS: What It Takes to Put Welfare Recipients to Work," Progressive Policy Institute Policy Briefing, 17 July 1995.

38. Michael Wiseman, "Research and Policy: A Symposium on the Family Support Act of 1988," *Journal of Policy Analysis and Management* 10, 4 (1991): 589.

39. Martin Tolchin, "Senate, 93-3, Votes Welfare Revision Mandating Work," *New York Times* 17 June 1988. (Tolchin was reporting on the first Senate vote before the House-Senate conference hammered out the final version.) Quoted in Szanton, "Remarkable 'Quango,' " 591.

40. Gideonese and Meyers, "Why the Family Support Act Will Fail," 33-39; Weinberg, "Workfare."

41. Garfinkel, McLanahan, and Robins, "Child Support and Child Well-Being," 2; Elaine Sorenson and Ariel Halpern, "Child Support Enforcement Is Working Better Than We Think" (Washington, DC: Urban Institute Assessing the New Federalism Project, 1999); Irwin Garfinkel and Sara McLanahan, "Single-Mother Families, Economic Insecurity, and Government Policy," in Danziger, Sandefur, and Weinberg, *Confronting Poverty*, 205-25; Sarah McLanahan, private communication to author, 5 September 1995. For an example of the situation in one state, see Rob Green, Wendy Zimmerman, Toby Douglas, Sheila Zedlewski, and Shelley Waters, *Income Support and Social Services for Low-Income People in California* (Washington, DC: Urban Institute, Assessing the New Federalism Program, 1998), 45-46.

42. Gideonese and Meyers, "Why the Family Support Act Will Fail," 35; Edelman, "The Politics of Welfare Reform," 82-83. For an excellent overview of the state of child support enforcement in early 2000, see the special issue on child support enforcement and low-income families: *Focus* 21, 1 (Spring 2000).

43. Jan L. Hagen, Irene Lurie, and Ling Wang, "Implementing Jobs: The Perspective of Front-Line Workers" (State University of New York at Albany, Nelson A. Rockefeller Institute of Government, 1993); Jan L. Hagen and Irene Lurie, "How 10 States Implemented JOBS," *Public Welfare* 50, 3 (1992): 13-22; Jan L. Hagen and Irene Lurie, "Implementing JOBS: Initial State Choices" (State University of New York at Albany, Nelson A. Rockefeller College of Public Affairs and Policy, 1993); Jan L. Hagen and Irene Lurie, "The JOB Opportunities and Basic Skills Training Program and Child Care: Initial State Developments," *Social Service Review* 67, 2 (1993): 199-216.

44. Grubb, *Learning to Work*, 6-7, 15.

45. Edelman, "The Passage of the Family Support Act," 120.

CHAPTER 4: GOVERNORS AS WELFARE REFORMERS

1. Tommy Thompson, *Power to the People: An American State at Work* (New York: HarperCollins, 1996), 4-7; Charles Mahtesian, "Captains of Conservatism," *Governing Magazine* 8, 5 (February 1995): 26.

2. For this story, see Michael B. Katz, *In the Shadow of the Poorhouse: A Social History of Welfare*, 10th anniversary ed. (New York: Basic Books, 1997), 3-113. On mental hospitals, see Gerald N. Grob, *Mental Institutions in America: Social Policy to 1875* (New York: Free Press, 1973). For the explosion of institutions to deal with deviance in the Jacksonian period, see David J. Rothman, *The Discovery of*

the Asylum: Social Order and Disorder in the New Republic (Boston: Little, Brown, 1971); Michael B. Katz, Michael J. Doucet, and Mark J. Stern, *The Social Organization of Early Industrial Capitalism* (Cambridge: Harvard University Press, 1982), 349–391. On reform schools, see Robert M. Mennel, *Thorns and Thistles: Juvenile Delinquents in the United States, 1825–1840* (Hanover, NH: University Press of New England, 1973); Barbara Brenzel, *Daughters of the State: Social Portrait of the First Reform School for Girls in North America, 1846–1905* (Cambridge: MIT Press, 1983); and Eric Schneider, *In the Web of Class: Delinquents and Reformers in Boston, 1810s to 1930s* (New York: New York University Press, 1992). On hospitals, see Charles Rosenberg, *The Care of Strangers: The Rise of America's Hospital System* (New York: Basic Books, 1987). See also Michael B. Katz, *Poverty and Policy in American History* (New York: Academic Press, 1983).

3. William R. Brock, *Investigation and Responsibility: Public Responsibility in the United States, 1865–1900* (Cambridge: Cambridge University Press, 1984), 88–115, quote from the New York Board on 91; Grob, *Mental Hospitals*; Katz, *In the Shadow of the Poorhouse*, 89, 102–4.

4. James T. Patterson, *The New Deal and the States: Federalism in Transition* (Princeton: Princeton University Press, 1969), 12; Roy Lubove, *The Struggle for Social Security, 1900–1935* (Pittsburgh: University of Pittsburgh, 1986); James Weinstein, "Big Business and the Origins of Workmen's Compensation," *Labor History* 8, 2 (Spring 1967): 156–74; Carl Gersuny, *Work Hazards and Industrial Conflict* (Hanover, NH: University Press of New England, 1981); Edward Berkowitz and Kim McQuaid, *Creating the Welfare State: The Political Economy of Twentieth-Century Reform* (New York: Praeger, 1980); Daniel Nelson, *Unemployment Insurance: The American Experience, 1915–1935* (Madison: University of Wisconsin Press, 1969); Andrew Achenbaum, *Old Age in the New Land: The American Experience since 1870* (Baltimore: Johns Hopkins University Press, 1978); Ann Shola Orloff, *The Politics of Pensions: A Comparative Analysis of Britain, Canada, and the United States, 1880–1940* (Madison: University of Wisconsin Press, 1993); William Graebner, *A History of Retirement: The Meaning and Function of an American Institution, 1885–1978* (New Haven: Yale University Press, 1980); Katz, *In the Shadow of the Poorhouse*, chap. 7; Theda Skocpol, *Protecting Soldiers and Mothers: The Political Origins of Social Policy in the United States* (Cambridge: Harvard University Press, 1992); Joanne L. Goodwin, *Gender and the Politics of Welfare: Mothers' Pensions in Chicago, 1911–1929* (Chicago: University of Chicago Press, 1997); Alexander Keyssar, *Out of Work: The First Century of Unemployment in the United States* (New York: Cambridge University Press, 1986); Patterson, *The New Deal and the States*, 6–9.

5. Patterson, *The New Deal and the States*, 12.

6. Blanche D. Coll, *Safety Net: Welfare and Social Security; 1929–1979* (New Brunswick, NJ: Rutgers University Press, 1995), 167; John D. Morris, "Government Aims on Relief Limited," *New York Times*, 1 March 1949.

7. Martha Derthick, *The Influence of Federal Grants: Public Assistance in Massachusetts* (Cambridge: Harvard University Press, 1970), 69, 242; Patterson, *The New Deal and the States*.

8. Advisory Commission on Intergovernmental Relations, *The Question of State Government Capability* (Washington, DC, 1985), (report), 1; Jill S. Quadagno, *The Transformation of Old Age Security: Class and Politics in the American Welfare State* (Chicago: University of Chicago Press, 1988); Robert C. Leiberman, *Shifting*

the Color Line: Race and the American Welfare State (Cambridge: Harvard University Press, 1998).

9. Mary Mann Reeves, "The States as Polities: Reformed, Reinvigorated, Resourceful," *Annals, American Academy of Political and Social Science* 509 (May 1990): 84–86; J. Richard Aronson and John L. Hilley, *Financing State and Local Governments*, 4th ed. (Washington, DC: Brookings Institution Press, 1986), 1.

10. *Pennsylvania 1997–1998 General Fund Budget*, http://www.state.pa.us/PA_Exec/Budget/1997–1998/CAFR.

11. Richard Nathan, Fred C. Doolittle, et al., *Reagan and the States* (Princeton: Princeton University Press, 1987), 38–41. On the history of grants-in-aid and federal aid to cities, see also Advisory Commission on Intergovernmental Relations (ACIR), *The Question of State Government Capability* (Washington, DC: 1985) (report), 5–25; E. Blaine Liner, ed., *A Decade of Devolution: Perspectives on State-Local Relations* (Washington, DC: Urban Institute Press, 1989), 3–25.

12. Richard Nathan, "American Federalism—the Great Experiment," *Spectrum: The Journal of State Government* 68, 3 (Summer 1995): 47–51; Nathan et al., *Reagan and the States* 5, 64, 45–66. In 1981, his block grants, the Omnibus Budget Reconciliation Act, and the Economic Recovery Tax Act all devolved authority and reduced funding. Liner, *Decade of Devolution*, 9–10; J. Richard Aronson and John L. Hilley, *Financing State and Local Governments*, 3–4; Jack A. Brizius, "An Overview of the State-Local Fiscal Landscape," in Liner, *Decade of Devolution*, 64; Ann O'M. Bowman and Richard C. Kearney, *The Resurgence of the States* (Englewood Cliffs, NJ: Prentice-Hall, 1985), 8–9.

13. Brizius, "An Overview of the State-Local Fiscal Landscape," 57; Nathan et al., *Reagan and the States*, 7.

14. Nathan et al., *Reagan and the States*, 74–75.

15. Bowman and Kearney, *Resurgence of the States*, 10, 20, 85–93; ACIR, *State Government Capability* 2, 98, 138, 144, 364; Reeves, "States as Polities."

16. Reeves, "States as Polities," 86–87; Nathan, "American Federalism"; Bowman and Kearney, *Resurgence of the States*, 17.

17. R. Scott Fosler, "Revitalizing State-Local Economies," in Liner, *Decade of Devolution*, 90–91.

18. Peter Overby, "The Michigan Experiment: Cut Taxes! Throw the Deadbeats Off Welfare! Take Control of the Schools! All This and More—Or Is That Less?" *Common Cause Magazine*, January 1994.

19. Greg Kaza, "Can Michigan's Engler Pull Off His Taxpayer's Revolution?" *Policy Review* 57 (Summer 1991): 74; R-Beal City, "John M. Engler: Governor," www.migov.state.mi.us/govbio.htm.

20. Governor John Engler, "First Principles in the Public Arena," First Russell Kirk Memorial Lecture, the Heritage Foundation, Washington, DC, 26 September 1995. See chapter 12 for a discussion of the specious but widely used $5 trillion figure.

21. Engler, "First Principles in the Public Arena."

22. Governor John Engler, "CATO Institute Remarks," Washington, DC, 14 March 1995, http://www.cato.org/.

23. John Engler, "Be Not Afraid: Look the Adversary in the Eye," Keynote Address to Catholic Campaign for America's First National Convention, Washington, DC, 18 November 1995; National Conference of Catholic Bishops, *Economic Justice for All: Pastoral Letter on Catholic Social Teaching and the U.S. Economy* (Washington DC: U.S. Catholic Conference, 1986); Engler, "First Principles in the Public Arena"; Engler, "Be Not Afraid: Look the Adversary in the Eye."

24. Michael deCourcy Hinds, "To Victors Go the Trials after Races against Taxes," *New York Times*, 19 November 1990.

25. Kaza, "Can Michigan's Engler Pull Off His Taxpayer's Revolution?"; Hinds, "To Victors Go the Trials"; Ronald Brownstein, "Partisan Struggle Waged over Michigan Deficit," *Los Angeles Times*, 9 March 1991.

26. Robert Greenstein, "The States and the Poor," News Conference, Center on Budget and Policy Priorities, National Press Club (Washington, DC: Federal News Service, 18 December 1991).

27. Helen B. O'Bannon, ". . . It Deserves Legislative Support," *Philadelphia Inquirer*, 23 February 1981; Dick Thornburgh, "Welfare Could Collapse of Its Own Weight," *Philadelphia Bulletin*, 22 June 1980; Terry E. Johnson, "Can Welfare Rolls Be Cut? Republicans Ponder It," *Philadelphia Inquirer*, 7 June 1980; Christopher Berglund et al., "Report on House Bill 2044: Consequences for the General Assistance Population" (University of Pennsylvania, Department of City and Regional Planning, 30 May 1980) (report); Walter F. Roche., Jr., "State Readies Rules for Welfare, Raises Restrictions," *Philadelphia Inquirer*, 3 June 1982; Marc Kaufman and Walter F. Roche, Jr., "What the Welfare Cuts Have Wrought," *Philadelphia Inquirer*, 17 June 1984; Walter F. Roche, Jr., "Welfare Changes Criticized," *Philadelphia Inquirer*, 9 September 1984.

28. Sandra K. Danziger and Sherrie A. Kossoudji, "When Welfare Ends: Subsistence Strategies of Former GA Recipients," Final Report of the General Assistance Project (University of Michigan, School of Social Work, February 1995), 8; Don Terry, "To Avoid Deficit, Michigan Ends Welfare to Some Adults," *New York Times*, 7 October 1991. For background on Detroit, see Thomas J. Sugrue, *Origins of the Urban Crisis: Race and Inequality in Postwar Detroit* (Princeton: Princeton University Press, 1996).

29. Rick Pluta, "Protesters Erect 'Englerville' on Capital Lawn," U.I., 5 December 1991, Thursday, B.C. Cycle; Rick Pluta, "Jackson Leads 3,000 in March on Lansing," U.I., 15 January 1992, Wednesday, B.C. Cycle; "Michigan Governor John Engler to Go on Trial," *PR Newswire*, 28 April 1992; "UAW Says General Assistance Cuts Are 'Inhumane and Senseless,' " *PR Newswire*, 30 September 1991; Rick Pluta, "Judge Restores GA as Engler Unveils $129 Million in Vetoes," U.I., 11 October 1991, Friday, B.C. Cycle; "Court Upholds a Welfare Cutoff in Michigan," *New York Times*, 9 November 1991.

30. L. Jerome Gallagher, "A Shrinking Portion of the Safety Net: General Assistance from 1989 to 1998" (Washington, DC: Urban Institute, Assessing the New Federalism Project, 1999).

31. Overby, "The Michigan Experiment"; Jason DeParle, "Off the Rolls—a Special Report," *New York Times*, 14 April 1992; Danziger and Kossoudji, "When Welfare Ends," 7; "The Cruel Side of Welfare Reform," editorial, *St. Louis Post-Dispatch*, 30 December 1995. While the share of SSI expenses borne by states rose 6 percent nationally, in Michigan it dropped 11 percent.

32. Danziger and Kossoudji, "When Welfare Ends," 1–3; Center on Social Welfare Law and Policy, *Jobless, Penniless, Often Homeless: State General Assistance Cuts Leave "Employables" Struggling for Survival* (1994), prepublication copy, 5; Anthony Halter, "Welfare Reform: One State's Alternative," *Journal of Sociology and Social Welfare* 16, 2 (1989): 151–61.

33. Danziger and Kossoudji, "When Welfare Ends," 3–7.

34. Rick Pluta, "Engler Recall Effort Begins Counting Signatures," U.I., 19 August

1991; "Engler's Popularity Faltering, Says Poll," U.I., 10 November 1991; Engler, "CATO Institute Remarks."

35. Rusty Hills, Director of Public Affairs, Office of the Governor, "Engler's Agenda Keeps Rolling Along," *Detroit News*, 14 May 1996, letter to the editor; "Engler's Stand Pat Budget," editorial, *Detroit News*, 9 February 1996; Frank Reeves, "Warfare on Welfare," *Pittsburgh Post-Gazette*, 6 December 1995; Governor John Engler, "Promises Made, Promises Kept—1996 Accomplishments," April 1996, http://www.migov.state.mi.us/issues/accomplishments.html; Governor John Engler, "Advancing Michigan's Renaissance," Sixth State of the State Address, Michigan State Capitol, Lansing, 17 January 1996, http://www.migov.state.mi.us/speeches/sos1996.html.

36. Paul N. Courant and Susanna Loeb, "Centralization of School Finance in Michigan," *Journal of Policy Analysis and Management* 16, 1 (1997): 114–36; Mahtesian, "Captains of Conservatism."

37. Robyn Meredith, "Michigan Welfare Reform Draws Unlikely Support," *New York Times*, 22 January 1996; Governor John Engler, "Response to President Clinton's Weekly Radio Address," 25 May 1996, http://www.migov.state.mi.us/prs/9605/radiores2.html; Center on Social Welfare Law and Policy, *Overview of the Law Governing Waiver of Federal Requirements Applicable to State AFDC Programs*, Publication no. 170 (1993), 2–3.

38. Michael Wiseman, "State Strategies for Welfare Reform: The Wisconsin Story," WP no. 1066-95, rev. ed. (University of Wisconsin-Madison, Institute for Research on Poverty, 1995), 10; emphasis in original. Quotation from *New York Times*, 29 January 1992, is cited in Wiseman, *State Strategies* 1; Center on Social Welfare Law and Policy, *Summary of AFDC Waiver Activity since February 1993*, Publication no. 169-2 (1995), 2, 3.

39. Robert Pear, "Dole Reversal: A Welfare Revolution Hits Home, but Quietly," *New York Times*, 13 August 1995; "Welfare Reform under President Clinton" (state summaries of welfare innovation prepared by Clinton administration, 1966, no month and day, unbound sheets); Alison Mitchell, "Clinton and Dole Present Programs to Alter Welfare," *New York Times*, 31 July 1995.

40. Jodie Levin-Epstein and Mark Greenberg, *The Rush to Reform: 1992 State AFDC Legislative and Waiver Actions* (Washington, DC: Center on Social Welfare Law and Policy, 1992), 1; Richard Nathan, *Turning Promises into Performance: The Management Challenge of Implementing Workfare* (New York: Columbia University Press, 1993), 3–5; Pear, "Dole Reversal"; Center on Social Welfare Law and Policy, *Summary of AFDC Waiver Activity since February 1993*; Lawrence M. Mead, *The New Politics of Poverty: The Nonworking Poor in America* (New York: Basic Books, 1992).

41. There are summaries of Engler's welfare activities in various state documents titled "Michigan's Welfare Reform Changes—a Chronology" and issued at various times. See also Engler's official account, "Issue Update: Welfare Reform. Michigan Leads the Nation in Reforming Welfare" (n.d., Fall 1996), http://www.migov.state.mi.us/issues/welfareissue.html.

42. Michigan Family Independence Agency, "New Name, New Focus, Clear Expectations, Contingency Plan" (1995), http://www.mfia.state.mi.us/; Michigan Family Independence Agency, "Statewide Highlights," 23 June 1997, http://www.mfia.state.mi.us/.

43. Ruth Conniff, "Welfare, Ground Zero: Michigan Tries to End It All," *Nation*, 27

May 1996, 16–20. For a more annecdotal criticism along the same lines see Benjamin Morrison, "Ballyhooed Reforms Also Criticized as Harsh," *Cleveland Plain Dealer*, 18 May 1997; Sheldon Danziger and Jeffrey Lehman, "How Will Welfare Recipients Fare in the Labor Market?" *Challenge* 39, 2 (March–April 1996): 30–36; see also Sheldon Danziger, Prepared Testimony before the Senate Finance Committee, *Federal News Service*, 29 February 1996. Danziger served on the task force that prepared Michigan's block grant proposal. He directed his criticism toward proposed federal welfare reform bills, not Michigan's—but the warning can be extrapolated.

44. Wendy Wedland and Jack Kresnak, "In Metro Detroit, Too Many Kids Are Still Growing Up in Poverty," *Free Press*, 11 December 1996.
45. Nathan, "American Federalism."
46. Rogers Worthington, "Wisconsin's Big Cheese," *Chicago Tribune*, 10 April 1994, Sunday magazine, 8; Thompson, *Power to the People*, 16.
47. Thompson, *Power to the People*, 17–20.
48. Thompson, *Power to the People*, 21.
49. Michael Wiseman, "State Strategies for Welfare Reform: The Wisconsin Story," *Journal of Policy Analysis and Management* 15, 4 (1996): 518–19.
50. Wiseman, "State Strategies," 519.
51. Wiseman, "State Strategies," 520–24.
52. Wiseman, "State Strategies," 525–27.
53. University of Wisconsin-Milwaukee, Employment and Training Institute, "The Impact of Learnfare on Milwaukee County Social Service Clients," March 1990, http://www.uwm.edu/Dept/ETI/pages/surveys/each/learn390.htm.
54. Ronald Brownstein, "Tough Love Comes to Politics," *Los Angeles Times*, 19 November 1991; Employment and Training Institute, "Impact of Learnfare"; John Pawasarat, Lois Quinn, and Frank Stetzer, "Evaluation of the Impact of Wisconsin's Learnfare Experiment on the School Attendance of Teenagers Receiving Aid to Families with Dependent Children," report submitted to the Wisconsin Department of Health and Social Services and the U.S. Department of Health and Human Services by the Employment and Training Institute of the University of Wisconsin-Milwaukee, 5 February 1992; Dirk Johnson, "Wisconsin Welfare Effort on Schools Is a Failure, Study Says," *New York Times*, 19 May 1996.
55. Jonathan Rabinovitz, "Rowland Seeks to Cut Welfare for Parents of Truant Children," *New York Times*, 15 February 1996; Alexander Nguyen, "No Fanfare for Learnfare," *American Prospect*, 28 February 2000, 16–17.
56. Brownstein, "Tough Love Comes to Politics"; Lawrence Mead, "Growing a Smaller Welfare State; Wisconsin's Reforms Show That to Cut the Rolls, You Need More Bureaucrats," *Washington Post*, 3 December 1995.
57. Wiseman, "State Strategies," 25–31; Isabel Wilkerson, "Wisconsin Welfare Plan: To Reward the Married," *New York Times*, 12 February 1991; Tommy Thompson, report to Senate Finance Committee Hearing on States' Perspective on Welfare Reform, 3 March 1995.
58. Thompson, *Power to the People*, 63–68.
59. Thompson, *Power to the People*, 73.
60. Elisabeth Boehnen and Thomas Corbett, "Work-Not-Welfare: Time Limits in Fond du Lac County, Wisconsin," *Focus* 18, 1 (1996): 79, 80–81.
61. Jennifer A. Galloway, "The Politics of Welfare Reform," *(Madison, WI) Capital Times*, 7 May 1994; Matt Pommer, "Panel Backs Work Not Welfare," *(Madison, WI) Capital Times*, 15 October 1993.

62. Wiseman, "State Strategies," 532; Thompson, *Power to the People*, 73–76; Galloway, "The Politics of Welfare Reform."

63. Arthur L. Srb, "Search to Begin for Alternatives to Welfare," *(Madison, WI) Capital Times*, 14 December 1993.

64. Wisconsin Department of Workforce Development, "W-2 Fact Sheets—Overview," 19 May 1997; http://www.dwd.state.wi.us/desw2/wisworks.htm; Wiseman, "State Strategies," 532. For criticisms of W-2 on these grounds, see Peter Steinfels, "Beliefs: Debate on Welfare Mixes Politics and Principle," *New York Times*, 27 July 1996.

65. Wiseman, "State Strategies," 536; Wisconsin Department of Workforce Development, "Introducing the End of Welfare," 28 May 1996, http://www.dwd. state.wi.us/; Thomas Corbett, "Understanding Wisconsin Works (W-2)," *Focus* 18, 1 (1996): 53–55; Department of Workforce Development, "W-2 Fact Sheets— Overview."

66. Thompson, *Power to the People*, 78–83; David Callender, "Fed OK of W-2 Expected," *(Madison, WI) Capital Times*, 30 September 1996; David Callender, "Estimate of W-2 Cost Now Up to 1.3 billion," *(Madison WI) Capital Times*, 6 June 1997.

67. Wiseman, "State Strategies," 33–39; University of Wisconsin–Milwaukee, Employment and Training Institute, "Financial Impact of W-2 and Related Welfare Reform Initiatives on Milwaukee County AFDC Cases," April 1996, http://www.uwm.edu/Dept/ETI/pages/surveys/each/execsum.htm; Edward Walsh, "Homelessness and Hunger Rise in Milwaukee: Is Welfare Reform to Blame?" *Washington Post*, 27 December 1996.

68. Harriet Brown, "Wisconsin's Welfare Boomerang," *New York Times*, 7 May 1996.

69. "Wisconsin Has Gone Too Far," editorial, *St. Louis Post-Dispatch*, 24 June 1996; "AFSCME President Takes Stand against 'Wisconsin Works' for Welfare Reform," press release, AFSCME, 8 July 1996; "Wisconsin's Bold, Risky Welfare Plan," editorial, *New York Times*, 3 May 1996; Wiseman, "State Strategies," 542; Mark H. Greenberg, "Wisconsin Works: Significant Experiment, Troubling Features" (Washington, DC: Center for Law and Social Policy, 1996).

70. Wisconsin Council 10 AFSCME, "Wisconsin Works, or W-2," June 1996, electronic text ed.; "Bob and Tommy Celebrate Union Busting," editorial, *(Madison, WI) Capital Times*, 23 May 1996; Matt Pommer, "Is Governor 'Laundering' Fed Welfare Funds?" *(Madison, WI) Capital Times*, 16 December 1996; Amy Rinard, "Two Senators Say State Is Using W-2 Surplus to Balance Budget," *(Madison, WI) Capital Times*, 17 December 1996; David Callender, "Estimate of W-2 Cost Now Up to 1.3 billion," *(Madison, WI) Capital Times*, 6 June 1997; Wiseman, "State Strategies," 538–39, 541.

71. "Massachusetts," in *The Almanac of American Politics 1996* (National Journal, Inc.), 627, electronic text ed.

72. "Massachusetts Governor: Cut Unwed Teen Moms' Aid," *Orlando Sentinel Tribune*, 16 October 1995; Meg Vaillancourt, "Weld: Welfare Battle Looms," *Boston Globe*, 6 August 1995.

73. Michael Cooper, "Massachusetts Governor Signs Bill Overhauling Welfare," *New York Times*, 10 February 1995.

74. "Virginia Votes 2-year Limit on Welfare," *New York Times*, 26 February 1995.

75. President Bill Clinton, weekly radio address to the nation, Office of the Press Secretary, 18 May 1996, http://www.pub.whitehouse.gov/urites/12R?urn:pdi:// oma.eop.gov.us/1996/5/19/5.text.l; Robert Pear, "Administration Backs Off Support of Wisconsin Welfare Plan," *New York Times*, 15 June 1996; Robyn Meredith,

"Michigan Welfare Plan Draws Unlikely Support," *New York Times*, 22 January 1996; Rochelle L. Stanfield, "Just Do It," *National Journal* 28, 13 (30 March 1996): 692.

CHAPTER 5: URBAN SOCIAL WELFARE IN AN AGE OF AUSTERITY

1. Historians have by and large missed the activist side of local government and the drain of poverty on local finances in earlier periods of American history. Robin L. Einhorn, for example, in an interesting and significant study, presents a very restricted view of city government functions in nineteenth-century Chicago. She is able to do this only by ignoring education (except for the management of the school fund) and not considering the role of county government, which bore most of the poverty-related expenses. Combining city and county governments, which together governed and financed the city, gives a different picture. Robin L. Einhorn, *Property Rules: Political Economy in Chicago, 1833–1872* (Chicago: University of Chicago Press, 1991). Reading municipal budgets often gives a misleading account of city expenses because functions such as poor relief and hospitals frequently have been county responsibilities; city residents and businesses pay a large share of county taxes, however. Take as an example Chicago and Cook County (which paid most of the city's poverty-related expenses) in the mid-1890s. Cook County maintained a public hospital for the poor, which in 1895 treated 15,655 patients at a cost (including a "detention hospital" for the insane and dependent children awaiting examination) of $251,000. Together the poorhouse, the care of the insane, and outdoor relief cost $316,000. The county agent supplied outdoor relief to 42,788 persons; the county physicians, who treated the poor, made 28,899 visits. The agent also adjudicated the commitment of 1,294 insane and dependent children, and he heard the cases of 485 other dependent children, whom he mostly placed in residential schools and homes. In all, the agent spent $100,000 on relief. Between 1875 and 1893, the county paid an average of 72.8 percent of the cost of outdoor relief. This pattern persisted into the twentieth century. In 1928, almost two-thirds of the amount spent on relief came from public sources. *Handbook of Cook County Institutions: Review of Its Business Transactions and Financial Affairs for Year 1895* (Chicago: William C. Hollister and Brothers, 1896), 50, 89–90, 94; Joanne L. Goodwin, *Gender and the Politics of Welfare Reform: Mothers' Pensions in Chicago, 1911–1929* (Chicago: University of Chicago Press, 1997), 83–84, 226.

2. Terrence J. McDonald, *The Parameters of Urban Fiscal Policy: Socioeconomic Change and Political Culture in San Francisco, 1860–1906* (Berkeley and Los Angeles: University of California Press, 1986), 12.

3. Gary Burtless, "Public Spending on the Poor: Historical Trends and Economic Limits," in *Confronting Poverty: Prescriptions for Change*, eds. Sheldon H. Danziger, Gary D. Sandefur, and Daniel H. Weinberg (Cambridge: Harvard University Press, 1994), 57; William E. Parshall, Deputy Managing Director for Special Needs Housing, Testimony, House Ways and Means Committee, 2 February 1995.

4. Janet Rothenberg Pack, "Poverty and Urban Public Expenditures," Working Paper no. 215 (University of Pennsylvania, Wharton Real Estate Center, September 1995); Citizens Budget Commission, *The State of Municipal Services in the 1990s: Social Services in New York City*, 11 August 1997, http://epn.org/cbc/socserv2.html; Anita A. Summers and Lara Jakubowski, "The Fiscal Burden of Unreimbursed Poverty Expenditures in the City of Philadelphia, 1985–1995," Working

Paper no. 238 (University of Pennsylvania, Wharton Real Estate Center, August 1996). Primary poverty expenses are those "unambiguously associated with addressing the needs of the poverty population," which means that they exclude police, fire, courts, and schools.

5. Carolyn Adams, David Bartelt, David Elesh, Ira Goldstein, Nancy Kleniewski, and William Yancey, *Philadelphia: Neighborhoods, Division, and Conflict in a Postindustrial City* (Philadelphia: Temple University Press, 1991), 30–65, 81–87; Dale Russakoff, "Another Kind of Help," *Washington Post*, 20 March 1994; Patrick Harveson, "Survey of Greater Philadelphia," *Financial Times*, 4 May 1994; Ben Yagoda, "Mayor on a Roll," *New York Times*, 22 May 1994; Scott Minerbrook, "The Bonfire of Fiscal Realities," *U.S. News and World Report*, 107, 21 (1989): 31; Michael Abramowitz and Marcia Slacum Greene, "City Faces Struggle over Budget Drained by Social Costs," *Washington Post*, 8 January 1989; "National League of Cities Press Conference by Alan Beals, Executive Director, Regarding Annual Report on Fiscal Conditions in 1989" (Washington, DC: Federal News Service, 10 July 1989).

6. Demetrios Caraley, "Washington Abandons the Cities," *Political Science Quarterly*, 107, 1 (1992) 7–12; Ronald F. Gibbs, "An Urban Agenda When D.C. Turns Its Back on Cities," *Chicago Tribune*, 9 June 1989.

7. Lester A. Salamon, *Partners in Public Service: Government-Nonprofit Relations in the Modern Welfare State* (Baltimore: Johns Hopkins University Press, 1995), 76–79.

8. Caraley, "Washington Abandons the Cities," 12–13.

9. Paul A. Jargowsky, *Ghetto Poverty in the United States, 1970 to 1990*, chaps. 3 and 4.

10. Minerbrook, "The Bonfire of Fiscal Realities"; Christopher S. Wren, "Cost of Substance Abuse Put at $20 Billion," *New York Times*, 29 February 1996; Citizens' Budget Commission, *State of Municipal Services*.

11. Summers and Jakubowski, "Fiscal Burden," apps. A and B; Citizens' Budget Commission, *State of Municipal Services*; Jeff Gelles, "Shredding City Safety Net Shows Shift in Public Policy," *Philadelphia Inquirer*, 21 July 1996; Dennis P. Culhane, Stephen Metraux, and Susan Wachter, "Homeless and Public Shelter Provision in New York City" (MS 2d rev., June 1997).

12. *Human Services in Philadelphia and Other Cities*, Current Urban Documents 1992–1993 no. 2299, table 1; "Our Troubled Cities; We've Taken a Beating over the Last Eight Years," interview with Terry Goddard, *USA Today*, 14 March 1989; Robert A. Hamilton, "Tough Times Pinch Welfare Programs," *New York Times*, 3 February 1991.

13. Statement of Joseph Ganim, Mayor of Bridgeport, CT, Hearings before the Committee on Banking, Housing, and Urban Affairs, U.S. Senate, 30 January 1992, "The Economic Conditions of Our Nation's Cities" (Washington, DC: GPO, 1993), 181; Minerbrook, "The Bonfire of Fiscal Realities"; Robert Inman, "How to Have a Fiscal Crisis: Lessons from Philadelphia," *American Economic Review* 85, 2 (1995): 381–83; David Johnston, "How Government Pensions Are Robbing You," *Money*, October 1994, 138; Abromowitz and Greene, "City Faces Struggle." In Philadelphia the cost of wages and employee benefits rose $15.45 per resident per year from 1972 to 1990; benefits alone increased 23 percent.

14. On New York's fiscal crisis of the 1970s, see Roger E. Alcaly and David Mermelstein, eds., *The Fiscal Crisis of American Cities: Essays on the Political Economy of Urban America with Special Reference to New York* (New York: Random House, 1977); William K. Tabb, *The Long Default: New York and the Urban Fiscal Crisis* (New York: Monthly Review Press, 1982); Martin Shefter, *Political Crisis/Fiscal Crisis: The Collapse and Revival of New York City* (New York: Basic Books, 1985).

15. *National League of Cities Press Conference;* Kevin Sack, "U.S. Cities Reaping Benefits of Economic Growth," *New York Times,* 12 July 1997; Adam Cohen, "City Boosters: A New Breed of Activist Mayors Is Making City Hall a Hothouse for Innovation," *Time,* 18 August 1997, 20; Richard L. Berke, "Politicians Even a Voter Could Love," *New York Times,* 9 November 1997, "Week in Review."

16. Stephen Goldsmith, *The Twenty-first Century City* (Washington, DC: Regnery Publishing, 1997), 194

17. Peter Beinart, "The Pride of the Cities," *New Republic,* 30 June 1997, 30; Michael E. Porter, "The Competitive Advantage of the Inner City," *Harvard Business Review,* May–June 1995, 55. Porter's thesis has generated considerable controversy. For a critical discussion that reviews the issue and the major literature it has spawned, see Merrill Goozner, "The Porter Prescription," *American Prospect* 38 (May–June 1988): 56–64.

18. Henry Goldman, "N.Y. Think Tank Is Making Waves with Conservative Agenda," *Philadelphia Inquirer,* 13 October 1997; "National Press Club Luncheon Speakers: New York City Mayor Rudolph Giuliani," Federal News Service, 30 March 1995.

19. William D. Eggers, "Righting City Hall," *National Review,* 46, 16 (1994): 378–83; Buzz Bissinger, *A Prayer for the City* (New York: Random House, 1977), 279. Bissinger provides a unique and absorbing account of Rendell's first term based on the unprecedented access Rendell allowed him.

20. Inman, "How to Have a Fiscal Crisis," 378–83.

21. Bissinger, *A Prayer for the City* 30, 35–37, 101–54. Bissinger claims that Rendell and his chief of staff, David Cohen, discovered that the annual deficit was far greater than they had been led to believe, and that the long-range deficit was $1.24 billion. Lorri Grube, "Urban Guerrillas: Re-inventing Our Cities," *Chief Executive* 98 (October 1994): 50.

22. Excerpts from the City of Philadelphia's FY 1994–FY 1999 Financial Plan, in Edward G. Rendell, Testimony before House Ways and Means Committee, 12 January 1995; "PNC President Outlines How Business Can Play a Major Role in the Economic Renewal of Philadelphia," *PR News Wire,* State and Regional News, 20 April 1994; Janet Ward, "Philadelphia Mayor Ed Rendell: 1996 Municipal Leader of the Year," *American City and Country,* 111, 12 (November 1996): 28.

23. Anthony Flint, "New Mayors Bring Similar Hopes, Plans, to the Job of Governing Cities," *Boston Globe,* 19 November 1993; Parshall, Testimony; Robert Lenzner and Lisa Coleman, "The Philadelphia Story," *Forbes,* 9 November 1992, 52–54; Russakoff, "Another Kind of Help"; Christopher Matthews, "A Tale of Two Cities," *San Francisco Examiner,* 17 April 1994; Arndt, "Ed Rendell"; Peirce, "Fearless Ed Rendell"; Neal R. Peirce, "A New Agenda to Rescue the Cities," *Baltimore Sun,* 26 April 1994; Harveson, "Survey of Greater Philadelphia"; Yagoda, "Mayor on a Roll."

24. Peirce, "Fearless Ed Rendell"; Bissinger, *A Prayer for the City,* 375–76; Randy Arndt, "Ed Rendell Calls for 'a New Urban Agenda,' " *Nation's Cities Weekly,* 25 April 1994, 1; Lorri Grube, "Urban Guerrillas"; "Mr. Rendell Challenges the Fed," *Washington Post,* 17 April 1994; Edward G. Rendell, Testimony, Senate Government Affairs Committee Hearing on Mandates on State and Local Government, 3 November 1993.

25. Interview with Ed Rendell, "Morning Edition," National Public Radio, 15 April 1994; Bob Edwards, interviewer.

26. Eggers, "Righting City Hall"; Thomas McArdle, "Rendell," *Investor's Business*

Daily, 20 June 1994, 1; Brett Pulley, "Privatization and Public Unions," *New York Times News Service*, America Online edition, 4 September 1995.

27. Craig R. McCoy, "People and Jobs Are Leaving the City," *Philadelphia Inquirer*, 24 March 1996; Peter Nicholas, "Council Rebuts Merits of Gambling," *Philadelphia Inquirer*, 27 March 1996; Howard Goodman and Craig R. McCoy, "Suddenly Rendell Is Trumpeting Philadelphia's Many Problems," *Philadelphia Inquirer*, 5 August 1996; Robert P. Casey, Edward G. Rendell, Christine Todd Whitman, and Arnold W. Webster, "The Strategic Plan (III)," *Philadelphia and Camden Empowerment Zone Strategic Plan* (24 June 1994), 13–14.

28. Goodman and McCoy, "Rendell Trumpeting Philadelphia's Problems"; Bissinger, *A Prayer for the City*, 371–73; Jere Downs, "Philadelphia Led Big Cities in Loss of Its People," *Philadelphia Inquirer*, 19 November 1997; Howard Goodman, "Economic Slide of City 'Precipitous,'" *Philadelphia Inquirer*, 17 October 1996; Andrew Cassel, "City Stems Job Loss, Suburbs Gain," *Philadelphia Inquirer*, 19 March 1997.

29. Jere Downs, "Philadelphia in Straits during Recession," *Philadelphia Inquirer*, 2 April 1997; Bissinger, *A Prayer for the City*, 244–49, 372. For one example, see Nathan Gorenstein, "Rendell Urges Firms to Create Jobs for Ex-Welfare Recipients," *Philadelphia Inquirer*, 6 February 1997; Larry Lewis, "Rendell, Doctors Seek Help for Health Crisis," *Philadelphia Inquirer*, 23 March 1997; Suzette Parmley, "Rendell to Outline Jobs Plan for Poor," *Philadelphia Inquirer*, 12 April 1998.

30. Bissinger, *A Prayer for the City*, 280, 291; Thomas Ferrick, Jr., "Redefining Philadelphia's Ailing Neighborhoods," *Philadelphia Inquirer*, 25 February 1997. There were a few promising examples of programs directed toward revitalizing troubled neighborhoods—for example, a joint city, community, and federal effort to attract a middle class back to an area of North Philadelphia once called "the Ruins." Thomas Ferrick, Jr., "Building a Middle Class in North Philadelphia," *Philadelphia Inquirer*, 12 November 1997; Sara Rimer, "Philadelphia: Marching to the Beat of Hope," *New York Times*, 12 January 1998; Michael Janofsky, "Philadelphia Neighborhood Reborn," *New York Times*, 24 February 1998.

31. Peter Nicholas, "Passing Grade for Housing Authority," *Philadelphia Inquirer*, 1 November 1997. In the fall of 1997, Section 8 itself became controversial as neighborhood groups objected to subsidized housing. Peter Nicholas, "PHA Hit with More Criticism," *Philadelphia Inquirer*, 10 November 1997; Peter Nicholas and Craig R. McCoy, "Section 8: A Racist Rallying Cry," *Philadelphia Inquirer*, 16 November 1997; Suzette Parmley, "At City Council Hearing, Sharp Words over Section 8," *Philadelphia Inquirer*, 19 November 1997; Elis Lotozo, "It's Hopelessly Confusing, Racially Explosive, and Crazy 8," *Philadelphia Weekly*, 19 November 1997, 22–28; Laura Bruch, "Vacant Towers Coming Down amid Hope of Better Housing," *Philadelphia Inquirer*, 2 December 1996; Craig McCoy, "How PHA Lost Out on $40 Million," *Philadelphia Inquirer*, 17 February 1997; Peter Nicholas, "PHA's Far-Flung Failings," *Philadelphia Inquirer*, 23 July 1997.

32. National Law Center on Homelessness and Poverty, *No Homeless People Allowed*, (Washington, DC, December 1994), i–ii; "Homelessness in America, Part 5," "Morning Edition," National Public Radio, 29 December 1995. For an exploration of the legal issues surrounding the use of city streets by panhandlers and the homeless, see Robert C. Ellickson, "Controlled Chronic Misconduct in City Spaces: Of Panhandlers, Skid Rows, and Public-Space Zoning," *Yale Law Journal* 105 (March 1996): 1165.

33. Carey Goldberg, "The Homeless Huddle at City's Margins," *New York Times*, 12 November 1995; "Little Help for the Homeless," *New York Times*, 20 November 1995; Joe Conason, "Police Mayor in FIRE City: Mayor Rudolph Giuliani of New York, New York," *Nation,* 18 December 1995, 779; Jodi Wilgoren, "Panhandlers Facing L.A. Crackdown," *Philadelphia Inquirer*, 29 January 1997; Carol Morello, "Tough L.A. Panhandling Law Aims for Hassle-Free Streets," *Philadelphia Inquirer*, 8 July 1997; Don Terry, "L.A. Redevelopment Plans May Hem in Skid Row," *New York Times*, 23 October 1997.

34. Craig R. McCoy, "Rendell Promises to Add Jobs, Fight Crime, and Aid Schools," *Philadelphia Inquirer*, 24 January 1997; "Out of Room," *Philadelphia Inquirer*, 10 July 1996; Howard Goodman, "City Turns Away Single Homeless," *Philadelphia Inquirer*, 17 July 1996; Michael Janofsky, "Welfare Cuts Raise Fears for Mayors," *Philadelphia Inquirer*, 30 July 1996; Jeff Gelles, "Shredding City Safety Net Shows Shift in Public Policy," *Philadelphia Inquirer*, 21 July 1996; Philadelphia/Delaware Valley Union of the Homeless, letter to the editor, *Philadelphia Inquirer*, 23 July 1996; Jeff Gelles, "Homeless Shelters Ease Admissions," *Philadelphia Inquirer*, 14 August 1996; Howard Goodman, "$2 Million More for the Homeless," *Philadelphia Inquirer*, 28 September 1996; Linda Wertheimer, interview with William Parshall, Deputy Managing Director, Special Needs Housing, Philadelphia, "All Things Considered," National Public Radio, 8 August 1996; Lewis, "Help for Health Crisis," *Philadelphia Inquirer*, 23 March 1997.

35. William D. Eggers, "City Lights: America's Boldest Mayors," *Policy Review* 65 (Summer 1993): 67; Jonathan Riskind, "Why Indy Has More Than the 500," *Columbus (Ohio) Dispatch*, 26 January 1992; Norm Heikens, "Business vs. Bureaucracy: Goldsmith Taps Private Sector to Dissect City Government," *Indianapolis Business Journal* (17 February 1992).

36. Ronald E. Yates, "Public Verdict on 'Private' City," *Chicago Tribune*, 6 November 1995; "Competition Keys Indy's Privatization," excerpts from comments by Stephen Goldsmith at the American Banker/Bond Buyer First Annual Midwest Regional Public Finance Conference, *Public Finance/Washington Watch* 6, 18 (11 May 1992): 8; Teri Sforza, "Public Problems, Private Solutions," *Orange County Register*, 28 February 1995; Stephen Goldsmith, Testimony, House Ways and Means, Contract with America, 12 January 1995; Mary Francis, "City Proposes to Ease Labor Market," *Indianapolis Star*, 17 April 1997.

37. Bill Beck, "The Prince of Privatization," *Indiana Business Magazine* 39, 4 (April 1995): 61; "Competition Keys Indy Privatization"; Goldsmith, *Twenty-first Century City*, 18.

38. Stephen Goldsmith, "Can Business Really Do Business with Government?" *Harvard Business Review* (May–June 1997): 110; Richard Wolf, "Local Governments Discover Competition Is Key to Reducing Costs," *USA Today*, 22 June 1995; Stephen Goldsmith, Testimony, Senate Banking Committee, "Housing Opportunity and Community Development," 29 March 1995; David Broder, "A Mayor Shows Gore's Team the Way," *Washington Post*, 25 August 1993; George F. Will, "A Minimalist Mayor," *Washington Post*, 12 May 1994; Goldsmith, *Twenty-first Century City*, 22.

39. S. Goldsmith, transcript, Remarks; Kathleen Schuckel, "Stigma of Pregnancy Exists Now, Says Unwed Teen-ager," *Indianapolis Star*, 22 October 1995.

40. Stephen Goldsmith, "We Can Save America's Cities—and Here's How," *Washington Times*, 18 November 1994; S. R. Goldsmith, Testimony, Senate Banking Committee.

41. S. Goldsmith, *Twenty-first Century City*, 78–79.
42. S. Goldsmith, Testimony, Senate Banking Committee.
43. S. Goldsmith, "We Can Save America's Cities."
44. Gerry Lanosga, "Families, Welfare Reform at Top of Goldsmith's Agenda," *Indianapolis Star*, 4 January 1996; Steve Goldsmith, "Toward a Welfare System with Flexibility and Heart," *Indianapolis Star*, 23 August 1996; Larry MacIntyre, "Goldsmith's Agenda Falters in Statehouse," *Indianapolis Star*, 2 February 1996; Kevin Morgan, "America Works Gets 100 off Welfare," *Indianapolis Star*, 21 December 1994; Eliza Newlin Carney, "Do Welfare Recipients Need Salvation?" *National Journal* 27, 43 (28 October 1995): 2652; "A Role for Churches," *Indianapolis Star*, 21 January 1996; Stephen Goldsmith, "Who Owns Our Sidewalks?" *Policy Review*, September–October 1996; Stephen Goldsmith, "Revamping Welfare, Rebuilding Lives," *New York Times*, 4 August 1996; Goldsmith, *Twenty-first Century City*, 96.
45. Yates, "Public Verdict"; John Ketzenberger, "Privatization or Competition to Provide Government Services," *Gannett News Service*, 20 September 1996; Rozelle Boyd, Susan Williams, Monroe Gray, Jeff Golc, "Bad News on City's Privatized Services," *Indianapolis Star*, 25 August 1996; Sforza, "Public Problems, Private Solutions"; "Bus Privatization," *Indianapolis Star*, 23 June 1996; John Bittner, "Privatization and the Pot O'Gold: Will Privatization Become a Campaign Cash Grab?" Utility Workers Union of America, Local 433, http:/www.nauticom.net/www/uwua; slgold.htm.
46. Fran Quigley, "Where Are They Going to Live?" *NUOVO Weekly*, 2–9 April 1998, 16. On the problem of affordable housing in Indianapolis see also "A Focus Group Study Prepared for Community Service Council," prepared for United Way of Central Indiana, May–July 1997; and "Linkages: A Strategy for Housing and Employment," Executive Summary, A Homeless Prevention Plan Prepared by the United Way/Community Service Council for the Coalition for Human Services Planning, January 1996. In 1992, the Indiana State Department of Health stopped providing detailed county-level estimates of poverty and near poverty in the years between national censuses. This makes tracking poverty in Indianapolis extremely difficult. *Kids Count in Indiana, 1996: Data Book*, 11; Michael Greenwald, "The Myth of the Supermayor," *American Prospect* 4 (September–October 1998): 20–27.
47. Greenwald, "Supermayor," 20–27.
48. Greenwald, "Supermayor," 27.
49. Jacob A. Riis, *How the Other Half Lives: Studies among the Tenements of New York* (New York: C Scribners's Sons, 1904); Roy Lubove, *The Progressives and the Slums: Tenement House Reform in New York City, 1890–1917* (Pittsburgh: University of Pittsburgh Press, 1962); U.S. House of Representatives, Committee on Ways and Means, *1996 Green Book* (Washington, DC: GPO, 1996), 919–21.
50. John C. Weicher, ed., *Maintaining the Safety Net: Income Redistribution Programs in the Reagan Administration* (Washington, DC: American Enterprise Institute, 1984), 93; Jason DeParle, "Slamming the Door on Affordable Housing," *Journal of Housing and Community Development* 54, 1 (January–February 1997): 9–21, repr. from *New York Times Magazine*.
51. On the commission, see R. Allen Hays, *The Federal Government and Urban Housing: Ideology and Change in Public Policy* (Albany: State University of New York Press, 1985), 246–49; William F. McKenna, chair, *Report of the President's Commission on Housing* (Washington, DC: GPO, 1982), xvii.

52. McKenna, *President's Commission*, xxii–xxiii, xxviii. For an excellent description of how Section 8 works, see Judith D. Feins, W. Eugene Rizor, Paul Elwood, and Linda Noel, *State and Metropolitan Administration of Section 8: Current Models and Potential Resources*, final report, prepared for U.S. Department of Housing and Urban Development, Office of Policy Development and Research (Cambridge, MA: Abt Associates, April 1997), 1.4–1.12.

53. Paul Pierson, *Dismantling the Welfare State? Reagan, Thatcher, and the Politics of Retrenchment* (New York: Cambridge University Press, 1994), 90–91.

54. McKenna, *President's Commission*, xiv, xxx–xxxi, 31–32, 63–64, 180–183.

55. McKenna, *President's Commission*, 71, 75–87; Barry Bluestone and Bennett Harrison, *The Deindustrialization of America* (New York: Basic Books, 1982), 226.

56. Margery Austin Turner and Raymond J. Struyk, *Urban Housing in the 1980s: Markets and Policies* (Washington, DC: Urban Institute Press, 1984), 37–39; Pierson, *Dismantling the Welfare State?*, 89; Charles H. Moore and Patricia A. Hoban-Moore, "Some Lessons from Reagan's HUD: Housing Policy and Public Service," *PS: Political Science and Politics* (March 1990): vol. 14. For an excellent summary of the change in federal urban program outlays from 1978 to 1994, see John Mollenkopf, "Urban Policy at the Crossroads," in *The Social Divide: Political Parties and the Future of Activist Government*, ed. Margaret Weir (Washington, DC: Brookings Institution Press; New York: Russell Sage Foundation, 1998), 470, table 11-1.

57. 1990 Housing Act, HOME and HOPE programs; U.S. Senate, "Summary of S.566, the Cranston-Gonzalez National Affordable Housing Act," 6 November 1990; "Senator Alan Cranston Conference Report on S.566, the Cranston-Gonzalez National Affordable Housing Act," 25 October 1990 (mimeo); Pierson, *Dismantling the Welfare State?*, 92–93.

58. U.S. Senate, "Summary of S.566"; "Cranston Conference Report"; Pierson, *Dismantling the Welfare State?*, 92–93; Steven A. Holmes, "Kemp's Legacy as Housing Secretary: One of Ideas, Not Accomplishments," *New York Times*, 20 April 1996.

59. One of the best studies of homelessness in this period is Martha R. Burt, *Over the Edge: The Growth of Homelessness in the 1980s* (New York: Russell Sage Foundation, 1992). See also Mary K. Nenno, "H/CD after Reagan: A New Cycle of Policies and Partners," *Journal of Housing* (March–April 1990): 76; Moore and Hoban-Moore, "Some Lessons," 13.

60. Moore and Hoban-Moore, "Some Lessons," 16.

61. The best overview of Clinton urban policy is Mollenkopf, "Urban Policy"; see p. 477, figure 11-1, for a chart of Clinton administration urban policy initiatives.

62. Lori Montgomery and Vanessa Gallman, "As Cisneros Departs, HUD Faces Crisis," *Philadelphia Inquirer*, 7 December 1996. By early 1998, HUD, which had fired thousands of employees, had made significant progress in improving its internal and external management. Judith Havemann, "Consultant Backs Plan for HUD Restructuring," *Washington Post*, 27 March 1998; Statement by Hon. Henry G. Cisneros, former Secretary of Housing and Urban Development; Senate Committee on Banking, Housing, and Urban Affairs, "Confirmation Hearing on the Nomination of Andrew Cuomo to become HUD Secretary," 22 January 1997.

63. U.S. Department of Housing and Urban Development, Office of Policy Development and Research, *Empowerment: A New Covenant with America's Communities: President Clinton's National Urban Policy Report* (July 1995), 7–9.

64. HUD, *Empowerment*, 34. The Clinton administration also advocated continuing

project-based assistance where circumstances made it the most appropriate option. Secretary Andrew Cuomo, Statement before the Senate Committee on Banking, Housing and Urban Affairs Subcommittee on Housing Opportunity and Urban Development, 17 June 1997; *1996 Green Book*, percentages calculated from table 16-25.

65. "HUD Housing Vouchers Expand Residence Choices for Section 8 Recipients," *CUPReport* 8, 3 (Winter 1997): 1, 5; John Goering and Judie Feins, "The Moving to Opportunity Social 'Experiment': Early Stages of Implementation and Research Plans," *Poverty Research News* 1, 2 (Spring 1997): 4-6; U.S. Department of Housing and Urban Development, Office of Policy Development and Research, "Residential Mobility Programs," no. 1 (Spring 1994); *Moving to Opportunity News*, (Abt Associates) 3, 1 (January 1998); Moving to Opportunity for Fair Housing Demonstration, U.S. Department of Housing and Urban Development, Office of Policy Development and Research, *Expanding Housing Choices for HUD-Assisted Families: First Biennial Report to Congress* (April 1996); "Public Housing Residents Move to Opportunity," *Recent Research Results: A Newsletter from HUD USER* (September 1999): 1, 3; U.S. Department of Housing and Urban Development, *V. The Moving to Opportunity Demonstration*, U.S. Department of Housing and Urban Development, 30 June 1999, www.huduser.org:80/publications/affhsg/expand/sec5 html.

66. *1996 Green Book*, 919-21; "The Clinton Administration and Homelessness: From Attack to Retreat," *Safety Network* (February–March 1997); Association of Community Organizations for Reform Now, Center for Community Change, National Housing Law Project, National Low-Income Housing Coalition; "Critical Issues in Pending Public Housing Reform Legislation: HR 2 and S.462. A Briefing Paper—Revised 6/24/97"; National Low Income Housing Coalition, "HUD FY99 Appropriations Bill," *Weekly Housing Update: Memo to Members* 3, 37 (9 October 1998); David Stout, "Congressional Negotiators Agree to Create More Rent Subsidies," *New York Times*, 6 October 1998; Michael Janofsky, "Mayors Applaud President and His Urban Proposal," *New York Times*, 30 January 1999; Robert A. Rankin and Jodi Edna Rankin, "Clinton Targets Abandoned Buildings," *Philadelphia Inquirer*, 29 January 1999; "President Clinton Announces $900 Million in Homeless Assistance," press release, HUD no. 99-273, 25 December 1999; "President Clinton Proposes $28 Billion HUD Budget—a $2.5 Billion Increase—to Open Doors for More Americans," press release, HUD no. 99-22, 1 February 1999; "President Clinton Proposes $32.1 Billion HUD Budget—Strongest in More Than 20 Years, and a $6 Billion Increase," press release, HUD no. 00-26, 7 February 2000.

67. Mollenkopf, "Urban Policy," 482-84; HUD, *Empowerment*, 37; E. M. Gramlich, "A Policy in Lampman's Tradition: The Community Reinvestment Act," *Focus* 20, 3 (Fall 1999): 11-14.

68. HUD, *Empowerment* 39, 44; U.S. Department of Housing and Urban Development, *The State of the Cities*, June 1997 [available online from huduser.org], 48-49. The initiative encompassed a number of distinct strategies: lowering homeownership costs for city home buyers through reduced premiums on mortgage insurance; offering incentives for police officers to live in the communities in which they worked; intensifying attacks on discrimination in housing; funding "homeownership zones" in inner cities; targeting urban lending through federal mortgage insurance; and introducing homeownership empowerment vouchers, which would allow households to use Section 8 certificates and vouchers for mortgage pay-

ments. National Low Income Housing Coalition, "1998 Housing Reform Act," *Weekly Housing Update* 3, 37 (9 October 1998); Stout, "Congressional Negotiators."

69. McKenna, *President's Commission*, 106–7; Bluestone and Harrison, *Deindustrialization*, 225–26; Jeffrey S. Lehman, "Updating Urban Policy," in Danziger, Sandefur, and Weinberg, *Confronting Poverty*, 229. Kemp, who became Bush's secretary of HUD, insisted on limiting incentives in enterprise zones to tax cuts, especially lower capital gains. Skeptics in cities and Congress wanted a broader approach that included a mix of tax incentives, public funds, and social services. Kemp's refusal to compromise with Congress doomed his enterprise zone proposal. Richard H. Cowden, executive director of the American Association of Enterprise Zones, claimed that Kemp lacked credibility "because at every opportunity to choose between practical political compromise to benefit low-income communities and his supply side dogma, he consistently chose the latter"; his rigid position guaranteed a policy "stalemate." Holmes, "Kemp's Legacy."

70. HUD, *Empowerment*, 44; *State of the Cities*, 51; "Empowerment Zones: Program Highlights," 17 February 1998, http://www.hud.gov/budget99/justif99/cpd; shbcpdzone.html.

71. Gerry Riposa, "From Enterprise Zones to Empowerment Zones: The Community Context of Urban Economic Development," *American Behavioral Scientist* 39, 5 (March–April 1996); *State of the Cities*, 51.

72. "Trouble in the Zones," *Philadelphia Inquirer*, 1 June 1999; "Just the Sort City Needs," *Philadelphia Inquirer*, 2 June 1999; Scott Martelle, "Can Santa Ana Make Urban-Aid History? Renewal: For Its Empowerment Zone to Succeed, the City Must Heed Painful Lessons Learned Elsewhere," *Los Angeles Times*, 23 August 1999; U.S. Department of Housing and Urban Development, "Empowerment Zones: Program Highlights."

73. "An Overview of President Clinton's Trip to America's New Markets" (White House, 6 July 1999), www.whitehouse.gov/WH/New/New_Markets/tripoverview. html; U.S. Department of Housing and Urban Development, "New Markets: The Untapped Retail Buying Power in America's Inner Cities," 6 July 1999, www. huduser.org/publications/newmarkets/execsum.html; John Broder, "A Pledge of Federal Help for the Economic Byways," *New York Times*, 6 July 1999; President Bill Clinton, "Remarks by the President to the Newark Community" (White House Office of the Press Secretary, 4 November 1999), http://www.whitehouse. gov/WH/New/html/99991104_1.html; Sonya Ross, "He Wants to Highlight the New Jersey Nets' Good Deeds off the Basketball Court," *Philadelphia Inquirer*, 4 November 1999; David E. Sanger, "In Newark and Hartford, Clinton Says Cities Are Untapped Markets," *New York Times*, 5 November 1999.

74. Curt Anderson, "House Passes a Bill to Share the Wealth," *Philadelphia Inquirer*, 26 July 2000; Caren Benjamin, "Bill Targets Investment in Poor Areas," *Philadelphia Inquirer*, 23 June 2000.

75. *State of the Cities*, 60–61; *National Urban Policy Report*, 4.

76. Adam Nagourney, "Dole Calls Public Housing One of 'Last Bastions of Socialism,'" *New York Times*, 30 April 1996; Ronald D. Utt, "Time for New Management at America's Troubled Public Housing Projects," *Heritage Foundation Reports*, Backgrounder Update no. 247, 17 May 1995.

77. Nicholas Lemann, "The Public Housing That Succeeds," *New York Times*, 5 May 1996.

78. David Hess, "House Votes to Restructure Federal Role in Public Housing,"

Philadelphia Inquirer, 10 May 1996; Lemann, "Public Housing"; Stuart A. Gabriel, "Urban Housing Policy in the 1990s," *Housing Policy Debates* 7, 4 (1996): 687. For a defense of mixed-income public housing using the idea of social capital, see Lynn H. Spence, "Rethinking the Social Role of Public Housing," *Housing Policy Debates* 4, 3 (1993): 355–68. For reports of successes in mixed-income housing, see Judith Havemann, "Public Housing's Upscale Idea," *Washington Post*, 18 April 1998.

79. Lori Nitschke, "Housing Overhaul Still Looking for a Home in GOP Congress," *Weekly Report of February 21, 1998, Congressional Quarterly*, 425.

80. *State of the Cities*, 62.

81. HUD secretary Henry G. Cisneros, "Leave No One Behind, Extend Opportunity to All," National Press Club, 7 January 1997; Henry G. Cisneros, "To the Congress of the United States," in U.S. Department of Housing and Urban Development, Office of Policy Development and Research, *Rental Housing Assistance at a Crossroads: A Report to Congress on Worst-Case Housing Needs*, March 1996; Ian Fisher, "G.O.P. Fights More Housing Aided by U.S.," *New York Times*, 3 March 1996.

82. David Stout, "Odds Worsen in Hunt for Low-Income Rentals," *New York Times*, 24 September 1999; "Housing Needs Report Shows Crisis Worsening," *Recent Research Results: A Newsletter from HUD USER* (May 2000): 1–3.

83. National Low Income Housing Coalition, *NLHC Weekly Housing Update* 2, 33 (10 October 1997); National Coalition for the Homeless, "FY98 Budget and Homelessness: Housing and Shelter," 11 October 1997.

84. The White House, Office of the Press Secretary, "President Clinton's Next Budget Will Include 120,000 New Housing Vouchers for America's Working Families," 29 December 1999.

85. "1998 Housing Reform Act"; "A Win-Win on Housing," *New York Times*, 12 October 1998; "House Passes Bill to Broaden Kind of Housing-Project Tenants," *Philadelphia Inquirer*, 7 October 1998.

86. Joel Blau, *The Visible Poor: Homelessness in the United States* (New York: Oxford University Press, 1992), 113.

87. Blau, *Visible Poor*, 113–14.

88. "The Clinton Administration and Homelessness." Emergency Shelter continued existing policies; Supportive Housing emphasized transitional living arrangements, permanent housing for the homeless disabled, and supportive services; Shelter Plus Care provided supportive permanent housing and services for people with disabilities; SRO Section 8 increased the supply of single-room-occupancy apartments. Ester Fuchs and William McAllister, Barnard-Colombia Center for Urban Policy, Columbia University, *The Continuum of Care: A Report on the New Federal Policy to Address Homelessness* (U.S. Department of Housing and Urban Development, December 1996), 11–14.

89. Nonetheless, HUD exaggerated its accomplishment when it boasted inaccurately that a 1995 Columbia University study found HUD programs served fourteen times more homeless people than in 1992 at only twice the cost in federal funds. HUD secretary Andrew Cuomo, Testimony before the Appropriations Subcommittee, 13 May 1997; Fuchs and McAllister, *Continuum of Care*, 29 and appendix B.

90. "The Clinton Administration and Homelessness: From Attack to Retreat," *Safety Network: The Newsletter of the National Coalition for the Homeless* (February–March 1997); Fuchs and McAllister, *Continuum of Care*, 158, 168, 178.

91. The most recent major survey reports that 44 percent of the homeless had worked the previous month. Their great problems were poverty and poor health—their mean income for the previous thirty days was $348; 46 percent had chronic health problems; 55 percent lacked medical insurance; and 66 percent claimed indications of problems related to mental health, drugs, or alcohol. "Homelessness: Programs and the People They Serve (Highlights)," National Survey of Homeless Assistance Providers and Clients (NSHAPC), 1999, www.huduser.org; shpublications/homelessness/highlights.html.

92. "Misguided Shelter Reform," *New York Times*, 28 October 1999.

93. *State of the Cities*, 17–20; Steven A. Holmes, "Budget Woes Ease for Cities in U.S.," *New York Times*, 8 January 1995; Timothy Egan, "Urban Mayors Share the (Not Unwelcome) Burden of Coping with Prosperity," *New York Times*, 13 June 2000.

94. *State of the Cities*, 28–39. For two very different perspectives on the availability of affordable housing, see Kathryn P. Nelson, "*Whose* Shortage of Affordable Housing?" *Housing Policy Debates* 5, 4 (1994): 401–43, and James E. Wallace, "Financing Affordable Housing in the United States," *Housing Policy Debates* 6, 4 (1995): 785–815. See also Bluestone and Harrison, *Deindustrialization*, 227–29; U.S. Conference of Mayors, *Implementing Welfare Reform in America's Cities: A 34-City Survey* (November 1997), 9; G. Thomas Kingsley, *Federal Housing Assistance and Welfare Reform: Uncharted Territory*, Urban Institute, Assessing the New Federalism Project, ser. A, no. A-19 (December 1997); Lori Nitschke, "The Rocky Relationship of Housing and Welfare," *Weekly Report of February 21, 1998, Congressional Quarterly*, 424; Bissinger, *A Prayer for the City*, 373. "One authority" quoted in Holmes, "Budget Woes Ease."

CHAPTER 6: THE INDEPENDENT SECTOR, THE MARKET, AND THE STATE

1. See the statement by Ralph Reed, executive director of the Christian Coalition, quoted in Elizabeth Greene, John Murawski, and Grant Williams, "Charities and the Republican Revival," *Chronicle of Philanthropy* 22, 26 (January 1995): 23. The major book-length statement of this position is an unreliable book by a journalism professor from Texas, principal domestic policy adviser to governor and presidential candidate George W. Bush, on which Republican House Speaker Newt Gingrich lavished praise. Marvin Olasky, *The Tragedy of American Compassion* (Washington, DC: Regnery Gateway, 1992). For reviews of Olasky, comments about the use of the book, and Gingrich's praise see David C. Hammack, review, *H-NET Book Review*, February 1996, h-net2.msu.edu; shreviews/show.eu.cgi? path=3672851041828; Peter Steinfels, "Beliefs," *New York Times*, 28 October 1995; Martin Hochbaum, "Charity Alone Can't Provide for the Poor," *New York Times*, 5 November 1995; Suzanne Gamboa, "Being GOP's Guru is UT Prof's Latest Turn," *Austin American-Statesman*, 10 July 1995; Adam Wolfson, "Welfare Fixers: Three Perspectives on Changing the Welfare System," *Commentary* 101, 4 (April 1996): 4; David Van Biema, Ann Blackman, Jenifer Mattos, Jeanne McDowell, and Lisa H. Towle, "Can Charity Fill the Gap?" *Time*, 4 December 1995, 4. Olasky has summarized his position in various places, for example: "Thinking Long-Term about Welfare," *Washington Times*, 9 August 1995; "Thinking about Welfare Replacement," *Philanthropy, Culture, and Society* (September 1995); "History's Solutions," *National Review*, 7 February 1994, 45.

2. I have reconstructed some of the stories of very poor families from charitable organizations' case records. See Michael B. Katz, *Poverty and Policy in American History* (New York: Academic Press, 1983), 17–24; Michael B. Katz, "The History of an Impudent Poor Woman in New York City from 1918 to 1923," in *The Uses of Charity*, ed. Peter Mandler (Philadelphia: University of Pennsylvania Press, 1991), 227–46; Michael B. Katz, *Improving Poor People: The Welfare State, the "Underclass," and Urban Schools as History* (Princeton: Princeton University Press, 1995), 144–72; Olasky, *Tragedy of American Compassion*, 4, 219–23.

3. The discussion of charity, voluntarism, and the social services in this section is based on my book *In the Shadow of the Poorhouse: A Social History of Welfare in America*, 10th anniversary ed. (New York: Basic Books, 1997); there were, of course, innumerable voluntary organizations not concerned with the poor. On the role of voluntarism in the antebellum period the classic statement is Alexis de Tocqueville, *De la démocratie en Amérique* (1835). On the role of voluntarism in the nineteenth century, a particularly helpful work is Stuart M. Blumin, *The Emergence of the Middle Class: Social Experience in the American City, 1760–1900* (New York: Cambridge University Press, 1989), 66–107. An important and stimulating discussion is Gerald Gamm and Robert Putnam, "Association-Building in America, 1840–1900," *Journal of Interdisciplinary History* (forthcoming). The most recent history of Catholic charities is Dorothy K. Brown and Elizabeth McKeown, *The Poor Belong to Us: Catholic Charities and American Welfare* (Cambridge: Harvard University Press, 1998).

4. Paul Boyer, *Urban Masses and Moral Order in America, 1820–1920* (Cambridge: Harvard University Press, 1978). Boyer refers to Sunday schools as an example of the "moral–social control" tradition.

5. William J. Novak, *The People's Welfare: Law and Regulation in Nineteenth-Century America* (Chapel Hill: University of North Carolina Press, 1996), ix, 1–2, points out that mainstream historiography obscures the activist role of local government in the first three-quarters of the nineteenth century. "Public responses to destitution and dependence paralleled regulation of public safety, economy, space, health, and morals in a reigning theory and practice of governance committed to the pursuit of the people's welfare and happiness in a well-ordered society and polity."

6. For an excellent discussion of the private-public relations in the case of orphanages, see Timothy A. Hacsi, *Second Home: Orphan Asylums and Poor Families in America* (Cambridge: Harvard University Press, 1998).

7. Katz, *Improving Poor People*, 38–39; for an extended discussion of scientific charity, see Katz, *In the Shadow of the Poorhouse*, 60–87.

8. Olasky, *Tragedy of American Compassion*, 72.

9. Judith Havemann, "Heads of Nation's Largest Charities See Rise in Their Salaries," *Philadelphia Inquirer*, 6 July 1998.

10. The independent sector includes women's groups; religious and social welfare organizations; programs in education, conservation, ecology, and preservation; religious and social welfare organizations; minority civil rights activism; and health and rehabilitation agencies. Virginia Ann Hodgkinson, Murray S. Weitzman, et al., *Nonprofit Almanac, 1996–1997: Dimensions of the Independent Sector* (San Fracisco: Jossey-Bass Publishers, 1996), 23; David R. Stevenson, Thomas H. Pollak, and Linda M. Lampkin, *State Nonprofit Almanac, 1997* (Washington, DC: Urban Institute Press, 1997), 1; Jacob France Center, "Baltimore City Nonprofit Sector: A Study of Its Economic and Programmatic Impacts on the City of Balti-

more" (Maryland Association of Nonprofit Organizations, 29 May 1977), 3; Jon Pratt and Chris Sullivan, "Minnesota's Nonprofit Economy 1997" (Minnesota Council of Nonprofits, 6 October 1997), 3.

11. Elizabeth T. Boris, "Myths about the Nonprofit Sector," Charting Civil Society Series, no. 4 (Washington, DC: Urban Institute, July 1998), 1–3; Burton A. Weisbrod, "The Future of the Nonprofit Sector: Its Entwining with Private Enterprise and Government," *Journal of Policy Analysis and Management* 16, 4 (1997): 542; Hodgkinson, Weitzman, et al., *Nonprofit Almanac 1996–1997, Dimensions of the Independent Sector*, 3–4, 193, 211, 244.

12. Lester M. Salamon, "The Marketization of Welfare: Changing Nonprofit and For-Profit Roles in the American Welfare State," *Social Service Review* 27, 1 (March 1993): 19–20.

13. Jacob France Center, "Baltimore City Nonprofit Sector," i–ii.

14. Tax-exempt organizations have more legal flexibility in advocacy than most realize. Karen M. Paget, "The Big Chill: Foundations and Political Passion," *American Prospect* 44 (May–June 1999): 26–33.

15. Stevenson, Pollak, and Lampkin, *State Nonprofit Almanac, 1997*, xvii. Because the IRS requires only organizations with annual revenues of more than $25,000 to file reporting forms, the number of reporting public charities—164,429 in 1992—is much smaller than the total. Detailed information about sources of funding is available only for these charities that file reports.

16. Hodgkinson, Weitzman, et al., *Nonprofit Almanac, 1996–1997*, 46, 48; Wilmer L. Kerns, "Role of the Private Sector in Financing Social Welfare Programs, 1977–1992," *Social Security Bulletin* 58, 1 (1995): 66.

17. Greene, Murawski, and Williams, "Charities and the Republican Revival," 22; Steven Rathgeb Smith and Michael Lipsky, *Nonprofits for Hire: The Welfare State in an Age of Contracting* (Cambridge: Harvard University Press, 1993), 6, 9–10.

18. For observations on Reagan's policies toward the nonprofit center, see Peter Dobkin Hall, *Inventing the Nonprofit Sector and Other Essays on Philanthropy, Voluntarism, and Nonprofit Organizations* (Baltimore: Johns Hopkins University Press, 1992), 88–90; Salamon, "The Marketization of Welfare," 22–23; Smith and Lipsky, *Nonprofits for Hire*, 63. Nonetheless, some categories of federal spending increased in the 1980s; these included child welfare, foster care, and care for the homeless. If the tricounty Detroit area serves as a representative example, the geography as well as the funding patterns of nonprofits also tilted social services toward the middle class. Although "nonprofit employing organizations" there doubled in number between 1982 and 1992, the number increased 58 percent within the city of Detroit, compared to 232 percent in the rest of the county, that is, primarily in the suburbs. F. K. Marsh, "Survival of the Fittest: Nonprofit Development in Metropolitan Detroit" (Ph.D. diss., University of Michigan, 1996), 84–85, 106; "The Federal Budget and the Nonprofit Sector," *Snapshots: Research Highlights from the Nonprofit Sector Research Fund* 7 (October 1999); Alan J. Abramson, Lester M. Salamon, and C. Eugene Steurle, *The Nonprofit Sector and the Federal Budget in the 1980s and 1990s* (Nonprofit Sector Research Fund, 23 December 1999), available from www.aspenistitute.org/dir/polpro/NSRF/Summaries/Abramson.html.

19. Greene, Murawski, and Williams, "Charities and the Republican Revival," 26; Hodgkinson, Weitzman, et al., *Nonprofit Almanac, 1996–1997*, 160–61; Lester M. Salamon, "Holding the Center: America's Nonprofit Sector at a Crossroads," report to Nathan Cummings Foundation (1997), www.ncf.org/ncf/publications/

reports/holding_the _center/hc.contents.html; Alan J. Abramson and Lester M. Salamon, "The Nonprofit Sector and the Federal Budget: FY 1998 Congressional Budget Resolution," prepared for Independent Sector, November 1997, www.indpsec.org/whatsnew/budget.html. Very useful, as well, is Lester A. Salamon, *America's Nonprofit Sector: A Primer* (Foundation Center, 1992); "The Federal Budget and the Nonprofit Sector"; John Cordes, John O'Hare, and Eugene Steuerle, "Extending the Charitable Deduction to Nonitemizers: Policy Issues and Options" (Urban Institute, Center on Nonprofits and Philanthropy, 2000).

20. Sarah Jay, "Government Safety Net Cut, Charities Turn to Public," *New York Times*, 3 December 1995; Van Biema et al., "Can Charity Fill the Gap?" 44; Alice Lipowicz, "Future Looks Uncharitable for Nonprofits," *Crain's New York Business*, 4 December 1995; Catholic Charities USA, "Economic Recovery Bypasses Working Families and Poor," press release, 12 December 1995; Rachel L. Swarns, "Bare Pantries in New York as Cuts Loom," *New York Times*, 31 December 1995; Milt Freudenheim, "Charities Aiding Poor Fear Loss of Government Subsidies," *New York Times*, 5 February 1996; Marsh, "Survival of the Fittest: Nonprofit Development in Metropolitan Detroit," 116.

21. Weisbrod, "The Future of the Nonprofit Sector," 542.

22. Smith and Lipsky, *Nonprofits for Hire*, 66.

23. "Total Giving Increased 10.7% in 1998 Announces Giving USA," press release, AAFRC Press Office, 25 May 1999, http://aafrc.org /NEWS.HTM; Karen W. Arenson, "Charitable Giving Surged Again in '99, by an Estimated 9%," *New York Times*, 5 May 2000; Karen Arenson, "Charitable Giving Set Record in '98, Report Says," *New York Times*, 26 May 1999.

24. David Cay Johnston, "United Way Faced with Fewer Donors Giving Less Money," *New York Times*, 9 November 1997; Salamon, "The Marketization of Welfare," 24–26; "Non-Profit Groups Tell Congress That They Cannot 'Do It All,'" *Chronicle of Philanthropy*, 23 February 1995, 47.

25. Hodgkinson, Weitzman et al., *Nonprofit Almanac, 1996–1997*, 56–57, 65–66, 71; Salamon, "Holding the Center"; National Commission on Philanthropy and Civic Renewal, *Giving Better, Giving Smarter* (1997) (report), 14; U.S. House of Representatives Committee on Ways and Means, *1996 Green Book* (Washington DC: GPO, 1996), 1271; Arenson, "Charitable Giving"; "Total Giving Reaches $190.16 Billion," AAFRC Press Office, 24 May 2000.

26. Boris, "Myths about the Nonprofit Sector," 1–3; Sara Mosle, "The Vanity of Voluntarism," *New York Times Magazine*, 2 July 2000, 22.

27. Salamon, "The Marketization of Welfare," 16–17.

28. Lester M. Salamon, *Partners in Public Service: Government-Nonprofit Relations in the Modern Welfare State* (Baltimore: Johns Hopkins University Press, 1995), 25.

29. Salamon, "The Marketization of Welfare," 24–26; Salamon, "Holding the Center"; Bob Tedeschi, "E-Commerce: Charitable Groups Discover New Revenue in Retailing Goods via Their Own Web Sites," *New York Times*, 27 March 2000; Burton A. Weisbrod, "The Nonprofit Mission and Its Financing: Growing Links between Nonprofits and The Rest of the Economy," in *To Profit or Not to Profit: The Commercial Transformation of the Nonprofit Sector*, ed. Burton A. Weisbrod (New York: Cambridge University Press, 1998), 1.

30. Smith and Lipsky, *Nonprofits for Hire*, 67–68. The chapters in Weisbrod, *To Profit or Not to Profit*, describe many of the types of commercialization.

31. Douglas Frantz, "Elizabeth Dole: Her Power and Tenure as Leader of Red Cross," *New York Times*, 30 May 1996.

32. Frantz, "Elizabeth Dole."

33. Karen Stark, "Small Nonprofit Agencies Fear Becoming Extinct," *Philadelphia Inquirer*, 18 June 1998; Thomas DiLorenzo, "Hocking the Halo: Are America's Charities for Sale?" *Washington Times*, 17 August 1996; Weisbrod, "The Future of the Nonprofit Sector," 543–44.

34. Reed Abelson, "Charities Use For-Profit Units to Skirt Rules," *New York Times*, 9 February 1998.

35. Salomon, "The Marketization of Welfare," 26–27. For a good discussion of the dilemmas posed by commercialization for social services, based on six case histories, see Dennis R. Young, "Commercialism in Nonprofit Social Service Associations: Its Character, Significance, and Rationale," in Weisbrod, *To Profit or Not to Profit*, 195–216.

36. Salomon, "Holding the Center"; see also Judith E. Bell, "Saving Their Assets: How to Stop Plunder at Blue Cross and Other Nonprofits," *American Prospect*, no. 26 (May–June 1966): 60–66.

37. Salomon, "The Marketization of Welfare," 28–33; Salomon, "Holding the Center."

38. Salomon, "Holding the Center"; Nina Bernstein, "Giant Companies Entering Race to Run State Welfare Programs," *New York Times*, 15 September 1996. Bernstein also wrote about the galloping privatization in the foster care system in "Welfare Bill Has Opened Foster Care to Big Business," *New York Times*, 4 May 1997. See also Barbara Ehrenreich, "Spinning the Poor into Gold: How Corporations Seek to Profit from Welfare Reform," *Harper's*, August 1997, 44; Sam Howe Verhovek, "White House Rejects Texas Plan for Business Role in Welfare," *New York Times*, 11 May 1997; Steven Thomma, "Privatization Jackpot Eyed: Takeover of Texas Welfare," *Philadelphia Inquirer*, 24 March 1997; William D. Hartung and Jennifer Washburn, "Lockheed Martin: From Warfare to Welfare," *Nation*, 2 March 1998; Nina Bernstein, "Squabble Puts Welfare Deal under Spotlight in New York," *New York Times*, 22 February 2000.

39. Bernstein, "Giant Companies Entering Race to Run State Welfare Programs"; Edward Walsh, "Michigan Still Pays for Shelter after Welfare Cutoff," *Washington Post*, 23 December 1995; Amy L. Sherman, "Michigan Lessons of Looking to God for Welfare Reform," *Detroit News*, 29 October 1995; Robin T. Edwards, "Changes Raise Church-State Question," *National Catholic Reporter* 32, 10 (29 December 1995): 4; Lynette Holloway, "Private Nonprofit Groups Reshape NYC Homeless Shelters," *New York Times*, 12 November 1997. Food assistance offers an instructive example of the assimilation of charity to the state and some of its consequences. For a scathing criticism of food banks, see Theresa Funiciello, *The Tyranny of Kindness: Dismantling the Welfare System to End Poverty in America* (New York: Atlantic Monthly Press, 1993), 123–61. For an example of the changing relations in food banks in one Delaware city, see Karen A. Curtis, "Urban Poverty and the Social Consequences of Privatized Food Assistance," *Journal of Urban Affairs* 19, 2 (1997): 207–26.

40. For thoughtful comments on this theme, see Weisbrod, "The Future of the Nonprofit Sector," 544–53; Sherman, "Michigan Lessons of Looking to God for Welfare Reform"; Kimberly Dennis, "Charities on the Dole"; Salomon, "Holding the Center"; National Commission on Philanthropy and Civic Renewal, *Giving Better, Giving Smarter*, *Policy Review: The Journal of American Citizenship*, 76 (March–April 1996), 5.

41. Salomon, "Holding the Center"; Funiciello, *The Tyranny of Kindness*, 119–22; John McKnight, *The Careless Society: Community and Its Counterfeits* (New York:

Basic Books, 1995), 10, 97. Freedman's comments reported by Bernstein, "Giant Companies Entering Race to Run State Welfare Programs." Smith and Lipsky, *Nonprofits for Hire*; 9–14, 204–5.

42. Both quotations from Greene, Murawski, and Williams, "Charities and the Republican Revival," 23; Ken Rankin, "50 Nonprofit Leaders Call on Government to Do More," *Nonprofit Times* (November 1997).

43. Weisbrod, "The Future of the Nonprofit Sector," 545; Gwen Florio, "In Colorado, a Move to Tax Nonprofits," *Philadelphia Inquirer*, 24 September 1996; John Murawski and Grant Williams, "Turning to Charities for Taxes," *Chronicle of Philanthropy* 18 May 1995: 1, 34–37. In Pennsylvania, the controversy reached the state legislature, which threatened to pass legislation making it harder for cities to exact payments from nonprofits. A compromise bill allowed cities to continue to virtually require large nonprofits to make "voluntary" contributions in lieu of property taxes. Ken Dilanian, "State Fine-Tunes Charities Bill to Cities' Liking," *Philadelphia Inquirer*, 20 November 1997; Christina Asquith, "Longwood Ruling a Big Relief to Nonprofits," *Philadelphia Inquirer*, 22 July 1998.

44. Michael Matza, "Hartford Curbs Agencies for Poor as U.S. Watches," *Philadelphia Inquirer*, 20 August 1996; Jonathan Rabinovitz, "Fighting Poverty Programs: Hartford Faces Vote to Bar New Nonprofit Services," *New York Times*, 24 March 1996; "Sharing the Stress," *Philadelphia Inquirer*, 26 August 1996.

45. John A. Coleman, "Under the Cross and the Flag: Reflections on Discipleship and Citizenship in America," *America* 174, 16 (11 May 1996): 6; John D. Davis, "Social Needs Overwhelming Catholic Charities, Leader Warns," *Sun-Sentinel (Fort Lauderdale, FL)*, 13 September 1997.

46. Mark Chaves, "Congregations' Social Service Activities" (Urban Institute Center on Nonprofits and Philanthropy, 1999); David O'Reilly, "Urban Study Affirms Value of Religious Congregations," *Philadelphia Inquirer*, 31 October 1997; Diane Cohen and A. Robert Jager, *Sacred Places at Risk: New Evidence on How Endangered Older Churches and Synagogues Service Communities* (Philadelphia: Partners for Sacred Places, 1977), 14. Calculations are from Hodgkinson, Weitzman, et al., *Nonprofit Almanac; 1996–1997*, 175–76, 209–11, table 4.17.

47. Davis, "Social Needs Overwhelming Catholic Charities"; George M. Anderson, "Catholic Charities and the Poor: An Interview with Fred Kammer, President of Catholic Charities USA," *America* 177, 4 (16 August 1997): 9.

48. John J. DiIulio, Jr., "The Church and the 'Civil Society Sector,'" *Brookings Review* 15, 4 (Fall 1997): 27–35; Brent B. Coffin, "Charitable Choice: Faith-Based Organizations Furthering or Countering Inequality?" (Harvard University Divinity School, Center for the Study of Values in Public Life, 1999); Dennis R. Hoover, "Yes to Charitable Choice," *Nation*, 7–14 August 2000, 6–7, 28.

49. Isaac Kramnick and R. Laurence Moore, "Can the Churches Save the Cities? Faith-Based Services and the Constitution," *American Prospect* 35 (November–December 1997): 53.

50. Hoover, "Yes to Charitable Choice."

51. Kevin Sack, "Gore Backs Federal Money for Church Social Service Program," *New York Times*, 25 May 1999; Adam Clymer, "Filter Aid to Poor through Churches, Bush Urges," *New York Times*, 23 July 1999; Henry G. Cisneros, "Higher Ground: Faith Communities and Community Building," *Cityscape* (December 1996): 71–84.

52. Cisneros, "Higher Ground," 74.

53. Wendy Zoba Murray, "Separate and Equal: Boston Minister Eugene Rivers

Dreams of a Separate but Equal Society," *Christianity Today* 40, 2 (5 February 1996): 14; see also Joe Klein, "In God They Trust," *New Yorker*, 16 June 1997: 40–48; also Richard A. Kauffman, "Apostle to the City," *Christianity Today* 41, 3 (3 March 1997): 36.

54. Andres Tapias, "Soul Searching: How Is the Black Church Responding to the Urban Crisis?" *Christianity Today* 40, 3 (4 March 1996): 26.

55. Tapias, "Soul Searching."

56. Glen C. Loury and Linda Datcher Loury, "Not by Bread Alone: The Role of the African-American Church in Inner-City Development," *Brookings Review* 15, 1 (Winter 1997): 10–13; DiIulio, "The Church and the 'Civil Society Sector' "; Kramnick and Moore, "Can the Churches Save the Cities?" 50. One of the most important researchers on the impact of faith-based activities is Mark Chaves. See his "Religious Congregations and Welfare Reform: Who Will Take Advantage of 'Charitable Choice'?" *American Sociological Review* 64, 6 (December 1999): 836–47.

57. Cisneros, "Higher Ground," 74–75; Kramnick and Moore, "Can the Churches Save the Cities?" 47.

58. Coleman, "Under the Cross and the Flag"; Research and Policy Committee, *Rebuilding Inner-City Communities* (New York: Committee for Economic Development, 1995), 25. A particularly interesting and successful example of economic development blends community organizing with faith-based action. This is the work of the Industrial Areas Foundation, founded in the 1960s by Saul Alinsky. The IAF assembles church-based networks in cities. The most well known are COPS in San Antonio and the Nehemiah Homes project in East Brooklyn, New York. Jeremy Nowak, A. Robert Jager, J. Randall Cotton, and Catherine Goulet, *Religious Institutions and Community Renewal* (Philadelphia: Pew Charitable Trusts, December 1981), 70–71. The focus of IAF work on churches developed gradually and represented a significant departure from Alinsky's approach. Robert Fisher, *Let the People Decide: Neighborhood Organizing in America*, rev. ed. (New York: Twayne, 1994), 146–47, 191–97; Michael A. Fletcher, "Diverse Interfaith Group Finds a Common Voice," *Washington Post*, 22 June 1995; "Housing Project Launched," *B.C. Cycle, U.I.*, 23 February 1993; Suzanne Sataline, "Offering Neighborhood Hope," *Philadelphia Inquirer*, 7 August 1995.

59. Kramnick and Moore, "Can the Churches Save the Cities?" 52; Public Law 105-285 [S.2206], 27 October 1998 (Community Opportunities, Accountability, and Training and Educational Services Act of 1998); Coffin, "Charitable Choice."

60. National Commission on Philanthropy and Civic Renewal, *Giving Better, Giving Smarter*, 90–91.

61. AmeriCorps is one of three programs run by the Corporation for National Service, created by an act of Congress in 1993. The other two are Learn and Save America and National Senior Service Corps. AmeriCorps sends people of all ages and backgrounds into community service work. Currently, there are more than twenty thousand AmeriCorps members serving full- or part-time in more than 350 AmeriCorps programs nationwide. The program provides a living allowance and a postservice award to help with higher education or vocational training.

62. Todd S. Purdum, "Clinton, Bush, and Powell to Share Ideas about Volunteerism," *New York Times*, 25 January 1997; Steve Goldstein, "Sharing Vision on Summit," *Philadelphia Inquirer*, 25 January 1997; Andrea Knox, "Corporate Promises Are Pouring In," *Philadelphia Inquirer*, 13 April 1997; Jason DeParle, "Does Voluntarism Do Any Good?" *New York Times*, 26 April 1997.

63. Benjamm R. Barber, "Service Is Good, But When Is It Most Effective?" *Philadelphia Inquirer*, 20 April 1997. Social capital is a concept given prominence in the 1990s by the work of political scientist Robert Putnam. Within inner cities, in this argument, the erosion of social capital, along with the attenuation of civil society, has compounded the effects of poverty by weakening initiative and reinforcing passivity and dependence. G. Thomas Kinsley and James O. Gibson, "Civil Society, the Public Sector, and Poor Communities," *Future of the Public Sector Series,* no. 12 (Urban Institute, August 1997); Robert D. Putnam, *Making Democracy Work: Civic Traditions in Modern Italy* (Princeton: Princeton University Press, 1993); John Kretzman and John L. McKnight, *Building Communities from the Inside Out: A Path toward Finding and Mobilizing a Community's Assets* (Evanston, IL: Center for Urban Affairs and Policy Research, Northwestern University, 1993).

64. Robert A. Rankin, "With Volunteerism Push, a Warning It Has Limits," *Philadelphia Inquirer*, 4 February 1997; Dick Polman, "For Summit, Parties Rush toward Middle," *Philadelphia Inquirer*, 16 April 1997; DeParle, "Does Voluntarism Do Any Good?"; David O'Reilly, "The Presidents' Summit: Religious Leaders Skeptical," *Philadelphia Inquirer*, 26 April 1997.

65. See sources in note 62.

66. Henry J. Holcomb, "Volunteerism in Area Thrives," *Philadelphia Inquirer*, 26 April 1998. For less rosy views see Karen E. Quinones Miller, "Stepping In and Stepping Up: A Year after the Summit, a West Philadelphia Drill Team Is Waiting for Promised Help," *Philadelphia Inquirer*, 26 April 1998; Gwen Florio, "A Year Later, Few Gains for Colorado Volunteerism," *Philadelphia Inquirer*, 27 April 1998; Knox, "Corporate Promises Are Pouring In"; Marc Kaufman, "2,000 Delegates, but the Big Names Take Center Stage," *Philadelphia Inquirer*, 27 April 1997; James Bennet, "Leaders Paint Picture of Need for Voluntarism," *New York Times*, 28 April 1997; Marc Kaufman, "Summit's Plea: Help a Child," *Philadelphia Inquirer*, 29 April 1997; Marc Kaufman, "A Spotty Summit Graffiti Cleanup," *Philadelphia Inquirer,* 4 May 1997; Dick Polman, "Seeing 'a Civil Society' beyond the Summit," *Philadelphia Inquirer*, 4 May 1997; Judith Miller, "Push for Voluntarism Brings No Outpouring," *New York Times*, 23 September 1997; Murray Dubin, "A Year Later, Volunteer Spark Still Glows," *Philadelphia Inquirer*, 24 April 1998; Alexandra Zavis, "Powell Says Campaign Is Aiding Youth," *Philadelphia Inquirer*, 28 April 1998; Steve Goldstein, "Powell May Extend Youth Mission," *Philadelphia Inquirer*, 28 April 1998; "Promises to Keep," *Philadelphia Inquirer*, 27 April 1998; Reed Abelson, "Charity Led by General Powell Comes under Heavy Fire, Accused of Inflating Results," *New York Times*, 8 October 1999.

67. Nowak et al., *Religious Institutions and Community Renewal*, I-8-9; Alvis C. Vidal, *Rebuilding Communities: A National Study of Urban Community Development Corporations* (New York: New School for Social Research, Graduate School of Management and Urban Policy, Community Development Research Center, 1992), 34; Robert O. Zdenek, *Taking Hold: The Growth and Support of Community Development Corporations* (Washington, DC: National Congress for Community Economic Development, 1990), 2-6.

68. National Congress for Community Economic Development, *Tying It All Together* (Washington, DC: NCCED, 1995), 1, 19; Vidal, *Rebuilding Communities*, 87.

69. Zdenek, *Taking Hold*, 5-15.

70. Zdenek, *Taking Hold*, 7-8; Neal R. Peirce and Carol F. Steinbach, *Enterprising Communities: Community-Based Development in America, 1990* (Washington, DC: Council for Community-Based Development, 1990), 27-30.

71. Peirce and Steinbach, *Enterprising Communities*; 23; Zdenek, *Taking Hold*, 12.

72. Peirce and Steinbach, *Enterprising Communities*; 35, 41–61.

73. The involvement of nonprofits and social reformers in housing construction has a long history. See, for example, Eugenie Ladner Birch and Deborah S. Gardner, "The Seven-Percent Solution: A Review of Philanthropic Housing, 1870–1910," *Journal of Urban History* 7, 4 (August 1981) 403–38; Peter Dreier, "Philanthropy and the Housing Crisis: The Dilemmas of Private Charity and Public Policy," *Housing Policy Debate* 8, 1 (1997): 235–93; Peirce and Steinbach, *Enterprising Communities*; 17; National Congress for Community Economic Development, *Tying It All Together*, 9–13.

74. Nowak, *Religious Institutions and Community Renewal*, 1–9.

75. For a discussion that emphasizes the oppositional character of CDCs, see Tony Robinson, "Inner-City Innovator: The Non-Profit Community Development Corporation," *Urban Studies* 33, 9 (November 1996): 1647; Fisher, *Let the People Decide*, 181.

76. Peirce and Steinbach, *Enterprising Communities*, 33.

77. Jeremy Nowak, "Neighborhood Initiative and the Regional Economy," *Economic Development Quarterly* 11, 1 (February 1997): 3–10.

78. Norman J. Glickman and Lisa J. Servon, *More Than Bricks and Sticks: What Is Community Development 'Capacity'?* (New Brunswick, NJ: Rutgers University, Center for Urban Policy Research, September 1997), 4.

79. Randy Stoecker, "The CDC Model of Urban Redevelopment: A Critique and an Alternative," *Journal of Urban Affairs* 19, 1 (1997): 1–22; Rachel G. Bratt, "CDCs: Contributions Outweigh Contradictions: A Reply to Randy Stoecker," *Journal of Urban Affairs* 19, 1 (1997) 23–38; see also W. Dennis Keating, "The CDC Model of Urban Development: A Reply to Randy Stoecker," and Randy Stoecker, "Should We . . . Could We . . . Change the CDC Model? A Rejoinder," *Journal of Urban Affairs* 19, 1(1997): 29–33, 35–44.

80. Peirce and Steinbach, *Enterprising Communities*, 12.

CHAPTER 7: THE PRIVATE WELFARE STATE AND THE END
OF PATERNALISM

1. Steven A. Sass, *The Promise of Private Pensions: The First Hundred Years* (Cambridge: Harvard University Press, 1997), 6–17, 54; Jill Quadagno, *The Transformation of Old Age Security: Class and Politics in the American Welfare State* (Chicago: University of Chicago Press, 1988), 80–85; William Graebner, *A History of Retirement: The Meaning and Function of an American Institution, 1885–1978* (New Haven: Yale University Press, 1980), 91–93; Teresa Ghilarducci, *Labor's Capital: The Economics and Politics of Private Pensions* (Cambridge: MIT Press, 1992), 9–24.

2. Sass, *The Promise of Private Pensions*, 54–55.

3. This paragraph is based on the sources in note 1. See also Christopher Howard, *The Hidden Welfare State: Tax Expenditures and Social Policy in the United States* (Princeton: Princeton University Press, 1997), 61–62.

4. Howard, *The Hidden Welfare State*, 61–62; Andrea Tone, *The Business of Benevolence: Industrial Paternalism in Progressive America* (Ithaca: Cornell University Press, 1997), 1–15; Daniel Nelson, *Managers and Workers: Origins of the New Factory System in the United States* (Madison: University of Wisconsin Press, 1975), 91–95, 117–18; Edward Berkowitz and Kim McQuaid, *Creating the Welfare State:*

The Political Economy of Twentieth-Century Reform, 2d ed. (New York: Praeger, 1988), 4–11; Stanley Buder, *Pullman: An Experiment in Industrial Order and Community Planning, 1880–1930* (New York: Oxford University Press, 1967); Stuart D. Brandes, *American Welfare Capitalism, 1880–1940* (Chicago: University of Chicago Press, 1976), 23–32; David Brody, *Workers in Industrial America: Essays on the Twentieth-Century Struggle* (New York: Oxford University Press, 1980), 54–74.

5. Tone, *Business of Benevolence*, 141–44.

6. Tone, *Business of Benevolence*, 244. See references for note 7.

7. Brody, *Workers in Industrial America*, 59, 61, 74; Brandes, *American Welfare Capitalism*, 138; Gerald Zahavi, "Negotiated Loyalty: Welfare Capitalism and the Shoeworkers of Endicott Johnson, 1920–1940," *Journal of American History* 71, 3 (December 1983): 602–20; Lizabeth Cohen, *Making a New Deal: Industrial Workers in Chicago, 1919–1939* (New York: Cambridge University Press, 1990), 209, 246, 249; Stanford M. Jacoby, *Modern Manors: Welfare Capitalism since the New Deal* (Princeton: Princeton University Press, 1997), 31–32; Tone, *Business of Benevolence*, 209.

8. Jacoby, *Modern Manors*, 5.

9. Frank R. Dobbin, "The Origins of Private Social Insurance: Public Policy and Fringe Benefits in America, 1920–1950," *American Journal of Sociology* 97, 5 (March 1992): 1424; Bartholomew H. Sparrow, *From the Outside In: World War II and the American State* (Princeton: Princeton University Press, 1996), 49–52; Sass, *The Promise of Private Pensions*, 90.

10. Sass, *The Promise of Private Pensions*, 67–76, is an excellent discussion of the early important role of insurance companies. The integration of pensions with Social Security was permitted by legislation in 1942. The result has worked against the interests of low-income workers by capping their potential retirement incomes. Patricia E. Dilley, "The Evolution of Entitlement: Retirement Income and the Problem of Integrating Private Pensions and Social Security," *Loyola of Los Angeles Law Review* 30 (April 1997): 1063–1198; Dobbin, "The Origins of Private Social Insurance," 1432–44; Beth Stevens, "Labor Unions, Employee Benefits, and the Privatization of the American Welfare State," *Journal of Policy History* 2, (1990) 233–60. See also Beth Stevens, "Blurring the Boundaries: How the Federal Government Has Influenced Welfare Benefits in the Private Sector," in *The Politics of Social Policy in the United States*, ed. Margaret Weir, Ann Shola Orloff, and Theda Skocpol (Princeton: Princeton University Press, 1988), 123–48; Marilyn J. Field and Harold T. Shapiro, eds., *Employment and Health Benefits: A Connection at Risk* (Washington, DC: National Academy Press, 1993), 52.

11. Dobbin, "The Origins of Private Social Insurance," 1434–45; Stevens, "Labor Unions, Employee Benefits, and the Privatization of the American Welfare State," 236–54; Sass, *The Promise of Private Pensions*, 99–100.

12. Ghilarducci, *Labor's Capital*, 16.

13. Section 23 (p) of the 1942 Revenue Act; Sass, *The Promise of Private Pensions*, 108–11, 144–78, 184–85.

14. Howard, *The Hidden Welfare State*, 123; Nelson Lichtenstein, "Labor in the Truman Era: Origins of the Private Welfare State," in *The Truman Presidency*, ed. Michael J. Lacey (New York: Cambridge University Press, 1989), 153–54. See also Hugh Mosley, "Corporate Social Benefits and the Underdevelopment of the American Welfare State," *Contemporary Crises* 5 (1981): 139–54; Stevens, "Labor Unions, Employee Benefits, and the Privatization of the American Welfare State,"

254; Charles Noble, *Welfare As We Knew It: A Political History of the American Welfare State* (New York: Oxford University Press, 1997), 85.

15. Lichtenstein, "Labor in the Truman Era"; Noble, *Welfare As We Knew It*, 88.

16. Stevens, "Blurring the Boundaries," 126.

17. *1997 Hay Benefit Report* (HayGroup), executive summary, x–3.

18. Gregory Acs and Eugene Steuerle, "The Corporation as a Dispenser of Welfare and Security," in *The American Corporation Today*, ed. Carl Kaysen (New York: Oxford University Press, 1996), 368; Celia Silverman, Carolyn Pemberton, and Deborah Holmes, *EBRI Databook on Employee Benefits*, 3d ed. (Washington, DC: Employee Benefit Research Institute, 1995), 15, 18; Ken McDonnell, Paul Fronstin, Kelly Olsen, Pamela Ostuw, Jack VanDerher, and Paul Yakoboski, *EBRI Databook on Employee Benefits*, 4th ed. (Washington, DC: Employee Benefit Research Institute, 1997), 9–10, 100, 106; David M. Walker, "Testimony before House Ways and Means Committee Re: Savings and Investment," Federal News Service, 1 February 1995.

19. *Fundamentals of Employee Benefit Programs*, 5th ed. (Washington, DC: Employee Benefit Research Institute, 1997), 3. On the provisions and significance of ERISA, see Sass, *The Promise of Private Pensions*, 219–26.

20. *Fundamentals of Employee Benefit Programs*, 35–36, 439. *EBRI Databook on Employee Benefits*, 4th ed., 503–10, contains a useful summary of federal legislation concerning employee benefits. Daniel J. B. Mitchell, "Social Insurance and Benefits," in *Research Frontiers in Industrial Relations and Human Resources*, ed. David Lewin, Olivia S. Mitchell, and Peter D. Sherer (Madison, WI: Industrial Relations Research Association, 1992), 593; Howard, *The Hidden Welfare State*, 37.

21. Ghilarducci, *Labor's Capital*, 23; Mitchell, "Social Insurance," 593–94; Howard, *The Hidden Welfare State*, 132.

22. Graebner, *A History of Retirement*; Jacoby, *Modern Manors*. "Vesting: a process in a qualified retirement plan where participants earn a nonforfeitable right to accrued benefits (under a defined benefit plan) or account balances (under a defined contribution plan) by completion of years of service as specified under the plan's vesting provisions. Nonvested benefits are forfeited by participants on separation from service. Employee contributions are immediately vested." *EBRI Databook on Employee Benefits*, 4th ed., 517; Mitchell, "Social Insurance," 593–94; Marilyn J. Field and Harold T. Shapiro, eds., *Employment and Health Benefits: A Connection at Risk* (Washington, DC: National Academy Press, 1993), 85.

23. *1997 Hay Benefit Report*, 2, 5, 9.

24. The statistics represent "private-sector wage and salary workers age 18–64, with at least 20 weekly hours and 26 weeks of work." Lawrence Mishel, Jared Bernstein, and John Schmitt, *The State of Working America, 1996–1997* (Armonk, NY: M. E. Sharpe, 1997), 159. See also U.S. Government General Accounting Office, *Employment-Based Health Insurance Cost Increases and Family Coverage Decreases*, GAO/HEHS-97-35, February 1997; Paul Fronstin, "Trends in Health Insurance Coverage," EBRI Issue Brief no. 185 (Employee Benefit Research Institute, May 1997); Mishel, Bernstein, and Schmitt, *State of Working America*, 160. For useful and detailed statistics on benefits, see also the relevant publications of the U.S. Bureau of Labor Statistics, especially *Employee Benefits in Small Private Establishments, 1994* (April 1996); *Employee Benefits in a Changing Economy: A BLS Chartbook* (September 1992); *Employee Benefits Survey: A BLS Reader* (February 1995); *Employee Benefits in State and Local Governments, 1994* (May 1996); *Employee Benefits in Medium and Large Private Establishments, 1993* (November 1994).

25. The figure for pensions refers to employers who sponsored a plan rather than employees participating in one. Not all employees participate in their employers' plans. Unless otherwise noted, statistics are from *EBRI Databook on Employee Benefits*, 4th ed., chaps. 10 and 27. Pension figures are for workers employed in nonagricultural occupations. Acs and Steuerle, "The Corporation," 476–77.
26. Mishel, Bernstein, and Schmitt, *Working America*, 199.
27. Acs and Steuerle, "The Corporation," 477.
28. Peter M. Kelly, "Downsizing and Other Related Workforce Trends: An Employee Benefit Perspective," *Benefits Quarterly* 11, 12 (Third Quarter 1996): 8–42; Dennis A. Toth, "After the UPS Strike: The Impact on Compensation and Benefits," *ACA News* (October 1997): 14; Bernstein, Mishel, and Schmitt, *Working America*, 258; Dallas Salisbury, Ken McDonnell, and Edina Rheem, "The Changing World of Work and Employee Benefits," EBRI Issue Brief no. 173 (Employee Benefit Research Institute, April 1996); Walker, "Testimony"; Mitchell, "Social Insurance," 594.
29. For examples see: Bill Jacobs, "Deere and Co., UWA Illustrate Big Labor Questions of the '90s," *Quad City Times*, 18 October 1994; Rebecca Kuzins, "Unions, Marriott Disagree over Health Benefits," *Business Journal-Sacramento*, 5 June 1995; Ghilarducci, *Labor's Capital: The Economics and Politics of Private Pensions*, 23; Linda A. Bell, "Union Wage Concessions in the 1980s: The Importance of Firm-Specific Factors," *Industrial and Labor Relations Review* 8, 2 (1995): 58; Christopher R. Conte, "Retirement Prospects in a Defined Contribution World: A Report on EBRI's April 30, 1997, Policy Forum," in *Retirement Contributions in a Defined Contribution World*, ed. Dallas L. Salisbury (Washington, DC: Employee Benefit Research Institute, 1997), 6.
30. Barry B. Burr, "UAW-Ford Pact Has Retiree Inflation Link," *Pensions and Investments* 30 (September 1996): 6; Keith Bradsher "U.A.W.'s Pact at Ford Aims at Downsizing," *New York Times*, 18 September 1996; David Cay Johnston, "Pension Concerns Move to the Picket Line," *New York Times*, 10 August 1997; "Labor Unrest: Strike May Signal Return of a More Balanced Playing Field," *Pittsburgh Post-Gazette*, 5 August 1997; "All Things Considered," National Public Radio, 5 August 1997. For a good discussion of the UPS issues see Sandra Livingston, "UPS, Teamsters in Tug-of-War over Control of Pension Plan," *Cleveland Plain Dealer*, 17 August 1997; see also Bureau of National Affairs, "Teamsters Claim Victory over UPS on Health Coverage, Pension Control," *Pension and Benefits Reporter* 24, 34 (25 August 1997): 1983–84; "BNA Surveys Employers on 1997 Aims for Pensions, Other Employee Benefits," *BNA Pension and Benefits Reporter*, 2 December 1996; Steven Greenhouse, "Labor, Revitalized with New Recruiting, Has Regained Power and Prestige," *New York Times*, 9 October 1999.
31. U.S. General Accounting Office, *Employment-Based Health Insurance: Cost Increase and Family Coverage Decrease*, February 1997, GAO/HEHS-97-35, 2; *EBRI Databook on Employee Benefits*, 4th ed., 13; "Group Health Covers Most Americans, Takes Large Piece of Compensation Pie," *BNA Management Briefing*, 29 August 1995; Robert Pear, "6-Month Rule Set on Mental Health Insurance," *New York Times*, 16 December 1997.
32. *EBRI Databook on Employee Benefits*, 3d ed., 7–10; Salisbury, McDonnell, and Rheem, "Changing World of Work"; John A. Turner, "Facing the Inevitable: Demographics and Retirement Income," *Benefits Quarterly* 12, 3 (Third Quarter, 1996): 58–62; David Hale, "How the Rise of Pension Funds Will Change the Global Economy in the 21st Century," in *The Coming of the Global Pension Crisis*,

comp. Council on Foreign Relations, New York City, 15–16 November 1996, 86–89; John H. Briggs, "Implications of Demographic Change for the Design of Retirement Programs," Working Paper ser. 91-5 (University of Pennsylvania, Wharton School, May 1995); "Employment Benefits, Retirement Patterns, and Implications for Increased Work Life," EBRI Issue Brief no. 184 (Employee Benefit Research Institute, April 1997).

33. Salisbury, McDonnell, and Rheem, "Changing World of Work"; Jerry Geisel, "EBRI Execs See Silver Lining Here, Others See Dark Clouds," *Business Insurance*, 15 May 1995, 12. See also Anna M. Rappaport, "The New Employment Contract and Employee Benefits: A Road Map for the Future," *ACS Journal* (Summer 1997): 7; Andrew Cassel, "The New Rules of Employment," *Philadelphia Inquirer*, 9 July 1999.

34. *EBRI Databook on Employee Benefits*, 3d ed., 704.

35. Conte, "Retirement Prospects," 2–3.

36. *1997 Hay Benefit Report*, 8; Kelly Olsen and Jack VanDerhei, "Defined Contribution Plan Dominance Grows Across Sectors and Employer Sizes, While Mega Defined Benefit Plans Remain Strong: Where We Are and Where We Are Going," EBRI Special Report SR-33 and EBRI Issue Brief, No. 190 (Employee Benefit Research Institute, October 1997), 18.

37. Olsen and VanDerhei, "Defined Contribution Plan," 3; "EBRI Hybrid Sponsor Survey Results: Full Report" (MS, n.d.); Margaret Boitano, "Revised Pension Plans Suit Younger Workers," *Philadelphia Inquirer*, 23 August 1998. By 1999, problems with these cash-balance plans surfaced and prompted calls for legislation. Albert B. Crenshaw, "Debate on Capitol Hill over Pension Plans," *Philadelphia Inquirer*, 25 July 1999; Richard A. Oppel, Jr., "Cash-Balance Pension Plans under Scrutiny by Tax Agency," *New York Times*, 17 September 1999; Richard A. Oppel, Jr., "Clinton Seeks Disclosure Rules on Changes to Pension Plans," *New York Times*, 14 July 1999.

38. James S. Ray, "Employee Benefits and Labor Law Reform," in *EBRI-ERF Policy Forum: Business, Work, and Benefits* (Washington, DC: Employee Benefit Research Institute, 1989), 267–70; "Remarks of Robert A. Georgine, President, Building and Construction Trades Department, AFL-CIO," EBRI Policy Forum, 4 May 1988, mimeo; Johnston, "Pension Concerns."

39. "Contribution Rates and Plan Features: An Analysis of Large 401(k) Plan Data," EBRI Issue Brief no. 174 (June 1996), 3, 12; "Workers Investment Decisions: An Analysis of Large 401(k) Plan Data," EBRI Issue Brief no. 176 (August 1996).

40. Paul Fronstin, Testimony before House Ways and Means Committee on Medicare Revisions, 19 May 1995, *Health Line; EBRI Databook on Employee Benefits*, 4th ed., 241, 256; *1997 Hay Benefit Report*, 1.

41. *EBRI Databook on Employee Benefits*, 4th ed., 211; "Employment-Based Health Insurance and the Changing Workforce," *EBRI Education and Research Fund Monthly Newsletter* 18, 6 (June 1997): 2–3; Paul Fronstin and Sarah C. Snider, "An Examination of the Decline in Employment-Based Health Insurance between 1988 and 1993," *Inquiry* 33 (Winter 1996–97): 317–25.

42. "Employee Benefits, Retirement Patterns," 19; *EBRI Databook on Employee Benefits*, 4th ed., 308.

43. Frank Swoboda and Albert Crenshaw, "Court Says GM Can Cut Benefits," *Washington Post*, 9 January 1998; Stephen Franklin, "Justices Shun GM Retirees' Appeal," *Chicago Tribune*, 9 June 1998.

44. See source for note 38.

45. Randolph Wayne, "The Ongoing Revolution in Benefits Administration: The Forces of Change Unleashed," *Benefits Quarterly* 11, 4 (Fourth Quarter 1995): 41–47; Buck Consultants, "Buck Survey: Outsourcing of Human Resource and Employee Benefit Function to Increase," news release, New York, 26 June 1996.
46. Wendy Rhodes, "Separation Anxiety: Will You Lose Touch with Employees by Outsourcing?" *Benefits Quarterly* 13, 1 (First Quarter 1997): 21–26.
47. Jason Jeffay, Stephen Bohannon, and Esther K. Laspia, "Beyond Benefits: The Changing Face of HR Outsourcing," *Benefits Quarterly* 13, 1 (First Quarter 1997): 41–46; Bureau of National Affairs, "Employers Groping for Answers to Outsourcing, Benefit Costs," Special Report no. 16, June 1997; Lynn Brenner, "The Disappearing HR Department: Reengineering Human Resources," *CFO* (March 1996): 61–64.
48. The discussion of Southwestern Bell is based on Cassandra Carr, "Changes in the Employment Climate at SBC Corporation," paper presented at "The Changing World of Work and Employee Benefits," a policy forum sponsored by the Employee Benefit Research Institute, 7 December 1995.
49. This discussion of DuPont is based on Steven A. Harrison, "The Changing World of Work and Employee Benefits: DuPont Experience," paper presented at "The Changing World of Work and Employee Benefits," a policy forum sponsored by the Employee Benefit Research Institute, 7 December 1995.
50. The discussion of Mead is based on Charles A. Mazza, "Changes in the Employment Climate: Mead Case Study," paper presented at "The Changing World of Work and Employee Benefits," a policy forum sponsored by the Employee Benefit Research Institute, 7 December 1995, and the transcript of Mazza's remarks.

CHAPTER 8: INCREASED RISKS FOR THE INJURED, DISABLED, AND UNEMPLOYED

1. All risks, historian Paul Johnson points out, fall into one of four categories: "health, life-cycle stage, economy, and environment." The "strategies adopted to accommodate these risks . . . form the welfare structures of any society." Paul Johnson, "Private and Public Social Welfare in Britain, 1870–1939," in *The Mixed Economy of Social Welfare: Public/Private Relations in England, Germany and the United States, the 1870s to the 1930s,* ed. Michael B. Katz and Christoph Sachsse (Baden-Baden: Nomos, 1996), 31.
2. Tom Baker, "On the Genealogy of Moral Hazard," *Texas Law Review* 75, 237, (December 1996).
3. Baker, "Genealogy."
4. For a comprehensive introduction to workers' compensation, see Edward M. Welch, *Employer's Guide to Workers' Compensation* (Washington, DC: Bureau of National Affairs, 1994). A useful overview is in the *1996 Green Book,* 945–50. For a list of machine-readable sources, see Fay Hansen, "Where to Find Compensation and Benefits Sources on the Web," *Compensation and Benefits Review* 4, 29 (17 July 1997), 16. For an outstanding analysis of the assumptions underlying workers' compensation, see Martha T. McCluskey, "The Illusion of Efficiency in Workers' Compensation 'Reform,' " *Rutgers Law Review* 50, 3 (Spring 1998): 657–941; Emily A. Spieler, "Perpetuating Risk? Workers' Compensation and the Persistence of Occupational Injuries," *Houston Law Review* 31, 119 (Summer 1994): 170. For a stinging criticism of the no-fault system, see also Lawrence White, *Human Debris* (New York: Seaview/Putnam, 1983).

5. For statistics on the cost of workers' compensation over time, including the $43 trillion figure, see *EBRI Databook*, 4th ed. (Washington: Employee Benefit Research Institute, 1997), 421–22; Kathleen M. Rest, Charles Levenstein, and James Ellenberger, "A Call for Worker-Centered Research in Workers' Compensation," *New Solutions* (Spring 1995): 72.

6. James Weinstein, "Big Business and the Origins of Workmen's Compensation," *Labor History* 8, 2 (Spring 1967): 157–58; Carl Gersuny, *Work Hazards and Industrial Conflict* (Hanover, NH: University Press of New England, 1981), 20, 28; Roy Lubove, *The Struggle for Social Security, 1900–1935* (Cambridge: Harvard University Press, 1968), 49–64; Edward Berkowitz and Kim McQuaid, *Creating the Welfare State: The Political Economy of Twentieth-Century Reform* (New York: Praeger, 1980), 33–41; Theda Skocpol, *Protecting Soldiers and Mothers: The Political Origins of Social Policy in the United States* (Cambridge: Harvard University Press, 1992), 293–99.

7. Quoted in Michael B. Katz, *In the Shadow of the Poorhouse: A Social History of Welfare in America*, 10th anniversary ed. (New York: Basic Books, 1997), 198.

8. Paul B. Bellamy, *A History of Workmen's Compensation, 1898–1915: From Courtroom to Boardroom* (New York: Garland Publishing, 1997), 170.

9. *The Report of the National Commission on State Workmen's Compensation Laws* (Washington, DC: July 1972), 15–17; Price V. Fishback and Shawn Everett Kantor, "Did Workers Pay for the Passage of Workers' Compensation Laws?" National Bureau of Economic Research Working Paper no. 4947 (December 1994).

10. Spieler, "Perpetuating Risk?" 179; *Annual Supplement to 1994 Analysis of Workers' Compensation Laws* (U.S. Chamber of Commerce, 1994), 13–15.

11. *Report of the National Commission, passim.*

12. *EBRI Databook*, 4th ed. 422; Ruth Gaskell, ed., "Workers' Compensation," in *Insurance Issues Update* (Insurance Information Institute, November 1997), 3; National Conference of State Legislatures, *The State of Workers' Compensation*, (January 1994), vii.

13. *Workers' Compensation: A Resource Manual from the AFL-CIO* [n.d.], 12; *EBRI Databook*, 4th ed., 422; Gaskell, "Workers' Compensation"; Spieler, "Perpetuating Risk?" 134, 139, 150.

14. On the rise in costs, see McCluskey, "Illusion of Efficiency," 683–90; "Drop in Workers' Compensation Has Helped Reduce Costs of Risk," *Solutions* (July–August 1996): 10; Tina Royter, "Injured on Duty," *Plan Sponsor* (June 1996): 39, 42, 52; Fay Hansen, "Who Gets Hurt and How Much Does It Cost? Workplace Injuries," *Compensation and Benefits Review* 3, 29 (May 1997): 6; Spieler, "Perpetuating Risk?" 117, 119, 145.

15. Spieler, "Perpetuating Risk?" 216, 226–27. The greater number of claims filed in union than in comparable nonunion workplaces supports the argument that a sense of job security encourages workers to file workers' compensation claims.

16. Rest, Levenstein, and Ellenberger, "A Call," 72; Mary Fricker, "Insult to Injury: Workers Compensation" *(Santa Rosa) Press Democrat*, 7–10 December 1997; John G. Kilgour, "California's Experience: Addressing Workers' Compensation Fraud and Abuse," *Compensation and Benefits Review* 29, 3 (May 1997): 44. Kilgour's numbers come from Gary T. Schwartz, "Waste, Fraud, and Abuse in Workers' Compensation: The Recent California Experience," *Maryland Law Review* 52: 987. Kilgour recounts the successful attempt to curb fraud and abuse in California in the early 1990s. For a statement discounting the importance of fraud in workers' compensation costs, see, e.g., Meg Fletcher, "Face of Workers Comp to Change

Significantly in Next Decade," *Business Insurance*, 17 March 1997, 2, 54; McCluskey, "Illusion of Efficiency," 874–93; CAPR: The Compensation and Prevention Research Institute, "Fraud in the Workers' Compensation System: How Much Is There and Who Is Responsible" (mimeo, n.d.); Spieler, "Perpetuating Risk?" 216.

17. Baker, "Genealogy," 276, 279, 280, 283.
18. *AFL-CIO Resource Manual*, 23; Rachel Kaganoff Stern, Mark A. Peterson, and Mary E. Vaiana, *Findings and Recommendations on California's Permanent and Partial Disability System: Executive Summary* (Santa Monica, CA: Rand Corporation Institute for Civil Justice, 1997). For particularly egregious examples of delays, see David Cay Johnston, "Paralyzed since the Fall in 1962, Man Still Seeking Benefits," *New York Times*, 5 May 1997; and White, *Human Debris*.
19. Gaskell, "Workers' Compensation," 3; "New Academy Study Shows Benefits Decline in Workers' Compensation," *Social Insurance Update* 11, 3 (2000): 1, 7.
20. "Workers' Compensation: Back from the Brink? The Power of Specialists" (Conning and Company, 1994), 9, 48; *Reality Testing: Assessing the Performance of Workers Compensation Cost-Management Initiatives*, Tillinghast-Towers Perrin, 3d Biennial Survey (1995), 3, 9, 11; Kelly Ossewaarde, "Workers' Compensation Costs Continue to Drop," *Solutions* (June 1997): 20–22; Gaskell, "Workers' Compensation"; "Back from the Brink?" 48; Royter, "Injured on Duty," 43; Robert Kazel, "Unions Reject Managed Care in Comp," *Business Insurance* (17 October 1996): 34; CAPRI: The Compensation and Prevention Research Institute, "Workers' Compensation Managed Care: Proceed with Caution" (mimeo, n.d.); *AFL-CIO Resource Manual*, 50; James N. Ellenberger, "Comment," in *Disability: Challenges for Social Insurance, Health Care Financing, and Labor Market Policy*, ed. Virginia P. Reno, Jerry L. Mashaw, Bill Gradison (Washington DC: National Academy of Social Insurance, 1997), 156; Valerie Peters, "Workers' Compensation: Under New Management," *Solutions* (September 1996): 22–24; "State of Workers' Compensation," 21; Spieler, "Perpetuating Risk?" 249.
21. William Molmen and Thomas Parry, "Integrating Employee Benefits: Giving Up the Moat Mentality," *Compensation and Benefits Review* 3, 29 (May 1997): 31; Gaskell, "Workers' Compensation."
22. Spieler, "Perpetuating Risk?" 47. Spieler notes that official Bureau of Labor Statistics figures undercounted workplace injury and occupational illness (84). Hansen, "Who Gets Hurt"; Alan B. Kruger, "Fewer Workplace Injuries and Illnesses Adding to Economic Strength," *New York Times*, 14 September 2000.
23. Fricker, "Insult to Injury," 6.
24. Gaskell, "Workers' Compensation"; Spieler, "Perpetuating Risk?" 160, 161, 243–44, 249.
25. John F. Burton, Jr., Florence Blum, and Elizabeth H. Yates, "Workers' Compensation Benefits Continue to Decline," *John Burton's Workers' Compensation Monitor*, 10, 4 (July/August 1997): 8; Gaskell, "Workers' Compensation." Looked at another way, the insurance carriers' profitability ratios increased 5.1 percent in 1992, 11.9 percent in 1993, and 6.4 percent in 1994. Burton, Blum, and Yates, "Workers' Compensation Benefits," 7; Royter, "Injured on Duty," 40; "The Impact of Oregon's Cost Containment Program," Workers' Compensation Research Institute Research Brief, Vol. 12, no. 2 (February 1996), table C; Spieler, "Perpetuating Risk?" 157; Robert Hartwig, "Riding the Economic Cycles: How Growth and Recession Affect Workers' Compensation," *Compensation and Benefits Review* 29, 3 (May 1997): 12.

26. "Impact of Oregon's Cost Containment Program." Unless otherwise noted, the discussion of Oregon in the following paragraphs is based on this research brief. Spieler, "Perpetuating Risk?" 243; Steven Hecker, Patricia A. Gwartney, and Amy E. Barlow, *Declining Occupational Injury Rates in Oregon: A Preliminary Investigation of Variables, Data Sources, and Directions for Research* (University of Oregon, Labor Education Research Center and Oregon Survey Research Laboratory, July 1995); "The 1991 Reforms in Massachusetts: An Assessment of Impact," Workers' Compensation Research Institute Research Brief, vol. 12, no. 5 (May 1996).

27. Thomas Suddes and Benjamin Marrison, "House GOP Pushes through Workers' Comp Reform Bill," *Cleveland Plain Dealer*, 17 April 1997; Marcia Pledger, "Coalition Seeks Referendum to Overturn Comp Reform," *Plain Dealer*, 26 April 1997; Tom Ford, "Battle Looming in the Fall," *Crain's Cleveland Business*, 30 June 1997.

28. Robert Weissman, "Bad Claims on Workers' Comp," *Nation*, 10 November 1997, 25; Mark Tatge, "Workers' Comp Battle Threatens to Be Ugly," *Plain Dealer*, 9 October 1997.

29. Andrew Doehrel, "Does Workers' Comp Reform Target Waste or Workers?" *Cincinnati Enquirer*, 22 October 1997; "State Wrap-Up 1997: Action in the Legislatures: Workers' Comp Stable," *Business Insurance*, 30 June 1997, 12; Tom Ford, "Business Groups Unite in Workers' Comp Fight," *Crain's Cleveland Business*, 11 August 1997, 3; Meg Fletcher, "Ballot Battle in Ohio," *Business Insurance*, 8 September 1997; Alan Johnson, "State Looks to Reduce Carpal Tunnel Claims," *Crain's Cleveland Business*, 15 September 1997, 13; Tom Ford, "Issue 2 Ads Elicit Lawyers' Wrath," *Crain's Cleveland Business*, 6 October 1997, 2; Mark Tatge, "Voters Have Final Say on Workers' Comp Law; Changes Target Carpal Tunnel Syndrome," *Plain Dealer*, 30 October 1997; Weissman, "Bad Claims," 22–26. The AFL-CIO resource manual notes, "Both the AMA and the National Commission on State Workmen's Compensation Laws urged states not to use the *Guides* to determine the extent of **disability** (an **economic** consequence of an injury), but rather to limit their use to extent of **impairment** (a **medical** consequence of an injury.)" The language in the AMA *Guides* is very clear: "The accurate and proper use of medical information to assess impairment in connection with disability determinations depends on the recognition that, whereas impairment is a medical matter, disability arises out of the interaction between impairment and external demands. Consequently, as used in the *Guides*, 'impairment' means an alteration of an individual's health status that is assessed by medical means; 'disability,' which is assessed by nonmedical means, means an alteration of an individual's capacity to meet personal, social, or occupational demands, or to meet statutory or regulatory requirements. Simply stated, 'impairment' is what is wrong with the individuals; 'disability' is the gap between what the individual can do and what the individual needs or wants to do." Quoted in *AFL-CIO Resource Manual*, 41–42; Weissman, "Bad Claims," 25.

30. Weissman, "Bad Claims," 25; "State Wrap-Up 1997"; Michael Hawthorne, "Battle over Workers' Comp Law Is Clash of Titans," *Cincinnati Enquirer*, 30 September 1997.

31. "Statewide Coalition Reaffirms Commitment to Workers' Compensation," *PR Newswire*, 21 July 1997.

32. Doehrel, "Does Workers' Comp Reform Target Waste or Workers?"; Hawthorne, "Battle over Workers' Comp Law"; Tom Ford, "Business Groups Unite in Workers' Comp Fight," *Crain's Cleveland Business*, 11 August 1997; Alan Johnson,

"Business, Labor Spend Big on Issue 2," *Columbus Dispatch*, 24 October 1997; "Predictable Propaganda," *Plain Dealer*, 28 July 1997.

33. McCluskey, "Illusion of Efficiency," 914, 918, 940.

34. Johnson, "Business, Labor Spend Big"; Sandra Livingston, "Labor Takes Its Message Directly to Voters," *Plain Dealer*, 27 July 1977; Weissman, "Bad Claims," 22.

35. Elizabeth Auster, "Voinovich, Clinton Fail to Sell Nervous Workers," *Plain Dealer*, 13 November 1997. On the referendum see also Mary Beth Lane and Thomas Suddes, "Issue 2 Tests Clout of Unions, Democrats," *Plain Dealer*, 1 November 1997; Mark Tatge and Benjamin Marrison, "Overhaul of Workers' Comp Law Rejected," *Plain Dealer*, 5 November 1997; James Bradshaw, "Issue 2 Loses Decisively," *Columbus Dispatch*, 5 November 1997; Debra Jasper, "Labor Big Winner—or Not," *Dayton Daily News*, 6 November 1997; Sandy Theis and Michael Hawthorne, "Gentler Revision to Law Sought," *Cincinnati Enquirer*, 6 November 1997; Meg Fletcher, "Ohio Workers' Compensation Reforms Fail to Garner Voter Approval," *Business Insurance*, 10 November 1997, 1.

36. Deborah A. Stone, *The Disabled State* (Philadelphia: Temple University Press, 1984), 12–13, 21, 100–103. On the issues in disability insurance and its history, see also Matthew Diller, "Entitlement and Exclusion: The Role of Disability in the Social Welfare System," *UCLA Law Review* 44, (1996): 361–465.

37. Edward D. Berkowitz, *Disabled Policy: America's Programs for the Handicapped* (New York: Cambridge University Press, 1987), 4. Also very useful on the history of disability and its differences from other social insurance programs in America is Edward Berkowitz and Wendy Wolff, "Disability Insurance and the Limits of American History," *Public Historian* 8, 2 (Spring 1986): 65–82. An excellent account of the ADA is Edward Berkowitz, "George Bush and the Americans with Disability Act," in *The Bush Presidency, Part Two: Ten Intimate Perspectives of George Bush*, ed. Kenneth Thompson (Lanham, MD: Miller Center and University of Virginia Press, 1998), 131–48.

38. Berkowitz, *Disabled Policy*, 4–5. On the definitional problems in disability, see Monroe Berkowitz and Edward Berkowitz, "Labor Force Participation among the Disabled," *Labor Economics* 11 (1990): 181–200.

39. Stone, *Disabled State*, 24, italics in original.

40. Recall that Disability Insurance applies only to individuals under age sixty-five with enough covered work experience to be insured. Jerry L. Mashaw and Virginia P. Reno, eds., *Balancing Security and Opportunity: The Challenge of Disability Policy*, Report of the Disability Policy Panel (Washington, DC.: National Academy of Social Insurance, 1996), 59–60. Recall that SSI supports disabled persons who do not qualify for Disability Insurance. *1996 Green Book*, 17, 259–263, 292. For background, see Lenna Kennedy, "SSA Programs That Benefit Children," *Social Security Bulletin* 3, 59 (September 1996): 64.

41. Mashaw and Reno, *Balancing Security and Opportunity*, 60–62, 63, 67, 71. "Rising Disability Rolls Raise Questions That Must Be Answered," Statement of Jane L. Ross, Associate Director, Income Security Issues, Human Resources Division, before the House of Representatives, Committee on Ways and Means, Subcommittee on Social Security, 22 April 1993 (GAO/T-HRD-93-15).

42. Mashaw and Reno, *Balancing Security and Opportunity*, 63–67.

43. Mashaw and Reno, *Balancing Security and Opportunity*, 68–71.

44. Stone, *Disabled State*, 181–86.

45. Susan Gluck Mezey, *No Longer Disabled: The Federal Courts and the Politics of Social Security Disability* (Wesport, CT: Greewood Press, 1988), 60, 71; Martha

Derthick, *Agency under Stress: The Social Security Administration in American Government* (Washington, DC: Brookings Institution Press, 1990), 33–34; Donald E. Chambers, "The Reagan Administration's Welfare Retrenchment Policy: Terminating Social Security Benefits for the Disabled," *Policy Studies Review* 5, 2 (November 1985): 230.

46. Mezey, *No Longer Disabled*, 82; Derthick, *Agency under Stress*, 44.

47. Derthick, *Agency under Stress*, 145.

48. Mezey, *No Longer Disabled*, 82; Derthick, *Agency under Stress*, 211.

49. Mezey, *No Longer Disabled*, 121; Derthick, *Agency under Stress*, 140–141; Chambers, "Welfare Retrenchment," 237. The conflict between the SSA and the courts centered around the question of "nonacquiescence"—that is, the refusal of the agency to accept court decisions as precedents.

50. Mezey, *No Longer Disabled*, 148–68.

51. Jerry Mashaw, "Findings of the Disability Policy Panel," in Reno, Mashaw, and Gradison, *Disability*, 17–21.

52. U.S. General Accounting Office, Report to Congressional Committees, *Social Security: Disability Programs Lag in Promoting Return to Work*, March 1997; GAO/HEHS-97-46, p. 2. The report suggested learning from the experience of employers and other countries, notably Germany and Sweden. On the same issue, see Jane L. Ross, "Social Security Disability: Improving Return-to-Work Outcomes Important, but Trade-Offs and Challenges Exist," Testimony before the U.S. House of Representatives, Committee on Ways and Means, Subcommittee on Social Security, 23 July 1997, GAO/T-HEHS-97-186; U.S. General Accounting Office, Report to the Chairman, U.S. Senate, Special Committee on Aging, *SSA Disability: Program Redesign Necessary to Encourage Return to Work*, April 1996, GAO/HEHS-96-62; U.S. General Accounting Office, Report to the Chairman, U.S. Senate, Special Committee on Aging, *SSA Disability: Return-to-Work Strategies from Other Systems May Improve Federal Programs*, July 1996; GAO/HEHS-96-133; Mashaw, "Findings," 24; Monroe Berkowitz, "Linking Beneficiaries with Return-to-Work Services," in Reno, Mashaw, and Gradison, *Disability*, 41–46.

53. Heather MacDonald, "SSI Fosters Disabling Dependency," *Wall Street Journal*, 20 January 1995; Robert S. Stein, "Does Spending Cripple America? Disability Programs May Lure Many onto Dole," *Investor's Business Daily*, 5 October 1994, 19; *1996 Green Book*, 298–300; Dee Mukherjee, "New Drug Law Denies SSI, SSDI to Those with Alcoholism and Drug Addiction," NAMI (no date); *Social Security Disability Notes*, No. 17, Social Security Administration, Office of Disability, Pub. no. 64-040, 10 March 1997; Reese Erlich, "Study Tracks What Happened to Disabled People Who Were Eliminated from SSI in 1996," "Morning Edition," National Public Radio, 1999.

54. Jerry L. Mashaw, James M. Perrin, and Virginia P. Reno, eds., *Restructuring the SSI Disability Program for Children and Adolescents*, Report of the Committee on Childhood Disability of the Disability Policy Panel (Washington, DC: National Academy of Social Insurance, 1996), 2.

55. Consortium for Citizens with Disabilities, Testimony before the U.S. House Ways and Means Committee, Subcommittee on Human Resources. "Welfare Overhaul," 23 May 1996.

56. Christopher Georges, "A Media Crusade Gone Haywire," *Forbes Media Critics*, September 1995, 66–71; Molly Ivins, "Disabled Poor Kids Get No Help from Media," *Fort Worth Star-Telegram*, 19 September 1995.

57. Georges, "A Media Crusade," 67; Jocelyn Y. Stewart, "For Thousands of Chil-

dren, Aid Rides on a Definition," *Los Angeles Times*, 17 October 1996, quoted in MacDonald, "SSI Fosters Disabling Dependency."

58. Stewart, "For Thousands of Children"; Jane L. Ross, "Supplemental Security Income: Long-Standing Problems Put Program at Risk for Fraud, Waste, and Abuse," Testimony before the House of Representatives, Committee on Ways and Means, Subcommittee on Oversight, 4 March 1997, GAO/T-HEHS-97-88.

59. Pamela J. Loprest, "Supplemental Security Income for Children with Disabilities," Urban Institute, Issues Brief, ser. A, no. A-10, July 1997, 1-2; Cheryl Weitzstein, "103,000 Children Cut from SSI Rolls under New Policy," *Washington Times*, 25 August 1997. These less severe disabilities included: attention deficit, personality, mood, developmental/emotional, anxiety-related, developmental, learning, and organic mental disorders, as well as loss of voice and asthma.

60. Loprest, "Supplemental Security Income," 1; Stewart, "For Thousands of Children."

61. Mashaw, Perrin, and Reno, *Restructuring SSI*, 12-13.

62. Consortium for Citizens with Disabilities, Testimony; Loprest, "Supplemental Security Income," 3. Stein also played an important role in the disability review litigation in the 1980s.

63. Barbara Vobejda, "Aid for Disabled Children Hinges on New Definition," *Washington Post*, 7 November 1996.

64. Susan Daniels, Social Security Administration, on "CNN Early Prime," 4 December 1996; Mark V. Nadel, for Jane L. Ross, Director, Income Security Issues, letter to Hon. William V. Roth, Jr., and Hon. E. Clay Shaw, U.S. Senate; re: Supplemental Security Income: Review of SSA Regulations Governing Children's Eligibility for the Program, GAO; shHEHS-97-220R, 16 September 1997, 2; Robert A. Rosenblatt and Melissa Healy, "Welfare Bill Will Exclude 135,000, Disabled Children," *Los Angeles Times*, 7 February 1997; Nadel, "Supplemental Security Income," 4. The SSA reported progress on dealing with its backlog of reviews. Jane L. Ross, "Social Security Disability: SSA Is Making Progress toward Eliminating Continuing Disability Review Backlogs," Testimony before the House of Representatives, Committee on Ways and Means, Subcommittee on Social Security, 25 September 1997, GAO/T-HEHS-97-222; "100,000 Kids Lose Welfare," *Orlando Sentinel*, 15 August 1997.

65. Robert Pear, "U.S. Challenges Courts on Disabilities," *New York Times*, 21 April 1997. For an explanation of the sources of the tension between the disability determination services and administrative law judges, see Jane L. Ross, "Social Security Disability: SSA Must Hold Itself Accountable for Continued Improvement in Decision-Making," Report to the Chairman, House of Representatives, Committee on Ways and Means, Subcommittee on Social Security, August 1997, GAO/HEHS-97-102.

66. Robert Pear, "After a Review, 95,180 Children Will Lose Cash Disability Benefits," *New York Times*, 14 August 1997; "Morning Edition," National Public Radio, 18 September 1997; Weitzstein, "103,000 Children," Melissa Healy, "Social Security Says Neediest Disabled Children Not Cut," *Los Angeles Times*, 18 September 1997. In a modest extension of disability benefits, in 1999 Congress extended the length of time former Social Security disability beneficiaries could receive Medicare after returning to work and gave states new options that allowed disabled workers to buy into Medicaid. It also improved return-to-work services. "President Signs Disability Bill," *Social Insurance Update* 11, 1 (2000): 1,4. For a terrible

story about one child cut off from SSI, see, Charles P. Pierce. "The Era of Big Government Is Over and Marcus Stephens Is Dead: A True Chronicle of Waste, Fraud, and Abuse," *Esquire*, April 2000, 144–52, 64.

67. Barbara Vobejda, "Quick Review Promised for SSI Rules," *Washington Post*, 11 September 1997; Robert Pear, "U.S. Mistakenly Cuts Benefits for Many Disabled Children," *New York Times*, 16 Novembetr 1997; Robert Pear, "Fearing Errors, U.S. Will Review Cutoff in Aid to Disabled Youth," *New York Times*, 18 December 1997; Bazelon Center for Mental Health Law, "Children Who Lost Disability Benefits Get a Second Chance," news release, 23 December 1997; Thomas Yates, "The Aftermath of Welfare Reform: SSI Childhood Disability," *Clearinghouse Review*, November–December 1997, 358–72.

68. This figure is the "wage replacement ratio"; it is based on the average weekly benefit, not the maximum allowable by law. It is an average across the states. Christopher J. O'Leary and Murray A. Rubin, "Adequacy of the Weekly Benefit Amount," in *Unemployment Insurance in the United States: Analysis of Policy Issues*, eds. Christopher J. O'Leary and Stephen A. Wandner (Kalamazoo, MI: W. E. Upjohn Institute for Employment Research, 1997), 171, table 5.1; Laurie J. Bassi and Daniel P. McMurrer, "Coverage and Recipiency," in O'Leary and Wandner, *Unemployment Insurance*, 51–89.

69. Advisory Council on Unemployment Compensation, *Unemployment Insurance in the United States: Benefits, Financing, Coverage*, a Report to the President and Congress, February 1995, 8; *1996 Green Book*, 329.

70. Saul Blaustein, Christopher J. O'Leary, and Stephen A. Wandner, "Policy Issues: An Overview," in O'Leary and Wandner, *Unemployment Insurance*, 2, 28; James R. Storey and Jennifer A Niesner, "Unemployment Compensation in the Group of Seven Nations," in O'Leary and Wandner, *Unemployment Insurance*, 599–667.

71. These historical observations on unemployment insurance are based on Alexander Keyssar, *Out of Work: The First Century of Unemployment in Massachusetts* (New York: Cambridge University Press, 1986); Don D. Lescohier, *The Labor Market* (New York: Macmillan, 1919); Lubove, *Struggle for Social Security*; Daniel Nelson, *Unemployment Insurance: The American Experience, 1915–1935* (Madison: University of Wisconsin Press, 1969); John A. Garraty, *Unemployment in History: Economic Thought and Public Policy* (New York: Harper and Row, 1978); Ohio Commission on Unemployment Insurance, *Report* (Columbus, Ohio: 1932); Robert C. Lieberman, *Shifting the Color Line: Race and the American Welfare State* (Cambridge: Harvard University Press, 1998), 56–64.

72. Blaustein, O'Leary, and Wandner, "Policy Issues," 4; Saul J. Blaustein, *Unemployment Insurance in the United States: The First Half Century* (Kalamazoo, MI: W E. Upjohn Institute, 1993), 170; William Haber and Merrill G. Murray, *Unemployment Insurance in the American Economy: An Historical Review and Analysis* (Homewood, IL: Richard D. Irwin, 1966), 121.

73. Bassi and McMurrer, "Coverage and Recipiency," 54.

74. Baldwin, "Benefit Recipiency," 67; Haber and Murray, *Unemployment Insurance*, 47–75, 143; Blaustein, *Unemployment Insurance*, tables 4.1 and 4.2, pp. 82–83. The Committee on Economic Security believed that workers who used up their unemployment benefits should be supported by public works programs, not extended benefits or poor relief.

75. Phillip B. Levine, "Financing Benefit Payments," in O'Leary and Wandner, *Unemployment Insurance*, 321; General Accounting Office, "Unemployment Insurance: Program's Ability to Meet Objectives Jeopardized," September 1993,

GAO/HRD-93-107, 3; Baldwin, "Benefit Recipiency," 82–94; Blaustein, *Unemployment Insurance*, 232–35.

76. Haber and Murray, *Unemployment Insurance*, 312–13; *Monthly Labor Review* 117, 1 (January 1994): 70; *Monthly Labor Review* 119, 1 (January 1996): 74. See for instance, the 1993 Kansas rule. *Monthly Labor Review* 117, 1 (January 1994) 67; and "States Clarify Testing-Benefits Relationship," *Employment Testing—Law and Policy Reporter*, June 1996, 93; "Courts Weigh Drug Testing's Impact on Worker Privacy under State Law," *Employment Testing—Law and Policy Reporter*, January 1997, 1; Walter Nicholson, "Initial Eligibility for Unemployment Compensation," in O'Leary and Wandner, *Unemployment Insurance*, 104; Baldwin, "Benefit Recipiency Rates," 92–93; Advisory Council on Unemployment, 1995, 115.

77. This figure includes all unemployment programs, that is to say, state programs plus a number of special programs such as supplemental federal benefits and benefits for former armed service members and railroad employees. Christopher J. O'Leary and Stephen A. Wandner, "Summing Up: Achievements, Problems, and Prospects," in O'Leary and Wandner, *Unemployment Insurance*, 683, table 15.6. Some analysts of declining ratios focus on the declining number of people who apply for unemployment insurance in the first place. This begs the question of why they do not apply. The reasons reflect the same factors that leave fewer people eligible. Young-Hee Yoon, Roberta Spalter-Roth, and Marc Baldwin, "Unemployment Insurance: Barriers to Access for Women and Part-Time Workers," National Commission for Employment Policy Research Report no. 95–06, July 1995, 14; Bassi and McMurrer, "Coverage and Recipiency," 69–70. For an example of how union strength moderated business demands to restrict and cut unemployment insurance, see Marc Baldwin, "Benefit Recipiency Rates under the Federal/State Unemployment Insurance Program: Explaining and Reversing Decline" (Ph.D. diss., MIT, 1993), 114–18. In a regression analysis, Baldwin found that union membership is a significant factor in the decline of unemployment insurance recipiency. An example of the AFL-CIO in action on behalf of workers' unemployment claims is "AFL-CIO Sues to Fix Unemployment Insurance for 120,000 Workers," *Business Wire*, 15 January 1997.

78. Greg Jaffe, "South Takes Aim at Jobless Insurance Tax," *Wall Street Journal*, 27 January 1997. Wayne Vroman, an expert on unemployment insurance at the Urban Institute, warned, "These states will face the consequences of the cuts in the next recession." AFL-CIO president John Sweeney observed, "States like Virginia, Florida, and Georgia have UI taxes below the national average, pay benefits to one-fourth or fewer of their unemployed, and are now proposing tax giveaways" (MS, 1977).

79. On the mismatch between labor force trends and public program design, see General Accounting Office, "Workers at Risk: Increased Numbers in Contingent Employment Lack Insurance, Other Benefits," March 1991, GAO/HRD-91-56; Yoon, Spalter-Roth, and Baldwin, "Unemployment Insurance," 20–29; Lieberman, *Shifting the Color Line*, 192–93.

80. The extended benefits are activated by the unemployment rate. The federal government pays the same benefits as the state; half of the money comes from federal funds and half from state unemployment reserves.

81. Stephen A. Woodbury and Murray Rubin, "The Duration of Benefits," in O'Leary and Wandner, *Unemployment Insurance*, 227.

82. Advisory Council on Unemployment Compensation, 1995, 181, 198 200; Bruce D. Meyer, "Lessons from the U.S. Unemployment Insurance Experiments," *Journal of Economic Literature* 5, 33 (March 1995): 91–131.

83. Mark Wilson, "Putting America Back to Work: Reforming the Employment Security System," Heritage Foundation, Roe Backgrounder no. 1120. 10 June 1997; Richard Miniter, "Reforming Unemployment Insurance," *Washington Times*, 24 April 1997.

84. Wilson, "Putting America Back to Work"; Miniter, "Reforming Unemployment Insurance"; Blaustein, *Unemployment Insurance*, 326.

85. Baldwin quoted in Miniter, "Reforming Unemployment Insurance"; personal conversation with Marc Baldwin, 21 January 1998. See also the AFL-CIO's position paper, "Unemployment Insurance Administrative Finance: Problems with Devolution" (photocopy), January 1998; Advisory Council on Unemployment Compensation, *Defining Federal and State Roles in Unemployment Insurance, A Report to the President and Congress*, January 1996, 4, 8.

86. "Unemployment Compensation: The One Payroll Tax You Can Control Directly," *Solutions*, April–May 1994, 31–32.

87. Janet Kidd Stewart, "More Firms Appeal Insurance Claims, *Chicago Sun-Times*, 16 December 1996.

88. There are suggestions for reform in O'Leary and Wandner, *Unemployment Insurance*; Advisory Council on Unemployment Compensation, *Defining Federal and State Roles*; and Baldwin, "Benefit Recipiency."

CHAPTER 9: NEW MODELS FOR SOCIAL SECURITY

1. Steven Ruggles, *Prolonged Connections: The Rise of the Extended Family in Nineteenth-Century England and America* (Madison: University of Wisconsin Press, 1987); Andrew Achenbaum, *Old Age in the New Land: The American Experience since 1870* (Baltimore: Johns Hopkins University Press, 1978); Carol Haber, *Beyond Sixty-Five: The Dilemma of Old Age in America's Past* (New York: Cambridge University Press, 1983); Carol Haber and Brian Gratton, *Old Age and the Search for Security: An American Social History* (Bloomington: Indiana University Press, 1994); Brian Gratton, "Boston's Elderly, 1890–1950: Work, Family, and Dependency" (Ph.D. diss., Boston University, 1980); Michael B. Katz, *Poverty and Policy in American History* (New York: Academic Press, 1983).

2. Theda Skocpol, *Protecting Soldiers and Mothers: The Political Origins of Social Policy in the United States* (Cambridge: Harvard University Press, 1992), 102–51.

3. Skocpol, *Protecting Soldiers and Mothers*, 272–78; Ann Shola Orloff, "The Political Origins of America's Belated Welfare State," in *The Politics of Social Policy in the United States*, ed. Margaret Weir, Ann Shola Orloff, and Theda Skocpol (Princeton: Princeton University Press, 1988), 37–80; Ann Shola Orloff, *The Politics of Pensions: A Comparative Analysis of Britain, Canada, and the United States, 1880–1940* (Madison: University of Wisconsin Press, 1993).

4. Achenbaum, *Old Age in the New Land*, 48.

5. The idea that pensions developed because businesses and public employers wanted to move old people out of the workforce is the thesis of William Graebner, *A History of Retirement: The Meaning and Function of an American Institution, 1885–1978* (New Haven: Yale University Press, 1980).

6. Roy Lubove, *The Struggle for Social Security, 1900–1935* (Cambridge: Harvard University Press, 1968), 136–37, 142; Orloff, "The Political Origins of America's Belated Welfare State," 68–69, 72–73.

7. *Report to the President of the Committee on Economic Security* (Washington, DC: GPO, 1935); Arthur J. Altmeyer, *The Formative Years of Social Security* (Madison:

University of Wisconsin Press, 1968); Edward D. Berkowitz, *America's Welfare State: From Roosevelt to Reagan* (Baltimore: Johns Hopkins University Press, 1991), 13–38. For an argument in support of the pay-as-you-go system, see Dimitri B. Papadimitriou and L. Randall Wray, "More Pain, No Gain: Breaux Plan Slashes Social Security Benefits Unnecessarily" (Jerome Levy Economics Institute of Bard College, 1999).

8. Henry J. Aaron and Robert D. Reischauer, *Countdown to Reform: The Great Social Security Debate* (New York: Century Foundation, 1998), 57; Michael K. Brown, *Race, Money, and the American Welfare State* (Ithaca: Cornell University Press, 1999), 71.

9. Brown, *Race, Money, and the American Welfare State*, 91; Berkowitz, *America's Welfare State*, 39–149.

10. Jerry Cates, *Insuring Inequality* (Ann Arbor: University of Michigan Press, 1983); Robert M. Ball with Thomas N. Bethell, "Bridging the Centuries: The Case for Traditional Social Security," in *Social Security in the 21st Century*, eds. Eric R. Kingson and James H. Schulz (New York: Oxford University Press, 1977).

11. Lawrence H. Thompson and Melina M. Upp, "The Social Insurance Approach and Social Security," in Kingson and Schulz, *Social Security*, 7–8.

12. "The Importance of Social Security to Seniors" (Economic Policy Institute, 28 April 1999), available from http://www/epinet.org/webfeatures.snapshots/archives/042899/snapshot042899.html; Ball with Bethell, "Bridging the Centuries," 259–60.

13. Marilyn Moon, "Are Social Security Benefits Too High or Too Low?" in Kingson and Schulz, *Social Security*, 52, 67; Robert M. Ball, Edith U. Fierst, Gloria T. Johnson, Thomas W. Jones, George Kourpias, and Gerald M. Shea, "Social Security for the 21st Century: A Strategy to Maintain Benefits and Strengthen America's Family Protection Plan," in *Report of the 1994–1996 Advisory Council on Social Security* (Washington, DC: GPO, 1997), 1: 59; Ball with Bethell, "Bridging the Centuries" 263.

14. The major statement of the historical case against the social insurances from a feminist point of view is Linda Gordon, *Pitted but Not Entitled: Single Mothers and the History of Welfare* (New York: Free Press, 1994), e.g., 6, 145, 271. See also the important book by Susan Mettler, *Dividing Citizens: Gender and Federalism in New Deal Public Policy* (Ithaca: Cornell University Press, 1998). An excellent article on gender issues in Social Security is Marianne A. Ferber, "Women's Employment and the Society Security System," *Social Security Bulletin* 56, 3 (Fall 1993): 33–55. The ways in which current benefits work against the interests of women are described in Edith U. Fierst, "Supplemental Statement," in *Report of the 1994–1996 Advisory Council on Social Security*, 1: 135–51; statistics on widows and widowers are from p. 142. An excellent, concise statement of the problem is Christina Smith FitzPatrick and Joan Entmacher, "Widows, Poverty, and Social Security Policy Options" (National Academy of Social Insurance, 2000).

15. U.S. Department of Health and Human Services, Social Security Administration, *Annual Statistical Supplement, 1993, to the Social Security Bulletin* (Washington, DC: Social Security Administration, 1993), 138; Berkowitz, *America's Welfare State*; Blanche D. Coll, *Safety Net: Welfare and Social Security, 1929–1979* (New Brunswick, NJ: Rutgers University Press, 1995); Michael B. Katz, "Segmented Visions: Recent Historical Writing on American Welfare," *Journal of Urban History* 24, 2 (January 1998): 244–55; "Social Security Reduces Proportion of Elderly Who Are Poor from Nearly One in Two to Less Than One in Eight" (Center on

Budget and Policy Priorities, 8 April 1999), available from www.cbpp.org/4-8-99socsec.htm; Trudy Lieberman, "Social Security for Women," *Nation*, 19 July 1999, 6.

16. Eric. A. Patashnik, "Unfolding Promises: Trust Funds and the Politics of Commitment," *Political Science Quarterly* 112, 3 (1997): 431–52; Max J. Skidmore, *Social Security and Its Enemies: The Case for America's Most Efficient Insurance Program* (Boulder, CO: Westview Press, 1999), 2; Kathryn Olson and Virginia Reno, "Social Security Finances: Findings of the 2000 Trustees Report" (National Academy of Social Insurance, 2000).

17. Edward D. Berkowitz, "The Historical Development of Social Security in the United States," in Kingson and Schulz, *Social Security in the 21st Century*, 36–37; Julian Emanuel Zelizer, "Where Is the Money Coming From? The Reconstruction of Social Security Financing, 1939–1950," *Journal of Policy History* 9, 4 (1997): 399–424.

18. Theodore R. Marmor, Jerry L. Mashaw, and Philip L. Harvey, *America's Misunderstood Welfare State: Persistent Myths and Enduring Realities* (New York: Basic Books, 1990).

19. *Report of the National Commission on Social Security Reform, January 1983* (Washington, DC: GPO, 1983), chapter 2-2. "The National Commission considered, but rejected, proposals to make the Social Security program a voluntary one, or to transform it into a program under which benefits are a product exclusively of the contributions paid, or to convert it into a fully-funded program, or to change it to a program under which benefits are conditioned on the showing of financial need."

20. Berkowitz, "Historical Development," 37; *Report of the National Commission on Social Security Reform*; Patashnick, "Unfolding Promises," 450; U.S. House of Representatives Committee on Ways and Means, *1996 Green Book*, 59.

21. Editorial, *New York Times*, 11 April 1988, quoted in Marmor, Mashaw, and Harvey, *America's Misunderstood Welfare State*, 129–30. The commission was appointed by President Bill Clinton and chaired by Senators J. Robert Kerrey and John C. Danforth. "Reform Proposal of Commissioner Peter G. Peterson," in *Bipartisan Commission on Entitlement and Tax Reform* (Washington, DC: GPO, January 1995), ii, 2, 8.

22. Theodore R. Marmor, Fay Lomax Cook, and Stephen Scher, "Social Security Politics and the Conflict between Generations: Are We Asking the Right Questions?" in Kingson and Schulz, *Social Security in the 21st Century*, 204; Henry Fairlie, "Talkin 'bout My Generation; Government Assistance to Those over 65 and the Pampered Lifestyle," *New Republic*, 28 March 1988, 9.

23. Marmor, Cook, and Scher, "Social Security Politics," 195–205, quotation on 204. For a review of Peterson's work, as well as an excellent overview of the issues in the Social Security debate, see Jeff Madrick, "Social Security and Its Discontents," *New York Review*, 19 December 1996: 68–72. See also "Reform Proposal of Commissioner Peter G. Peterson," 55.

24. Dean Baker and Mark Weisbrot, *Social Security: The Phony Crisis* (Chicago: University of Chicago Press, 1999).

25. This is a less straightforward number to calculate than first appears. It is affected not only by fertility and mortality, but by retirement age. The trend toward early retirement could be changed fairly dramatically by public policy through tax laws and other measures. For an alternative view of dependency ratios, see "How Many People Does Each Worker Support?" *Social Insurance Update* 4, 2 (April 1997): 1, 12–13; Yung-Ping Chen and Stephen C. Goss, "Are Returns on Payroll Taxes

Fair?" in Kingson and Schulz, *Social Security in the 21st Century*, 83; Baker and Weisbrot, *Social Security*, 34–35; Aaron and Reischauer, *Countdown to Reform*, 51 (italics in original); Eisner, *Social Security: More Not Less* (New York: Century Foundation, 1998), 10.

26. Aaron and Reischauer, *Countdown to Reform*, 93; Social Security Administration, "How Does Social Security Benefit Low-Wage Workers?" (1999).

27. *Social Security Privatization* (National Committee to Preserve Social Security and Medicare, February 1998), available from http://www.ncpssm.org/vp_privatiza-tion.html; Eisner, *Social Security: More, Not Less*, 9; Ball and Bethel, "Bridging the Centuries," write: "Smoothing out lifetime income somewhat by shifting income from wages to the periods of retirement or disability, or to the family after the death of a wage earner, is the most basic program objective" (265). See the interesting discussions of generational issues in Jerry R. Green, "Demographics, Market Fail-ure, and Social Security"; Alan S. Blinder, "Why Is the Government in the Pen-sion Business?"; and Andrew W. Abel, "Comment," all in *Social Security and Private Pensions: Providing Retirement for the 21st Century*, ed. Susan M. Wachter, (Lexington, MA: Lexington Books, 1988), 3–40.

28. Aaron and Reischauer, *Countdown to Reform*, 2.

29. Robert Eisner, *Social Security: More, Not Less*, 5; Richard W. Stevenson, "Fed Chief Sees Hard Choices to Preserve Social Security," *New York Times*, 29 Janu-ary 1999. On the 1972 episode, see, for instance, Peter J. Ferrara and Michael Tan-ner, *A New Deal for Social Security* (Washington, DC: Cato Institute, 1998), 30.

30. The Employee Benefit Research Institute is formulating a more sophisticated model for use in developing polices for Social Security. For a first discussion of the model with reactions from scholars and policy analysts, see Dallas L. Salisbury, ed., *Assessing Social Security Reform Alternatives* (Washington, DC: Employee Benefit Research Institute, 1997); Dimitri B. Papdimitriou and Randall Wray, "Does Social Security Need Saving?" Jerome Levy Economics Institute of Bard College, Public Policy Brief 55A (August 1999). A counterargument to the optimistic dependency ratio is that the elderly cost a lot more to support than children do. Aaron and Reis-chauer, *Countdown to Reform*, 62; Alex Berenson, "Rising Productivity Challenges Notions on Limits of Growth," *New York Times*, 10 September 2000.

31. Doug Henwood, "Antisocial Insecurity," *Left Business Observer*, no. 87 (31 December 1998): 1–2, 4; Eisner, *Social Security: More, Not Less*, 12; Baker and Weisbrot, *Social Security*, 1–2.

32. Henwood, "Antisocial Insecurity," 1–2, 4. For a comparison of major proposals for modifying Social Security, see Aaron and Reischauer, *Countdown to Reform*, 117, 147, 161–68.

33. Peter Passell, "Partial Privatization of Social Security Very Possible," *New York Times*, 9 April 1998.

34. For a convincing rebuttal of the charge that Social Security represents a pyramid or "Ponzi" scheme, see Aaron and Reischauer, *Countdown to Reform*, 44–45; Fer-rara and Tanner, *A New Deal*, 7–10, 65, 110.

35. William G. Shipman, "Retiring with Dignity: Social Security vs. Private Markets"; and Karl Borden, "Dismantling the Pyramid: The Why and How of Privatizing Social Security," in *The Cato Project on Social Security Privatization*, SSP no. 1 and SSP no. 2, 14 August 1995; Joseph Collins and John Lear, *Chile's Free Market Miracle: A Second Look* (Oakland, CA: Institute for Food and Development Policy, 1995), 181; Skidmore, *Social Security and Its Enemies*, 99–100.

36. Clifford Krauss, "Social Security, Chilean Style," *New York Times*, 16 August 1998.

37. Ferrara and Tanner, *A New Deal*, 154; Richard Stevenson, "Britons Govern Their Own Retirement," *New York Times*, 19 July 1998; Skidmore, *Social Security and Its Enemies*, 154.

38. Robert Dreyfus, "The Real Threat to Social Security," *Nation*, 8 February 1999, 15–21; Aaron and Reischauer, *Countdown to Reform*, 85–90. For other criticisms of privatization, see Baker and Weisbrot, *Social Security*, 88–104; Walter M. Cadette, "Social Security Privatization: A Bad Idea" (Jerome Levy Economics Institute of Bard College, 1999).

39. "Reform Proposal of Commissioner Peter G. Peterson," 58–59; *Report of the 1994–1996 Advisory Council on Social Security*, 18. The Advisory Council labeled its three options: (1) maintenance of benefits (MB); (2) publicly held individual accounts (IA); and (3) two-tiered system with privately held accounts (PSA). The maintenance of benefits option proposed to tax all Social Security benefits that exceeded contributions; bring all new state and local government employees under the Social Security system; require a slightly longer period of work for full benefits; raise payroll taxes 1.6 percent after fifty years; and, tentatively, invest 40 percent of the Trust Fund in equities rather than government bonds. (Raising the return on money in the Fund from an inflation-adjusted 2 percent to 4 percent would generate income to offset some of the decline in the ratio of workers to retirees.)

The Private Security Account option proposed a two-tiered system. The first tier, funded with a 5 percent payroll tax (contrasted with the current 12.4 percent rate shared equally by employers and employees), would provide a flat retirement benefit for all retirees, set in 1996 at $410/month, 65 percent of the current poverty level for an elderly person, or 76 percent of the benefit payable to a low-wage worker retiring in 1996. The second tier would consist of fully funded, individually owned, defined-contribution retirement accounts (called personal security accounts) with few restrictions on the choice of investments. These accounts would be funded with 5 percentage points of the payroll tax. The plan also called for accelerating the increase in the age of eligibility for benefits and increasing it to 70 by 2083; eliminating the retirement earnings test, which reduces benefits on earnings above an exempt amount; changing benefit rules for spouses, survivors, and disabled workers; introducing new rules for taxation; and covering all new state and local government employees. The private account option promised to be expensive, at least for the seventy-two years during which it would be phased in. The federal government would have to pay existing benefits to older workers grandfathered into the program while it allowed younger workers to accumulate funds in their personal accounts. To finance the transition, advocates of the PSA option proposed adding 1.52 percent to the payroll tax and forty years' worth of new government bonds valued at $1.9 trillion in 1995 dollars.

The publicly held individual account option (IA) mixed elements from the other two. It proposed to protect the adequacy of Social Security benefits while slowing their growth. The principal mechanism was a 1.6 percent additional payroll tax, whose proceeds would be deposited in individual defined-contribution accounts held for investment by the federal government. Individuals would have a limited number of investment choices, and when they retired, their funds would be converted into guaranteed indexed annuities (the PSA plan did not require the conversion of individual accounts to annuities). Supporters of the IA option proposed to rein in the growth of benefits through a number of measures: increasing the age of eligibility for full retirement benefits; slowing the growth in benefits for middle- and high-wage workers; taxing Social Security benefits under regular income-tax principles; and extending the computation period for benefits. Like the other plans, it called for covering all new state and local government employees. It also proposed changes in benefits for two-earner couples and dependent spouses. Like the individual account option, it moved Social Security toward a defined-contribution model, but it put a much smaller share of payroll taxes into individual accounts, while it preserved existing benefits essentially unchanged for lower-paid workers.

40. *Report of the 1994–1996 Advisory Council on Social Security*, 59–60 (italics in original), 75–76.
41. *Report of the 1994–1996 Advisory Council on Social Security*, 103, 106, 134.
42. *Report of the 1994–1996 Advisory Council on Social Security*, 156–57.
43. Richard Stevenson, "Social Security Proposal Will Suggest Private Investment, Later Retirement," *New York Times*, 19 May 1998.
44. Andrew Cassell, "Whatever Happened to the Looming Emergency over Social Security?" *Philadelphia Inquirer*, 19 May 1999; "CBO Says Improving Economy Would Help Ensure Future Social Security Benefits," *New York Times*, 24 February 1999; Kilolo Kijakazi, Wendell Primus, and Robert Greenstein, "Understanding the Financial Status of the Social Security System in Light of the 1999 Trustees' Report" (Center on Budget and Policy Priorities, 30 March 1999), available from http://www.cbpp,org/3-30-99socsec.htm; "Social Security Trust Funds Gain Two Additional Years of Solvency" (Social Security Administration, 30 March 1999), available from http://www/ssa/gov/pressoficce/trus399.htm; David E. Rosenbaum, "Longer Solvency for Medicare and Social Security," *New York Times*, 31 March 1999; Olson and Reno, "Social Security Finances," 2.
45. James Bennet, "Unbowed, Clinton Presses Social Security Plan," *New York Times*, 20 January 1999; Associated Press, "A Look at the Social Security Plan," *New York Times*, 20 January 1999; Richard W. Stevenson, "House Backs End to Earnings Limit on Social Security," *New York Times*, 2 March 2000.
46. David E. Rosenbaum, "Social Security: The Basics, with a Tally Sheet," *New York Times*, 28 January 1999.
47. Richard W. Stevenson, "Domestic Issues: Clinton Plan to Strengthen Social Security Runs into Opposition," *New York Times*, 20 January 1999; Michael M. Weinstein, "Clinton's Plan for Social Security," *New York Times*, 21 January 1999; L. Randall Wray, "The Emperor Has No Clothes: President Clinton's Proposed Social Security Reform" (Jerome Levy Economics Institute of Bard College, 1999).
48. Weinstein, "Clinton's Plan"; David E. Rosenbaum, "Greenspan Sees Harm in Proposal," *New York Times*, 21 January 1999; Diana B. Henriques, "Social Security Investment Plan Raises a Debate," *New York Times,* 24 January 1999.
49. David E. Rosenbaum, "When Ideology Goes Where Actuaries Tread," *New York Times,* 2 May 1999.
50. Robert Reischauer, "The 75-Year Plan," *New York Times*, 9 April 1999. The plan in one sense represented a retreat for Aaron and Reischauer, who in *Countdown to Reform* had recommended investing part of the reserves in stock index funds. Despite partisan sniping, by midsummer 1999 it appeared that Clinton and the Republicans had reached a broad agreement on Social Security, although many specific details remained unresolved. "Clinton, GOP Reach Broad Social Security Agreement" (CNN Interactive, 13 July 1999), available from http://www.cnn.com/ALLPOLITICS/stories/1999/07/13/budget; Richard W. Stevenson, "Clinton Abandons Idea of Investing Retirement Funds," *New York Times*, 24 October; 1999.

51. Steven A. Holmes, "Law Removes an Earnings limit on Recipients of Social Security," *New York Times*, 8 April 2000.
52. Henry J. Aaron, Alan S. Blinder, Alicia H. Munnell, and Peter R. Orszag, "Governor Bush's Individual Account Proposal Implications for Retirement Benefits," Century Foundation: Social Security Network, 2000; Alison Mitchell and James Dao, "Bush Presents Social Security as Crucial Test," *New York Times*, 16 May 2000; Richard Stevenson "Bush to Advocate Private Accounts in Social Security," *New York Times*, 1 May 2000; Richard Stevenson, "Challenges to Bedrock of Retirement," *New York Times*, 16 May 2000.
53. James Dao, "Gore Proposes New Benefits for Parents and Widows," *New York Times*, 5 April 2000; James Dao and Alison Mitchell, "Gore Denounces Bush Social Security Plan as Too Risky," *New York Times*, 17 May 2000; Richard Stevenson, "Gore Is Pursuing His Case for Retirement Savings Plan," *New York Times*, 21 June 2000.
54. Sheila Burke, Eric Kingson, and Uwe Reinhardt, eds., *Social Security and Medicare: Individual vs. Collective Risk and Responsibility* (Washington, DC: Brookings Institution Press, 2000).

CHAPTER 10: THE ASSIMILATION OF HEALTH CARE
TO THE MARKET

1. Ronald L. Numbers, *Almost Persuaded: American Physicians and Compulsory Health Insurance, 1912–1920* (Baltimore: Johns Hopkins University Press, 1978), 19; Michael B. Katz, *Improving Poor People: The Welfare State, the "Underclass," and Urban Schools as History* (Princeton: Princeton University Press, 1995), 160–61.
2. The paragraphs on the history of health insurance that follow are based on the following sources: Numbers, *Almost Persuaded*; Daniel S. Hirshfield, *The Lost Reform: The Campaign for Compulsory Health Insurance in the United States from 1932 to 1943* (Cambridge: Harvard University Press, 1970); Monte M. Poen, *Harry S. Truman versus the Medical Lobby: The Genesis of Medicare* (Columbia: University of Missouri Press, 1979); Theodore R. Marmor, *The Politics of Medicare* (London: Routledge and Kegan Paul, 1970); Paul Starr, *The Social Transformation of American Medicine* (New York: Basic Books, 1982); James A. Morone and Gary S. Belkin, eds., *The Politics of Health Care Reform: Lessons from the Past, Prospects for the Future* (Durham, NC: Duke University Press, 1994); Rosemary Stevens, *In Sickness and in Wealth: American Hospitals in the Twentieth Century* (Baltimore: Johns Hopkins University Press, 1999).
3. The most recent study of Blue Cross and Blue Shield is Robert Cunningham, *The Blues: A History of the Blue Cross and Blue Shield System* (DeKalb: Northern Illinois University Press, 1997).
4. Stevens, *In Sickness and in Wealth*, 295–96.
5. Starr, *Social Transformation of American Medicine*, 309; Rosemary Stevens, Foreword to Cunningham, *The Blues*, ix.
6. On Mills and Medicare, see Julian E. Zelizer, *Wilbur E. Mills, Congress, and the State, 1945–1975* (New York: Cambridge University Press, 1998), 212–54.
7. On Medicare and Medicaid as great cash cows for the medical industry, see Howard Wolinsky and Tom Brune, *Serpent on the Staff: The Unhealthy Politics of the American Medical Association* (New York: G. Putnam's Sons, 1994), 44–67.
8. There is useful background on Medicaid in Barbara Wolfe, "A Medicaid Primer," *Focus* 17, 3 (Spring 1996): 1–6.

9. Starr, *Social Transformation of American Medicine*, 377.

10. Marilyn Moon, *Medicare Now and in the Future* (Washington, DC: Urban Institute Press, 1993), 30; Michael B. Katz, *In the Shadow of the Poorhouse: A Social History of Welfare in America* (New York: Basic Books, 1986), 272.

11. Starr, *Social Transformation of American Medicine*, 381, 449.

12. Starr, *Social Transformation of American Medicine*, 395–96, 404–45.

13. Starr, *Social Transformation of American Medicine*, 394; Moon, *Medicare Now and in the Future*, 40, 43–44; U.S. House of Representatives Committee on Ways and Means, *1996 Green Book*, table 16-13, 896 and table 16-14, 897–98; Randall R. Bovbjerg and John Holahan, *Medicaid in the Reagan Era: Federal Policy and State Choices* (Washington, DC: Urban Institute Press, 1982), 3: Teresa A. Coughlin, Leighton Ku, and John Holahan, *Medicaid since 1980: Costs, Coverage, and the Shifting Alliance Between the Federal Government and the States* (Washington, DC: Urban Institute Press, 1994), 11.

14. Theodore R. Marmor, Jerry L. Mashaw, and Philip L. Harvey, *America's Misunderstood Welfare State: Persistent Myths, Enduring Realities* (New York: Basic Books, 1990), 185–86.

15. Moon, *Medicare Now and in the Future*, 24–30; Coughlin, Ku, and Holahan, *Medicaid since 1980*, 35.

16. Keith Bradsher, "Rise in Uninsured Becomes an Issue in Medicaid Fight," *New York Times*, 27 August 1995; U.S. House of Representatives, *1996 Green Book*, table 16-18, 905. States raised "donations" from providers, such as hospitals. They then counted these donations as matching funds with which to leverage more money from the federal government. When the federal government reimbursed them, states returned part of the money to the providers. Together, these arrangements involved about $25 billion in 1992 (1991 legislation that became effective in 1993 set limits on these schemes). Coughlin, Ku, and Holahan, *Medicaid since 1980*, 88, 90. The Catastrophic Coverage Act required Medicaid to pay Medicare coinsurance, deductibles, and premiums for elderly people with incomes below the poverty line and raised the amount of assets that one spouse could retain when another turned to Medicaid to pay for a nursing home. These measures also increased the cost of Medicaid. Economist Walter M. Cadette argues persuasively that the only solution to the cost of long-term care is for compulsory long-term care insurance to replace Medicaid. Walter M. Cadette, "Financing Long-Term Care" (Jerome Levy Economics Institute of Bard College, 2000).

17. Jacob S. Hacker, *The Road to Nowhere: The Genesis of President Clinton's Plan for Health Security* (Princeton: Princeton University Press, 1997), 14–15; Starr, *The Social Transformation of American Medicine*, 401, 402, 417.

18. Coughlin, Ku, and Holahan, *Medicaid since 1980*, 14.

19. Moon, *Medicare Now and in the Future*, 48–50. For an excellent discussion of prospective payment and its influence, see Stevens, *In Sickness and in Wealth*, 322–27.

20. Moon, *Medicare Now and in the Future*, 40–41, 55–56, 64–65, 72, 76; James A. Morone, "The Bureaucracy Empowered," in Morone and Belkin, *The Politics of Health Care Reform*, 155.

21. Theodore R. Marmor, *Understanding Health Care Reform* (New Haven: Yale University Press, 1994,) 23; Stevens, *In Sickness and in Wealth*, 324.

22. Moon, *Medicare Now and in the Future*, 107–36.

23. Starr, *The Social Transformation of American Medicine*, 419, 421, 428, 429. The phrase was used in Arnold S. Relman, "The New Medical-Industrial Complex,"

New England Journal of Medicine 321, 43 (23 October 1980): 963–70. Relman was the journal's editor.

24. This is one of the themes in Dave Lindorff, *Marketplace Medicine: The Rise of the For-Profit Hospital Chains* (New York: Bantam Books, 1992), 27, 101–3.

25. Lawrence D. Weiss, *No Benefit: Crisis in America's Health Insurance Industry* (Boulder, CO: Westview Press, 1992), 19; Moon, *Medicare Now and in the Future*, 11.

26. My understanding and interpretation of the history of Clinton's health plan draws principally on four books: Hacker, *The Road to Nowhere*; Nicholas Laham, *A Lost Cause: Bill Clinton's Campaign for National Health Insurance* (Westport, CT: Praeger, 1996); Theda Skocpol, *Boomerang: Health Care Reform and the Turn against Government* (New York: Norton, paperback edition 1997); Haynes Johnson and David Broder, *The System: The American Way of Politics at the Breaking Point* (Boston: Little, Brown, paperback edition 1997).

27. James J. Mongan, comment, in Henry J. Aaron, ed., *The Problem That Won't Go Away: Reforming U.S. Health Care Financing* (Washington, DC: Brookings Institution Press, 1996), 59; Daniel Yankelovich, "The Debate That Wasn't: The Public and the Clinton Health Care Plan," in Aaron, *The Problem That Won't Go Away*, 76; Skocpol, *Boomerang*, 21–22; *The President's Health Security Plan* (New York: Times Books, 1993), 9.

28. Skocpol, *Boomerang*, 174–75.

29. Hacker, *The Road to Nowhere*, 12–18; from a speech by President Bill Clinton, 27 October 1993, in *President's Health Security Plan*, xiii.

30. Skocpol, *Boomerang*, 25–37; Hacker, *The Road to Nowhere*, 10–11; Laham, *A Lost Cause*, 43–44; Johnson and Broder, *The System*, 58–61.

31. On Magaziner's background, see Johnson and Broder, *The System*, 105–8, 113, 610–11.

32. Weiss, *No Benefit*, 97–98; Hacker, *The Road to Nowhere*, 52–60 and 91–95.

33. Robert G. Evans, "Canada: The Real Issues," in Morone and Belkin, *The Politics of Health Care Reform*, 473–86; Marmor, Mashaw, and Harvey, *America's Misunderstood Welfare State*, 203–9.

34. *The President's Health Security Plan*, 33; Laham, *A Lost Cause*, 184.

35. Laham, *A Lost Cause*, 29–31, 76–78. Everyone would be required to join an alliance, except for workers in firms with more than five thousand employees, which could form their own corporate alliances. Medicaid beneficiaries would enroll in an alliance; Medicare recipients could choose to enroll in one as long as it offered the same minimum benefits as Medicare. Private insurers would have to offer the same package of benefits to everyone. They could not deny coverage because of chronic ill health ("prexisting conditions"); their premiums would have to reflect the cost of providing health care to the entire community; and they all would use a single form. The federal government would subsidize small employers who could not afford premiums and families with incomes up to 150 percent of the poverty line. The bill also proposed to extend Medicare to cover prescription drugs and expand coverage of home health care. Alliances would have to offer members the option of joining health maintenance organizations. Expanded HMO enrollment also would help contain costs. Other savings would come from limits on the rising costs of Medicare and Medicaid. The growth of Medicare spending would slow from 11.6 percent in 1994 to 4.1 percent in 2000, and Medicaid's would decline from 16.5 percent to 4.1 percent in the same years. Increases in private health insurance premiums would not be allowed to exceed the consumer price

index. A National Health Board would administer the act and regulate costs for each health alliance. *The President's Health Security Plan*, 64.

36. On the role of interest groups in the debate on Clinton's bill, see Graham K. Wilson, "Interest Groups in the Health Care Debate," in Aaron, *The Problem That Won't Go Away*, 110–30; Laham, *A Lost Cause*, 47, 51, 55–58, provides tables that show the rising contribution of the health care industry to key members of Congress, including key committee members. For other statistics showing the contribution of the American Medical Association to national politics, see Wolinsky and Brune, *Serpent on the Staff*, 79–80. Compare the timing of the contributions listed in Hacker with the change in public sentiment. Hacker, *Road to Nowhere*, 12–18.

37. Wolinsky and Brune, *Serpent on the Staff*, 41; Laham, *A Lost Cause*, 75, 73–79; Johnson and Broder, *The System*, 204–6; Skocpol, *Boomerang*, 134–39; Hacker, *The Road to Nowhere*, 145–46.

38. Small businesses would receive a premium that would cap their costs for employee insurance at 3.5 percent of their payroll, and they probably would pay less for insurance for themselves and their families. Laham, *A Lost Cause*, 126–40; Skocpol, *Boomerang*, 156–157; Johnson and Broder, *The System*, 215–24; 215.

39. Johnson and Broder, *The System*, 39; Skocpol, *Boomerang*, 147–48; Laham, *A Lost Cause*, 82–105.

40. Laham, *A Lost Cause*, 160, 174–76.

41. Hacker, *Road to Nowhere*, 178–79.

42. Laham, *A Lost Cause*, 211–14; Johnson and Broder, *The System*, 153–54, 656.

43. Randall R. Bovbjerg and Jill A. Marsteller, "Health Care Market Competition in Six States: Implications for the Poor" (Washington, DC: Urban Institute, Assessing the New Federalism Project, 1998), quoted in Lindorff, *Marketplace Medicine*, 88; Marmor, *Understanding Health Care*, 75; Yankelovich, "The Debate That Wasn't," 86–87. For a stunning critique of market models in medicine see Robert Kuttner, *Everything for Sale: The Virtues and Limits of Markets* (New York: Alfred A. Knopf, 1997), 110–58.

44. Skocpol, *Boomerang*, 184.

45. Martin Gottlieb, "Battle over the Budget: Medical Care," *New York Times*, 18 November 1995; Nick Taylor, "Purgatory Revisited," *New York Times*, 20 October 1995.

46. Gottlieb, "Battle"; Martin Gottlieb and Robert Pear, "Beneath Surface, Health Care Plan Is Offering Boons," *New York Times*, 15 October 1995.

47. David Rosenbaum, "Washington Memo: The Medicare Brawl: Finger-Pointing, Hyperbole, and the Facts behind Them," *New York Times*, 1 October 1995; Robert Pear, "Bill Would Sever Medicaid Benefits from Welfare Aid," *New York Times*, 12 December 1995.

48. Ken Dilanian, "Ridge to Seek Big U.S. Funding for Child Health," *Philadelphia Inquirer*, 1 October 1997; Carole Burns, "Insurance for Working Poor May Provide Measure of Relief," *New York Times*, 26 May 1997.

49. John Holahan, Joshua Wiener, and Susan Wallin, "Health Policy for the Low-Income Population: Major Findings from the 'Assessing the New Federalism' Case Studies" (Washington, DC: Urban Institute, Assessing the New Federalism Project, 1998), 1; Martin Gottlieb, "A Managed Care Cure-All with Flaws and Potential," *New York Times*, 1 October 1995; Martin Gottlieb, "A Free-for-All in Swapping Medicaid for Managed Care," *New York Times*, 2 October 1995; Timothy Egan, "Federal Cap Could Limit Oregon's Medicaid Test," *New York Times*, 30 September 1995. On state level reform efforts, see also Debra J. Lipson, Stephen

Norton, Lisa Dubay, and Peter T. Kilborn, "Tuscon HMOs May Offer Model for Medicare's Future," *New York Times*, 26 March 1996; "Health Policy for Low-Income People in Florida" (Washington, DC: Urban Institute, Assessing the New Federalism Project, 1997); Leighton Ku, Alicia Berkowitz, Frank Ullman, and Marsha Regenstein, "Health Policy for Low-Income People in Mississippi" (Washington, DC: Urban Institute, Assessing the New Federalism Project, 1997); "HealthQuest Plan Moves Health Coverage in Hawaii to the Next Level of Improved Access, Stabilized Costs," *Business Wire*, 12 July 1994; Weiss, *No Benefit*, 109–11.

50. Milt Freudenheim, "Health Care in the Era of Capitalism," *New York Times*, 7 April 1996; Milt Freudenheim, "For Blue Cross, Fight to Save Traditional Role," *New York Times*, 12 June 1996; Thomas Weil and Norman E. Jorgenson, "The Tripartite Regulation of America's Health Services," *Spectrum: The Journal of State Government* 69, 1 (Winter 1996): 39–43; Robert E. Hurley and Susan Wallin, "Adopting and Adapting Managed Care for Medicaid Beneficiaries: An Imperfect Translation" (Washington, DC: Urban Institute, Assessing the New Federalism Project, 1998); Holihan, Wiener, and Wallin, "Health Care for the Low-Income Population," 2. See also Bovbjerg and Marsteller, "Health Care Market Competition," 58–59.

51. Weil and Jorgenson, "Tripartite Regulation," quoted in Cunningham, *The Blues*, 235. The movement of the Blues toward commercialism started with their development of health maintenance organizations. On this story, see Irwin Miller, *American Health Care Blues: Blue Cross, HMOs, and Pragmatic Reform since 1960* (New Brunswick, NJ: Transaction Publishers, 1996). See also Weiss, *No Benefit*, 24–25; Stevens, "Foreword," xi; Cunningham, *The Blues*, 247; Robert Sherrill, "The Madness of the Market: Dangerous to Your Health," *Nation* 9 January 1995, 245. Califano quote in source.

52. "New York Wants to Privatize Its Hospitals," "Morning Edition," National Public Radio, 5 September 1995, transcript no. 1687-3; Elizabeth Rosenthal, "Private NYC Hospitals Signal Deepening Financial Crisis," *New York Times*, 4 June 1996; Katherine Dowling, "The Latest Victims of Cut-Rate Care: Highly Trained Registered Nurses," *Philadelphia Inquirer*, 19 April 1996; Elisabeth Rosenthal, "Studies Say HMOs Will Eliminate Jobs and Hospital Beds in New York," *New York Times*, 7 April 1996; Andrea Gerlin, "Financial Prognosis for Hospitals Declines," *Philadelphia Inquirer*, 16 July 1997; Peter T. Kilborn, "Philadelphia Shaken by Collapse of Health-Care Giant," *New York Times*, 22 August 1998; Karl Stark, "How Hospital Systems Bled Red Ink Last Year," *Philadelphia Inquirer*, 11 April 1999.

53. Tony Pugh, "Community Health Centers Struggling," *Philadelphia Inquirer*, 10 November 1997.

54. Lindorff, *Marketplace Medicine*, 19, 127–34, 202–5, 209–10, 262–66. On similarities between for-profit and not-for-profit hospitals, see also Stevens, *In Sickness and in Wealth*, 335–36.

55. Milt Freudenheim, "Drug Substitutions Add to Discord over Managed Care," *New York Times*, 8 October 1996; "Consumers and Managed Care," *New York Times*, 9 February 1997; Robert Pear, "HMO Contracts: The Tricky Business of Keeping Doctors Quiet," *New York Times*, 22 September 1996.

56. Milt Freudenheim, "Insurers Tighten Rules and Reduce Fees for Doctors," *New York Times*, 28 June 1998; Milt Freudenheim, "HMOs Cope with a Backlash on Cost Cutting," *New York Times*, 19 May 1996.

57. Peter T. Kilborn, "Devalued by Managed Care, Doctors Seek Union Banner," *New York Times*, 30 May 1996; Andrea Gerlin, "Doctors' Drive to Unionize Spurred by 'Desperation,' " *Philadelphia Inquirer*, 4 November 1997; Ken Dilanian, "Gov. Ridge Calls for Regulations on Managed Care," *Philadelphia Inquirer*, 11 March 1998; Steven Greenhouse, "Doctors, under Pressure from HMO's, Are Ready Union Recruits," *New York Times*, 4 February 1999; Ewart Rouse, "Doctors Again Denied a Union," *Philadelphia Inquirer*, 25 May 1999; Steven Greenhouse, "AMA's Delegates Decide to Create Union of Doctors," *New York Times*, 24 June 1999; Robert Pear, "House Votes Doctors' Collective Bargaining," *New York Times*, 30 June 2000.

58. Weiss, *No Benefit*, 69–70; Cunningham, *The Blues*, 138–39; Martin Gottlieb and Kurt Eichenwald, "A Hospital Chain's Brass Knuckles, and the Backlash," *New York Times*, 11 May 1997; Kurt Eichenwald, "Two Leaders Are Out at Health Giant as Inquiry Goes On," *New York Times*, 26 July 1997; Kurt Eichenwald, "Whistle-Blower Lawsuits Aim at Big Provider of Health Care," *New York Times*, 19 August 1997; Kurt Eichenwald, "Columbia/HCA Cites Talks with Potential Buyers," *New York Times*, 16 August 1997; Milt Freudenheim, "Columbia/HCA Says Its 3d-Quarter Earnings Will Fall," *New York Times*, 10 September 1997; Kurt Eichenwald, "Columbia/HCA's Use of Special Medicare Units under Scrutiny," *New York Times*, 26 September 1997; Kurt Eichenwald, "Reshaping the Culture at Columbia/HCA," *New York Times*, 4 November 1997; Kurt Eichenwald, "Columbia Ouster Costs Nearly $10 Million," *New York Times*, 14 November 1997; Kurt Eichenwald, "Columbia/HCA Planning to Cut Network by at Least a Third," *New York Times*, 4 November 1997; Kurt Eichenwald, "Columbia/HCA Is Said to Settle Tax Case for $71 Million," *New York Times*, 3 December 1997; David J. Morrow, "Hospital Giant Expects to Post a Huge Loss," *New York Times*, 7 February 1988. For background on Frist, see Lindorff, *Marketplace Medicine* 39–42; Karen L. Shaw, "Columbia/HCA Executives Convicted of Fraud," *Philadelphia Inquirer*, 3 July 1999.

59. Reed Abelson, "Struggling Oxford Health Posts $507.6 Million Loss," *New York Times*, 12 August 1998; "HMOs Still Losing Money: Industry Is $490 Million in the Red," *Philadelphia Inquirer*, 10 August 1999; Milt Freudenheim, "United Healthcare Agrees to Buy Humana," *New York Times*, 29 May 1998; Stacey Burling, "A Health-Care Sea Change Is on the Horizon," *Philadelphia Inquirer*, 26 July 1998; Milt Freudenheim, "Bitter Pills for Ailing Hospitals," *New York Times*, 31 October 1999; Karl Stark, "Penn to Cut 1,700 in Health," *Philadelphia Inquirer*, 22 October 1999; Milt Freudenheim, "Oxford Health Plans Posts Its First Profit in Two Years," *New York Times*, 3 November 1999.

60. Peter T. Kilborn, "HMO's Are Cutting Back Coverage of the Poor and Elderly,"*New York Times*, 6 July 1998; Robert Pear, "HMO's Will Drop 327,000 Medicare Patients, U.S. Says," *New York Times*, 16 July 1999; Robert Pear, "Medicare HMOs to Cut Free Prescription Coverage," *New York Times*, 22 September 1999; Robert Pear, "Estimate of Ousters by HMOs Is Raised," *New York Times*, 25 July 2000.

61. *Highlights, National Health Expenditures, 1998* (HCFA, 10 January 2000), available from www.hcfa.gov/stats/nhe-oact-hilites.htm; Robert A. Rosenblatt, "Medicare HMO Patients to Face Higher Charges," *Los Angeles Times*, 16 September 1999; Robert Pear, "Annual Spending on Medicare Dips for the First Time," *New York Times*, 14 November 1999.

62. Robert Pear, "Spending on Health Grew Slowly in 1996," *New York Times*, 13 Jan-

uary 1998; Robert Pear, "Survey Paints Bleak Medical-Care Picture for Many Americans," *New York Times*, 23 October 1996; David J. Morrow, "The High Cost of Plugging the Gaps in Medicare," *New York Times*, 12 May 1996; Rhonda L. Rundle, "Can Managed Care Manage Costs?" *Wall Street Journal*, 9 August 1999.

63. Steven Findlay and Joel Miller, "Down a Dangerous Path: The Erosion of Health Insurance Coverage in the United States" (National Coalition on Health Care, 1999). Counting the uninsured is far from a straightforward or unambiguous task. See Kimball Lewis, Marilyn Ellwood, and John L. Czajka, "Counting the Uninsured: A Review of the Literature" (Washington, DC: Urban Institute, Assessing the New Federalism Project, 1998); U.S. Census Bureau, *Health Insurance Coverage: 1999,* 4 October 1999.

64. Todd S. Purdum, "Clinton Signs Bill Expanding Access to Health Insurance," *New York Times*, 12 August 1996; David Hess and James Kuhnhenn, "Senate Debate on HMOs Is Clash of Monied Titans," *Philadelphia Inquirer*, 9 July 1999; Robert Pear, "Clinton to Push Health Insurers Who Deny Coverage to Sick," *New York Times*, 7 July 1998.

65. Robert Pear, "Six-Month Rule Set on Mental Health Insurance," *New York Times*, 16 December 1997; John Hendren, "Loophole Undermines Law on Parity for Mental Health Care," *Philadelphia Inquirer*, 10 August 1998; Robert Pear, "Federal Workers Promised Gains in Mental-Health Coverage," *New York Times*, 25 May 1999.

66. John M. Broder, "Clinton Proposes Allowing Some Uninsured to Buy Medicare Coverage," *New York Times*, 7 January 1998; Robert Pear, "Clinton to Call for Extensive Regulation of Health Plans," *New York Times*, 20 November 1997; Robert Pear, "Health Panel at a Standstill in Enforcing Rights," *New York Times*, 9 March 1998; "Legislating a Patient's Rights," *New York Times*, 10 March 1998; Alissa J. Rubin, "Business Joins Fight against Health Reform Legislation: Lawmakers Can Expect a Full-Court Press by Lobbyists Who Fear Passage of a Patients' Bill of Rights in Congress," *Los Angeles Times*, 8 August 1999; Laura Meckler, "Business to Counter HMO Curbs," *Philadelphia Inquirer*, 11 March 1998; Robert Pear, "Series of Rulings Eases Constraints on Suing HMO's," *New York Times*, 15 August 1999; Robert Pear, "Court Backs Protections for Medicare Patients Denied by HMOs," *New York Times*, 14 August 1998; Robert Pear, "President to Announce New Protections for HMO Patients," *New York Times*, 17 September 1998; Linda Greenhouse, "Managed Care Challenge to Be Heard by High Court," *New York Times*, 29 September 1999; Milt Freudenheim, "Managed Care Companies Seek to Build a Legal Victory," *New York Times*, 19 August 2000; Milt Freudenheim, "Under Legal Attack, HMO's Face a Supreme Court Test," *New York Times*, 4 January 2000.

67. "Clinton Pushes Democratic Patients' Bill," CNN, 13 July 1999; available from www.cnn.com/ALLPOLITICS/stories/1999/07/13/healthcare.01/; Hess and Kuhnhenn, "Senate Debate on HMOs Is Clash of Monied Titans"; Alison Mitchell, "Senate Approves Republican Plan for Health Care," *New York Times*, 16 July 1999; Alison Mitchell, "House Leaders Try to Stem Dissent over Managed Care," *New York Times*, 28 July 1999; Robert Pear, "Most in HMOs Wouldn't Benefit from Senate Bill," *New York Times*, 28 July 1999; Robert Pear, "House Passes Bill to Expand Rights on Medical Care," *New York Times*, 8 October 1999; Robert Pear, "Health Care Bill Passed by House Intensifies Furor," *New York Times*, 7 October 1999; Robert Pear, "Stung by Defeat in House, HMOs Seek Compromise," *New York Times*, 9 October 1999; Milt Freudenheim, "Big HMOs to Give

Decisions on Care Back to Doctors," *New York Times*, 9 November 1999; Milt Freudenheim, "Medical Insurers Revise Cost-Control Efforts," *New York Times*, 3 December 1999; "In Senate, GOP Backs Bill of Rights for Patients," *New York Times*, 30 June 2000; Neil Lewis, "Patients' Bill Set to Become an Issue for Campaign," *New York Times*, 7 July 2000; Robert Pear, "Clinton Plans to Issue Rules Expanding Patients' Rights," *New York Times*, 9 October 2000.

68. Carey Goldberg, "Maine Will Cap Drug Prices with a Groundbreaking Law," *New York Times*, 12 April 2000; Carey Goldberg, "State Referendums Seeking to Overhaul Health Care System," *New York Times*, 11 June 2000; Todd S. Purdum, "California to Set Level of Staffing for Nursing Care," *New York Times*, 12 October 1999; James Sterngold, "Trailblazing California Broadens the Rights of Its HMO Patients," *New York Times*, 20 September 1999; Carey Goldberg, "For Many States, Health Care Bills Are Top Priority," *New York Times*, 23 January 2000.

69. Ron Winslow and Carol Gentry, "A Reaction to Managed Care," *Wall Street Journal*, 8 February 2000.

70. For Web-based sources of information on the Balanced Budget Act of 1997, see KRT News Service; "Budget Details on the Web," *Newark, NJ, Star-Ledger*, 1 August 1997; Robert Pear, "$24 Billion to Be Set Aside for Children's Medical Care," *New York Times*, 30 July 1997; Douglas J. Besharov, "Beware the Real Agenda," *New York Times*, 5 August 1997; Frank Ullman, Brian Bruen, and John Holahan, "The State Children's Health Insurance Program: A Look at the Numbers" (Washington, DC: Urban Institute, Assessing the New Federalism Project, 1998).

71. Robert Pear, "President Set to Establish a Toll-Free Number to Enroll Children in Health Insurance Plans," *New York Times*, 23 February 1999; Robert Pear, "Many States Slow to Use Child Health Plan," *New York Times*, 9 May 1999; "Providing ACCESS," *Philadelphia Inquirer*, 6 July 1999; Robert Pear, "Clinton to Chide States for Failing to Cover Children," *New York Times*, 8 August 1999; Robert Pear and Robin Toner, "President Urges Government to Reach Uninsured Children," *New York Times*, 1999; Robert Pear, "Clinton to Broaden Effort in Children's Health Coverage," *New York Times*, 11 January 2000.

72. Robert Pear, "Beyond Medicare: New Choices in Health Insurance," *New York Times*, 10 August 1997; "Some Adjustments Are Needed in Medicare before Recent Belt-Tightening Affects In-Home Care" (editorial), *Philadelphia Inquirer*, 27 February 1998; Robert Pear, "Medicare Wrongly Denies Elderly Home Health Coverage," *New York Times*, 15 February 1998.

73. Robert Pear, "With Budget Cutting, Medicare Spending Fell Unexpectedly," *New York Times*, 4 May 1999; Laurie McGinley, "Congress Moves to Ease Medicare Cuts with Bills Increasing Reimbursements," *Wall Street Journal*, 14 October 1999; Robert Pear, "Republicans Plan to Restore Billions Cut from Medicare," *New York Times*, 14 October 1999.

74. Milt Freudenheim, "So Far, 'Medicare Plus Choice' Is Minus Most of the Options," *New York Times*, 4 October 1998; "Focus Groups Show Beneficiaries Need Help with Medicare Choices," *Social Insurance Update* 9, 2 (September 1998): 1–2. For an example of a pamphlet explaining Medicare, see J. Robert Treanor, Dale R. Detfels, and Robert J. Myers, *2000 Medicare* (Washington. DC: Social Security Administration, 1999).

75. Associated Press, "Congress Seeks to Restore Money to Home Health Care Agencies," *New York Times*, 6 August 1998; Michael Vitez, "New Rules Hurt Home Health-Care Agencies, Doctors Told," *Philadelphia Inquirer*, 5 December 1998; see sources in preceding note. For an account of the moral and ethical conse-

quences of changes in home health care, see Deborah Stone, "Care and Trembling," *American Prospect*, no. 43 (March–April 1999); Robert Pear, "Medicare Spending for Care at Home Plunges by 45%," *New York Times*, 21 April 2000.

76. Alice Ann Love, "States Get New Freedom to Cut Medicaid for Nursing Homes," *Philadelphia Inquirer*, 16 August 1997; Joshua M. Weiner and David G. Stevenson, "Repeal of the 'Boren Amendment': Implications for the Quality of Care in Nursing Homes" (Washington, DC: Urban Institute, Assessing the New Federalism Project, 1998); Eric Bates, "The Shame of Our Nursing Homes," *Nation*, 29 March 1999, 11–19.

77. John Stamper, "Medicare Gaps Put Burden of Expense on Poor, Study Finds," *Philadelphia Inquirer*, 5 March 1998; Robert Pear, "Study Offered in Bid to Block Medicare Cuts," *New York Times*, 5 March 1998; Robert Pear, "Clinton's Plan to Have Medicare Cover Drugs Means a Big Debate Ahead in Congress," *New York Times*, 24 January 1999; Milt Freudenheim, "Patients Facing Higher Costs for Prescription Drugs," *New York Times*, 25 January 1999; Michael E. Gluck, "A Medicare Prescription Drug Benefit" (Washington, DC: National Academy of Social Insurance, 1999); Robert Toner, "Prescription Drug Coverage Dominates Fight Brewing on Medicare Overhaul," *New York Times*, 16 June 1999. Clinton proposed that Medicare pay for half of a beneficiary's drug costs up to $5,000 each year when the plan phased in fully in 2008. Medicare also would offer beneficiaries discounts similar to those in many employer plans, and it would ensure that beneficiaries with incomes below 135 percent of the poverty line would not pay premiums or cost sharing and that those with incomes between 135 and 150 percent of the poverty line would receive help with premiums as well. Employers would receive incentives to retain retiree health coverage if they added a prescription drug benefit. The new benefit would cost roughly $24 a month when it started in 2002 and rise to $44 a month in 2008. Beneficiaries also would pay a new charge, 20 percent of the cost of laboratory tests, which could amount to a very sizable increase in their medical expenses. Michael Weinstein, "Two Medicare Plans, But Not So Far Apart," *New York Times*, 1 July 1999; Jennifer Steinhauer, "Rising Costs of Medications Take Bigger Share of Insurance Outlays," *New York Times*, 29 October 1999; David E. Rosenbaum, "The Gathering Storm over Prescription Drugs," *New York Times*, 14 November 1999.

78. Robert Pear, "Drug Makers and Insurers Lock Horns over Medicare," *New York Times*, 21 February 2000; Robert Pear, "White House Raises Expected Cost of Medicare Drug Plan," *New York Times*, 10 February 2000; Robert Pear, "Drug Makers Drop Their Opposition to Medicare Plan," *New York Times*, 14 January 2000; Robert Pear, "Studies Doubt Effectiveness of Drug Plan by President," *New York Times*, 7 March 2000.

79. Robert Pear, "Senator Offers Proposal to Change Medicare," *New York Times*, 23 January 1999; Robert Pear, "Panel on Medicare Disbands after Clinton Denunciation," *New York Times*, 17 March 1999; Robert Pear, "Kennedy Opens Attack on Plan by Chief of Medicare Panel," *New York Times*, 28 January 1999.

80. Robin Toner, "The Hard Lessons of Health Reform," *New York Times*, 4 July 1999; Robert Pear, "Drug Makers Fault the Details of Clinton Medicare Proposal," *New York Times*, 16 July 1999; Robert Pear, "Drug Company Ads Attack Coverage of Drugs," *New York Times*, 29 July 1999; "Clinton Proposes a Discount System on Medicare Costs," *New York Times*, 19 October 1999; Robert Pear, "Congress Rejects Idea of Using Managed Care for Medicare," *New York Times*, 22 October 1999; Milt Fruedenheim, "In Clinton's Derailed Proposal for Medicare, a Ques-

tion of Savings," *New York Times*, 24 October 1999; Robert Pear, "Budget Office Says Clinton Underestimated Cost of Drug Plan," *New York Times*, 23 July 1999; Robert Pear, "House Approves Medicare Extension for the Disabled," *New York Times*, 20 October 1999; "Panel of Bipartisan Health Experts Agree: U.S. Must Consider New Revenues for Medicare's Long Term," *Social Insurance Update* 10, 3 (November 1999): 1–2.

81. "America's Unmet Obligation," *New York Times*, 12 September 1999; James Dao, "Bradley Presents Health Plan for Almost All the Uninsured," *New York Times*, 29 September 1999; Robin Toner, "Rx Redux: Fevered Issues, Second Opinion," *New York Times*, 10 October 1999; Charles Babbington, "Clinton Issues Health Care Plan: $110 Billion Proposal Aims to Expand Coverage," *Washington Post*, 20 January 2000; "Clinton-Gore Administration Unveils Major New Health Insurance Initiative (White House Office of the Press Secretary, 19 January 2000).

82. Kevin Sack, "Gore, Sensing Edge, Pushes Bush for More Specifics on Health Care," *New York Times*, 28 August 2000; Robin Toner, "Political Battle Lines Are Clearly Drawn in Fight over Medicare Drug Coverage," *New York Times*, 24 July 2000.

83. Toner, "Political Battle Lines"; Sack, "Gore, Sensing Edge"; Robin Toner, "Experts See Fix for Medicare as One Tough Proposition," *New York Times*, 12 September 2000.

CHAPTER 11: FIGHTING POVERTY 1990S STYLE

1. Iris J. Lav and Edward B. Lazere, *A Hand Up. How State Earned Income Credits Help Working Families Escape Poverty* (Washington, DC: Center on Budget and Policy Priorities, January 1996), 3–4; Isaac Shapiro and Sharon Parrott, "An Unraveling Consensus? An Analysis of the Effect of the New Congressional Agenda on the Working Poor" (Washington: Center on Budget and Policy Priorities, 1995).

2. Congress enacted the EITC in 1975 to combine welfare reform with tax relief for low-income workers. It offered conservative members of Congress an acceptable alternative to the guaranteed income implicit in President Richard Nixon's Family Assistance Plan, and it reduced or eliminated rising Social Security taxes for low-income wage earners. Taxpayers claim a credit against their income tax; if the credit exceeds their liability, they receive a check for the difference. Christopher Howard, *The Hidden Welfare State: Tax Expenditures and Social Policy in the United States* (Princeton: Princeton University Press, 1997), 69, 74; Testimony, 15 June 1995, Robert Greenstein, Executive Director, Center for Budget and Policy Priorities, House Ways and Means Oversight, "Earned Income Tax Credit"; Saul D. Hoffman and Laurence S. Seidman, *The Earned Income Tax Credit: Antipoverty Effectiveness and Labor Market Effects* (Kalamazoo, MI: W. E. Upjohn Institute for Employment Research, 1990), 4; John Karl Scholz, "Tax Policy and the Working Poor: The Earned Income Tax Credit," *Focus* 15, 3 (Winter 1993–94): 1–2; Lav and Lazere, *A Hand Up*, 15–17; *1996 Green Book*, 804; Rebecca M. Blank, "The Employment Strategy: Public Policies to Increase Work and Earnings," in *Confronting Poverty: Prescriptions for Change*, eds. Sheldon H. Danziger, Gary D. Sandefur, and Daniel H. Weinberg (Cambridge: Harvard University Press; New York: Russell Sage Foundation, 1994), 192–95. The EITC expanded with little support, or opposition, from the usual players—corporations and other major interest groups. Outside Congress, its major support came from Robert

Greenstein and his Center for Budget and Policy Priorities. Howard, *Hidden Welfare State*, 139, 147.

3. *1996 Green Book*, 809, table 14–14; Scholz, "Alternatives," 41; Richard W. Stevenson, "Clinton Wants $2 Billion in Expansion in Tax Credit for Working Poor," *New York Times*, 12 January 2000.

4. For an example of Republican moderation on the EITC, see, Testimony, 26 September 1995, William Roth, Jr., Chairman, Senate Finance Full Committee Markup, "Budget Reconciliation."

5. Howard, *Hidden Welfare State*, 139–40; Tim Weiner, "G.O.P. Plan Would Delay a Tax Credit for Workers," *New York Times*, 30 September 1999.

6. Howard, *Hidden Welfare State*, 142, 156; "Clinton's Economic Plan: The Speech; Text of the President's Address to a Joint Session of Congress," *New York Times*, 18 February 1993.

7. Testimony, 15 June 1995, Leslie Samuels, Assistant Secretary, Tax Policy, Department of the Treasury, House Ways and Means Oversight, "Earned Income Tax Credit"; Testimony, 8 May 1997, American Institute of Certified Public Accountants, House Ways and Means, "Earned Income Tax Credit Compliance Study"; Testimony, 8 May 1997, Bill Archer, Congressman, House Ways and Means, "Earned Income Tax Credit Compliance Study"; Testimony, 29 January 1998, Stefan F. Tucker, Chair-Elect on Behalf of the Section of Taxation of the American Bar Association, Senate Finance, IRS Restructuring and Oversight; Testimony, 15 June 1995, Jonathan Forman, Professor, University of Oklahoma Law School, House Ways and Means Oversight, "Earned Income Tax Credit"; Testimony, 10 February 1997, Dr. Joseph E. Stiglitz, Chairman, President's Council of Economic Advisors, "House Joint 1997 Economic Report of the President." For an argument that problems of noncompliance and inaccuracy are inherent in tax-based transfer programs such as the EITC, see Anne L. Alstott, "The Earned Income Tax Credit and the Limitations of Tax-Based Welfare Reform," *Harvard Law Review* 108 (January 1995): 533–92. Testimony, 8 May 1997, John Karl Scholz, Deputy Assistant Secretary for Tax Analysis, Department of the Treasury, House Ways and Means, "Earned Income Tax Credit Compliance Study"; Testimony, 8 May 1997, Michael P. Dolan, Deputy Commissioner, Internal Revenue Service, House Ways and Means, "Earned Income Tax Credit Compliance Study"; Testimony, 8 May 1997, Lynda D. Willis, Director, Tax Policy and Administration Issues, General Government Division, U.S. General Accounting Office, House Ways and Means, "Earned Income Tax Credit Compliance Study."

8. Lisa Schiffren, "America's Best Kept Welfare Secret," *American Spectator*, April 1995, 25. For other conservative criticism, see Testimony, 8 June 1995, Marvin H. Kosters, American Enterprise Institute, Senate Finance, "Earned Income Tax Credit"; and Testimony, 26 September 1995, Orrin G. Hatch, Senator, Senate Finance Full Committee Markup, "Budget Reconciliation." On the marriage penalty, see Testimony, 28 January 1998, Bruce Bartlett, Senior Fellow, National Center for Policy Analysis, House Ways and Means, "Proposals to Reduce Taxes"; and Testimony, 28 January 1998, Michael J. Graetz, Justus S. Hotchkiss Professor of Law, Yale Law School, House Ways and Means, "Proposals to Reduce Taxes"; Testimony, 15 June 1995, Robert Greenstein, Executive Director, Center for Budget and Policy Priorities, House Ways and Means Oversight, "Earned Income Tax Credit"; John Karl Scholz, "Alternatives to Welfare Income: The EITC," *Welfare Reform in the 104th Congress: Goals, Options and Tradeoffs*.

Strategies for Self-Sufficiency: Jobs, Earnings, Child Support and Earned Income Tax Credit, Institute for Research on Poverty, special report no. 65 (28 April 1995), 41–43.

9. Other means-tested transfer programs reduced the depth of poverty by closing the poverty gap (the distance between income and the poverty line) more effectively— about 21 percent, compared to 8.7 percent for the EITC. It reduced poverty among children who were white non-Hispanic by 5.5 percent, among black non-Hispanic by 8.1 percent, and among Hispanic by 14.8 percent. The EITC proved especially effective among Hispanic children, whose parents often were employed, but at low wages. "Strengths of the Safety Net: How the EITC, Social Security, and Other Government Programs Affect Poverty," 9 March 1998, Center on Budget and Policy Priorities; Howard, *Hidden Welfare State*, 159; "Congressional Briefing. The Earned Income Tax Credit: Help for Poor Working Families," Joint Center for Policy Research, 23 June 1999, http://www.jcpr.org/EITCbriefing.html; Gene B. Spirling, "The Clinton Administration's Anti-Poverty Agenda," 1 October 1999, http://whitehouse.gov/WH/New/html/poverty.html.

10. For more on the near sacrilization of work, see Daniel T. Rodgers, *The Work Ethic in Industrializing America, 1850–1920* (Chicago: University of Chicago Press, 1978); for an application of the glorification of work to welfare, see Lawrence M. Mead, *Beyond Entitlement: The Social Obligations of Citizenship* (New York: Free Press, 1986).

11. Robert Rankin, "Minimum Wage Raise Looks Likely," *Philadelphia Inquirer*, 22 April 1996; Louis Uchitelle, "Pros and Cons Acknowledged in Higher Minimum Wage," *New York Times*, 20 March 1998; Testimony, 10 February 1997; David E. Rosenbaum, "Notebook—the Minimum Wage: A Portrait," *New York Times*, 19 April 1996; Dr. Joseph E. Stiglitz, Chairman, President's Council of Economic Advisors, "House Joint 1997 Economic Report of the President"; Robert Greenstein, "Raising Families with a Full-Time Worker Out of Poverty: The Role of an Increase in the Minimum Wage" (Washington, DC: Center for Budget and Policy Priorities, May 8, 1996), http://epn.org/cbpp/cbrafa.html; Bob Herbert, "In America, Sliding Pay Scale," *New York Times*, 5 February 1996. Social science research helped Clinton's case. Orthodox economists had argued more on the basis of theory than empirical evidence that raising the minimum wage increased unemployment. A study by two economists, David Card of the University of California at Berkeley and Alan B. Krueger of Princeton, effectively refuted the argument with evidence from New Jersey, where modest increases in low-skilled work had followed an increase in the minimum wage. The experience of the economy after the Clinton administration increase confirmed their findings and underlined the failure of the minimum wage either to fuel inflation or throw people out of work. Other research revealed that the combination of the minimum wage and EITC constituted an effective antipoverty strategy. Rebecca Blank, "The Employment Strategy: Public Policies to Increase Work and Earnings," in Danziger, Sandefur, and Weinberg, *Confronting Poverty*, 195; E. J. Dionne, Jr., "A Strong Economy and Principles of Social Justice Can Provide Incentives to Workers," *Philadelphia Inquirer*, 21 July 1998.

12. This argument is influenced by the framework developed in James Weinstein, *The Corporate Ideal in the Liberal State, 1900–1918* (Boston: Beacon Press, 1968). Resident aliens also could claim the EITC. However, the Clinton administration excluded illegal aliens from benefits.

13. Howard, *Hidden Welfare State*, 160.
14. Howard, *Hidden Welfare State*, 160; David T. Ellwood, "Anti-Poverty for Families in the Next Century: From Welfare to Work—and Worried" (1999).
15. Michael Hout, "Inequality at the Margins: The Effects of Welfare, the Minimum Wage, and Tax Credits on Low-Wage Labor Markets" (Russell Sage Foundation, March 1997); Spirling, "Clinton Administration's Anti-Poverty Agenda."
16. Victor Oliveira, "Food-Assistance Spending Held Steady in 1996," *Food Assistance*, January–April 1997, 49–56.
17. On federal agricultural relief policies in the 1930s, see Janet Popendieck, *Breadlines Knee Deep in Wheat: Food Assistance in the Great Depression* (New Brunswick, NJ: Rutgers University Press, 1986). On the history of food stamps and issues in program design and management, see Maurice MacDonald, *Food, Stamps, and Income Maintenance* (New York: Academic Press, 1977); James C. Ohls and Harold Beebout, *The Food Stamp Program: Design Tradeoffs, Policy, and Impacts* (Washington, DC: Urban Institute Press, 1993); Ardith L. Maney, *Still Hungry after All These Years: Food Assistance Policy from Kennedy to Reagan* (New York: Greenwood Press, 1989).
18. MacDonald, *Food, Stamps, and Income Maintenance*; Ohls and Beebout, *The Food Stamp Program*; Maney, *Still Hungry; Physician Task Force on Hunger in America: The Growing Epidemic* (Boston: Harvard University School of Public Health, 1985); John E. Schwarz, *America's Hidden Success: A Reassessment of Twenty Years of Public Policy* (New York: Norton, 1983).
19. The Hunger Prevention Act of 1988; the 1990 Food, Agriculture, Conservation, and Trade Act; and the 1992 Mickey Leland Childhood Hunger Act. *1996 Green Book*, 877–78, 861, table 16–4.
20. *1996 Green Book*, 856–67.
21. The numbers are drawn from U.S. Department of Agriculture, Food and Nutrition Service, Office of Analysis and Evaluation, *Characteristics of Food Stamp Households, Fiscal Year 1996* (March 1998).
22. Viviana A. Zelizer, *The Social Meaning of Money* (New York: Basic Books, 1994), 195–96. For a criticism of the restriction of food stamp purchases to other than "junk" foods, see Testimony, 10 May 1995, C. Manly Molpus, President and Chief Executive Officer, Grocery Manufacturers of America, House Agricultural Department Operations, Nutrition and Foreign Agriculture Food Stamp Program; Department Operations and Nutrition Subcommittee, House Agriculture Committee; Ohls and Beebout, *The Food Stamp Program*, 172: A switch from coupons to cash "could significantly erode public support for the program. Indeed, it might well end the program as a separate entity." Some states have received waivers to operate pilot cash-out programs.
23. Testimony, 10 May 1995, Dwain J. Kyles, Attorney and Consultant for the Jane Addams Hull House Association, House Committee on Agriculture, Subcommittee on Department Operations. For one comment on the progress of EBT, see Testimony, 12 May 1997, Mary Ann Keefe, Acting Undersecretary, Food, Nutrition, and Consumer Services, U.S. Department of Agriculture. House Committee on Agriculture. Subcommittee on Department Operations, Nutrition, and Foreign Agriculture.
24. Testimony, 5 February 1998, Christo M. Tola, President, United Council on Welfare Fraud, House Agriculture Department Operations, Nutrition and Foreign Agriculture Food Stamp Fraud, Committee on Agriculture, Subcommittee on Department Operations; Testimony, 1 February 1995, Hon. Pat Roberts, Chair-

man, House Agriculture, Food Stamps Program Revision; Testimony, 30 October 1997, Robert A. Robinson, Director, Food and Agriculture Issues, General Accounting Office, Agriculture Department Operations, Nutrition and Foreign Agriculture Food Stamp Program Abuses, before Subcommittee on Department Operations.

25. Ed Gillespie and Bob Schellhas, eds., *Contract with America: The Bold Plan by Rep. Newt Gingrich, Rep. Dick Armey, and the House Republicans to Change the Nation* (New York: Times Books, 1994), 72–73; Testimony, 8 June 1995, Ellen Haas, Undersecretary, Food, Nutrition, and Consumer Services, U.S. Department of Agriculture, before the Subcommittee on Department Operations, Nutrition and Foreign Agriculture, Committee on Agriculture; Robert Pear, "House Leaders and Republican Governors Agree on an Alternative to Food Stamps," *New York Times*, 2 March 1995; Robert Pear, "House Republicans Propose Using a Work Requirement to Help Cut Food Stamp Costs," *New York Times*, 6 March 1995; Robert Pear, "House Panel Votes to Cut Food Stamps," *New York Times*, 8 March 1995; Robert Pear, "2 Nutrition Programs Win Crucial Backing in Senate," *New York Times*, 10 June 1995; AP, "Panel Trims Nutrition Spending, but Keeps Food Stamps Benefits," *New York Times*, 14 June 1995; Robert Pear, "House and Senate Leaders Compromise to Soften Welfare Bill," *New York Times*, 10 November 1995.

26. Rachel L. Swarns, "Denied Food Stamps, Many Immigrants Scrape for Meals," *New York Times*, 8 December 1997. For an eloquent criticism of the food stamp provisions in the 1996 legislation, see Bob Herbert, "In America, Get Real on Food Stamps," *New York Times*, 21 February 1997. Center on Budget and Policy Priorities, "Who Will Lose Food Stamps under the Three-Month Cut-Off?" rev. 5 March 1997 and "The Depth of the Food Stamp Cuts in the Final Welfare Bill," rev. 14 August 1996.

27. *1996 Green Book*, 379–80. For example, see Karl Stark, "USDA Grants Food-Stamp Waivers, Benefits Are Saved for 29,000 in PA," *Philadelphia Inquirer*, 16 January 1997. This paragraph is based in part on a conversation with Steven Carlson of the Food and Nutrition Service, 24 March 1998. See also editorial "An Uneven Budget Agreement," *New York Times*, 3 May 1997; Peter T. Kilborn, "In Budget Deal, Clinton Keeps Welfare Pledge," *New York Times*, 1 August 1997.

28. Robert Pear, "GOP Governors Seek to Restore Immigrant Aid," *New York Times*, 25 January 1997; Robert Pear, "Limit Change on Welfare, Governors Say," *New York Times*, 3 February 1997; Marjorie Valbrun, "Pressure on Ridge to Fund Food Stamps," *Philadelphia Inquirer*, 11 March 1998. See, for example, Joe Sexton, "Merchants with Stubborn Hopes," *New York Times*, 19 July 1997; Thomas Ginsberg, "N.J. Will Restore Food Aid For 20,000 Immigrants Set to Lose Food Stamps Next Week," *Philadelphia Inquirer*, 27 August 1997; Jennifer Lyon, "Signs of Hunger after Cuts in Aid," *Philadelphia Inquirer*, 5 January 1998; Stacy Dean and Kelly Carmody, "States Now Have the Option to Purchase Food Stamps to Provide Assistance to Legal Immigrants," Center on Budget and Policy Priorities, 4 December 1997 [http://www.cbpp.org/statepor.htm]; Tony Pugh, "Law to End Food Stamps for 900,000," *Philadelphia Inquirer*, 18 August 1997; James Dao, "Aliens Would Get Food Stamps Back in Clinton Budget," *New York Times*, 2 February 1998; Lizette Alvarez, "Senate Approves Restoration of Food Stamps for Some Legal Immigrants," *New York Times*, 13 May 1998; Curt Anderson "House Passes Food Stamp Bill," *Washington Post*, 6 May, 1998; Helen Dewar, "Bill to Restore Food Stamps Struggles Despite 71 Senators' Support," *Washing-*

ton Post, 28 April 1998; Michael Janofsky, "Legal Immigrants Would Regain Aid in Clinton's Plan," *New York Times*, 25 January 1999; Sandra Sobieraji, "Clinton Signs Bill to Restore Food Stamps to Some Immigrants," *Philadelphia Inquirer*, 24 June 1998. Congress approved food stamps for immigrants in this country before the passage of the August 1996 "welfare reform" legislation, and to those who were elderly, under eighteen, or came to the United States to escape religious or political persecution.

29. "Food Stamp Program Qs and As," U.S. Department of Agriculture, Food and Consumer Service, December 1997, worldwide Web edition; "Some Food Stamp Facts," U.S. Department of Agriculture, Food and Consumer Service, undated, worldwide Web edition; interview with Steven Carlson; "The Food Stamp Fracas in New York," *New York Times*, 12 November 1999; Nina Bernstein, "Burial Plots, Bingo and Blood in the Quest for Food Stamps," *New York Times*, 12 August 2000; Dana Milbank, "Spare a Dime?, Review of *Sweet Charity? Emergency Food and the End of Entitlement*, by Janet Poppendieck," *New York Times*, 18 October 1998; Andrew C. Revkin, "Plunge in Use of Food Stamps Causes Concern," *New York Times*, 25 February 1999; Rachel L. Swarns, "In an Odd Turn, Officials Are Pushing Welfare," *New York Times*, 22 November 1998; Robert Pear, "Clinton Plan to Seek Out Those Eligible for Food Stamps," *New York Times*, 14 July 1999.

30. William L. Hamilton et al., "Household Food Security in the United States in 1995," Summary Report of the Food Measurement Project, U.S. Department of Agriculture, Food and Consumer Service, Office of Analysis and Evaluation, September 1997; Margaret Andrews, Mark Nord, Gary Bickel, and Steven Carlson, "Household Food Security in the United States, 1999" (U.S. Department of Agriculture, 2000).

31. Rachel L. Swarns, "Cut Off from Food Stamps but Not Flocking to Soup Kitchens," *New York Times*, 6 July 1997; David Firestone, "Rise in Hunger Prompts City to Approve $2 Million for Food," *New York Times*, 27 November 1997; "Long Lines at Soup Kitchens after Idaho Welfare Cuts," *New York Times*, 7 December 1997; Jennifer Loven, "Signs of Hunger after Cuts in Aid," *Philadelphia Inquirer*, 5 January 1998. Hunger remained a problem among the elderly, too. See Trudy Lieberman, "Hunger in America," *Nation*, 30 March 1998, 11–16; Monica Yant, "Food Banks Face Possible Crisis," *Philadelphia Inquirer*, 10 June 1999. See also Mark Forrest, "Measuring Social Costs at a Basic Level: Food Banks," *Philadelphia Inquirer*, 21 March 1999; Andrew C. Revkin, "As Demand for Food Donations Grows, Supplies Steadily Dwindle," *New York Times*, 27 February 1999; Andrew C. Revkin, "Welfare Policies Altering Face of Lines at Charities Offering Food," *New York Times*, 26 February 1999.

32. Tony Pugh, "Study: Face of Hunger Is Changing," *Philadelphia Inquirer*, 11 March 1998.

33. On the history of legal services, see John A. Dooley and Alan W. Houseman, "Legal Services History" (MS, November 1984), and Linda E. Perle, "History of Legal Services," MS (Center for Law and Social Policy, December 1992); Alan W. Houseman, "Can Legal Services Achieve Equal Justice?" (Center for Law and Social Policy).

34. Houseman, "Can Legal Services Achieve Equal Justice?"

35. Perle, "History," 3; Dooley and Houseman, "Legal Services History." On the history of welfare rights cases and the debates among poverty-law attorneys, see Martha F. Davis, *Brutal Need: Lawyers and the Welfare Rights Movement*,

1960–1973 (New Haven: Yale University Press, 1993). Houseman, "Can Legal Services Achieve Equal Justice?"

36. Alexander Forger, Testimony, Committee on Labor and Human Resources, U.S. Senate, 23 June 1995.

37. Anthony Lewis, "Abroad at Home, Thumb on the Scales," *New York Times*, 29 May 1996; William Booth, "Attacked as Left-Leaning, Legal Services Suffers Deep Cuts," *Washington Post*, 1 June 1996.

38. Mary Wisniewski-Holden, "Clipped Wings and Budget Cuts Tax Legal Aid," *Chicago Lawyer*, August 1997.

39. Robert Pear, "U.S. Issues Rules to Tighten Legal Aid to Poor and Elderly," *New York Times*, 4 September 1983; Stuart Taylor, "Battle over Legal Services May Now Begin in Earnest," *New York Times*, 16 June 1985; John A. Dooley and Alan W. Houseman, "Refine, Don't Destroy Legal Services," *ABA Journal*, May 1983, 606; Anne Kornhauser, "Reagan Administration's Legal Legacy: Last-Gasp Lobbying Push by Legal Services Board," *Legal Times*, 10 October 1988, 5; on tensions between the Legal Services Corporation and local offices during the 1980s, see Kenneth Jost, " 'Past Actions Not Defensible'; The Legal Services Corporation Chief Haunted by Own Critique of Agency," *Legal Times*, 18 November 1991, 22; Kenneth H. Boehm, "The Legal Services Corporation: New Funding, New Loopholes, Old Games," Heritage Foundation Backgrounder Update no. 276 (17 May 1996).

40. Kenneth F. Boehm and Peter T. Flaherty, "Why the Legal Services Corporation Must Be Abolished," Heritage Foundation Backgrounder no. 1057 (18 October 1995); David Wilkinson, "Legal Services for the Poor: Is Federal Support Necessary?" *Alternatives in Philanthropy* (November 1996), www.savers.org/crc/ap/ap§1196.html. Wilkinson was the first inspector general of the Legal Services Corporation (1989–91) and Utah attorney general (1981–89).

41. Dooley and Houseman, "Legal Services History"; Forger, Testimony.

42. Stephen Labaton, "House Panel Opts to Kill Agency Giving Legal Advice to the Poor," *New York Times*, 14 September 1995; Carol Horowitz, "Activism of Legal Services Corp.," *Investor's Business Daily*, 24 July 1995, A1; Rhonda McMillion, "The Legal Services Corporation, Down but Not Out: With Reauthorizations Smiling, ABA Carries on Fight for Legal Services," *ABA Journal*, August 1996; "No Legal Services for the Undocumented," *Washington Post*, 24 June 1996; Judith Resnik and Emily Bazelon, "Legal Services: Then and Now," *Yale Law and Policy Review* 17, 1 (1 November 1998): 291–303.

43. David Cole, "Confining Compromise," *Recorder*, 12 February 1997, 5; Houseman, "Can Legal Services Achieve Equal Justice?"; Lewis, "Thumb on the Scales"; Nina Bernstein, "Suit Challenges Accord That Bars Legal Services Class-Action Cases for Poor," *New York Times*, 1 August 1996; Jan Hoffman, "Counseling the Poor, but Now One by One," *New York Times*, 15 September 1996; Don Van Natta, Jr., "Legal Services Wins on Suit for the Poor," *New York Times*, 27 December 1996; Don Van Natta Jr., "Lawyers Split on Impact of Ruling on Suits for the Poor," *New York Times*, 29 January 1996; Linda Greenhouse, "Court Questions Congress' Limits on Legal Aid Arguments," *New York Times*, 5 October 2000.

44. Henry Weinstein, "Legal Aid for the Impoverished Faces Budget Ax," *Los Angeles Times*, 29 December 1995; Booth, "Attacked as Left Leaning"; David S. Udell, "The Legal Services Restrictions: Lawyers in Florida, New York, Virginia, and Oregon Describe the Costs," *Yale Law and Policy Review* 17, 1 (November 1998): 337–68.

45. Houseman, "Can Legal Services Achieve Equal Justice?"; and Alan W. House-man, "Devolution: The Legal Services Response" (Center for Law and Social Policy, February 1998), www.clasp.org/pubs/legalservices/MIEJAN_DR.htm; Supreme Court of the United States, *"Saenz v. Roe,"* no. 98–97 (1999); Tom Avril, "N.J. Residency Law to Limit Welfare Pay Is Struck Down," *Philadelphia Inquirer*, 9 July 1998; Linda Greenhouse, "The Court Resurrects a Civil War Era Ideal," *New York Times*, 23 May, 1999; Linda Greenhouse, "Justices Bar Two-Tiered Welfare," *New York Times*, 18 May 1999.

46. Catherine C. Carr and Alison E. Hirschel, "The Transformation of Community Legal Service, Inc., of Philadelphia: One Program's Experience since the Federal Restrictions," *Yale Law and Policy Review* 17, 1 (November 1998): 319–35; Rinat Fried, "Legal Aid Groups Divide and Conquer," *Legal Times*, 9 September 1996, 14.

47. Boehm, "New Funding, New Loopholes"; Wilkinson, "Is Federal Support Necessary?"; Julie Stoiber, "Legal Services to Get a Badly Needed Financial Lift," *Philadelphia Inquirer*, 28 August 1996; "Lawyers Deliver Record 500,000 to Local Legal Aid Agencies," *PR Newswire*, 18 December 1996; April White, "Arbitration Donations Benefit Foundation, Community Legal Services to Tune of $22,000," *Legal Intelligencer*, 9 September 1996; Michael A. Riccardi, "IOLTA Means Neighborhood Law Office Stays Open," *Legal Intelligencer*, 30 July 1996, 3; Telephone interview with Catherine Carr, Community Legal Services, 19 March 1998; "The Price of Equality? A Court That Should Back Equal Justice for All Undercuts the Funding of Legal-Aid Programs," *Philadelphia Inquirer*, 22 June 1998; Linda Greenhouse, "Court Ruling Could Jeopardize Funding of Legal Services," *New York Times*, 16 June 1998; Lorna K. Blake, "The IOLTA Fund and LSC Restrictions," *Yale Law and Policy Review* 17, 1 (1 November 1998): 455–67; Joseph S. Genova, "Thankfully, the Status Quo Continues for IOLTA," *Welfare News* 5, 1 (2000): 1–3.

48. Alan Fram, "$250 Million for Legal Services is Voted," *Philadelphia Inquirer*, 5 August 1998; David Rohde, "Decline Is Seen in Legal Help for City's Poor," *New York Times*, 26 August 1998; Karen Gullo, "Legal-aid Cases Overstated by Agency," *Philadelphia Inquirer*, 8 April 1999; Karen Gullo, "Federal Legal Agency Overstated Its Workload by 75,000 Cases," *Philadelphia Inquirer*, 26 June 1999; Houseman, "Can Legal Services Achieve Equal Justice?"; Greg Winter, "Legal Firms Cutting Back on Free Services for Poor," *New York Times*, 17 August 2000.

49. For an excellent discussion of survival strategies in the mid-nineteenth century, including the use of agriculture, see Alexander Keyssar, *Out of Work: The First Century of Unemployment in Massachusetts* (New York: Cambridge University Press, 1986). I have studied survival strategies among the poorest of New York's families at the turn of the century. For one essay based on that research, see Michael B. Katz, "Surviving Poverty," in *Improving Poor People: The Welfare State, the "Underclass," and Urban Schools as History* (Princeton: Princeton University Press, 1995), chap. 4.

50. Kathryn Edin and Laura Lein, *Making Ends Meet: How Single Mothers Survive Welfare and Low-Wage Work* (New York: Russell Sage Foundation, 1997), 143, 150; Louis Uchitelle, "The Quiet Help of Family Members," *New York Times*, 24 October 1999.

51. Doug Henwood, *Wall St.*, updated ed. (London and New York: Verso, 1997), 64–66.

52. Edward J. Bird, Paul A. Hagstrom, and Robert Wild, "Credit Cards and the Poor," *Focus* 20, 2 (Spring 1999): 40–43; Doug Henwood, "Debts Everywhere," *Nation*, 19 July 1999; Robert B. Reich, "No Easy Answers to Easy Credit Fallout" (first published in *USA Today*), available from http://www.epn.org/reich/rr990608.html; Teresa A. Sullivan, Elizabeth Warren, and Jay Lawrence Westbrook, *As We Forgive Our Debtors: Bankruptcy and Consumer Credit in America* (Cambridge: Harvard University Press, 1989); David E. Rosenbaum and Stephen Labaton, "Bankruptcy Bill Is Blocked in Fight over Minimum Pay," *New York Times*, 22 September 1999.

CHAPTER 12: THE END OF WELFARE

1. Ed Gillispie and Bob Schellhas, eds., *Contract with America: The Bold Plan by Rep. Newt Gingrich, Rep. Dick Armey, and the House Republicans to Change the Nation* (New York: Times Books, 1994), 65–77.

2. Robert Rector and William F. Lauber, *America's Failed $5.4 Trillion War on Poverty* (Washington, DC: Heritage Foundation, 1995), 2–3; *Congressional Record—House*, 31 July 1996, H9396, H9398, H9404.

3. Sharon Parrott, "How Much Do We Spend on Welfare?" (Center on Budget and Policy Priorities, 4 August 1995); Mark J. Stern, "Poverty and Family Composition since 1940," in *The "Underclass" Debate: Views from History*, ed. Michael B. Katz (Princeton: Princeton University Press, 1993), 220–53.

4. U.S. House of Representatives, *1996 Green Book*, 447–48, table 8–15.

5. Lawrence M. Mead, *The New Politics of Poverty: The Nonworking Poor in America* (New York: Basic Books, 1992); Mary Jo Bane and David T. Ellwood, *Welfare Realities: From Rhetoric to Reform* (Cambridge: Harvard University Press, 1994), 67; Daniel Patrick Moynihan, *Family and Nation* (San Diego: Harcourt, Brace, Jovanovich, 1986); Daniel Patrick Moynihan, *Miles to Go: A Personal History of Social Policy* (Cambridge: Harvard University Press, 1996); Kristin A. Moore, Executive Summary, in *Report to Congress*, pp. v–vi; *1996 Green Book*, 104–14, 1230, table H-6, 1329; Background Material and Data on Programs Within the Jurisdiction of the Committee on Ways and Means, 4 November 1996, 104th Congress, 2d session, 104–14; Paul E. Barton, "Welfare: Indicators of Dependency" (Princeton: Policy Information Center, Research Division, Educational Testing Service, 1998).

6. Rector and Lauber, *America's Failed $5.4 Trillion War*, 23, 25.

7. Most of the literature on teenage motherhood accepts that growing up with a young mother is bad for children—they do worse in school, they have more behavior problems. In a very interesting article, Arline T. Geronimus challenges this view. She points out that most studies of the impact of teenage mothers on children do not use a control group. They do not ask whether outcomes would have been similar if the same mothers had postponed childbearing to an older age. What evidence can be teased out argues that there would be no difference. She also argues for the "rationality" of teenage births among low-income African American young women. Arline T. Geronimus, "Teenage Childbearing and Personal Responsibility: An Alternative View," *Political Science Quarterly* 112, 3 (1997); Santorum, quoted in Dan Meyers and Jeffrey Fleishman, "Reform Poses Consequences for Poor," *Philadelphia Inquirer*, 22 January 1995.

8. *1996 Green Book*, 473, 1193; *Welfare Myths: Fact or Fiction?* (Center for Social Welfare Policy and Law, 1996), 19. There is a very large literature on out-of-wedlock

births and on teenage pregnancy. For a very good summary of research see, U.S. Department of Health and Human Services, *Report to Congress on Out-of-Wedlock Childbearing*, DHHS Pub. No. (PHHS) 95–1227, September 1995. The report's executive summary is written by Kristin A. Moore and the report contains a number of expert papers by authorities in the field—William Julius Wilson and Kathryn Neckerman, for instance.

9. One study found that only 19 percent of black women and 26 percent of whites who had lived in a "highly dependent" household were themselves "highly dependent." Another study found that 75 percent of AFDC "caretakers" had not received AFDC as children. Wilson quoted in Daniel Patrick Moynihan, "The Devolution Revolution," *New York Times*, 6 August 1995. *1996 Green Book*, 510. For a useful summary of research on the relation between welfare benefits and nonmarital fertility that stresses the inconclusive state of current knowledge, see Saul D. Hoffman, "Could It Be True after All? AFDC Benefits and Non-Marital Births to Young Women," *Poverty Research News* 1, 2 (Spring 1997): 1–3.

10. *Welfare Myths*, 7; *1996 Green Book*, 501–8.

11. For an excellent criticism of the argument that states should have full control of welfare, see Sheryll D. Cashin, "Federalism, Welfare Reform, and the Minority Poor: Accounting for the Tyranny of State Majorities," *Columbia Law Review* 99, 3 (April 1999): 552–627; *Congressional Record—House*, 31 July 1996, H9393.

12. Martin Gilens, *Why Americans Hate Welfare: Race, Media, and the Politics of Antipoverty Policy* (Chicago: University of Chicago Press, 1999), 3; *Congressional Record—House*, 31 July 1996, H9415.

13. Gilens, *Why Americans Hate Welfare*, 102–53; *1996 Green Book*, 474, table 8–28, 483–84, table 8–33.

14. David T. Ellwood, "Welfare Reform as I Knew It: When Bad Things Happen to Good Policies," *American Prospect*, no. 26 (May–June 1996): 22–29. Ellwood is one of the leading academic authorities on poverty and welfare. Jason DeParle, "In Welfare Debate, It's Not 'How?' but 'Why?'" *New York Times*, 8 May 1994; Peter T. Kilborn and Sam Howe Verhovek, "Clinton Welfare Shift and Tortuous Journey," *New York Times*, 2 August 1996.

15. For an excellent discussion of the political logic of Clinton's position see R. Kent Weaver, "Ending Welfare as We Know It," in *The Social Divide: Political Parties and the Future of Activist Government*, ed. Margaret Weir (Washington, DC: Brookings Institution; New York: Russell Sage Foundation, 1998), 363. *Contract with America*, 68. Peter Edelman, "The Worst Thing Bill Clinton Has Done," *Atlantic Monthly*, March 1997, 43–58; Robert Pear, "House Backs Bill Undoing Decades of Welfare Policy," *New York Times*, 25 March 1995.

16. Pear, "House Backs Bill"; Alison Mitchell, "Clinton and Dole Present Programs to Alter Welfare," *New York Times*, 1 August 1995; Edelman, "The Worst Thing."

17. Robert Pear, "Dole Offers Welfare Bill, but Conservatives Reject It," *New York Times*, 5 August 1995; Robert Pear, "White House Seeks Areas of Welfare Accord with G.O.P.," *New York Times*, 6 August 1995; Alison Mitchell, "Clinton Prods Senate on Welfare Overhaul," *New York Times*, 9 September 1995; Robin Toner, "Senators Gain on Welfare Bill but Delay Vote," *New York Times*, 5 September 1995; "The Conference Agreement on the Welfare Bill" (Center on Budget and Policy Priorities, 1995), http://epn.org/cbpp/cbconf.html; "Senate Approves Welfare Bill," "Morning Edition," National Public Radio, 20 September 1995, transcript #1698–1; "Senate Republicans Basking in Glow of Welfare Reform," "All Things Considered," National Public Radio, 21 September 1995, transcript

#1977–11; Robert Pear, "G.O.P. Seek Compromise on Welfare Bill," *New York Times*, 25 October 1995; Alison Mitchell, "Greater Poverty Toll Is Seen in Welfare Bill," *New York Times*, 10 November 1995; Robert Pear, "House and Senate Leaders Compromise to Soften Welfare Bill," *New York Times*, 10 November 1995; Robert Pear, "As Welfare Compromise Emerges, Clinton Aide Says Veto It," *New York Times*, 13 November 1995; Alison Mitchell, "Clinton in Political Quandary on Welfare," *New York Times*, 20 November 1995; Robert Pear, "Battle over the Budget: The Legislation; Clinton Vetoes G.O.P. Plan to Change Welfare System," *New York Times*, 10 January 1996.

18. Robert Pear, "Republicans Finish with Welfare Measure, Clinton Ambivalent," *New York Times*, 31 July 1996; Vanessa Gallman, "Republicans Offer Welfare Bill Compromise," *Philadelphia Inquirer*, 31 July 1996; Robert Pear, "Clinton Says He'll Sign Bill Overhauling Welfare System," *New York Times*, 1 August 1996.

19. Weaver, "Ending Welfare," 375, table 9–1; *Congressional Record—House*, 31 July 1996, H9396.

20. *Congressional Record—House*, 31 July 1996, H9393, H9398.

21. Concern with the cost of entitlements was, of course, bipartisan. See, for example, "Remarks of President Clinton to the Future of Entitlements Conference, Bryn Mawr, Pennsylvania" (White House Briefing, Federal News Service, 13 December 1993).

22. Edelman, "The Worst Thing," 45.

23. *1996 Green Book*, 1325; 1325–1410 offer an excellent summary of the PRWO Act, and the following discussion is based on it.

24. *1996 Green Book*, 1339. The secretary of HHS is charged with implementing a strategy for preventing teen births and annually ranking states on their success.

25. Jessica Yates, "Child Support Enforcement and Welfare Reform" (Welfare Information Network, May 1997), http://www/welfareinfo.org/yates2.htm.

26. Michael Janofsky, "Legal Immigrants Would Regain Aid in Clinton's Plan," *New York Times*, 25 January 1999; Lizette Alvarez, "Senate Approves Restoration of Food Stamps for Some Legal Immigrants," *New York Times*, 13 May 1998.

27. Robert Pear, "Congress Adopts Sweeping Changes in Welfare Policy," *New York Times*, 1 August 1996. Shaw quoted in, "With Welfare Transformed, Some Are Optimistic, Others Fearful," *New York Times*, 4 August 1996; Dirk Johnson, "Most Governors Laud Clinton's Decision to Sign Welfare Bill," *New York Times*, 1 August 1996.

28. Quoted in Kilborn and Verhjovek, "Welfare Shift"; Robert Pear, "Clinton Says Cuts Are Too Deep in GOP Welfare Plan," *New York Times*, 18 July 1996; David T. Ellwood, "Welfare Reform in Name Only," *New York Times*, 22 July 1996; Michael Janofsky, "Welfare Cuts Raise Fears for Mayors," *New York Times*, 30 July 1996.

29. Margaret Weir, "Is Anybody Listening? The Uncertain Future of Welfare Reform in the Cities," *Brookings Review* 15, 1 (Winter 1997): 30–33; Rachel L. Swarns, "New York's New Strategy Sharply Cuts Welfare Applications at Two Offices," *New York Times*, 22 June 1998; "Federal Court Finds New York City Illegally Deters and Denies Food Stamps, Medicaid, and Cash Assistance Applications and Bars Expansion of Job Centers," *Welfare News* 4, 1 (February 1999): 1–3.

30. Edelman, "The Worst Thing," 46–47.

31. An interview with Olivia Golden suggested changes in public opinion following the passage of the 1996 bill.

32. Jeanette M. Hercik, "Organizational Culture Change in Welfare Reform" (Wel-

fare Information Network, March 1998); Elena Lahr-Vivaz, "Putting Work First in Washington State," *Public Welfare* (Fall 1997): 22–23; Marjorie Valbrun, "State Welfare Workers Now Pushing Jobs, Not Paper," *Philadelphia Inquirer*, 12 April 1998.

33. John Nordheimer, "Welfare-to-Work Effort Is Off to Slow Start," *New York Times*, 13 February 1997; James Bennett, "Clinton Urges Companies to Hire off Welfare Rolls," *New York Times*, 18 November 1997; Robert Rankin, "A Showcase on Hiring Ex-Welfare Recipients," *Philadelphia Inquirer*, 10 January 1997; Robert Pear, "10,000 Welfare Recipients Hired by Federal Agencies," *New York Times*, 1 March 1999; Robert Pear, "President Orders Agencies to Train Those on Welfare," *New York Times*, 6 March 1997; Sandra Sobieraj, "Clinton Tells U.S. Agencies to Hire off Welfare Rolls," *Philadelphia Inquirer*, 9 March 1997; Irving Molotsky, "President Says the Government Will Hire 10,000 off Welfare," *New York Times*, 11 April 1997; Pear, "10,000 Welfare Recipients"; Bureau of Labor Statistics, "National Employment, Hours, and Earnings," Series Catalog: Series ID: EE09199991 (not seasonally adjusted), http://146.1424.24/cgi-bin/surveymost; Robert Pear, "White House Releases New Figures on Welfare," *New York Times*, 1 August 1999.

34. Rachel L. Swarns, "Acute Lack of Day Care Hinders Shift to Workfare," *New York Times*, 14 April 1998; Robyn Meredith, "Job-Seeking Detroiters Cannot Get to Where the Jobs Are," *New York Times*, 26 May 1998; Margaret Pugh, "Barriers to Work: The Spatial Divide between Jobs and Welfare Recipients in Metropolitan Areas" (Washington, DC: Brookings Institution, 1998); Demetra Smith Nightingale and Kathleen Brennan, "The Welfare-to-Work Grants Program: A New Link in the Welfare Reform Chain" (Washington, DC: Urban Institute, Assessing the New Federalism Project, 1998); Laura Meckler, "Strict Rules Leave Welfare Money Untapped," *Philadelphia Inquirer*, 2 June 1999.

35. Keith Watson and Steven D. Gold, "The Other Side of Devolution: Shifting Relationships between State and Local Governments," Urban Institute, Assessing the New Federalism Project, Occasional Papers, August 1997; Jason DeParle, "U.S. Welfare System Dies as State Programs Emerge," *New York Times*, 30 June 1997.

36. Gallman, "Reports Say Welfare Law Too Optimistic"; Sandra J. Clark et al., "Income Support and Social Services for Low-Income People in Alabama," Urban Institute, Assessing the New Federalism Project, n.d., http://newfederalism.urban.org/html/Alincome.html; L. Jerome Gallagher et al., "One Year after Federal Welfare Reform: A Description of State Temporary Assistance for Needy Families (TANF) Decision as of October 1997" (Washington, DC: Urban Institute, Assessing the New Federalism Project, 1998); "State Welfare Reform Strategies Show Promise," *Urban Research Monitor* 3, 4 (1998): 1–3, 11.

37. Barbara Vobejda and Judith Havemann, "Sanctions Fuel Drop in Welfare Rolls," *Washington Post*, 23 March 1998.

38. Jason DeParle, "Wisconsin Welfare Rolls Crumble as Workfare Settles In," *New York Times*, 7 May 1997; Robert Pear, "States Given More Latitude in Following Welfare Law," *New York Times*, 1 February 1997; "APWA/NGA Comments on Proposed TANF Regulations," 18 February 1998, http://www.apwa.org/comments.htm; Hans Bos et al., "New Hope for People with Low Incomes: Two-Year Results of a Program to Reduce Poverty and Reform Welfare" (New York: Manpower Demonstration Research Corporation, 1999); Jason DeParle, "Project to

Rescue Needy Stumbles against Persistence of Poverty," *New York Times*, 15 May 1999.

39. Robert Lerman, Pamela Loprest, and Caroline Ratcliffe, "How Well Can Urban Labor Markets Absorb Welfare Recipients?" (Washington, DC: Urban Institute, Assessing the New Federalism Project, 1999); Rebecca M. Blank and David E. Card, "The Labor Market and Welfare Reform," in *Finding Jobs: Work and Welfare Reform*, ed. Rebecca M. Blank and David E. Card (New York: Russell Sage Foundation, 2000), 7–8; Steven Greenhouse, "Many Workfare Participants Are Taking Place of City Workers," *New York Times*, 13 April 1998.

40. Steven Greenhouse, "Labor Leaders Seek to Unionize Welfare Recipients Who Must Go to Work," *New York Times*, 19 February 1997; Steven Greenhouse, "Labor Rewriting Rules in Organizing Workfare Participants," *New York Times*, 7 July 1997; Laura Meckler, "Minimum Wage Must Be Paid," *Philadelphia Inquirer*, 30 July 1997.

41. "Clinton Cites Record Dip in U.S. Welfare Rolls," *Philadelphia Inquirer*, 6 July 1997; Jason DeParle, "Cutting Welfare Rolls but Raising Questions," *New York Times*, 7 May 1997; "Clinton: Welfare Rolls Fall Again," *New York Times*, 11 April 1999; Laura Meckler, "Welfare Rolls Drop to 30-Year Low, but Pace of Decline Slows," *Philadelphia Inquirer* 25 January 1999.

42. "The State of Welfare Caseloads in America's Cities: 1999" (Washington, DC: Brookings Institution, Center on Urban and Metropolitan Policy, 1999); Jason DeParle, "Welfare Rolls Show Growing Racial and Urban Imbalance," *New York Times*, 27 July 1998.

43. Pear, "Welfare Rolls Lowest."

44. Council of Economic Advisors, "Explaining the Decline in Welfare Receipt, 1993–1996" (May 9, 1997).

45. Rebecca Blank, lecture at University of Pennsylvania, Wharton School (March 18, 1999); Geoffrey Wallace and Rebecca M. Blank, "What Goes Up Must Come Down? Explaining Recent Changes in Public Assistance Caseloads" (Evanston, IL: Joint Center for Policy Research, 1999).

46. Gene B. Spirling, *The Clinton Administration's Anti-Poverty Agenda*, (1 October 1999), http://whitehouse.gov/WH/New/html/poverty.html; Marjorie Valbrun, "U.S. Grants to States Target Hard-to-Place Welfare Recipients," *Philadelphia Inquirer*, 4 September 1997; "Fact Sheet. U.S. Department of Labor. Welfare-to-Work Grants," http://wtw.doleta.gov/resources/factsheet.htm; "Implementation of Welfare-to-Work Grants," http:sh/wtw.doleta.gov/resources/whtpap7.htm; Pear, "Welfare Rolls Lowest." For an example of how a state bundled funds, see "U.S. Increases Help in Getting off Welfare," *Philadelphia Inquirer*, 29 January 1998. "President Clinton Announces Child Care Initiative" (White House, 7 January 1998), http:sh/waisgate.hhs.gov/cgi-bin/waisgate? . . . ocID=424623076+ 40+0+0&WAISaction=retrieve; Department of Health and Human Services Administration for Children and Families, "State Spending under the New Welfare Reform Law" (31 December 1999), wysiwyg://205/http://www.acf.dhhhs. gov/programs/ofa/data/q199/fy1999.htm; Department of Health and Human Services Administration for Children and Families, "President Clinton Announces New Grants for After-School Programs" (12 November 1999), http://www. acf.dhhs.gov/news/press/1998/whccn12.htm; Department of Health and Human Services Administration for Children and Families, "Fact Sheet" (18 June 1999), http://www.acf.dhhs.gov/programs/opa/facts/ccfund.htm; Blank, "Remarks."

47. Jason DeParle, "Life after Welfare: Spending the Savings Leftover Money for Welfare Baffles, or Inspires, States," *New York Times*, 29 August 1999; Tim Weiner, "Leaders in House Covet States' Unspent Welfare Money," *New York Times*, 28 July 1999; Jere Downs, "Transit Aid for the Needy Is Sitting Idle," *Philadelphia Inquirer*, 13 February 2000. In 2000, Congress also threatened to cut welfare block grant funding for sixteen states by eliminating "supplemental grants" promised by the 1996 legislation. Kristina Daugirdas, Wendell Primus, and Robert Greenstein, "Appropriations Bills Would Cut Welfare Reform Block Grant Funding for 16 States, Undoing Compromise in Welfare" (Washington, DC: Center on Budget and Policy Priorities, 2000).

48. A number of important studies are tracking the impact of the 1996 legislation. For the most part, these are being conducted by private research organizations or by universities. The Urban Institute's Assessing the New Federalism project, for one, should yield a mass of important data. Barbara Vobejda and Robert Haveman, "States' Welfare Data Disarray Clouds Analysis," *Washington Post*, 13 April 1998; DeParle, "Cutting Welfare Rolls"; Melissa Healy, "Reports on Welfare Stir Debate on Whether Reform Is Working," *Philadelphia Inquirer*, 28 May 1999.

49. "State Efforts to Track and Follow Up on Welfare Recipients" (Information provided by participants at the NGA/NSCL/APWA Meeting on Tracking and Follow-up Under Welfare Reform, February 26–27, 1998); Cary Goldberg, "No Benefits, but No Jobs: Welfare's Missing-in-Action," *New York Times*, 2 May 1999; Sarah Brauner and Pamela Loprest, "Where Are They Now? What States' Studies of People Who Left Welfare Tell Us" (Washington, DC: Urban Institute, Assessing the New Federalism Project, 1999).

50. DeParle, "Cutting Welfare Rolls"; "U.S. Welfare System Dies"; "Wisconsin Welfare Rolls Crumble"; "Getting Opal Caples to Work," *New York Times Magazine*, 24 August 1997; "Incentives Do Little to Coax People from Welfare, Study Suggests," *New York Times*, 28 August 1997; Jason DeParle, "Tougher Welfare Limits Bring Surprising Results," *New York Times*, 30 December 1997; Raymond Hernandez, "People Not Going from Welfare into Jobs, New York Survey Says," *New York Times*, 23 March 1998; "Most Former Welfare Recipients Are Working," *New Federalism: Policy Research and Resources* 6 (July 1999); Mark Greenberg, "Beyond Welfare: New Opportunities to Use TANF To Help Low-Income Working Families" (Washington, DC: Center for Law and Social Policy, 1999).

51. Janet Raffel, Erin Mooney, and Graham S. Finney, "Roadmap from Welfare to Work" (Philadelphia: 21st Century League, 1999); Paul Kane, "Preparing for the Welfare Job Crunch," *New York Times*, 24 November 1997. For problems encountered implementing welfare reform in Philadelphia during its first years, see Janet E. Raffel, "TANF, Act 35, and Pennsylvania's New Welfare System: A Review of the First Year of Implementation in Greater Philadelphia" (Philadelphia: 21st Century League, 1998).

52. DeParle, "Tougher Welfare Limits"; Hernandez, "People Not Going from Welfare into Jobs"; Ellen Nakashima, "Welfare-to-Work May Fall Short for Most in VA," *Washington Post*, 22 November 1997; "Most Former Welfare Recipients Are Working"; Greenberg, "Beyond Welfare"; Monica Yant, "Jobs Push Has Spotty Resume," *Philadelphia Inquirer*, 28 February 2000.

53. Michael Massing, "The End of Welfare?" *New York Review*, 7 October 1999, 22–26; Michael Wiseman, "In the Midst of Reform: Wisconsin in 1997," *Focus* 20, 3 (Fall 1999): 15–21.

54. Virginia Knox, Cynthia Miller, and Lisa A. Gennetian. "Reforming Welfare and Rewarding Work: A Summary of the Final Report on the Minnesota Family Investment Program" (New York: Manpower Demonstration Research Corporation, 2000). Robert Pear. "Changes in Welfare Bring Improvements for Families," *New York Times*, 1 June 2000.

55. "Average Incomes of Very Poor Families Fell during Early Years of Welfare Reform, Study Finds" (Center on Budget and Policy Priorities, 22 August 1999), www.cbpp.org/secure/8-22-99wel.htm; Kathryn Porter and Wendell Primus, "Recent Changes in the Impact of the Safety Net on Child Poverty" (Washington, DC: Center on Budget and Policy Priorities, 1999).

56. DeParle, "Tougher Welfare Limits."

57. "Hunger amid Plenty," *Philadelphia Inquirer*, 6 May 1998; Raymond Hernandez, "N.Y. State Welfare Rolls Cut by Seeking Child Support," *New York Times*, 19 April 1998; Jason DeParle, "As Welfare Rolls Shrink, Burden on Relatives Grows,"*New York Times*, 21 February 1999; Peter Eisinger, "Food Pantries and Welfare Reform: Estimating the Effect," *Focus* 20, 3 (Fall 1999): 23–27; Tamar Lewin, "Study Finds Welfare Changes Lead a Million into Child Care," *New York Times*, 4 February 2000.

58. Clare Nolan, "Downside of Welfare Reform—No Safety Net" (13 April 1999), available from www.stateline.org/story.cfm?StoryID=12021. See also the sobering results of Milwaukee's New Hope project. Hans Bos et al., "New Hope for People with Low Incomes: Two-year Results of a Program to Reduce Poverty and Reform Welfare" (New York: Manpower Demonstration Research Corporation, 1999); Jason DeParle, "Project to Rescue Needy Stumbles against Persistence of Poverty," *New York Times*, 15 May 1999; Peter Edelman, "Making Welfare Work," *New York Times*, 8 June 1999.

59. DeParle, "Tougher Welfare Limits"; see also Massing, "End of Welfare?" 25–26.

EPILOGUE: WORK, DEMOCRACY, AND CITIZENSHIP

1. For a stunning example of provider fraud, see Robert Pear, "Fraud in Medicare Increasingly Tied to Calims Payers," *New York Times*, 20 September 1999.

2. Martin Gilens, *Why Americans Hate Welfare: Race, Media, and the Politics of Antipoverty Policy* (Chicago: University of Chicago Press, 1999). A superb essay pointing out the ambiguities of fraud as a category and its manipulation by authorities is Lucie E. White, "Subordination, Rhetorical Survival Skills, and Sunday Shoes: Notes on the Hearing of Mrs. G.," *Buffalo Law Review* 38, no. 1 (Winter 1990): 1–58.

3. Eric Schlosser, "The Prison-Industrial Complex," *Atlantic Monthly*, December 1999, 51–77.

4. T. H. Marshall, "Citizenship and Social Class" [1950]," in *Citizenship and Social Class*, ed. T. H. Marshall and Tom Bottomore (London and Concord, MA: Pluto Press, 1992), 8. Lawrence Mead argues, correctly, that Marshall stressed the importance of work in his concept of citizenship. But I think Mead misses Marshall's essential point, that citizenship was a status, not a privilege. Lawrence M. Mead, "Citizenship and Social Policy: T. H. Marshall and Poverty," *Social Philosophy* 14, no. 2 (Summer 1997).

5. Raymond Plant, "So You Want to Be a Citizen?" *New Statesman* 127, no. 4371 (6 February 1998): 30; Jocelyn Pixley, *Citizenship and Employment: Investigating Post-Industrial Options* (Cambridge: Cambridge University Press, 1993), 201.

6. For Marshall, social citizenship, points out political scientist Hugh Heclo, "aimed not merely at attacking poverty at the bottom of society but at restructuring the overall provision of welfare in a more equal and just manner so as to express the solidarity of a national community." Hugh Heclo, "The Social Question," in *Poverty and the Future of Social Policy: Western States in the New World Order*, ed. Katherine McFate, Roger Lawson, and William Julius Wilson (New York: Russell Sage Foundation, 1995), 670–72.

7. Tom Bottomore, "Citizenship and Social Class, Forty Years On," in Marshall and Bottomore, *Citizenship and Social Class*, 55–92; Nora V. Demleitner, "The Fallacy of Social 'Citizenship,' or the Threat of Exclusion," *Georgetown Immigration Law Journal* 12 (Fall 1997): 35–65; Anthony Giddens, "T. H. Marshall, the State, and Democracy," in *Citizenship Today: The Contemporary Relevance of T. H. Marshall*, eds. Martin Bulmer and Anthony M. Rees (London: University College of London, 1996), 65–80; Eric Gorham, "Social Citizenship and Its Fetters," *Polity* 28, 1 (Fall 1995): 25–47; Jytte Klausen, "Social Rights Advocacy and State Building: T. H. Marshall in the Hands of Social Reformers," *World Politics* 47, 2 (1995): 244–68. On the implications of the EU for citizenship, see John Grahl and Paul Teague, "Economic Citizenship in the New Europe," *Political Quarterly* 65 (December–October 1994): 379–96.

8. Marshall, "Citizenship and Social Class," 8.

9. On the attack on the assumptions underlying the welfare state, see Robert Henry Cox, "The Consequences of Welfare Reform: How Conceptions of Social Rights Are Changing," *Journal of Social Policy* 27, 1 (1998): 1–16. See also William E. Nelson, "Two Models of Welfare: Private Charity versus Public Duty," *Southern California Interdisciplinary Law Journal* 7 (Fall 1998): 295–313.

10. Ralf Dahrendorf, "Citizenship and Social Class," in Bulmer and Rees, *Citizenship Today*, 31.

11. Demleitner, "Fallacy of Social 'Citizenship,' " 36; Rogers Smith, *Civic Ideals Conflicting Visions of Citizenship in U.S. History* (New Haven: Yale University Press, 1997), 15.

12. James H. Kettner, *The Development of American Citizenship, 1608–1870* (Chapel Hill: University of North Carolina Press, 1978); James W. Fox, Jr., "Citizenship, Poverty, and Federalism, 1787–1882," *University of Pittsburgh Law Review*, 60, 2 (Winter 1999): 421–577.

13. The relation of race to early welfare state benefits is explored in Robert C. Lieberman, *Shifting the Color Line: Race and the American Welfare State* (Cambridge: Harvard University Press, 1998). It appears that states discriminated much less with Old Age Assistance. There is excellent data in Richard Sterner, *The Negro's Share: A Study of Income, Consumption, Housing and Public Assistance* (New York: Harper and Brothers, 1943). On race and the welfare state see also the superb work of Michael K. Brown, *Race, Money, and the American Welfare State* (Ithaca: Cornell University Press, 1999). Linda Gordon, *Pitied but Not Entitled: Single Mothers and the History of Welfare, 1890–1935* (New York: Free Press, 1994), 303, stresses the impact of leaving public assistance with the states.

14. Julia S. O'Connor, "From Women in the Welfare State to Gendering Welfare State Regimes," *Current Sociology* 44 (Summer 1996): 1–30; Carole Pateman, "The Patriarchal Welfare State," in *Democracy and the Welfare State*, ed. Amy Gutmann (Princeton: Princeton University Press, 1988), 237; Pixley, *Citizenship and Employment*, 219.

15. Julia Parker, *Citizenship, Work, and Welfare: Search for the Good Society* (London: Macmillan, 1998), 146.

16. Judith Shklar, *American Citizenship: The Quest for Inclusion* (Cambridge: Harvard University Press, 1991), 62–63; Lawrence M. Mead, *Beyond Entitlement: The Social Obligations of Citizenship* (New York: Free Press, 1986).

17. Doug Henwood, "Work and Its Future," *Left Business Observer*, no. 72 (April 1996); David R. Howell, "Institutional Failure and the American Worker: The Collapse of Low-Skill Wages," Public Policy Brief, the Jerome Levy Economics Institute of Bard College (1997), 21. For a prediction of a relatively jobless future, see Jeremy Rifkin, *The End of Work: The Decline of the Global Labor Force and the Dawn of the Post-Market Era* (New York: G. P. Putnam's Sons, 1995). Doug Henwood refutes this view in "Work and Its Future" and in "How Jobless the Future?" *Left Business Observer*, no. 75 (December 1996). For the argument that jobs are available for everyone, even young minority men in inner cities and women on public assistance, see Mead, *Beyond Entitlement*; and Lawrence M. Mead, *The New Politics of Poverty: The Nonworking Poor in America* (New York: Basic Books, 1992).

18. Paul Osterman, *Securing Prosperity: The American Labor Market: How It Has Changed and What to Do about It* (Princeton: Princeton University Press, 1999), 56, 60, 80, 73, 197; Henwood, "How Jobless."

19. Osterman, *Securing Prosperity*, 84; Henwood, "How Jobless"; David Bollier, "Work and Future Society: Where Are the Economy and Technology Taking Us?" report of the Aspen Institute's Domestic Strategy Group (Washington, DC: 1998), 17.

20. Osterman, *Securing Prosperity*, 90–91.

21. Robert B. Reich, *The Work of Nations: Preparing Ourselves for the Twenty-first Century* (New York: Knopf, 1991); Henwood, "Work and Its Future"; Richard Rothstein, "Shortage of Skills? A High-Tech Myth," *New York Times*, 27 October 1999.

22. Michael J. Handel, "Is There a Skills Crisis? Trends in Job Skill Requirements, Technology, and Wage Inequality in the United States," Jerome Levy Economics Institute of Bard College Working Paper no. 295, February 2000; Howell, "Institutional Failure," 19. For what is probably the most well-known statement of the skills mismatch, see William B. Johnston and Arnold E. Packer, *Workforce 2000: Work and Workers for the 21st Century* (Indianapolis: Hudson Institute, 1987); Henwood, "Work and Its Future."

23. James K. Galbraith, *Created Unequal: The Crisis in American Pay* (New York: Simon and Schuster, 1998), 34–35, 209; Handel, "Is There a Skills Crisis?"

24. Howell, "Institutional Failure," 23–25; Osterman, *Securing Prosperity*, 74; "Basement Living," *Left Business Observer*, no. 84 (July 1998); Doug Henwood, "Welfare and Wages," *Left Business Observer*, report, 18 October 1993.

25. Kenneth L. Karst, "The Coming Crisis of Work in Constitutional Perspective," *Cornell Law Review* 82 (March 1997): 533–34; Robert E. Lane, *The Market Experience* (New York: Cambridge University Press, 1991), 335.

26. Dahrendorf, "Citizenship and Social Class," 32–33. See also Robert Henry Cox, "The Consequences of Welfare Reform: How Conceptions of Social Rights Are Changing," *Journal of Social Policy* 27, 1 (1998): 1–16; James W. Fox, Jr., "Liberalism, Democratic Citizenship, and Welfare Reform: The Troubling Case of Workfare," *Washington University Law Quarterly* 74 (Spring 1996): 103–78; Mara

Schoen Lindsay, "Working Welfare Recipients: A Comparison of the Family Support Act and the Personal Responsibility and Work Opportunity Reconciliation Act," *Fordham Urban Journal* 24 (Spring 1997): 635–62; Mary E. O'Connell, "On the Fringe: Rethinking the Link between Wages and Benefits," *Tulane Law Review* 67 (May 1993): 1422–1529.

27. Paterman, "Patriarchal Welfare State"; O'Connor, "From Women in the Welfare State"; Edgar S. Cahn, *Thinking Outside the Box: Redefining Work to Redefine Welfare* (Time Dollar Institute, 1998), available from http://www.timedollar.org/welfarefinal.htm.

28. On grass-roots movements see Harry C. Boyte, *The Backyard Revolution: Understanding the New Citizen Movement* (Philadelphia: Temple University Press, 1980); Manuel Castells, *The City and the Grassroots: A Cross-Cultural Theory of Urban Social Movements* (Berkeley: University of California Press, 1983); Robert Fisher, *Let the People Decide: Neighborhood Organizing in America*, rev. ed. (New York: Twayne Publishers, 1994).

29. Richard M. Titmuss, *Gift Relationship: From Human Blood to Social Policy* (London: Allen and Unwin, 1970); Will Hutton, *The State We're In* (London: J. Cape, 1995); Robert Kuttner, *Everything for Sale: The Virtues and Limits of Markets* (New York: Knopf, 1997), 39.

30. "The problem is not solely, or perhaps even primarily, how to fund welfare institutions: it is how to re-order those institutions so as to make them mesh with the much more active, reflexive lives that most of us now lead." Giddens, "T. H. Marshall," 80. See also Nelson, "Two Models," 295.

31. Linda Kerber, "The Meanings of Citizenship," *Dissent* (Fall 1997): 35; see also Linda K. Kerber, *No Constitutional Right to Be Ladies: Women and the Obligations of Citizenship* (New York: Hill and Wang, 1998); Kuttner, *Everything for Sale*, 351. See also Bruce E. Tonn and Carl Petrich, "Everyday Life's Constraints on Citizenship in the United States," *Futures* 30, 8 (1998): 783–813; Dahrendorf, "Origins of Inequality," 39; Giddens, "T. H. Marshall," 66–67, 80. For an alternative concept of democracy, see the interesting and provocative C. Douglas Lummis, *Radical Democracy* (Ithaca: Cornell University Press, 1996).

32. Barbara Cruikshank, *The Will to Empower: Democratic Citizens and Other Subjects* (Ithaca: Cornell University Press, 1999). Offers a brilliant critique of definitions of citizenship based solely on market considerations. Instead, she argues for a multidimensional notion of citizenship "realized" only through an array of what she terms "technologies."

ACKNOWLEDGMENTS

Many people generously helped me with advice and information during the research and writing of this book. I would like to thank the following and to ask the forgiveness of anyone whose name I have inadvertently omitted. Marc Baldwin, Elizabeth Boris, Steven Carlson, Catherine Carr, Sheryll Cashin, Faye Lomax Cooke, Susan Crawford, Denise Dunbar, Peter Edelman, James Ellenberger, David Ellwood, Paul Fronstin, Evelyn Ganzglass, Olivia Golden, Mark Greenberg, Robert Inman, Andrea Kane, Tracy Kauffman, Anna Kondratas, Sanders Korenman, Richard Larson, Julia Paley, Linda Perle, Robert Reischauer, Lauren Rich, Rev. Eugene Rivers, Jonathan Stein, Mark Stern, Thomas Sugrue, Amy Tucci, Barry Van Lare, Richard Weishaupt, Robert Weissman, Paul Yakoboski, Ethel Zelinske.

I presented some of the ideas for this book on various occasions and received excellent suggestions. For allowing me the opportunity to share the work, I thank the following organizations, the individuals there who arranged for the presentations, the commentators, and the audiences. Institute for Policy Research, Northwestern University; Council of Economic Advisors (staff brown-bag lunch); Social Inequality Seminar, Kennedy School, Harvard University; Woodrow Wilson International Center for Scholars (fellows' lunch); Heller School, Brandeis University; Liman Symposium, Yale University Law School; University of Texas at San Antonio; Public Policy Program, Vanderbilt University; Faculty-Graduate Student Colloquium, Urban Studies Graduate Certificate Program, University of Pennsylvania; Twentieth-Century American History Group, History Department, University of Pennsylvania.

Exceptionally helpful and knowledgeable librarians proved essential to the research for this book. My thanks to the superb reference staff at the University of Pennsylvania and also to the librarians at the Employee Benefit Research Institute, the Woodrow Wilson Center, and the Rangeley, Maine, Public Library.

A number of research assistants performed crucial work. At the Woodrow Wilson Center, I was helped by Maria-Stella Gatzoulis. At the University of Pennsylvania, Lorrin Thomas's creative research helped shape the prologue and the coauthored journal article on which it is based. Joseph (Trey) Fitzpatrick III did splendid research on Michigan under John Engler, and Josh Gottheimer did the same on Wisconsin under Tommy Thompson. Michael Larson's work on the footnotes and bibliography was heroic. Thanks, as well, to Brennan Maier and Jason Parkin.

Three colleagues read large sections of this book and offered essential comments. Edward Berkowitz's close attention to several chapters and vast knowledge of the subject not only sharpened my ideas but saved me from many embarrassing errors. With his wisdom about cities and economic development, Jeremy Nowak has for years taught me a great deal about urban policy, and I appreciate his astute reading of chapters. Viviana Zelizer was both an acute reader, with a keen eye for problems, and the primary source of my education about the sociology of markets.

Without generous financial support that freed me from teaching, I could not have written this book. My deep gratitude, therefore, goes to the Open Society Institute, which awarded me an Individual Fellowship, and to the Woodrow Wilson International Center for Scholars, which provided both a fellowship and a stimulating, helpful setting—lively colleagues, research and administrative support, and an office with a great view over the Washingon Mall.

Steven Fraser, then at Basic Books, first encouraged me to turn the chapter written for the tenth anniversary edition of *In the Shadow of the Poorhouse* into a book. And I thank him for encouragement over the years. Thanks, too, to my agent John Wright for teaching me about book proposals, finding a home for the book, and support during the writing. At Metropolitan Books, Sara Bershtel as always proved a tough and astute editor; her red and green pencils have reminded me that I will always have a lot to learn about writing. Thanks also to her staff and especially to Tim Moss. For excellent copyediting, I am once again indebted to Cindy Crumrine.

My friends and neighbors in Oquossoc, Maine, undoubtedly have heard a lot more about the trials of writing this book than they want, and, as in the past, I appreciate their companionship and patience. My daughter, Sarah, not only took an interest in the subject but applied her creative talents to help me find a title. My other children, Paul and Rebecca, and their families provided not only support but, especially in the summer of 1999, a wonderful and needed distraction. My wife Edda has had to live with my preoccupation over this book and the emotional roller coaster it has occasioned. For her patience, understanding, and support I am very grateful. Throughout my life, my parents, Beatrice and George Katz, have been unfailing in their faith in my abilities and in their support. They also have always been interested in the intellectual substance of my work. I will be forever thankful that they were able to attend my presentation of the book's ideas at Harvard's Kennedy School in October 1999. I only regret that my father is not here to see it published.

INDEX

ABOUT THE AUTHOR

MICHAEL B. KATZ is the Sheldon and Lucy Hackney Professor in the Department of History at the University of Pennsylvania and author of ten books including *The Underserving Poor: From the War on Poverty to the War on Welfare, In the Shadow of the Poorhouse,* and *Improving Poor People.* He has held fellowships from the Guggenheim Foundation, the Institute for Advanced Studies, the Shelby Cullom Davis Center, the Russell Sage Foundation, the Woodrow Wilson Center, and the Open Society Institute. He lives in Philadelphia and Oqquossoc, Maine.